An Anthology of
Canadian Literature
in English

Volume II

An Anthology of Canadian Literature in English

Volume II

Edited by

Donna Bennett

and

Russell Brown

Scarborough College, University of Toronto

Toronto
OXFORD UNIVERSITY PRESS
1983

TO RUSSELL MORTON BROWN, Sr.

CANADIAN CATALOGUING IN PUBLICATION DATA
Main entry under title:
An Anthology of Canadian literature in English

Includes index.
ISBN 0-19-540311-8 (v. 1). - ISBN 0-19-540394-0 (v. 2).

1. Canadian literature (English).* I. Brown,
Russell, 1942- II. Bennett, Donna, 1945-

PS8233.A57   C813'.8   C82-094580-3
PR9194.4.A57

OXFORD is a trademark of Oxford University Press

© Oxford University Press Canada 1983
1 2 3 4-6 5 4 3
Printed in Canada by
John Deyell Company

CONTENTS

ACKNOWLEDGEMENTS xi

INTRODUCTION xiii

SHEILA WATSON
And the four animals   2

P.K. PAGE
The Stenographers   6
Stories of Snow   7
If It Were You   8
Portrait of Marina   10
Photos of a Salt Mine   11
Cry Ararat!   13
Arras   16
Preparation   17
Another Space   18
After Reading 'Albino Pheasants'   19
Chinese Boxes   20
For Mstislav Rostropovich with Love   21

MIRIAM WADDINGTON
My Lessons in the Jail   24
Looking for Strawberries in June   25
Icons   27
Advice to the Young   28
The Nineteen Thirties Are Over   29
Ten Years and More   31

MARGARET AVISON
Neverness   33
The Butterfly   35
Perspective   35
Snow   36
Butterfly Bones; or Sonnet Against
   Sonnets   37
The Apex Animal   37

Meeting Together of Poles and Latitudes
   (In Prospect)   38
Tennis   39
Strong Yellow, for Reading Aloud   39
Light (I)   41
Light (II)   42
Light (III)   42

LOUIS DUDEK
From a Library Window   45
A Child Blowing Bubbles   46
Coming Suddenly to the Sea   46
Old Song   47
A Torn Record   48
Within the Walls of the Visible   48
Poetry Reading   48
Tao   49

AL PURDY
Winter Walking   51
Pause   52
The Cariboo Horses   52
The Country North of Belleville   53
Trees at the Arctic Circle   55
Notes on a Fictional Character   56
Wilderness Gothic   57
Lament for the Dorsets   59
Roblin's Mills (2)   61
Married Man's Song   63
Alive or Not   64
A Handful of Earth   65
The Nurselog   67

RAYMOND SOUSTER
Flight of the Roller-Coaster   70
Boldt's Castle   70
Get the Poem Outdoors   72
Queen Anne's Lace   72
Like the Last Patch of Snow   73
The Trillium Returns   73
Eight Pears   74

MAVIS GALLANT
About Geneva   76
The Ice Wagon Going Down the Street   81

HENRY KREISEL
The Broken Globe   98
The Prairie: A State of Mind   105

ELI MANDEL
Two Part Exercise on a Single Image   116
Day of Atonement: Standing   117
Houdini   117
The Meaning of the *I Ching*   118
On the 25th Anniversary of the
   Liberation of Auschwitz   120
Instructions   123
Doors of Perception   125
In My 57th Year   126
Ventriloquists   127
The City in Canadian Poetry   128

MARGARET LAURENCE
The Tomorrow-Tamer   139
To Set Our House in Order   154
A Place to Stand On   165

JAMES REANEY
The School Globe   170
Dream Within Dream   172
The Bicycle   173
The Lost Child   174
Writing and Loving   175
The Alphabet   175
From 'A Message to Winnipeg'   177

Starling with a Split Tongue   178
A Table of Contents   179
From The Preface to *Masks of
   Childhood*   180
The Easter Egg   182

PHYLLIS WEBB
Lear on the Beach at Break of Day   226
Marvell's Garden   226
The Glass Castle   228
To Friends Who Have Also Considered
   Suicide   229
From *Naked Poems*
   Suite I   230
   Suite II   232
For Fyodor   234
Spots of Blood   235
Eschatology of Spring   236

ROBERT KROETSCH
Stone Hammer Poem   238
Poem of Albert Johnson   243
F.P. Grove: The Finding   244
Unhiding the Hidden: Recent Canadian
   Fiction   246

HUGH HOOD
Flying a Red Kite   251
The Woodcutter's Third Son   259

D.G. JONES
Beautiful Creatures Brief as These   275
I Thought There Were Limits   275
For Eve   276
From 'Kate, These flowers . . .
   (The Lampman Poems)'   277
The Diamond Sutra   280
Introduction to *Butterfly on Rock*   282

JAY MACPHERSON
From *The Boatman*
   The Thread   289
   The Third Eye   290

Eurynome I   290
Eurynome II   291
The Old Enchanter   291
The Boatman   292
The Anagogic Man   292
The Fisherman   293
From *Welcoming Disaster*
   Substitutions   294
   A Lost Soul   295
   After the Explosion   296
   Orion   296
   Surrogate   297
   Visiting   297
   Old Age of the Teddy-Bear   298
   Notes & Acknowledgements   299

ALICE MUNRO
Something I've Been Meaning To Tell
   You   301
The Moons of Jupiter   314

MORDECAI RICHLER
The Summer My Grandmother Was
   Supposed to Die   327

ALDEN NOWLAN
Dancer   337
Canadian Love Song   338
The Sleepwalker   338
Temptation   339
The First Stirring of the Beasts   340
Country Full of Christmas   341
Hymn to Dionysus   341
Canadian January Night   342
Survival   342
The Broadcaster's Poem   343
On the Barrens   344

LEONARD COHEN
For Anne   348
You Have the Lovers   348
A Kite Is a Victim   349
Another Night with Telescope   350

In the Bible Generations Pass . . .   350
Suzanne Takes You Down   350
Priests   352
Welcome to these lines . . .   352
From *Death of a Lady's Man*
   I Decided   353
   I Decided   353

LEON ROOKE
Sixteen-year-old Susan March
   Confesses to the Innocent Murder of
   All the Devious Strangers Who Would
   Drive Her Down   355

RUDY WIEBE
The Naming of Albert Johnson   366

GEORGE BOWERING
Harbour Beginnings & That Other
   Gleam   376
Thru   376
From *Autobiology*
   The Raspberries   377
Desert Elm   378

W.P. KINSELLA
First Names and Empty Pockets   386

AUDREY THOMAS
Green Stakes for the Garden   399
Initram   402

ALISTAIR MacLEOD
The Lost Salt Gift of Blood   414

JOHN NEWLOVE
Four Small Scars   428
Crazy Riel   428
The Double-Headed Snake   430
Samuel Hearne in Wintertime   431
Ride Off Any Horizon   433
The Prairie   436
The Green Plain   437

JACK HODGINS
The Lepers' Squint   441

MARGARET ATWOOD
This is a Photograph of Me   456
Pre-Amphibian   457
The Reincarnation of Captain Cook   458
Progressive Insanities of a Pioneer   459
From *The Journals of Susanna Moodie*
    Disembarking at Quebec   461
    Further Arrivals   462
    First Neighbours   463
    The Planters   464
    The Wereman   465
    Paths and Thingscape   465
    The Two Fires   466
    Departure from the Bush   467
    Dream 2: Brian the Still-Hunter 469
    Thoughts from Underground   470
    Afterword to *The Journals*
        of Susanna Moodie   471
Procedures for Underground   472
Dream: Bluejay or Archeopteryx   473
Tricks with Mirrors   474
Siren Song   476
Marrying the Hangman   477
Variation On The Word *Sleep*   480
Last Poem   480
From *Murder in the Dark*
    Making Poison   481
    Strawberries   482
The Resplendent Quetzal   482

PATRICK LANE
Because I Never Learned   493
Unborn Things   493
The Hustler   494
The Children of Bogota   495
At the Edge of the Jungle   496
Albino Pheasants   497
Stigmata   498
The Witnesses   499
Thinking on That Contest   500

A Murder of Crows   501
CPR Station—Winnipeg   502
The Long Coyote Line   503
Weasel   503

DENNIS LEE
When I Went Up to Rosedale   505
The Death of Harold Ladoo   507
From 'Cadence, Country, Silence:
    Writing in Colonial Space'   521

W.D. VALGARDSON
God is Not a Fish Inspector   534

CLARKE BLAISE
Eyes   543

FRANK DAVEY
From *Weeds*
    The Garden   549
    The Bandit   549
    Weeds   550
    The Reading   550
    What Is in the Sky Is Not Brown   550
    Mealtimes   551
    The Place   551
    A Yellow Page   551
    The Rock   552
    Them Apples   552
    I Do Not Write Poems   552
    Red   553
    The Mirror   553

GWENDOLYN MacEWEN
Icarus   560
A Breakfast for Barbarians   562
Manzini: Escape Artist   563
The Portage   564
Dark Pines under Water   565
A Lecture to the Flat Earth Society   565
The Real Name of the Sea   566
The Golden Hunger   567
From *The T.E. Lawrence Poems*

The Real Enemies 567
The Void 568

MICHAEL ONDAATJE
The Time Around Scars 570
Elizabeth 571
Near Elginburg 572
Billboards 573
Burning Hills 574
Letters & Other Worlds 576
Pig Glass 578
Light 579
Sallie Chisum/Last Words on Billy
  the Kid. 4 A.M. 581
From Running in the Family
  The Cinnamon Peeler 583
  Lunch Conversation 584

bp NICHOL
From The Martyrology
  From Book 1 589
  From Book 3 594
  From Book 5 600
  From Continental Trance 603

POETS FOR FURTHER READING

DAVID DONNELL
The Canadian Prairies View
  of Literature 607
Hound 608

GARY GEDDES
Letter of the Master of Horse 609

DAPHNE MARLATT
From Steveston
  Imagine: a town 615
  Coming Home 616
  At Birch Bay 616

ANDREW SUKNASKI
Homestead, 1914
  (Sec. 32, Tp4, Rge2, W3rd, Sask.) 617

ROBERT BRINGHURST
Deuteronomy 623
Essay on Adam 626
These Poems, She Said 626

MARY DI MICHELE
The City is a Village 627
A Fiction of Edvard Munch 628

ROO BORSON
Blue 630
The Creation 630
Gray Glove 631

ERIN MOURÉ
It Is Only Me 632
Barrington 633
Reading Nietzsche 634

INDEX 635

ACKNOWLEDGEMENTS

MARGARET ATWOOD. 'This Is a Photograph of Me', 'Pre-Amphibian' © Margaret Atwood 1966, from *The Circle Game* (Toronto: House of Anansi Press). 'The Resplendent Quetzal' from *Dancing Girls* by Margaret Atwood used by permission of The Canadian Publishers, McClelland and Stewart Limited, Toronto. 'Making Poison', 'Strawberries' from *Murder in the Dark* (Coach House Press), © Margaret Atwood, reprinted by permission. Reprinted by permission of Oxford University Press Canada: 'Progressive Insanities of a Pioneer', 'The Reincarnation of Captain Cook' from *The Animals in That Country*; 'Disembarking at Quebec', 'Further Arrivals', 'First Neighbours', 'The Planters', 'The Wereman', 'Paths and Thingscape', 'The Two Fires', 'Departure from the Bush', 'Dream 2: Brian the Still-Hunter', 'Thoughts from Underground', 'Afterword to *The Journals of Susanna Moodie*' from *The Journals of Susanna Moodie*; 'Dream: Bluejay or Archeopteryx', 'Procedures for Underground' from *Procedures for Underground*; 'Tricks with Mirrors', 'Siren Song' from *You Are Happy*; 'Marrying the Hangman' from *Two-Headed Poems*; 'Last Poem', 'Variation on the Word *Sleep*' from *True Stories*. MARGARET AVISON. 'Neverness', 'Perspective', 'Snow', 'Butterfly Bones; or Sonnet Against Sonnets', 'The Apex Animal', 'The Butterfly', 'Meeting Together of Poles and Latitudes', 'Tennis', 'Strong Yellow, for Reading Aloud' from *Winter sun/The dumbfounding: poems 1940-66* by Margaret Avison used by permission of The Canadian Publishers, McClelland and Stewart Limited, Toronto. 'Light I', 'Light II', 'Light III' from *sunblue* by Margaret Avison, reprinted by permission of Lancelot Press Limited. CLARK BLAISE. 'Eyes' by Clark Blaise from *A North American Education*. Copyright © 1973 by Clark Blaise. Reprinted by permission of Doubleday & Company, Inc. ROO BORSON. All poems reprinted by permission of the author. GEORGE BOWERING. 'Harbour Beginnings & That Other Gleam' and 'Thru' reprinted by permission of the author. From *Autobiology*, 'The Raspberries', 'Desert Elm' from *The Catch* by George Bowering reprinted by permission of The Canadian Publishers, McClelland and Stewart Limited, Toronto. 'Against Description' from *West Window* reprinted by permission of General Publishing Co. Limited. ROBERT BRINGHURST. 'Deuteronomy', 'These Poems, She Said', 'Essay on Adam' from *The Beauty of Weapons* by Robert Bringhurst used by permission of The Canadian Publishers, McClelland and Stewart Limited, Toronto. LEONARD COHEN. Reprinted by permission of The Canadian Publishers, McClelland and Stewart Limited, Toronto: 'A Kite is a Victim', 'You Have the Lovers', 'For Anne', 'Another Night with Telescope', 'In the Bible Generations Pass . . .', 'Suzanne Takes You Down' from *Selected Poems* by Leonard Cohen; 'Priests' from *The Songs of Leonard Cohen* by Leonard Cohen; 'Welcome to these lines . . .' from *The Energy of Slaves* by Leonard Cohen; and 'I Decided', '*I Decided*' from *Death of a Lady's Man*. FRANK DAVEY. All poems reprinted by permission of the author. MARY DI MICHELE. 'The City is a Village' by Mary di Michele is reprinted from *Bread and Chocolate* by permission of Oberon Press. 'A Fiction of Edvard Munch' from *Mimosa and Other Poems* by Mary di Michele reprinted by permission of Mosaic Press. DAVID DONNELL. Both poems reprinted by permission of the author. LOUIS DUDEK. All poems reprinted by permission of the author. MAVIS GALLANT. 'About Geneva'—reprinted by permission of Georges Borchardt, Inc., copyright © 1951 Mavis Gallant—first appeared in *The New Yorker*. 'The Ice Wagon Going Down the Street'—reprinted by permission of Georges Borchardt, Inc., copyright © 1963 Mavis Gallant—first appeared in *The New Yorker*. GARY GEDDES. 'Letter of the Master of Horse' from *The Acid Test* reprinted by permission of the author. JACK HODGINS. 'The Lepers' Squint' reprinted by permission of the author. HUGH HOOD. 'The Woodcutter's Third Son' and 'Flying a Red Kite' reprinted by permission of the author. D. G. JONES. 'Beautiful Creatures Brief as These', 'From "Kate, These Flowers . . ."', and 'The Diamond Sutra' reprinted by permission of the author. 'I Thought There Were Limits', 'For

Eve' from *Phrases from Orpheus* reprinted by permission of Oxford University Press Canada. 'Introduction to *Butterfly on Rock*' reprinted from *Butterfly on Rock*, by D. G. Jones, by permission of University of Toronto Press. © University of Toronto Press 1970. W. P. KINSELLA. 'First Names and Empty Pockets' by W. P. Kinsella is reprinted from *Shoeless Joe Jackson Comes to Iowa* by permission of Oberon Press. HENRY KREISEL. 'The Broken Globe' and 'The Prairie: A State of Mind' reprinted by permission of NeWest Press and Henry Kreisel. ROBERT KROETSCH. 'Poem of Albert Johnson', 'Stone-hammer Poem', 'F. P. Grove: The Finding', 'Unhiding the Hidden: Recent Canadian Fiction' reprinted by permission of Robert Kroetsch. PATRICK LANE. All poems reprinted by permission of the author. MARGARET LAURENCE. Reprinted by permission of The Canadian Publishers, McClelland and Stewart Limited, Toronto: 'The Tomorrow Tamer' from *The Tomorrow Tamer* by Margaret Laurence; 'To Set Our House in Order' from *A Bird in the House* by Margaret Laurence; 'A Place to Stand On' from *Heart of a Stranger* by Margaret Laurence. DENNIS LEE. 'When I Went up to Rosedale', 'The Death of Harold Ladoo' from *The Gods* by Dennis Lee reprinted by permission of The Canadian Publishers, McClelland and Stewart Limited, Toronto. 'From "Cadence, Country, Silence"' © Dennis Lee, reprinted by permission. GWENDOLYN MacEWEN. 'Icarus', 'A Breakfast for Barbarians', 'Manzini: Escape Artist', 'The Portage', 'Dark Pines Under Water' from *Magic Animals* by Gwendolyn MacEwen. © Gwendolyn MacEwen 1974. Reprinted by permission of Macmillan of Canada A Division of Gage Publishing Limited. 'The Void', 'The Real Enemies' from *T. E. Lawrence Poems* by Gwendolyn MacEwen, reprinted by permission of Mosaic Press. 'A Lecture to the Flat Earth Society', 'The Golden Hunger', 'The Real Name of the Sea' from *Earth Light*, reprinted by permission of General Publishing Co. Limited. ALISTAIR MacLEOD. 'The Lost Salt Gift of Blood' from *The Lost Salt Gift of Blood* by Alistair MacLeod reprinted by permission of The Canadian Publishers, McClelland and Stewart Limited, Toronto. JAY MACPHERSON. All poems from *Poems Twice Told* reprinted by permission of Oxford University Press Canada. ELI MANDEL. 'Two Part Exercise on a Single Image', 'Day of Atonement: Standing', 'The Meaning of the I CHING' by Eli Mandel, from *Crusoe: Poems Selected and New* (Toronto: House of Anansi Press, 1973). 'On the 25th Anniversary of the Liberation of Auschwitz', 'Doors of Perception', 'Instructions', 'The City in Canadian Poetry', reprinted by permission of Press Porcépic. Reprinted by permission of Eli Mandel: 'Houdini' from *An Idiot Joy* and 'In My 57th Year', 'Ventriloquists' from *Life Sentence: Poems and Journals, 1976-1980* (Press Porcépic). DAPHNE MARLATT. 'Imagine: a town', 'Coming Home', and 'At Birch Bay' from *Net Work: Selected Writing* (Talonbooks, 1980). Reprinted by permission of the author. ERIN MOURÉ. 'It is Only Me', 'Barrington', 'Reading Nietzsche' by Erin Mouré, from *Wanted Alive*, (Toronto: House of Anansi Press, 1983). ALICE MUNRO. 'The Moons of Jupiter' © 1982 Alice Munro. All rights reserved. From the book *The Moons of Jupiter* by Alice Munro. Originally published in *The New Yorker*. Reprinted by permission of Virginia Barber Literary Agency. 'Something I've Been Meaning to Tell You' copyright © 1974 by Alice Munro. All rights reserved. From the book *Something I've Been Meaning to Tell You* by Alice Munro. Reprinted by permission of Virginia Barber Literary Agency. JOHN NEWLOVE. Reprinted by permission of The Canadian Publishers, McClelland and Stewart Limited, Toronto: 'Ride Off Any Horizon' from *Black Night Window* by John Newlove; 'Four Small Scars', 'Crazy Riel', 'The Double-Headed Snake', 'Samuel Hearne in Wintertime', 'The Prairie' from *The Fat Man* by John Newlove. Reprinted by permission of John Newlove: 'The Green Plain', from *The Green Plain*. bp NICHOL. All poems reprinted by permission of the author. ALDEN NOWLAN. 'Canadian Love Song' from *The Things Which Are* and 'Dancer' from *Playing the Jesus Game* reprinted by permission of the author. All other poems are from *Between Tears and Laughter* by Alden Nowlan © 1971 by Clarke, Irwin & Company Limited. Used by permission. MICHAEL ONDAATJE. All poems reprinted by permission of the author: 'Time Around Scars', 'Elizabeth', 'Billboards', 'Letters & Other Worlds', 'Near Elginburg', 'Burning Hills', 'Pig Glass', Sallie Chisum/Last Words on Billy the Kid, 4 A.M.', 'Light' from *There's a Trick with a Knife I'm Learning to Do* (McClelland and Stewart Limited) © Michael Ondaatje; 'The Cinnamon Peeler', 'Lunch Conversations' from *Running in the Family* (McClelland and Stewart Limited) © Michael Ondaatje. P. K. PAGE. All poems reprinted by permission of the author. AL PURDY. 'Winter Walking' by Al Purdy, from *Poems for all the Annettes* (Toronto: House of Anansi Press, 1973). Reprinted by permission of House of Anansi Press and the author. Reprinted by permission of The Canadian Publishers, McClelland and Stewart Limited, Toronto: 'Pause', 'Wilderness Gothic', 'Notes on a Fictional Character', 'The Cariboo Horses', 'Trees at the Arctic Circle', 'Lament for the Dorsets', 'Roblin's Mills (2)', 'Married Man's Song', 'Alive or Not', 'A Handful of Earth' from *Being Alive* by Al Purdy; 'The

Country North of Belleville' from *Selected Poems* by Al Purdy; 'The Nurselog' from *The Stone Bird* by Al Purdy. JAMES REANEY. Reprinted with the kind permission of the author, publisher, and Sybil Hutchison, literary agent: 'A Table of Contents', 'Writing and Loving', 'Winnipeg Seen as a Body of Time and Space', 'The Bicycle', 'Starling with a Split Tongue', 'The Alphabet', 'The Lost Child', 'The School Globe', and 'Dream within Dream' from *Poems* by James Reaney, New Press, Toronto, copyright by James Reaney, 1972, Canada; 'Preface to *Masks of Childhood*' and 'The Easter Egg' from *Masks of Childhood* (New Drama 2), edited by Brian Parker, copyright 1972, published by New Press, Toronto. MORDECAI RICHLER. 'The Summer My Grandmother Was Supposed to Die' from *The Street* by Mordecai Richler reprinted by permission of The Canadian Publishers, McClelland and Stewart Limited, Toronto. LEON ROOKE. Reprinted by permission of E.C.W. Press. RAYMOND SOUSTER. All poems reprinted from *Collected Poems of Raymond Souster* by permission of Oberon Press. ANDREW SUKNASKI. 'Homestead, 1914 (Sec. 32, Tp4, Rge 2, W3rd, Sask.)' from *Wood Mountain Poems* by Andrew Suknaski © Andrew Suknaski 1976. Reprinted by permission. AUDREY THOMAS. 'Green Stakes for the Garden' and 'Initram' from *Two in the Bush and Other Stories* by Audrey Thomas used by permission of The Canadian Publishers, McClelland and Stewart Limited, Toronto. W. D. VALGARDSON. 'God Is Not a Fish Inspector' by W. D. Valgardson is reprinted from *God Is Not a Fish Inspector* by permission of Oberon Press. SHEILA WATSON. 'And the four animals' (Coach House Press, Manuscript Editions, 1980) reprinted by permission of Sheila Watson. MIRIAM WADDINGTON. 'Ten Years and More' © Miriam Waddington from *The Price of Gold* (Oxford University Press, 1976) reprinted by permission of Miriam Waddington. All other poems reprinted from *Driving Home* by Miriam Waddington by permission of Oxford University Press Canada. PHYLLIS WEBB. All poems reprinted by permission of the author. RUDY WIEBE. 'The Naming of Albert Johnson' from *Where Is the Voice Coming From?* by Rudy Wiebe reprinted by permission of The Canadian Publishers, McClelland and Stewart Limited, Toronto.

INTRODUCTION

Volume I of this anthology contains works by forty English-Canadian writers born no later than 1914. This second volume features thirty-eight writers, all of whom (with the exception of Sheila Watson) were born after that date, plus a supplementary section presenting eight additional poets. As in Volume I, authors are arranged chronologically by birth year, and their selections are preceded by introductions that locate them in the contexts of Canadian literary history and of each writer's career and place in the literary community. Footnotes throughout give additional information and elucidate points that might otherwise remain obscure.

We have sought to provide enough space to give readers a sense of the overall accomplishment of most of these writers, and have avoided excerpting works of fiction, drama, and poetry—except for the extract made, with its author's approval, from bp Nichol's ongoing poem, *The Martyrology*. Certain works of non-fiction (James Reaney's Preface to *Masks of Childhood*, D.G. Jones's *Butterfly on Rock*, and Dennis Lee's 'Cadence, Country, Silence') have been excerpted because their chief function in this volume is to shed light on other texts. In addition to the several full-length selections in Volume I, this second volume contains the whole of Reaney's play *The Easter Egg*, all of 'Desert Elm' by George Bowering, and all of Lee's long poem *The Death of Harold Ladoo*. When choosing poems from a poetic sequence—a form important to many Canadian writers—we have taken special care to select those that can stand by themselves and have indicated the sequence from which they come. (Sequences represented in this volume include James Reaney's 'Twelve Letters to a Small Town', Jay Macpherson's *The Boatman* and *Welcoming Disaster*, Leonard Cohen's *The Energy of Slaves* and *Death of a Lady's Man*, George Bowering's *Autobiology*, Margaret Atwood's *The Journals of Susanna Moodie* and *Murder in the Dark*, Frank Davey's *Weeds* and *Arcana*, and Gwendolyn MacEwen's *The T.E. Lawrence Poems*.)

It has been impossible to include all writers we might have wished, so we have chosen for this second volume a broadly representative group to suggest the recent history, as well as the range, variety, and continuing development, of English-Canadian literature. Some authors—among them Timothy Findley, Graeme Gibson, Robert Harlow, and Adele Wiseman—are not represented here because their chief works are full-length novels, and there are a number of fiction writers (such as Matt Cohen, Dave Godfrey, John Metcalf, David Adams Richards, Kent Thompson, and Guy Vanderhaghe) who were not included for reasons of space but who also deserve the reader's attention. The presence at the end of this volume of a section called 'Poets for Further Reading' serves to suggest that the anthologist's task is always, by its very nature, unfinished, and that all who are interested in Canadian writing ought to go beyond the bounds of this, or any, anthology.

The authors and works in Volume I documented three stages in the development of English-Canadian literature: the first beginnings of a literary culture, in the eighteenth and early nineteenth centuries; the emergence of a national literature, in the years following Confederation; and the establishment of literary modernism, in the first part of the twentieth century, by poets such as A.J.M. Smith, F.R. Scott, A.M. Klein, Dorothy Livesay, Earle Birney, and Irving Layton, and fiction writers such as Morley Callaghan, Sinclair Ross, and Ethel Wilson. Most of these writers are still alive and active, and some—like Birney—have not only influenced the writers in Volume II but have been influenced by them in turn.

Because the time covered in the second volume is briefer and the literary activity more intense and diverse, no such well-defined division into periods is possible. It is clear, however, that this volume records the progress of Canadian writers in consolidating the modernism of their predecessors; in exploring and developing the range of possibilities that had been opened up to them; and, in some cases, in reacting against or seeking to go beyond this inheritance. Modernism as a literary movement has an interesting history in Canada. On the one hand it arrived rather late (not until the twenties), largely stripped of the revolutionary character associated with it elsewhere; on the other hand, almost from the beginning the Canadian literary community manifested aspects of what later became the modernist temperament: the need to find new forms and philosophies because old ones had ceased to provide meaning; a sense of alienation and displacement as an inevitable part of existence; and an interest in myth as one possible source of meaning where a controlling vision has otherwise been lost.

Modernism, like most new aesthetic movements, had as one of its chief impulses the drive to provide a new version of 'realism'; that is, it has sought a new way of coming to terms with what is 'true'. Breaking with the nineteenth-century heritage of romantic idealism—which saw reality as unified, as part of an identifiable overall plan that the mind could perceive and understand—modernists saw truth as partial, internal, and subjective. In Canada, as elsewhere, this new vision produced divergent responses. One group of writers sought the real world internally, through investigation of the psyche, especially the unconscious, and of the worlds that the mind can construct, such as literature and myth; a second group looked for reality instead in the local and immediate world of physical experience. In Canada that first response is initially made by the poets of the 'Montreal group', and it is later seen in the mythopoeic writing that, while it had early exemplars in Joyce and Eliot, later received—especially in Canada—tremendous impetus in the critical theories of Northrop Frye. The other kind of modernist writing has its roots in the rural realism of Raymond Knister, W.W.E. Ross, and the early work of Dorothy Livesay; in the forties it emerges full-blown in the writers who, reacting against the 'Montreal Group', gathered around John Sutherland and his little magazine, *First Statement*. These writers tended to identify themselves with, and write about, the everyday world and the common man; to adopt a style close to normal speech; and to simplify their writing wherever possible. In Volume II the reader may see the continuation of both traditions—the former apparent in the work of Sheila Watson, James Reaney, Jay Macpherson, and those who came after them; the latter in the writings of the *Tish* group, of recent Prairie poets, and others.

In all parts of the world today we hear statements about the end of modernism and about the beginning of a 'post-modern' era characterized by literary forms that are self-conscious and self-reflexive, but that also express considerable ironic doubt about the self as an object of inquiry. As was earlier true of modernism, many Canadian writers responded to post-modernism because its concerns are strikingly congruent with preoccupations—such as the Canadian anxiety about self-identity—that existed already in this country. Similarly, post-modern anxieties about, and fascination with, language—which is seen as becoming increasingly elusive in meaning and yet as having a previously unrecognized power to shape its users—have particular significance for Canadians today, since, as the essays by Kroetsch and Lee suggest, language may be the most pervasive yet least visible remnant of a colonial heritage. In this context the work of bp Nichol takes on increased importance, for he has anticipated the current post-modern desire to 'deconstruct' existing literary forms and even language itself in order to find new means of expression. In the light of this Canadian affinity for post-modern concerns, it should come as no surprise to discover that one of our writers, Robert Kroetsch, is a founding editor and shaping influence for a leading international journal of post-modern theory.

Of course post-modern literature may turn out to be a transitional movement. If so, what is to come may already be contained in the most recent work in this volume, though that will be apparent only in retrospect. In any case Canadian writers will continue to play a role in new developments.

The essays in this volume by Henry Kreisel, Eli Mandel, Kroetsch, Jones, and Lee make interesting generalizations about several works, or about the Canadian literary tradition itself and the cultural milieu from which it springs. Some readers might want to begin with these commentaries and test them against their own perceptions as they read; others might wish to compare the concerns expressed in these pieces with those found in the critical essays contained in Volume I (by Daniel Wilson, E.H. Dewart, E.K. Brown, Hugh MacLennan, Northrop Frye, and George Woodcock). In all cases, of course, readers should let these critical statements carry them back to a living body of work rather than come between them and the texts.

The technical apparatus of this anthology has been kept as simple and accessible as possible. The notes provide information rather than interpretation. They are not intended to replace a dictionary, but it has sometimes seemed desirable to provide definitions for obscure terms or for words used in an unfamiliar sense. Major literary and historical figures—especially those in the English-language tradition—and recognizable literary allusions have usually been left unexplained. To distract the reader as little as possible, more than one item is sometimes glossed in a single note; in such cases the superscript appears in the text appended to the first reference, and the additional words being glossed are repeated within the note. When we were uncertain about the need for annotation we consulted students in Canadian-literature and in first-year English courses and have been guided by their responses. For their help and patience we here express our gratitude.

We have attempted to provide reliable texts throughout. Where more than one version of a text exists, we have usually chosen the author's most recent revision. We have silently corrected obvious typographical errors; where any doubt about texts existed we have, when possible, consulted the authors. All selections are dated according to first book publication. If substantive changes were later made, we have indicated the date of the revised publication (e.g. '1962, rev. 1968'). When we thought it helpful to indicate a significantly earlier date of prior (journal) publication, two dates are provided (e.g. '1974, 1983'); if a date of composition is indicated, it has been placed in square brackets (e.g. '[1956], 1972'). In some cases writers have themselves appended dates to their poems; these have usually been retained and appear at the end and to the right.

Since the texts in this volume have never previously been annotated, we have drawn on the knowledge of a great many people for help: friends, acquaintances, librarians, and colleagues have all shown their patience in tolerating our questions. Many of the people acknowledged in Volume I were of assistance again as we worked on Volume II, and in addition a great many of the authors were themselves consulted. Although we cannot possibly list all who made themselves helpful in various ways, we would like to express especial gratitude to George Bowering, Frank Davey, Jack David, L.E. Doucette, Hugh Hood, D.G. Jones, Robert Kroetsch, David Lambden, Sheila Latham, Dennis Lee, Don Le Pan, Eli Mandel, Bruce Meyer, Peter Nicholson, Michael Ondaatje, P.K. Page, James Reaney, Peter Styrmo, John Warden, Jan Whitehouse, and Rudy Wiebe. We would also like to thank the reference librarians at the Metropolitan Toronto Library, and at the Robarts Library and the Scarborough campus of the University of Toronto. We received valuable research assistance from Ann Wilson and help in manuscript preparation from Penny Moore and Phyllis Wilson of Oxford and from Ellen Pekilis and Ian Chunn. Finally we are grateful for the patient support given us by William Toye and Pat Sillers of Oxford University Press Canada.

Donna Bennett
Russell Brown
Toronto, 28 June 1983

Sheila Watson

b. 1909

Sheila Watson, née Sheila Martin Doherty, was born in New Westminster, B.C. She grew up in the mental hospital there (her father was the presiding physician) and did not enter school until she was ten. After receiving a Catholic education, she enrolled at the University of British Columbia and completed a B.A. in 1931. Two years later, after taking a teaching certificate and an M.A., Watson began her career as a teacher. Until the end of the Second World War she taught in schools in small B.C. communities, including a tiny settlement in the Cariboo region, where she spent two years. In 1941 she married the poet Wilfred Watson, and after the war they taught in Ontario, British Columbia, and Alberta.

From 1949 to 1951, while an instructor at UBC, Watson wrote a series of four mythic short stories; two of them appeared in *Queen's Quarterly* (1954 and 1956) and another in the *Tamarack Review* (1959). Her novel *The Double Hook*, which grew out of her experiences in the Cariboo, was finished in Calgary in the early fifties (although the book was not published until 1959). After a year in Paris, Watson began graduate studies in 1957 at the University of Toronto, where she worked under Marshall McLuhan on a study of the English novelist-painter Wyndham Lewis. In 1961 she returned to Alberta and became a member of the University of Alberta's English Department. She completed her Ph.D. in 1965 and continued to teach at Alberta until she retired in 1975 as full professor. She now lives in British Columbia.

Watson's active involvement in the liter-ary community in Edmonton led her to help found, with her husband among others, the little magazine, the *White Pelican* (1970-5). In 1975 the journal *Open Letter* ran a special issue of her work, collecting her essays, a brief commentary by her on *The Double Hook*, and the four stories, which were also published in book form as *Four Stories* (1979). Reprinted below is a fifth piece of fiction, 'And the four animals'. Although it was written early in Watson's career, it did not appear until 1980, when it was published as a Coach House Press 'manuscript edition' (normally a form of pre-publication that allows an author to make changes in a work before final publication).

Watson is a singular figure in Canadian literature. Although her fictional output—one novel, five pieces of short fiction—has been small, she has had a large influence on the contemporary Canadian novel. The publication of *The Double Hook* was of especial importance because it marked the first appearance in Canada of a work of modernist fiction in which form and idea took precedence over narrative event. This novel also broke the constraints of regionalism that had hitherto bound Canadian fiction. Paradoxically Watson accomplished this by focusing on a definite region and—abandoning the conventions of realism—giving it a symbolic and allegorical cast, transforming it into a region of the mind.

Written in a voice that recalls both Greek tragedy and Biblical narratives and that, in its terse statements, lends itself to allegory and fable, Watson's novel and stories employ a style best described as 'prophetic'. 'And the four animals' has much in common with her other fiction. Like *The Double Hook*, it is located in a specific environment—the colours and the emptiness of the landscape evoke a picture of the West—and in both the short story and the novel the Indian trickster-god of appetite, Coyote, is a controlling element. Coyote represents a necessary but omnivorous part of existence, the source of the destruction and regeneration that maintain the eternal cycles of life and death. Thus, like Watson's other short fiction, 'And the four animals' draws its meaning, significance, and energy from the structure of myth. The characters, which are but aspects of their environment, exist in a non-historical context—the realm of myth—and are both the source of events in time and the emblematic explanation of them. Man in this story replaces Coyote as creator and destroyer. Identified with a volcanic near-wasteland, man is the cause of both the dogs' corrupt, time-bound condition—which has broken their link to their primitive forebear, Coyote—and their reabsorption back into the eternal landscape itself. 'And the four animals', recalling the allegoric narratives of Revelation, is perhaps *the* myth of the West, in which time and space, the finite and the infinite, civilization and wilderness, vie for control and yet remain in a state of dynamic equilibrium.

And the four animals[1]

The foothills slept. Over their yellow limbs the blue sky crouched. Only a fugitive green suggested life which claimed kinship with both and acknowledged kinship with neither.

Around the curve of the hill, or out of the hill itself, came three black dogs. The watching eye could not record with precision anything but the fact of their presence. Against the faded contour of the earth the things were. The watcher could not have said whether they had come or whether the eye had focused them into being. In the place of the hills before and after have no more meaning than the land gives. Now there were the dogs where before were only the hills and the transparent stir of the dragonfly.

Had the dogs worn the colour of the hills, had they swung tail round leg, ears oblique and muzzles quivering to scent carrion, or mischief, or the astringency of grouse mingled with the acrid smell of low-clinging sage, the eye might have recognized a congruence between them and the land. Here Coyote, the primitive one, the god-baiter and troublemaker, the thirster after power, the vainglorious,

---

[1]The four animals appear in The Jerusalem Bible. (In other translations, such as the King James version, 'four animals' is translated as 'four beasts'.) They first appear in Revelation 5:13-14: 'Then I heard all the living things in creation—everything that lives in the air, and on the ground, and under the ground, and in the sea, crying "To the One who is sitting on the throne and to the Lamb, be all praise, honour, glory and power, for ever and ever". And the four animals said, "Amen"; and the elders prostrated themselves to worship.' The phrase, 'and the four animals', recurs in Revelation 7:11 and 19:4. The four animals are described in Revelation 4:6-8 as *'four animals with many eyes*, in front and behind. *The first* animal was like *a lion, the second* like *a bull, the third* animal had *a human face*, and *the fourth* animal was like a flying *eagle. Each* of the four animals had *six wings* and had *eyes all the way round* as well as inside.' Traditionally this image is interpreted as suggesting the ceaseless worship that should be rendered to God by the chief representative of his creation. Watson also follows a tradition in which the four animals are associated with the four apostles.

might have walked since the dawn of creation—for Coyote had walked early on the first day.

The dogs, however, were elegant and lithe. They paced with rhythmic dignity. In the downshafts of light their coats shone ebony. The eye observed the fineness of bone, the accuracy of adjustment. As the dogs advanced they gained altitude, circling, until they stood as if freed from the land against the flat blue of the sky.

The eye closed and the dogs sank back into their proper darkness. The eye opened and the dogs stood black against the blue of the iris for the sky was in the eye yet severed from it.

In the light of the eye the dogs could be observed clearly—three Labrador retrievers, gentle, courteous, and playful with the sedate bearing of dogs well schooled to know their worth, to know their place, and to bend willingly to their master's will. One stretched out, face flattened. Its eyes, darker than the grass on which it lay, looked over the rolling hills to the distant saw-tooth pattern of volcanic stone. Behind it the other two sat, tongues dripping red over the saw-tooth pattern of volcanic lip.

The dogs were against the eye and in the eye. They were in the land but not of it. They were of Coyote's house, but became aristocrats in time which had now yielded them up to the timeless hills. They, too, were gods, but civil gods made tractable by use and useless by custom. Here in the hills they would starve or lose themselves in wandering. They were aliens in this spot or exiles returned as if they had never been.

The eye closed. It opened and closed again. Each time the eye opened the dogs circled the hill to the top and trained their gaze on the distant rock. Each time they reached the height of land with more difficulty. At last all three lay pressing thin bellies and jaws against the unyielding earth.

Now when the eye opened there were four dogs and a man and the eye belonged to the man and stared from the hill of his head along the slope of his arm on which the four dogs lay. And the fourth which he had whistled up from his own depths was glossy and fat as the others had been. But this, too, he knew in the end would climb lackluster as the rest.

So he opened the volcanic ridge of his jaws and bit the tail from each dog and stood with the four tails in his hand and the dogs fawned graciously before him begging decorously for food. And he fed the tail of the first dog to the fourth and the tail of the fourth to the first. In the same way he disposed of the tails of the second and the third. And the dogs sat with their eyes on his mouth.

Then he bit the off-hind leg from each and offered it to the other; then the near-hind leg, and the dogs grew plump and shone in the downlight of his glance. Then the jaw opened and closed on the two forelegs and on the left haunch and the right and each dog bowed and slavered and ate what was offered.

Soon four fanged jaws lay on the hill and before them the man stood rolling the amber eyes in his hands and these he tossed impartially to the waiting jaws. Then he fed the bone of the first jaw to the fourth and that of the second to the third. And taking the two jaws that lay before him he fed tooth to tooth until one tooth remained and this he hid in his own belly.

1980

P.K. Page

b. 1916

Patricia Kathleen Page calls herself a traveller without a map. Certainly journeys have played an important role in her life and work. Born in England and raised in Calgary, Winnipeg, and Saint John, N.B., she moved in the 1940s to Montreal, where she worked first as a clerk and then as a scriptwriter for the National Film Board. There she met its head, W. Arthur Irwin, whom she later married; and when Irwin entered the Department of External Affairs, his diplomatic career took the two of them abroad in the early fifties to Australia, Brazil, and Mexico. It was not until 1964 that they returned to Canada and settled in Victoria, B.C.

Although P.K. Page began to write in her teens, her work did not receive public recognition until Alan Crawley published her poetry, beginning with the first issue of his *Contemporary Verse* (1941-52). Shortly after submitting her work to Crawley, Page moved to Montreal and began an association with Patrick Anderson's *Preview* (1942-5). Though she has never been a political poet, the influence of Anderson and of the social movements in Montreal in the forties is evident in her poetry of this period: her early verse expresses her concerns about the dehumanizing effect of social institutions. In 1944 Page's work appeared in *Unit of Five*, a collection of a small group of poets—including Louis Dudek, Raymond Souster, James Wreford, and its editor, Ronald Hambleton—which, like the thirties anthology, *New Provinces*, showed the artistic and philosophical positions of Canada's emerging poets. These poets were also among those included in

John Sutherland's *Other Canadians* (1947), a larger anthology that was published in response to the 1943 edition of A.J.M. Smith's *Book of Canadian Poetry*, which itself contained four poems by Page. During this period she also produced her own volume of poetry, *As Ten As Twenty* (1946), and shortly after she left Canada a second volume appeared, *The Metal and the Flower* (1954), which won a Governor General's Award.

Page continued to produce poetry during her three years in Australia, but after moving to Latin America she found herself unable to write; drawing and painting became her chief creative outlet until she returned to Canada. In 1967 *Cry Ararat: Poems New and Selected* was published, followed by *The Sun and the Moon and Other Fictions* (1973), which contains short stories and a novella, *The Sun and the Moon*, written when Page was twenty-one (it was originally published in 1944 under the pseudonym 'Judith Cape'). Another collection, *Poems Selected and New*, appeared in 1974. Her latest book, *Evening Dance of the Grey Flies* (1981), contains new poems, and a short story, 'Unless the eye catch fire . . .'. She has also edited an anthology of very brief poems, *To Say the Least: Canadian Poets from A to Z* (1979).

Page's poetry owes what she calls 'nourishment' to several different lyric traditions: that of the English poets of the thirties, particularly Spender, Wilfred Owen, and Auden; of certain continental writers, such as Rainer Maria Rilke and Federico García Lorca; and of Middle Eastern poets, especially those who are part of the mystical Sufi tradition. Central also to Page's use of imagery and to her philosophy are the writings of Jung and Yeats who, along with the Sufi writers, have provided the basis for her markedly Platonic poetics. She believes that poetry is an inspired creativity that calls not only for craft but also for 'a state of purity . . . a burning with some clear enough light' from which the poet receives poetic vision. This Delphic attitude—that 'the theme chooses you' and that 'You have to be worthy of being chosen'—is central to an understanding of her poetry. Underlying her work is the image of the poet as dreamer, one who has a lifeline to the 'collective unconscious', to a 'memory of Eden or heaven'—which, as she expresses it, gives the artist the 'seed' of his work and allows him access to another dimension in which he must search for the dismembered parts of his poem before he can assemble them in the real world. Images of the individual on a spiritual quest appear in both her poems and her fiction: her characters tend to journey to a remembered garden only to find that it is not the Edenic ideal of their dreams. They exist in a fractured reality controlled by the poet's magic vision, a reality that 'makes spinach of space and time' and that often contains magical, other-worldly events:

I seem to be attempting to copy exactly something which exists in a dimension where worldly senses are inadequate. As if a thing only felt had to be extracted from invisibility and transposed into a seen thing, a heard thing. The struggle is to fit the 'made' to the 'sensed' in such a way that the whole can occupy a world larger than the one I normally inhabit. (Canadian Literature, No. 46, 1970)

Despite her preoccupation with 'invisibility', her poems are neither vague nor abstract; her highly sensual images integrate the mystical and worldly dimensions so effectively that mystery becomes a necessary part of sensory experience. Page achieves this integration chiefly by means of visual cues—references to eyes and seeing, to space and shape, and to colour—but she also makes her images dissolve into one another so as to alter the reader's concept of the nature of reality. Page's reader, along with the travellers in her poems, discovers that entrancing visual images can be distorting lenses that obscure the truth; nevertheless sensory experience remains necessary as the only pathway to revelation, the departure-point of a lifelong spiritual quest. The effect of stimulating the sensory faculties can be that described in a poem by Theodore Roszak to which Page has several times referred:

Unless the eye catch fire
The God will not be seen
Unless the ear catch fire
The God will not be heard
Unless the tongue catch fire
The God will not be named
Unless the heart catch fire
The God will not be loved
Unless the mind catch fire
The God will not be known
(Where the Wasteland Ends, 1973)

The Stenographers

After the brief bivouac of Sunday,
their eyes, in the forced march of Monday to Saturday,
hoist the white flag, flutter in the snow-storm of paper,
haul it down and crack in the mid-sun of temper.

In the pause between the first draft and the carbon
they glimpse the smooth hours when they were children—
the ride in the ice-cart, the ice-man's name,
the end of the route and the long walk home;

remember the sea where floats at high tide
were sea marrows growing on the scatter-green vine   10
or spools of grey toffee, or wasps' nests on water;
remember the sand and the leaves of the country.

Bell rings and they go and the voice draws their pencil
like a sled across snow; when its runners are frozen
rope snaps and the voice then is pulling no burden
but runs like a dog on the winter of paper.

Their climates are winter and summer—no wind
for the kites of their hearts—no wind for a flight;
a breeze at the most, to tumble them over
and leave them like rubbish—the boy-friends of blood.   20

In the inch of the noon as they move they are stagnant.
The terrible calm of the noon is their anguish;
the lip of the counter, the shapes of the straws
like icicles breaking their tongues, are invaders.

Their beds are their oceans—salt water of weeping
the waves that they know—the tide before sleep;
and fighting to drown they assemble their sheep
in columns and watch them leap desks for their fences
and stare at them with their own mirror-worn faces.

In the felt of the morning the calico-minded,   30
sufficiently starched, insert papers, hit keys,
efficient and sure as their adding machines;
yet they weep in the vault, they are taut as net curtains
stretched upon frames. In their eyes I have seen
the pin men[1] of madness in marathon trim
race round the track of the stadium pupil.

1946

---

[1] 'Stick figures, such as children draw' (Page).

Stories of Snow

Those in the vegetable rain retain
an area behind their sprouting eyes
held soft and rounded with the dream of snow
precious and reminiscent as those globes—
souvenir of some never-nether land—
which hold their snow-storms circular, complete,
high in a tall and teakwood cabinet.

In countries where the leaves are large as hands
where flowers protrude their fleshy chins
and call their colours,   10
an imaginary snow-storm sometimes falls
among the lilies.
And in the early morning one will waken
to think the glowing linen of his pillow
a northern drift, will find himself mistaken
and lie back weeping.
And there the story shifts from head to head,
of how in Holland, from their feather beds
hunters arise and part the flakes and go
forth to the frozen lakes in search of swans—   20
the snow-light falling white along their guns,
their breath in plumes.
While tethered in the wind like sleeping gulls
ice-boats wait the raising of their wings
to skim the electric ice at such a speed
they leap jet strips of naked water,
and how these flying, sailing hunters feel
air in their mouths as terrible as ether.
And on the story runs that even drinks
in that white landscape dare to be no colour;   30
how flasked and water clear, the liquor slips
silver against the hunters' moving hips.
And of the swan in death these dreamers tell
of its last flight and how it falls, a plummet,
pierced by the freezing bullet
and how three feathers, loosened by the shot,
descend like snow upon it.
While hunters plunge their fingers in its down
deep as a drift, and dive their hands
up to the neck of the wrist   40
in that warm metamorphosis of snow
as gentle as the sort that woodsmen know
who, lost in the white circle, fall at last
and dream their way to death.

And stories of this kind are often told
in countries where great flowers bar the roads
with reds and blues which seal the route to snow—
as if, in telling, raconteurs unlock

the colour with its complement and go
through to the area behind the eyes   50
where silent, unrefractive whiteness lies.

1946

If It Were You

If it were you, say, you
who scanning the personal map one day knew
your sharp eyes water and grow colour blind,
unable to distinguish green from blue
and everything terribly run together as if rain
had smudged the markings on the paper—
a child's painting after a storm—
and the broad avenue erased,
the landmarks gone;
and you, bewildered—not me this time and not   10
the cold unfriendly neighbour or the face in the news—
who walked a blind circle in a personal place;

and if you became lost, say, on the lawn,
unable to distinguish left from right
and that strange longitude that divides the body
sharply in half—that line that separates
so that one hand could never be the other—
dissolved and both your hands were one,
then in the garden though birds went on with their singing
and on the ground   20
flowers wrote their signatures in coloured ink—
would you call help like a woman assaulted,
cry to be found?

No ears would understand. Your friends and you
would be practically strangers, there would be no face
more familiar than this unfamiliar place
and there would be walls of air, invisible, holding
you single and directionless in space.

First you would be busy as a woodsman marking
the route out, making false starts and then   30
remembering yesterday when it was easy
you would grow lazy.
Summer would sit upon you then as on a stone
and you would be tense for a time beneath the morning sun
but always lonely
and birds perhaps would brush your coat and become
angels of deliverance
for a moment only;
clutching their promising wings you would discover

they were illusive and gone   40
as the lost lover.
Would you call Ariel,[1] Ariel, in the garden,
in a dream within a dream be Orpheus[2]
and for a certain minute take a step
delicately across the grass?

If so, there would be no answer nor reply
and not one coming forward from the leaves.
No bird nor beast with a challenging look
or friendly.
Simply nothing but you and the green garden,   50
you and the garden.

And there you might stay forever, mechanically
occupied, but if you raised your head
madness would rush at you from the shrubbery
or the great sun, stampeding through the sky
would stop and drop—
a football in your hands
and shrink as you watched it
to a small dark dot
forever escaping focus   60
like the injury to the cornea which darts
hard as a cinder across the sight but dims
fading into the air like a hocus-pocus
the minute that you are aware
and stare at it.

Might you not, if it were you,
bewildered, broken,
slash your own wrists, commit
an untidy murder in the leafy lane

and scar the delicate air with your cries or sit   70
weeping, weeping in the public square
your flimsy butterfly fingers in your hair
your face destroyed by rain?

If it were you, the person you call 'I',
the one you loved and worked for,
the most high
now become Ishmael,[3]
might you not
grow phobias about calendars and clocks,
stare at your face in the mirror, not knowing it   80

[1]Prospero's servant in Shakespeare's *The Tempest*; an airy spirit who assists his master with his magic.
[2]Poet and musician of Greek legend whose singing enchanted all who heard it.
[3]Abraham's son (by Sarah's handmaiden, Hagar), who was cast out of Abraham's household; thus, an outcast (Genesis 21:8-21).

and feel an identity with idiots and dogs
as all the exquisite unborns of your dreams
deserted you to snigger behind their hands?

1946

Portrait of Marina

Far out the sea has never moved. It is
Prussian[1] forever, rough as teazled wool
some antique skipper worked into a frame
to bear his lost four-master.
                               Where it hangs
now in a sunny parlour, none recalls
how all his stitches, interspersed with oaths
had made his one pale spinster daughter grow
transparent with migraines—and how his call
fretted her more than waves.   10
                               Her name
Marina, for his youthful wish—
boomed at the font of that small salty church
where sailors lurched like drunkards, would, he felt
make her a water woman, rich with bells.
To her the name Marina simply meant
he held his furious needle for her thin
fingers to thread again with more blue wool
to sew the ocean of his memory.
Now, where the picture hangs, a dimity[2]   20
young inland housewife with inherited
clocks under bells and ostrich eggs on shelves
pours amber tea in small rice china cups
and reconstructs
how great-great-grandpapa at ninety-three
his fingers knotted with arthritis, his
old eyes grown agatey with cataracts
became as docile as a child again—
that fearful salty man—
and sat, wrapped round in faded paisley shawls   30
gently embroidering.
While Aunt Marina in grey worsted, warped
without a smack of salt, came to his call
the sole survivor of his last shipwreck.

                    *

Slightly off shore it glints. Each wave is capped
with broken mirrors. Like Marina's head

---

[1]Prussian blue, i.e., dark blue; 'teazled': teased or roughened.
[2]Crisp cotton fabric.

the glinting of these waves.
She walked forever antlered with migraines
her pain forever putting forth new shoots
until her strange unlovely head became   40
a kind of candelabra—delicate—
where all her tears were perilously hung
and caught the light as waves that catch the sun.
The salt upon the panes, the grains of sand
that crunched beneath her heel
her father's voice, 'Marina!'—all these broke
her trembling edifice. The needle shook
like ice between her fingers.
In her head
too many mirrors dizzied her and broke.   50

*

But where the wave breaks, where it rises green
turns into gelatine, becomes a glass
simply for seeing stones through, runs across
the coloured shells and pebbles of the shore
and makes an aspic of them
then sucks back
in foam and undertow—
this aspect of the sea
Marina never knew.
For her the sea was Father's Fearful Sea   60
harsh with sea serpents
winds and drowning men.
For her it held no spiral of a shell
for her descent to dreams,
it held no bells.
And where it moved in shallows it was more
imminently a danger, more alive
than where it lay off shore full fathom five.

1954

Photos of a Salt Mine

How innocent their lives look,
how like a child's
dream of caves and winter, both combined;
the steep descent to whiteness
and the stope[1]
with its striated walls
their folds all leaning as if pointing to
the greater whiteness still,
that great white bank

[1]An excavation in the form of steps made as ore is mined from vertical or steeply inclined veins.

with its decisive front,   10
that seam upon a slope,
salt's lovely ice.

And wonderful underfoot the snow of salt
the fine
particles a broom could sweep,
one thinks
muckers might make angels in its drifts
as children do in snow,
lovers in sheets,
lie down and leave imprinted where they lay   20
a feathered creature holier than they.

And in the outworked stopes
with lamps and ropes
up miniature matterhorns
the miners climb
probe with their lights
the ancient folds of rock—
syncline[2] and anticline—
and scoop from darkness an Aladdin's cave:
rubies and opals glitter from its walls.   30

But hoses douse the brilliance of these jewels,
melt fire to brine.
Salt's bitter water trickles thin and forms,
slow fathoms down,
a lake within a cave,
lacquered with jet—
white's opposite.
There grey on black the boating miners float
to mend the stays and struts of that old stope
and deeply underground   40
their words resound,
are multiplied by echo, swell and grow
and make a climate of a miner's voice.

So all the photographs like children's wishes
are filled with caves or winter,
innocence
has acted as a filter,
selected only beauty from the mine.
Except in the last picture,
it is shot   50
from an acute high angle. In a pit
figures the size of pins are strangely lit
and might be dancing but you know they're not.

[2]Low, troughlike fold in stratified rock, the opposite of 'anticline': fold with strata sloping downwards on both sides away from a common crest.

Like Dante's vision of the nether hell[3]
men struggle with the bright cold fires of salt,
locked in the black inferno of the rock:
the filter here, not innocence but guilt.

1954

[3]Lower part of hell that contains both fire and ice.

Cry Ararat![1]

I
In the dream the mountain near
but without sound.
A dream through binoculars
seen sharp and clear:
the leaves moving, turning
in a far wind
no ear can hear.

First soft in the distance,
blue in blue air
then sharpening, quickening   10
taking on green.
Swiftly the fingers
seek accurate focus
(the bird
has vanished so often
before the sharp lens
could deliver it)
then as if from the sea
the mountain appears
emerging new-washed   20
growing maples and firs.
The faraway, here.

Do not reach to touch it
nor labour to hear.
Return to your hand
the sense of the hand;
return to your ear
the sense of the ear.
Remember the statue,
that space in the air   30

[1]Mountain range on which Noah's ark landed. As the flood-waters began to recede, Noah—believing
that God would once again provide a fertile earth—sent out the dove which, on its second excursion,
returned bearing an olive branch.

which with nothing to hold
what the minute is giving
is through each point
where its marble touches air.

Then will each leaf and flower
each bird and animal
become as perfect as
the thing its name evoked
when busy as a child
the world stopped at the Word   40
and Flowers more real than flowers
grew vivid and immense;
and Birds more beautiful
and Leaves more intricate
flew, blew and quilted all
the quick landscape.

So flies and blows the dream
embracing like a sea
all that in it swims
when dreaming, you desire   50
and ask for nothing more
than stillness to receive
the I-am animal,
the We-are leaf and flower,
the distant mountain near.

II
So flies and blows the dream that haunts us when we wake
to the unreality of bright day:
the far thing almost sensed by the still skin
and then the focus lost, the mountain gone.
This is the loss that haunts our daylight hours   60
leaving us parched at nightfall
blowing like last year's leaves
sibilant on blossoming trees
and thirsty for the dream of the mountain
more real than any event:
more real than strangers passing on the street
in a city's architecture white as bone
or the immediate companion.

But sometimes there is one
raw with the dream of flying: 70
'I, a bird,
landed that very instant
and complete—
as if I had drawn a circle in my flight
and filled its shape—
find air a perfect fit.

But this my grief,
that with the next tentative lift
of my indescribable wings
the ceiling looms   80
heavy as a tomb.

'Must my most exquisite and private dream
remain unleavened?
Must this flipped and spinning coin that sun
could gild and make miraculous become
so swiftly pitiful?
The vision of the flight it imitates
burns brightly in my head as if a star
rushed down to touch me where I stub against
what must forever be my underground.'   90

III
These are the dreams that haunt us,
these the fears.
Will the grey weather wake us,
toss us twice in the terrible night to tell us
the flight is cancelled
and the mountain lost?

O, then cry Ararat!

The dove believed
in her sweet wings and in the rising peak
with such a washed and easy innocence   100
that she found rest on land for the sole of her foot
and, silver, circled back,
a green twig in her beak.

The leaves that make the tree by day,
the green twig the dove saw fit
to lift across a world of water
break in a wave about our feet.
The bird in the thicket with his whistle
the crystal lizard in the grass
the star and shell   110
tassel and bell
of wild flowers blowing where we pass,
this flora-fauna flotsam, pick and touch,
requires the focus of the total I.

A single leaf can block a mountainside;
all Ararat be conjured by a leaf.

1967

16 | P.K. Page

Arras[1]

Consider a new habit—classical,
and trees espaliered on the wall like candelabra.
How still upon that lawn our sandalled feet.

But a peacock rattling his rattan tail and screaming
has found a point of entry. Through whose eye
did it insinuate in furled disguise
to shake its jewels and silk upon that grass?

The peaches hang like lanterns. No one joins
those figures on the arras.
             Who am I   10
or who am I become that walking here
I am observer, other, Gemini,
starred for a green garden of cinema?

I ask, what did they deal me in this pack?
The cards, all suits, are royal when I look.
My fingers slipping on a monarch's face
twitch and grow slack.
I want a hand to clutch, a heart to crack.

No one is moving now, the stillness is
infinite. If I should make a break. . . .   20
take to my springy heels. . . . ? But nothing moves.
The spinning world is stuck upon its poles,
the stillness points a bone[2] at me. I fear
the future on this arras.
             I confess:

It was my eye.
Voluptuous it came.
Its head the ferrule[3] and its lovely tail
folded so sweetly; it was strangely slim
to fit the retina. And then it shook   30
and was a peacock—living patina,
eye-bright, maculate!
Does no one care?

I thought their hands might hold me if I spoke.
I dreamed the bite of fingers in my flesh,
their poke smashed by an image, but they stand

---

[1]Wall hanging, particularly a tapestry.
[2]'Aboriginal projective magic. A prepared human or kangaroo bone is pointed by a sorcerer at an intended victim (who may be miles away) to bring about his death' (from Page's glossary of Australian terms in *Cry Ararat!*).
[3]Metal cap used to reinforce or secure the end of a pole or handle—here belonging to an umbrella.

as if within a treacle,[4] motionless,
folding slow eyes on nothing. While they stare
another line has trolled the encircling air,
another bird assumes its furled disguise   40

1967

[4]Molasses or sweet syrup; used here as that which entraps the insects it attracts.

Preparation

Go out of your mind.
Prepare to go mad.
Prepare to break
split along cracks
inhabit the darks of your eyes
inhabit the whites.

Prepare to be huge.
Be prepared to be small
the least molecule
of an unlimited form.   10
Be a limited form
and spin in your skin
one point in its whole.

Be prepared to prepare
for what you have dreamed
to burn and be burned
to burst like a pod
to break at your seams.

Be pre-pared. And pre-pare.
But its never like that.   20
It is where you are not
that the fissure occurs
and the light crashes in.

1974

Another Space

Those people in a circle on the sand
are dark against its gold
turn like a wheel
revolving in a horizontal plane
whose axis—do I dream it?—
vertical
invisible
immeasurably tall
rotates a starry spool.

Yet *if* I dream   10
why in the name of heaven are fixed parts
within me set in motion
like a poem?

Those people in a circle reel me in.
Down the whole length of golden beach I come
willingly pulled by their rotation
slow
as a moon pulls waters
on a string
their turning circle winds around its rim.   20

I see them there in three dimensions yet
their height implies another space
their clothes'
surprising chiaroscuro[1] postulates
a different spectrum.
What kaleidoscope
does air construct
that all their movements make a compass rose
surging and altering?
I speculate   30
on some dimension I can barely guess.

Nearer I see them dark-skinned.
They are dark. And beautiful.
Great human sunflowers spinning in a ring
cosmic as any bumble-top
the vast
procession of the planets in their dance.
And nearer still I see them—"a Chagall"[2]—
each fiddling on an instrument—its strings
of some black woollen fibre   40
and its bow—feathered—
an arrow almost.
                      Arrow *is*.

[1]The use of light and shade in painting.
[2]Marc Chagall (b.1887). Russian-Jewish painter and illustrator, resident of Paris; many of his paintings contain images of dancing fiddlers.

For now the headman—one step forward shoots
(or does he bow or does he lift a kite
up and over the bright pale dunes of air?)
to strike the absolute centre of my skull
my absolute centre somehow
with such skill
such staggering lightness   50
that the blow is love.

And something in me melts.
It is as if a glass partition melts—
or something I had always thought was glass—
some pane that halved my heart
is proved, in its melting, ice.

And to-fro all the atoms pass
in bright osmosis
hitherto
in stasis locked   60
where now a new
direction opens like an eye.

1974

After Reading 'Albino Pheasants'[1]

For Pat Lane

Pale beak . . . pale eye . . . the dark imagination
flares like magnesium. Add but *pale flesh*
and I am lifted to a weightless world:
watered cerulean,[2] chrome-yellow (light)
and green, veronese[3]—if I remember—a soft wash
recalls a summer evening sky.

At Barro de Navidad[4] we watched the sky
fade softly like a bruise. Was it imagination
that showed us Venus phosphorescent in a wash
of air and ozone?—a phosphorescence flesh   10
wears like a mantle in bright moonlight,
a natural skin-tone in that other world.

Why should I wish to escape this world?
Why should three phrases alter the colour of the sky

[1]A poem by Patrick Lane (see page 497). Page's poem originally appeared in 1978 as 'Sestina for Pat Lane after Reading "Albino Pheasants" '
[2]Sky blue; light, slightly greenish blue.
[3]'Rich but light green' (Page).
[4]The west coast of Mexico, which Page describes as 'wild and unbelievable'.

the clarity, texture even, of the light?
What is there about the irrepressible imagination
that the adjective *pale* modifying *beak, eye* and *flesh*
can set my sensibilities awash?

If with my thickest brush I were to lay a wash
of thinnest water-color I could make a world   20
as unlike my own dense flesh
as the high-noon midsummer sky;
but it would not catch at my imagination
or change the waves or particles of light

yet *pale* can tip the scales, make light
this heavy planet. If I were to wash
everything I own in mercury, would imagination
run rampant in that suddenly silver world—
free me from gravity, set me floating sky-
ward—thistledown—permanently disburdened of my flesh?   30

Like cygnets hatched by ducks, our minds and flesh
are imprinted[5] early—what to me is light
may be dark to one born under a sunny sky.
And however cool the water my truth won't wash
without shrinking except in its own world
which is one part matter, nine parts imagination.

I fear flesh which blocks imagination,
the light of reason which constricts the world.
Pale beak . . . pale eye . . . pale flesh . . . My sky's awash.

1981

[5] A young animal is said to 'imprint' on the adult animal it most often sees in the period after its birth; that is, to identify it as its parent and therefore identify itself as a member of the same species.

Chinese Boxes

Box within box.
I know the order, know
large to small diminishing until
that cube the size of sugar—like a die—
is cast within its core
and therein set—dimensionless—
an all-ways turning eye—
a dot, an aleph,[1] which

[1] First letter in the Hebrew alphabet; here Page uses it in the same way as Jorge-Luis Borges does in his story 'The Aleph', where 'an Aleph is one of the points in space containing all points', and when looked into, reveals 'all points in the universe'.

with one swift glance
sees heaven and hell united   10
as a globe
in whose harmonious spinning
day and night
and birth and death are conjured into one,
where seasons lie like compass points
and where, twinned with its answer,
question is born null.

Box within box.
From small to large increasing—
angles, blocks,   20
enormous, made of plexiglass,
the sky
filling with them,
visible as air
is visible when briefly smoked with breath
until their structures grow too large and sheer
for sight to encompass—
cellophane box kites
huge as the Kaaba[2]
luminous as ice   30
and imperceptible to any sense
more coarse than sightings of that inner eye
which sees the absolute
in emptiness.

1981

[2] A cubical stone building standing in the court of the Great Mosque of Mecca; it is considered by Muslims to be the oldest and most sacred sanctuary of Allah. Page has described it as 'dwarfing humanity'.

For Mstislav Rostropovich[1] with Love

Listening ear
a conduit for these sounds,
I watch your bowing arm
and see beneath
your sleeve, shirtcuff
and pliant sheath of skin,
a wrist of stainless steel
precision-turned,
fluid with bearings,

[1] (b.1927). Well-known cellist, now conductor of the Washington National Symphony Orchestra. Page wrote this poem after attending a concert in which he played a Dvořák cello concerto.

bright as adamant   10
with power to blind us
like a silver sun;
while gazing fearless
fire into fire
the enduring pupil
of my inner eye
made in the manner
that you made your wrist—
of matter primal and alchemical
impervious to accident   20
or hurt.

This is already much.
But there is more:
what falls apart is held together
each
atom aligned
and in its proper place.
So great an order interlocks my flesh
that I, as centred
as a spinning top   30
am perfectly asleep
(which, in this sense
means, if not *perfectly*
then *more* awake).

And as an atom—
one among these rapt
like-centred listeners—
I am part
of that essential
intricate design   40
which forms a larger unit—
mutable
around its sleeping core—
while it, in turn,
part of a vaster
one I barely glimpse—
already cosmic—
leads us to the stars.

Maestro, *salud*.
Perfection in an art   50
can heal an open wound,
a broken heart
or fuse fragmented man.

Tonight, are we not proof?

1981

Miriam Waddington

b. 1917

Born into Winnipeg's Russian-Jewish immigrant community, Miriam Dworkin Waddington grew up in a climate of socialism and European traditions. In 1931 her parents moved to Ottawa; there, and in Montreal, she became acquainted with artists and intellectuals, many of them part of Montreal's Jewish community. During the Depression, Waddington was an undergraduate student at the University of Toronto (1936-9). After marrying, she remained in Toronto until the end of the Second World War. Although she had been writing poems since childhood, her poetry written during the war gained her public recognition. In 1943 John Sutherland offered to publish her work in his magazine, *First Statement* (1942-5); subsequently her first book, *Green World* (1945), was published by his First Statement Press. These poems, while lyrical and concerned with man's relationship to the natural world— they have been compared to those of Dylan Thomas—also reflect the social interests that led Waddington to take a diploma in social work from the University of Toronto (1942) and a Master's degree in the same field from the University of Pennsylvania (1945).

After the war Waddington moved, with her husband, to Montreal where she pursued a career in social work. While a caseworker in hospitals, prisons, and social agencies, she continued to write, publishing *The Second Silence* (1955) and *The Season's Lovers* (1958). Many poems of this period are angry responses to social conditions that Waddington observed. The strongest of these are self-reflective poems, such as 'My Lessons in the Jail'.

In 1960 Waddington, just divorced, moved back to Toronto with her young children, leaving social work to begin a new career—as a university teacher of literature, instructing evenings while she worked on a Master's in English at the University of Toronto (1968). In 1964 she accepted a full-time teaching position at York University, remaining there until her retirement as professor in 1983.

In the last twenty years Waddington has published five books of poetry: *The Glass Trumpet* (1966), *Say Yes* (1969), *Driving Home: Poems New and Selected* (1972), *The Price of Gold* (1976), and *The Visitants* (1981). While commonplace experience has always been important to her writing, her later work has moved from a poetry emanating from social experience to a more personal, introspective one. Social inequity has been displaced as a major topic by themes of loss and mortality. While close in overall structure to the meditations on nature that appear in *Green World*, these later poems have short lines rather than long, loose ones and a simplified, less dramatic diction.

Waddington's writing has not been limited to poetry. Her short stories have recently been collected in *Summer at Lonely Beach and Other Stories* (1982), and she has produced a body of academic and critical work. Of particular importance to her have been her studies on A.M. Klein—her Master's thesis on him was published in 1970—and John Sutherland. She has edited a collection of Klein's poems (1974), and a volume of Sutherland's prose and poetry (1972).

Both Klein and Sutherland, members of the socially active Montreal writers' movement in the forties of which Waddington was also a part, moved in their careers from a near religious faith in the efficacy of poetry for effecting social change to a profound disillusionment with their old goals. Waddington has come to share their sense of an empty and valueless world, but she has not been led to retreat from her earlier positions. While she has been greatly influenced by her European background, and her poetry has largely been determined by her being both a woman and a Jew, these aspects are overshadowed in her work by a more generalized sense of displacement. Throughout her later poems one finds accounts of a 'darkening world' in which beliefs, traditions, and relationships become fragmented and are lost. Yet for Waddington the loss is always mitigated, for she retains threads of traditions that still anchor her, memories that keep her company, and an ironic sense of humour.

My Lessons in the Jail

Walk into the prison, that domed citadel
that yellow skull of stone and sutured steel,
walk under their mottoes, show your pass,
salute their Christ to whom you cannot kneel.

In the white-tiled room arrange the interview
with the man who took his daughter and learn
that every man is usual but none are equal
in the dark rivers that in them burn.

And take this man's longest bleakest year
between done act and again-done act, and take   10
his misery and need, stand against his tears
and transform them to such a truth as slakes

The very core of thirst and be sure
the thirst is his and not your own deep need
to spurt fine fountains; accept accept
his halting words—since you must learn to read

Between the lines his suffering and doubt.
Be faithful to your pity, be careworn,
though all this buffet you and beat and cruelly
test you—you chose this crown of thorns.   20

Wear it with grace and when you rise to go
thank him and don't let yourself forget
how hard it is to thank and to beholden be
one to another and spin your role out yet

For moments in the hallway, compose your face
to sale good humour, conceal your sex:
smile at the brute who runs the place
and memorized the banner *Christus Rex*.

1958

Looking for Strawberries in June

I have to tell you
about the words I
used to know, such
words, so sheer, thin
transparent, so light
and quick, I had such
words for wind for
whatever grew
I knew a certain
leaf-language from   10
somewhere, but now

it is all used up
I have come to the
end of some line or
other like walking
on railroad ties in
the country looking
for strawberries in
June and suddenly
the ties end in the   20
middle of no-place
and I stop to look
around to take my
direction but I

don't recognize the
landscape. It is all
grey, feathery, the
voices of birds are
foreign, yet I used
to know such words   30
japanned, brushed and
papery, whitefolded
Russian flowerwords

cabbage roses, huge
holes in the head of
the universe pouring
out rosy revolutions:

and I used to know
swarthy eastern words
heavy with Hebrew, then   40
I was kidnapped by
gypsies, I knew the
up and down of their
dark-blue anger, the
leathery touch of
the fortune-telling
begging wandering
words, but what's
become of them?
I don't know, I'm   50

just standing here
on the threshold of
a different country,
everything is made
of plastic and silence;
what month is it any-
way? I'm knocking at
the door but nobody
answers. I mutter *Lenin
Karl Marx, Walt Whitman*   60
Chaucer, Hopkins, even
Archibald Lampman, but
nobody comes, I don't

know the password
I only know it has
nothing to do with
being good or true
nothing to do with
being beautiful.

1968

Icons

Suddenly
in middle age
instead of withering
into blindness
and burying myself
underground
I grow delicate
and fragile
superstitious;
I carry icons   10
I have begun
to worship
images.

I take them out
and prop them up
on bureau tops
in hotel rooms
in Spain
I study them
in locked libraries   20
in Leningrad
I untie them
from tourist packages
in Italy
they warm me
in the heatless winters
of London in the
hurry-up buses
of Picadilly.

My icons are not   30
angels or holy
babies they have
nothing to do
with saints or
madonnas, they
are mostly of
seashores summer
and love which I no
longer believe in
but I still believe   40
in the images,
I still preserve
the icons:

a Spanish factory
worker talks to me

in a street behind
the cathedral he
offers me *un poco*
amor, the scars on
his hand, his wounded   50
country and the black-
jacketed police; he
touches me on the
arm and other places,
and the alcoholic
in the blazing square
drinks brandy, confides
that fortunes can still
be made in Birmingham
but he has a bad   60
lung is hard of
hearing and owns
an apartment in Palma.

1969

Advice to the Young

1
Keep bees and
grow asparagus,
watch the tides
and listen to the
wind instead of
the politicians
make up your own
stories and believe
them if you want to
live the good life.   10

2
All rituals
are instincts
never fully
trust them but
study to im-
prove biology
with reason.

3
Digging trenches
for asparagus
is good for the   20
muscles and

waiting for the
plants to settle
teaches patience
to those who are
usually in too
much of a hurry.

4
There is morality
in bee-keeping
it teaches how   30
not to be afraid
of the bee swarm
it teaches how
not to be afraid of
finding new places
and building in them
all over again.

1972

The Nineteen Thirties
Are Over

The nineteen thirties
are over; we survived
the depression, the Sacco-
Vanzetti[1] of childhood
saw Tom Mooney[2] smiling
at us from photographs,
put a rose on the grave
of Eugene Debs,[3] listened
to our father's stories
of the Winnipeg strike[4] and   10
joined the study groups
of the OBU[5] always keeping
one eye on the revolution.

[1]Nicola Sacco (1891-1927) and Bartolomeo Vanzetti (1888-1927), Italian-born political activists living in the U.S., were tried, convicted, and executed for murder; it has been widely held that their conviction, which became emblematic of an extreme misuse of a legal system, rested more on their political activities and national origins than on evidence related to the murder.

[2]American anarchist and labour agitator, whose controversial conviction and imprisonment for a 1916 bombing in San Francisco ended with his pardon in 1939, after years of leftist activity to gain his freedom; his story was celebrated in song by folk-singer and union supporter, Woody Guthrie.

[3](1855-1926), American labour leader and five-time Socialist candidate for President of the United States (1900-20).

[4]Winnipeg General Strike, a bloody and bitter dispute (following the demobilization at the end of the First World War) that paralysed Winnipeg between 15 May and 25 June 1919.

[5]'One Big Union'; one of the many factors that played a part in the Winnipeg strike, it was based on the concept that groups of workers could achieve their goals by collectively refusing to work.

Later we played records
with thorn needles, Josh
White's *Talking Union*[6] and
Prokofief's *Lieutenant Kije*,[7]
shuddered at the sound of
bells and all those wolves
whirling past us in snow   20
on the corner of Portage
and Main, but in my mind
summer never ended on the
shores of Gimli where we
looked across to an Icelandic
paradise we could never see
the other side of; and I
dreamed of Mexico and shining
birds who beckoned to me
from the gold-braided lianas   30
of my own wonder.

These days I step out
from the frame of my wind-
battered house into Toronto
city; somewhere I still
celebrate sunlight, touch
the rose on the grave of
Eugene Debs but I walk
carefully in this land
of sooty snow; I pass the   40
rich houses and double
garages and I am not really
this middle-aged professor
but someone from
Winnipeg whose bones ache
with the broken revolutions
of Europe, and even now
I am standing on the heaving
ploughed-up field
of my father's old war.   50

1972

[6]Josh White (1915-1969), American folk singer and guitarist, recorded an album entitled *Talking Union*, with Pete Seeger and Woody Guthrie; 'Talking Union' is a protest song written in 1941 by Lee Hays, Mill Lampell, and Seeger.
[7]Symphonic suite for orchestra, Op. 60, from a film score of the same title (1934) by Sergei Prokofief (or Prokofiev) (1891-1953), a Soviet composer noted for his stirring and heroic compositions.

Ten Years and More

When my husband
lay dying a mountain
a lake three
cities ten years
and more
lay between us:

There were our
sons my wounds
and theirs,
despair loneliness,   10
handfuls of un-
hammered nails
pictures never
hung all

The uneaten
meals and unslept
sleep; there was
retirement, and
worst of all
a green umbrella   20
he can never
take back.

I wrote him a
letter but all
I could think of
to say was: do you
remember Severn
River, the red canoe
with the sail
and lee-boards?   30

I was really saying
for the sake of our
youth and our love
I forgave him for
everything
and I was asking him
to forgive me too.

1976

Margaret Avison

b. 1918

Margaret Avison was born in Galt, Ont., and grew up there and in Alberta. She took her B.A. in English literature from Victoria College, University of Toronto, in 1940, and attended schools of creative writing at the Universities of Indiana (1955) and Chicago (1956-7)—the latter on a Guggenheim Fellowship. She returned to the University of Toronto as a graduate student in 1963. Since then Avison has worked as a librarian; as a lecturer at Scarborough College, University of Toronto; as a social worker at the Presbyterian Mission in Toronto; and as a secretary for a Southeast Asia mission. She has also been a writer-in-residence at the University of Western Ontario (1972-3) and has written book reviews, translated poems, and composed a school text on Canadian history. Meanwhile, she has worked steadily at her poetry, producing a small corpus of excellence.

Although her poems began to appear as early as the late thirties, Avison has always been diffident about collecting them for book publication. Encouraged by friends, in 1960 she finally published her first book, *Winter Sun* (which won a Governor General's Award). Two years later the American literary magazine *Origin* featured her poetry, printing thirteen poems and a letter she wrote to its editor, Cid Corman, in which she expressed her thoughts on the writing of poetry. She has since produced two more volumes, *The Dumbfounding* (1966) and *Sunblue* (1978).

Avison has written two distinct but related types of poetry. The first of these— written up to the early sixties— included poems that inquired into the nature and purpose of man, his world, and the universe. In 1963 Avison's life changed dramatically when she embraced Christianity and committed herself to contemplation and service; the poetry that followed reflects this commitment. The seeds of her religious concerns may, however, be seen in some of her earlier works, which depict a fallen world where spacious, open landscapes and awesome skies (like those she experienced growing up on the Prairies) are lost to a darker world of urban decay and atrophy. These poems struggle with the question of a creator who seems omnipotent but absent or unresponding. After her conversion there is a reassessment of the distance between man and God and an attempt to show the effects of a closer relationship between the two.

Avison's earlier poems—much like those of T.S. Eliot and Wallace Stevens— depend upon a wide knowledge of history and poetic tradition, of contemporary events and universal myths. A.J.M. Smith described her diction in this period as 'erudite, complex, archaic, simple, modern— an amalgam of the scientific and philosophical with the familiar and the new, a high style and low, pillaged and put to work'. This kind of poetry is dense and challenging, full of both difficulties and rewards. Witty and complex, it can juxtapose the painter's rules of vanishing-point perspective with our view of the world as we move through it; or it can turn the sonnet into a weapon against all sonnets. Among these earlier poems 'The Apex Animal' remained obscure enough that Avison later composed 'Strong Yellow' to explain it to an English class. (Both poems appear below.)

Since *The Dumbfounding* Avison has progressively simplified the form of her poetry. The syntax and diction of the later poems sometimes catch the inflection of her own speech and sometimes recall the oracular voice of such visionary poets as Dickinson, Hopkins, Herbert, and Traherne. The contemplative life Avison has chosen creates a tension that replaces the intricacies of her earlier, more philosophical verse: under the text of these poems the reader senses a struggle between the natural ego of a writer and the self-effacement demanded by a religious life. She still believes, as she did in her early work, that the act of seeing is not passive, that an 'optic heart' must continue to labour intellectually and spiritually to retain its passionate Christian perspective. Her poems, especially those in *Sunblue*, provide an ongoing meditation—a chronicle not only of a vision found but of the wonder and struggle it subsequently engenders.

Neverness

OR, THE ONE SHIP BEACHED
ON ONE FAR DISTANT SHORE

Old Adam,[1] with his fist-full of plump earth,
His sunbright gaze on his eternal hill
Is not historical:
His tale is never done
For us who know a world no longer bathed
In harsh splendor of economy.
We millions hold old Adam in our thoughts
A pivot for the future-past, a core
Of the one dream that never goads to action
But stains our entrails with nostalgia   10
And wrings the sweat of death in ancient eyes.

The one-celled plant is not historical.
Leeuwenhoek[2] peered through his magic window
And in a puddle glimpsed the tiny grain
Of firmament that was before the Adam.

I'd like to pull that squinting Dutchman's sleeve
And ask what were his thoughts, lying at night,
And smelling the sad spring, and thinking out
Across the fullness of night air, smelling
The dark canal, and dusty oat-bag, cheese,   20
And wet straw-splintered wood, and rust-seamed leather
And pearly grass and silent deeps of sky
Honey-combed with its million years' of light
And prune-sweet earth
Honey-combed with the silent worms of dark.
Old Leeuwenhoek must have had ribby thoughts
To hoop the hollow pounding of his heart
Those nights of spring in 1600-odd.

[1]Fallen man; Adam expelled from Eden, as opposed to the 'New Adam', or Christ.
[2]Anton van Leeuwenhoek (1632-1723), Dutch naturalist, was an important pioneer in microscopy.

It would be done if he could tell it us.
The tissue of our metaphysic cells   30
No magic window yet has dared reveal.
Our bleared world welters on
Far past the one-cell Instant. Points are spread
And privacy is unadmitted prison.

Why, now I know the lust of omnipresence!
You thousands merging lost,
      I call to you
Down the stone corridors that wall me in.

I am inside these days, snug in a job
In one of many varnished offices   40
Bleak with the wash of daylight
And us, the human pencils wearing blunt.
Soon I'll be out with you,
Another in the lonely unshut world
Where sun blinks hard on yellow brick and glazed,
On ads in sticky posterpaint
      And fuzzy
         At midday intersections.
The milk is washed down corded throats at noon
Along a thousand counters, and the hands   50
That count the nickel from a greasy palm
Have never felt an udder.
      The windy dark
That thrums high among towers and nightspun branches
Whirs through our temples with a dry confusion.
We sprawl abandoned into disbelief
And feel the pivot-picture of old Adam
On the first hill that ever was, alone,
And see the hard earth seeded with sharp snow
And dream that history is done.   60

         *

And if that be the dream that whortles[3] out
Into unending night
Then must the pivot Adam be denied
And the whole cycle ravelled and flung loose.
Is this the Epoch[4] when the age-old Serpent
Must writhe and loosen, slacking out
To a new pool of Time's eternal sun?
O Adam, will your single outline blur
At this long last when slow mist wells
Fuming from all the valleys of the earth?   70
Or will our unfixed vision rather blind
Through agony to the last gelid stare
And none be left to witness the blank mist?

1943

[3]Here, 'hurtles'.
[4]i.e. Armageddon, as described in Revelation; 'Serpent': Satan, see Revelation 12 ff.

The Butterfly

An uproar,
a spruce-green sky, bound in iron,
the murky sea running a sulphur scum,
I saw a butterfly, suddenly.
It clung between the ribs of the storm, wavering,
and flung against the battering bone-wind.
I remember it, glued to the grit of that rain-strewn beach
that glowered around it, swallowed its startled design
in the larger iridescence of unstrung dark.

That wild, sour air, those miles of crouching forest, that moth   10
when all enveloping space
is a thin glass globe, swirling with storm
tempt us to stare, and seize analogies.
The Voice that stilled the sea of Galilee[1]
overtoned by the new peace, the fierce subhuman peace
of such an east sky, blanched like Eternity.

The meaning of the moth, even the smashed moth, the
meaning of the moth—
can't we stab that one angle into the curve of space
that sweeps so unrelenting, far above,   20
towards the subhuman swamp of under-dark?

1943

[1]Christ, aboard a boat with his disciples, calmed a great storm. Mark 4: 36-41; Matt. 8: 23-7.

Perspective[1]

A sport,[2] an adventitious sprout
These eyeballs, that have somehow slipped
The mesh of generations since Mantegna?[3]

Yet I declare, your seeing is diseased
That cripples space. The fear has eaten back
Through sockets to the caverns of the brain
And made of it a sifty habitation.

We stand beholding the one plain
And in your face I see the chastening
Of its small tapering design   10
That brings up *punkt.*[4]
(The Infinite, you say,
Is an unthinkable—and pointless too—
Extension of that *punkt.*)

[1]This poem and the two preceding poems received their book publication in *The Book of Canadian Poetry* edited by A.J.M. Smith: 'Neverness' and 'The Butterfly' in the First Edition (1943), and 'Perspective' in the Second Edition (1948).
[2]A mutation, used later in the poem in the more familiar sense of the word.
[3]Andrea Mantegna (1431-1506), Italian painter and engraver famous for his use of perspective of great depth.
[4]Point; the vanishing point in perspective.

But do you miss the impact of that fierce
Raw boulder five miles off? You are not pierced
By that great spear of grass on the horizon?
   You are not smitten with the shock
     Of that great thundering sky?

Your law of optics is a quarrel   20
Of chickenfeet on paper. Does a train
Run pigeon-toed?

I took a train from here to Ottawa
On tracks that did not meet. We swelled and roared
Mile upon mightier mile, and when we clanged
Into the vasty station we were indeed
Brave company for giants.

   Keep your eyes though,
You, and not I, will travel safer back
        To Union station.   30

Your fear has me infected, and my eyes
That were my sport so long, will soon be apt
Like yours to press out dwindling vistas from
The massive flux massive Mantegna knew
And all its sturdy everlasting foregrounds.

1948

Snow

Nobody stuffs the world in at your eyes.
The optic heart must venture: a jail-break
And re-creation. Sedges and wild rice
Chase rivery pewter. The astonished cinders quake
With rhizomes.[1] All ways through the electric air
Trundle candy-bright disks; they are desolate
Toys if the soul's gates seal, and cannot bear,
Must shudder under, creation's unseen freight.
But soft, there is snow's legend: colour of mourning
Along the yellow Yangtze[2] where the wheel   10
Spins an indifferent stasis that's death's warning.
Asters of tumbled quietness reveal
Their petals. Suffering this starry blur
The rest may ring your change,[3] sad listener.

1960

[1]Rootlike stems running along or under the ground, from which roots, stalks, and leaves grow.
[2]River in China, the longest in Asia.
[3]Change ringing is the ringing of church bells in all the permutations of a given pattern; thus, to ring changes is to play with permutations.

Butterfly Bones; or Sonnet Against Sonnets

The cyanide jar seals life, as sonnets move
towards final stiffness. Cased in a white glare
these specimens stare for peering boys, to prove
strange certainties. Plane dogsled and safari
assure continuing range. The sweep-net skill,
the patience, learning, leave all living stranger.
Insect—or poem—waits for the fix, the frill
precision can effect, brilliant with danger.
What law and wonder the museum spectres
bespeak is cryptic for the shivery wings,   10
the world cut-diamond-eyed, those eyes' reflectors,
or herbal grass, sunned motes, fierce listening.
Might sheened and rigid trophies strike men blind
like Adam's lexicon locked in the mind?

1960

The Apex Animal

A Horse, thin-coloured as oranges ripened in freight-cars
which have shaken casements through the miles of night
across three nights of field and waterfront warehouses—
rather, the narrow Head of the Horse
with the teeth shining and white ear-tufts:
It, I fancy, and from experience
commend the fancy to your inner eye,
It is the One, in a patch of altitude
troubled only by clarity of weather,
Who sees, the ultimate Recipient   10
of what happens, the One Who is aware
when, in the administrative wing
a clerk returns from noon-day, though
the ointment of mortality
for one strange hour, in all his lustreless life,
has touched his face.

(For that Head of a Horse there is no question
whether he spent the noon-hour with a friend,
below street-level, or on the parapet—
a matter which may safely rest   20
in mortal memory.)

1960

Meeting Together of Poles
and Latitudes (In Prospect)

Those who fling off, toss head,
   Taste the bitter morning, and have at it—
   Thresh, knead, dam, weld,
   Wave baton, force
   Marches through squirming bogs,
   Not from contempt, but
   From thrust, unslakeably thirsty,
   Amorous of every tower and twig, and
   Yet like railroad engines with
   Longings for their landscapes (pistons pounding)   10
   Rock fulminating through
   Wrecked love, unslakeably loving—

   Seldom encounter at the Judgment Seat
Those who are flung off, sit
   Dazed awhile, gather concentration,
   Follow vapour-trails with shrivelling wonder,
   Pilfer, mow, play jongleur[1]
   With mathematic signs, or
   Tracing the forced marches make
   Peculiar cats-cradles of telephone wire,   20
   Lap absently at sundown, love
   As the stray dog on foreign hills
   A bone-myth, atavistically,
   Needing more faith, and fewer miles, but
   Slumber-troubled by it,
   Wanting for death that
   Myth-clay, though
   Scratch-happy in these (foreign) brambly wilds;

But when they approach each other
   The place is an astonishment: 30
   Runways shudder with little planes
   Practising folk-dance steps or
   Playing hornet,
   Sky makes its ample ruling
   Clear as a primary child's exercise-book
   In somebody else's language,
   And the rivers under the earth
   Foam without whiteness, domed down,
   As they foam indifferently every
   Day and night (if you'd call that day and night)   40
   Not knowing how they wait, at the node,[2] the
   Curious encounter.

1960

[1]Juggler.
[2]Central point; in mathematics, the point at which a continuous curve crosses itself; also the complication or dilemma of a story.

Tennis

Service is joy, to see or swing. Allow
All tumult to subside. Then tensest winds
Buffet, brace, viol and sweeping bow.
Courts are for love and volley. No one minds
The cruel ellipse of service and return,
Dancing white galliardes[1] at tape or net
Till point, on the wire's tip, or the long burn-
ing arc to nethercourt marks game and set.
Purpose apart, perched like an umpire, dozes,
Dreams golden balls whirring through indigo.   10
Clay blurs the whitewash but day still encloses
The albinos, bonded in their flick and flow.
Playing in musicked gravity, the pair
Score liquid Euclids[2] in foolscaps of air.

1960

[1]'Galliard', a spirited dance in triple time, popular in Elizabethan England.
[2]Geometric figures; Euclid was a Greek mathematician of the third century who systematized the essentially undefined concepts of point, line, and plane.

Strong Yellow, for Reading Aloud:
*written for and read to English 385's
class when asked to comment on my
poem 'The Apex Animal', etc.*

A painted horse,
a horse-sized clay horse, really,
like blue riverclay, painted,
with real mural eyes—or a
Clydesdale with his cuff-tufts
barbered—the mane
marcelled like a conch and cropped and plastered down like a
merry-go-round pony's
without the varnish—
all kinds confounding,   10
yet a powerful presence
on the rainy Sunday diningroom wall,
framed by a shallow niche . . .

Q: 'Miss Avison could you
          relate that to the "head of a horse"?'

No.   No.   That one
was strong yellow—almost tangerine, with

white hairs, the eyes
whited too as if
pulled back by the hair   20
so the eyeballs would water with wind in them,
one you'd call Whitey, maybe,
though he was not, I say,
white . . .

Q: 'Auburn?'

It was not a horse-shaped horse,
or sized.   It loomed.   Only the
narrow forehead part, the
eyes starting   loose and appled,
and shoulder-streaming part. . . .   30
Colour? a stain on the
soiled snow-mattress-colour of
the office-day noon-hour mezzanine
                      that is the sky downtown.

Q: 'The Head of the Horse
         "sees", you say in that poem.
         Was that your vision of
         God, at that period
         in your development?'

Who I was then we   40
both approach timorously—
or I do, believe me!
But I think, reading the lines,
the person looking *up* like that
was all squeezed solid, only a crowd-pressed
mass of herself at shoulder-
level, as it were, or at least
nine to noon, and the p.m. still to come
day *in* day *out*   as the saying goes
which pretty well covers everything   50
or seems to, in *and* out then,
          when it's like that: no heart, no surprises, no
people-scope, no utterances,
no strangeness, no nougat of delight
                      to touch, and worse,
no secret cherished in the
midriff then.
Whom you look up from that to
is Possibility not
God.   60
         I'd think . . .

Q: 'Strong yellow.'

Yes!   Not the clay-blue
with rump and hoof and all and almost
eyelashes, the pupil
fixed on you, on that wall of
fake hunt, fake aristocracy
in this fake Sunday
diningroom I was telling
about. . . .   70

1978

Light (I)

The stuff of flesh and bone
is given, *datum*. Down
the stick-men, plastiscene-
people, clay-lump children, are strewn,
each casting shadow in the eye of day.

Then—listen!—I see
breath of delighting rise from
those stones the sun touches
and hear a snarl of breath
as a mouth sucks air. And with   10
shivery sighings—see: they stir
and turn and move, and power
to build, to undermine, is theirs,
is ours.

The stuff, the breath, the power to move even thumbs
and with them, things: *data*. What is
the harpsweep on the heart for?
What does the constructed power
of speculation reach for?
Each of us casts a shadow in the bewildering day,   20
                    an own-shaped shadow only.

The light has looked on Light.

He from elsewhere
speaks; he breathes impasse-
crumpled hope even
in us:
that near.

1978

Light (II)

That picture, taken from the
wing window, shows a shadow.

High up, between
the last clouds and the airless
light/dark, any shadow is
—apart from facing sunlessness—
self, upon
self.

Nights have flowed;
tree shadows gather; the sundial   10
of a horizoning hill in Lethbridge measures the
long grassy afternoon.

Still, freed from swallowing downtown blocks of shadow,
I note self-shadow on
        stone, cement, brick,
relieved; and look to the sunblue.

So, now.

1978

Light (III)

Flying Air Canada over
the foxed[1] spread snowy land,
we look where light is shed
from lucid sky on
waters that mirror light.

The magical reflectors there belie
factory   and fall-out   and run-off effluvia.

Where is the purity then,
except from so
feebly far aloft?   10
Is it a longing, but to be brought to earth,
an earth so poisoned and yet precious to us?

The source of light is high

---

[1]Marked with brown stain caused by damp (as of linen, pages, etc.); with a play on 'fox-inhabited'.

above the plane.   The window-passengers
eye those remote bright waters.

Interpreters and spoilers since the four
rivers flowed out of Eden,[2]
men have nonetheless
learned that the Pure can bless
on earth *and* from on high   20
ineradicably.

1978

[2]Genesis 2:10; the four rivers, two of which are historically known—the Tigris and the Euphrates—
and two of which are not—The Pishon ('Gusher') and the Gihon ('Bubbler')—were said to have originated from an underground ocean. They flowed out from under the Tree of Life to the four corners
of the known historical world.

Louis Dudek

b. 1918

Montreal has been central to Louis Dudek's life. Born on its east side to Polish immigrant parents, he attended its Protestant English-language school system and later McGill University, from which he graduated in 1940. As a student he worked on the *McGill Daily*; there, and in the Quebec *Chronicle*, his first poems were published. After graduation he was employed as a copywriter, and in 1943 he and Irving Layton joined John Sutherland in editing and contributing to *First Statement* (1942-5). The literary activity in Montreal in this period—particularly Sutherland's and Layton's commitment to a poetry of social protest—led Dudek to see poetry as a social weapon and the publication of creative writing as a political act.

In the fall of 1943 Dudek moved to New York, beginning his only significant absence from Montreal and leaving behind a career in advertising. The year following he enrolled in the graduate program of Columbia University (M.A., 1945; Ph.D., 1955), where he studied under the American critic Lionel Trilling. There Dudek moved away from the *First Statement*

Marxist poetics, adopting instead Trilling's notion that art is inherently inimical to proletarian values and is essentially an ideational, historical, and philosophic activity. *Literature and the Press* (1960), a book that developed from his dissertation, supported this position; it argues that for an artist's work to be a viable antidote to society's ills, it must be kept separate from both popular literary forms and from commercial publication. Dudek came to admire writers who avoided commercialism, especially Carlyle in the nineteenth century and Ezra Pound in the twentieth. He became acquainted with Pound in 1949 and worked as his assistant for several years. During that period Dudek began 'Poetry Grapevine', a 'mailbag' of poetry and criticism, which each participating poet received and added to before passing it on. Among the contributors were Pound, Charles Olson, William Carlos Williams, Harold Norse, Paul Blackburn, and Raymond Souster, whom Dudek had met through Sutherland before leaving Canada.

Dudek returned to Montreal in 1951 to teach at McGill, where he continues to lecture in modern poetry, Canadian literature, and European literature. He started a Canadian mailbag, a 'postal round table', which again included Souster, and began to contribute poems and editorials to Souster's Toronto magazine *Contact* (1951-4); he was also advisory editor to *CIV/n* (1953-5). Contact Press (1952-67) was founded by Souster and Dudek, together with Layton (who did not play an active editorial role) and—as Frank Davey has observed in *Louis Dudek & Raymond Souster* (1980)— was more an imprimatur than an organized publishing house: its editors usually selected manuscripts separately and sometimes even proceeded to press without consultation. Because many of the books were paid for in part or in whole by their authors, each editor was able to maintain a significant degree of independence. Contact Press's first book, *Cerberus* (1952; rpt. 1967), an anthology of its editors' poetry, was followed by several books by each editor; the Press also published early books by most of the major poets to emerge in the fifties and sixties. D.G. Jones, Gael Turnbull, Eli Mandel, Phyllis Webb, Margaret Atwood, and other writers found support from Souster or Dudek in the formative stages of their careers.

In the late fifties Dudek, one of the earliest and most enthusiastic supporters of Irving Layton, began to express his distaste for the bombast and high-flown rhetoric he found in Layton's poetry and for his self-created celebrity status. Around the same time Dudek also strongly objected to Souster's interest in the U.S. Black Mountain poets, and in the new Canadian poetry movements they influenced, such as *Tish*. In 1956 Dudek founded the McGill Poetry Series (chapbooks by McGill students), which he not only edited but financed; a year later he started *Delta* (1957-66) in reaction to the internationalism of Souster's new magazine *Combustion* (1957-60), which had replaced *Contact*. *Delta* was a personal journal in which Dudek's editorial statements, by this time essentially aphorisms, were inserted between carefully chosen contributions by Canadian writers.

In particular Dudek placed himself in opposition to the mythopoeic poets associated with Northrop Frye, supporting instead a poetics of rational, intellectual, and non-emotive writing, a poetry that processed reality rather than abstracting universal themes from a mythic unconscious. He was able to promulgate those ideas through Contact Press and Delta Canada Press (1964-1970), which he started (after a dispute with Souster) in association with Montreal writers Michael Gnarowski and Glen Siebrasse. In 1970 Delta Press split into Golden Dog (edited by Gnarowski), Delta Can (edited by Siebrasse), and DC books (edited by Dudek and Aileen Collins).

There has been no real division between Dudek's activities as editor, publisher, critic, and poet. Each role enables him to implement his poetics and its accompanying social philosophy. Although often identified as a social realist, Dudek has disclaimed that role, seeing realism as a 'springboard' to truth-telling:

The artist's function is not to make decorative verses . . . but to record in words the results of his personal explorations in the various dimensions of actuality and to share with the world his search for new depths of truth and beauty in human experience. (Canadian Literature, *No. 22, 1964*)

In *The First Person in Literature* (1967), *Selected Essays and Criticism* (1978), *Technology and Culture* (1979), and in a special Dudek issue of *Open Letter* (Series 4, Nos. 8-9, 1981), Dudek applies his aesthetics to practical criticism. The critic, whose purpose is to invigorate art, must evaluate the writer; he must praise the poet who aligns himself with 'universal order and value' by writing a rational imagist poetry without sentiment or rhetoric, and he must condemn all who forgo sensible, realistic poetry.

Much of the poetry Dudek wrote before 1955—some of which appeared in the anthology *Unit of Five* (1944) and in *East of the City* (1946), *The Searching Image* (1952), and *Europe* (1954), and some of which was not published until later in *The Transparent Sea* (1956), *Collected Poetry* (1971), and *Selected Poetry* (1975)—exemplifies the kind of imagism he called for. In these poems intense and structured images expressed in the natural rhythms of language produce an effective and accessible poetry.

Europe, as Dudek has acknowledged, is his last work to express social goals for poetry:

Europe *was the culmination of the public voice, the voice that seemed to be related to the audience in a healthy kind of way, in terms of the reality about which I was writing. From that point on, I moved inward and into a meditative sort of writing.* (Essays on Canadian Writing, *No. 3, 1975*)

Europe also begins a type of writing that has absorbed Dudek's interest for nearly thirty years:

. . . *separate individual short poems are not the form one wants. How much more interesting if one could document the real continual process of poetry-making that* goes on inside the mind. (The Tamarack Review, *No. 69, 1976*)

This documentation of the creative process is what he attempted in his book-length meditative poems *En México* (1958) and *Atlantis* (1967), and in his ongoing work *Continuations*. They are part of

an infinite poem in progress, in which the main job is simply recording the words that come to you and writing them down continually in a book, and then reworking them— rarely, very rarely altering the position of the lines. (The Tamarack Review, *No. 69, 1976*)

For many readers it is generally Dudek's short poems, written early in his career, that remain most attractive. The later work often seems more like homiletic prose journals set as poetry. However, even as Dudek the editor and publisher influenced the development of Canadian poetry, Dudek the poet has continued to influence its direction through his exploration of the extended stream-of-consciousness poem, since many younger writers have adopted this form.

From a Library Window

The scene is paper-thin, pastel pale and white,
the tennis courts are horizontally smooth
chalked with flat lines; the players strike
the ball with abstract sticks;
now the field tilts to an experimental plane,
the players' faces grow light red:
this is a platform, for the play of intellect.

A wind rises and sweeps the pale sand,
a Mongolian storm taking away the land.
It thrashes at the feet of the men;   10
yet all is simple and light-swept, the wind
sounds like the singing of humming birds,

a feeble flight we can allow or end
with a motion of the hand.

At this distance, closed in glass shelves,
leaning against each other, the realities
past and present are easy,
dispersed on a level plane, in an order of line, under the
        rule of play:
but we miss the muscle wrenched from the thigh,   20
the eye slit by the sun racing the pin ball,
and the active brain broken by fight and defeat.

1946

A Child Blowing Bubbles

Against the storefronts, by the loud buses whose
blue exhaust in its clean colored worlds
made moving clouds and many a blossoming rose,
the child laughed, blowing its small breath
into a curved wire, a magic circle for a cent.

Blowing more, and catching the globes, it laughed
at me bemused in wheels of floating foam,
crisp and crystal fortune balls about my head—
when looking at the future there I lost my thread
of childlike sense, and brutish saw each bubble burst.   10

1952

Coming Suddenly to the Sea

Coming suddenly to the sea in my twenty-eighth year,
to the mother of all things that breathe, of mussels and whales,
I could not see anything but sand at first
and burning bits of mother-of-pearl.
But this was the sea, terrible as a torch
which the winter sun had lit,
flaming in the blue and salt sea-air
under my twenty-eight-year infant eyes.
And then I saw the spray smashing the rocks
and the angry gulls cutting the air,   10
the heads of fish and the hands of crabs on stones:
the carnivorous sea, sower of life,
battering a granite rock to make it a pebble—

love and pity needless as the ferny froth on its long smooth waves.
The sea, with its border of crinkly weed,
the inverted Atlantic of our unstable planet,
froze me into a circle of marble, sending the icy air out in lukewarm waves.
And so I brought home, as an emblem of the day
ending my long blind years, a fistful of blood-red weed in my hand.

1956

Old Song

Since nothing so much is
as the present kiss
don't let an old kiss
so disconcert you,
but know it is no crime
to give a new kiss time
and reason to convert you.

The first you ever had
was an eternal lad
whose smile was very May   10
no other mouth replaces,
but this today
has an October way
to harvest his embraces.

Loves are the fruits of time
different and the same
the perfect and imperfect,
and in the body's branches
where old kisses hang
and sweet birds sang   20
the wind fills his paunches.

And any kiss at all
is present after all
for now is all we have
now when we want them,
so grant your kisses leave
to give and to receive
nor waste your lips to count them.

1956

A Torn Record

Nothing that man makes, or believes, is permanent.
I have seen the ruins of cathedrals—
it is only a question of how long
          what is left of them can stand.
A thousand, two thousand years later, they lie forgotten.

Nothing matters forever, what matters now
is desire, at the center of the whirlwind
          where our two pleasures are folded in one rose.
What matters always is energy, how you can laugh,
          your mouth wide and wonderful against the wind.   10

1980

Within the Walls of the Visible

Caught in the chicken-wire of dreams,
eternity mumbles a little in our poems.

1980

Poetry Reading

I like to be at a meeting of poets
          where they read
Each proud of his art, stands up
and works his high effect

different from any other
                    strange, separate
as the grasses, or the species

Some declaim, others jest
some seem to suffer—for the sake of the game
          (as all do in fact)   10
some in the very clouds, some in dirt
but all devotional in their secular praise

of the actual and the endless ways
their syllables turn and return to contain themselves.

1980

Tao[1]

For F.R.S.

Things that are blown or carried by a stream
seem to be living—not in that they oppose the wind
or oppose the water, but in that they move
                                    lightly blown,
lightly flowing, like things that live.

We who are actually living do best when we do not resist,
    do not insist, when winds and waters blow,
but go gently with them, being of their kind,
in the secret of wind and water, the thought of flow.

1980

[1]The Way; in the Taoist religion, the eternal and substantive universe; the 'course', which is nothing in itself but which is the regulator of all movements. 'F.R.S.' is F.R. Scott.

Al Purdy

b. 1918

In the opening lines of 'The Country North of Belleville' Al Purdy maps out his home territory—a 'Bush land scrub land' near the eastern end of Lake Ontario, a landscape that gives a man 'some sense of what beauty/is', yet is also 'the country of our defeat'. Although this is a region 'where the young/leave quickly', Purdy himself has spent most of his life in this contradictory landscape, making it the subject of some of his most powerful poetry. Born in Wooler, a small town a little west of Belleville (described by Purdy as 'mythological because the same village could not now be found'), he attended school in nearby Trenton and held his first jobs there and in Belleville, where he met his wife. Although he left the area to serve in the RCAF during the Second World War, and moved to Vancouver in 1950, since 1957 he has made his home in Ameliasburg, a small town on Roblin Lake, a few miles south of Belleville. Purdy has frequently travelled away from that home base, however, utilizing his journeys—to Europe, the Cariboo country of British Columbia, Baffin Island, Hiroshima, South America—to reinvigorate his poetry and to further his reflections on the meaning of place.

Purdy began writing poetry in his teens. In 1944 he paid to have his first book, *The Enchanted Echo*, published (only a few copies still exist) and in the fifties he produced three more collections of apprenticeship work. After spending time in the later fifties in Montreal—where, with the poet Milton Acorn, he founded a little magazine, *Moment*—Purdy began to find a sure and distinctive voice, publishing *Poems for All the Annettes* (1962) and *The Cariboo Horses* (1965; winner of a Governor General's Award). In 1968 *Poems for All the Annettes* was reissued in an expanded edition, in which Purdy collected and revised all the poetry up to 1965 that he wished to preserve. He has published some twenty more collections since then, including three more retrospective volumes: *Selected Poems* (1972), *Being Alive: Poems 1958-1978* (1978), and *Bursting into Song: An Al Purdy Omnibus* (1982). His most recent book of new poems, *The Stone Bird* (1981), published when he was sixty-three, was felt by many readers to contain some of his best work. An unpretentious writer who once described himself as 'a cynical Canadian nationalist, a lyrical Farley Mowat', he writes poems that are accessible, easy in diction, relaxed in tone; yet beneath their apparently simple surfaces they are often complexly affecting. Though he did not continue his formal education beyond grade 10, Purdy has always read widely and is an intense student of his craft. A full-time writer for more than twenty years now, he has several times taught creative writing and been writer-in-residence at various universities. In his poetry he often draws upon the jobs he took during his early years, which he describes as 'a little of everything . . . Bata Shoe Factory, picking apples, six years in the

R.C.A.F., store clerk in a foundry, in a Vancouver mattress factory, six months making box springs in Montreal'.

The most striking feature of Purdy's poetry is the sense it conveys of a mind in motion: a mind synthesizing its environment and looking for connection and meaning—even (as in 'Trees at the Arctic Circle') a mind engaged in composing the poem that we are now reading. Often the connections that the poet makes in these poems are temporal ones, for time is no less important than place to Purdy, and his poems tend to move from present to past and back again, seeking to restore lost continuities. In poems such as 'Elegy for a Grandfather' and 'Roblin Mills (2)', Purdy struggles to understand the vanished era he remembers glimpsing in his childhood. The origins of family and place even became the subject of a book-length poem, *In Search of Owen Roblin* (1974). In other poems the time span is much longer, for Purdy—like Pratt and many other modern Canadian writers—finds in the present vestiges of a more primitive era, a prehistoric past that gives meaning to 'The Cariboo Horses' and poignancy to 'Lament for the Dorsets'. For Purdy the past is a living thing, carried within us all, and a source of strength. Because we often lose sight of our past, one of Purdy's goals is to recover and respond to it. Thus 'Lament for the Dorsets' is an exemplary poem: the poet showing us the continuing life of an old work of art—'the ivory thought still warm'—while at the same time revealing how that work contains its own history, stretching back to the earliest human moments.

Winter Walking

Sometimes I see churches
like tons of light,
triangles and hexagons
sideways in air.
Sometimes an old house
holds me watching, still,
with no idea of time,
waiting for the grey shape
to reassemble in my mind,
and I carry it away   10
(translated back
to drawing board, concept,
mathematic and symbol);
I puzzle myself
with form and line
of an old house
that goes where man goes.
A train's violent anapest
(- - —! - - —!)
cries in my ears,   20
and leaves me a
breathless small boy.
What entered me trembling
was not the steel's dream.
And walking by,
in a pile of old snow
under a high wall
a patch of brilliant
yellow dog piss
glows, and joins   30
things in the mind.
Sometimes I stand still,
like a core at the centre
of my senses, hidden and still—
All the heavy people,
clouds and tangible buildings,
enter and pass thru me:
stand like a spell
of the wild gold sunlight,
knowing the ache stones have,   40
how mountains suffer,
and a wet blackbird feels
flying past in the rain.
This is the still centre,
an involvement in silences—

1962, rev. 1968

Pause

Uneasily the leaves fall at this season,
forgetting what to do or where to go;
the red amnesiacs of autumn
drifting thru the graveyard forest.

What they have forgotten they have forgotten:
what they meant to do instead of fall
is not in earth or time recoverable—
the fossils of intention, the shapes of rot.

1962, rev. 1968

The Cariboo Horses

At 100 Mile House[1] the cowboys ride in rolling
stagey cigarettes with one hand reining
half-tame bronco rebels on a morning grey as stone
—so much like riding dangerous women
        with whiskey coloured eyes—
such women as once fell dead with their lovers
with fire in their heads and slippery froth on thighs
—Beaver or Carrier women maybe or
        Blackfoot squaws far past the edge of this valley
on the other side of those two toy mountain ranges   10
        from the sunfierce plains beyond

But only horses
        waiting in stables
hitched at taverns
        standing at dawn
pastured outside the town with
jeeps and fords and chevvys and
busy muttering stake trucks rushing
importantly over roads of man's devising
over the safe known roads of the ranchers   20
families and merchants of the town
        On the high prairie
are only horse and rider
        wind in dry grass
clopping in silence under the toy mountains
dropping sometimes and
        lost in the dry grass
        golden oranges of dung

Only horses
        no stopwatch memories or palace ancestors   30

[1]Town in the British Columbia Cariboo region.

not Kiangs[2] hauling undressed stone in the Nile Valley
and having stubborn Egyptian tantrums or
Onagers racing thru Hither Asia[3] and
the last Quagga[4] screaming in African highlands
        lost relatives of these
        whose hooves were thunder
the ghosts of horses battering thru the wind
whose names were the wind's common usage
whose life was the sun's
        arriving here at chilly noon   40
        in the gasoline smell of the
        dust and waiting 15 minutes
        at the grocer's

1965

[2]Species of wild Asian ass, as are onagers.
[3]The Near East.
[4]A zebra-like animal of southern Africa that became extinct in the nineteenth century.

The Country North of Belleville

Bush land scrub land—
        Cashel Township and Wollaston
Elzevir McClure and Dungannon
green lands of Weslemkoon Lake
where a man might have some
        opinion of what beauty
is and none deny him
            for miles—

Yet this is the country of defeat
where Sisyphus rolls a big stone   10
year after year up the ancient hills
picnicking glaciers have left strewn
with centuries' rubble
        backbreaking days
        in the sun and rain
when realization seeps slow in the mind
without grandeur or self deception in
        noble struggle
of being a fool—

A country of quiescence and still distance   20
a lean land
        not like the fat south
with inches of black soil on
        earth's round belly—
And where the farms are
        it's as if a man stuck

both thumbs in the stony earth and pulled

        it apart
        to make room
enough between the trees   30
for a wife
        and maybe some cows and
        room for some
of the more easily kept illusions—
And where the farms have gone back
to forest
        are only soft outlines
        shadowy differences—

Old fences drift vaguely among the trees
        a pile of moss-covered stones   40
gathered for some ghost purpose
has lost meaning under the meaningless sky
        —they are like cities under water
and the undulating green waves of time
        are laid on them—

This is the country of our defeat
        and yet
during the fall plowing a man
might stop and stand in a brown valley of the furrows
        and shade his eyes to watch for the same   50
        red patch mixed with gold
        that appears on the same
        spot in the hills
        year after year
        and grow old
plowing and plowing a ten-acre field until
the convolutions run parallel with his own brain—

And this is a country where the young
        leave quickly
unwilling to know what their fathers know   60
or think the words their mothers do not say—

Herschel Monteagle and Faraday
lakeland rockland and hill country
a little adjacent to where the world is
a little north of where the cities are and
sometime
we may go back there
        to the country of our defeat
Wollaston Elzevir and Dungannon
and Weslemkoon lake land   70
where the high townships of Cashel
        McClure and Marmora once were—

But it's been a long time since
and we must enquire the way
         of strangers —

1965, rev. 1972

Trees at the Arctic Circle

(Salix Cordifolia—Ground Willow)

They are 18 inches long
or even less
crawling under rocks
grovelling among the lichens
bending and curling to escape
making themselves small
finding new ways to hide
Coward trees
I am angry to see them
like this   10
not proud of what they are
bowing to weather instead
careful of themselves
worried about the sky
afraid of exposing their limbs
like a Victorian married couple

I call to mind great Douglas firs
I see tall maples waving green
and oaks like gods in autumn gold
the whole horizon jungle dark   20
and I crouched under that continual night
But these
even the dwarf shrubs of Ontario
mock them
Coward trees

And yet—and yet—
their seed pods glow
like delicate grey earrings
their leaves are veined and intricate
like tiny parkas   30
They have about three months
to make sure the species does not die
and that's how they spend their time
unbothered by any human opinion
just digging in here and now
sending their roots down down down
And you know it occurs to me
         about 2 feet under

those roots must touch permafrost
ice that remains ice forever   40
and they use it for their nourishment
they use death to remain alive

I see that I've been carried away
in my scorn of the dwarf trees
most foolish in my judgments
To take away the dignity
        of any living thing
even tho it cannot understand
        the scornful words
is to make life itself trivial   50
and yourself the Pontifex Maximus[1]
        of nullity
I have been stupid in a poem
I will not alter the poem
but let the stupidity remain permanent
as the trees are
in a poem
the dwarf trees of Baffin Island
              Pangnirtung
1967

[1]The chief priest in ancient Rome; in later use, the Pope.

Notes on a Fictional Character

With cobwebs between elbows and knees,
I say that I hate violence:
there have been street fights;
two wills glaring eye to eye arm
wrestling—;
hours struggling for my soul or hers
with a woman in a taxi;
whacked and bloody and beaten in a poolroom,
playing pool with the winner and winning,
then the walk home, and fall down like a broken chair,   10
that kind of pride.
All violence,
the inner silent implacable defiance
of money or god or damn near anything:
but it was useful once
to the middle-aged man with belly and ballpoint
getting drunk on words but sobering ah sobering.
Remember the factory manager Arthur Watt,
big, charming smile, attractive personality,
who worked alongside his crew,   20
wearing a white shirt and tailored trousers,
to increase production:

one day Watt and four others
pulled against three of us across a table,
hauling the cover onto a mattress
much too big for the cover, with ropes,
a workday job delightfully turned to a tug-o-war:
me, digging up more strength than I had,
aimed it at Watt especially,
yanked the bastard toward me,   30
dragged an extra ten pounds of myself
from the guts and yanked
the boss till his head banged wood with
both arms stretched toward me on the table praying
to Allah there is no god but Allah
                              W. Purdy . . .
The trick was to keep an absolutely straight face,
no expression whatever hold
the chortle to a goddam whimper
of pure joy that started in the balls   40
and raced 90-miles-per-hour to the angels' antennae
where it sang sweet songs to female cherubs
emerging in the factory dust as a deprecating tsk-tsk,
a normal cigarette cough,
successfully dishonestly solicitous.
As a matter of course he hated me,
which I accepted modestly as my just due:
I've drawn it after me down the years,
that sobbing violence,
ropes to the mattress past like cobwebs   50
that break with a sudden movement or gentle smile:
or, tough as steel hawsers,
the ropes drag me inch by inch
to the other side of the table,
where the factory manager waits
his unruly workman with a gun,
to watch with amazed eyes
while I write this poem,
like blossoming thistle.

1968, rev. 1972

Wilderness Gothic

Across Roblin Lake, two shores away,
they are sheathing the church spire
with new metal. Someone hangs in the sky
over there from a piece of rope,
hammering and fitting God's belly-scratcher,
working his way up along the spire
until there's nothing left to nail on—

Perhaps the workman's faith reaches beyond:
touches intangibles, wrestles with Jacob,[1]
replacing rotten timber with pine thews,   10
pounds hard in the blue cave of the sky,
contends heroically with difficult problems of
gravity, sky navigation and mythopeia,
his volunteer time and labour donated to God,
minus sick benefits of course on a non-union job—

Fields around are yellowing into harvest,
nestling and fingerling are sky and water borne,
death is yodelling quiet in green woodlots,
and bodies of three young birds have disappeared
in the sub-surface of the new county highway—   20

That picture is incomplete, part left out
that might alter the whole Dürer[2] landscape:
gothic ancestors peer from medieval sky,
dour faces trapped in photograph albums escaping
to clop down iron roads with matched greys:
work-sodden wives groping inside their flesh
for what keeps moving and changing and flashing
beyond and past the long frozen Victorian day.
A sign of fire and brimstone? A two-headed calf
born in the barn last night? A sharp female agony?   30
An age and a faith moving into transition,
the dinner cold and new-baked bread a failure,
deep woods shiver and water drops hang pendant,
double yolked eggs and the house creaks a little—
Something is about to happen. Leaves are still.
Two shores away, a man hammering in the sky.
Perhaps he will fall.

1968

---

[1]Jacob wrestled with an angel until he was given a blessing; see Genesis 32: 24-29. In this line 'with' should probably be understood in the sense of 'alongside'.
[2]Albrecht Dürer (1471-1528), painter and engraver, the greatest artist of the northern Renaissance; caught up in a period of intense change, and influential in bringing Italian Renaissance styles into Germany, Dürer also maintained some of the dominant Gothic style of earlier German art.

Lament for the Dorsets

(Eskimos extinct in the 14th century A.D.)[1]

Animal bones and some mossy tent rings
scrapers and spearheads   carved ivory swans
all that remains of the Dorset giants
who drove the Vikings back to their long ships
talked to spirits of earth and water
—a picture of terrifying old men
so large they broke the backs of bears
so small they lurk behind bone rafters
in the brain of modern hunters
among good thoughts and warm things   10
and come out at night
to spit on the stars

The big men with clever fingers
who had no dogs and hauled their sleds
over the frozen northern oceans
awkward giants
              killers of seal
they couldn't compete with little men
who came from the west with dogs
Or else in a warm climatic cycle   20
the seals went back to cold waters
and the puzzled Dorsets scratched their heads
with hairy thumbs around 1350 A.D.
—couldn't figure it out
went around saying to each other
plaintively
              'What's wrong? What happened?
              Where are the seals gone!'
And died

Twentieth century people   30
apartment dwellers
executives of neon death
warmakers with things that explode
—they have never imagined us in their future
how could we imagine them in the past
squatting among the moving glaciers
six hundred years ago
with glowing lamps?
As remote or nearly

[1]The date of the mysterious disappearance of the Dorset, who were probably absorbed or expelled by the Thule Inuit, is now placed at around A.D. 1000, during a gradual warming period that began around then. To preserve good relations with the spirits of the animals they hunted, Dorset craftsmen carved finely detailed miniature replicas.

as the trilobites[2] and swamps   40
when coal became
or the last great reptile hissed
at a mammal the size of a mouse
that squeaked and fled

Did they ever realize at all
what was happening to them?
Some old hunter with one lame leg
a bear had chewed
sitting in a caribou-skin tent
—the last Dorset?   50
Let's say his name was Kudluk
and watch him sitting there
carving 2-inch ivory swans
for a dead grand-daughter
taking them out of his mind
the places in his mind
where pictures are
He selects a sharp stone tool
to gouge a parallel pattern of lines
on both sides of the swan   60
holding it with his left hand
bearing down and transmitting
his body's weight
from brain to arm and right hand
and one of his thoughts
turns to ivory
The carving is laid aside
in beginning darkness
at the end of hunger
and after a while wind   70
blows down the tent and snow
begins to cover him

After 600 years
the ivory thought
is still warm

1968

---

[2]Extinct arthropods from the Paleozoic period (600 million to 230 million years ago).

Roblin's Mills (2)[1]

The wheels stopped
and the murmur of voices
behind the flume's tremble
stopped
    and the wind-high ships
that sailed from Rednersville[2]
to the sunrise ports of Europe
are delayed somewhere
in a toddling breeze
The black millpond   10
turns an unreflecting eye
to look inward
like an idiot child
locked in the basement
when strangers come
whizzing past on the highway
above the dark green valley
a hundred yards below
The mill space is empty
even stones are gone   20
where hands were shaken
and walls enclosed laughter
saved up and brought here
from the hot fields
where all stories
are rolled into one
And white dust floating
above the watery mumble
and bright human sounds
to shimmer among the pollen   30
where bees dance now
Of all these things
no outline remains
no shadow on the soft air
no bent place in the heat glimmer
where the heavy walls pressed
And some of those who vanished
lost children of the time
kept after school
left alone in a graveyard   40
who may not change
or ever grow six inches
in one hot summer
or turn where the great herons

---

[1]Originally published as 'Roblin's Mills: Circa 1842'. Purdy later retitled this poem 'Roblin's Mills (2)' to distinguish it from an earlier poem entitled 'Roblin's Mills'. Purdy also used 'Roblin's Mills (2)' as the conclusion of his long poem *In Search of Owen Roblin* (1974).
[2]Town on the Bay of Quinte, not far from Roblin Mills.

graze the sky's low silver
—stand between the hours
in a rotting village
near the weed-grown eye
that looks into itself
deep in the black crystal   50
that holds and contains
the substance of shadows
manner and custom
        of the inarticulate
departures and morning rumours
gestures and almost touchings
announcements and arrivals
gossip of someone's marriage
when a girl or tired farm woman
whose body suddenly blushes   60
beneath a faded house dress
with white expressionless face
turns to her awkward husband
to remind him of something else
The black millpond
                holds them
movings and reachings and fragments
the gear and tackle of living
under the water eye
all things laid aside   70
                discarded
                        forgotten
but they had their being once
and left a place to stand on

1968, rev. 1972

Married Man's Song

When he makes love to the young girl
what does the middleaged long-married
man say to himself and the girl?
—that lovers live and desk clerks perish?

When neons flash the girl into light and shadow
the room vanishes and all those others
guests who checked out long ago
are smiling
and only the darkness of her may be touched
only the whiteness looked at   10
she stands above him as a stone goddess
weeping tears and honey
she is half his age and far older
and how can a man tell his wife this?

Later they'll meet in all politeness
not quite strangers but never friends
and hands touched elsewhere may shake together
with brush of fingers and casual eyes
and the cleanser cleans to magic whiteness
and love survives in the worst cologne   20
(but not girls' bodies that turn black leather)
for all believe in the admen's lies

In rare cases among the legions of married men
such moments of shining have never happened
and whether to praise such men for their steadfast virtue
or condemn them as fools for living without magic
answer can hardly be given

There are rooms for rent in the outer planets
and neons blaze in Floral Sask
we live with death but it's life we die with   30
in the blossoming earth where springs the rose
In house and highway in town and country
what's given is paid for blood gifts are sold
the stars' white fingers unscrew the light bulbs
the bill is due and the desk clerk wakes
outside our door the steps are quiet
light comes and goes from a ghostly sun
where only the darkness may be remembered
and the rest is gone

1970

Alive or Not

It's like a story
because it takes so long to happen:

a block away on an Ottawa street
I see this woman about to fall
and she collapses slowly
in sections the way you read about
and there just might be time
for me to reach her
running as fast as I can
before her head hits the sidewalk   10
Of course it's my wife
I am running toward her now
and there is a certain amount of horror
a time lag in which other things happen
I can almost see flowers break into blossom
while I am running toward the woman
my wife it seems
orchids in the Brazilian jungle
exist like unprovable ideas
until a man in a pith helmet   20
steps on one and yells Eureka or something
—and while I am thinking about this
her body splashes on the street
her glasses fall broken beside her
with a musical sound under the traffic
and she is probably dead too
Of course I cradle her in my arms
a doll perhaps without life
while someone I do not know
signals a taxi   30
as the bystanders stare
What this means years later
as I grow older and older
is that I am still running toward her:
the woman falls very slowly
she is giving me more and more time
to reach her and make the grab
and each time each fall she may die
or not die and this will go on forever
this will go on forever and ever   40
As I grow older and older
my speed afoot increases
each time I am running and reach
the place before she falls every time
I am running too fast to stop
I run past her farther and farther
it's almost like a story
as an orchid dies in the Brazilian jungle
1976   and there is a certain amount of horror

A Handful of Earth

To René Lévesque

Proposal:
let us join Quebec
if Quebec won't join us
I don't mind in the least
being governed from Quebec City
by Canadiens instead of Canadians
in fact the fleur-de-lis
                and maple leaf
are only symbols
and our true language   10
speaks from inside
the land itself

Listen:
you can hear soft wind blowing
among tall fir trees on Vancouver Island
it is the same wind we knew
whispering along Côte des Neiges
on the island of Montreal
when we were lovers and had no money
Once flying in a little Cessna 180   20
above that great spine of mountains
where a continent attempts the sky
I wondered who owns this land
and knew that no one does
for we are tenants only

Go back a little:
to hip-roofed houses on the Isle d'Orléans
and scattered along the road to Chicoutimi
the remaining few log houses in Ontario
sod huts of sunlit prairie places   30
dissolved in rain long since
the stones we laid atop of one another
a few of which still stand
those origins
in which children were born
in which we loved and hated
in which we built a place to stand on
and now must tear it down?
—and here I ask all the oldest questions
of myself   40
the reasons for being alive
the way to spend this gift and thank the giver
but there is no way

I think of the small dapper man
chain-smoking at PQ headquarters

Lévesque
on Avenue Christophe Colomb in Montreal
where we drank coffee together six years past
I say to him now: my place is here
whether Côte des Neiges Avenue Christophe Colomb   50
Yonge Street Toronto Halifax or Vancouver
this place is where I stand
where all my mistakes were made
when I grew awkwardly and knew what I was
and that is Canadian or Canadien
it doesn't matter which to me

Sod huts break the prairie skyline
then melt in rain
the hip-roofed houses of New France as well
but French no longer   60
nor are we any longer English
—limestone houses
lean-tos and sheds our fathers built
in which our mothers died
before the forests tumbled down
ghost habitations
only this handful of earth
for a time at least
I have no other place to go

1977, rev. 1978

The Nurselog[1]

These are my children
these are my grandchildren
they have green hair
their bones grow from my bones
when rain comes they drink the sky
I am their mother and grandmother
I am their past
their memory is my thousand years
of growing and waiting for them

Four hundred rings past   10
in my body count
there was fire
it touched me and I glowed

[1]'When a fallen log in the B.C. rain forest begins to decay, its trunk becomes a nursery for hundreds of tiny tree seedlings, all of them aligned in the same direction as the fallen tree. Decay within the log raises temperature, hastening growth of seedlings. Compressed annual rings in their heartwood record the seedlings' growth before their roots reach soil; and then they continue on toward the sky' [Purdy's note].

with blue fire from the sky
the sky was so close
it hissed and shimmered in me
then rain fell
Three hundred and fifty rings
past there was no rain
for many growing times   20
but when it came I heard
the forest talking together
How great a time ago
is lost but I remember
long-necked animals eating me
one great-jawed creature eating them
everything consumed everything else
and wondered if living was eating
Then the birds came
but strange birds like reptiles   30
with broad leathery wings
flapping and crashing through me
they changed to specks of blue
and orange and green and yellow
little suns sleeping in me
I remember this in a dream
when we all dreamed
as if I were an old repeated story
once told to me that I retell
And now the little green ones   40
nesting cleverly in a row
some love the shade and some the sun
another is growing crookedly
but she will straighten given time
one grows more slowly than the others
and has my own special affection
They are so different these small ones
their green hair shines
they lift their bodies high in light
they droop in rain and move in unison   50
toward some lost remembered place
we came from like a question
like a question and the answer
nobody remembers now
no one can remember . . .

1981

Raymond Souster

b. 1921

Raymond Holmes Souster was born and educated in Toronto. After high school he began a career in banking in which, with the exception of four years' wartime service in the RCAF, he has remained. Over the last forty years he has, through his poetry, chronicled his own life as a middle-class white-collar worker and the lives of the people he sees on his way to work, over the lunch-counter, and in his Toronto neighbourhood.

Souster began writing poetry as a boy: his first poem, 'an attempt to write a typical Lampman sonnet', was published in the Toronto *Star* in the early thirties. During the Second World War his poems appeared in John Sutherland's *First Statement* (1942-5), in *Direction* (1943-6), a little magazine he edited with Bill Goldberg from their RCAF station in Sydney, N.S., and in the anthology *Unit of Five* (1944). After the war he published his first two books, *When We Are Young* (1946), and the Ryerson chapbook *Go to Sleep World* (1947); but then, frustrated over what he felt was a growing bias for safe, conventional poetry in Canadian literary magazines and presses, Souster began his own journal, *Contact* (1952-4). In it he published the poetry of Canadians—including Irving Layton, Louis Dudek, and Phyllis Webb—and of Americans such as the Black Mountain writers Charles Olson and Robert Creeley, as well as poems by modern European poets in translation. With Dudek and Layton, Souster also began Contact Press (1952-67), a loosely organized publishing operation that not only printed the work of its editors—its first

book, *Cerberus* (1952, rpt. 1967), was an anthology of their poetry—but of writers such as D.G. Jones, F.R. Scott, W.W.E. Ross, Peter Miller (who replaced Layton as editor in 1959 and served as director of the press until 1967), Gael Turnbull, Eli Mandel, and Margaret Atwood. In 1957 Souster began his third journal, *Combustion* (1957-60), to replace Cid Corman's *Origin*, a U.S. literary magazine that had temporarily ceased publication. Like *Contact* and *Origin, Combustion* was an international magazine, publishing the innovative poetry of Europe, Britain, and North America. Souster's support of new poetry in Canada also manifested itself in his anthology *New Wave Canada* (1966), which brought together poetry of the west-coast *Tish* movement and the work of young Ontario poets; this volume, like *New Provinces* and *Unit of Five* before it, gave a united voice to a new generation of Canadian writers.

After Contact Press ceased publication Souster co-edited several school anthologies and helped to found the League of Canadian Poets (of which he has twice served as chairman). Since the mid-sixties many collections of his own poetry have appeared under the imprint of commercial publishers, including *The Colour of the Times* (1964), winner of a Governor General's Award; *As Is* (1967); *Selected Poems* (1972); *Extra Innings* (1977); and *Hanging In: New Poems* (1979). Oberon Press has published his collected poems in four volumes.

Souster is a poet of surfaces, a romantic realist who relies upon intuitive, empathetic observations of external circumstances and outward behaviour to animate his work. As he once said in an interview with Jon Pearce:

When I write a poem, I'm first of all concerned with my own reaction to the subject matter, how it affects me, and I'm also concerned with communicating the emotion that subject matter arouses in me.

(Twelve Voices, *1980*) Rather than relying upon rhetoric or conceptualized 'ideas' to express the feelings his observations arouse, Souster usually employs images. His technique owes much to that of the imagist poets William Carlos Williams and W.W.E. Ross (one of the first modernist poets in Canada).

Although Souster has always shown interest in experimental writing, his own poetry has never much departed from its imagist origins. Except for some experiments with the long poem ('Death Chants for Mr Johnson's America', 'Pictures of a Long Lost World'), and the novel (he published, under the pseudonyms 'Raymond Holmes' and 'John Holmes', two novels dealing with the Second World War), he has written mainly short, unornate poems—each devoted to a single observation—that are colloquial in tone and diction. When viewed cumulatively as part of an enormous body of work, the individual poems gain in interest, taking on the character of journal entries in an ongoing chronicle of Souster's life.

Many of Souster's poems make social statements. They are concerned with the dehumanization and degradation that our mechanized society inflicts upon its members, and with the need to seek out the simple pleasures of nature and of the pre-industrial past. These poems are not written as polemical strategies but as 'gut reactions'. Souster's impulse, more reportorial than revolutionary, acknowledges the imperfections of the world but offers no plan for social change.

A recurrent Souster image is that of the baseball game, which has played an important role in both his work and his life. In 'Waiting for the Poem to Come Through' (from *Extra Innings*) the poet-as-batter, waiting for the pitch, tells the reader more about Souster's poetics and philosophy of life than any discursive statement could:

Then you're ready,
the umpire behind you
growls 'play ball'
you give that last little wiggle,
look straight ahead at the kid
standing tall on the rubber,
murmur under your breath
'throw it over and duck',

wait for the poem to come whipping
curving
sinking in.

Flight of the Roller-Coaster

Once more around should do it, the man confided . . .

And sure enough, when the roller-coaster reached the peak
Of the giant curve above me—screech of its wheels
Almost drowned by the shriller cries of the riders—

Instead of the dip and plunge with its landslide of screams
It rose in the air like a movieland magic carpet, some
    wonderful bird,

And without fuss or fanfare swooped slowly across the
    amusement park,
Over Spook's Castle, ice-cream booths, shooting-gallery;   10
    and losing no height

Made the last yards above the beach, where the cucumber-cool
Brakeman in the last seat saluted
A lady about to change from her bathing-suit.

Then, as many witnesses duly reported, headed leisurely
    over the water,
Disappearing mysteriously all too soon behind a low-lying
    flight of clouds.

1955

Boldt's Castle

The ruins of the castle,
abandoned, half-finished,
are no sadder than
each fat sunfish that toys
with the garbage tourists
toss into the dockside's
tepid water. Both are prisoners
of this island, this river,
island with grotesque gingerbread
of Rhinish castle, river   10
with its thousand islands
strung out, maze
without beginning or end.

Boldt,[1] so the story goes,
began this castle

[1]George C. Boldt, who emigrated from Prussia to New York State in the 1860s.

as a wedding present for his bride,
but death took her voyaging
before she'd set eyes on it.
No further work was done. The rooms
remain unfinished, the walls   20
worked over by time and sun and rain
begin to crumble. The dream
of the young German immigrant
come to New York to make his fortune
sits here to impress or start a smile.

Another New World dream
begun with power and careless wealth
ending in sorrow, in ruin. As if a man
had no business to let
his imagination soar too grandly.   30
As if a conspiracy
of forces lurked in the wings
to bring the curtain down on tragedy.
As if the island finally chosen
to house this fantasy had from the first
hated the honour, the river sliding
lordly by had felt the same way,
and both schemed together: how to bring
this upstart down, how to ensure
laughter would never ring   40
in those rooms, life would never flow
on those staircases, boats
never dock with happy passengers
to fill those battlements. . . .

Well, they had their way,
or something had its way.
I stand on this wharf
ignoring the sunfish, deaf to the hum
from the souvenir shop, counting the minutes
before I crowd back with sightseers   50
onto the Rockport launch, to circle back
through more island mazes, with our driver
continuing like someone in a sideshow,

but the castle far behind men then,
the ghosts well back there who watch
the sun striking walls with no glass
in their hundred windows to throw back the flames.

Heart Island, Thousand Islands, August 1964

1967

Get the Poem Outdoors

Get the poem outdoors under any pretext,
reach through the open window if you have to,
    kidnap it right off the poet's desk,
then walk the poem in the garden, hold it up
    among the soft yellow garlands of the
    willow,
command of it no further blackness, no silent
    cursing at midnight, no puny whimpering
    in the endless small hours, no more
    shivering in the cold-storage room of the   10
    winter heart,
tell it to sing again, loud and then louder so it
    brings the whole neighbourhood out, but
    who cares,
ask of it a more human face, a new tenderness,
    even the sentimental allowed between the
    hours of nine to five,
then let it go, stranger in a fresh green world, to
    wander down the flower beds, let it go to
    welcome each bird that lights on the still   20
    barren mulberry tree.

1969

Queen Anne's Lace

It's a kind of flower
that if you didn't know it
you'd pass by the rest of your life.

But once it's pointed out
you'll look for it always,
even in places
where you know it can't possibly be.

You will never tire
of bending over to examine,
to marvel at this,   10
the shyest filigree of wonder
born among grasses.

You will imagine poems
as brief, as spare,
so natural with themselves
as to take breath away.

1972

Like the Last Patch of Snow

That's the way
we've got to hang on—

like the last patch of snow
clinging to the hillside
crouching at the wood edge
with April done

dirty-white
but defiant

lonely
fighting death.   10

1972

The Trillium[1] returns

Imagine her in the Sixties
moored in some Island lagoon,
slowly rotting through the summer,
aching, shivering through the winter,
her paddle-wheels broken, sides peeled of paint,
boiler rusting, only the cries
of birds, the padding of rodents
to remind her she still lived, served a humble need.

(My father's fondest thought of her
one hot summer evening   10
when she had hundreds more
than her usual passengers
coming back from Hanlan's[2]
and a Maple Leafs ball-game,
the year 1913,
and how at the city side
she keeled over badly
and for a long minute
Dad thought he'd get
a free swim in the bay,   20

and my dearest memory
another summer night
in a much later summer,

[1]The ferry that connects Toronto Island to the mainland. It ran from 1910 to 1956 and was returned to service in 1976.
[2]Hanlan's Point Stadium (1897-1925) was the home of the Toronto 'Maple Leafs' baseball team. See also 'Hanlan's Point Amusement Park' (1954), another poem in which Souster refers to his father's enthusiasm for baseball.

when I stood at her railing
coming back from the Point,
and fancied I could make out
City Hall's clock-tower
through the mixed hell-black
and hell-flaming crimson
of Toronto's skyline). . . .   30

Now imagine her next year (1976)
tied up at Queen's Quay dockside, nervous
as a new bride to have the gang-plank lowered,
the first holidayers come aboard!
New paddle-wheels, shining new superstructure,
new steam-plant! Imagine her joy
when the warning cast-off whistle sounds,
as she clears the dock, heads out into the bay,
feeling her paddle-wheels churning again,
the pulse-beat of her engines!   40
                    Fairer than ever
this flower of our city's water-gardens,
reborn again, still kindling the dream!

1977

Eight Pears

Placed there
in the big picture-window
to catch the morning
and afternoon sun,

eight yellow-green
slightly rotund &
very solemn pears

continue to be stubborn
stay hard

fearing our greedy   10
two sets of teeth
eager to pierce their skins
dig deep into heavenly juices.

Eight pears
sit there in that window

hating the sun
& fighting time
that ripens everything.

1977

Mavis Gallant

b. 1922

Mavis Gallant, born Mavis de Trafford Young in Montreal, entered at the age of four a strict French-Catholic boarding school where, a Protestant child of Scots heritage, she was something of an anomaly. Her father's early death and her peripatetic education (she attended over seventeen schools in Canada and the United States) prepared her for an independent and, by choice, solitary life. After high school she worked briefly for the National Film Board and then became a reporter for the *Montreal Standard*. Gallant had begun to write fiction during these years but was disinclined to submit her work for publication. Although two of her stories—'Good Morning and Goodbye' and 'Three Brick Walls'—were published as early as 1944 in the Montreal little magazine *Preview* (because a friend forwarded them to its editor, Patrick Anderson), she sent out her manuscripts herself only after she had decided in 1950 to quit reporting and become a full-time writer. At twenty-eight, after a brief marriage, Gallant left Canada for Europe, settling eventually in Paris. She submitted her first story to the *New Yorker*, which returned it, saying that it was too Canadian for their readers but that they wanted to see more of her work. (That story, 'The Flowers of Spring', was subsequently published in *Northern Review* in its issue of June/July 1950.) The *New Yorker*, however, did publish her second submission in its issue of September 1, 1951; since then most of her stories—even her 'Canadian' ones—have appeared first in that magazine.

Over the years Gallant has written highly polished, urbane short stories and novellas. They have been collected in *The Other Paris* (1956); *My Heart Is Broken* (British title: *An Unmarried Man's Summer*, 1964); *The Pegnitz Junction* (1973), linked stories about the sources of German fascism; *The End of the World and Other Stories* (1974), selected by Robert Weaver; *From the Fifteenth District* (1979); and a collection of stories about Canadians, *Home Truths* (1981), which won a Governor General's Award. Some of Gallant's most recent short fiction has moved away from the deliberately brittle, ironic story that has formed the bulk of her writing; these very short post-modern pieces, on the whole humorous and non-narrative in nature, have yet to be collected. She has also written two novels, *Green Water, Green Sky* (1959) and *A Fairly Good Time* (1970), which, like her stories, are subtle yet penetrating character studies. She occasionally writes non-fiction as well, reporting and reviewing from her position as an observer of France. Her long essay in *The Affair of Gabrielle Russier* (1971), a book about a complex French legal scandal involving a teacher and her student, led to her current project: a non-fiction book about another famous episode in French law and history, the Dreyfus case.

Gallant, who has immersed herself in French culture and life for over twenty-five years and has been bilingual from childhood, writes only in English, believing that 'one needs a strong, complete language, fully understood, to anchor one's understanding'. She has always been concerned with the individual's experience of an unfamiliar culture, and her decision to write in English while seeking out the nature and differences of other cultures is a key to understanding her work. Her stories, which capture the universal sense of alienation that has dominated modern society, are often about exiled and isolated people. To survive emotionally, her characters struggle—while hanging on to threads of their former cultures— to understand foreign environments that are alien both literally and psychologically. They are cut off not simply from their physical homeland but also from other people. Even at home they stand apart, unable to make contact, unable to join those around them. In 'About Geneva' the sense of psychic distance between generations is intensified by the loss of traditional codes. As in the fiction of Henry James, the truncated form of communication that prevails takes place in the twilight of an obsolescent world.

Gallant's method of portraying characters obliquely, often by focusing on specific social customs and on unconscious behaviour, recalls Proust as well as James.

Little is said directly—communication is an elaborate, unspoken ritual—but what *is* said is of great importance. Consequently her dialogue is filled with nuances. Gallant's detached characters, unable to make outspoken judgements, are akin to those found in stories by Sinclair Ross, Alice Munro, Margaret Atwood, and Clarke Blaise. They share a malady often portrayed in modern Canadian fiction: burdened by history yet isolated by it, they find society moving away from the familiar patterns that both bind and reassure them. Gallant, like other Canadian writers, shows her characters reacting with restraint and surviving, without comment or evaluation 'because there was no help for it'.

Although the setting of much of Gallant's writing takes place outside of the Canadian locale, she has continued many associations with Canada and has retained, along with her English language, a cultural identity with her homeland. In 1982 she returned to Canada for the première of her first play, *What Is to Be Done?*, at the Tarragon Theatre in Toronto, and for 1983-4 she has accepted a position as writer-in-residence at the University of Toronto.

About Geneva

Granny was waiting at the door of the apartment. She looked small, lonely, and patient, and at the sight of her the children and their mother felt instantly guilty. Instead of driving straight home from the airport, they had stopped outside Nice for ice cream. They might have known how much those extra twenty minutes would mean to Granny. Colin, too young to know what he felt, or why, began instinctively to misbehave, dragging his feet, scratching the waxed parquet. Ursula bit her nails, taking refuge in a dream, while the children's mother, Granny's only daughter, felt compelled to cry in a high, cheery voice, 'Well, Granny, here they are, safe and sound!'

'Darlings,' said Granny, very low. 'Home again.' She stretched out her arms to Ursula, but then, seeing the taxi driver, who had carried the children's bags up the stairs, she drew back. After he had gone she repeated the gesture, turning this time to Colin, as if Ursula's cue had been irrevocably missed. Colin was wearing a beret. 'Wherever did that come from?' Granny said. She pulled it off and stood still, stricken. 'My darling little boy,' she said, at last. 'What have they done to you? They have cut your hair. Your lovely golden hair. I cannot believe it. I don't want to believe it.'

'It was high time,' the children's mother said. She stood in the outer corridor, waiting for Granny's welcome to subside. 'It was high time someone cut Colin's hair. The curls made such a baby of him. We should have seen that. Two women can't really bring up a boy.'

Granny didn't look at all as if she agreed. 'Who cut your hair?' she said, holding Colin.

'Barber,' he said, struggling away.

'Less said the better,' said Colin's mother. She came in at last, drew off her gloves, looked around, as if she, and not the children, had been away.

'He's not my child, of course,' said Granny, releasing Colin. 'If he were, I can just imagine the letter I should write. Of all the impudence! When you send a child off for a visit you expect at the very least to have him return exactly as he left. And you,' she said, extending to Ursula a plump, liver-spotted hand, 'what changes am I to expect in you?'

'Oh, Granny, for Heaven's sake, it was only two weeks.' She permitted her grandmother to kiss her, then went straight to the sitting room and hurled herself into a chair. The room was hung with dark engravings of cathedrals. There were flowers, red carnations, on the rickety painted tables, poked into stiff arrangements by a maid. It was the standard seasonal Nice *meublé*. [1] Granny spent every winter in rented flats more or less like this one, and her daughter, since her divorce, shared them with her.

Granny followed Ursula into the room and sat down, erect, on an uncomfortable chair, while her daughter, trailing behind, finally chose a footstool near the empty fireplace. She gave Granny a gentle, neutral look. Before starting out for the airport, earlier, she had repeated her warning: There were to be no direct questions, no remarks. It was all to appear as natural and normal as possible. What, indeed, could be more natural for the children than a visit with their father?

'What, indeed,' said Granny in a voice rich with meaning.

It was only fair, said the children's mother. A belief in fair play was so embedded in her nature that she could say the words without coloring deeply. Besides, it was the first time he had asked.

'And won't be the last,' Granny said. 'But, of course, it is up to you.'

Ursula lay rather than sat in her chair. Her face was narrow and freckled: She resembled her mother who, at thirty-four, had settled into a permanent, anxious-looking, semi-youthfulness. Colin, blond and fat, rolled on the floor. He pulled his mouth out at the corners, then pulled down his eyes to show the hideous red underlids. He looked at his grandmother and growled like a lion.

'Colin has come back sillier than ever,' Granny said. He lay prone, noisily snuffing the carpet. The others ignored him.

'Did you go boating, Ursula?' said Granny, not counting this as a direct question. 'When I visited Geneva, as a girl, we went boating on the lake.' She went on about white water birds, a parasol, a boat heaped with colored cushions.

'Oh, Granny, no,' said Ursula. 'There weren't even any big boats, let alone little ones. It was cold.'

[1] Furnished apartment.

'I hope the house, at least, was warm.'

But evidently Ursula had failed to notice the temperature of her father's house. She slumped on her spine (a habit Granny had just nicely caused her to get over before the departure for Geneva) and then said, unexpectedly, 'She's not a good manager.'

Granny and her daughter exchanged a look, eyebrows up.

'Oh?' said Ursula's mother, pink. She forgot about the direct questions and said, 'Why?'

'It's not terribly polite to speak that way of one's hostess,' said Granny, unable to resist the reproof but threatening Ursula's revelation at the source. Her daughter looked at her, murderous.

'Well,' said Ursula, slowly, 'once the laundry didn't come back. It was her fault, he said. Our sheets had to be changed, he said. So she said Oh, all right. She took the sheets off Colin's bed and put them on my bed, and took the sheets off my bed and put them on Colin's. To make the change, she said.'

'Dear God,' said Granny.

'Colin's sheets were a mess. He had his supper in bed sometimes. They were just a mess.'

'Not true,' said Colin.

'Another time . . . ,' said Ursula, and stopped, as if Granny had been right, after all, about criticizing one's hostess.

'Gave us chocolate,' came from Colin, his face muffled in carpet.

'Not every day, I trust,' Granny said.

'For the plane.'

'It might very well have made you both airsick,' said Granny.

'Well,' said Ursula, 'it didn't.' Her eyes went often to the luggage in the hall. She squirmed upright, stood up, and sat down again. She rubbed her nose with the back of her hand.

'Ursula, do you want a handkerchief?' said Granny.

'No,' said Ursula. 'Only it so happens I'm writing a play. It's in the suitcase.'

Granny and the children's mother looked at each other again. 'I *am* pleased,' Granny said, and her daughter nodded, agreeing, for, if impertinence and slumping on one's spine were unfortunate inherited tendencies, this was something else. It was only fair that Ursula's father should have bequeathed her *something* to compensate for the rest. 'What is it about?' said Granny.

Ursula looked at her feet. After a short silence she said, 'Russia. That's all I want to tell. It was her idea. She lived there once.'

Quietly, controlled, the children's mother took a cigarette from the box on the table. Granny looked brave.

'Would you tell us the title, at least?' said Granny.

'No,' said Ursula. But then, as if the desire to share the splendid thing she had created were too strong, she said, 'I'll tell you one line, because they said it was the best thing they'd ever heard anywhere.' She took a breath. Her audience was gratifyingly attentive, straining, nearly, with attention and control. 'It goes like this,' Ursula said. ' "The Grand Duke enters and sees Tatiana all in gold." '

'Well?' said Granny.

'Well, what?' said Ursula. 'That's it. That's the line.' She looked at her mother and grandmother and said, '*They* liked it. They want me to send it to them, and everything else, too. She even told me the name Tatiana.'

'It's lovely, dear,' said Ursula's mother. She put the cigarette back in the box. 'It sounds like a lovely play. Just when did she live in Russia?'

'I don't know. Ages ago. She's pretty old.'

'Perhaps one day we shall see the play after all,' said Granny. 'Particularly if it is to be sent all over the Continent.'

'You mean they might act in it?' said Ursula. Thinking of this, she felt sorry for herself. Ever since she had started 'The Grand Duke' she could not think of her own person without being sorry. For no reason at all, now, her eyes filled with tears of self-pity. Drooping, she looked out at the darkening street, to the leafless trees and the stone facade of a public library.

But the children's mother, as if Granny's remark had for her an entirely different meaning, not nearly so generous, said, 'I shall give you the writing desk from my bedroom, Ursula. It has a key.'

'Where will you keep your things?' said Granny, protesting. She could not very well say that the desk was her own, not to be moved. Like everything else—the dark cathedrals, the shaky painted tables—it had come with the flat.

'I don't need a key,' said the children's mother, lacing her fingers tightly around her knees. 'I'm not writing a play, or anything else I want kept secret. Not any more.'

'They used to take Colin for walks,' said Ursula, yawning, only vaguely taking in the importance of the desk. 'That was when I started to write this thing. Once they stayed out the whole afternoon. They never said where they'd been.'

'I wonder,' said her mother, thoughtful. She started to say something to Ursula, something not quite a question, but the child was too preoccupied with herself. Everything about the trip, in the end, would crystallize around Tatiana and the Grand Duke. Already, Ursula was Tatiana. The children's mother looked at Ursula's long bare legs, her heavy shoes, her pleated skirt, and she thought, I must do something about her clothes, something to make her pretty.

'Colin, dear,' said Granny in her special inner-meaning voice, 'do you remember your walks?'

'No.'

'I wonder why they wanted to take him alone,' said Colin's mother. 'It seems odd, all the same.'

'Under seven,' said Granny, cryptic. 'Couldn't influence girl. Too old. Boy different. Give me first seven years, you can have rest.'

'But it wasn't seven years. He hasn't been alive that long. It was only two weeks.'

'Two very impressionable weeks,' Granny said.

'I understand everything you're saying,' Ursula said, 'even when you talk that way. They spoke French when they didn't want us to hear, but we understood that, too.'

'I fed the swans,' Colin suddenly shouted.

There, he had told about Geneva. He sat up and kicked his heels on the carpet as if the noise would drown out the consequence of what he had revealed. As he said it, the image became static; a gray sky, a gray lake, and a swan wonderfully turning upside down with the black rubber feet showing above the water. His father was not in the picture at all; neither was *she*. But Geneva was fixed for the rest of his life: gray, lake, swan.

Having delivered his secret he had nothing more to tell. He began to invent. 'I was sick on the plane,' he said, but Ursula at once said that this was a lie, and he lay down again, humiliated. At last, feeling sleepy, he began to cry.

'He never once cried in Geneva,' Ursula said. But by the one simple act of creating Tatiana and the Grand Duke, she had removed herself from the ranks of reliable witnesses.

'How would you know?' said Granny bitterly. 'You weren't always with him. If you had paid more attention, if you had taken care of your little brother, he wouldn't have come back to us with his hair cut.'

'Never mind,' said the children's mother. Rising, she helped Colin to his feet and led him away to bed.

She stood behind him as he cleaned his teeth. He looked male and self-assured with his newly cropped head, and she thought of her husband, and how odd it was that only a few hours before Colin had been with him. She touched the tender back of his neck. 'Don't,' he said. Frowning, concentrating, he hung up his toothbrush. 'I told about Geneva.'

'Yes, you did.' He had fed swans. She saw sunshine, a blue lake, and the boats Granny had described, heaped with colored cushions. She saw her husband and someone else (probably in white, she thought, ridiculously bouffant, the origin of Tatiana) and Colin with his curls shorn, revealing ears surprisingly large. There was nothing to be had from Ursula—not, at least, until the Grand Duke had died down. But Colin seemed to carry the story of the visit with him, and she felt the faintest stirrings of envy, the resentfulness of the spectator, the loved one left behind.

'Were you really sick on the plane?' she said.

'Yes,' said Colin.

'Were they lovely, the swans?'

But the question bore no relation to anything he had seen. He said nothing. He played with toothpaste, dawdling.

'Isn't that child in bed yet?' called Granny. 'Does he want his supper?'

'No,' said Colin.

'No,' said his mother. 'He was sick on the plane.'

'I thought so,' Granny said. 'That, at least, is a fact.'

They heard the voice of Ursula, protesting.

But how can they be trusted, the children's mother thought. Which of them can one believe? 'Perhaps,' she said to Colin, 'one day, you can tell me more about Geneva?'

'Yes,' he said perplexed.

But, really, she doubted it; nothing had come back from the trip but her own feelings of longing and envy, the longing and envy she felt at night, seeing, at a crossroad or over a bridge, the lighted windows of a train sweep by. Her children had nothing to tell her. Perhaps, as she had said, one day Colin would say something, produce the image of Geneva, tell her about the lake, the boats, the swans, and why her husband had left her. Perhaps he could tell her, but, really, she doubted it. And, already, so did he.

1956

The Ice Wagon
Going Down the Street

Now that they are out of world affairs and back where they started, Peter Frazier's wife says, 'Everybody else did well in the international thing except us.'

'You have to be crooked,' he tells her.

'Or smart. Pity we weren't.'

It is Sunday morning. They sit in the kitchen, drinking their coffee, slowly, remembering the past. They say the names of people as if they were magic. Peter thinks, *Agnes Brusen,* but there are hundreds of other names. As a private married joke, Peter and Sheilah wear the silk dressing gowns they bought in Hong Kong. Each thinks the other a peacock, rather splendid, but they pretend the dressing gowns are silly and worn in fun.

Peter and Sheilah and their two daughters, Sandra and Jennifer, are visiting Peter's unmarried sister, Lucille. They have been Lucille's guests seventeen weeks, ever since they returned to Toronto from the Far East. Their big old steamer trunk blocks a corner of the kitchen, making a problem of the refrigerator door; but even Lucille says the trunk may as well stay where it is, for the present. The Fraziers' future is so unsettled; everything is still in the air.

Lucille has given her bedroom to her two nieces, and sleeps on a camp cot in the hall. The parents have the living-room divan. They have no privileges here; they sleep after Lucille has seen the last television show that interests her. In the hall closet their clothes are crushed by winter overcoats. They know they are being judged for the first time. Sandra and Jennifer are waiting for Sheilah and Peter to decide. They are waiting to learn where these exotic parents will fly to next. What sort of climate will Sheilah consider? What job will Peter consent to accept? When the parents are ready, the children will make a decision of their own. It is just possible that Sandra and Jennifer will choose to stay with their aunt.

The peacock parents are watched by wrens. Lucille and her nieces are much the same—sandy-colored, proudly plain. Neither of the girls has the father's insouciance or the mother's appearance—her height, her carriage, her thick hair, and sky-blue eyes. The children are more cautious than their parents; more Canadian. When they saw their aunt's apartment they had been away from Canada nine years, ever since they were two and four; and Jennifer, the elder, said, 'Well, now we're home.' Her voice is nasal and flat. Where did she learn that voice? And why should this be home? Peter's answer to anything about his mystifying children is, 'It must be in the blood.'

On Sunday morning Lucille takes her nieces to church. It seems to be the only condition she imposes on her relations: the children must be decent. The girls go willingly, with their new hats and purses and gloves and coral bracelets and strings of pearls. The parents, ramshackle, sleepy, dim in the brain because it is Sunday, sit down to their coffee and privacy and talk of the past.

'We weren't crooked,' says Peter. 'We weren't even smart.'

Sheilah's head bobs up; she is no drowner. It is wrong to say they have nothing to show for time. Sheilah has the Balenciaga.[1] It is a black afternoon dress, stiff and boned at the waist, long for the fashions of now, but neither Sheilah nor Peter would change a thread. The Balenciaga is their talisman, their treasure; and after they remember it they touch hands and think that the years are not behind them but hazy and marvelous and still to be lived.

The first place they went to was Paris. In the early 'fifties the pick of the international jobs was there. Peter had inherited the last scrap of money he knew he was ever likely to see, and it was enough to get them over: Sheilah and Peter and the babies and the steamer trunk. To their joy and astonishment they had money in the bank. They said to each other, 'It should last a year.' Peter was fastidious about the new job; he hadn't come all this distance to accept just anything. In Paris he met Hugh Taylor, who was earning enough smuggling gasoline to keep his wife in Paris and a girl in Rome. That impressed Peter, because he remembered Taylor as a sour scholarship student without the slightest talent for life. Taylor had a job, of course. He hadn't said to himself, I'll go over to Europe and smuggle gasoline. It gave Peter an idea; he saw the shape of things. First you catch your fish. Later, at an international party, he met Johnny Hertzberg, who told him Germany was the place. Hertzberg said that anyone who came out of Germany broke now was too stupid to be here, and deserved to be back home at a desk. Peter nodded, as if he had already thought of that. He began to think about Germany. Paris was fine for a holiday, but it had been picked clean. Yes, Germany. His money was running low. He thought about Germany quite a lot.

That winter was moist and delicate; so fragile that they daren't speak of it now. There seemed to be plenty of everything and plenty of time. They were living the dream of a marriage, the fabric uncut, nothing slashed or spoiled. All winter they spent their money, and went to parties, and talked about Peter's future job. It lasted four months. They spent their money, lived in the future, and were never as happy again.

After four months they were suddenly moved away from Paris, but not to Germany—to Geneva. Peter thinks it was because of the incident at the Trudeau wedding at the Ritz. Paul Trudeau was a French-Canadian Peter had known at school and in the Navy. Trudeau had turned into a snob, proud of his career and his Paris connections. He tried to make the difference felt, but Peter thought the difference was only for strangers. At the wedding reception Peter lay down on the floor and said he was dead. He held a white azalea in a brass pot on his chest, and sang, 'Oh, hear us when we cry to Thee for those in peril on the sea.' Sheilah bent over him and said, 'Peter, darling, get up. Pete, listen, every single person who can do something for you is in this room. If you love me, you'll get up.'

'I do love you,' he said, ready to engage in a serious conversation. 'She's so beautiful,' he told a second face. 'She's nearly as tall as I am. She was a model in London. I met her over in London in the war. I met her there in the war.' He lay

---

[1]A dress designed by Spanish couturier Cristobal Balenciaga. His creations were noted for their elegance.

on his back with the azalea on his chest, explaining their history. A waiter took the brass pot away, and after Peter had been hauled to his feet he knocked the waiter down. Trudeau's bride, who was freshly out of an Ursuline convent, became hysterical; and even though Paul Trudeau and Peter were old acquaintances, Trudeau never spoke to him again. Peter says now that French-Canadians always have that bit of spite. He says Trudeau asked the Embassy to interfere. Luckily, back home there were still a few people to whom the name 'Frazier' meant something, and it was to these people that Peter appealed. He wrote letters saying that a French-Canadian combine was preventing his getting a decent job, and could anything be done? No one answered directly, but it was clear that what they settled for was exile to Geneva: a season of meditation and remorse, as he explained to Sheilah, and it was managed tactfully, through Lucille. Lucille wrote that a friend of hers, May Fergus, now a secretary in Geneva, had heard about a job. The job was filing pictures in the information service of an international agency in the Palais des Nations. The pay was so-so, but Lucille thought Peter must be getting fed up doing nothing.

Peter often asks his sister now who put her up to it—what important person told her to write that letter suggesting Peter go to Geneva?

'Nobody,' says Lucille. 'I mean, nobody in the way *you* mean. I really did have this girl friend working there, and I knew you must be running through your money pretty fast in Paris.'

'It must have been somebody pretty high up,' Peter says. He looks at his sister admiringly, as he has often looked at his wife.

Peter's wife had loved him in Paris. Whatever she wanted in marriage she found that winter, there. In Geneva, where Peter was a file clerk and they lived in a furnished flat, she pretended they were in Paris and life was still the same. Often, when the children were at supper, she changed as though she and Peter were dining out. She wore the Balenciaga, and put candles on the card table where she and Peter ate their meal. The neckline of the dress was soiled with make-up. Peter remembers her dabbing on the make-up with a wet sponge. He remembers her in the kitchen, in the soiled Balenciaga, patting on the make-up with a filthy sponge. Behind her, at the kitchen table, Sandra and Jennifer, in buttonless pajamas and bunny slippers, ate their supper of marmalade sandwiches and milk. When the children were asleep, the parents dined solemnly, ritually, Sheilah sitting straight as a queen.

It was a mysterious period of exile, and he had to wait for signs, or signals, to know when he was free to leave. He never saw the job any other way. He forgot he had applied for it. He thought he had been sent to Geneva because of a misdemeanor and had to wait to be released. Nobody pressed him at work. His immediate boss had resigned, and he was alone for months in a room with two desks. He read the *Herald-Tribune,* and tried to discover how things were here—how the others ran their lives on the pay they were officially getting. But it was a closed conspiracy. He was not dealing with adventurers now but civil servants waiting for pension day. No one ever answered his questions. They pretended to think his questions were a form of wit. His only solace in exile was the few happy weekends he had in the late spring and early summer. He had met another old acquaintance, Mike Burleigh. Mike was a serious liberal who had married a serious heiress. The Burleighs had two guest lists. The first was composed of stuffy people they felt obliged to entertain, while the second was made up of their real friends, the friends they wanted. The real friends strove hard to become stuffy and dull and thus achieve the first guest list, but few succeeded. Peter went on the first list straight away. Possibly Mike didn't understand, at the beginning, why Peter was pretending to be a file clerk. Peter had such an air—he might have been sent by a universal inspector to see how things in Geneva were being run.

Every Friday in May and June and part of July, the Fraziers rented a sky-blue Fiat and drove forty miles east of Geneva to the Burleighs' summer house. They brought the children, a suitcase, the children's tattered picture books, and a token bottle of gin. This, in memory, is a period of water and water birds; swans, roses, and singing birds. The children were small and still belonged to them. If they remember too much, their mouths water, their stomachs hurt. Peter says, 'It was fine while it lasted.' Enough. While it lasted Sheilah and Madge Burleigh were close. They abandoned their husbands and spent long summer afternoons comparing their mothers and praising each other's skin and hair. To Madge, and not to Peter, Sheilah opened her Liverpool childhood with the words 'rat poor'. Peter heard about it later, from Mike. The women's friendship seemed to Peter a bad beginning. He trusted women but not with each other. It lasted ten weeks. One Sunday, Madge said she needed the two bedrooms the Fraziers usually occupied for a party of sociologists from Pakistan, and that was the end. In November, the Fraziers heard that the summer house had been closed, and that the Burleighs were in Geneva, in their winter flat; they gave no sign. There was no help for it, and no appeal.

Now Peter began firing letters to anyone who had ever known his late father. He was living in a mild yellow autumn. Why does he remember the streets of the city dark, and the windows everywhere black with rain? He remembers being with Sheilah and the children as if they clung together while just outside their small shelter it rained and rained. The children slept in the bedroom of the flat because the window gave on the street and they could breathe air. Peter and Sheilah had the living-room couch. Their window was not a real window but a square on a well of cement. The flat seemed damp as a cave. Peter remembers steam in the kitchen, pools under the sink, sweat on the pipes. Water streamed on him from the children's clothes, washed and dripping overhead. The trunk, upended in the children's room, was not quite unpacked. Sheilah had not signed her name to this life; she had not given in. Once Peter heard her drop her aitches. 'You kids are lucky,' she said to the girls. 'I never 'ad so much as a sit-down meal. I ate chips out of a paper or I 'ad a butty out on the stairs.' He never asked her what a butty was. He thinks it means bread and cheese.

The day he heard 'You kids are lucky' he understood they were becoming in fact something they had only *appeared* to be until now—the shabby civil servant and his brood. If he had been European he would have ridden to work on a bicycle, in the uniform of his class and condition. He would have worn a tight coat, a turned collar, and a dirty tie. He wondered then if coming here had been a mistake, and if he should not, after all, still be in a place where his name meant something. Surely Peter Frazier should live where 'Frazier' counts? In Ontario even now when he says 'Frazier' an absent look comes over his hearer's face, as if its owner were consulting an interior guide. What is Frazier? What does it mean? Oil? Power? Politics? Wheat? Real estate? The creditors had the house sealed when Peter's father died. His aunt collapsed with a heart attack in somebody's bachelor apartment, leaving three sons and a widower to surmise they had never known her. Her will was a disappointment. None of that generation left enough. One made it: the granite Presbyterian immigrants from Scotland. Their children, a generation of daunted women and maiden men, held still. Peter's father's crowd spent: they were not afraid of their fathers, and their grandfathers were old. Peter and his sister and his cousins lived on the remains. They were left the rinds of income, of notions, and the memories of ideas rather than ideas intact. If Peter can choose his reincarnation, let him be the oppressed son of a Scottish parson. Let Peter grow up on cuffs and iron principles. Let him make the fortune! Let him flee the manse! When he was small his patrimony was squandered under his nose. He remembers people dancing in his father's house. He remembers seeing and nearly understanding adultery in a guest room, among a pile of wraps. He thought he had seen a murder; he never told. He remembers licking glasses wherever he found them—on window sills, on stairs, in the pantry. In his room he listened while Lucille read Beatrix Potter. The bad rabbit stole the carrot from the good rabbit without saying please, and downstairs was the noise of the party—the roar of the crouched lion. When his father died he saw the chairs upside down and the bailiff's chalk marks. Then the doors were sealed.

He has often tried to tell Sheilah why he cannot be defeated. He remembers his father saying, 'Nothing can touch us,' and Peter believed it and still does. It has prevented his taking his troubles too seriously. 'Nothing can be as bad as this,' he will tell himself. 'It is happening to me.' Even in Geneva, where his status was file clerk, where he sank and stopped on the level of the men who never emigrated, the men on the bicycles—even there he had a manner of strolling to work as if his office were a pastime, and his real life a secret so splendid he could share it with no one except himself.

In Geneva Peter worked for a woman—a girl. She was a Norwegian from a small town in Saskatchewan. He supposed they had been put together because they were Canadians; but they were as strange to each other as if 'Canadian' meant any number of things, or had no real meaning. Soon after Agnes Brusen came to the office she hung her framed university degree on the wall. It was one of the gritty, prideful gestures that stand for push, toil, and family sacrifice. He thought, then, that she must be one of a family of immigrants for whom education is everything. Hugh Taylor had told him that in some families the older children never marry until the youngest have finished school. Sometimes every second child is sacrificed and made to work for the education of the next born. Those who finish college spend years paying back. They are white-hot Protestants, and they live with a load of work and debt and obligation. Peter placed his new colleague on scraps of information. He had never been in the West.

She came to the office on a Monday morning in October. The office was overheated and painted cream. It contained two desks, the filing cabinets, a map of the world as it had been in 1945, and the Charter of the United Nations left behind by Agnes Brusen's predecessor. (She took down the Charter without asking Peter if he minded, with the impudence of gesture you find in women who wouldn't say boo to a goose; and then she hung her college degree on the nail where the Charter had been.) Three people brought her in—a whole committee. One of them said, 'Agnes, this is Pete Frazier. Pete, Agnes Brusen. Pete's Canadian, too, Agnes. He knows all about the office, so ask him anything.'

Of course he knew all about the office: he knew the exact spot where the cord of the venetian blind was frayed, obliging one to give an extra tug to the right.

The girl might have been twenty-three: no more. She wore a brown tweed suit with bone buttons, and a new silk scarf and new shoes. She clutched an unscratched brown purse. She seemed dressed in going-away presents. She said, 'Oh, I never smoke,' with a convulsive movement of her hand, when Peter offered his case. He was courteous, hiding his disappointment. The people he worked with had told him a Scandinavian girl was arriving, and he had expected a stunner. Agnes was a mole: she was small and brown, and round-shouldered as if she had always carried parcels or younger children in her arms. A mole's profile was turned when she said goodbye to her committee. If she had been foreign, ill-favored though she was, he might have flirted a little, just to show that he was friendly; but their being Canadian, and suddenly left together, was a sexual damper. He sat down and lit his own cigarette. She smiled at him, questioningly, he thought, and sat as if she had never seen a chair before. He wondered if his smoking was annoying her. He wondered if she was fidgety about drafts, or allergic to anything, and whether she would want the blind up or down. His social compass was out of order because the others couldn't tell Peter and Agnes apart. There was a world of difference between them, yet it was she who had been brought in to sit at the larger of the two desks.

While he was thinking this she got up and walked around the office, almost on tiptoe, opening the doors of closets and pulling out the filing trays. She looked inside everything except the drawers of Peter's desk. (In any case, Peter's desk was locked. His desk is locked wherever he works. In Geneva he went into Personnel one morning, early, and pinched his application form. He had stated on the form that he had seven years' experience in public relations and could speak French, German, Spanish, and Italian. He has always collected anything important about himself—anything useful. But he can never get on with the final act, which is getting rid of the information. He has kept papers about for years, a constant source of worry.)

'I know this looks funny, Mr Ferris,' said the girl. 'I'm not really snooping or anything. I just can't feel easy in a new place unless I know where everything is. In a new place everything seems so hidden.'

If she had called him 'Ferris' and pretended not to know he was Frazier, it could only be because they had sent her here to spy on him and see if he had repented and was fit for a better place in life. 'You'll be all right here,' he said. 'Nothing's hidden. Most of us haven't got brains enough to have secrets. This is Rainbow Valley.' Depressed by the thought that they were having him watched now, he passed his hand over his hair and looked outside to the lawn and the parking lot and the peacocks someone gave the Palais des Nations years ago. The peacocks love no one. They wander about the parked cars looking elderly, bad-tempered, mournful, and lost.

Agnes had settled down again. She folded her silk scarf and placed it just so, with her gloves beside it. She opened her new purse and took out a notebook and a shiny gold pencil. She may have written

Duster for desk
Kleenex
Glass jar for flowers
Air-Wick because he smokes
Paper for lining drawers

because the next day she brought each of these articles to work. She also brought a large black Bible, which she unwrapped lovingly and placed on the left-hand corner of her desk. The flower vase—empty—stood in the middle, and the Kleenex made a counterpoise for the Bible on the right.

When he saw the Bible he knew she had not been sent to spy on his work. The conspiracy was deeper. She might have been dispatched by ghosts. He knew everything about her, all in a moment: he saw the ambition, the terror, the dry pride. She was the true heir of the men from Scotland; she was at the start. She had been sent to tell him, 'You can begin, but not begin again.' She never opened the Bible, but she dusted it as she dusted her desk, her chair, and any surface the cleaning staff had overlooked. And Peter, the first days, watching her timid movements, her insignificant little face, felt, as you feel the approach of a storm, the charge of moral certainty round her, the belief in work, the faith in undertakings, the bread of the Black Sunday. He recognized and tasted all of it: ashes in the mouth.

After five days their working relations were settled. Of course, there was the Bible and all that went with it, but his tongue had never held the taste of ashes long. She was an inferior girl of poor quality. She had nothing in her favor except the degree on the wall. In the real world, he would not have invited her to his house except to mind the children. That was what he said to Sheilah. He said that Agnes was a mole, and a virgin, and that her tics and mannerisms were sending him round the bend. She had an infuriating habit of covering her mouth when she talked. Even at the telephone she put up her hand as if afraid of losing anything, even a word. Her voice was nasal and flat. She had two working costumes, both dull as the wall. One was the brown suit, the other a navy-blue dress with changeable collars. She dressed for no one; she dressed for her desk, her jar of flowers, her Bible, and her box of Kleenex. One day she crossed the space between the two desks and stood over Peter, who was reading a newspaper. She could have spoken to him from her desk, but she may have felt that being on her feet gave her authority. She had plenty of courage, but authority was something else.

'I thought—I mean, they told me you were the person . . .' She got on with it bravely: 'If you don't want to do the filing or any work, all right, Mr Frazier. I'm not saying anything about that. You might have poor health or your personal reasons. But it's got to be done, so if you'll kindly show me about the filing I'll do it. I've worked in Information before, but it was a different office, and every office is different.'

'My dear girl,' said Peter. He pushed back his chair and looked at her, astonished. 'You've been sitting there fretting, worrying. How insensitive of me.

How trying for you. Usually I file on the last Wednesday of the month, so you see, you just haven't been around long enough to see a last Wednesday. Not another word, please. And let us not waste another minute.' He emptied the heaped baskets of photographs so swiftly, pushing 'Iran—Smallpox Control' into 'Irish Red Cross' (close enough), that the girl looked frightened, as if she had raised a whirlwind. She said slowly, 'If you'll only show me, Mr Frazier, instead of doing it so fast, I'll gladly look after it, because you might want to be doing other things, and I feel the filing should be done every day.' But Peter was too busy to answer, and so she sat down, holding the edge of her desk.

'There,' he said, beaming. 'All done.' His smile, his sunburst, was wasted, for the girl was staring round the room as if she feared she had not inspected everything the first day after all; some drawer, some cupboard, hid a monster. That evening Peter unlocked one of the drawers of his desk and took away the application form he had stolen from Personnel. The girl had not finished her search.

'How could you *not* know?' wailed Sheilah. 'You sit looking at her every day. You must talk about *something*. She must have told you.'

'She did tell me,' said Peter, 'and I've just told you.'

It was this: Agnes Brusen was on the Burleighs' guest list. How had the Burleighs met her? What did they see in her? Peter could not reply. He knew that Agnes lived in a bed-sitting room with a Swiss family and had her meals with them. She had been in Geneva three months, but no one had ever seen her outside the office. 'You *should* know,' said Sheilah. 'She must have something, more than you can see. Is she pretty? Is she brilliant? What is it?'

'We don't really talk,' Peter said. They talked in a way: Peter teased her and she took no notice. Agnes was not a sulker. She had taken her defeat like a sport. She did her work and a good deal of his. She sat behind her Bible, her flowers, and her Kleenex, and answered when Peter spoke. That was how he learned about the Burleighs—just by teasing and being bored. It was a January afternoon. He said, '*Miss* Brusen. Talk to me. Tell me everything. Pretend we have perfect rapport. Do you like Geneva?'

'It's a nice clean town,' she said. He can see to this day the red and blue anemones in the glass jar, and her bent head, and her small untended hands.

'Are you learning beautiful French with your Swiss family?'

'They speak English.'

'Why don't you take an apartment of your own?' he said. Peter was not usually impertinent. He was bored. 'You'd be independent then.'

'I am independent,' she said. 'I earn my living. I don't think it proves anything if you live by yourself. Mrs Burleigh wants me to live alone, too. She's looking for something for me. It mustn't be dear. I send money home.'

Here was the extraordinary thing about Agnes Brusen: she refused the use of Christian names and never spoke to Peter unless he spoke first, but she would tell anything, as if to say, 'Don't waste time fishing. Here it is.'

He learned all in one minute that she sent her salary home, and that she was a friend of the Burleighs. The first he had expected; the second knocked him flat.

'She's got to come to dinner,' Sheilah said. 'We should have had her right from the beginning. If only I'd known! But *you* were the one. You said she looked like—oh, I don't even remember. A Norwegian mole.'

She came to dinner one Saturday night in January, in her navy-blue dress, to which she had pinned an organdy gardenia. She sat upright on the edge of the sofa. Sheilah had ordered the meal from a restaurant. There was lobster, good wine, and a *pièce-montée*[2] full of kirsch and cream. Agnes refused the lobster; she had never eaten anything from the sea unless it had been sterilized and tinned, and said so. She was afraid of skin poisoning. Someone in her family had skin poisoning after having eaten oysters. She touched her cheeks and neck to show where the poisoning had erupted. She sniffed her wine and put the glass down without tasting it. She could not eat the cake because of the alcohol it contained. She ate an egg, bread and butter, a sliced tomato, and drank a glass of ginger ale. She seemed unaware she was creating disaster and pain. She did not help clear away the dinner plates. She sat, adequately nourished, decently dressed, and waited to learn why she had been invited here—that was the feeling Peter had. He folded the card table on which they had dined, and opened the window to air the room.

'It's not the same cold as Canada, but you feel it more,' he said, for something to say.

'Your blood has gotten thin,' said Agnes.

Sheilah returned from the kitchen and let herself fall into an armchair. With her eyes closed she held out her hand for a cigarette. She was performing the haughty-lady act that was a family joke. She flung her head back and looked at Agnes through half-closed lids; then she suddenly brought her head forward, widening her eyes.

'Are you skiing madly?' she said.

'Well, in the first place there hasn't been any snow,' said Agnes. 'So nobody's doing any skiing so far as I know. All I hear is people complaining because there's no snow. Personally, I don't ski. There isn't much skiing in the part of Canada I come from. Besides, my family never had that kind of leisure.'

'Heavens,' said Sheilah, as if her family had every kind.

I'll bet they had, thought Peter. On the dole.

Sheilah was wasting her act. He had a suspicion that Agnes knew it was an act but did not know it was also a joke. If so, it made Sheilah seem a fool, and he loved Sheilah too much to enjoy it.

'The Burleighs have been wonderful to me,' said Agnes. She seemed to have divined why she was here, and decided to give them all the information they wanted, so that she could put on her coat and go home to bed. 'They had me out to their place on the lake every weekend until the weather got cold and they moved back to town. They've rented a chalet for the winter, and they want me to come there, too. But I don't know if I will or not. I don't ski, and, oh, I don't know—I don't drink, either, and I don't always see the point. Their friends are too rich and I'm too Canadian.'

She had delivered everything Sheilah wanted and more: Agnes was on the first

[2] Show-piece.

guest list and didn't care. No, Peter corrected; doesn't know. Doesn't care and doesn't know.

'I thought with you Norwegians it was in the blood, skiing. And drinking,' Sheilah murmured.

'Drinking, maybe,' said Agnes. She covered her mouth and said behind her spread fingers, 'In our family we were religious. We didn't drink or smoke. My brother was in Norway in the war. He saw some cousins. Oh,' she said, unexpectedly loud, 'Harry said it was just terrible. They were so poor. They had flies in their kitchen. They gave him something to eat a fly had been on. They didn't have a real toilet, and they'd been in the same house about two hundred years. We've only recently built our own home, and we have a bathroom and two toilets. I'm from Saskatchewan,' she said. 'I'm not from any other place.'

Surely one winter here had been punishment enough? In the spring they would remember him and free him. He wrote Lucille, who said he was lucky to have a job at all. The Burleighs had sent the Fraziers a second-guest list Christmas card. It showed a Moslem refugee child weeping outside a tent. They treasured the card and left it standing long after the others had been given the children to cut up. Peter had discovered by now what had gone wrong in the friendship— Sheilah had charged a skirt at a dressmaker to Madge's account. Madge had told her she might, and then changed her mind. Poor Sheilah! She was new to this part of it—to the changing humors of independent friends. Paris was already a year in the past. At Mardi Gras, the Burleighs gave their annual party. They invited everyone, the damned and the dropped, with the prodigality of a child at prayers. The invitation said 'in costume', but the Fraziers were too happy to wear a disguise. They might not be recognized. Like many of the guests they expected to meet at the party, they had been disgraced, forgotten, and rehabilitated. They would be anxious to see one another as they were.

On the night of the party, the Fraziers rented a car they had never seen before and drove through the first snowstorm of the year. Peter had not driven since last summer's blissful trips in the Fiat. He could not find the switch for the windshield wiper in this car. He leaned over the wheel. 'Can you see on your side?' he asked. 'Can I make a left turn here? Does it look like a one-way?'

'I can't imagine why you took a car with a right-hand drive,' said Sheilah.

He had trouble finding a place to park; they crawled up and down unknown streets whose curbs were packed with snow-covered cars. When they stood at last on the pavement, safe and sound, Peter said. 'This is the first snow.'

'I can see that,' said Sheilah. 'Hurry, darling. My hair.'

'It's the first snow.'

'You're repeating yourself,' she said. 'Please hurry, darling. Think of my poor shoes. My *hair*.'

She was born in an ugly city, and so was Peter, but they have this difference: she does not know the importance of the first snow—the first clean thing in a dirty year. He would have told her then that this storm, which was wetting her feet and destroying her hair, was like the first day of the English spring, but she made a frightened gesture, trying to shield her head. The gesture told him he did not understand her beauty.

'Let me,' she said. He was fumbling with the key, trying to lock the car. She took the key without impatience and locked the door on the driver's side; and then, to show Peter she treasured him and was not afraid of wasting her life or her beauty, she took his arm and they walked in the snow down a street and around a corner to the apartment house where the Burleighs lived. They were, and are, a united couple. They were afraid of the party, and each of them knew it. When they walk together, holding arms, they give each other whatever each can spare.

Only six people had arrived in costume. Madge Burleigh was disguised as Manet's 'Lola de Valence',[3] which everyone mistook for Carmen. Mike was an Impressionist painter, with a straw hat and a glued-on beard. 'I am all of them,' he said. He would rather have dressed as a dentist, he said, welcoming the Fraziers as if he had parted from them the day before, but Madge wanted him to look as if he had created her. 'You know?' he said.

'Perfectly,' said Sheilah. Her shoes were stained and the snow had softened her lacquered hair. She was not wasted; she was the most beautiful woman here.

About an hour after their arrival, Peter found himself with no one to talk to. He had told about the Trudeau wedding in Paris and the pot of azaleas, and after he mislaid his audience he began to look round for Sheilah. She was on a window seat, partly concealed by a green velvet curtain. Facing her, so that their profiles were neat and perfect against the night, was a man. Their conversation was private and enclosed, as if they had in minutes covered leagues of time and arrived at the place where everything was implied, understood. Peter began working his way across the room, toward his wife, when he saw Agnes. He was granted the sight of her drowning face. She had dressed with comic intention, obviously with care, and now she was a ragged hobo, half tramp, half clown. Her hair was tucked up under a bowler hat. The six costumed guests who had made the same mistake—the ghost, the gypsy, the Athenian maiden, the geisha, the Martian, and the apache—were delighted to find a seventh; but Agnes was not amused; she was gasping for life. When a waiter passed with a crowded tray, she took a glass without seeing it; then a wave of the party took her away.

Sheilah's new friend was named Simpson. After Simpson said he thought perhaps he'd better circulate, Peter sat down where he had been. 'Now look, Sheilah,' he began. Their most intimate conversations have taken place at parties. Once at a party she told him she was leaving him; she didn't, of course. Smiling, blue-eyed, she gazed lovingly at Peter and said rapidly, 'Pete, shut up and listen. That man. The man you scared away. He's a big wheel in a company out in India or someplace like that. It's gorgeous out there. Pete, the *servants*. And it's warm. It never never snows. He says there's heaps of jobs. You pick them off the trees like . . . orchids. He says it's even easier now than when we owned all those places, because now the poor pets can't run anything and they'll pay *fortunes*. Pete, he says it's warm, it's heaven, and Pete, they pay.'

A few minutes later, Peter was alone again and Sheilah part of a closed, laugh-

[3]A painting by Edouard Manet (1832-83) of the Spanish dancer whom he and Baudelaire admired as being '*un bijou rose et noir*'. 'Carmen': entrancing but heartless Spanish *femme fatale*, the heroine of Bizet's renowned opera of the same name (1875).

ing group. Holding her elbow was the man from the place where jobs grew like orchids. Peter edged into the group and laughed at a story he hadn't heard. He heard only the last line, which was, 'Here comes another tunnel.' Looking out from the tight laughing ring, he saw Agnes again, and he thought, I'd be like Agnes if I didn't have Sheilah. Agnes put her glass down on a table and lurched toward the doorway, head forward. Madge Burleigh, who never stopped moving around the room and smiling, was still smiling when she paused and said in Peter's ear, 'Go with Agnes, Pete. See that she gets home. People will notice if Mike leaves.'

'She probably just wants to walk around the block,' said Peter. 'She'll be back.'

'Oh, stop thinking about yourself, for once, and see that that poor girl gets home,' said Madge. 'You've still got your Fiat, haven't you?'

He turned away as if he had been pushed. Any command is a release, in a way. He may not want to go in that particular direction, but at least he is going somewhere. And now Sheilah, who had moved inches nearer to hear what Madge and Peter were murmuring, said, 'Yes, go, darling,' as if he were leaving the gates of Troy.

Peter was to find Agnes and see that she reached home: this he repeated to himself as he stood on the landing, outside the Burleighs' flat, ringing for the elevator. Bored with waiting for it, he ran down the stairs, four flights, and saw that Agnes had stalled the lift by leaving the door open. She was crouched on the floor, propped on her fingertips. Her eyes were closed.

'Agnes,' said Peter. '*Miss* Brusen, I mean. That's no way to leave a party. Don't you know you're supposed to curtsey and say thanks? My God, Agnes, anybody going by here just now might have seen you! Come on, be a good girl. Time to go home.'

She got up without his help and, moving between invisible crevasses, shut the elevator door. Then she left the building and Peter followed, remembering he was to see that she got home. They walked along the snowy pavement, Peter a few steps behind her. When she turned right for no reason, he turned, too. He had no clear idea where they were going. Perhaps she lived close by. He had forgotten where the hired car was parked, or what it looked like; he could not remember its make or its color. In any case, Sheilah had the key. Agnes walked on steadily, as if she knew their destination, and he thought, Agnes Brusen is drunk in the street in Geneva and dressed like a tramp. He wanted to say, 'This is the best thing that ever happened to you, Agnes; it will help you understand how things are for some of the rest of us.' But she stopped and turned and, leaning over a low hedge, retched on a frozen lawn. He held her clammy forehead and rested his hand on her arched back, on muscles as tight as a fist. She straightened up and drew a breath but the cold air made her cough. 'Don't breathe too deeply,' he said. 'It's the worst thing you can do. Have you got a handkerchief?' He passed his own handkerchief over her wet weeping face, upturned like the face of one of his little girls. 'I'm out without a coat,' he said, noticing it. 'We're a pair.'

'I never drink,' said Agnes. 'I'm just not used to it.' Her voice was sweet and quiet. He had never seen her so peaceful, so composed. He thought she must surely be all right, now, and perhaps he might leave her here. The trust in her tilted face had perplexed him. He wanted to get back to Sheilah and have her explain something. He had forgotten what it was, but Sheilah would know. 'Do you live around here?' he said. As he spoke, she let herself fall. He had wiped her face and now she trusted him to pick her up, set her on her feet, take her wherever she ought to be. He pulled her up and she stood, wordless, humble, as he brushed the snow from her tramp's clothes. Snow horizontally crossed the lamplight. The street was silent. Agnes had lost her hat. Snow, which he tasted, melted on her hands. His gesture of licking snow from her hands was formal as a handshake. He tasted snow on her hands and then they walked on.

'I never drink,' she said. They stood on the edge of a broad avenue. The wrong turning now could lead them anywhere; it was the changeable avenue at the edge of towns that loses its houses and becomes a highway. She held his arm and spoke in a gentle voice. She said, 'In our house we didn't smoke or drink. My mother was ambitious for me, more than for Harry and the others.' She said, 'I've never been alone before. When I was a kid I would get up in the summer before the others, and I'd see the ice wagon going down the street. I'm alone now. Mrs Burleigh's found me an apartment. It's only one room. She likes it because it's in the old part of town. I don't like old houses. Old houses are dirty. You don't know who was there before.'

'I should have a car somewhere,' Peter said. 'I'm not sure where we are.'

He remembers that on this avenue they climbed into a taxi, but nothing about the drive. Perhaps he fell asleep. He does remember that when he paid the driver Agnes clutched his arm, trying to stop him. She pressed extra coins into the driver's palm. The driver was paid twice.

'I'll tell you one thing about us,' said Peter. 'We pay everything twice.' This was part of a much longer theory concerning North American behavior, and it was not Peter's own. Mike Burleigh had held forth about it on summer afternoons.

Agnes pushed open a door between a stationer's shop and a grocery, and led the way up a narrow inside stair. They climbed one flight, frightening beetles. She had to search every pocket for the latchkey. She was shaking with cold. Her apartment seemed little warmer than the street. Without speaking to Peter she turned on all the lights. She looked inside the kitchen and the bathroom and then got down on her hands and knees and looked under the sofa. The room was neat and belonged to no one. She left him standing in this unclaimed room—she had forgotten him—and closed a door behind her. He looked for something to do—some useful action he could repeat to Madge. He turned on the electric radiator in the fireplace. Perhaps Agnes wouldn't thank him for it; perhaps she would rather undress in the cold. 'I'll be on my way,' he called to the bathroom door.

She had taken off the tramp's clothes and put on a dressing gown of orphanage wool. She came out of the bathroom and straight toward him. She pressed her face and rubbed her cheek on his shoulder as if hoping the contact would leave a scar. He saw her back and her profile and his own face in the mirror over the fireplace. He thought, This is how disasters happen. He saw floods of sea water moving with perfect punitive justice over reclaimed land; he saw lava covering vineyards and overtaking of dogs and stragglers. A bridge over an abyss snapped in two and the long express train, suddenly V-shaped, floated like snow. He thought amiably of every kind of disaster and thought, This is how they occur.

Her eyes were closed. She said, 'I shouldn't be over here. In my family we didn't drink or smoke. My mother wanted a lot from me, more than from Harry and the others.' But he knew all that; he had known from the day of the Bible, and because once, at the beginning, she had made him afraid. He was not afraid of her now.

She said, 'It's no use staying here, is it?'

'If you mean what I think, no.'

'It wouldn't be better anywhere.'

She let him see full on her blotched face. He was not expected to do anything. He was not required to pick her up when she fell or wipe her tears. She was poor quality, really—he remembered having thought that once. She left him and went quietly into the bathroom and locked the door. He heard taps running and supposed it was a hot bath. He was pretty certain there would be no more tears. He looked at his watch: Sheilah must be home, now, wondering what had become of him. He descended the beetles' staircase and for forty minutes crossed the city under a windless fall of snow.

The neighbor's child who had stayed with Peter's children was asleep on the living-room sofa. Peter woke her and sent her, sleepwalking, to her own door. He sat down, wet to the bone, thinking, I'll call the Burleighs. In half an hour I'll call the police. He heard a car stop and the engine running and a confusion of two voices laughing and calling goodnight. Presently Sheilah let herself in, rosy-faced, smiling. She carried his trenchcoat over her arm. She said, 'How's Agnes?'

'Where were you?' he said. 'Whose car was that?'

Sheilah had gone into the children's room. He heard her shutting their window. She returned, undoing her dress, and said, 'Was Agnes all right?'

'Agnes is all right. Sheilah, this is about the worst . . .'

She stepped out of the Balenciaga and threw it over a chair. She stopped and looked at him and said, 'Poor old Pete, are you in love with Agnes?' And then, as if the answer were of so little importance she hadn't time for it, she locked her arms around him and said, 'My love, we're going to Ceylon.'

Two days later, when Peter strolled into his office, Agnes was at her desk. She wore the blue dress, with a spotless collar. White and yellow freesias were symmetrically arranged in the glass jar. The room was hot, and the spring snow, glued for a second when it touched the window, blurred the view of parked cars.

'Quite a party,' Peter said.

She did not look up. He sighed, sat down, and thought if the snow held he would be skiing at the Burleighs' very soon. Impressed by his kindness to Agnes, Madge had invited the family for the first possible weekend.

Presently Agnes said, 'I'll never drink again or go to a house where people are drinking. And I'll never bother anyone the way I bothered you.'

'You didn't bother me,' he said. 'I took you home. You were alone and it was late. It's normal.'

'Normal for you, maybe, but I'm used to getting home by myself. Please never tell what happened.'

He stared at her. He can still remember the freesias and the Bible and the heat in the room. She looked as if the elements had no power. She felt neither heat nor cold. 'Nothing happened,' he said.

'I behaved in a silly way. I had no right to. I led you to think I might do something wrong.'

'*I* might have tried something,' he said gallantly. 'But that would be my fault and not yours.'

She put her knuckle to her mouth and he could scarcely hear. 'It was because of you. I was afraid you might be blamed, or else you'd blame yourself.'

'There's no question of any blame,' he said. 'Nothing happened. We'd both had a lot to drink. Forget about it. Nothing *happened.* You'd remember if it had.'

She put down her hand. There was an expression on her face. Now she sees me, he thought. She had never looked at him after the first day. (He has since tried to put a name to the look on her face; but how can he, now, after so many voyages, after Ceylon, and Hong Kong, and Sheilah's nearly leaving him, and all their difficulties—the money owed, the rows with hotel managers, the lost and found steamer trunk, the children throwing up the foreign food?) She sees me now, he thought. What does she see?

She said, 'I'm from a big family. I'm not used to being alone. I'm not a suicidal person, but I could have done something after that party, just not to see any more, or think or listen or expect anything. What can I think when I see these people? All my life I heard, Educated people don't do this, educated people don't do that. And now I'm here, and you're all educated people, and you're nothing but pigs. You're educated and you drink and do everything wrong and you know what you're doing, and that makes you worse than pigs. My family worked to make me an educated person, but they didn't know you. But what if I didn't see and hear and expect anything any more? It wouldn't change anything. You'd all be still the same. Only *you* might have thought it was your fault. You might have thought you were to blame. It could worry you all your life. It would have been wrong for me to worry you.'

He remembered that the rented car was still along a snowy curb somewhere in Geneva. He wondered if Sheilah had the key in her purse and if she remembered where they'd parked.

'I told you about the ice wagon,' Agnes said. 'I don't remember everything, so you're wrong about remembering. But I remember telling you that. That was the best. It's the best you can hope to have. In a big family, if you want to be alone, you have to get up before the rest of them. You get up early in the morning in the summer and it's you, you, once in your life alone in the universe. You think you know everything that can happen . . . Nothing is ever like that again.'

He looked at the smeared window and wondered if this day could end without disaster. In his mind he saw her falling in the snow wearing a tramp's costume, and he saw her coming to him in the orphanage dressing gown. He saw her drowning face at the party. He was afraid for himself. The story was still unfinished. It had to come to a climax, something threatening to him. But there was no climax. They talked that day, and afterward nothing else was said. They went on in the same office for a short time, until Peter left for Ceylon; until somebody read the right letter, passed it on for the right initials, and the Fraziers began the Oriental tour that should have made their fortune. Agnes and Peter were too tired to speak after that morning. They were like a married couple in danger, taking care.

But what were they talking about that day, so quietly, such old friends? They talked about dying, about being ambitious, about being religious, about different kinds of love. What did she see when she looked at him—taking her knuckle slowly away from her mouth, bringing her hand down to the desk, letting it rest there? They were both Canadians, so they had this much together—the knowledge of the little you dare admit. Death, near-death, the best thing, the wrong thing—God knows what they were telling each other. Anyway, nothing happened.

When, on Sunday mornings, Sheilah and Peter talk about those times, they take on the glamor of something still to come. It is then he remembers Agnes Brusen. He never says her name. Sheilah wouldn't remember Agnes. Agnes is the only secret Peter has from his wife, the only puzzle he pieces together without her help. He thinks about families in the West as they were fifteen, twenty years ago—the iron-cold ambition, and every member pushing the next one on. He thinks of his father's parties. When he thinks of his father he imagines him with Sheilah, in a crowd. Actually, Sheilah and Peter's father never met, but they might have liked each other. His father admired good-looking women. Peter wonders what they were doing over there in Geneva—not Sheilah and Peter, *Agnes* and Peter. It is almost as if they had once run away together, silly as children, irresponsible as lovers. Peter and Sheilah are back where they started. While they were out in world affairs picking up microbes and debts, always on the fringe of disaster, the fringe of a fortune, Agnes went on and did—what? They lost each other. He thinks of the ice wagon going down the street. He sees something he has never seen in his life—a Western town that belongs to Agnes. Here is Agnes—small, mole-faced, round-shouldered because she has always carried a younger child. She watches the ice wagon and the trail of ice water in a morning invented for her: hers. He sees the weak prairie trees and the shadows on the sidewalk. Nothing moves except the shadows and the ice wagon and the changing amber of the child's eyes. The child is Peter. He has seen the grain of the cement sidewalk and the grass in the cracks, and the dust, and the dandelions at the edge of the road. He is there. He has taken the morning that belongs to Agnes, he is up before the others, and he knows everything. There is nothing he doesn't know. He could keep the morning, if he wanted to, but what can Peter do with the start of a summer day? Sheilah is here, it is a true Sunday morning, with its dimness and headache and remorse and regrets, and this is life. He says, 'We have the Balenciaga.' He touches Sheilah's hand. The children have their aunt now, and he and Sheilah have each other. Everything works out, somehow or other. Let Agnes have the start of the day. Let Agnes think it was invented for her. Who wants to be alone in the universe? No, begin at the beginning: Peter lost Agnes. Agnes says to herself somewhere, Peter is lost.

1964

Henry Kreisel

b. 1922

When Henry Kreisel wrote his doctoral thesis, 'The Problem of Exile and Alienation in Modern Literature', he was treating themes central to his own experience. Born in Vienna in 1922, Kreisel—a Jew—fled the Nazi invasion in 1938, taking refuge in England, where he found work in a clothing factory in Leeds. After Britain declared war on Germany, however, Kreisel was interned as an 'enemy alien'; the internment camp he was sent to in 1940 was in Canada. Fortunately, because of writings smuggled out of the camp, he was recognized as a promising student and allowed to complete his high-school education at Jarvis Collegiate, Toronto. In 1942 he enrolled at the University of Toronto, where he led his class and was awarded several scholarships.

Kreisel was deeply affected during his undergraduate studies by the poetry of A.M. Klein. He later said that 'having left Austria . . . as a refugee, I wanted to identify myself emotionally with Canada. Klein gave me [both] the courage to do this and to use everything that belonged to my total tradition' (*The Sphinx*, II, 3, 1977). Kreisel's interest in Canadian and other modern literatures led him to help found—with James Reaney and Robert Weaver—a Modern Letters Club in the university. After completing his B.A. in 1946 and his M.A. the following year, he accepted a teaching position in the English department at the University of Alberta. Except for two years at the University of London completing his Ph.D. (1952-4), Kreisel has remained at Alberta, and in 1975 he was named University Professor.

Kreisel is the author of two novels, *The Rich Man* (1948) and *The Betrayal* (1964), both dealing not only with the problems of the immigrant experience but also with the ethical complexities and difficult choices created by the moral chaos of the Nazi era. He has also written eight short stories, collected in *The Almost Meeting and Other Stories* (1981), which treat these subjects as well as Kreisel's experience of western Canada. His best-known story, 'The Broken Globe', has been translated into German, Italian, and Swedish, and adapted for the stage. Kreisel describes the particular event that inspired it in 'The Prairie: A State of Mind'. In this influential essay, which locates 'The Broken Globe' in a regional tradition that stretches back to the novels of Frederick Philip Grove and Martha Ostenso, Kreisel becomes an important spokesman for the idea that writing is shaped by the physical aspects of a writer's milieu: he believes that his own part in the literary tradition of the Prairies was created not by a knowledge of earlier writers but by the impact of place itself.

The Broken Globe

Since it was Nick Solchuk who first told me about the opening in my field at the University of Alberta, I went up to see him as soon as I received word that I had been appointed. He lived in one of those old mansions in Pimlico[1] that had once served as town houses for wealthy merchants and aristocrats, but now housed a less moneyed group of people—stenographers, students, and intellectuals of various kinds. He had studied at Cambridge and got his doctorate there and was now doing research at the Imperial College and rapidly establishing a reputation among the younger men for his work on problems which had to do with the curvature of the earth.

His room was on the third floor, and it was very cramped, but he refused to move because he could look out from his window and see the Thames and the steady flow of boats, and that gave him a sense of distance and of space also. Space, he said, was what he missed most in the crowded city. He referred to himself, nostalgically, as a prairie boy, and when he wanted to demonstrate what he meant by space he used to say that when a man stood and looked out across the open prairie, it was possible for him to believe that the earth was flat.

'So,' he said, after I had told him my news, 'you are going to teach French to prairie boys and girls. I congratulate you.' Then he cocked his head to one side, and looked me over and said: 'How are your ears?'

'My ears?' I said. 'They're all right. Why?'

'Prepare yourself,' he said. 'Prairie voices trying to speak French—that will be a great experience for you. I speak from experience. I learned my French pronunciation in a little one-room school in a prairie village. From an extraordinary girl, mind you, but her mind ran to science. Joan McKenzie—that was her name. A wiry little thing, sharp-nosed, and she always wore brown dresses. She was particularly fascinated by earthquakes. "In 1755 the city of Lisbon, Portugal, was devastated. Sixty-thousand persons died; the shock was felt in Southern France and North Africa; and inland waters of Great Britain and Scandinavia were agitated." You see, I still remember that, and I can hear her voice too. Listen: "In common with the entire solar system, the earth is moving through space at the rate of approximately 45,000 miles per hour, toward the constellation of Hercules. Think of that, boys and girls." Well, I thought about it. It was a lot to think about. Maybe that's why I became a geophysicist. Her enthusiasm was infectious. I knew her at her peak. After a while she got tired and married a solid farmer and had eight children.'

'But her French, I take it, was not so good,' I said.

'No,' he said. 'Language gave no scope to her imagination. Mind you, I took French seriously enough. I was a very serious student. For a while I even practiced French pronunciation at home. But I stopped it because it bothered my father. My mother begged me to stop. For the sake of peace.'

'Your father's ears were offended,' I said.

'Oh, no,' Nick said, 'not his ears. His soul. He was sure that I was learning French so I could run off and marry a French girl . . . . Don't laugh. It's true.'

[1]District in West London.

When once my father believed something, it was very hard to shake him.'

'But why should he have objected to your marrying a French girl anyway?'

'Because,' said Nick, and pointed a stern finger at me, 'because when he came to Canada he sailed from some French port, and he was robbed of all his money while he slept. He held all Frenchmen responsible. He never forgot and he never forgave. And, by God, he wasn't going to have that cursed language spoken in his house. He wasn't going to have any nonsense about science talked in his house either.' Nick was silent for a moment, and then he said, speaking very quietly, 'Curious man, my father. He had strange ideas, but a strange kind of imagination, too. I couldn't understand him when I was going to school or to the university. But then a year or two ago, I suddenly realized that the shape of the world he lived in had been forever fixed for him by some medieval priest in the small Ukrainian village where he was born and where he received an education of sorts when he was a boy. And I suddenly realized that he wasn't mad, but that he lived in the universe of the medieval church. The earth for him was the centre of the universe, and the centre was still. It didn't move. The sun rose in the East and it set in the West, and it moved perpetually around a still earth. God had made this earth especially for man, and man's function was to perpetuate himself and to worship God. My father never said all that in so many words, mind you, but that is what he believed. Everything else was heresy.'

He fell silent.

'How extraordinary,' I said.

He did not answer at once, and after a while he said, in a tone of voice which seemed to indicate that he did not want to pursue the matter further, 'Well, when you are in the middle of the Canadian West, I'll be in Rome. I've been asked to give a paper to the International Congress of Geophysicists which meets there in October.'

'So I heard,' I said. 'Wilcocks told me the other day. He said it was going to be a paper of some importance. In fact, he said it would create a stir.'

'Did Wilcocks really say that?' he asked eagerly, his face reddening, and he seemed very pleased. We talked for a while longer, and then I rose to go.

He saw me to the door and was about to open it for me, but stopped suddenly, as if he were turning something over in his mind, and then said quickly, 'Tell me—would you do something for me?'

'Of course,' I said. 'If I can.'

He motioned me back to my chair and I sat down again. 'When you are in Alberta,' he said, 'and if it is convenient for you, would you—would you go to see my father?'

'Why, yes,' I stammered, 'why, of course. I—I didn't realize he was still. . . .'

'Oh, yes,' he said, 'he's still alive, still working. He lives on his farm, in a place called Three Bear Hills, about sixty or seventy miles out of Edmonton. He lives alone. My mother is dead. I have a sister who is married and lives in Calgary. There were only the two of us. My mother could have no more children. It was a source of great agony for them. My sister goes to see him sometimes, and then she sometimes writes to me. He never writes to me. We—we had—what shall I call it—differences. If you went to see him and told him that I had not gone to the devil, perhaps . . .' He broke off abruptly, clearly agitated, and walked over to his window and stood staring out, then said, 'Perhaps you'd better not. I—I don't want to impose on you.'

I protested that he was not imposing at all, and promised that I would write to him as soon as I had paid my visit.

I met him several times after that, but he never mentioned the matter again.

I sailed from England about the middle of August and arrived in Montreal a week later. The long journey West was one of the most memorable experiences I have ever had. There were moments of weariness and dullness. But the very monotony was impressive. There was a grandeur about it. It was monotony of a really monumental kind. There were moments when, exhausted by the sheer impact of the landscape, I thought back with longing to the tidy, highly cultivated countryside of England and of France, to the sight of men and women working in the fields, to the steady succession of villages and towns, and everywhere the consciousness of nature humanized. But I also began to understand why Nick Solchuk was always longing for more space and more air, especially when we moved into the prairies, and the land became flatter until there seemed nothing, neither hill nor tree nor bush, to disturb the vast unbroken flow of land until in the far distance a thin, blue line marked the point where the prairie merged into the sky. Yet over all there was a strange tranquillity, all motion seemed suspended, and only the sun moved steadily, imperturbably West, dropping finally over the rim of the horizon, a blazing red ball, but leaving a superb evening light lying over the land still.

I was reminded of the promise I had made, but when I arrived in Edmonton, the task of settling down absorbed my time and energy so completely that I did nothing about it. Then, about the middle of October, I saw a brief report in the newspaper about the geophysical congress which had opened in Rome on the previous day, and I was mindful of my promise again. Before I could safely bury it in the back of my mind again, I sat down and wrote a brief letter to Nick's father, asking him when I could come out to visit him. Two weeks passed without an answer, and I decided to go and see him on the next Saturday without further formalities.

The day broke clear and fine. A few white clouds were in the metallic autumn sky and the sun shone coldly down upon the earth, as if from a great distance. I drove south as far as Wetaskiwin and then turned east. The paved highway gave way to gravel and got steadily worse. I was beginning to wonder whether I was going right, when I rounded a bend and a grain elevator hove like a signpost into view. It was now about three o'clock and I had arrived in Three Bear Hills, but, as Nick had told me, there were neither bears nor hills here, but only prairie, and suddenly the beginning of an embryonic street with a few buildings on either side like a small island in a vast sea, and then all was prairie again.

I stopped in front of the small general store and went in to ask for directions. Three farmers were talking to the storekeeper, a bald, bespectacled little man who wore a long, dirty apron, and stood leaning against his counter. They stopped talking and turned to look at me. I asked where the Solchuk farm was.

Slowly scrutinizing me, the storekeeper asked, 'You just new here?'

'Yes,' I said.

'From the old country, eh?'

'Yes.'

'You selling something?'

'No, no,' I said. 'I—I teach at the University.'

'That so?' He turned to the other men and said, 'Only boy ever went to University from around here was Solchuk's boy, Nick. Real brainy young kid, Nick. Two of 'em never got on together. Too different. You know.'

They nodded slowly.

'But that boy of his—he's a real big-shot scientist now. You know them addem bombs and them hydrergen bombs. He helps make 'em.'

'No, no,' I broke in quickly. 'That's not what he does. He's a geophysicist.'

'What's that?' asked one of the men.

But before I could answer, the little storekeeper asked excitedly, 'You know Nick?'

'Yes,' I said, 'we're friends. I've come to see his father.'

'And where's he now? Nick, I mean.'

'Right now he is in Rome,' I said. 'But he lives in London, and does research there.'

'Big-shot, eh,' said one of the men laconically, but with a trace of admiration in his voice, too.

'He's a big scientist, though, like I said. Isn't that so?' the storekeeper broke in.

'He's going to be a very important scientist indeed,' I said, a trifle solemnly.

'Like I said,' he called out triumphantly. 'That's showing 'em. A kid from Three Bear Hills, Alberta. More power to him!' His pride was unmistakable. 'Tell me, mister,' he went on, his voice dropping, 'does he remember this place sometimes? Or don't he want to know us no more?'

'Oh no,' I said quickly. 'He often talks of this place, and of Alberta, and of Canada. Some day he plans to return.'

'That's right,' he said with satisfaction. He drew himself up to full height, banged his fist on the table and said, 'I'm proud of that boy. Maybe old Solchuk don't think so much of him, but you tell him old Mister Marshall is proud of him.' He came from behind the counter and almost ceremoniously escorted me out to my car and showed me the way to Solchuk's farm.

I had about another five miles to drive, and the road, hardly more now than two black furrows cut into the prairie, was uneven and bumpy. The land was fenced on both sides of the road, and at last I came to a rough wooden gate hanging loosely on one hinge, and beyond it there was a cluster of small wooden buildings. The largest of these, the house itself, seemed at one time to have been ochre-colored, but the paint had worn off and it now looked curiously mottled. A few chickens were wandering about, pecking at the ground, and from the back I could hear the grunting and squealing of pigs.

I walked up to the house and, just as I was about to knock, the door was suddenly opened, and a tall, massively built old man stood before me.

'My name is . . . ' I began.

But he interrupted me. 'You the man wrote to me?' His voice, though unpolished, had the same deep timbre as Nick's.

'That's right,' I said.

'You a friend of Nick?'

'Yes.'

He beckoned me in with a nod of his head. The door was low and I had to stoop a bit to get into the room. It was a large, low-ceilinged room. A smallish window let in a patch of light which lit up the middle of the room but did not spread into the corners, so that it seemed as if it were perpetually dusk. A table occupied the centre, and on the far side there was a large wood stove on which stood a softly hissing black kettle. In the corner facing the entrance there was an iron bedstead, and the bed was roughly made, with a patchwork quilt thrown carelessly on top.

The old man gestured me to one of the chairs which stood around the table. 'Sit.'

I did as he told me, and he sat down opposite me and placed his large calloused hands before him on the table. He seemed to study me intently for a while, and I scrutinized him. His face was covered by a three-day's stubble, but in spite of that, and in spite of the fact that it was a face beaten by sun and wind, it was clear that he was Nick's father. For Nick had the same determined mouth, and the same high cheekbones and the same dark, penetrating eyes.

At last he spoke. 'You friend of Nick.'

I nodded my head.

'What he do now?' he asked sharply. 'He still tampering with the earth?'

His voice rose as if he were delivering a challenge, and I drew back involuntarily. 'Why—he's doing scientific research, yes,' I told him. 'He's . . . '

'What God has made,' he said sternly, 'no man should touch.'

Before I could regain my composure, he went on, 'He sent you. What for? What he want?'

'Nothing,' I said, 'nothing at all. He sent me to bring you greetings and to tell you he is well.'

'And you come all the way from Edmonton to tell me?'

'Yes, of course.'

A faint smile played about his mouth, and the features of his face softened. Then suddenly he rose from his chair and stood towering over me. 'You are welcome in this house,' he said.

The formality with which he spoke was quite extraordinary and seemed to call for an appropriate reply, but I could do little more than stammer a thank you, and he, assuming again a normal tone of voice, asked me if I cared to have coffee. When I assented he walked to the far end of the room and busied himself about the stove.

It was then that I noticed, just under the window, a rough little wooden table and on top of it a faded old globe made of cardboard, such as little children use in school. I was intrigued to see it there and went over to look at it more closely. The cheap metal mount was brown with rust, and when I lifted it and tried to turn the globe on its axis, I found that it would not rotate because part of it had been squashed and broken. I ran my hand over the deep dent, and suddenly the old man startled me.

'What you doing there?' Curiosity seemed mingled with suspicion in his voice and made me feel like a small child surprised by its mother in an unauthorized raid on the pantry. I set down the globe and turned. He was standing by the table with two big mugs of coffee in his hands.

'Coffee is hot,' he said.

I went back to my chair and sat down, slightly embarrassed.

'Drink,' he said, pushing one of the mugs over to me.

We both began to sip the coffee, and for some time neither of us said anything.

'That thing over there,' he said at last, putting down his mug, 'that thing you was looking at—he brought it home one day—he was a boy then—maybe thirteen-year-old—Nick. The other day I found it up in the attic. I was going to throw it in the garbage. But I forgot. There it belongs. In the garbage. It is a false thing.' His voice had now become venomous.

'False?' I said. 'How is it false?'

He disregarded my question. 'I remember,' he went on, 'he came home from school one day and we was all here in this room—all sitting around this table eating supper, his mother, his sister and me and Alex, too—the hired man like. And then sudden-like Nick pipes up, and he says, we learned in school today, he says, how the earth is round like a ball, he says, and how it moves around and around the sun and never stops, he says. They learning you rubbish in school, I say. But he says no, Miss McKenzie never told him no lies. Then I say she does, I say, and a son of mine shouldn't believe it. Stop your ears! Let not Satan come in!' He raised an outspread hand and his voice thundered as if he were a prophet armed. 'But he was always a stubborn boy—Nick. Like a mule. He never listened to reason. I believe it, he says. To me he says that—his father, just like that. I believe it, he says, because science has proved it and it is the truth. It is false, I cry, and you will not believe it. I believe it, he says. So then I hit him because he will not listen and will not obey. But he keeps shouting and shouting and shouting. She moves, he shouts, she moves, she moves!'

He stopped. His hands had balled themselves into fists, and the remembered fury sent the blood streaming into his face. He seemed now to have forgotten my presence and he went on speaking in a low murmuring voice, almost as if he were telling the story to himself.

'So the next day, or the day after, I go down to that school, and there is this little Miss McKenzie, so small and so thin that I could have crush her with my bare hands. What you teaching my boy Nick? I ask her. What false lies you stuffing in his head? What you telling him that the earth is round and that she moves for? Did Joshua tell the earth to stand still, or did he command the sun?[2] So she says to me, I don't care what Joshua done, she says, I will tell him what science has discovered. With that woman I could get nowhere. So then I try to keep him away from school, and I lock him up in the house, but it was not good. He got out, and he run to the school like, and Miss McKenzie she sends me a letter to

---

[2] Joshua 10:12-13: 'Then spake Joshua . . . and he said in the sight of Israel, Sun, stand thou still upon Gibeon . . . So the sun stood still in the midst of heaven, and hasted not to go down about a whole day.' From the time Copernicus first advanced his heliocentric theory, this biblical passage has been used to defend the earlier geocentric view.

say she will send up the inspectors if I try to keep him away from the school. And I could do nothing.'

His sense of impotence was palpable. He sat sunk into himself as if he were still contemplating ways of halting the scientific education of his son.

'Two, three weeks after,' he went on, 'he comes walking in this door with a large paper parcel in his hand. Now, he calls out to me, now I will prove it to you, I will prove that she moves. And he tears off the paper from the box and takes out this—this thing, and he puts it on the table here. Here, he cries, here is the earth, and look, she moves. And he gives that thing a little push and it twirls around like. I have to laugh. A toy, I say to him, you bring me a toy here, not bigger than my hand, and it is supposed to be the world, this little toy here, with the printed words on colored paper, this little cardboard ball. This Miss McKenzie, I say to him, she's turning you crazy in that school. But look, he says, she moves. Now I have to stop my laughing. I'll soon show you she moves, I say, for he is beginning to get me mad again. And I go up to the table and I take the toy thing in my hands and I smash it down like this.'

He raised his fists and let them crash down on the table as if he meant to splinter it.

'That'll learn you, I cry. I don't think he could believe I had done it, because he picks up the thing and he tries to turn it, but it don't turn no more. He stands there and the tears roll down his cheeks, and then, sudden-like, he takes the thing in both his hands and he throws it at me. And it would have hit me right in the face, for sure, if I did not put up my hand. Against your father, I cry, you will raise up your hand against your father. Asmodeus![3] I grab him by the arm, and I shake him and I beat him like he was the devil. And he makes me madder and madder because he don't cry or shout or anything. And I would have kill him there, for sure, if his mother didn't come in then and pull me away. His nose was bleeding, but he didn't notice. Only he looks at me and says, you can beat me and break my globe, but you can't stop her moving. That night my wife she make me swear by all that's holy that I wouldn't touch him no more. And from then on I never hit him again nor talk to him about this thing. He goes his way and I go mine.'

He fell silent. Then after a moment he snapped suddenly, 'You hold with that?'

'Hold with what?' I asked, taken aback.

'With that thing?' He pointed behind him at the little table and at the broken globe. His gnarled hands now tightly interlocked, he leaned forward in his chair and his dark, brooding eyes sought an answer from mine in the twilight of the room.

Alone with him there, I was almost afraid to answer firmly. Was it because I feared that I would hurt him too deeply if I did, or was I perhaps afraid that he would use violence on me as he had on Nick?

I cleared my throat. 'Yes,' I said then. 'Yes, I believe that the earth is round and that she moves. That fact has been accepted now for a long time.'

I expected him to round on me but he seemed suddenly to have grown very

[3]An evil demon, sometimes regarded as king of demons.

tired, and in a low resigned voice he said, 'Satan has taken over all the world.' Then suddenly he roused himself and hit the table hard with his fist, and cried passionately, 'But not me! Not me!'

It was unbearable. I felt that I must break the tension, and I said the first thing that came into my mind. 'You can be proud of your son in spite of all that happened between you. He is a fine man, and the world honors him for his work.'

He gave me a long look, 'He should have stayed here,' he said quietly. 'When I die, there will be nobody to look after the land. Instead he has gone off to tamper with God's earth.'

His fury was now all spent. We sat for a while in silence, and then I rose. Together we walked out of the house. When I was about to get into my car, he touched me lightly on the arm. I turned. His eyes surveyed the vast expanse of sky and land, stretching far into the distance, reddish clouds in the sky and blue shadows on the land. With a gesture of great dignity and power he lifted his arm and stood pointing into the distance, at the flat land and the low-hanging sky. 'Look,' he said, very slowly and very quietly, 'she is flat, and she stands still.'

It was impossible not to feel a kind of admiration for the old man. There was something heroic about him. I held out my hand and he took it. He looked at me steadily, then averted his eyes and said, 'Send greetings to my son.'

I drove off quickly, but had to stop again in order to open the wooden gate. I looked back at the house, and saw him still standing there, still looking at his beloved land, a lonely, towering figure framed against the darkening evening sky.

1965, 1981

The Prairie: A State of Mind

Soon after I first arrived in Alberta, now over twenty years ago, there appeared in the *Edmonton Journal* a letter in which the writer, replying to some article which appeared sometime earlier, asserted with passionate conviction that the earth was flat. Now in itself that would have been quite unremarkable, the expression merely of some cranky and eccentric old man. Normally, then, one would not have been likely to pay very much attention to such a letter, and one would have passed it over with an amused smile. Nothing pleases us more than to be able to feel superior to pre-scientific man, secure behind the fortress of our own knowledge. I am no different in this respect from most other people. But there was something in the tone of that letter that would not allow me that kind of response. Far from feeling superior, I felt awed. Even as I write these lines, the emotion evoked in me by that letter that appeared in a newspaper more than twenty years ago comes back to me, tangible and palpable.

The tone of the letter was imperious. Surveying his vast domains, a giant with feet firmly rooted in the earth, a lord of the land asserted what his eyes saw, what his heart felt, and what his mind perceived. I cut the letter out and for some time carried it about with me in my wallet. I don't really know why I did that. I do know that in my travels round the prairie in those early years of my life in the Canadian west I looked at the great landscape through the eyes of that unknown man. At last I threw the clipping away, but the imagined figure of that giant remained to haunt my mind.

Years later I finally came to terms with that vision in a story that I called 'The Broken Globe.'[1] This story deals with the clash between a father and his young son. The son, who is eventually to become a scientist, comes home from school one day and tells his father that the earth moves. The father, a Ukrainian settler, secure in something very like a medieval faith, asserts passionately that it does not and that his son is being tempted and corrupted by the devil. The story is told by a narrator, an academic who goes to visit the father, now an old man, to bring him greetings from his estranged scientist-son. At the end of the story, after the narrator has heard from the father about the conflict that alienated him from his son, the narrator rises to leave:

Together we walked out of the house. When I was about to get into my car, he touched me lightly on the arm. I turned. His eyes surveyed the vast expanse of sky and land, stretching far into the distance, reddish clouds in the sky and blue shadows on the land. With a gesture of great dignity and power he lifted his arm and stood pointing into the distance, at the flat land and the low-hanging sky.

'Look,' he said, very slowly and very quietly, 'she is flat and she stands still.'

It was impossible not to feel a kind of admiration for the old man. There was something heroic about him. I held out my hand and he took it. He looked at me steadily, then averted his eyes and said, 'Send greetings to my son.'

I drove off quickly, but had to stop again in order to open the wooden gate. I looked back at the house, and saw him still standing there, still looking at his beloved land, a lonely, towering figure framed against the darkening evening sky.

You will have noticed that the images I used to describe my imagined man seem extravagant—'a lord of the land,' 'a giant.' These were in fact the images that came to me and I should myself have regarded them as purely subjective, if I had not afterward in my reading encountered similar images in the work of other writers who write about the appearances of men on the prairie at certain times. Thus in Martha Ostenso's *Wild Geese*[2] a young school teacher sees 'against the strange pearly distance . . . the giant figure of a man beside his horse,' and when he comes closer she recognizes Fusi Aronson, 'the great Icelander. . . . He was grand in his demeanor, and somehow lonely, as a towering mountain is lonely, or as a solitary oak on the prairie.' On the very first page of *Settlers of the Marsh*, Philip Grove,[3] describing two men 'fighting their way through the gathering

[1]Preceding.

[2]1925; Martha Ostenso (1900-63) was born in Norway and came to the U.S. when she was two. After living in Minnesota and North Dakota she spent her adolescence and young adulthood in Manitoba, before returning to the States. Of her many novels, *Wild Geese*—now considered a classic of prairie realism—was the only one written while she was in Canada.

[3]1879-1948; Grove was also an immigrant, coming to North America from Germany around 1909 and arriving on the Prairies around 1912. (See Vol. I, pp. 257-8.) He published *Settlers of the Marsh* in 1925, *In Search of Myself* in 1946, and *Fruits of the Earth* in 1933.

dusk,' calls one of them, Lars Nelson, 'a giant, of three years' standing in the country'. And in his autobiography, *In Search of Myself*, Grove, recalling the origin of *Fruits of the Earth* and his first encounter with the figure who was to become Abe Spalding, describes the arresting and startling sight of a man plowing land generally thought to be unfit for farming. 'Outlined as he was against a tilted and spoked sunset in the western sky,' he writes, 'he looked like a giant. Never before had I seen, between farm and town, a human being in all my drives.' Grove goes on to tell how he stopped his horses and learned that this man had only that very afternoon arrived from Ontario, after a train journey of two thousand miles, had at once filed a claim for a homestead of a hundred and sixty acres, had unloaded his horses from the freight-car, and was now plowing his first field. And when Grove expresses his surprise at the speed with which this newcomer set to work, the man replies, 'Nothing else to do'.

I set the image of the giant in the landscape over against the more familiar one of man pitted against a vast and frequently hostile natural environment that tends to dwarf him, at the mercy of what Grove calls, in *Settlers of the Marsh*, 'a dumb shifting of forces'. Man, the giant-conqueror, and man, the insignificant dwarf always threatened by defeat, form the two polarities of the state of mind produced by the sheer physical fact of the prairie.

There are moments when the two images coalesce. So the observant Mrs Bentley, whose diary forms the substance of Sinclair Ross's novel *As for Me and My House*,[4] records the response of a prairie congregation during the bleak and drought-haunted 1930s:

> The last hymn was staidly orthodox, but through it there seemed to mount something primitive, something that was less a response to Philip's sermon and scripture reading than to the grim futility of their own lives. Five years in succession now they've been blown out, dried out, hailed out; and it was as if in the face of so blind and uncaring a universe they were trying to assert themselves, to insist upon their own meaning and importance.

All discussion of the literature produced in the Canadian west must of necessity begin with the impact of the landscape upon the mind. 'Only a great artist,' records Mrs Bentley, 'could ever paint the prairie, the vacancy and stillness of it, the bare essentials of a landscape, sky and earth.' W.O. Mitchell, in the opening sentences of *Who Has Seen the Wind*,[5] speaks of the 'least common denominator of nature, the skeleton requirements simply, of land and sky'. He goes on to describe the impact of the landscape on Brian O'Connal, a four-year-old boy, living in a little prairie town and venturing for the first time to the edge of town:

> He looked up to find that the street had stopped. Ahead lay the sudden emptiness of the prairie. For the first time in his four years of life he was alone on the prairie.
> He had seen it often, from the veranda of his uncle's farmhouse, or at the end of a long street, but till now he had never heard it. The hum of telephone

---

[4] 1941; Ross (b. 1908) was born in Saskatchewan and lived there and in Manitoba until 1942. (See Vol. I, pp. 448-9.)

[5] 1947; Mitchell (b. 1914) lived in Saskatchewan until moving to the United States when he was twelve. He returned to the Prairies at seventeen and has lived there since. (See Vol. I, pp. 665-6.)

wires along the road, the ring of hidden crickets, the stitching sound of grass-hoppers, the sudden relief of a meadow lark's song, were deliciously strange to him. . . .

A gopher squeaked questioningly as Brian sat down upon a rock warm to the back of his thigh. . . . The gopher squeaked again, and he saw it a few yards away, sitting up, and watching him from his pulpit hole. A suave-winged hawk chose that moment to slip its shadow over the face of the prairie.

And all about him was the wind now, a pervasive sighing through great emptiness, unhampered by the buildings of the town, warm and living against his face and in his hair.

Only one other kind of landscape gives us the same skeleton requirements, the same vacancy and stillness, the same movement of wind through space—and that is the sea. So when Mrs Bentley records in her diary that 'there's a high, rocking wind that rattles the window and creaks the walls. It's strong and steady like a great tide after the winter pouring north again, and I have a queer, helpless sense of being lost miles out in the middle of it', she might well be tossing in heavy seas, protected only by a small and fragile little bark. In Grove's *Over Prairie Trails*, that remarkable book of impressionistic essays describing seven trips that Grove made in 1917 and 1918 between Gladstone and Falmouth near the western shore of Lake Manitoba, the prairie as sea becomes one of the controlling patterns shaping the imagination of the observer. On one of these trips—in the dead of winter—Grove prepares his horse-drawn cutter as if it were a boat being readied for a fairly long and possibly dangerous journey:

Not a bolt but I tested it with a wrench; and before the stores were closed, I bought myself enough canned goods to feed me for a week should through any untoward accident the need arise. I always carried a little alcohol stove, and with my tarpaulin I could convert my cutter within three minutes into a wind-proof tent. Cramped quarters, to be sure, but better than being given over to the wind at thirty below![6]

Soon the cutter, the horses, and the man meet the first test—very like a Conradian crew coming to grips with a storm at sea. A mountainous snowdrift bars the way. The horses, Dan and Peter, who become wonderful characters in their own right, panic. They plunge wildly, rear on their hind legs, pull apart, try to turn and retrace their steps. 'And meanwhile the cutter went sharply up at first, as if on the vast crest of a wave, then toppled over into a hole made by Dan, and altogether behaved like a boat tossed on a stormy sea. Then order returned into the chaos. . . . I spoke to the horses in a soft, quiet, purring voice; and at last I pulled in.'

He becomes aware of the sun, cold and high in the sky, a relentless, inexorable force, and suddenly two Greek words come into his mind: Homer's *pontos airy-getos*—the barren sea. A half hour later he understands why:

This was indeed like nothing so much as like being out in rough waters and in a troubled sea, with nothing to brace the storm with but a wind-tossed nutshell

[6]From the sketch called 'Snow', reprinted in Vol. I, pp. 259-76. *Over Prairie Trails*, Grove's first book, was published in 1922.

of a one-man sailing craft. . . . When the snow reached its extreme depth, it gave you the feeling which a drowning man may have when fighting his desperate fight with the salty waves. But more impressive than that was the frequent outer resemblance. The waves of the ocean rise up and reach out and batter against the rocks and battlements of the shore, retreating again and ever returning to the assault. . . . And if such a high crest wave had suddenly been frozen into solidity, its outline would have mimicked to perfection many a one of the snow shapes that I saw around.

And when, at the end of another journey, the narrator reaches home, he is like a sailor reaching harbor after a long voyage:

there was the signal put out for me. A lamp in one of the windows of the school. . . . And in the most friendly and welcoming way it looked with its single eye across at the nocturnal guest.

I could not see the cottage, but I knew that my little girl lay sleeping in her cosy bed, and that a young woman was sitting there in the dark, her face glued to the window-pane, to be ready with a lantern which burned in the kitchen whenever I might pull up between school and house. And there, no doubt, she had been sitting for a long while already; and there she was destined to sit during the winter that came, on Friday nights—full often for many and many an hour—full often till midnight—and sometimes longer.

The prairie, like the sea, thus often produces an extraordinary sensation of confinement within a vast and seemingly unlimited space. The isolated farmhouses, the towns and settlements, even the great cities that eventually sprang up on the prairies, become islands in that land-sea, areas of relatively safe refuge from the great and lonely spaces. In *Wild Geese* Martha Ostenso describes a moment when the sensation of safety and of abandonment are felt to be evenly balanced:

Fine wisps of rain lashed about the little house, and the wind whistled in the birch trees outside, bleak as a lost bird. These sounds defined the feelings of enclosed warmth and safety. . . . But they did also the opposed thing. They stirred the fear of loneliness, the ancient dread of abandonment in the wilderness in the profounder natures of these two who found shelter here. For an imponderable moment they sought beyond each other's eyes, sought for understanding, for communion under the vast terrestrial influence that bound them, an inevitable part and form of the earth, inseparable one from the other.

At the same time the knowledge of the vast space outside brings to the surface anxieties that have their roots elsewhere and thus sharpens and crystallizes a state of mind. In *As for Me and My House* Mrs Bentley uses the prairie constantly as a mirror of her own fears, frustrations, and helplessness:

It's an immense night out there, wheeling and windy. The lights on the street and in the houses are helpless against the black wetness, little unilluminating glints that might be painted on it. The town seemed huddled together, cowering on a high, tiny perch, afraid to move lest it topple into the wind. Close to the parsonage is the church, black even against the darkness, towering ominously up through the night and merging with it. There's a soft steady swish of rain on the roof, and a gurgle of eave troughs running over. Above, in the high cold night, the wind goes swinging past, indifferent, liplessly mournful. It frightens me, makes me feel lost, dropped on this little perch of town and abandoned. I wish Philip would waken.

That, however, is not the only, perhaps not even the most significant response to the challenge of lonely and forbidden spaces. It is easy to see Mrs Bentley's reaction as prototypical of the state of mind induced by the prairie, but it would not be altogether accurate. It is one kind of response, but set over against it there is the response typified in Grove's *Settlers of the Marsh* by Niels Lindstedt, who, like a Conradian adventurer, a Lord Jim or a Stein, is driven to follow a dream. It expresses itself in 'a longing to leave and go to the very margin of civilization, there to clear a new place; and when it is cleared and people began to settle about it, to move on once more, again to the very edge of pioneerdom, to start it all over anew. . . . That way his enormous strength would still have a meaning.'

To conquer a piece of the continent, to put one's imprint upon virgin land, to say, 'Here I am, for that I came,' is as much a way of defining oneself, of proving one's existence, as is Descartes's *cogito, ergo sum*. That is surely why that man whom Grove saw plowing a field barely two hours after his arrival was driven to do it. He had to prove to himself that he was in some way master of his destiny, that he was fully alive, and that his strength had meaning. When he told Grove that he was doing what he was doing because there was nothing else to do, he was telling him the simple truth, but leaving a more complex truth unspoken, and probably even unperceived.

The conquest of territory is by definition a violent process. In the Canadian west, as elsewhere on this continent, it involved the displacement of the indigenous population by often scandalous means, and then the taming of the land itself. The displacement, the conquest of the Indians, and later the rising of the Métis under Louis Riel, are events significantly absent from the literature I am discussing. Occasionally Riel breaks into the consciousness of one or another of the characters, usually an old man or an old woman remembering troubled times; occasionally the figure of an Indian appears briefly, but is soon gone. No doubt that is how things appeared to the European settlers on the prairie; no doubt our writers did not really make themselves too familiar with the indigenous people of the prairie, seeing them either as noble savages or not seeing them at all, but it is likely that a conscious or subconscious process of suppression is also at work here.

The conquest of the land itself is by contrast a dominant theme, and the price paid for the conquest by the conqueror or the would-be conqueror is clearly and memorably established. The attempt to conquer the land is a huge gamble. Many lose, and there are everywhere mute emblems testifying to defeat. 'Once I passed the skeleton of a stable,' Grove records in *Over Prairie Trails*, 'the remnant of the buildings put up by a pioneer settler who had to give in after having wasted effort and substance and worn his knuckles to the bone. The wilderness uses human material up.' But into the attempted conquest, whether ultimately successful or not, men pour an awesome, concentrated passion. The breaking of the land becomes a kind of rape, a passionate seduction. The earth is at once a willing and unwilling mistress, accepting and rejecting her seducer, the cause of his frustration and fulfilment, and either way the shaper and controller of his mind, exacting servitude.

The most powerful statement of that condition in the literature of the Canadian west is, I think, to be found in Martha Ostenso's *Wild Geese*, the story of Caleb Gare, a tyrannical man who, himself enslaved to the land, in turn enslaves his whole family to serve his own obsession. Characteristically, Ostenso sees him as a gigantic figure. 'His tremendous shoulders and massive head, which loomed forward from the rest of his body like a rough projection of rock from the edge of a cliff,' she writes, 'gave him a towering appearance.' He is conceived in a way which makes it difficult to speak of him in conventional terms of human virtue or human vice, for he is conceived as 'a spiritual counterpart of the land, as harsh, as demanding, as tyrannical as the very soil from which he drew his existence'. He can only define himself in terms of the land, and paradoxically it is the land and not his children that bears testimony to his potency and manhood. As he supervises his sons and daughters, grown up, but still only extensions of himself, working in the fields, he is gratified by the knowledge that what they are producing is the product of *his* land, the result of *his* industry, 'as undeniably his as his right hand, testifying to the outer world that Caleb Gare was a successful owner and user of the soil'. At night he frequently goes out with a lantern swinging low along the earth. No one knows where he goes or why he goes, and no one dares to ask him, but his daughter Judith once remarks scornfully 'that it was to assure himself that his land was still all there'. Only the land can ultimately give him the assurance that he is alive: 'Before him glimmered the silver grey sheet of the flax—rich, beautiful, strong. All unto itself, complete, demanding everything, and in turn yielding everything—growth of the earth, the only thing on the earth worthy of respect, of homage.'

Being so possessed by the prairie, his mind and body as it were an extension of it, he cannot give himself to anyone else. Since he is incapable of loving another human being, he can receive no love in return. He marries his wife knowing that she has had a child born out of wedlock because this gives him the power of blackmail over her and, in a stern and puritan society, chains her forever to him and to his land. He knows that she once gave herself to another man in a way in which she can never give herself to him, but he cannot see that he chose her because he wanted someone who could not demand from him a love he is incapable of giving. Having committed his mind and his body to the land, greedily acquiring more and more, he can only use other human beings as instruments to help feed an appetite that can never be satisfied. His human feelings must therefore be suppressed, and the passion of his blood must remain forever frustrated, sublimated in his passion for the acquisition of more and more land. Man, the would-be conqueror, is thus also man, the supreme egoist, subordinating everything to the flow of a powerful ambition. 'Caleb Gare—he does not feel,' says Fusi Aronson, the Icelander. 'I shall kill him one day. But even that he will not feel.'

He does feel for his land. But the land is a fickle mistress, and he must live in perpetual fear, for he can never be sure that this mistress will remain faithful. She may, and indeed she does, with hail and fire destroy in minutes all that he has labored to build.

Caleb Gare's obsession may be extreme, and yet a measure of egocentricity, though more often found in less virulent form, is perhaps necessary if the huge task of taming a continent is to be successfully accomplished. At the same time the necessity of survival dictates cooperative undertakings. So it is not surprising that the prairie has produced the most right-wing as well as the most left-wing provincial governments in Canada. But whether conservative or radical, these governments have always been puritan in outlook, a true reflection of their constituencies.

The prairie settlements, insecure islands in that vast land-sea, have been austere, intensely puritan societies. Not that puritanism in Canada is confined to the prairie, of course, but on the prairie it has been more solidly entrenched than even in rural Ontario, and can be observed in something very like a distilled form.

It can be argued that in order to tame the land and begin the building, however tentatively, of something approaching a civilization, the men and women who settled on the prairie had to tame themselves, had to curb their passions and contain them within a tight neo-Calvinist framework. But it is not surprising that there should be sudden eruptions and that the passions, long suppressed, should burst violently into the open and threaten the framework that was meant to contain them. In the literature with which I am dealing this violence often takes the form of melodrama, and though this sudden eruption of violence sometimes seems contrived for the sake of a novel's plot, it is also clearly inherent in the life the novelists observed. It is natural that novelists should exploit the tensions which invariably arise when a rigid moral code attempts to see strict limits on the instinctual life, if not indeed to suppress it altogether. Thus illicit love affairs, conducted furtively, without much joy, quickly begun and quickly ended, and sometimes complicated by the birth of illegitimate children, can be used as a perhaps obvious but nevertheless effective centre for a novel's structure, as for example in Stead's *Grain*,[7] in Ostenso's *Wild Geese*, in Laurence's *A Jest of God*, in Ross's *As for Me and My House*.

It is because *As for Me and My House* contains the most uncompromising rendering of the puritan state of mind produced on the prairie that the novel has been accorded a central place in prairie literature. In the figure of Philip Bentley, a Presbyterian minister and artist *manqué*, we have—at least as he emerges from the diary of his wife—an embodiment of the puritan temperament, the product of his environment and much more a part of it than he would ever admit, angry not really because the communities in which he serves are puritan, but because they are not puritan enough, because they expect him to purvey a genteel kind of piety that will serve as a respectable front to hide a shallow morality. But his own emotions remain frozen within the puritan framework from which he cannot free his spirit. So he draws more and more into himself, becomes aloof and unknowable, not in the end so different from Caleb Gare, though in temperament and sensibil-

---

[7]Robert Stead (1880-1959) was born in Ontario but lived in Manitoba from the time he was two. Between 1914 and 1931 he wrote eight novels; *Grain* (1926) is regarded as the most important of these. Margaret Laurence (b. 1926) has written five works of fiction about characters from Manawaka, a fictionalized version of her hometown of Neepawa, Man. *The Stone Angel* (1964) and *A Jest of God* (1966) are the first two of these. (See pp. 000-00.)

ity they seem at first glance to move in totally different worlds. Philip's wife is certain that 'there's some twisted, stumbling power locked up within him, so blind and helpless still it can't find outlet, so clenched with urgency it can't release itself.' His drawing and painting reflect an inner paralysis. He draws endless prairie scenes that mirror his own frustration—the false fronts on the stores, doors and windows that are crooked and pinched, a little schoolhouse standing lonely and defiant in a landscape that is like a desert, 'almost a lunar desert, with queer, fantastic pits and drifts of sand encroaching right to the doorstep'. Philip Bentley's emotional paralysis affects of course his relationship with his wife. Thus she describes in her diary how he lies beside her, his muscles rigid, and she presses closer to him, pretending to stir in her sleep, 'but when I put my hand on his arm there was a sharp little contraction against my touch, and after a minute I shifted again, and went back to my own pillow'.

Only once does the twisted power that's locked up within him find some kind of outlet—and then disastrously, when he seduces the young girl Judith who has come to help in the house during his wife's illness.

Prairie puritanism is one result of the conquest of the land, part of the price exacted for the conquest. Like the theme of the conquest of the land, the theme of the imprisoned spirit dominates serious prairie writing, and is connected with it. We find this theme developed not only in Ross's novel, where it is seen at its bleakest and most uncompromising, not only in Grove's and Ostenso's work, but also in more recent novels, such as Margaret Laurence's two novels, *The Stone Angel* and *A Jest of God*, and in George Ryga's *Ballad of a Stone Picker*,[8] and, surprisingly perhaps, in W.O. Mitchell's *Who Has Seen the Wind*, which is conceived as a celebration and lyrical evocation of a prairie childhood. Brian O'Connal is initiated into the mysteries of God and nature, of life and death, but he is also brought face to face with the strange figure of the young Ben, a curious amalgam of noble savage and Wordsworthian child of nature. Again and again he appears, seemingly out of nowhere, soundlessly, the embodiment of a kind of free prairie spirit. His hair is 'bleached as the dead prairie grass itself', his trousers are always torn, he never wears shoes. He has 'about as much moral conscience as the prairie wind that lifted over the edge of the prairie world to sing mortality to every living thing'. He does not play with other children, takes no part in organized school games. Though he can run 'with the swiftness of a prairie chicken,' and jump like an antelope, he refuses to have anything to do with athletic competitions. School itself is 'an intolerable incarceration for him, made bearable only by flights of freedom which totaled up to almost the same number as the days he attended'. The solid burghers of the town, strait-laced and proper, try desperately to tame him, for his wild spirit represents a danger to them. But they cannot control him any more than they can control the wind. Brian O'Connal is drawn to the young Ben, and though they rarely speak to each other, there grows up between them a strong bond, what Mitchell calls 'an extrasensory brothership'. The young Ben is Brian's double, the free spirit Brian would like to be, but dare not be. For Brian, one feels, will ultimately conform to the demands of his society and he will subdue the young Ben within himself.

[8] 1966; Ryga (b. 1932) grew up in Alberta but has lived in British Columbia since 1962.

Most of the works that I have dealt with were conceived and written more than a quarter of a century ago. There have been social and industrial changes on the prairie since then, and the tempo of these changes has been rapidly accelerating in the past ten years or so. Yet it is surprising that such novels as Adele Wiseman's *The Sacrifice*[9] and John Marlyn's *Under the Ribs of Death*, published in the 1950s, and Margaret Laurence's *The Stone Angel* and *A Jest of God* and George Ryga's *Ballad of a Stone Picker*, published in the 1960s, should still adhere to the general pattern of the earlier works. The Winnipeg of Wiseman and Marlyn is the city of the 1920s and 1930s, a city of newly arrived immigrants, and the small towns of the Laurence and Ryga novels are clearly the small towns Ross and Ostenso knew.

For though much has changed in the west, much also still remains unchanged. Prairie puritanism is now somewhat beleaguered and shows signs of crumbling, but it remains a potent force still, and the vast land itself has not yet been finally subdued and altered. On a hot summer day it does not take long before, having left the paved streets of the great cities where hundreds of thousands of people now live, one can still see, outlined against the sky, the lonely, giant-appearing figures of men like Caleb Gare or the Ukrainian farmer in my story. And on a winter day one can turn off the great superhighways that now cross the prairies and drive along narrow, snow-covered roads, and there it still lies, the great, vast land-sea, and it is not difficult to imagine Philip Grove in his fragile cutter, speaking softly to Dan and Peter, his gentle, faithful horses, and preparing them to hurl themselves once more against that barren sea, those drifts of snow.

1968

[9]1956; Wiseman (b. 1928) grew up in Winnipeg and now lives in Toronto. John Marlyn (b. 1912) was born in Hungary and came to Winnipeg with his family as an infant; *Under the Ribs of Death* was published in 1957.

Eli Mandel

b. 1922

Elias Wolf Mandel grew up in the small western-Canadian town of Estevan, Sask., which, with the neighbouring towns of Hoffer and Hirsch, provided him not only with a strong sense of Russian-Jewish culture but with the *idea* of the Prairie West—both important elements in his poetry. He left Estevan to attend the University of Saskatchewan. After serving as an army medical corpsman in the Second World War he returned to the university for graduate work, completing an M.A. in 1949 and then beginning Ph.D. studies at the University of Toronto. During this period Mandel began to publish poetry in John Sutherland's *Northern Review*, Raymond Souster's *Contact*, and the Montreal journal *CIV/n*. In 1954 his work—along with that of Gael Turnbull and Phyllis Webb—was featured in *Trio*, published by Souster's Contact Press. In the same year Mandel joined the staff of the Collège Militaire Royal de Saint-Jean (where he taught until the completion of his Ph.D. in 1957) and became part of the literary community in nearby Montreal.

In 1957 Mandel returned west to join the University of Alberta's English faculty. Ten years later he became a member of the Humanities and English departments at York University, Toronto. In 1978 he was writer-in-residence for the city of Regina, in 1979 visiting professor at the University of Victoria, and in spring 1983 visiting professor at the University of Rome.

As well as being a teacher, a poet, and a critic, Mandel has also been an important editor. His anthologies include *Poetry 62/Poésie 62* (1961, edited with Jean-Guy

Pilon), *Poets of Contemporary Canada: 1960-1970* (1972), *Five Modern Canadian Poets* (1970), and *Eight More Canadian Poets* (1972). His anthology of essays, *Contexts of Canadian Criticism* (1971), provides an overview of the influences of culture and theory on the criticism of Canadian literature.

Mandel's own poetry is a further reflection of his interest in the range of Canadian literary activity. His early work, the 'Minotaur Poems' in *Trio* as well as *The Fuseli Poems* (1960), tends toward abstract, mythopoeic meditations, a type of writing associated with Canadian poets of this period who were influenced by Northrop Frye. His next collection, *Black and Secret Man* (1964), was followed by *An Idiot Joy* (1967), which won a Governor General's Award. (In 1973 Mandel included poems from these volumes in *Crusoe: Poems New and Selected*.) While continuing to reflect Mandel's belief in man's inherently dark and deceptive side, these books showed—in their increased social awareness and in their spare, more accessible, style—the influence of his earlier contact with the Montreal poets. In *Stony Plain* (1973), *Out of Place* (1977), and *Life Sentence* (1981) Mandel's poetry is concerned with observation and event, and its style is even more stripped-down—features it shares with the work of west-coast writers such as those in the *Tish* movement, and with the prairie poetry of John Newlove.

The drive to make connections—to create a poetry that draws together widely varied places, individuals, and periods, and to find meaning in their relationships—

informs all of Mandel's work. Even his criticism tends to unite divergent elements of culture and literature into a personal vision. In the lectures and critical essays collected in *Criticism: The Silent-Speaking World* (1966) and *Another Time* (1977), he allows the reader to follow the development of his thought from his initial consideration of a problem, through his processes of associating seemingly unrelated elements, to a final synthesizing of these elements in his conclusion. This method of associative thought is as important as Mandel's initial subject, offering the reader not so much new answers to existing questions as new questions. 'The City in Canadian Poetry', reprinted below, is an example of this kind of phenomenological criticism.

Mandel's best poems develop in the same associative manner, describing a pattern of response and a process of moving from perception of a single event or thing to a growing understanding of its real importance, its hidden meaning. He maps—in poems such as 'The Meaning of the I CHING' and 'Doors of Perception'—the non-linear pathways the mind takes to unite perception with memory: in effect he tells us his dreams. Appropriately the title of his collected poems, *Dreaming Backwards* (1981), is a metaphor for the general meditative nature of his poetry. For Mandel the writer is a kind of healer, a shaman, who through the trickery of words and syntax tears away the confusion and complexity of a duplicitous present to reveal a truth that lies beyond self and time.

Two Part Exercise on a Single Image

I
I come into the desolation
Of this calm September town
Which slants out of morning
Into the wild disaster of sunlight,
And I see that my street is a tree
Split into a thousand sentences
Any one of which can hang me.
The sun shatters my tree
In a wind of light
Into a torch in the unexplained   10
Interior, luminous with volcanoes,
Dark fig trees, and the white
Question mark of a polar bear.

II
You think it's easy? A matter of words?
You wonder that I'm a poor speller?
Let me tell you this has nothing to do with
Teaching, or even the love of poetry.
It is an eyesore, a stye,
A social disaster. Look for once
At the real, ridiculous self   20
Crouched in the unexplained interior.
See it looming in the light of
Exploding volcanoes, dark fig trees,

Like the hunched white question mark of
A polar bear.
        Oh my friend
I too like company
And have ambitions in business.

1960

Day of Atonement:[1] Standing

My Lord, how stands it with me now
Who, standing here before you
(who, fierce as you are, are also just),
Cannot bow down. You order this.
Why, therefore, I must break
If bend I will not, yet bend I must.

But I address myself to you thus,
Covered and alert, and will not bare
My self. Then I must bear you,
Heavy as you are.   10
        This is the time
The bare tree bends in the fierce wind
And stripped, my God, springs to the sky.

1964

[1] Yom Kippur, the ritual day in the Jewish calendar on which man seeks reconciliation with God for his transgressions. In Jewish ceremonies a man traditionally stands in prayer and meditation with his head covered by a prayer shawl; such prayer often takes the form of conversing with God.

Houdini[1]

I suspect he knew that trunks are metaphors,
could distinguish between the finest rhythms
unrolled on rope or singing in a chain
and knew the metrics of the deepest pools

I think of him listening to the words
spoken by manacles, cells, handcuffs,
chests, hampers, roll-top desks, vaults,
especially the deep words spoken by coffins

escape, escape: quaint Harry in his suit

[1] Harry Houdini, born Ehrich Weiss (1874-1926), stage magician and escape artist; his most dramatic escapes were those from chains while inside a trunk under water and from a buried coffin.

his chains, his desk, attached to all attachments   10
how he'd sweat in that precise struggle
with those binding words, wrapped around him
like that mannered style, his formal suit

and spoken when? by whom? What thing first said
'there's no way out?'; so that he'd free himself,
leap, squirm, no matter how, to chain himself again,
once more jump out of the deep alive
with all his chains singing around his feet
like the bound crowds who sigh, who sigh.

1967

The Meaning of the *I Ching*[1]

i
unopened
          book of old men
          orange-blossom book
                         before me
you were
          how could you contain me?

do you not see I am the mouths
of telegraphs and cemeteries?
my mother groaned like the whole
of Western Union to deliver   10
my message
               and yelling birthdays
that unrolled from my lungs
like ticker-tape for presidents
about to be murdered
                  I sped
on a line that flew
to the vanishing point of the west

before I was
               you were   20

[1]The *I Ching* (pronounced 'E Jing') or *Book of Changes*, an ancient Taoist book of wisdom that was incorporated into Confucianism and remained, until fairly recently, part of Chinese education. A book of oracular pronouncements, long associated with occult practices, the *I Ching* is a collection of interpretations and commentary on the permutations of pairs of 'trigrams' (combinations of three broken or unbroken lines) that result in sixty-four 'hexagrams' obtained randomly, often by throwing coins. These hexagrams, all of which have names, and their commentaries symbolically express a complete philosophy of life that teaches the individual how to respond to flux or change, partly by affirming that the natural order of the universe is constant. (Mandel says that he wrote this poem upon first getting the *I Ching*, before he opened the book, and that the phrase 'earth upon earth' in line 46 was coincidentally also the name of the first hexagram he 'threw' after writing the poem.)

unopened book
      do not craze me
with the odour of orange-blossom

do not sit there
like smiling old men

    how could you contain me?

ii
under my fingers words form themselves
it's crazy to talk of temples in this day
but light brightens on my page
like today moving against the wooden house   30
all shapes change and yet stay
as if they were marble in autumn
as if in the marbled yellow autumn
each western house becomes a shrine
stiff against the age of days
under my fingers stiffly formed

I will walk in streets that vanish
noting peculiar elms like old women
who will crash under the storm of sun
that breaks elm, woman, man   40
into a crumble of stump and bark
until the air is once more clear
in the sane emptiness of fall

iii
my body speaks to me
as my arms say: two are one
as my feet say: earth upon earth
as my knees say: bow down, unhinge yourself
as my cells say: we repeat the unrepeatable

the book speaks: arrange yourself in the form
                that will arrange you   50

before I was: colours that hurt me
                arranged themselves in me

before I was: horizons that blind me
                arranged themselves in me

before I was: the dead who speak to me
                arranged themselves in me

iv
I am the mouths
of smiling old men

there rises from me
the scent of orange-blossoms   60

I speak in the words
of the ancient dead

arranged
in the raging sun
in the stiffening age of days

and in the temple of my house

1967

On the 25th Anniversary of the
Liberation of Auschwitz:[1]

MEMORIAL SERVICES, TORONTO, JANUARY 25, 1970
YMHA BLOOR & SPADINA

the name is hard
a German sound made out of
the gut guttural throat
y scream yell ing open
voice mouth growl
                    and sweat
'the only way out of Auschwitz
is through the chimneys'[2]
                    of course
that's second hand   that's told   10
again   Sigmund Sherwood (Sobolewski)[3]
twisting himself into that sentence
before us on the platform
                    the poem

---

[1]The German name for Oswiecim, a southern Polish city and the location of the notorious Nazi exter-
mination camp in which prisoners—Polish, Russian, and, beginning in 1941, Jewish—were tortured,
experimented upon, and killed *en masse* in acid showers that produced cyanide gas. They were then
cremated in ovens to keep the soil from being poisoned by the burial of this large number of corpses.
The German commander of the camp, Rudolf Hess, admitted to the murder of over 2,500,000; Allied
Forces estimated the figure to be as high as four million.
[2]Deputy Commandant Karl Fritzsch—who first tried Zyklon B, the commercial form of hydrocyanic
acid preferred by the Nazis for exterminating human beings—was fond of greeting incoming prisoners with this expression.
[3]A survivor of five years' imprisonment at Auschwitz who spoke at the Toronto Memorial Service; a
socialist, Sherwood (his Polish name was Sobolewski) was one of the earliest prisoners brought to
Auschwitz, where few inmates survived more than several months.

shaping itself late in the after
noon later than it would be:

Pendericki's 'Wrath of God'[4]
moaning electronic Polish theatric
the screen silent
                    framed by the name   20
looking away from/pretending not there
no   name   no   not   name no

            Auschwitz
        in GOTHIC lettering [5]
                    the hall
a parody a reminiscence a nasty memory
the Orpheum in Estevan before Buck Jones[6]
the Capitol in Regina before Tom Mix
waiting for the guns
waiting for the cowboy killers   30
one two three
            Legionnaires
Polish ex-prisoners Association
Legions
        their medals their flags

so the procession, the poem gradual
ly insistent beginning to shape itself
with the others
            walked with them
into the YMHA Bloor & Spadina   40
thinking apocalypse shame degradation
thinking bones and bodies melting
thickening thinning melting bones and bodies
thinking not mine / must speak clearly
the poet's words / Yevtyshenko[7] at Baba-Yar

    there   this January   snow

[4]*Dies Irae*, for soloist, choir, and orchestra, was composed in 1967 by Krysztof Penderecki (b.
1933), Polish composer of experimental music that employs unconventional sounds, including electronic ones, along with unusual vocal articulation; his music is often freakish and eerie.
[5]Gothic letters over the entrance-way to Auschwitz spelled out the words '*Arbeit Macht Frei*' ('Work
Makes One Free')—an ironic motto, because those who were not immediately destroyed in the death
chambers were worked to death. Mandel has indicated that he was here also invoking other senses of
the word 'gothic', including its particular association with German art and architecture as well as the
word's original meaning of 'primitive' or 'barbaric'.
[6]Cowboy hero in silent movies, as was Tom Mix. Mandel is here ironically counterpointing the memory of himself as a Jewish youngster cheering for the cowboy—that is, for the 'white man' against the
Indian—with the genocide that he as an adult later confronted.
[7]Russian poet Yevgeny Yevtushenko (b. 1933) wrote a poem entitled 'Babi Yar' about a ravine near
Kiev in which many thousands of Jews were massacred and buried during the Second World War.
Writing of the Russian pogroms against the Jews in pre-Revolutionary Russia and against anti-semi-
tism in Europe and Russia, Yevtushenko sees all who struggle against totalitarianism as being under
similar attack.

heavy wet   the wind   heavy wet
the street grey white slush melted concrete
bones and bodies melting slush
saw   50
with the others
        the prisoner
in the YMHA hall Bloor & Spadina
arms wax stiff body stiff unnatural
coloured face blank eyes
           walked
with the others toward the screen
toward the pictures
        SLIDES
        this is mother   60
        this is father
        this is
        the one who is
waving her arms like that
is the one who
      like
I mean running with her breasts bound
ing
  running
      with her hands here and there   70
with her here and
        there
hands
  that   that is
the poem becoming the body
becoming the faint hunger
ing body
    prowling
      through
words the words words the words   80
opening   mouths ovens
the generals smiling saluting
in their mythic uniforms god-like
generals uniforms with the black leather
with the straps and the intricate leather
the phylacteries[8] and the prayer shawl
corsets and the boots and the leather straps

and the shining faces of the generals in their boots
and their stiff wax bodies their unnatural faces
and their blank eyes and their hands their stiff hands   90
and the generals in their straps and wax and stiff
staying standing
      melting bodies and thickening

---

[8]Small leather boxes containing scriptures on parchments that are bound to the forehead and left forearm of orthodox Jews during morning worship, except on the Sabbath and on holidays.

quick flesh on flesh handling
hands
the poem flickers, fades
the four Yarzeit candles[9] guttering one
each four million lights dim
my words drift
        smoke from chimneys and ovens   100
a bad picture, the power failing
pianist clattering on and over and through
the long Saturday afternoon in the Orpheum
    while the whitehatted star spangled cowboys
      shot the dark men and shot the dark men
      and we threw popcorn balls and grabbed
      each other and cheered:
                me jewboy yelling
for the shot town and the falling men
    and the lights come on   110
            and
    with the others
standing in silence

the gothic word hangs
over us on a shroud-white screen

and we drift away
        to ourselves
           to the late Sunday Times
           the wet snow
           the city   120

        a body melting

1973

[9]Candles burned on the anniversary of a death, usually lighted by children commemorating the death of parents or close relatives.

Instructions:

(ON THE NATURE OF DOUBLES AND DOUBLING)

all mirrors should be covered[1]
do not look deeply into a sink of hot water
ditto cold
wear rings on only two fingers

[1]After a family member's death, mirrors in a Jewish home are covered until the end of Shivah, the solemn period of mourning lasting seven days after the funeral—an ancient practice that stems in part from an old belief that the soul of the newly dead could become trapped in a reflection.

your eyes are doubles doubled
everything divides by two or is uneven
poetry consists in the doubling of words
doubled words are poetic words
this is the true meaning of duplicity
each poem speaks to another poem   10
the language of poetry is a secret language
these are the true doubles

false doubles are ones and threes
four is a good number

doubled names are: eli[2]   elijah
                      jesse   jesus
                      paul   saul
                      joseph pharoah
                                        etc.

in Hebrew this is common   20
no one knows the jewish name of god
indian names are secret
poetry is the naming of secret names
among these are:
                god
                spirit
                alphabets

                names in stone
                doubled names
                the psalms   30
                hoodoos
                animals
                eyes
                jewels

the place of no shadows called badlands
the place of shadows called badlands
you begin to see the difficulties

1977

[2]The high priest of Israel who, having lost the favour of God, did not hear God's voice when he spoke in the night to Samuel, Eli's young assistant (1 Samuel); in contrast, Elijah the prophet not only heard and saw God but was granted miraculous powers (1 and 2 Kings). (Mandel's first name, Elias, is a variant form of Elijah—though he is usually known as Eli.) 'Jesse': the father of David and ancestor of Jesus (1 Samuel 16; Matthew 1). 'Paul': the apostle who as Saul of Tarsus was a bitter persecutor of the early Christians before experiencing a sudden conversion when he heard the voice of God on the road to Damascus; he became the leading Christian missionary and theologian (Acts 9ff). 'Joseph': the youngest son of Jacob who, after being sold into bondage by his brothers, rose to become the prime minister of Egypt when he was the only person able to interpret the Pharaoh's prophetic dreams.

Doors of Perception:[1]

roads lead here   there
on the prairie Ann[2] holds the Pinto
along great swoops of highway down
from Lloydminster past Batoche
rebellion Rudy's book researched[3]
prophetic voices as a guide

in Huxley's version time curves
upon itself
                    cities of the mescal dream
turned biblical   jeweled places   10
palaces of John in Revelation[4]
Blake's engraving the drunkenness
of Smart's madness   prophecy

our history is in motion   curved
like straight correction lines[5]
earth-measured on a western grid
place known through time   time
measuring place
                    Thompson[6] walked
through unafraid for knowing   20

---

[1]An allusion to Aldous Huxley's *The Doors of Perception* (1954), which takes its title from a line in William Blake's *The Marriage of Heaven and Hell* :
  If the doors of perception were cleansed
  every thing would appear to man as it is, infinite.
In *Doors of Perception* Huxley gives an account of an experiment in which he took mescalin or mescal, the psychoactive substance found in peyote. He discussed his experiences and his theory of why drug-taking—like meditation and hypnosis—changes the way we perceive the world. Huxley agreed with C.D. Broad, Cambridge philosopher, that
  Each person is at each moment capable of remembering all that is happening everywhere in the universe. The function of the brain and nervous system is to protect us from being overwhelmed and confused by this mass of largely useless and irrelevant knowledge, by shutting out most of what we should otherwise perceive or remember at any moment, and leaving only that very small and special selection which is likely to be practically useful.
For Huxley certain persons are able to avoid the linear perception we have of history and see it as curved—in the same way that Einstein saw space and time—so that every moment exists at once.
[2]Ann Mandel—critic, English professor, and photographer—is Eli Mandel's wife.
[3]Northwest Rebellion of 1885, which followed the tensions depicted in Rudy Wiebe's *The Temptations of Big Bear* (1973); Wiebe continued to write about the Métis uprisings in *The Scorched-Wood People* (1977). See also p. 428, n.1.
[4]See particularly Chapter 21; the Book of Revelation is a spiritual vision in which John sees heaven and the future of the earth and mankind. William Blake, a visionary poet and artist, depicted in his prophetic texts and his illustrations for other writers a similar foretelling of man's fate (see especially *Jerusalem*, and Blake's illustrations for Milton's poems). Blake illustrated several poems by the English poet Christopher Smart (1722-71), who eventually became a religious visionary and believed that he brought messages from God; owing to the combined effects of drink and religious mania, he sank into a period of insanity and was placed in asylums and eventually in debtor's prison, where he died in a state of madness remembling schizophrenia.
[5]Roads and boundaries in the Canadian Prairies developed along rectangular grids laid out in the original surveys. Correction lines occur when the north-south lines are turned at right angles for a distance sufficient to compensate for the curvature of the earth.
[6]David Thompson (1770-1857), early mapmaker of Western Canada. See Vol. I, pp. 33-41.

measurement and lore
            ignorant
of clocks and vision we accelerate
a sweep through dying towns and farms

now is the badlands   measure
our choices random we believe
whatever we can find or where the map
of our own voices leads us listening to

the road to the cancer clinic
past the sundial's didacticism   30
toward the language of shadows
bedlam the alcoholic's nightmare
uses of wheat and rye and mould[7]

strict farms die
beside the rails the roads
the sons construct
the rules of mind

the jewish exodus from shtetl[8] to the plains
leads to this eygpt abraham learned
dream-sickness and the way to heal   40
a place of bread and chemistry

madness is neither east nor north
Riel[9] was hung in streets
I walked on every day to school

1977

---

[7]Ergot, a fungoid parasite on wheat and rye, is a naturally occurring hallucinogen; scientific investigation of ergot led to the synthesizing of LSD. Some historians have suggested that bread made from ergot-contaminated rye was responsible for epidemics of madness in the Middle Ages.
[8]Small town or village (Yiddish term particularly used by the Ashkenazic Jewish community of eastern Europe); specifically the restricted ghettos in which Jews had to live.
[9]See p. 428, n.1.

In My 57th Year

This is the year my mother lay dying
knocked down by tiny strokes she claimed
never once hit her though when she lay
crib-like where they laid her there she wept
for shame to be confined so near her death.
This is the year the cancer inside my father's
groin began its growth to knock him down

strong as he was beside his stricken wife.
This is the year I grew, ignorant of politics,
specious with law, careless of poetry.   10
There were no graves. The prairie rolled on
as if it were the sea. Today my children make
their way alone across those waves.
Do lines between us end as sharply
as lines our artists draw upon the plains?
I cry out. They keep their eye upon
their politics, their myths,
careful of lives as I was careless.

What shall I say? It is too late to tell again
tales we never knew. The legends of ourselves   20
spill into silence. All we never said, father
to daughter, son to unmanned man, we cannot say
to count the years.
                    I no longer know time or age
thinking of parents, their time, their grave of names.
Telling the time fiction consumes me.

1981

Ventriloquists

There is so much to be said—imitating
one another: the act of love,
say, speaking with tongues. Yet it was a while
before I saw we gave these words
to one another and heard our voices
elsewhere than the place they were
speaking beside oneself, throwing voices
away across the room, to other places.

Now seeing him this way I know
myself an imitation. I hear   10
his voice reading my poems written by him.
Later in darkness
on the question of love
it is more complex.

Do you love me?
The question ontological now,
She hears only his words
asking a question about me.

How do you do that?
It is a trick with my tongue   20

he says and with your ear
Look closely and you'll see
I don't move my lips.
The way the blade enters
is just as mysterious as the tongue,
perhaps not as deadly
though he has nothing more to say
not even questions now.

As for myself I remain
wondering where I have gone.   30

1981

The City in Canadian Poetry

'I don't know whether you know Mariposa. If not, it is of no consequence, for if you know Canada at all, you are probably well acquainted with a dozen towns just like it.' The opening lines of Leacock's *Sunshine Sketches*[1] take us back to a world we think we once knew: elm-shaded streets; Post Office, Fire Hall, and YMCA on the main intersection; two banks, the hardware and general store, and 'On all the side streets . . . maple trees and broad sidewalks, trim gardens with upright calla lilies, houses with verandahs, which are here and there being replaced by residences with piazzas.' The 'deep and unbroken peace' of the small town at the turn of the century before the great move to the city began, before urbanization, before the megalopolis, before parkways and thruways, before traffic and jackhammers and subways and noise:

> Can someone turn off the noise?
>
> The streets yearn for action nobler than traffic
> red lights want to be flags
> policemen want their arms frozen in loud movies:
> ask a man for the time
> your voice is ruined with static:
>   What a racket! What strange dials!
> Only Civil War can fuse it shut—[2]

It seems obvious. It seems true. Once we were at 'home' in the world, in the definable, local place. Once we knew the little town with its square streets and trim maple trees, almost within echo of the primeval forest. Or did we dream it? 'Mariposa,' Leacock says, 'is not a real town.' And he goes on to suggest in the 'Envoi' to *Sunshine Sketches* where he dreams of how one returns to that other place, other time, that it exists only as a version of a town that we in the cities

[1]See Vol. I, pp. 222-58.
[2]Leonard Cohen, 'Montreal 1964' (*Flowers for Hitler*, 1968).

think we remember. Mariposa is not a place; it is a state of mind. It is the dream of innocence that we attach to some place other than here and now.

In the burlesque mythology of *Sunshine Sketches*, Leacock plays on this dream of town and city: the city as an image of the small-town mind; the small-town as an image of the city-mind. And in so playing, he gives us a clue as to how in poem and story, town and city are metaphors. Some readers, of course, mistake them for real places. The particulars, the local colour, the details are there. Robert Creeley says, 'locale is both a geographic term and an inner sense of being.'[3] Raymond Souster[4] gives us the feel, taste, smell, sense of the city of Toronto, its sensuous quality, though I, for one, have long felt his city some remembered place, a fantasy Torontonians particularly cherish of Yonge Street as a setting for a serious version of 'Guys and Dolls'. Souster is much more interesting as a poet concerned with the process of perception than as a poet of place.

To begin with Mariposa, then, is to begin at the beginning, the point where city and town intersect. Of course, historically, city and town exist before the turn of the century in Canada. Montreal glitters in half a dozen novels of the *ancien régime*. For Susanna Moodie,[5] arriving in Canada in the 1830s, Quebec city appears as fortress, glorious crown of the citadel, and cholera-stricken charnel house.[6] Halifax alternately thrives with a kind of animal vitality or sickens in a gloomy winter of poverty, following a rhythm that Haliburton's Sam Slick[7] finds in its half-insect, half-human life. History does make demands upon poetry; places exist outside of the poem which describes them. But in poetry, place is metaphor, city is image, location is mythic. And so one begins, not with history, but with story; not with geography but with geographics—earth pictures, the line and model.

But what sort of model of a city could we find in a poem? James Reaney,[8] who is a kind of Benjamin Franklin of Canadian poetry, sets out provisional answer in the 'Second Letter' of *Twelve Letters to a Small Town* where he provides 'Instructions: How to Make a Model of the Town':

> First take two sticks and two leafy branches.
> Put their ends together so they form spokes.
> The spokes of an invisible wheel.
> Coming together at the centre and fanning out—
> These sticks and branches are
> The principal through streets of the town.
> Huron Street and Ontario Street can be leafy branch streets.
> Downie and Erie can be the bare stick streets.
> We'll make model houses out of berries.
> Take some berries. Ripe gooseberries for red houses.
> White raspberries for yellow brick houses. . . .
> And trees can be represented by their leaves.

[3]From *A Quick Graph: Collected Notes and Essays* (1970).
[4]See pp. 68-74.
[5]New France before the British conquest.
[6]Described in *Roughing It in the Bush*; See Vol. I, pp. 81-9.
[7]Central character of *The Clockmaker* sketches; see Vol. I, pp. 55-69.
[8]See pp. 168-224.

One elm leaf for a whole elm tree,
And streets laid out with rows of berry houses.
From the air, you know, a small town
Must look like rows of berries in the grass.

Now take some red apples and some russet apples,
Put these along the main streets for the business places.
Three potatoes each for the Court House
St Joseph's Church (R.C.) and St James's (C of E).
Buildings around the Market Square—ditto.

With a rather sharpside brick-coloured tomato in the centre
of the Market Square—to stand for the three towered
City Hall.[9]

Well, anyone who has been there will recognize Stratford, Ont., in Reaney's model of a town, I expect, though obviously no one will want to call the model realistic. But then why would Reaney want to build a model rather than attempt to show us the town itself in his poem? The answer seems to have something to do with things like totem poles and tribal clans, at least according to the anthropologist Claude Levi-Strauss.[1] Writing about the complex ways in which totemic classifications work, Strauss is led to wonder whether 'the small-scale model . . . may . . . in fact be the universal type of the work of art.' The peculiar pleasure we derive from models seems to be particularly related to their dimensions, Strauss notes, and he goes on to say that 'In the case of miniatures, in contrast to what happens when we try to understand an object or living creature of real dimensions, knowledge of the whole precedes knowledge of the parts. And even if this is an illusion, the point of the procedure is to create or sustain the illusion, which gratifies the intelligence and gives rise to a sense of pleasure which can already be called aesthetic on these grounds alone.' From our own perspective, looking at the model, we see the whole of it at once: it is a universe, a universal, and we, as gods, play at creation, making and destroying cities, peoples, civilizations. Reaney's instructions on how to make a model town turn out to be instructions on how to write a poem.

But his poetic city or town holds a surprise. Its form is a natural form, since it is a town made out of objects of nature: leaf, branch, berry, fruit, food. At first glance, this is puzzling because we tend to think of the city as an unnatural rather than a natural form. Maybe Reaney wants us to think the city ought to be human rather than mechanical and so he uses images we associate with life, like images of nature, rather than images of artificial things, to suggest what a city is. Or should be. Or maybe, as a small town boy he simply associates the city in its best form with natural forms. Anyhow, in a poem called 'Winnipeg Seen as a Body of Space and Time', part of a longer poem called 'A Message to Winnipeg', Reaney contrasts two human bodies of Winnipeg, one made out of the objects of

---

[9]'This presents a condensed version of a portion of Reaney's poem, itself actually in the form of a dialogue'—(Mandel's note).
[1](b. 1908), chief exponent of structuralism; Mandel refers here to Levi-Strauss's observations in *The Savage Mind* (1966).

nature, the other made out of man's products. The natural body of Winnipeg Reaney obviously approves of, but the mechanical one horrifies him. The first is good because it humanizes nature or is a human nature; the second is bad because it turns man into a machine, or at least mechanizes a city. The good city is a projection of life into nature; the bad one projects a mechanism into life.

As good city of the past, Winnipeg had the shape of a human body with arms of burr oaks and ash-leaf maples; its backbone a crooked silver muddy river; its thoughts ravens in flocks; its bones, snow. As bad city of the present, its shape can be described best as collapsed mechanical:

> A boneyard wrecked auto gent, his hair
> Made of rusted car door handles, his fingernails
> Of red Snowflake Pastry signs, his belly
> Of buildings downtown, his arms of sewers,
> His nerves electric wires, his mouth a telephone,
> His backbone—a cracked cement street.

I suppose there is some history in all this about the development of a natural site into a machine for living, and Reaney's poem does seem to work with the familiar contrasts of city and country, innocence and experience, naivety and sophistication, the organic and the mechanical. So it becomes possible to think that cities like Winnipeg once were organic, vital human places to live but now have collapsed into boneyards of used cars, the cemetery of the mechanical, a brittle, littered inhuman junkyard, 'crawling with the human fleas/Of a so-so civilization—half gadget, half flesh.' But if Reaney means this to be any kind of fact about Winnipeg, obviously he hasn't read Frederick Philip Grove, let alone any sociologists.

Actually, Reaney's 'boneyard Winnipeg' suggests something more than a fall from pastoral innocence and simplicity as the explanation of contemporary ills. The collapsed or broken giant recalls figures in Blake and the Bible and it is these Reaney wants us to remember rather than any simple-minded theory about 19th century spontaneity in the small town and 20th century wickedness at the corner of Portage and Main. To see what he wants to evoke, we can look at another version of the same image. It is one which appears in Canadian poetry as early as Lampman's City of the End of Things,[2] a poem of astonishing power and an eerie kind of prophetic force. In Lampman's vision of an automated city, an unholy trio rules, while a fourth, more hideous, figure guards the city's gates. Within its walls, the city burns with a thousand furnaces, and somewhere there sounds incessantly an inhuman music. These motifs—the blazing furnace, the three who walk there accompanied by a shadowy fourth, the city built to music—belong to the magic cities of legend and poem: Troy and Camelot, and the fiery furnace of the Bible where three walked unharmed protected by the angel of god.[3] But just as Pandemonium, Milton's version of Hell,[4] is a parody or upside-down version

---

[2] See Vol. I, pp. 187-9.
[3] In Daniel 3, Shadrach, Meshack, and Abednego, sent by Daniel to help rule Babylon, were condemned by its king, Nebuchadnezzar, to a 'fiery furnace' for failing to worship his golden idol; saved by God, they emerged from the fire unharmed.
[4] In Paradise Lost, Book I.

of the city of God, so Lampman's city parodies divine and magic places. Ultimately, it takes a single shape—or rather everything else falls away to reveal one
shape alone:

> One thing alone the hand of Time shall spare
> For the grim Idiot at the gate
> Is deathless and eternal there.

I doubt that Lampman intends to frighten us with stories of mechanical monsters.
The poem, by means of parody, evokes the horror of a *mindless* world. In other
words, Lampman sees the real opposition not between the nature and machine,
but between nature and imagination. The machine he is writing about is nature
itself.

The model we started with has now changed shape several times: it has been
leaf, twig, fruit, berry; boneyard auto gent; mechanical man; fiery furnace; fallen
giant—and in the process of changing shape it seems to have changed position
too, not only geographically, from Stratford to Winnipeg, but mentally, from the
image of city as technological horror to the image of nature itself as a machine.
Now, the problem before the poet is twofold: first, whether it is possible to put
together the world and the model, nature and imagination; and second, if it is not
possible, how to get past nature itself. For both parts of the question the city
seems to be a crucial image.

For example, the effort to put the world and the model together is made in one
of the most eloquent poems we possess, A.M. Klein's *Autobiographical*,[5] the
crucial setting for which is the city of Montreal.

We live always in duplicity, in a double world of memory and fantasy, time
and imagination, event and dream. And it is out of this duplicity that Klein
weaves a double image of Montreal. Like the double-exposure in a photograph,
the image places one pattern over another, one being occupying two spaces at the
same time. Perhaps one could have expected to find paradoxical pictures of Montreal simply because of its complicated French-English-Jewish ethos; or it may
be that the paradoxes emerge only from Klein's own Talmudic[6] and legalistic
mind, his vivid memories, his extraordinary awareness of the tradition in which
he writes, at once Hebraic, English, literary, and visionary, domestic and fabulous. No matter, Klein's Montreal is, on the one hand, a memory of his boyhood;
on the other, a fabled city of Jewish lore, imagination, and scripture. Interweav-
ing Oriental, Yiddish, European, and local images, the poem transforms and
transmutes all that it touches: ghettoes become pleasant bible land; the candy
store, a treasure cave of spices and jewels; and yet everything remains as it was,
living again in memory. Concentrating on childhood remembrance, Klein recalls
Wordsworth's approach to poetry, but only to reject the Wordsworthian notion of
poetry as tranquil recollection; and where Wordsworth equated childhood with
nature, Klein equates it with the city of his boyhood. That city recalls another
poet's effort to disengage from nature a timeless moment. It is like Yeats's

[5]See Vol. I, pp. 507-9.
[6]Literally, of the Talmud, a collection of Rabbinical writings constituting the religious authority for
traditional Judaism; having encyclopedic knowledge of arguments and counter-arguments.

Byzantium,[7] like the sacred palaces of romantic poetry, like the goal of the messianic quest; and yet in recalling Yeats, the poem rejects him. Where Yeats seeks to be gathered into the artifice of eternity and to burn away the mortal body, Klein turns to his own youth there to find the fabled city. Where Yeats turns away from youth to age, the 'sages standing in God's holy fire', the 'Monuments of unaging intellect', Klein turns away from age to youth,

> . . . the first flowering of the senses five,
> Discovering birds, or textures, or a star,
> Or tastes sweet, sour, acid, those that cloy;
> And perfumes.

And where Byzantium stands outside of nature, Klein's Montreal exists both in and out of time: as memory, in time; and as fable, out of time, poised somewhere between the world of eternal forms and the world of transient human memory, between pure image and event. The magical city of boyhood thus becomes the possibility of God's city promised in scripture:[8] the jargoning city (Babel, perhaps) becomes the fabled city (the New Jerusalem). Therefore, the past validates the future. History moves to the fulfillment of God's purposes. The fabled city of the past, of memory and scripture, was once and will be again, and the poet can write:

> I am no old man fatuously intent
> On memories, but in memory I seek
> The strength and vividness of nonage days,
> Not tranquil recollection of event.
> It is a fabled city that I seek;
> It stands in Space's vapours and Time's haze.

Montreal, of course, shows up as setting and symbol in a host of novels and poems. There is Richler's Montreal, and Cohen's Montreal, MacLennan's, Layton's, Gabrielle Roy's,[9] Dudek's, Scott Symons's. But whatever the reason, it seldom appears as the magical city it is in Klein's poem. In fact, few cities in Canada tempt the poet with imagery of the fabulous or magical. And a surprising number are seen in flames or as cities of the dead or as doomsday towns. Reaney's *Message to Winnipeg* concludes with a horrendous warning of dreadful things about to happen to Child's and Eaton's and Hudson's Bay. In a splendid and justly praised poem,[1] Wilfred Watson sees Calgary as Golgotha,[2] and as the

---

[7]In his poems, 'Sailing to Byzantium' and 'Byzantium'.
[8]In Revelation.
[9](b. 1909), the distinguished French-Canadian novelist, born in Manitoba, whose novels *Bonheur d'occasion (The Tin Flute)* and *Alexandre Chenevert* deal with Montreal life. Scott Symons (b. 1933) wrote *Place d'Armes* (1969), a novel about Montreal.
[1]'In the Cemetery of the Sun' in *Friday's Child* (1955), which won a Governor General's Award; Wilfred Watson (b. 1911) is a poet, dramatist, and former professor of English at the University of Alberta.
[2]Calvary, the place where Christ was crucified; the word Calvary, from the Latin *calvaria*, meaning 'skull', is the translator's word for the Aramaic *gulgultha*. Ezekiel, prophet and priest of the sixth century B.C., watched over the Israelites during their exile in Babylon. In response to God's question of whether dry bones in a valley could live, Ezekiel phrophesied that a wind would shake the bones together and they would live—an allegory for the restoration of Israel (Ezekiel 37:1-14).

valley of dry bones where clothes flapping on clotheslines are ghastly remini-
scences of crucifixions and of Ezekiel's prophecy that these dry bones shall
live:

> . . . In the cemetery of the sun below
> All the houses of the living were tombs;
> And I saw Calgary a hill of tombstones
> Rising under a coast of mountains
> Washed in the cold of my sun of cloud.
> When I walked to the wither of my day
> In this city where every backyard had
> Its cross and clothesline white and sere
> With sereclothes shining in the sun
> Of my first despair of resurrection
>
> Came my first Monday of darkness. It
> Was the week's hanging and drying noon.
> All the drought of my bones was for water.
> And the ghosts of my people flapped about
> Me in this washday blow and weather.

Through the poet's visionary eyes, his improved binoculars, as Layton calls
them, the whole city takes fire. Montreal explodes, prophetically enough we
might now say, at the corner of Peel and St Catherine, and the poet, looking
down on the holocaust, takes oddly detached notice of the behaviour of citizens
in that fire. Is it by the way to observe that the most sustained and finely articulated piece of prose description in the Canadian novel is Hugh MacLennan's
account of the Halifax explosion in 1917?[3] Winnipeg, Calgary, Montreal, Halifax, a fair enough list, one supposes. Of course, from another perspective the
fires of the city can be seen as something quite different from a natural holocaust
or a doomsday vision. Earle Birney, to judge from his verse play *The Trial of a
City* or *The Damnation of Vancouver*, has no great love to spare for that coastal
place, and indeed by the end of the play the suggestion seems fairly clear that
doomsday is at hand for Vancouver too. But looking down at the city from the
mountains around, in 'Vancouver Lights' he sees it as a Promethean defiance of
darkness, as the spark of human creativity, and as a mirror or model of the universe itself, a human galaxy answering or corresponding to the galaxies of light
in the great darkness of the heavens and amid the great dark of the earth itself.

The fire that burns in so many poems on Canadian cities now may be seen to
be the fire of the poet's own creativity burning away the dead husk of the city or
the machinery of the natural world. The answer to the question 'how to get past
nature?' is: by means of imagination. The furnace or forge symbolizes creative
energy, and in that forge new images are hammered into being. The flames of the
burning city turn out to be the golden or jewelled pavement of the redeemed city.
These are the flames that we see in the golden smithies of the emperor in Yeats's
'Byzantium', to take a famous example:

> At midnight on the Emperor's pavement flit

[3]*Barometer Rising* (1941).

Flames that no faggot feeds, nor steel has lit,
Nor storm disturbs, flames begotten of flame. . . .

Those images that yet
Fresh images beget. . . .

In that same fiery furnace of imagination, Layton's Montreal is transformed. After the explosion at Peel and St Catherine, where 'under the green neon sign' the poet sees only 'ruined corpses of corpulent singers', in a skeletal world of teeth and crosses, he seeks new eyes and another tree to supplant the fiery cross that inflames his city. Through the long night the fires burn until a new world emerges:

All night, all night the autos whizzed past me
into heaven, till I met men going there
    with golden nails and ravens whose wings
brushed the night up the tall sides of buildings
and behind them in the morninglight the windows shone
like saints pleased with the genius that had painted them.[4]

Cosmological transformations, like those we have been observing here, occur in the Bible where, for example, the jewels of Aaron's breastplate[5] form at one and the same time the pattern of the jewelled temple of Solomon, the tribal symbols, the blazing walls of the New Jerusalem, and the constellations of the Zodiac. It is tempting to think there may be a simple geographical explanation for Canadian poets' finding the pattern an appropriate one. One thinks, for example, of the perspective of Canadian cities seen from the air at night, jewels and stars strung out along a necklace of highways. Our cities enlarge or diminish remarkably as we leap toward or away from them at jet speed, and the contracting and expanding suggests at once the possibilities of total transformation. More than anything else, of course, the cities exist amid vast spaces, fortresses or garrisons in a wilderness, island universes in a sea of darkness, models of the universe itself. The transcanada flight seems irresistibly to suggest cosmic dimensions, as in Earle Birney's early version of it[6] in the old days of the North Star flights where prairie highways appear below the plane 'dim and miraculous as Martian lines' and Toronto is a galaxy. In F.R. Scott's 'Trans Canada',[7] the plane leaps away from Regina which falls below it like a pile of bones, and the poet meditates on the mystery and loneliness of space:

I have sat by night beside a cold lake
And touched things smoother than moonlight on still water,
But the moon on this cloud sea is not human,
And here is no shore, no intimacy,
Only the start of space, the road to suns.

Scott's cross-country flight returns us from the creative forge of imagination to actuality, to space. A curious fact about Canadian writing is the double presence

[4]'Winter Fantasy' in *The Improved Binoculars* (1956).
[5]See Exodus 28:15-26.
[6]'North Star West'
[7]See Vol. I, p. 349.

in it of ancient time and vast space. The one, time, appears as the folding into the present of the past: biblical or primitive or mythic or childhood time. The other, space, appears as the wilderness of the ocean. Even in Vancouver, near false-mouth creek, Birney walks brooding like a wanderer in an Anglo-Saxon poem about the eternal tides of time and darkness around him.[8] Our space is the emptiness between the cities and the stars, or even the emptiness in the modern city itself. If Montreal burns in the fires of time and poetry, Toronto is a void, an abyss. At least, it shows itself as the void to one of our most civilized poets, Dennis Lee.

Lee's remarkable *Civil Elegies*[9] is a book of seven brooding meditations on civility, civitas, the possibility of life in the modern city. Lee's symbol for the city is the civic square: an emptiness at the heart of the city, a form of space, a place to which people come:

> The light rides easy on people dozing at noon in Toronto, or
> here it does, in the square, with white jets hanging
> upward in plumes on the face of the pool and the
> Archer composing the distance, articulating
> pockets and whorls, in what heroic space?—
>
>   *   *   *
>
> Nothing is important.
> But if some man by the pool . . .
>   if that man comes upon the void he will
>   go under, or he
> must himself become void.

Like the hero of Cohen's *Beautiful Losers* who is most present at the point where he is most absent from himself, Lee finally conceives of absence as the creative point where anything is possible, all possibilities exist. And the city exists in its emptiness, giving us 'access to new nouns: as, tree, lintel, tower, body, cup'. A city and a country that are nothing, 'asymmetric pin points dotted at random/through tracts of emptiness' may be everything, says Lee:

> . . . and I learned to dwell among absence in jubilee,/declaring that all things which release us, all things which speed us into/calamity, as Canada, are blessed.

So space, place, city come to be defined:

> an open place   a square or market place
> extension in two (or three) directions
> a part of the earth
>   earth picture
> place of battle field
> city town village hamlet dwelling house
> seat mansion manor-house country-house
> fortress   or a strong place
> a place of amusement

---

[8] 'November Walk near False Creek Mouth'.
[9] (1968); Mandel quotes here from the Second and Seventh Elegies.

the apparent position of a heavenly body on the celestial sphere
'Who would kiss the place to make it well?'
'A falcon towering in her pride of place'
a proper appropriate or natural place
a fitting time   a room reasonable ground[1]

1977

[1] A collage of phrases assembled by Mandel as a conclusion to the essay.

Margaret Laurence

b. 1926

Born Jean Margaret Wemys in Neepawa, Man., Margaret Laurence has transformed this small prairie town in which she grew up into Manawaka, the backdrop for five interrelated works of fiction that begin with *The Stone Angel* (1964) and conclude with *The Diviners* (1974). Laurence's early years in Neepawa—in which she struggled to reconcile several deaths in her family (including her mother's when she was four and her father's when she was nine) with the powerful vision of a just God that was handed down from her Scots-Presbyterian grandparents—colour all her Manawaka fiction, especially the highly autobiographical Vanessa MacLeod stories, collected in *A Bird in the House* (1970). Like Vanessa, the adolescent Laurence felt herself trapped in her grandfather's house. The award in 1943 of a Manitoba scholarship that allowed her to attend United College in Winnipeg enabled her to escape and begin an independent life.

Marrying Jack Laurence in 1948, Margaret Laurence moved with her engineer husband to England in 1949 and in the following year to Africa, where they remained until 1957. In Africa Laurence began her career as a writer, first with *A Tree for Poverty* (1954), a translation and recasting of Somali poetry and tales, and then with a series of stories about the Africans she saw caught in a transitional moment between the old tribal world and the modern one. Her African stories, set in the Gold Coast (now Ghana), which began to appear in periodicals in 1954, were collected in *The Tomorrow-Tamer* (1963). Three other books grew out of Laurence's African years: *This Side Jordan* (1960), a novel that deals with Ghana's struggle for independence; *The Prophet's Camel Bell* (1963), an account of two years spent in Somaliland, prepared from the journal she kept while there; and *Long Drums and Cannons* (1968), a sensitive critical study of the English-language writers emerging in Nigeria. Although *This Side Jordan* remains an apprentice novel, Laurence's African short stories are among her best work, and her experience of the various African struggles for freedom and nationhood sharpened her sense of Canada as a new country that in its own way was still coming to terms with its colonial inheritance.

Laurence seems to have valued the perspective gained through expatriation. After five years back in Canada, she separated from her husband and moved to England, and it was there that the first three Manawaka novels—*The Stone Angel*, *A Jest of God* (1966), and *The Fire-Dwellers* (1969)—were written. These novels were influential in Canada in demonstrating the power and universality of regionalism and established Laurence as the foremost Canadian novelist of the decade. She returned to Canada to become writer-in-residence at the University of Toronto in 1969-70, and purchased a summer cottage in the Otonabee region. In 1971 she was named a Companion of the Order of Canada. The next year she made her return permanent, settling in Lakefield, Ont., near Peterborough.

In 1974 Laurence published *The Diviners*, her most ambitious work of fiction, which draws together characters and themes from the four other Manawaka novels and, by its use of reciprocal parallels with *The Stone Angel*, provides a formal close to the sequence. Like *A Jest of God*, *The Diviners* won a Governor General's Award. She has since published only children's stories and a few short nonfiction pieces. *Heart of a Stranger* (1976) is a selection of her essays from the previous twelve years.

From her early African writing through the later novels, and even in a children's book such as her marvelously whimsical tale of moles, *Jason's Quest* (1970), Laurence repeatedly chronicles a search for a life that is not only autonomous but that can be led with joy. However, powerful forces work against the individual in this search, as ninety-year-old Hagar Shipley at last realizes in the moving close to *The Stone Angel*:

This knowing comes upon me so forcefully, so shatteringly, and with such bitterness as I have never felt before. I must always, always, have wanted that—simply to rejoice. How is it I never could? . . .

Every good joy I might have held, in my man or any child of mine or even the plain light of morning, of walking the earth, all were forced to a standstill by some brake of proper appearances—oh, proper to whom? When did I ever speak the heart's truth?

Pride was my wilderness, and the demon that led me there was fear. I was alone, never anything else, and never free, for I carried my chains within me, and they spread out from me and shackled all I touched.

But even though Hagar and the women of her era seem unable to experience fully either freedom or joy, the Laurence protagonists who follow Hagar come closer to grasping that ideal—and, as we discover in *The Diviners*, Hagar's struggle (her name is the same as that of Abraham's bondswoman in the Bible) has served to free Morag (whose name is the Scottish equivalent of Sarah, Abraham's wife).

The way in which Hagar's experiences eventually touch and help Morag suggests the importance of *inheritance* as a theme for Laurence. Inheritance—which becomes not only genetic makeup, but also the unobserved but profoundly shaping influences of culture, society, and environment—is a prominent theme in all her Manawaka fiction. While our inheritance is often the restraint against which we must struggle, it is also our chief source of strength, the thing that allows us to survive in a world characterized by bewildering uncertainty.

Although Laurence announced her retirement as a writer of fiction after the publication of *The Diviners*, she is now said to be at work on a new novel. She has already given Canada, in *The Stone Angel* and *The Diviners*, two undisputed classics. In 1965 Northrop Frye wrote: 'There is no Canadian writer of whom we can say what we say of the world's major writers, that their readers can grow up inside their work without ever being aware of circumference.' Today the fully realized world contained in Margaret Laurence's work provides the unbounded pleasures that such a reading experience can give.

The Tomorrow-Tamer

The dust rose like clouds of red locusts around the small stampeding hooves of taggle-furred goats and the frantic wings of chickens with all their feathers awry. Behind them the children darted, their bodies velvety with dust, like a flash and tumble of brown butterflies in the sun.

The young man laughed aloud to see them, and began to lope after them. Past the palms where the tapsters got wine, and the sacred grove that belonged to Owura, god of the river. Past the shrine where Nana Ayensu poured libation to the dead and guardian grandsires. Past the thicket of ghosts, where the graves were, where every leaf and flower had fed on someone's kin, and the wind was the thin whisper-speech of ancestral spirits. Past the deserted huts, clay walls runnelled by rain, where rats and demons dwelt in unholy brotherhood. Past the old men drowsing in doorways, dreaming of women, perhaps, or death. Past the good huts with their brown baked walls strong against any threatening night-thing, the slithering snake carrying in its secret sac the end of life, or red-eyed Sasabonsam, huge and hairy, older than time and always hungry.

The young man stopped where the children stopped, outside Danquah's. The shop was mud and wattle, like the huts, but it bore a painted sign, green and orange. Only Danquah could read it, but he was always telling people what it said. *Hail Mary Chop-Bar & General Merchant*. Danquah had gone to a mission school once, long ago. He was not really of the village, but he had lived here for many years.

Danquah was unloading a case of beer, delivered yesterday by a lorry named *God Helps Those*, which journeyed fortnightly over the bush trail into Owurasu. He placed each bottle in precisely the right place on the shelf, and stood off to admire the effect. He was the only one who could afford to drink bottled beer, except for funerals, maybe, when people made a show, but he liked to see the bright labels in a row and the bottle-tops winking a gilt promise of forgetfulness. Danquah regarded Owurasu as a mudhole. But he had inherited the shop, and as no one in the village had the money to buy it and no one outside had the inclination, he was fixed here for ever.

He turned when the children flocked in. He was annoyed at them, because he happened to have taken his shirt off and was also without the old newspaper which he habitually carried.

The children chuckled surreptitiously, hands over mouths, for the fat on Danquah's chest made him look as though the breasts of a young girl had been stuck incongruously on his scarred and ageing body.

'A man cannot even go about his work,' Danquah grumbled, 'without a whole pack of forest monkeys gibbering in his doorway. Well, what is it?'

The children bubbled their news, like a pot of soup boiling over, fragments cast here and there, a froth of confusion.

Attah the ferryman—away, away downriver (half a mile)—had told them, and he got the word from a clerk who got it from the mouth of a government man. A bridge was going to be built, and it was not to be at Atware, where the ferry was, but—where do you think? At Owurasu! This very place. And it was to be the biggest bridge any man had ever seen—big, really big, and high—look, like this (as high as a five-year-old's arms).

'A bridge, eh?' Danquah looked reflectively at his shelves, stacked with jars of mauve and yellow sweets, bottles of jaundice bitters, a perfume called *Bint el Sudan*, the newly-arranged beer, two small battery torches which the village boys eyed with envy but could not afford. What would the strangers' needs be? From the past, isolated images floated slowly to the surface of his mind, like weed shreds in the sluggish river. Highland Queen whisky. De Reszke cigarettes. Chivers marmalade. He turned to the young man.

'Remember, a year ago, when those men from the coast came here, and walked all around with sticks, and dug holes near the river? Everyone said they were lunatics, but I said something would come of it, didn't I? No one listened to me, of course. Do you think it's true, this news?'

The boy grinned and shrugged. Danquah felt irritated at himself, that he had asked. An elder would not have asked a boy's opinion. In any event, the young man clearly had no opinion.

'How do I know?' the boy said. 'I will ask my father, who will ask Nana Ayensu.'

'I will ask Nana Ayensu myself,' Danquah snapped, resenting the implication that the boy's father had greater access to the chief than he did, although in fact this was the case.

The young man's broad blank face suddenly frowned, as though the news had at last found a response in him, an excitement over an unknown thing.

'Strangers would come here to live?'

'Of course, idiot,' Danquah muttered. 'Do you think a bridge builds itself?'

Danquah put on his pink rayon shirt and his metal-rimmed spectacles so he could think better. But his face remained impassive. The boy chewed thoughtfully on a twig, hoisted his sagging loincloth, gazed at a shelf piled with patterned tradecloth and long yellow slabs of soap. He watched the sugar ants trailing in amber procession across the termite-riddled counter and down again to the packed-earth floor.

Only the children did not hesitate to show their agitation. Shrilling like cicadas, they swarmed and swirled off and away, bearing their tidings to all the world.

Danquah maintained a surly silence. The young man was not surprised, for the villagers regarded Danquah as a harmless madman. The storekeeper had no kin here, and if he had relatives elsewhere, he never mentioned them. He was not son or father, nephew or uncle. He lived by himself in the back of his shop. He cooked his own meals and sat alone on his stoep[1] in the evenings, wearing food-smirched trousers and yellow shoes. He drank the costly beer and held aloft his ragged newspaper, bellowing the printed words to the toads that slept always in clusters in the corners, or crying sadly and drunkenly, while the village boys peered and tittered without pity.

The young man walked home, his bare feet making light crescent prints in the dust. He was about seventeen, and his name was Kofi. He was no one in particular, no one you would notice.

[1] Verandah (South African dialect; source of the English word 'stoop').

Outside the hut, one of his sisters was pounding dried cassava[2] into *kokonte* meal, raising the big wooden pestle and bringing it down with an unvaried rhythm into the mortar. She glanced up.

'I saw Akua today, and she asked me something.' Her voice was a teasing singsong.

Kofi pretended to frown. 'What is that to me?'

'Don't you want to know?'

He knew she would soon tell him. He yawned and stretched, languidly, then squatted on his heels and closed his eyes, miming sleep. He thought of Akua as she had looked this morning, early, coming back from the river with the water jar on her head, and walking carefully, because the vessel was heavy, but managing also to sway her plump buttocks a little more than was absolutely necessary.

'She wants to know if you are a boy or a man,' his sister said.

His thighs itched and he could feel the slow full sweetness of his amiable lust. He jumped to his feet and leapt over the mortar, clumsy-graceful as a young goat. He sang softly, so his mother inside the hut would not hear.

> *'Do you ask a question,*
> *Akua, Akua?*
> *In a grove dwells an oracle,*
> *Oh Akua——*
> *Come to the grove when the village sleeps——'*

The pestle thudded with his sister's laughter. He leaned close to her.

'Don't speak of it, will you?'

She promised, and he sat cross-legged on the ground, and drummed on the earth with his outspread hands, and sang in the cool heat of the late afternoon. Then he remembered the important news, and put on a solemn face, and went in the hut to see his father.

His father was drinking palm wine sorrowfully. The younger children were crawling about like little lizards, and Kofi's mother was pulling out yams and red peppers and groundnuts and pieces of fish from bowls and pots stacked in a corner. She said 'Ha—ei——' or 'True, true——' to everything the old man said, but she was not really listening—her mind was on the evening meal.

Kofi dutifully went to greet his grandmother. She was brittle and small and fleshless as the empty shell of a tortoise. She rarely spoke, and then only to recite in her tenuous bird voice her genealogy, or to complain of chill. Being blind, she liked to run her fingers over the faces of her grandchildren. Kofi smiled so that she could touch his smile. She murmured to him, but it was the name of one of his dead brothers.

'And when I think of the distance we walked,' Kofi's father was saying, 'to clear the new patch for the cocoyam, and now it turns out to be no good, and the yams are half the size they should be, and I ask myself why I should be afflicted in this way, because I have no enemies, unless you want to count Donkor, and he went away ten years ago, so it couldn't be him, and if it is a question of libation, who has been more generous than I, always making sure the gods drank before the planting——'

---

[2] An edible tuber; an important staple in Africa, where it is often ground into flour and baked as bread.

He went on in this vein for some time, and Kofi waited. Finally his father looked up.

'The government men will build a bridge at Owurasu,' Kofi said. 'So I heard.'

His father snorted.

'Nana Ayensu told me this morning. He heard it from Attah, but he did not believe it. Everyone knows the ferryman's tongue has diarrhoea. Garrulity is an affliction of the soul.'

'It is not true, then?'

'How could it be true? We have always used the Atware ferry. There will be no bridge.'

Kofi got out his adze and machete and went outside to sharpen them. Tomorrow he and his father would begin clearing the fallow patch beside the big baobab tree, for the second planting of cassava. Kofi could clear quickly with his machete, slicing through underbrush and greenfeather ferns. But he took no pride in the fact, for every young man did the same.

He was sorry that there would be no bridge. Who knows what excitement might have come to Owurasu? But he knew nothing of such things. Perhaps it was better this way.

A week later, three white men and a clerk arrived, followed by a lorry full of tents and supplies, several cooks, a mechanic and four carpenters.

'Oh, my lord,' groaned Gerald Wain, the Contractor's Superintendent, climbing out of the Land-Rover and stretching his travel-stiffened limbs, 'is this the place? Eighteen months—it doesn't bear thinking about.'

The silence in the village broke into turbulence. The women who had been filling the water vessels at the river began to squeal and shriek. They giggled and wailed, not knowing which was called for. They milled together, clambered up the clay bank, hitched up their long cloths and surged down the path that led back to the village, leaving the unfilled vessels behind.

The young men were returning from the farms, running all together, shouting hoarsely. The men of Owurasu, the fathers and elders, had gathered outside the chief's dwelling and were waiting for Nana Ayensu to appear.

At the *Hail Mary* Danquah found two fly-specked pink paper roses and set them in an empty jam jar on his counter. He whipped out an assortment of bottles—gin, a powerful red liquid known as Steel wine, the beer with their gleaming tops, and several sweet purple Doko-Doko[3] which the villagers could afford only when the cocoa crop was sold. Then he opened wide his door. In the centre of the village, under the sacred fire tree, Nana Ayensu and the elders met the new arrivals. The leader of the white men was not young, and he had a skin red as fresh-bled meat. Red was the favoured colour of witches and priests of witchcraft, as everyone knew, so many remarks were passed, especially when some of the children, creeping close, claimed to have seen through the sweat-drenched shirt a chest and belly hairy as the Sasabonsam's. The other two white men were

---

[3] According to 'The Perfumed Sea', an earlier story in *The Tomorrow-Tamer*, Doko-Doko is 'a lurid carbonated grape beverage'.

young and pale. They smoked many cigarettes and threw them away still burning, and the children scrambled for them.

Badu, the clerk-interpreter, was an African, but to the people of Owurasu he was just as strange as the white men, and even less to be trusted, for he was a coast man. He wore white clothes and pointed shoes and a hat like an infant umbrella. The fact that he could speak their language did not make the villagers any less suspicious.

'The stranger is like a child,' Nana Ayensu said, 'but the voice of an enemy is like the tail of a scorpion—it carries a sting.'

The clerk, a small man, slight and nervous as a duiker,[4] sidled up to weighty Opoku, the chief's spokesman, and attempted to look him in the eye. But when the clerk began to speak his eyes flickered away to the gnarled branches of the old tree.

'The wise men from the coast,' Badu bawled in a voice larger than himself, 'the government men who are greater than any chief—they have said that a bridge is to be built here, an honour for your small village. Workmen will be brought in for the skilled jobs, but we will need local men as well. The bungalows and labourers' quarters will be started at once, so we can use your young men in that work. Our tents will be over there on the hill. Those who want to work can apply to me. They will be paid for what they do. See to it that they are there tomorrow morning early. In this job we waste no time.'

The men of Owurasu stood mutely with expressionless faces. As for the women, they felt only shame for the clerk's mother, whoever she might be, that she had taught her son so few manners.

Badu, brushing the dust from his white sleeves, caught their soft deploring voices and looked defiant. These people were bush—they knew nothing of the world of streets and shops. But because they had once thrown their spears all along the coast, they still scorned his people, calling them cowards and eaters of fish-heads. He felt, as well, a dismal sense of embarrassment at the backwardness of rural communities, now painfully exposed to the engineers' eyes. He turned abruptly away and spoke in rapid stuttering English to the Superintendent.

With a swoosh and a rattle, the strangers drove off towards the river, scattering goats and chickens and children from the path, and filling the staring villagers' nostrils with dust. Then—pandemonium. What was happening? What was expected of them? No one knew. Everyone shouted at once. The women and girls fluttered and chattered like parrots startled into flame-winged flight. But the faces of the men were sombre.

Kofi came as close as he dared to the place where Nana Ayensu and the elders stood. Kofi's father was speaking. He was a small and wiry man. He plucked at his yellow and black cloth, twirling one end of it across his shoulder, pulling it down, flinging it back again. His body twitched in anger.

'Can they order us about like slaves? We have men who have not forgotten their grandfathers were warriors——'

---

[4] Small South African antelope; its name, which means 'diver', comes from its habit of disappearing suddenly into the bush.

Nana Ayensu merely flapped a desolate hand. 'Compose yourself, Kobla. Remember that those of our spirit are meant to model their behaviour on that of the river. We are supposed to be calm.'

Nana Ayensu was a portly man, well-fleshed. His bearing was dignified, especially when he wore his best *kente* cloth, as he did now, having hastily donned it upon being informed of the strangers' approach. He was, however, sweating a great deal—the little rivers formed under the gold and leather amulets of his headband, and trickled down his forehead and nose.

'Calm,' he repeated, like an incantation. 'But what do they intend to do with our young men? Will there be the big machines? I saw them once, when I visited my sister in the city. They are very large, and they feed on earth, opening their jaws—thus. Jaws that consume earth could consume a man. If harm comes to our young men, it is upon my head. But he said they would be paid, and Owurasu is not rich——'

Okomfo Ofori was leaning on his thornwood stick, waiting his turn to speak. He was older than the others. The wrinkled skin of his face was hard and cracked, as though he had been sun-dried like an animal hide. He had lived a long time in the forest and on the river. He was the priest of the river, and there was nothing he did not know. Watching him covertly, Kofi felt afraid.

'We do not know whether Owura will suffer his river to be disturbed,' Okomfo Ofori said. 'If he will not, then I think the fish will die from the river, and the oil palms will wither, and the yams will shrink and dwindle in the planting places, and plague will come, and river-blindness will come, and the snake will inhabit our huts because the people are dead, and the strangler vine will cover our dwelling places. For our life comes from the river, and if the god's hand is turned against us, what will avail the hands of men?'

Kofi, remembering that he had casually, without thought, wished the bridge to come, felt weak with fear. He wanted to hide himself, but who can hide from his own fear and from the eyes of a god?

That night, Kofi's father told him they were to go to the sacred grove beside the river. Without a word or question, the boy shook off sleep and followed his father.

The grove was quiet. The only sounds were the clicking of palm boughs and the deep low voice of Owura the river. Others were there—Kofi never knew who—young men and old, his friends and his uncles, all now changed, distorted, grown ghostly and unknown in the grey moonlight.

'Here is wine from our hands,' Okomfo Ofori said. 'God of the river, come and accept this wine and drink.'

The palm wine was poured into the river. It made a faint far-off splash, then the river's voice continued unchanged, like muted drums. The priest lifted up a black earthen vessel, an ordinary pot fashioned from river clay, such as the women use for cooking, but not the same, for this one was consecrated. Into the pot he put fresh river water, and leaves he had gathered from the thicket of ghosts, and eggs, and the blood and intestines of a fowl whose neck he wrung, and white seeds, and a red bead and a cowrie shell. He stirred the contents, and he stared for a long time, for this was the vessel wherein the god could make himself known to his priest. And no one moved.

Then—and the night was all clarity and all madness—the priest was possessed of his god, Owura the river. Kofi could never afterwards remember exactly what had happened. He remembered a priest writhing like a snake with its back broken, and the clothing trance-torn, and the god's voice low and deep. Finally, dizzied with sleeplessness and fear, he seemed to see the faces and trees blurred into a single tree face, and his mind became as light and empty as an overturned water vessel, everything spilled out, drained, gone.

Back at the hut, Kofi's father told him the outcome. Libation would be poured to the ancestors and to the god of the river, as propitiation for the disturbance of the waters. Also, one young man had been selected to go to the bridge work. In order that the village could discover what the bridgemen would do to the sons of Owurasu, one young man had been chosen to go, as a man will be sent to test the footing around a swamp.

Kofi was to be that young man.

He was put to work clearing a space for the bridgemen's dwellings. He knew his machete and so he worked well despite his apprehension, swinging the blade slowly, bending low from the waist and keeping his legs straight. The heat of the sun poured and filtered down the leaves and bushes, through the fronds and hairy trunks of the oil palms. The knotted grasses and the heavy clots of moss were warm and moist to the feet, and even the ferns, snapping easily under the blade, smelled of heat and damp. Kofi wore only his loincloth, but the sweat ran down his sides and thighs, making his skin glossy. He worked with his eyes half closed. The blade lifted and fell. Towards mid-day, when the river had not risen to drown him, he ventured to sing.

> 'We are listening, we are listening.
> Vine, do not harm us, for we ask your pardon.
> We are listening, River, for the drums.
> Thorn, do not tear us, for we ask your pardon.
> River, give the word to Crocodile.
> The crocodile, he drums in the river.
> Send us good word, for we ask your pardon.'

Before he left at nightfall, he took the gourd bottle he had brought with him and sprinkled the palm oil on the ground where his machete had cleared.

'Take this oil,' he said to the earth, 'and apply it to your sores.'

Kofi returned home whole, day after day, and finally Nana Ayensu gave permission for other young men to go, as many as could be spared from the farming and fishing.

Six bungalows, servants' quarters, latrines and a long line of labourers' huts began to take shape. The young men of Owurasu were paid for their work. The village had never seen so much cash money before. The white men rarely showed their faces in the village, and the villagers rarely ventured into the strangers' camp, half a mile upriver. The two settlements were as separate as the river fish from the forest birds. They existed beside one another, but there was no communication between them. Even the village young men, working on the bungalows, had nothing to do with the Europeans, whose orders filtered down to them through Badu or the head carpenter. The bridgemen's cooks came to the village market to buy fruit and eggs, but they paid good prices and although they were haughty they did not bother anyone. The carpenters and drivers came to Danquah's in the evening, but there were not many of them and the villagers soon took them for granted. The village grew calm once more in the prevailing atmosphere of prosperity.

In the *Hail Mary Chop-Bar* the young men of Owurasu began to swagger. Some of them now kept for themselves a portion of the money they earned. Danquah, bustling around his shop, pulled out a box of new shirts and showed them off. They were splendid; they shimmered and shone. Entranced, the young men stared. A bottle of beer, Danquah urged. Would the young men have another bottle of beer while they considered the new shirts? They drank, and pondered, and touched the glittering cloth.

Kofi was looked up to now by the other young men. Some of them called him the chief of the young men. He did not admit it, but he did not deny, either. He stretched to his full height, yawned luxuriously, drank his beer in mighty gulps, laughed a little, felt strength flooding through his muscles, walked a trifle crookedly across the room to Danquah, who, smiling, was holding up a blue shirt imprinted with great golden trees. Kofi reached out and grabbed the shirt.

When he left the *Hail Mary* that night, Kofi found Akua waiting for him in the shadows. He rememberd another purchase he had made. He drew it out and handed it to her, a green bottle with a picture of flowers. Akua seized it.

'For me? Scent?'

He nodded. She unstopped it, sniffed, laughed, grasped his arm.

'Oh, it is fine, a wonder. Kofi—when will you build the new hut?'

'Soon,' he promised. 'Soon.'

It was all settled between their two families. He did not know why he hesitated. When the hut was built, and the gifts given and received, his life would move in the known way. He would plant his crops and his children. Some of his crops would be spoiled by worm or weather; some of his children would die. He would grow old, and the young men would respect him. That was the way close to him as his own veins. But now his head was spinning from the beer, and his mouth was bitter as lime rind. He took Akua by the hand and they walked down the empty path together, slowly, in the dark, not speaking.

The next week the big machines came rolling and roaring into Owurasu. Lorries brought gangs of skilled labourers, more Europeans and more cooks. The tractor drivers laughed curses at the gaping villagers and pretended to run them down until they shrieked and fled in humiliation like girls or mice.

Gong-gong beat in Owurasu that night, and the drums did not stop their rumble until dawn. The village was in an uproar. What would the machines do? Who were these men? So many and so alien. Low-born coast men, northern desert men with their tribal marks burned in long gashes onto their cheeks and foreheads, crazy shouting city men with no shame. What would become of the village? No one knew.

Nana Ayensu visited the shrine where the carved and blackened state stools of dead chiefs were kept and where the ancestral spirits resided.

'Grandsires, we greet you. Stand behind us with a good standing. Protect us from the evils we know and from the evils we do not know. We are addressing you, and you will understand.'

Danquah sat at the counter of the *Hail Mary* with a hurricane lamp at his elbow. He was laboriously scrawling a letter to his cousin in the city, asking him to arrange for four cases of gin and ten of beer, together with fifty cartons of cigarettes, to be sent on the next mammy-lorry to Owurasu.

Okomfo Ofori scattered sacred *summe* leaves to drive away spirits of evil, and looked again into his consecrated vessel. But this time he could see only the weeping faces of his father and his mother, half a century dead.

When morning came, the big machines began to uproot the coconut palms in the holy grove beside the river. The village boys, who had been clearing the coarse grass from the river bank, one by one laid down their machetes and watched in horrified fascination as the bulldozers assaulted the slender trees. Everyone had thought of the river's being invaded by strangers. But it had never occurred to anyone that Owura's grove would be destroyed.

Kofi watched and listened. Under the noise of the engines he could hear the moaning of Owura's brown waters. Now would come the time of tribulation; the plague and the river-blindness would strike now. The bulldozer rammed another tree, and it toppled, its trunk snapping like a broken spine. Kofi felt as though his own bones were being broken, his own body assaulted, his heart invaded by the massive blade. Then he saw someone approaching from the village.

Okomfo Ofori was the river's priest, and there was nothing he did not know. Except this day, this death. Kofi stared, shocked. The old priest was running like a child, and his face was wet with his tears.

At the work site, the Superintendent listened wearily while the old man struggled to put his anguish into words.

'What's he saying, Badu? If it isn't one damn thing, it's another—what's the trouble now?'

'He says the grove belongs to the gods,' Badu explained.

'All right,' Wain sighed. 'Ask him how much he wants. It's a racket, if you ask me. Will ten pounds do it? It can be entered under Local Labour.'

The village boys looked towards Kofi, who stood unmoving, his machete dangling uselessly from his hand.

'What does it mean? What will happen?'

He heard their questioning voices and saw the question in their eyes. Then he turned upon them in a kind of fury.

'Why do you ask me? I know nothing, nothing, nothing!'

He dropped his machete and ran, not knowing where he was going, not seeing the paths he took.

His mother was a woman vast as mountains. Her blue cloth, faded and tinged with a sediment of brown from many washings in river water, tugged and pulled around her heavy breasts and hips. She reached out a hand to the head of her crouched son.

So the grove was lost, and although the pleas were made to gods and grandsires, the village felt lost, too, depleted and vulnerable. But the retribution did not come. Owura did not rise. Nothing happened. Nothing at all.

In the days following, Kofi did not go to the bridge work. He built the new hut, and when the gifts were given and taken, Akua made a groundnut stew and half the villagers were invited to share this first meal. Kofi, drinking palm wine and eating the food as though he could never get enough, was drawn into his new wife's smile and lapped around with laughter.

After a week, the young men of Owurasu went back to work for the bridge-men.

The approaches were cleared and the steamy river air was filled with the chunk-ing of the pile-driver and the whirr of the concrete-mixer, as the piers and anchor blocks went in.

To the villagers, the river bank no longer seemed bald without the grove. Kofi could scarcely remember how the palms had looked when they lived there. Grad-ually he forgot that he had been afraid of the machines. Even the Europeans no longer looked strange. At first he had found it difficult to tell them apart, but now he recognized each.

Akua bought a new cloth and an iron cooking-pot. On one memorable day, Kofi came home from the *Hail Mary* with a pocket torch. It was green and hand-some, with silver on its end and silver on the place one touched to make the light come on. Kofi flicked the switch and in the tiny bulb a faint glow appeared. Akua clapped her hands in pleasure.

'Such a thing. It is yours, Kofi?'

'Mine. I paid for it.'

The glow trembled, for the battery was almost worn out from the village boys' handling. Kofi turned it off hastily. Danquah had forgotten to tell him and so he did not know that the power could be replaced.

At the bridge, Kofi's work had changed. Now he helped in the pouring of con-crete as the blocks were made. He unloaded steel. He carried tools. He was everywhere. Sweat poured from him. His muscles grew tough as liana vines. He talked with the ironworkers, some of whom spoke his tongue. They were brash, easy-laughing, rough-spoken men, men of the city. Their leader was a man by the name of Emmanuel, a man with a mighty chest, hugely strong. Emmanuel wore a green felt hat enlivened with the white and lightly dancing feathers of the egrets that rode the cattle on the grasslands of the coast. He spoke often to Kofi, telling of the places he had been, the things he had seen.

'The money goes, but who cares? That's an ironworker's life—to make money and spend it. Someday I will have a car—you'll see. Ahh—it'll be blue, like the sea, with silver all over it. Buick—Jaguar—you don't known those names. Learn them, hear me? I'm telling them to you. Wait until you see me on the high steel. Then you'll know what an ironworker does. Listen—I'll tell you something— only men like me can be ironworkers, did you know that? Why? Because I know I won't fall. If you think you might fall, then you do. But not me. I'll never fall, I tell you that.'

Kofi listened, his mouth open, not understanding what Emmanuel was talking about, but understanding the power of the man, the fearlessness. More and more Kofi was drawn to the company of the bridgeman in the evenings at the *Hail Mary*. Akua would click her tongue disapprovingly.

'Kofi—why do you go there so much?'

'I am going,' he would reply, not looking into her eyes. 'It is not for you to say.'

He still went each evening to see his father and his mother. His father was morose, despite the money, and had taken to quoting proverbs extensively.

'Man is not a palm-nut that he should be self-centred. At the word of the elder, the young bends the knee. If you live in an evil town, the shame is yours.'

He would continue interminably, and Kofi would feel uneasy, not certain why his father was offended, not knowing where his own offence lay. But after he had returned to his own hut and had filled himself with bean soup and *kokonte*, he would feel better and would be off again to the *Hail Mary*.

One evening Kofi's father sent the women and younger children away and began to speak with his son. The old man frowned, trying to weave into some pattern the vast and spreading spider-web of his anxieties.

'The things which are growing from the river—we did not know the bridge would be like this, a defiance. And these madmen who go about our village—how many girls are pregnant by them already? And what will the children be like? Children of no known spirit——'

Kofi said nothing at all. He listened silently, and then he turned and walked out of the hut. It was only when he was halfway to the *Hail Mary* that he realized he had forgotten to greet or say farewell to the grandmother who sat, blind and small, in the darkened hut, repeating in her far-off voice the names of the dead.

At the *Hail Mary*, Kofi went over to Emmanuel, who was drinking beer and talking with Danquah. Danquah no longer complained about the village. These days he said that he had always known something wonderful would happen here; he had prayed and now his prayers had been answered. Emmanuel nodded and laughed, shrugging his shoulders rhythmically to the highlife music bellowed by the gramophone, a recent investment of Danquah's. Kofi put one hand on Emmanuel's arm, touching the crimson sheen of the ironworker's shirt.

'I am one of the bridgemen,' he said. 'Say it is true.'

Emmanuel clapped him on the shoulder.

'Sure,' he said. 'You are a bridgeman, bush boy. Why not?'

He winked at Danquah, who stifled a guffaw. But Kofi did not notice.

The dry *harmattan*[5] wind came down from the northern deserts and across the forest country, parching the lips and throats of fishermen who cast their moon-shaped nets into the Owura river, and villagers bent double as they worked with their hoes in the patches of yam and cassava, and labourers on the sun-hot metal of the bridge.

More than a year had passed, and the bridge had assumed its shape. The towers were completed, and the main cables sang in the scorching wind.

Kofi, now a mechanic's helper, scurried up and down the catwalks. He wore only a loincloth and he had a rag tied around his forehead as slight insulation against the fiery sun. He had picked up from the mechanics and ironworkers

---

[5] A hot, dry African wind that blows in December, January, and February, bringing with it severe dust storms.

some of the highlife songs, and now as he worked he sang of the silk-clad women of the city.

Badu, immaculate in white shirt and white drill trousers, called to him.

'Hey, you, Kofi!'

Kofi trotted over to him.

'The bridge will be completed soon,' Badu said. 'Do you want to stay on as a painter? We will not need so many men. But you have worked well. Shall I put your name down?'

'Of course,' Kofi said promptly. 'Am I not a bridgeman?'

Badu gave him a quizzical glance.

'What will you do when the bridge is finished? What will you do when we leave?'

Kofi looked at him blankly.

'You will be leaving? Emmanuel, he will be leaving?'

'Naturally,' Badu said. 'Did you think we would stay for ever?'

Kofi did not reply. He merely walked away. But Badu, watching him go, felt uneasily that something somewhere was disjointed, but he could not exactly put his finger on it.

To the people of Owurasu, the bridge was now different. It had grown and emerged and was an entity. And so another anxiety arose. Where the elders had once been concerned only over the unseemly disturbance of Owura's waters and grove, now they wondered how the forest and river would feel about the presence of this new being.

The forest was alive, and everywhere spirit acted upon spirit, not axe upon wood, nor herb upon wound, nor man upon steel. But what sort of spirit dwelt in the bridge? They did not know. Was it of beneficent or malicious intent? If a being existed, and you did not know whether it meant you good or ill, nor what it required of you, how could you possibly have peace of mind?

A series of calamities enforced the villagers' apprehension. Two of the pirogues[6] drifted away and were found, rock-battered and waterlogged, some distance downriver. A young child fell prey to the crocodile that dwelt under the river bank. Worst of all, three of the best fishermen, who worked downstream near the rapids where the waterflies flourished, developed river-blindness.

When the council of elders met, Kofi was told to attend. He was not surprised, for he had now been the spokesman of the village youth for some time. Nana Ayensu spoke.

'The bridge is beside us, and we live beside this bridge, but we do not know it. How are we to discover its nature?'

Danquah, who was there by reason of his wealth, flatly stated that the bridge had brought good fortune to the village. Business was brisk; money flowed. He could not see why anyone should be worried.

Kofi's father leapt to his feet, quavering with rage. The bridge might have brought good fortune to Danquah, but it had brought ill fortune to everyone else.

'What of my son, spending all his time in the company of strangers? What of

[6]Dug-out canoes.

Inkumsah's child, buried in the river mud until his limbs rot soft enough for the crocodile to consume? What of——'

'Kobla, Kobla, be calm,' Nana Ayensu soothed. 'Remember the river.'

'The river itself will not be calm,' Kofi's father cried. 'You will see—Owura will not suffer this thing to remain.'

Okomfo Ofori and Opoku the linguist were nodding their heads. They agreed with Kobla. Kofi looked from face to face, the wise and wizened faces of his father, his uncles, his chief and his priest.

'Something is dwelling in it—something strong as Owura himself.'

Silence. All of them were staring at him. Only then did Kofi realize the enormity of his utterance. He was terrified at what he had done. He could not look up. The strength was drained from his body. And yet—the belief swelled and grew and put forth the leaf. The being within the bridge was powerful, perhaps as powerful as Owura, and he, Kofi, was a man of the bridge. He knew then what was meant to happen. The other bridgemen might go, might desert, might falter, but he would not falter. He would tend the bridge as long as he lived. He would be its priest.

When the paint began to appear on the bridge, the people of Owurasu gathered in little groups on the river bank and watched. The men shook their heads and lifted their shoulders questioningly. The women chirped like starlings.

'What's the matter with them?' Gerald Wain asked. 'Don't they like the aluminium paint?'

'They like it,' Badu replied. 'They think it is real silver.'

'What next?' the Superintendent said. 'I hope they don't start chipping it off.'

But the villagers were not primarily concerned with monetary value. The bridge was being covered with silver, like the thin-beaten silver leaf on a great queen's chair. Silver was the colour of queen mothers, the moon's daughters, the king-makers. The villagers wondered, and pondered meanings, and watched the bridge grow moon-bright in the kingly sun.

Kofi, who had been shunned at home ever since his insolence, himself brightened and shone with every brushful of paint he splashed and slapped on the metal. He painted like one possessed, as though the task of garbing the bridge lay with him alone.

In the *Hail Mary* he questioned Emmanuel.

'Where will you go, when you go from here?'

'Back to the city. First I'll have a good time. Everything a man does in the city, I'll do it—hear me? Then I'll look around for another job.'

Kofi was amazed. 'You do not know where you will go?'

'I'll find out,' Emmanuel said easily. 'What about you, bush boy?'

'I will tend the bridge,' Kofi said in a low voice.

Emmanuel's laughter boomed. 'Do you think it needs looking after? Do you think it would fall down tomorrow if no one was here?'

That was not what Kofi had meant. But he did not perceive the difference in their outlooks. He heard only one thing—the bridge did not need a priest. Emmanuel must be wrong. But if he were not? Kofi thought once again of the bridgemen, coming together for a while and then separating once more, going away to look for other places, somewhere. The thought could not be borne. He clicked it off like the little light of the green and silver torch.

He could return to his father's farm. That would please Akua and his mother. His father would welcome another pair of hands at the planting. He thought of his machete and adze. They would need a lot of sharpening. He stood up indecisively, looking from the counter to the door and back again. In his pocket the silver shillings clashed softly as he moved. He pulled them out and held them in his hand, staring at the last of the thin bright discs. Then he grasped Emmanuel's arm, clutching it tightly.

'What will I do? What will I do now?'

Emmanuel looked at him in astonishment.

'Why ask me?'

The towers were painted from small platforms run up on pulleys, and the cables were painted from the catwalks. Then the day came for painting the cross-members at the top of the towers. It was not a job which many men would have wanted, for one had to leave the safety of the catwalk and crawl gingerly out onto the steel beam.

Kofi at once volunteered. He swung himself lightly over the catwalk and onto the exposed steel. He straddled the beam, two hundred feet above the river, and began to paint.

On either side of the brown waters lay the forest, green and dense, heavy-hanging, sultry and still at mid-day. The palms rose above the tangle of under-brush and fern, and the great buttressed hardwoods towered above the palms. Through and around it all, the lianas twisted and twined. Poinsettia and jungle lily blood-flecked the greens with their scarlet.

Kofi listened to the steely twanging of the cables. The sound, high and sweet as bees or bells, clear as rain, seemed to grow louder and louder, obscuring the bird-voiced forest, surpassing even the deep-throated roar of Owura the river.

Squinting, Kofi could make out other villages, huts like small calabashes in the sun. Then he saw something else. At a distance a straight red-gold streak pierced like a needle through the forest. It was the new road. He had heard about it but he had not seen it before and had not believed it was really there. Now he saw that it would emerge soon here and would string both village and bridge as a single bead on its giant thread.

Emmanuel would ride along there in a mammy-lorry, shouting his songs. At some other village, some other bridge, Emmanuel would find his brothers waiting for him, and he would greet them and be with them again.

Then Kofi knew what to do. He was no longer the bridge's priest, but now the thought could be borne. He was fearless, fearless as Emmanuel. He knew the work of the bridge. In the far places, men would recognize him as a bridgeman. The power of it went with him and in him. Exultant, he wanted to shout aloud his own name and his praises. There was nothing he could not do. Slowly, deliberately, he pulled himself up until he was standing there on the steel, high above the forest and the river. He was above even the bridge itself. And above him, there was only the sky.

Then he did something that Emmanuel would never have done on the high steel—he looked up. The brightness of the bridge seemed strangely to pale in the sunfire that filled his eyes. For an instant he looked straight into the sun. Then, blinded, he swayed and his foot slipped on the silver paint. He pitched forward, missing the bridge entirely, and arched into the river like a thrown spear.

The bridgeworkers' shouted alarm, as they saw him, was each man's cry of terror for himself, who might have been the one to fall. The pirogues went out, and the men of the village dragged the river. But Kofi's body was not found.

'What could have possessed the idiot?' the Superintendent cried, in anger and anguish, for it was the only fatal accident on the job.

'He did not believe the bridge would hurt him, perhaps,' Badu said.

'Did he think it was alive?' Wain said despairingly. 'Won't they ever learn?'

But looking up now, and hearing the metallic humming of the cables, it seemed to him that the damn thing almost was alive. He was beginning to have delusions; it was time he went on leave.

As for the people of Owurasu, they were not surprised. They understood perfectly well what had happened. The bridge, clearly, had sacrificed its priest in order to appease the river. The people felt they knew the bridge now. Kofi had been the first to recognize the shrine, but he had been wrong about one thing. The bridge was not as powerful as Owura. The river had been acknowledged as elder. The queenly bridge had paid its homage and was a part of Owurasu at last.

The boy's father quoted, stoically and yet with pride, the proverb—'A priest cannot look upon his god and live.' Kofi's mother and his widow mourned him, and were not much consoled by the praises they heard of him. But even they, as they listened, felt a certain awe and wondered if this was indeed the Kofi they had known.

Many tales were woven around his name, but they ended always in the same way, always the same.

'The fish is netted and eaten; the antelope is hunted and fed upon; the python is slain and cast into the cooking-pot. But—oh, my children, my sons—a man consumed by the gods lives forever.'

1963

To Set Our House in Order

When the baby was almost ready to be born, something went wrong and my mother had to go into hospital two weeks before the expected time. I was wakened by her crying in the night, and then I heard my father's footsteps as he went downstairs to phone. I stood in the doorway of my room, shivering and listening, wanting to go to my mother but afraid to go lest there be some sight there more terrifying than I could bear.

'Hello—Paul?' my father said, and I knew he was talking to Dr Cates. 'It's Beth. The waters have broken, and the fetal position doesn't seem quite—well, I'm only thinking of what happened the last time, and another like that would be—I wish she were a little huskier, damn it—she's so—no, don't worry, I'm quite all right. Yes, I think that would be the best thing. Okay, make it as soon as you can, will you?'

He came back upstairs, looking bony and dishevelled in his pyjamas, and running his fingers through his sand-coloured hair. At the top of the stairs, he came face to face with Grandmother MacLeod, who was standing there in her quilted black satin dressing gown, her slight figure held straight and poised, as though she were unaware that her hair was bound grotesquely like white-feathered wings in the snare of her coarse night-time hairnet.

'What is it, Ewen?'

'It's all right, Mother. Beth's having—a little trouble. I'm going to take her into the hospital. You go back to bed.'

'I told you,' Grandmother MacLeod said in her clear voice, never loud, but distinct and ringing like the tap of a sterling teaspoon on a crystal goblet, 'I did tell you, Ewen, did I not, that you should have got a girl in to help her with the housework? She would have rested more.'

'I couldn't afford to get anyone in,' my father said. 'If you thought she should've rested more, why didn't you ever—oh God, I'm out of my mind tonight—just go back to bed, Mother, please. I must get back to Beth.'

When my father went down to the front door to let Dr Cates in, my need overcame my fear and I slipped into my parents' room. My mother's black hair, so neatly pinned up during the day, was startingly spread across the white pillowcase. I stared at her, not speaking, and then she smiled and I rushed from the doorway and buried my head upon her.

'It's all right, honey,' she said. 'Listen, Vanessa, the baby's just going to come a little early, that's all. You'll be all right. Grandmother MacLeod will be here.'

'How can she get the meals?' I wailed, fixing on the first thing that came to mind. 'She never cooks. She doesn't know how.'

'Yes, she does,' my mother said. 'She can cook as well as anyone when she has to. She's just never had to very much, that's all. Don't worry—she'll keep everything in order, and then some.'

My father and Dr Cates came in, and I had to go, without ever saying anything I had wanted to say. I went back to my own room and lay with the shadows all around me. I listened to the night murmurings that always went on in that house, sounds which never had a source, rafters and beams contracting in the dry air, perhaps, or mice in the walls, or a sparrow that had flown into the attic through the broken skylight there. After a while, although I would not have believed it possible, I slept.

The next morning I questioned my father. I believed him to be not only the best doctor in Manawaka, but also the best doctor in the whole of Manitoba, if not in the entire world, and the fact that he was not the one who was looking after my mother seemed to have something sinister about it.

'But it's always done that way, Vanessa,' he explained. 'Doctors never attend members of their own family. It's because they care so much about them, you see, and—'

'And what?' I insisted, alarmed at the way he had broken off. But my father did not reply. He stood there, and then he put on that difficult smile with which adults seek to conceal pain from children. I felt terrified, and ran to him, and he held me tightly.

'She's going to be fine,' he said. 'Honestly she is. Nessa, don't cry—'

Grandmother MacLeod appeared beside us, steel-spined despite her apparent fragility. She was wearing a purple silk dress and her ivory pendant. She looked as though she were all ready to go out for afternoon tea.

'Ewen, you're only encouraging the child to give way,' she said. 'Vanessa, big girls of ten don't make such a fuss about things. Come and get your breakfast. Now, Ewen, you're not to worry. I'll see to everything.'

Summer holidays were not quite over, but I did not feel like going out to play with any of the kids. I was very superstitious, and I had the feeling that if I left the house, even for a few hours, some disaster would overtake my mother. I did not, of course, mention this feeling to Grandmother MacLeod, for she did not believe in the existence of fear, of if she did, she never let on. I spent the morning morbidly, in seeking hidden places in the house. There were many of these—odd-shaped nooks under the stairs, small and loosely nailed-up doors at the back of clothes closets, leading to dusty tunnels and forgotten recesses in the heart of the house where the only things actually to be seen were drab oil paintings stacked upon the rafters, and trunks full of outmoded clothing and old photograph albums. But the unseen presences in these secret places I knew to be those of every person, young or old, who had ever belonged to the house and had died, including Uncle Roderick who got killed on the Somme,[1] and the baby who would have been my sister if only she had managed to come to life. Grandfather MacLeod, who had died a year after I was born, was present in the house in more tangible form. At the top of the main stairs hung the mammoth picture of a darkly uniformed man riding upon a horse whose prancing stance and dilated nostrils suggested that the battle was not yet over, that it might indeed continue until Judgment Day. The stern man was actually the Duke of Wellington, but at the time I believed him to be my grandfather MacLeod, still keeping an eye on things.

We had moved in with Grandmother MacLeod when the Depression got bad

[1]One of the most costly campaigns of the First World War. The British offensive at the Somme, which began in July 1915, was joined by the 4th Canadian Division in September; despite severe losses on both sides, the results were indecisive.

and she could no longer afford a housekeeper, but the MacLeod house never seemed like home to me. Its dark red brick was grown over at the front with Virginia creeper that turned crimson in the fall, until you could hardly tell brick from leaves. It boasted a small tower in which Grandmother MacLeod kept a weedy collection of anaemic ferns. The verandah was embellished with a profusion of wrought-iron scrolls, and the circular rose-window upstairs contained glass of many colours which permitted an outlooking eye to see the world as a place of absolute sapphire or emerald, or if one wished to look with a jaundiced eye, a hateful yellow. In Grandmother MacLeod's opinion, their features gave the house style.

Inside a multitude of doors led to rooms where my presence, if not actually forbidden, was not encouraged. One was Grandmother MacLeod's bedroom, with its stale and old-smelling air, the dim reek of medicines and lavender sachets. Here resided her monogrammed dresser silver, brush and mirror, nail-buffer and button hook and scissors, none of which must even be fingered by me now, for she meant to leave them to me in her will and intended to hand them over in the same flawless and unused condition in which they had always been kept. Here, too, were the silver-framed photographs of Uncle Roderick—as a child, as a boy, as a man in his Army uniform. The massive walnut spool bed had obviously been designed for queens or giants, and my tiny grandmother used to lie within it all day when she had migraine, contriving somehow to look like a giant queen.

The living room was another alien territory where I had to tread warily, for many valuable objects sat just-so on tables and mantelpiece, and dirt must not be tracked in upon the blue Chinese carpet with its birds in eternal motionless flight and its water-lily buds caught forever just before the point of opening. My mother was always nervous when I was in this room.

'Vanessa, honey,' she would say, half apologetically, 'why don't you go and play in the den, or upstairs?'

'Can't you leave her, Beth?' my father would say. 'She's not doing any harm.'

'I'm only thinking of the rug,' my mother would say, glancing at Grandmother MacLeod, 'and yesterday she nearly knocked the Dresden shepherdess off the mantel. I mean, she can't help it, Ewen, she has to run around—'

'Goddamn it, I know she can't help it,' my father would growl, glaring at the smirking face of the Dresden shepherdess.

'I see no need to blaspheme, Ewen,' Grandmother MacLeod would say quietly, and then my father would say he was sorry, and I would leave.

The day my mother went to the hospital, Grandmother MacLeod called me at lunch-time, and when I appeared, smudged with dust from the attic, she looked at me distastefully as though I had been a cockroach that had just crawled impertinently out of the woodwork.

'For mercy's sake, Vanessa, what have you been doing with yourself? Run and get washed this minute. Here, not that way—you use the back stairs, young lady. Get along now. Oh—your father phoned.'

I swung around. 'What did he say? How is she? Is the baby born?'

'Curiosity killed a cat,' Grandmother MacLeod said, frowning. 'I cannot understand Beth and Ewen telling you all these things, at your age. What sort of vulgar person you'll grow up to be, I dare not think. No, it's not born yet. Your mother's just the same. No change.'

I looked at my grandmother, not wanting to appeal to her, but unable to stop myself. 'Will she—will she be all right?'

Grandmother MacLeod straightened her already-straight back. 'If I said definitely yes, Vanessa, that would be a lie, and the MacLeods do not tell lies, as I have tried to impress upon you before. What happens is God's will. The Lord giveth, and the Lord taketh away.'

Appalled, I turned away so she would not see my face and my eyes. Surprisingly, I heard her sigh and felt her papery white and perfectly manicured hand upon my shoulder.

'When your Uncle Roderick got killed,' she said, 'I thought I would die. But I didn't die, Vanessa.'

At lunch, she chatted animatedly, and I realised she was trying to cheer me in the only way she knew.

'When I married your Grandfather MacLeod,' she related, 'he said to me, "Eleanor, don't think because we're going to the prairies that I expect you to live roughly. You're used to a proper house, and you shall have one." He was as good as his word. Before we'd been in Manawaka three years, he'd had this place built. He earned a good deal of money in his time, your grandfather. He soon had more patients than either of the other doctors. We ordered our dinner service and all our silver from Birks' in Toronto. We had resident help in those days, of course, and never had less than twelve guests for dinner parties. When I had a tea, it would always be twenty or thirty. Never any less than half a dozen different kinds of cake were ever served in this house. Well, no one seems to bother much these days. Too lazy, I suppose.'

'Too broke,' I suggested. 'That's what Dad says.'

'I can't bear slang,' Grandmother MacLeod said. 'If you mean hard up, why don't you say so? It's mainly a question of management, anyway. My accounts were always in good order, and so was my house. No unexpected expenses that couldn't be met, no fruit cellar running out of preserves before the winter was over. Do you know what my father used to say to me when I was a girl?'

'No,' I said. 'What?'

'God loves Order,' Grandmother MacLeod replied with emphasis. 'You remember that, Vanessa. God loves Order—he wants each one of us to set our house in order. I've never forgotten those words of my father's. I was a MacInnes before I got married. The MacInnes is a very ancient clan, the lairds of Morven and the constables of the Castle of Kinlochaline. Did you finish that book I gave you?'[2]

'Yes,' I said. Then, feeling some additional comment to be called for, 'It was a swell book, Grandmother.'

[2]Vanessa would have discovered in Robert Bain's *The Clans and Tartans of Scotland* (1938, and many subsequent editions; the mottoes were added later) that the MacInnesses were 'a Celtic clan of ancient origin', their earliest-known territory that of Morven. Bain says that they 'remained in possession of Morven, and as late as 1645 it appears that a MacInnes was in command of the Castle of Kinlochaline when it was besieged and burnt. . . .'

This was somewhat short of the truth. I had been hoping for her cairngorm[3] brooch on my tenth birthday, and had received instead the plaid-bound volume entitled *The Clans and Tartans of Scotland.* Most of it was too boring to read, but I had looked up the motto of my own family and those of some of my friends' families. *Be then a wall of brass. Learn to suffer. Consider the end. Go carefully.* I had not found any of these slogans reassuring. What with Mavis Duncan learning to suffer, and Laura Kennedy considering the end, and Patsy Drummond going carefully, and I spending my time in being a wall of brass, it did not seem to me that any of us were going to lead very interesting lives. I did not say this to Grandmother MacLeod.

'The MacInnes motto is *Pleasure Arises from Work,*' I said.

'Yes,' she agreed proudly. 'And an excellent motto it is, too. One to bear in mind.'

She rose from the table, rearranging on her bosom the looped ivory beads that held the pendant on which a fullblown ivory rose was stiffly carved.

'I hope Ewen will be pleased,' she said.

'What at?'

'Didn't I tell you?' Grandmother MacLeod said. 'I hired a girl this morning, for the housework. She's to start tomorrow.'

When my father got home that evening, Grandmother MacLeod told him her good news. He ran one hand distractedly across his forehead.

'I'm sorry, Mother, but you'll just have to unhire her. I can't possibly pay anyone.'

'It seems distinctly odd,' Grandmother MacLeod snapped, 'that you can afford to eat chicken four times a week.'

'Those chickens,' my father said in an exasperated voice, 'are how people are paying their bills. The same with the eggs and the milk. That scrawny turkey that arrived yesterday was for Logan MacCardney's appendix, if you must know. We probably eat better than any family in Manawaka, except Niall Cameron's. People can't entirely dispense with doctors or undertakers. That doesn't mean to say I've got any cash. Look, Mother, I don't know what's happening with Beth. Paul thinks he may have to do a Caesarean. Can't we leave all this? Just leave the house alone. Don't touch it. What does it matter?'

'I have never lived in a messy house, Ewen,' Grandmother MacLeod said, 'and I don't intend to begin now.'

'Oh Lord,' my father said. 'Well, I'll phone Edna, I guess, and see if she can give us a hand, although God knows she's got enough, with the Connor house and her parents to look after.'

'I don't fancy having Edna Connor in to help,' Grandmother MacLeod objected.

'Why not?' my father shouted. 'She's Beth's sister, isn't she?'

'She speaks in such a slangy way,' Grandmother MacLeod said. 'I have never believed she was a good influence on Vanessa. And there is no need for you to raise your voice to me, Ewen, if you please.'

---

[3] Also called 'Scotch topaz'; a semi-precious stone frequently worn as part of the Highland Scots costume.

I could barely control my rage. I thought my father would surely rise to Aunt Edna's defence. But he did not.

'It'll be all right,' he soothed her. 'She'd only be here for part of the day, Mother. You could stay in your room.'

Aunt Edna strode in the next morning. The sight of her bobbed black hair and her grin made me feel better at once. She hauled out the carpet sweeper and the weighted polisher and got to work. I dusted while she polished and swept, and we got through the living room and front hall in next to no time.

'Where's her royal highness, kiddo?' she enquired.

'In her room,' I said. 'She's reading the catalogue from Robinson & Cleaver.'

'Good Glory, not again?' Aunt Edna cried. 'The last time she ordered three linen tea-cloths and two dozen serviettes. It came to fourteen dollars. Your mother was absolutely frantic. I guess I shouldn't be saying this.'

'I knew anyway,' I assured her. 'She was at the lace handkerchiefs section when I took up her coffee.'

'Let's hope she stays there. Heaven forbid she should get onto the banqueting cloths. Well, at least she believes the Irish are good for two things—manual labour and linen-making. She's never forgotten Father used to be a blacksmith, before he got the hardware store. Can you beat it? I wish it didn't bother Beth.'

'Does it?' I asked, and immediately realised this was a wrong move, for Aunt Edna was suddenly scrutinising me.

'We're making you grow up before your time,' she said. 'Don't pay any attention to me, Nessa. I must've got up on the wrong side of the bed this morning.'

But I was unwilling to leave the subject.

'All the same,' I said thoughtfully, 'Grandmother MacLeod's family were the lairds of Morven and the constables of the Castle of Kinlochaline. I bet you didn't know that.'

Aunt Edna snorted. 'Castle, my foot. She was born in Ontario, just like your Grandfather Connor, and her father was a horse doctor. Come on, kiddo, we'd better shut up and get down to business here.'

We worked in silence for a while.

'Aunt Edna—' I said at last, 'what about Mother? Why won't they let me go and see her?'

'Kids aren't allowed to visit maternity patients. It's tough for you, I know that. Look, Nessa, don't worry. If it doesn't start tonight, they're going to do the operation. She's getting the best of care.'

I stood there, holding the feather duster like a dead bird in my hands. I was not aware that I was going to speak until the words came out.

'I'm scared,' I said.

Aunt Edna put her arms around me, and her face looked all at once stricken and empty of defences.

'Oh, honey, I'm scared, too,' she said.

It was this way that Grandmother MacLeod found us when she came stepping lightly down into the front hall with the order in her hand for two dozen lace-bordered handkerchiefs of pure Irish linen.

I could not sleep that night, and when I went downstairs, I found my father in the den. I sat down on the hassock beside his chair, and he told me about the operation my mother was to have the next morning. He kept on saying it was not serious nowadays.

'But you're worried,' I put in, as though seeking to explain why I was.

'I should at least have been able to keep from burdening you with it,' he said in a distant voice, as though to himself. 'If only the baby hadn't got itself twisted around—'

'Will it be born dead, like the little girl?'

'I don't know,' my father said. 'I hope not.'

'She'd be disappointed, wouldn't she, if it was?' I said bleakly, wondering why I was not enough for her.

'Yes, she would,' my father replied. 'She won't be able to have any more, after this. It's partly on your account that she wants this one, Nessa. She doesn't want you to grow up without a brother or sister.'

'As far as I'm concerned, she didn't need to bother,' I retorted angrily.

My father laughed. 'Well, let's talk about something else, and then maybe you'll be able to sleep. How did you and Grandmother make out today?'

'Oh, fine, I guess. What was Grandfather MacLeod like, Dad?'

'What did she tell you about him?'

'She said he made a lot of money in his time.'

'Well, he wasn't any millionaire,' my father said, 'but I suppose he did quite well. That's not what I associate with him, though.'

He reached across to the bookshelf, took out a small leather-bound volume and opened it. On the pages were mysterious marks, like doodling, only much neater and more patterned.

'What is it?' I asked.

'Greek,' my father explained. 'This is a play called *Antigone*. See, here's the title in English. There's a whole stack of them on the shelves there. *Oepidus Rex*. *Electra*. *Medea*. They belonged to your Grandfather MacLeod. He used to read them often.'

'Why?' I enquired, unable to understand why anyone would pore over those undecipherable signs.

'He was interested in them,' my father said. 'He must have been a lonely man, although it never struck me that way at the time. Sometimes a thing only hits you a long time afterwards.'

'Why would he be lonely?' I wanted to know.

'He was the only person in Manawaka who could read these plays in the original Greek,' my father said. 'I don't suppose many people, if anyone, had even read them in English translations. Maybe he would have liked to be a classical scholar—I don't know. But his father was a doctor, so that's what he was. Maybe he would have liked to talk to somebody about these plays. They must have meant a lot to him.'

It seemed to me that my father was talking oddly. There was a sadness in his voice that I had never heard before, and I longed to say something that would make him feel better, but I could not, because I did not know what was the matter.

'Can you read this kind of writing?' I asked hesitantly.

My father shook his head. 'Nope. I was never very intellectual, I guess. Rod was always brighter than I, in school, but even he wasn't interested in learning Greek. Perhaps he would've been later, if he'd lived. As a kid, all I ever wanted to do was go into the merchant marine.'

'Why didn't you, then?'

'Oh well,' my father said offhandedly, 'a kid who'd never seen the sea wouldn't have made much of a sailor. I might have turned out to be the seasick type.'

I had lost interest now that he was speaking once more like himself.

'Grandmother MacLeod was pretty cross today about the girl,' I remarked.

'I know,' my father nodded. 'Well, we must be as nice as we can to her, Nessa, and after a while she'll be all right.'

Suddenly I did not care what I said.

'Why can't she be nice to us for a change?' I burst out. 'We're always the ones who have to be nice to her.'

My father put his hand down and slowly tilted my head until I was forced to look at him.

'Vanessa,' he said, 'she's had troubles in her life which you really don't know much about. That's why she gets migraine sometimes and has to go to bed. It's not easy for her these days, either—the house is still the same, so she thinks other things should be, too. It hurts her when she finds they aren't.'

'I don't see—' I began.

'Listen,' my father said, 'you know we were talking about what people are interested in, like Grandfather MacLeod being interested in Greek plays? Well, your grandmother was interested in being a lady, Nessa, and for a long time it seemed to her that she was one.'

I thought of the Castle of Kinlochaline, and of horse doctors in Ontario.

'I didn't know—' I stammered.

'That's usually the trouble with most of us,' my father said. 'You go on up to bed now. I'll phone tomorrow from the hospital as soon as the operation's over.'

I did sleep at last, and in my dreams I could hear the caught sparrow fluttering in the attic, and the sound of my mother crying, and the voices of the dead children.

My father did not phone until afternoon. Grandmother MacLeod said I was being silly, for you could hear the phone ringing all over the house, but nevertheless I refused to move out of the den. I had never before examined my father's books, but now, at a loss for something to do, I took them out one by one and read snatches here and there. After I had been doing this for several hours, it dawned on me that most of the books were of the same kind. I looked again at the titles.

Seven-League Boots. [4] *Arabia Deserta. The Seven Pillars of Wisdom. Travels*

[4]Five classic works of travel literature, published between the two world wars, by Richard Halliburton, C.M. Doughty, T.E. Lawrence, H. Harrier, and Lowell Thomas respectively.

in Tibet. Count Lucknor the Sea Devil. And a hundred more. On a shelf by themselves were copies of the *National Geographic* magazine, which I looked at often enough, but never before with the puzzling compulsion which I felt now, as though I were on the verge of some discovery, something which I had to find out and yet did not want to know. I riffled through the picture-filled pages. Hibiscus and wild orchids grew in a soft-petalled confusion. The Himalayas stood lofty as gods, with the morning sun on their peaks of snow. Leopards snarled from the vined depths of a thousand jungles. Schooners buffetted their white sails like the wings of giant angels against the great sea winds.

'What on earth are you doing?' Grandmother MacLeod enquired waspishly, from the doorway. 'You've got everything scattered all over the place. Pick it all up this minute, Vanessa, do you hear?'

So I picked up the books and magazines, and put them all neatly away, as I had been told to do.

When the telephone finally rang, I was afraid to answer it. At last I picked it up. My father sounded faraway, and the relief in his voice made it unsteady.

'It's okay, honey. Everything's fine. The boy was born alive and kicking after all. Your mother's pretty weak, but she's going to be all right.'

I could hardly believe it. I did not want to talk to anyone. I wanted to be by myself, to assimilate the presence of my brother, towards whom, without ever having seen him yet, I felt such tenderness and such resentment.

That evening, Grandmother MacLeod approached my father, who, still dazed with the unexpected gift of neither life now being threatened, at first did not take her seriously when she asked what they planned to call the child.

'Oh, I don't know. Hank, maybe, or Joe. Fauntleroy, perhaps.'

She ignored his levity.

'Ewen,' she said, 'I wish you would call him Roderick.'

My father's face changed. 'I'd rather not.'

'I think you should,' Grandmother MacLeod insisted, very quietly, but in a voice as pointed and precise as her silver nail-scissors.

'Don't you think Beth ought to decide?' my father asked.

'Beth will agree if you do.'

My father did not bother to deny something that even I knew to be true. He did not say anything. Then Grandmother MacLeod's voice, astonishingly, faltered a little.

'It would mean a great deal to me,' she said.

I remembered what she had told me—*When your Uncle Roderick got killed, I thought I would die. But I didn't die*. All at once, her feeling for that unknown dead man became a reality for me. And yet I held it against her, as well, for I could see that it had enabled her to win now.

'All right,' my father said tiredly. 'We'll call him Roderick.'

Then, alarmingly, he threw back his head and laughed.

'Roderick Dhu!' he cried. 'That's what you'll call him, isn't it? Black Roderick. Like before. Don't you remember? As though he were a character out of Sir Walter Scott, instead of an ordinary kid who—'

He broke off, and looked at her with a kind of desolation in his face.

'God, I'm sorry, Mother,' he said. 'I had no right to say that.'

Grandmother MacLeod did not flinch, or tremble, or indicate that she felt anything at all.

'I accept your apology, Ewen,' she said.

My mother had to stay in bed for several weeks after she arrived home. The
baby's cot was kept in my parents' room, and I could go in and look at the small
creature who lay there with his tightly closed fists and his feathery black hair.
Aunt Edna came in to help each morning, and when she had finished the housework, she would have coffee with my mother. They kept the door closed, but this
did not prevent me from eavesdropping, for there was an air register in the floor
of the spare room, which was linked somehow with the register in my parents'
room. If you put your ear to the iron grille, it was almost like a radio.

'Did you mind very much, Beth?' Aund Edna was saying.

'Oh, it's not the name I mind,' my mother replied. 'It's just the fact that Ewen
felt he had to. You know that Rod had only had the sight of one eye, didn't
you?'

'Sure, I knew. So what?'

'There was only a year and a half between Ewen and Rod,' my mother said,
'so they often went around together when they were youngsters. It was Ewen's
air-rifle that did it.'

'Oh Lord,' Aunt Edna said heavily. 'I suppose she always blamed him?'

'No, I don't think it was so much that, really. It was how he felt himself. I
think he even used to wonder sometimes if—but people shouldn't let themselves
think like that, or they'd go crazy. Accidents do happen, after all. When the war
came, Ewen joined up first. Rod should never have been in the Army at all, but
he couldn't wait to get in. He must have lied about his eyesight. It wasn't so very
noticeable unless you looked at him closely, and I don't suppose the medicals
were very thorough in those days. He got in as a gunner, and Ewen applied to
have him in the same company. He thought he might be able to watch out for
him, I guess, Rod being—at a disadvantage. They were both only kids. Ewen
was nineteen and Rod was eighteen when they went to France. And then the
Somme. I don't know, Edna, I think Ewen felt that if Rod had had proper sight,
or if he hadn't been in the same outfit and had been sent somewhere else—you
know how people always think these things afterwards, not that it's ever a bit of
use. Ewen wasn't there when Rod got hit. They'd lost each other somehow, and
Ewen was looking for him, not bothering about anything else, you know, just
frantically looking. Then he stumbled across him quite by chance. Rod was still
alive, but—'

'Stop it, Beth,' Aunt Edna said. 'You're only upsetting yourself.'

'Ewen never spoke of it to me,' my mother went on, 'until once his mother
showed me the letter he'd written to her at the time. It was a peculiar letter, almost formal, saying how gallantly Rod had died, and all that. I guess I shouldn't
have, but I told him she'd shown it to me. He was very angry that she had. And
then, as though for some reason he were terribly ashamed, he said—*I had to
write something to her, but men don't really die like that, Beth. It wasn't that
way at all.* It was only after the war that he decided to come back and study medicine and go into practice with his father.'

'Had Rod meant to?' Aunt Edna asked.

'I don't know,' my mother said slowly. 'I never felt I should ask Ewen that.'

Aunt Edna was gathering up the coffee things, for I could hear the clash of cups and saucers being stacked on the tray.

'You know what I heard her say to Vanessa once, Beth? *The MacLeods never tell lies.* Those were her exact words. Even then, I didn't know whether to laugh or cry.'

'Please, Edna—' my mother sounded worn out now. 'Don't.'

'Oh Glory,' Aunt Edna said remorsefully, 'I've got all the delicacy of a two-ton truck. I didn't mean Ewen, for heaven's sake. That wasn't what I meant at all. Here, let me plump up your pillows for you.'

Then the baby began to cry, so I could not hear anything more of interest. I took my bike and went out beyond Manawaka, riding aimlessly along the gravel highway. It was late summer, and the wheat had changed colour, but instead of being high and bronzed in the fields, it was stunted and desiccated, for there had been no rain again this year. But in the bluff where I stopped and crawled under the barbed wire fence and lay stretched out on the grass, the plentiful poplar leaves were turning to a luminous yellow and shone like church windows in the sun. I put my head down very close to the earth and looked at what was going on there. Grasshoppers with enormous eyes ticked and twitched around me, as though the dry air were perfect for their purposes. A ladybird laboured mightily to climb a blade of grass, fell off, and started all over again, seeming to be unaware that she possessed wings and could have flown up.

I thought of the accidents that might easily happen to a person—or, of course, might not happen, might happen to somebody else. I thought of the dead baby, my sister, who might as easily have been I. Would she, then, have been lying here in my place, the sharp grass making its small toothmarks on her brown arms, the sun warming her to the heart? I thought of the leatherbound volumes of Greek, and the six different kinds of iced cakes that used to be offered always in the MacLeod house, and the pictures of leopards and green seas. I thought of my brother, who had been born alive after all, and now had been given his life's name.

I could not really comprehend these things, but I sensed their strangeness, their disarray. I felt that whatever God might love in this world, it was certainly not order.

1970

A Place to Stand On

The creative writer perceives his own world once and for all in childhood and adolescence, and his whole career is an effort to illustrate his private world in terms of the great public world we all share.

—Graham Greene, *Collected Essays*

I believe that Graham Greene is right in this statement. It does not mean that the individual does not change after adolescence. On the contrary, it underlines the necessity for change. For the writer, one way of discovering oneself, of changing from the patterns of childhood and adolescence to those of adulthood, is through the explorations inherent in the writing itself. In the case of a great many writers, this explanation at some point—and perhaps at all points—involves an attempt to understand one's background and one's past, sometimes even a more distant past which one has not personally experienced.

This sort of exploration can be clearly seen in the works of contemporary African writers, many of whom re-create their people's past in novels and plays in order to recover a sense of themselves, an identity and a feeling of value from which they were separated by two or three generations of colonialism and missionizing. They have found it necessary, in other words, to come to terms with their ancestors and their gods in order to be able to accept the past and be at peace with the dead, without being stifled or threatened by their past.

Oddly enough, it was only several years ago, when I began doing some research into contemporary Nigerian writing and its background, that I began to see how much my own writing had followed the same pattern—the attempt to assimilate the past, partly in order to be freed from it, partly in order to try to understand myself and perhaps others of my generation, through seeing where we had come from.

I was fortunate in going to Africa when I did—in my early twenties—because for some years I was so fascinated by the African scene that I was prevented from writing an autobiographical first novel. I don't say there is anything wrong in autobiographical novels, but it would not have been the right thing for me—my view of the prairie town from which I had come was still too prejudiced and distorted by closeness. I had to get farther away from it before I could begin to see it. Also, as it turned out ultimately, the kind of novel which I can best handle is one in which the fictional characters are very definitely *themselves*, not me, the kind of novel in which I can feel a deep sense of connection with the main character without a total identification which for me would prevent a necessary distancing.

I always knew that one day I would have to stop writing about Africa and go back to my own people, my own place of belonging, but when I began to do this, I was extremely nervous about the outcome. I did not consciously choose any particular time in history, or any particular characters. The reverse seemed to be true. The character of Hagar in *The Stone Angel* seemed almost to choose me. Later, though, I recognized that in some way not at all consciously understood by me at the time I had had to begin approaching my background and my past through my grandparents' generation, the generation of pioneers of Scots-Presbyterian origin, who had been among the first to people the town I called Manawaka. This was where my own roots began. Other past generations of my father's family had lived in Scotland, but for me, my people's real past—my own real past—was not connected except distantly with Scotland; indeed, this was true for Hagar as well, for she was born in Manawaka.

The name Manawaka is an invented one, but it had been in my mind since I was about seventeen or eighteen, when I first began to think about writing something set in a prairie town. Manawaka is not my hometown of Neepawa—it has elements of Neepawa, especially in some of the descriptions of places, such as the cemetery on the hill or the Wachakwa valley through which ran the small brown river which was the river of my childhood. In almost every way, however, Manawaka is not so much any one prairie town as an amalgam of many prairie towns. Most of all, I like to think, it is simply itself, a town of the mind, my own private world, as Graham Greene says, which one hopes will ultimately relate to the outer world which we all share.

When one thinks of the influence of a place on one's writing, two aspects come to mind. First, the physical presence of the place itself—its geography, its appearance. Second, the people. For me, the second aspect of environment is the most important, although in everything I have written which is set in Canada, whether or not actually set in Manitoba, somewhere some of my memories of the physical appearance of the prairies come in. I had, as a child and as an adolescent, ambiguous feelings about the prairies. I still have them, although they no longer bother me. I wanted then to get out of the small town and go far away, and yet I felt the protectiveness of that atmosphere, too. I felt the loneliness and the isolation of the land itself, and yet I always considered southern Manitoba to be very beautiful, and I still do. I doubt if I will ever live there again, but those poplar bluffs and the blackness of that soil and the way in which the sky is open from one side of the horizon to the other—these are things I will carry inside my skull for as long as I live, with the vividness of recall that only our first home can have for us.

Nevertheless, the people were more important than the place. Hagar in *The Stone Angel* was not drawn from life, but she incorporates many of the qualities of my grandparents' generation. Her speech is their speech, and her gods their gods. I think I never recognized until I wrote that novel just how mixed my own feelings were towards that whole generation of pioneers—how difficult they were to live with, how authoritarian, how unbending, how afraid to show love, many of them, and how willing to show anger. And yet, they had inhabited a wilderness and made it fruitful. They were, in the end, great survivors, and for that I love and value them.

The final exploration of this aspect of my background came when I wrote—over the past six or seven years—*A Bird in the House,* a number of short stories set in Manawaka and based upon my childhood and my childhood family, the only semi-autobiographical fiction I have ever written. I did not realize until I had finished the final story in the series how much all these stories are dominated by the figure of my maternal grandfather, who came of Irish Protestant stock. Perhaps it was through writing these stories that I finally came to see my grandfather not only as the repressive authoritarian figure from my childhood, but also as a boy who had to leave school in Ontario when he was about twelve, after his father's death, and who as a young man went to Manitoba by sternwheeler and walked the fifty miles from Winnipeg to Portage la Prairie, where he settled for some years before moving to Neepawa. He was a very hard man in many ways, but he had had a very hard life. I don't think I knew any of this, really knew it, until I had finished those stories. I don't think I ever knew, either, until that moment how much I owed to him. One sentence, near the end of the final story,[1] may show what I mean. 'I had feared and fought the old man, yet he proclaimed himself in my veins.'

My writing, then, has been my own attempt to come to terms with the past. I see this process as the gradual one of freeing oneself from the stultifying aspect of the past, while at the same time beginning to see its true value—which, in the case of my own people (by which I mean the total community, not just my particular family), was a determination to survive against whatever odds.

The theme of survival—not just physical survival, but the preservation of some human dignity and in the end some human warmth and ability to reach out and touch others—this is, I have come to think, an almost inevitable theme for a writer such as I, who came from a Scots-Irish background of stern values and hard work and puritanism, and who grew up during the drought and depression of the thirties and then the war.

This theme runs through two of my novels other than *The Stone Angel* (in which it is, of course, the dominant theme). In *A Jest of God* and *The Fire-Dwellers*, both Rachel and Stacey are in their very different ways threatened by the past and by the various inadequacies each feels in herself. In the end, and again in their very different ways and out of their very different dilemmas, each finds within herself an ability to survive—not just to go on living, but to change and to move into new areas of life. Neither book is optimistic. Optimism in this world seems impossible to me. But in each novel there is some hope, and that is a different thing entirely.

If Graham Greene is right—as I think he is—in his belief that a writer's career is 'an effort to illustrate his private world in terms of the great public world we all share,' then I think it is understandable that so much of my writing relates to the kind of prairie town in which I was born and in which I first began to be aware of myself. Writing, for me, has to be set firmly in some soil, some place, some outer and inner territory which might be described in anthropological terms as 'cultural background'. But I do not believe that this kind of writing needs therefore to be parochial. If Hagar in *The Stone Angel* has any meaning, it is the same as that of an old woman anywhere, having to deal with the reality of dying. On the other hand, she is not an old woman anywhere. She is very much a person who belongs in the same kind of prairie Scots-Presbyterian background as I do, and it was, of course, people like Hagar who created that background, with all its flaws and its strengths. In a poem entitled *Roblin Mills, Circa 1842*,[2] Al Purdy said:

> They had their being once
> and left a place to stand on

---

[1]'Jericho's Brick Battlements'.
[2]Later retitled 'Roblin's Mills (2)'; see p. 62.

They did indeed, and this is the place we are standing on, for better and for worse.

I remember saying once, three or four years ago, that I felt I had written myself out of that prairie town. I know better now. My future writing may not be set in that town—and indeed, my novel, *The Fire-Dwellers*, was set in Vancouver. I may not always write fiction set in Canada. But somewhere, perhaps in the memories of some characters, Manawaka will probably always be there, simply because whatever I am was shaped and formed in that sort of place, and my way of seeing, however much it may have changed over the years, remains in some enduring way that of a small-town prairie person.

1970, 1976

James Reaney

b. 1926

In all his writing James Reaney has created a world in which the local and regional often reveal the mythic and universal. Not only are his poetry and drama grounded in his own experience (especially that of growing up in Perth County, Ont.) and in the history of his region, but he is so convinced of the need to know one's home place intimately that he sometimes teaches a course in Ontario culture and literature by beginning with a close consideration of the actualities of daily existence and a careful scrutiny of maps. At the same time Reaney has long been convinced of the importance of myth in human society. His contact with Northrop Frye when he was an undergraduate, and again when he worked on his doctoral thesis under Frye, led him to consider the theories of literature contained in Frye's *Anatomy of Criticism*, and to read Carl Jung and others who have written on the mythic dimensions of the mind. In an important essay on *Alphabet*, the literary magazine that Reaney founded and edited, Margaret Atwood points out that Reaney wrote of making a form that would be 'Documentary on one side and myth on the other: Life and Art'; she suggests that this tension between myth and documentary (which for her is parallel to 'the exchange between the observing and the observed') is both central to Reaney's poetic vision and peculiarly Canadian ('Eleven Years of "Alphabet" ', *Canadian Literature*, No. 49, 1971).

Reaney was born on a farm near Stratford, Ont., and attended a nearby one-room school and then Stratford Collegiate. In 1944 he enrolled in the University of Toronto and, while still an undergraduate, began publishing stories and poems in *Contemporary Verse*, *Northern Review*, *Canadian Forum*, and elsewhere. He received his B.A. in English in 1948 and an M.A. in 1949. In that same year he published his first collection of poems, *The Red Heart*, which won a Governor General's Award and brought him to early prominence at twenty-three. In the fall of 1949 Reaney joined the English department in the University of Manitoba; his years there (1949-56 and 1958-60) mark the only time he has ever lived outside Ontario. In 1958 he completed his doctoral degree at the University of Toronto, writing a thesis about Spenser's influence on Yeats. While involved in this scholarly study, Reaney wrote a playful imitation of *The Shepheardes Calender* entitled *A Suit of Nettles* (1958), a sequence of poems that transforms Spenser's dialogues between shepherds tending their flocks in an idealized pastoral landscape into conversations among geese on an Ontario farm. Dense and frequently witty, *A Suit of Nettles* won Reaney a second Governor General's Award.

Around this time Reaney also began to write pieces for performance. He composed a libretto for *Night-Blooming Cereus*, an opera by John Beckwith (performed on the CBC in 1959 and staged the next year) and wrote *The Killdeer* and *One-Man Masque* (both produced in 1960), as well as *The Sun and the Moon* (produced in 1965). In 1962, following the publication of *The Killdeer and Other Plays* and *Twelve Letters to a Small Town*, a sequence of poems about Stratford read on CBC radio, Reaney was awarded a third Governor General's Award. These works, and the prolific dramatic output that followed, established him as the leading dramatist of the sixties, and many of the plays—including *Colours in the Dark* (1969) and *Listen to the Wind* (1972)—were eventually published. *The Killdeer* (revised and shortened), *Three Desks*, and *The Easter Egg* were collected in *Masks of Childhood* (1972).

In the late sixties Reaney immersed himself in the exhaustive research, writing, and extensive revision that eventually led to the creation of his major theatrical achievement, *The Donnellys*, a trilogy of plays (*Sticks and Stones*, 1975; *The St Nicholas Hotel*, 1976; and *Handcuffs*, 1977) about a contumacious Irish family who lived near London, Ont., in the second half of the nineteenth century and were massacred by a suspicious and intolerant community. (When *The Donnellys* toured nationally in 1975, Reaney travelled with the NDWT company; his account of the tour was published in 1977 as *14 Barrels from Sea to Sea*.) Like all of Reaney's plays, *The Donnellys* often subverts the formal conventions of realistic theatre: it is poetic in style and frequently departs from traditional narrative exposition. Reaney has since collaborated with Beckwith on *The Shivaree* (1978), a second opera, and adapted John Richardson's nineteenth-century novel *Wacousta* for the stage.

In more than thirty dramatic pieces, Reaney has brought a new vitality to Canadian drama with his innovative and open forms as well as by his involvement in workshops and productions of his plays. At various times he has invited audience participation, allowed actors to improvise, and experimented with impressionistic sets, symbolic costuming, and choral speech. Because Reaney is less interested in objective reality than in the imaginative structures into which the mind orders that reality—that is, not in what happens but in what we make of what happens—the rural community provides him not so much with events as with examples of the power of words to transform reality into stories, songs, folktales, nursery rhymes, and individual flights of fancy. Indeed, in *The Easter Egg* (as in the poem 'Starling with a Split-Tongue'), the acquisition of language itself becomes an act of magic.

The extent of Reaney's interest in the creative dimension and power of the human mind is conveyed by the full title of his literary magazine: *Alphabet: A Semi-Annual Devoted to the Iconography of the Imagination* (1960-71). Begun the year Reaney moved from Manitoba to the University of Western Ontario, *Alphabet* was a significant influence on the Canadian literary scene. Not only did it help redirect the attention of contemporary writers to myth, but it suggested—by the often arbitrary juxtaposition of its diverse contents to the mythic figure announced for each issue— that the presence of myth in a work is derived as much from the mind's quest for meaning as from anything inherent in individual stories and poems. At the same time, title and subtitle when taken together set up an opposition between the universalizing tendency of myth and the particulars out of which language grows, the very letters themselves. (Before beginning to publish his magazine Reaney trained as a typesetter and for a time typeset each issue.) Among the many emerging writers of the decade published in *Alphabet* was bp Nichol, whose concrete poetry literally attempted to create art out of the alphabet by treating letters as things in themselves— an act that influenced Reaney in his later work.

Even while he was teaching, editing, and writing plays, Reaney never stopped working on his poetry. The sequence 'A Message to Winnipeg' (broadcast 1960) grew out of Reaney's decision to learn to read his new western landscape in a way that made it as meaningful to him as his native Ontario. It was followed by *The Dance of Death at London, Ontario* (1963), a satiric sequence of poems about his new home town. *Poems* (1972), edited and with an introduction by Germaine Warkentin, is a large selection of Reaney's poetry, including poems from his plays. In that same year Reaney wrote an introduction to a new reprint of *The Collected Poems* of Isabella Valancy Crawford, a poet whose early mythologizing of nature and its opposing forces had long interested him.

In Reaney's poetry, and in his plays, we sense a mind seeking to make the world comprehensible. But since both mind and world oscillate between innocence and experience, and between dreaming and waking—in ways that make it hard to say which is which—comprehension remains elusive. The figure of the child, which recurs throughout Reaney's work, holds the secret truths that we as adults yearn for, and it is to this child in all of us that Reaney, in his constant playfulness, is ultimately speaking.

The School Globe

Sometimes when I hold
Our faded old globe
That we used at school
To see where oceans were
And the five continents,
The lines of latitude and longitude,
The North Pole, the Equator and the South Pole—
Sometimes when I hold this
Wrecked blue cardboard pumpkin
I think: here in my hands   10
Rest the fair fields and lands
Of my childhood
Where still lie or still wander
Old games, tops and pets;
A house where I was little
And afraid to swear

Because God might hear and
Send a bear
To eat me up;
Rooms where I was as old   20
As I was high;
Where I loved the pink clenches,
The white, red and pink fists
Of roses; where I watched the rain
That Heaven's clouds threw down
In puddles and rutfuls
And irregular mirrors
Of soft brown glass upon the ground.
This school globe is a parcel of my past,
A basket of pluperfect[1] things.   30
And here I stand with it
Sometime in the summertime
All alone in an empty schoolroom
Where about me hang
Old maps, an abacus, pictures,
Blackboards, empty desks.
If I raise my hand
No tall teacher will demand
What I want.
But if someone in authority   40
Were here, I'd say
Give me this old world back
Whose husk I clasp
And I'll give you in exchange
The great sad real one
That's filled
Not with a child's remembered and pleasant skies
But with blood, pus, horror, death, stepmothers, and lies.

1949

---

[1]More than perfect; in grammar the tense that denotes completed action (expressed in English by the auxiliary *had*).

Dream Within Dream

I slept and dreamed
A collection of dreams
That fitted each into each other
Like the dungeons and cells
Of a great dark jail.
Dreamed! rode pillion[1] rather
With a demon in front of me
Upon a horse whose favourite hay
Was human hair.
Dream within dream dreamt I.   10
I dreamt a dream in which I woke
And, when awake, I killed a man.
Then, still in this dream, I fell asleep
And dreamt again that I woke
And pushed a woman over a cliff.
Next I choked a vivacious gentleman;
Then I stabbed a girl on an ottoman.
Each time the face of the man became
More like my father's face;
And that of the woman, of course,   20
Began to seem like my mother's,
As if I could have slain my parents
For that foul deed that struck
Me out of chaos, out of nothing.
At last I swam out of my nightmare
And managed to pray to Heaven
With its thousand white stars
To somehow stop my maddened mind
From making the reflection
Of reflection of my bad despair.   30
So then I dreamt my last dream.
I dreamt I was the bed
I slept upon and, lifeless, cared
Not what sack of blood and bones,
What pillar of dust
Made my springs creak
Or weighed me down.
At last I woke!

1949

[1]To 'ride pillion' is to sit on the rear of the saddle (frequently on a special cushion), behind the person holding the reins.

The Bicycle[1]

Halfway between childhood & manhood,
  More than a hoop but never a car,
The bicycle talks gravel and rain pavement
  On the highway where the dead frogs are.

Like sharkfish the cars blur by,
  Filled with the two-backed beast[2]
One dreams of, yet knows not the word for,
  The accumulating sexual yeast.

Past the house where the bees winter,
  I climb on the stairs of my pedals   10
To school murmuring irregular verbs
  Past the lion with legs like a table's.

Autumn blows the windfalls down
  With a twilight horn of dead leaves.
I pick them up in the fence of November
  And burs on my sweater sleeves.

Where a secret robin is wintering
  By the lake in the fir grove dark
Through the fresh new snow we stumble
  That Winter has whistled sharp.   20

The March wind blows me ruts over,
  Puddles past, under red maple buds,
Over culvert of streamling, under
  White clouds and beside bluebirds.

Fireflies tell their blinking player
  Piano hesitant tales
Down at the bridge through the swamp
  Where the ogre clips his rusty nails.

Between the highschool & the farmhouse
  In the country and the town   30
It was a world of love and of feeling
  Continually floating down

[1]The concluding 'letter' in *Twelve Letters to a Small Town*.
[2]Jocular Elizabethan description of a couple having sexual intercourse; compare *Othello* I.i: 'I am one, sir, that comes to tell you your daughter and the Moor are now making the beast with two backs.'

On a soul whose only knowledge
    Was that everything was something,
This was like that, that was like this—
    In short, everything was
    The bicycle of which I sing.

1962

The Lost Child

Long have I looked for my lost child.
I hear him shake his rattle
Slyly in the winter wind
In the ditch that's filled with snow.

He pinched and shrieked and ran away
At the edge of the November forest.
The hungry old burdock stood
By the dead dry ferns.

Hear him thud that ball!
The acorns fall by the fence.   10
See him loll in the St. Lucy sun,[1]
The abandoned sheaf in the wire.

Oh Life in Death! my bonny nursling
Merry drummer in the nut brown coffin,
With vast wings outspread I float
Looking and looking over the empty sea

And there! in the—on the rolling death
Rattling a dried out gourd
Floated the mysterious cradle
Filled with a source.

I push the shore and kingdom to you,
Oh winter walk with seedpod ditch:
I touch them to the floating child
And lo! Cities and gardens, shepherds and smiths.

1962[2]

[1]St Lucy's Day, 13 December, was traditionally thought of as the shortest day of the year and the beginning of the winter solstice.
[2]Originally the final poem in *One-man Masque*.

Writing and Loving

Grammar's mistake is Love's correctness:
She likes the fused sentence, the commafault kiss,
Abhors loving the interior of one's clothes, the period,
The colon, the semicolon . . . bars to conjunction.

The periodic sentence[1] definites the usually indefinite
Article; the paratactic[2] she-sentence, with her verb
At the beginning & 1000's of modifiers after,
Spreads wide her subordinate clauses & colours
His infinitive with her introductory modifier
Until after some careful parallelism,   10
Slowly breaking into phrases, words mere
Letters of the alphabet until a blank page of ecstasy.

[1956], 1972

---

[1] A complex sentence the sense of which remains incomplete until its conclusion.
[2] A paratactic sentence connects phrases and clauses without the use of conjunctions or other co-ordinating elements.

The Alphabet

Where are the fields of dew?
I cannot keep them.
They quip and pun
The rising sun
Who plucks them out of view:
But lay down fire-veined jasper!

For out of my cloudy head
Come Ay Ee I Oh and U,
Five thunders shouted;
Drive in sardonyx!   10

And Ull Mm Nn Rr and hisSsings
Proclaim huge wings;
Pour in sea blue sapphires!

Through my bristling hair
Blows Wuh and Yuh
Puh, Buh, Phuh and Vuh,
The humorous air:
Lift up skies of chalcedony!

Huh, Cuh, Guh and Chuh
Grunt like pigs in my acorn mind: 20

Arrange these emeralds in a meadow!

Come down Tuh, Duh and Thuh!
Consonantly rain
On the windowpane
Of the shrunken house of the heart;
Lift up blood red sardius!

Lift up golden chrysolite!
Juh, Quuh, Zuh and X
Scribble heavens with light,
Steeples take fright.   30

In my mouth like bread
Stands the shape of this glory;
Consonants and vowels
Repeat the story:
And sea-green beryl is carried up!

The candle tongue in my dark mouth
Is anguished with its sloth
And stung with self-scoff
As my eyes behold this treasure.
Let them bring up topaz now!   40

Dazzling chrysoprase!
Dewdrops tempt dark wick to sparkle.
Growl Spark! you whelp and cur,
Leap out of tongue kennel
And candle sepulchre.

I faint in the hyacinthine quarries!
My words pursue
Through the forest of time
The fading antlers of this dew.

A B C D E F G H I J K L M   50
Take captive the sun
Slay the dew quarry
Adam's Eve is morning rib
Bride and bridegroom marry
Still coffin is rocking crib
Tower and well are one
The stone is the wind, the wind is the stone
New Jerusalem[1]
N O P Q R S T U V W X Y Z!

1960, 1972

---

[1]The final paradise after Armageddon according to Revelation; see Revelation 21-2, which is the source of the imagery of the poem.

From 'A Message to Winnipeg'[1]

II) WINNIPEG SEEN AS A BODY OF TIME AND SPACE

Winnipeg, what once were you. You were,
Your hair was grass by the river ten feet tall,
Your arms were burr oaks and ash leaf maples,
Your backbone was a crooked silver muddy river,
Your thoughts were ravens in flocks, your bones were snow,
Your legs were trails and your blood was a people
        Who did what the stars did and the sun.

Then what were you? You were cracked enamel like
Into parishes and strips that come down to the river.
Convents were built, the river lined with nuns   10
Praying and windmills turning and your people
Had a blood that did what a star did and a Son.

Then on top of you fell
A boneyard wrecked auto gent, his hair
Made of rusted car door handles, his fingernails
Of red Snowflake Pastry signs, his belly
Of buildings downtown; his arms of sewers,
His nerves electric wires, his mouth a telephone,
His backbone—a cracked cement street. His heart
An orange pendulum bus crawling with the human fleas   20
Of a so-so civilization—half gadget, half flesh—
        I don't know what I would have instead—
        And they did what they did more or less.

1962

---

[1]A five-poem sequence, originally broadcast on CBC Radio in 1960 as 'Poet and City—Winnipeg'. A 'Speaker' provides the following three-line bridge between the first poem ('The Factory') and the second:
I walk down the street conscious that this has not alway been like this.
I walk down the street knowing that this has not always been so.
Once there could have been a burial mound instead of the factory.

Starling with a Split Tongue[1]

Some boys caught me
   In the yard
And with a jackknife they
Split my tongue into speech
So in a phrenological[2] cage
Here in the garage I stay
   And say
The cracklewords passersby taught.
I say I know not what
Though I pray I do not pray   10
Though I curse I do not curse
Though I talk I do not talk

'I thought that made it kinda nice'
I heard her say as she began slipping on the ice
   The the I am   An a am I
   I and am are the & a   Who is are? Who saw war?
I rock a little pronoun   It does instead of me
I rose as I   Nooned as you
Lay down as he or she   Begat we, you & they
My eggs are covered with commas   20

    'Yuh remember when she fell down in a fit?'
    Reveries Jake from the bottom of the pit.

Before beforeday   after St After's Massacre
While the while is on   Since since is since
Let's wait till till   Or until if you like
I come from from   to Whither Bay
Down Whence Road   but not To-day

As still as infinitives were the   Stones
Filled with adjectives were the   Trees
And with adverbs the   Pond   30
This all is a recorded announcement
         This all is a recorded announcement
'I thought that made it kinda nice'
'Yuh remember . . . . in a fit?'
              Darkness deep
Now fills the garage and its town
         With wordless sleep.

Who split their tongues? I ask.
Of Giant Jackknife in the sky.

---

[1]Folk belief holds that splitting the tongues of crows, ravens, and starlings makes it possible to teach them how to speak.
[2]i.e. 'skull-like'; phrenology (literally the study of the mental faculties) is the pseudo-scientific theory that the shape of the skull gives evidence of personality and mental ability.

Who split their tongues into lie mask   40
And lie face; split their hand
Into this way, that way, up and down,
Divided their love into restless hemispheres,
Split into two—one seeing left, one right
Their once one Aldebaran[3] all-seeing eye?
In the larger garage of the endless starlight
      Do they not croak as I?

1964, 1972

[3]One of the brightest stars in the sky (actually a double star).

A Table of Contents

I wish my poetry to be
A crowd of long ladies
Wandering through a paginated mist
Who are made of brambles
Laid horizontally
On top of each other
Each bramble
Stuck with many a strange
Plum and pear
Bur and Toad-eye.   10

I believe that poetry
Is the sound
Of the wound
With its red mouth
Speaking to itself.

1972[1]

[1]'A Table of Contents' is an early poem that remained in manuscript until printed in Warkentin's Introduction to *Poems*.

FROM THE PREFACE
to *Masks of Childhood*

* * *

Behind *Easter Egg* literally lies a collection of glass Easter eggs I made from 1945 to 1955, aet.[1] 19 and over. Found my first one in a store on Harbord Street, an old grocery and sundries store out of the 1910 era. Before Macdonald's Drug-store, neon and vitriolite,[2] was built, the U of T students used to come here in the twenties and thirties for variety purchases, coffee &c; after Macdonald's this place fell into a backwater. Occasionally old things from the attic above appeared in the window and I spent my entertainment allowance on the milk glass eggs that appeared, one at a time. In Stratford, Le Souder's Second Hand Store also kept getting a supply as attics from the eighties and nineties descended to the auc-tioneer's gavel. Have never been quite sure of their exact cultural use; I think they were given to children at Easter. Some of them are small as hen's eggs and I have heard of these being used as nest eggs; others are large—a bit larger than a goose egg. Could they have been made at the Hamilton Glass Works? Did the same glassman also blow the white lightning rod O's—objects of a like fascina-tion on my part? Milk glass blown or moulded, painted with flowers, rabbits, chickens (a cherub hatching out of one I didn't buy), glowing with trapped pearly light—such glass cannot fail to set the story-telling instinct free. So a godmother gives a boy a glass Easter egg; he is drowning in an evil world and the present could float him to a shore. Someone steals the egg and the boy goes under a wave of word-blindness and numbness. Fourteen years later the Easter egg is found again and. . . .

Bethel and her setting were suggested by stories told at an academic party in Kingston; stories about the past on a campus somewhat farther east. Nearby Gar-den Island supplied the ghost story of a girl tied to a fence for stealing a twig of small fruit. To my astonishment I ran across the basic for the story in the *London Times*, 9 October, 1846 (No. 84). I think the heading is 'Gooseberry Case on Garden Island' and the owner of the gooseberries had the child brought up in court for stealing one! Confinement beneath a cellar door rather than tying to the fence was the cruelty practised. Before you rush to the microfilm section in the stacks I should remind you that the *Times* in question was published in London, Ontario, or London Minor as it was sometimes called.

Kenneth's character came from actually seeing retarded children tied to veran-dahs and hearing of 'attic children'; of feebleminded relatives being secretly kept in specially constructed barn hideouts. 'Your Aunt Jenny is dead,' said an old lady to a friend of mine in the Ottawa Valley. 'Aunt Who?!' Never having been told about her existence out in the barn, the calm announcement of Aunt Jenny's death was too much all at once. Kenneth, however, is also *not* like these chil-dren.

Another impulse behind the play, and now I branch off into problems of direc-

---

[1] At the age of (Latin: *aetatis*).
[2] Variant of 'Vitrolite' (trademark), a thick structural glass often used on old storefronts to give them a new, shiny finish.

tion, was to write for Pamela Terry[3] a neat, tidy play, concentrated in time and place, with few characters. My previous play *Killdeer*, beautifully realized by her, had presented difficulties because of too much time, space and character. Originally I dreamed of a production with a real clock whose time matched the time of the actors. This, like the idea of a raked mirror over the fireplace, has never materialized in a production, probably for excellent reasons. But it might come out in other ways.

A very great deal depends on the actor who plays Kenneth. In general, the actors who have been the best Kenneths have been amateurs, even 'reading' the part rather than 'acting' it. Actors and directors frequently do too much work for the audience; *Egg*'s very first production was a rehearsed reading at Western with staff and student actors directed by Mary Brown. Something about Kenneth, all the glass and water images &c. responds to this treatment; sometimes I think of founding a theatre to get to the bottom of the 'cooled down' style and the effectiveness of innocence I first glimpsed here.

Since the early productions, I have noticed that audiences seem readier to accept the Kenneth situation than they seemed to, say, in the Toronto of 1962. I'd be the first to complain if the rules of logic were completely suspended, but it helps the play enormously if audiences can be cajoled into just 'listening' to the story. I know perfectly well that in real life no one marries somebody because she got him to kill a bat; but here, in this story, they *do*, you see.

Two other images occur to me. If you've ever seen Disney's almost perfect film *Pinocchio*, you may have noticed that for a great deal of the time the hero exists in the strange state of neither being a marionette nor a human being. Because of this, several worlds meet in his character with chilling precision; I'm thinking of the scenes with the young reveller Lampwick where Pinocchio keeps showing his ticket to Pleasure Island—an Ace of Spades. He is *so* innocent; he simply doesn't know. Pleasure Island, the boys who are turned into donkeys for the salt-mines (in the original aren't they skinned on the spot?) and the English Coachman are the last scenes, people and places he should meet or be in. Well, he does. And this feeling is what I want in Kenneth's characterization. Another example is the 1958 Christmas stamp for T.B. Sanatoriums. A snowball is just knocking the hat off a snowman who, of course, still smiles and will continue to do so forever. Both Christmas and Easter (my feelings for which I can't even begin to describe) are deeply concerned with the two images I have presented to you in this paragraph; also with Kenneth and of course every line of the play he is in.

After what I've just said above readers are bound to suspect that *Three Desks*, the second play in this collection, is also a liturgical mystery play . . .

[3]Director of the original production of *The Easter Egg* at the University Alumnae Dramatic Club in Toronto.

The Easter Egg

CHARACTERS:

BETHEL HENRY

KENNETH RALPH, her stepson

IRA HILL, M.D.

POLLEX HENRY, Bethel's stepdaughter

REV. GEORGE SLOAN

SCENE: The parlour of a large old house somewhere in the English part of Canada.

AUTHOR'S NOTE: Stage time is continuous even through audience intermissions, and stage time is real time: the whole action of the play takes place during the time it takes to perform the play, except for some of KENNETH's speeches in Act III, which are flashfronts and should be specially lit and emphasized. Act I: 30 minutes; Act II: 41 minutes; Act III: 42 minutes.

ACT ONE

SCENE ONE

BETHEL: [*She has just finished winding the clock on the mantel.*]
But I thought you were a seven day clock
You're supposed to stop on Saturdays, not
Fridays, do you hear. Eh? Strike!
Strike half past six now! Good for you!
Polly's hands are too weak to wind you well.
Don't ever dare stop like this again, or,
Little clock, I'll tell the clock-doctor to
Come and put all your little wheels to sleep.
[*Turning away, then turning back*] Or,
Little clock, I'll tell the clock-doctor to
Come and put all your little wheels to sleep.
Kenneth! Kenneth! what's Polly done to you,
Done to you while I was away in Europe!
It used to be I'd tinkle this bell and a
Positive apparition would enter that door
Like Santa Claus when he was eighteen
With a beard, lots of hair but no buttons.
Well she's taught you to shave—I wonder how?
And to keep yourself clean, even to walk.
It's not till you open your mouth that we
See you're an absolute ninny. Otherwise—
You're quite the model youth. Open that box.

KENNETH: [*Who has been standing perfectly still, slowly opens the box and says*] Pretty knives, forks and spoons.
BETHEL: No. They aren't pretty. Not pretty at all.
Not until you've polished them. Then—pretty,
Oh pretty, pretty, pretty, pretty, pretty!
So take this polish and take this rag
And start to earn your keep.
KENNETH: That's Polly.
BETHEL: Yes. This rag once was Polly's dress.
Does it smell of her? When she was twelve
And sane, and you were twelve and insane,
She went to Sunday School in this dress.
I use half of it to polish my silver
And half of it to polish my old purple shoes.
Show me how well you can polish, Kenneth.
KENNETH: I've done enough work for you. I dug in the garden all yesterday.
BETHEL: What did you say?
KENNETH: Pretty knives and forks and spoons.
BETHEL: Or Kenneth will not get his supper.
Unless he has everything polished for my party
Kenneth will get not even a bone.
At last—you're beginning to polish. What
I, Bethel Henry, have had to suffer
As the guardian of you, you great big lout.
Surely you can do some work for me
Even if your fontanelle[1] hasn't closed in yet.
And don't you dare look at me like that.
KENNETH: Pretty knives, forks and spoons.
BETHEL: That's better. I can't stand this phase
Where you can speak complete sentences and
Look me in the eye, button your pants up
Et cetera, et cetera, et cetera. Oh—
For the good old days when you resembled
A second rate, seedy tired out snowman
Made in mad March by the child at the
Institute for the Palsied and the Feeble-minded
And the College for the Blind. You a snowman?
Yes, almost as intelligent as a—
Yes—a snowman. My snowman that I rolled
And patted and knocked and stuck things in.
I made you as clumsy a snowman as I could
And the safest kind of snowman. And Polly
Has to meddle with you. Make you uppity
While I'm away resting up from your past

---

[1]The 'soft spot' on the top of an infant's head; it normally ossifies between twelve and eighteen months.

Dowdiness which was bad enough. Even
One's very own snowman can get nerve wracking.
Why are dinner parties at eight thirty?
I'm famished like a wolf and all I get
Is tea. I'll tell you one thing. I have not
Been blest in my stepchildren. Poor Bethel!
KENNETH: [catching sight of a bat] There's the mouse who flies.
BETHEL: All that's needed
Is for that bat to start charging around.
I see you up there you wee furry black devil.
[KENNETH clatters a spoon.]
Oh, twice a stepmother. Never a mother.
Not so much noise over there, Jangle!
I'm trying to think where I am. Where am I?
KENNETH: Pretty knives, forks and spoons.
BETHEL: Can't you polish any faster than that?
Yeah, yeah. Twice a stepmother, never mother.
Lucky too. Have that little beaver inside you,
Let in by that absurd male appendage,
Building and building its dam until
One day it floods itself out in blood.
Pah! No—and maybe it's like you. Pah!
Complete sentences indeed. What next!
You know enough to complain about work,
What else do you know? Do you know—?
Sometimes I wonder if some wonderful night
You'll lift up the trunk lid of gentleness
And come stealing out of your room—a tiger,
Stark beserk—out of your little room
Above the woodshed where you've stayed so long,
Except when I ring the bell for your meals.
Out beserk! and slay us all. Murder!
To tell the truth I was rather hoping,
While I was away, that you'd do in Polly.
Rape would do, but murder, preferably
With mutilation, would serve her so right,
Serve her so right. Rape's too pleasurable.
That silly Lucrece² woman didn't know
What a good time she was having, the stupid.
KENNETH: Pretty knives, forks and spoons.
BETHEL: [Finishing her tea] Yes. But for Heaven's sake spare Ada.
She's a hare lip but I'd never, never,
Get a cook like her again till—Till.
And what has Bethel's teacup got to say?
Poor old Bethel. Big, bad, ill-used girl with

²In Roman legend, the virtuous Lucrece was cruelly ravished by the son of the king of Rome.

Two stepchildren, twice a widow and—and—
My God! I see a box. A round squarish box.
I see a wedding ring. No, no, Not again.
I see a ladder. Teacup, you're crazy.
You're nuts. But there it is. A box.
A ring and a ladder. No visitor though.

SCENE TWO

IRA: [Entering] Bethel? Anything for me?
BETHEL: My dinner party's not till eight thirty, you know.
IRA: I know.
BETHEL: Stay awhile Ira, but then do go away and come back again. I still have to
dress and push Ada over the top.
IRA: You asked me to drop in about six thirty. Don't you remember?
BETHEL: Sure I do, Ira. I just like to see that little-boy-hurt look come into your
eyes, that's all. Now why did I ask you to come in about six thirty?
KENNETH: And the. And and The the A a . . .
BETHEL: Pretty knives, forks and spoons.
KENNETH: Pretty knives, forks and spoons.
BETHEL: Whew! Back on the tracks once more.
IRA: Hello, Kenneth.
KENNETH: H-hello, Ira.
IRA: Bethel,
I'm ashamed of myself. Why did I kiss you
In front of him as if he were a dog?
BETHEL: Why? Do you want to know why? Because
You haven't seen me for two months, have you?
IRA: I had to try it just once more, I guess.
BETHEL: Just once more?
IRA: Just once more, Bethel.
Has Kenneth been crying? His eyes are bright.
BETHEL: Ira, that's why I asked you to come over.
What has Polly done to Kenneth? He's changed.
And he's become unmanageable. Yes,
The moment I leave for Europe she drops
All her work at college, comes home here,
Turfs out the housekeeper I'd left, and starts
Tinkering with this incorrigible idiot.
IRA: Then you admit he's changed?
BETHEL: Admit it!
Well, you can shave and polish him but
You can also be terribly unkind to him.
IRA: Someone's cuffed him on the side of the face.
BETHEL: I did, Ira. I had to. When I came in here
He made a grab at my dress. I cuffed him.

IRA: That's not true, is it Bethel? He's a child still.
A baby.
BETHEL: Babies do things to people.
Listen Ira, I knew a lady I knew died
Of a baby's bite and I knew another
Baby, so-called, struck its mother's eye out
Because his fatness was not contented
With his suck! Take a baby's mind, put it
In a big lout of twenty-one's body, and
Beware! Polly has opened a box
She'll never be able to shut again.
IRA: Bethel,
You just don't like babies. You've put him
To polishing the silver. That's new too.
BETHEL: Even my teacup's been acting up lately.
Can't he work if Polly's trained him? Eh?
All the rest of us toil away at something.
I toil away at being beautiful,
And being his guardian. You toil away
At keeping the village and the college alive.
So why shouldn't he polish my silver?
IRA: You're going to make me keep my promise,
Aren't you?
BETHEL: It's the other way around, Ira.
You're going to make me keep my promise
By going down to your office, getting the form,
The proper form, and after the party committing
Him—Kenneth—to the mental place. Then,
Then you can have what you once so wanted.
Look at the way he stares at me!
I can't stand it one more day. He must go.
IRA: That's why you went away the two months.
I was in such a state for you already that
Two months more and I'd sign anything.
BETHEL: She even taught him how to shave himself.
I didn't know Polly knew how to shave.
She should have been put through Barber's College.
IRA: Mrs Fuller died today, did you know?
BETHEL: She would pick the day of my party to die.
What did she die of or can you tell me?
IRA: Did you know she was Kenneth's godmother?
BETHEL: Yes, and she chased every pretty girl there was
Up at the college right up to the death rattle.
IRA: You led the pack there, didn't you? She
Made a mention of you as she died.
BETHEL: How sweet of her.
IRA: She said there was something she'd given him

A long time ago and that you'd stolen it.
BETHEL: Oh, she's raving.
IRA: She also said that she
Blessed the day she persuaded Dr Birch
Not to commit Kenneth three years ago.
BETHEL: She beat me there. Did she have a—death wish?
IRA: That Kenneth come to live with me.
BETHEL: You're kidding.
IRA: I'm not.
BETHEL: His father also had a dying wish:
That I should always be the guardian.
That I decide always for and about Kenneth.
IRA: Is it a real father who kills himself
In front of his child—almost on purpose?
BETHEL: Well, it certainly changed Kenneth. Ira,
The mad have neither purpose nor purposelessness.
I know what's good for Kenneth though.
He's got too old to be an attic child.
You and Polly will just make him worse
So—it's off to the place and I, I visit him.
IRA: Very well. I guess that's it, Kenneth.
But you'll have to find another doctor.
KENNETH: Pretty knives, forks and spoons.
BETHEL: You know, I always thought idiot boys went
'Buz buz buz' like in Wordsworth,[3] but no—
They have quite a vocabulary. Ira,
Polly has made a list of all the words
He uses and taught him to write them
In chalk all over the walls of his room.
IRA: [Shifting] Yes.
BETHEL: Basic English.[4] Sir Winston Churchill should
Be informed. Do you want to know something?
IRA: [Drowsily] Yes.
BETHEL: The Dean of Women is coming here tonight!
IRA: The Dean of Women is coming here tonight!
Why Bethel, you've finally arrived. You've—
BETHEL: It's my wages for helping her save the girls
From Mrs Fuller's clutches and do you know
Fifteen years ago I was a girl in the kitchen here.
IRA: Clatter! Clash! Plop! Bang! Crash!

---

[3]Wordsworth's poem 'The Idiot Boy' is a sentimental narrative about a mother searching for her lost idiot son. The boy chiefly makes the sound 'burr, burr, burr', though after he is found he utters a clear sentence. Bethel seems here to confuse Wordsworth with Shakespeare, where 'Buzz, buzz' is a contemptuous sound (as, for example, in *Hamlet* II. ii).

[4]A vocabulary of 850 words developed by C.K. Ogden of Cambridge University between 1925 and 1932; its adoption was urged by many prominent people, including Winston Churchill, not only to facilitate language learning but to promote communication between nations.

BETHEL: Yeah, something like that.
My mother still bootlegs up over the hill
While I give dinner parties to the Dean of Women.
At twelve I could barely write my name,
Now I give travel talks to college girls.
IRA: Right. Did you really marry Kenneth's father?
Or, rather, did he really marry you?
BETHEL: Oh, Ira. Do you want the certificate?
How else did I get all his money, eh?
Eh? And that wide world's wonder over there.
KENNETH: Pretty knives, forks and spoons.
IRA: The rise and fall of Bethel Henry!
BETHEL: And fall?! No. Just rise and rise and rise!
IRA: It's like a loaf of bread. The Bethel Story!
One: comes down from the mountain
Two: scrubs the professor's kitchen
Three: scrubs the professor in his tub
Four: Kenneth's father blows head off
Five: comes into Kenneth and also money
And house and estate and status and—
BETHEL: So next—Polly's father, the Bishop of—
IRA: Montreal! He took some catching, didn't he?
BETHEL: I had to go to college to be smart enough
To catch a bishop. Oh, I was so proud of him.
He never learned to speak French.
IRA: Why bother
If you're the Bishop of Montreal?
BETHEL: He always said if Wolfe won that battle,
Then he won that battle, and that meant all
Should speak English.
IRA: Fortunately, Polly
Does not take after her father.
BETHEL: In one way
I wish she did. He was finally electrocuted
By a shaft of lightning.
IRA: Hurrah!
BETHEL: And then Kenneth got very big and then
You fell madly in love with me, yes me,
And next I climb up to the Dean of Women,
Dr Ewell and the Principal's wife for
Dinner, finally get rid of Kenneth—on—
IRA: On down.
BETHEL: On *up*! I'm King of the Castle! [*Leaps up on chair.*]
After the party tonight, you'll give in.
You're not that little a man. Not you!
IRA: Bethel, let me bring you down from there.
Your ward, Kenneth, *is perfectly sane.*

KENNETH: Pretty knives, forks and spoons. [BETHEL *laughs*.]
IRA: Your ward, Kenneth, is perfectly sane.
He's like a carp down in the village pond
That comes up to the surface and then as you
Throw him a piece of bread he sinks down
Because the piece of bread cast a shadow.
BETHEL: Down in the mud is the best place for him. [*Pause*]
If he's sane, Ira, what's the matter with him?
IRA: I don't know but it's *not insanity*.
BETHEL: Polly's been at you. I'll fix her.
Tonight with a good dinner you'll succumb
Just as you've succumbed before. Why, I'm
The reason Mrs Harrison's baby is a whole day
Younger than it should be. Think of that.
IRA: Bethel, I don't want to make love to you.
I want to help Kenneth get better.
BETHEL: So do I—and Polly's making him worse
And you will too. Leave my Kenny alone.
IRA: He's like a rider on a horse comes
Galloping down the road to the bridge
And suddenly stops. There's something there—
In the middle of the bridge.
BETHEL: A black pig—oinking and grunting. Oink oink oink!
No! there's no bridge now for Kenneth.
And I'll not have him Polly's plaything.
And he's getting sicker and sicker.
IRA: How sicker?
For the first time in his life he looks you
In the eye, says hello to me, calls me
By name.
BETHEL; There's been signs. What do you want?
A full-scale attack?
KENNETH: Pretty knives, forks and spoons.
IRA: In the inquietude you've caused this bachelor,
Bethel, there have been moments when I have
Escaped from my obsession with you and
Seen other visions some of them preferable.
[*She descends from chair.*]
When my brother was still alive, we as students
Went with butterfly nets to the woods
Around the Big Pond. Kenneth, Kenneth,
I looked up to see what my brother saw:
It was you. At five years old. Stark naked.
Out of a silk scarf of your mother's you'd
Made a turban. That was all your dress.
While your parents had their afternoon nap
You escaped from this house, ran naked,

Through the sleeping village, the meadow,
Naked through the forest—just for fun.
You saw us. You stopped. A naked child
With all green light and sun streams about you.
You turned and vanished. I'll take that.
So far as I see that's what it all means.
And that naked innocent who gave me God
Is still lost in the forest and I shall bring him
Back to powerful friends who love him.
KENNETH: Pretty knives, forks and spoons.
IRA: Pretty knives, forks and spoons.
BETHEL: At the age of five he was showing signs, eh?
IRA: Of course, you'd say that.
BETHEL: Before the suicide he was certainly showing tendencies I'd say.
IRA: Not in the least.
KENNETH: Pretty knives, forks and spoons.
BETHEL: Say something else, Kenneth, or I'll go right off my rocker.
KENNETH: I've done enough work for you. I dug in the garden all day yesterday.
BETHEL: Enough! Go out to the kitchen and get your tray.
KENNETH: I've done enough work for you. I dug in the garden all day yesterday.
BETHEL: Pretty knives, forks and spoons.
KENNETH: [*Pause*] Pretty knives, forks and spoons.
IRA: So, Bethel. Thank you for the tea. By the way, you're not wearing a dress, are you?
BETHEL: [*Laughing*] I meant he tore at my blouse. You wouldn't call a blouse a pair of trousers, would you?
IRA: Bethel, I've never worn a blouse but it occurs to me that it's not a dress. So why not call it a blouse? Also—I taught Kenneth to shave. While you were away.
BETHEL: With a straight razor?
IRA: An old electric razor of mine. Don't get your hopes up so high.
BETHEL: Then you won't commit him for me?
IRA: No. And I'll fight any attempt to do so. If it were a good place I'll bet you wouldn't send him.
BETHEL: Isn't it a good place for mental cases?
IRA: It is. But it's not a good place for Kenneth. He's not a mental case. He's something else again.
BETHEL: So—the other side of the bargain goes too.
IRA: No. If you'll let Kenneth come to me I'll make love to you.
BETHEL: Ho, ho, ho. Where are you going now?
IRA: Over to the college for a swim.
BETHEL: Do that spoon over again, Kenny. Ira, if this goes on I'm going to run away with Kenneth. Somewhere you and Polly will never find us. Never see him again.

IRA: Bethel, if someone could just knock you down it would be so good for you. [*Leaving*]

BETHEL: No one'll knock me down. None of you have the strength. I'm King of the Castle, now.

IRA: [*Returning briefly*] There's someone stronger than you. And they'll knock you down.

BETHEL: Show me. Show me this phenomenon. Today, this very hour, I don't believe it.

IRA: [*Laughing*] He polishes your silver.

KENNETH: Pretty knives, forks and spoons.

BETHEL: By the way, Ira, if you're thinking of marrying Polly I hope you know you've a very strong rival there.

IRA's *laughter is only reply to this. He is gone and* POLLY *enters.*

SCENE THREE

POLLY: Why on earth would I marry Ira?

BETHEL: I thought Kenneth had brought you two together while I was away.

POLLY: Whatever has she set you doing, Kenneth?

BETHEL: If you've taught him how to work, Polly, then he shall work.

POLLY: Hasn't he done enough work for you? He dug in the garden all yesterday.

BETHEL: So that's where that comes from.

POLLY: Bethel, did the garden used to be on the other side of the house?

BETHEL: Why do you ask?

POLLY: When you sent Kenneth out to dig in the garden yesterday he went out and began to dig in the centre of the lawn—out there.

BETHEL: Polly, when Kenneth was six his father took a gun and blew the top off his head in front of him. After that he hasn't been able to tell a man from a woman, a garden from a lawn, a tree from a cloud.

POLLY: I know. But how come the ghost of the little girl always appears on the lawn side of the house—out there—if the garden wasn't there at one time.

BETHEL: There is no ghost of a little girl.

POLLY: Oh yes, there is. It's one of the truest stories connected with this house. Even Kenneth can see the little girl. I've heard him talk to her.

BETHEL: I do not believe in apparitions.

POLLY: She used to put her hand through the picket fence to get berries and a wicked old man who lived here tied her hand to the fence.

BETHEL: She was lucky. I'd have bitten it right off.

POLLY: So you can see her tugging away at the fence in the twilight.

BETHEL: Can you see her now?

POLLY: I can see her even in daytime.

BETHEL: Can you see her now?

POLLY: Of course. There she is. Don't you see her?

BETHEL: I don't see anything. Only the lawn and the fence and the street and the college buildings and the walnut trees.

POLLY: Bethel, I'd like to give Kenneth the rest of his lessons right now before he has supper and goes to bed.

BETHEL: Why did you ask about which side of the house the garden used to be on?

POLLY: I'd just like to know in view of—

BETHEL: Oh, what's the use of lessons for him? He finished the bit he could learn years ago. Don't bother answering. [*Going out*] A ladder, a round squarish box and a wedding ring. [*Exit.*] A ladder, a box and a ring. A ladder . . .

SCENE FOUR

POLLY: Kenneth. Here I'll finish that. Kenneth, my fiancé will be calling in ten minutes or so if not sooner. So we'll more or less pass the time until he comes. Let's sit down, Kenneth. Well? First, we'll do our word lists. Recite me the twenty-seven words that one uses At Home.

KENNETH: house door room porch floor hall entry staircase wardrobe parlour closet pantry kitchen window cupboard threshold dining-room bathroom garret attic cellar chamber bedroom library veranda balcony piazza

POLLY: Good. Now Kenneth. Kenneth, do we understand these words? Sometimes I really wonder if after all our work you understand what I say. Really understand, or do you just go by the rise and fall of my voice and the words you did know before—before it happened.

KENNETH: Polly, Polly. Come and see the little girl.

POLLY: Can you see her, Kenneth?

KENNETH: I can see the little girl. She's tied to the picket.

POLLY: [*Looking at a notebook*] Oh shucks. Picket. You have used it before. I was hoping it might be our new word. Not fence, eh? Fence?

KENNETH: Picket.

POLLY: Kenneth—Look out at the little girl. What do you see on one side of the picket fence, Kenneth?

KENNETH: Garden. Flowers. A butterfly.

POLLY: Yes. To you the garden is on that side of the house. Bethel must have put a lawn over the old garden. Yes. Kenneth, last night I went out and dug in the place where she stopped you digging in the lawn. I took a covered lantern. It was very exciting like digging for treasure. I found—do you know what I found?—a rusty old metal box which I couldn't open. So my fiancé is taking it to the blacksmith's today to get it opened. Now what could be inside it? Well, we'll soon know. Now let's see what words you understand in the At Home list.

KENNETH: There's the mouse with wings.

POLLY: My golly, there's the bat. It knows there's going to be a party. I'll bet it will go for the Dean of Women. Get all tangled up in her hair or her hat. Shall we warn Bethel?

KENNETH: I—I—

POLLY: Yes!

KENNETH: Told Bethel.

POLLY: Then she's warned. Now—show me that you understand *house*.

KENNETH: House! [*He mimes or points out the words he understands.*]

POLLY: Show me a door.

KENNETH: Door!

POLLY: Where is the attic? [*He points.*] And where is the cellar? [*He points.*] Where is the threshold? [*He is undecided.*]

Show it to me, Kenneth. Show me the threshold! [*He stamps his foot and shakes his head.*] I see. You did say the word, but you won't use it. Oh my dear. If only you'd use the new words I give you, why, you'd be free. But if you only use the old words you knew before it happened you'll always be back before it happened.

KENNETH: Polly—

POLLY: Kenneth. I look at you and then I look only at your eyes and then I look down your eyes. I see at the bottom of the well of your eyes:

> A sleeping young clever and talkative
> Young man whom I can never wake
> No matter what whistle or bell or call I use.
> Sometimes he reaches up to me and I
> Reach down to him. But our hands touch the glass
> Of impossibility and you sink back to *sleep*.

They reach out their hands to each other. Just as she is about to touch him he turns away until his back is to her.

Oh, Kenneth. Once more. Say 'tumbler'.

KENNETH: 'Tumbler'.

POLLY: Now bring me a tumbler from the cabinet over there.

KENNETH *stands still.*

Never mind. Here—see if you can read this. [*Gives him a book.*]

KENNETH: [*After looking it over*]

> The Huntsman Night
> Rides down the Sky
> To usher in the Morn[5]

POLLY: [*Hands him a piece of paper.*] Now read this.

KENNETH: I cannot read it, Polly.

POLLY: But it's the same. Only it's in handwriting. You can't read handwriting very often, can you? Now here. Read this. (*She gives him another piece of paper.*)

KENNETH:

> The Huntsman Night
> Rides down the Sky
> To usher in the Morn.

POLLY: It's the same too. Only I printed it out. That's a good thing to know, Kenneth. That you can read my printing. By the way what is a Huntsman? [*He mimes someone taking aim and shooting.*] Good! And what is—Night? [*He squeezes his eyes shut and mimes drowsiness.*] Good! Oh we'll rev and rev and rev your mind up until with just our eight hundred words we'll suddenly be flying—up over the word barrier. Kenneth, someday I'll be teaching you just as I am today and I'll

[5]Reaney says he took these lines from the British film *Gone to Earth* (1951), where it appeared as an inscription on a sun-dial.

ask you—as I did today—what a tumbler is. You'll pause, then suddenly say: 'I know, Polly, I know what a tumbler is. And a threshold. And a piazza.' And then—you'll be a grown man, Kenneth, and the lessons—my lessons will be over. Let's do etiquette, rhyming and dancing next. Rhymes for scholar!

KENNETH: Beggar, bursar, vicar!

POLLY: Rhymes for pioneer!

KENNETH: Auctioneer, charioteer, mutineer, scrutineer.

POLLY: Nursery!

KENNETH: Surgery, nunnery, colliery, cemetery.

POLLY: Story!

KENNETH: Dormitory, factory, observatory, oratory.

POLLY: Ward!

KENNETH: Eastward westward northward southward heavenward homeward leeward thitherward whitherward downward upward

POLLY: [closing her book] Most of those words you've no idea of their meaning, but we're sowing them in your mind anyhow. Now Kenneth. Etiquette. Introduce me to Mr Chair.

KENNETH: Mr Chair, I—I should like you to meet Miss Henry.

POLLY: No, no. The other way around.

KENNETH: Miss Henry, I should like you to meet Mr Chair. Mr Chair, I should like you to meet Miss Henry.

POLLY: Very nice to meet you, Mr Chair.

KENNETH: Polly, who is Miss Henry?

POLLY: Why Kenneth, don't you know? It's me. It's my official name. Now make conversation with Mr Chair and me.

KENNETH: Mr Chair, have you been long in town?

POLLY: Oh, a day or two. Just tootling through, you know.

KENNETH: Mr Chair, how do you find our summers?

POLLY: A pleasant contrast to your winters, I must say.

KENNETH: [Laughs.] And, Mr Chair, how do you find our, our aut—fall?

POLLY: Say what you were going to say, Kenneth. It can be the new word.

KENNETH: Father says it's American to say fall. United Empire Loyalists say— say autumn.

POLLY: Gosh, five words I didn't know you'd bumped into. [Writes in notebook.] Not really new words though. Words floating up from before—huh—before the Deluge. I wonder if your father also thought that [to herself] that United Empire Loyalists should say: I autumn off the ladder. I autumned down.

[She winds up a victrola.] Now our dancing. This gives you poise, Kenneth, and helps you to walk more gracefully. Like this. [Mimes.] I hate to see people walking along like this [Mimes.]—every tromp of foot and clumsy thrust of shoulder a denial of love and beauty. On the other hand, young men shouldn't be too graceful. A certain amount of clumsiness. A certain amount of clumsiness is quite charming to a girl because it means she has something to work on. He needs her help. This music is called—Isn't it odd my fiancé's not arrived? This is a really pretty piece. It's 'The Japanese Sandman'. Come. [They dance. At first she leads. Then as he catches on, he leads.] Oh—let's rest for a while. Are you as breathless as I am? [He still wants to dance.] George is very late. No, I couldn't dance another step. It's time for our closing story. I thought I'd illustrate your story tonight. Perhaps you'll understand it better. See—I've brought down this old toy train. And I'll take down this doll from the mantelpiece. You get it for me, dear. The little doll made out of pipe cleaners and pieces of old hair ribbon. What are you staring at the clock for, Kenneth?

KENNETH: 'Little clock, I'll tell the clock-doctor to
    Come and put all your little wheels asleep.'

POLLY: Hmh? [*She hasn't heard, putting the toy train together having occupied her attention.*] Now. We'll put the doll and the toy train on this little coffee table in front of us and listen awfully hard and see if you can understand. Yesterday we finished the tales of Jane Austen and today I rather thought we might go on to the works of Tolstoi. Now Kenneth, I am going to tell you the story of Anna Karenina. Once there was a girl, Anna by name, who married a rich important man somewhat older than herself. She had children by him. He really bored her to tears—he was so bossy and cold. See, Kenneth, Anna is the little doll standing by the toy train tracks.

KENNETH: Anna.

POLLY: Yes. One day she fell in love with a young soldier named Vronsky. After you are married you are not supposed to fall in love again. You must work hard at trying to love your husband even if he is a turnip. But Anna could not really help herself. Young Vronsky became an obsession with her. Her husband noted that she loved this young man and he was most displeased. One day at the horse races Vronsky fell off his horse and she showed obvious concern in front of a great many people. [*Leaping up*] Vronsky! Anna's husband was terribly embarrassed—ashamed—because now everyone else would know that Anna loved this young man instead of himself. 'Take my arm, Anna. Take my arm, Anna.'

Anna made a journey by train from St Petersburg to Moscow in the depth of winter and her little son met her at the station. [*She lets the train circle the track once or twice.*] At the snowy station there was an old man, a railway worker, who was tapping snow and ice from the wheels. The train moved unexpectedly and pinned him down. [POLLY *illustrates this with a poker from the fireplace and the sofa as the locomotive.*] The old man was hurt. Anna saw him and cried out. She felt that she someday would die that way. And the old man with his metal tapping rod was Death.

Kenneth, she separated from her husband and went to live with the young man. They sat in a farmhouse looking at the fire together and roasting apples. The way we did last winter. They went to Venice and lived in a palace there by a canal. Gondolas went up and down. But back in Russia the train still went back and forth through the snow between St Petersburg and Moscow.

They went back to Russia. Somehow or other they quarrelled. They couldn't get married. That was the trouble because Anna's husband wouldn't give her a divorce. So Anna and Vronsky had to be in love all the time which is very hard on the nerves as I can tell you. And she couldn't see her children. One night she, Anna, and he, Vronsky, quarrelled terribly. She ran out of their house and as she slammed the door she said, 'You'll be sorry'. She walked to the railway station. There was a train leaving soon. In the darkness up and down beside the tracks she walked up and down. She knew what she must do. The train began to move out of the station—its headlight gets larger and larger. With her back to the train Anna stood over one of the tracks and waited. [*She puts the doll on the track and lets the train start up, holding it back with her hand a bit. He leaps forward and stops the train with his arms. He gets the doll away.*]

KENNETH: No! No!

POLLY: Oh Kenneth, Kenneth. You do understand. You do understand the story. You don't want Anna to die. And she won't die. There, there. I'll change the story. It's wonderful you understand. Kenneth. [*He lies quietly in her arms on the sofa and she rocks him.*] There, there—I'll change the story, Kenneth.

As the curtain falls we see the doll in his hand. The toy train still goes round and round the track.

CURTAIN

ACT II

SCENE FIVE

The scene is the same. Perhaps we are aware that during the interval, while we have been out in the lobby for the intermission, they have been sitting on the sofa, she quieting him as the toy train has run down more slowly and more slowly until eventually it has stopped. Just before the curtain went up POLLY *started to discuss the new signal they would use to each other.*

POLLY: [*She plays a simple uprushing series of chords on the piano that is* KEN-NETH's *whole slowly opening, now swiftly opening, mind and understanding.*] I'll teach that to you Kenneth, so you can signal to me some day. But right now if you ever hear this it means I want you to come to me. I'll never ring Bethel's little bell. Never. It's a dog and cat bell, a slave bell. But now instead of my going all the way up to your room I can play this [*Plays it.*] and you'll come to me.

KENNETH: Will you need me?

POLLY: [*Pause*] Yes, Kenneth. If I play it—I need you. And Kenneth, Bethel can't play the piano so it'll never be her. Now it's time you went to the kitchen to see if Ada has your supper ready.

KENNETH: Polly, could I go to the party? Could I watch? I found some clothes. [*He has them hidden behind the couch. They investigate them. The shoes are too large.*]

POLLY: Kenneth. No dear. You're too good for the party. But I'll come up afterwards and bring you something before you go to sleep. A piece of cake. [*He goes off.*] She'll want this in the kitchen, Kenneth. [*Hands him the box of silver.*]

BETHEL: [*Entering? Fading? Entering as if* KENNETH *might still be there*] Polly? Are you and Kenny through in there? [*She has changed into evening dress.*]

POLLY: Yes.

BETHEL: I've been debating whether to come and break it up or not.

POLLY: That's a lovely dress, Bethel. Where did you get it?

BETHEL: I made it.

POLLY: You didn't.

BETHEL: Out of old handkerchiefs.

POLLY: You did not. Well, you've certainly spent father's money wisely.

BETHEL: Thank you. And it's all spent too—Polly, are you coming to my party? Or have you made up your mind yet? You'd better hurry up. Ada's about to set the table.

POLLY: Of course I'm coming. I might as well get some of my father's money back. First of all. And second of all—I'm almost sure to have some very important news to break.

BETHEL: Oh? Oh! You're engaged! Engaged, Polly, at long last to Kenneth!

POLLY: You think that's so funny, don't you?

BETHEL: Well, aren't you going to be engaged to Kenneth? You've been paying so much attention to him lately.

POLLY: You know why, Bethel. Because I found him so neglected by you. And you are his guardian. Oh, for two cents I would marry Kenneth. That would spite you, wouldn't it?

BETHEL: Would you marry him?

POLLY: Bethel! Kenneth will always be a child probably. He'd have to change— you know very well it's George I'm in love with.

BETHEL: George?

POLLY: You've invited him to your party, Bethel. The Reverend George Sloan.

BETHEL: Yes, Polly. No, I was just teasing about Kenneth, Polly. Polly, I'm so grateful for what you're trying to do with Kenneth. Sometimes I wonder if you can see why I'm not on tip toe waiting for the big breakthrough with Kenneth suddenly recovering his wits and so on. I've had my turn with Kenneth—please, please just let me finish. Turn. He's had these patches of brightness before. His godmother and I, Mrs Fuller who died this morning at long last Ira tells me, his godmother and I, when we got along better—but that's as far as it got.

POLLY: You didn't try love. You didn't really like him at all, did you? You certainly don't like him now.

BETHEL: I'm so glad you mentioned love, Polly. Love is something—I'm afraid of love and Kenneth at his age. Indeed, I'm rather surprised there hasn't been some sort of outburst already—long ago.

POLLY: I'm not afraid. *He's instinctively civilized.*

BETHEL: Because you are you think he is, my dear. I know more about it, Polly. Why where I was born—up over the mountain, Polly, there was a farmer's boy who was like Kenneth.

They kept him in a wooden cage up in the attic. Up until eighteen he was quite harmless and sweet—until quite suddenly—it hit him. Even his own mother wasn't safe with him, and, my dear, what he did and what he said were simply dreadful.

POLLY: No!

BETHEL: Yes. I rather suspect—they had to send him away of course—that Kenneth will go that way too if he's disturbed—by a young woman.

POLLY: [*At window*] Oh look. His pigeons are at his window waiting to be fed and they're wheeling back and forth around his window before they come down to be fed.

BETHEL: He quite scared the wits out of me earlier on here.

POLLY: How could Kenneth scare anybody?

BETHEL: He took hold of my blouse up here and wouldn't let go. I had to cuff him to make him let go.

POLLY: That's what you get for working him like a dog, Bethel.

BETHEL: But it helps him to work.

POLLY: He grabbed you—because he was angry at you for bossing him.

BETHEL: No, no, no. Not angry. Not in anger.

POLLY: He's never touched me, Bethel.

BETHEL: Has that ever been your *forte?*

POLLY: To have men touch me?

BETHEL: Yes. [*Pause*] And so. Do you want him to be unhappy, Polly? Or else— become so disturbed that you might be unhappy? Telling him all those love stories.

POLLY: Jane Austen? Leo Tolstoi?

BETHEL: It's the Jane Austen that worries me most. If I were a young fellow and had to sit through those stories where nobody gets even a hug until the final chapter I'd go stark raving berserk and roam the countryside a priapic menace.

POLLY: Hmh. Are you going to send him off somewhere?

BETHEL: Well, it just happens I was appointed his guardian and if I see him being harmed by amateur enthusiasts I may have to.

POLLY: But what would be so bad about sending him off? They'd know how to help him far better than I do.

BETHEL: No one's going to take him from me—not you, not the mental doctors— Ira doesn't think they'd be so good at helping—why, Polly, I might just go off alone with him and maybe Ada. To some place where we'd all be safe and quit from you all.

POLLY: Oh. You're wearing my necklace.

BETHEL: Polly, I just have to wear it tonight. It's the only thing that goes with my dress.

POLLY: All right. But I must have it for the next half hour.

BETHEL: Why?

POLLY: George gave me that necklace. He's coming to talk about things before the party. You can have it after.

BETHEL: After its work is done, eh? George. Oh yes. You're getting engaged to George.

POLLY: So I hope. Expect.

BETHEL: You're going to marry George and be a minister's wife.

POLLY: Yes. So I hope. Expect. Bethel, do you remember when I first met you at college? Then, too, I lent you something, a pin, a brooch—for tea. We were such friends then. Do you remember—you were wearing the red skirt and the black sweater and I stopped you just in time? And you put on something of mine that was more suitable. We were such friends then. My God. You hated me for that, didn't you? I just see it now. And yet I couldn't have let you go to the tea dressed like that—we were such. Such. You were older than us at college and I was your first friend. And you were shy. But awfully smart. Here you'd lived all these years a widow in this old house with the mad boy and the deformed kitchen girl and no one knew what you were like.

I think I know now. Suddenly—you came out into the world—a shy, uncertain—young widow and I put out my hand and pulled you into the game. The middle class game. That dress. This party.

BETHEL: My dear, here's your necklace. Wear it all the evening if you like. (POLLY *doesn't take it.*) I do remember. Yes. And I forget. Polly, why did you throw up your library school training and come home in the middle of winter like that when I was away? You've used up all your money and so you pretty well will have to marry George, won't you?

POLLY: You—

BETHEL: Here I thought I had you nicely launched into life as a librarian somewhere.

POLLY: You don't want to remember us at college, do you? Nicely launched into life! Listen Bethel, you must know what libraries are like. I'll not end up in a place where you secretly don't want anyone to read the books. I *shall* marry George no matter how weak he looks. He will marry me.

BETHEL: Yes, for they say it's wise to marry as soon as ever one can. After twenty-seven your bones stiffen and it's harder to bear the children.

POLLY: Well, my bones haven't stiffened quite yet.

BETHEL: I'm glad to hear it.

POLLY: Your pelvic bones must be rather stiff by now.

BETHEL: No—there's still the odd—elastic moment there.

POLLY: Bethel! I'm sorry. It's no use my talking like this. I just get wilder and wilder. When I saw you taking father away from me—I first started to think like this and now—I talk like this. Oh, young girls whose mothers have died should be able to take out stepmother insurance.

BETHEL: Polly, aren't you through your Cinderella phase yet?

POLLY: Cinderella's the truest story ever written.

BETHEL: I can't help if I'm your stepmother. I can't help it if I'm Kenneth's stepmother. You never think of what I feel like. The poor old stepmother!

POLLY: I took you home and there it turned out that you couldn't take communion because you'd never been christened.

BETHEL: George Sloan. Polly. Polly Sloan.

POLLY: I should explain that my home also happened to be a bishop's palace. And when father knew that—he'd never met such a charming heathen and so close to the palace too. No need to go to Africa. So by slow degrees you allowed yourself to be converted and soon you and father were both paddling around in the baptismal font. Why I'm your godmother! You knew he liked his Anglicanism high off the incense stick so you put on a regular circus for him. You memorized all the saints' days, your accent changed, on St Cecilia's Day you sang,[6] on St Lawrence's Day you made griddle cakes, on St Andrew's Day you played noughts and crosses and on St Sebastian's Day you shot a bow and arrow.

---

[6]St Cecilia is the patron saint of music, and in England her festival day (November 22) was traditionally celebrated with music. The remainder of Polly's account of Bethel's celebration of saints' days is, however, comical rather than traditional: St Lawrence was martyred by being stretched on a gridiron and his dying words are supposed to have been, 'My flesh is well cooked on one side, turn the other and eat'; St Andrew is supposed to have died on a cross in the shape of an X ('noughts and crosses' is the same as tic-tac-toe); the martyrdom of St Sebastian, who was tied to a tree and shot full of arrows, is the subject of several medieval and Renaissance paintings.

And on St Valentine's Day—you moved in for the slaughter.

BETHEL: Isn't that all—just courtship?

POLLY: And Kenneth rotted away here and I stood by and watched.

BETHEL: But why shouldn't I marry your father? I'm civilized. I went to college.

POLLY: You went to college to see what you could do, didn't you?

BETHEL: Do—with my mind. I can read poetry too, you know. And tell it from prose.

POLLY: There's no reason why father shouldn't marry you. It's so absurd though. Do you still go to the earliest communion at chapel?

BETHEL: I've lost my faith somewhat, Polly, since your father died. I don't know—if a bishop can get struck by lightning I begin to wonder if there is a God.

POLLY: There isn't one. There's just us—and the spiders.

BETHEL: At times—there's not even the spiders.

POLLY: Have you seen your mother lately, Bethel?

BETHEL: No. Don't you dare bring her up. The whole—

POLLY: Sh! Sh! It wasn't a ploy. George happened to drive me past her shack last night and I saw her smoking on the stoop. She's tremendous.

BETHEL: But she's not in my life.

POLLY: Don't you even go to see her?

BETHEL: The whole village and the college knows, the very grass knows, I was born in a hovel and my mother is an old hag who runs a blind pig[7] and that I ran away—down the mountain into this valley I could see every morning with the beautiful college buildings and the chimneys here sticking up through the elms. I came down and I climbed. I'm mistress of the largest and oldest house in the village. I married a professor, I married a bishop. And it hasn't just been going to bed either. I'm really smart.

POLLY: Sure.

BETHEL: As I reminded you before, I can read poetry.

POLLY: Sure Kenneth's a poem and you can't read him.

BETHEL: I read him the way I can.

POLLY: Your mother must know what to do with you. I don't.

BETHEL: My mother used to knock the stuffing out of me.

POLLY: Oh Bethel—it's so good to hear you being slangy again. It always frightens me when you're college bred with me and something else with Ira and something else with—you're so smart you've got German for Germans, Bantu for Bantus, and Kenneth talk for Kenneth. You've even got two words for blouse. It can be a dress and it can be a blouse.

BETHEL: You overheard. You heard every word I said to Ira!

POLLY: And every word he said to you. I heard the story about being attacked by Kenneth and the two versions of that story. Bethel, I can't help but overhear. Everything comes up the fireplace into my fireplace.

BETHEL: I see. [Pause] There's that bat. He must have heard you mention fireplace. He always comes down the chimney in summer and has a good go in the parlour until I frighten the daylights out of him.

___
[7]Illegal saloon.

POLLY: Give me the necklace, Bethel.

They perform the transfer which has been hanging fire. GEORGE *enters, a plump, young, theological graduate. Somehow he is not completely human but a special combination of weakness and shyness and boldness, even cruelty. He carries a metal box wrapped up in brown paper.*

SCENE SIX

BETHEL: Good evening, George. Is that the cake from the bakery? Surely not. It feels like a hunk of rusty scrap iron. [*She has the parcel now and feels the wrapping deeply.* GEORGE *gets it back from her.*]
GEORGE: Indeed, Mrs Henry, it's not a cake. It's a box. Polly here had me take it to the blacksmith's to have the lock sawed off.

BETHEL *grabs it back again but* POLLY *makes a final desperate snatch and retrieves it.*

BETHEL: What the hell. Where does Polly get a box that has to have the lock sawed off by the blacksmith?
POLLY: Never you mind, Bethel. It's a present George is making me and don't you dare hang onto it so. Let go!
BETHEL: Well, Polly, if you're going to pinch.
GEORGE: Mrs Henry, I think I should point out to you that you are the first bishop's widow I have ever heard swear.
BETHEL: Is that so, Mr Sloan? Mr Sloan, there are going to be so many firsts between you and me.
POLLY: George, [*Kissing him*] do just stay here while I run upstairs with this and change.

GEORGE *and* BETHEL *have an uncomfortable minute alone with each other.* BETHEL *either stares at him or else follows the flutterings of her friend the bat. Since* GEORGE *has no idea there is a bat in the room he wonders what she is craning her neck about. Is he dressed properly? Suddenly she vanishes into another room.* KENNETH *enters with his supper tray on the way to his quarters.*

SCENE SEVEN

GEORGE: [*All nervousness gone*] Hello Kenny. Hello.
KENNETH: You You.
GEORGE: Yes, yes. Old old you you. Got your little tray for sup sup I see. [*Coming close*] Jello. Milk. Yum yum. Mashed fish. Hey, it's just the way they feed 'em up at Melvida at the asylum. Gee—they let you have a knife. Perhaps you're getting better. Though I shouldn't suppose you ever shall, you poor idiot. You don't understand a single thing I say, do you? It's just goo goo to you. Like a baby. [*Shakes the tray.*] Watch out—you'll spill it on the carpet, Kenny. You have spilled it on the carpet! Shame on Kenny. Made a mess on the carpet. [*He strokes a finger at* KENNETH.]

Someone bounces a large yellow ball into the parlour and GEORGE *bounces it to* KENNETH *who bounces it sadly.*

Say, Kenneth—times have sure changed since that time at the picnic when you won the race because I tripped over the tree root and you won the first prize which was the yellow ball and you wouldn't let me play with it afterwards, but then your papa said you were to give it to me and oh you so sweetly did—so when I took it they all said how unselfish you were and what a pig I was. And I couldn't enjoy the yellow ball so I ran away and threw it up in a tree and then I waited till you came down the river and it was I threw the rock that hit you low in the belly and you were sick. Say, Kenny, eh? Times have changed. [KENNETH *has set down the tray and slowly bounces the ball, his head hung down.*] I'm to become a responsible member of society, a priest whom hundreds look up to. I'm even the sort of priest who can marry and sire children. I should doubt very much if you'll ever have the chance to do that. Or be allowed to even try it. Not very likely. Well, Kenny—move on. Don't let me keep you. You've got important business up there in the little room above the woodshed. Munch munch. Goo goo. If I had the time to spare, which I haven't being involved in courtship and afterwards a dinner engagement, I'd come up to adjust your bib and wipe off your mouth.

KENNETH *throws away the ball and disappears behind a sofa. Suddenly he emerges from behind another piece of furniture and leaps at* GEORGE. GEORGE *calls on* POLLY *and* BETHEL *but not too loudly. He's too stunned.* KENNETH *neatly puts* GEORGE *flat on the floor, then raises the top half of him up and makes* GEORGE *punish himself by taking* GEORGE's *limp hands and hitting* GEORGE's *face with them. Then suddenly and neatly,* KENNETH *leaps up over the sofa, picks up his tray and disappears.*

You do understand, Kenny. G-golly, you do understand.

SCENE EIGHT

BETHEL: Did you call, Mr Sloan? Or is it Reverend Mr Sloan?
GEORGE: Uh—not that I know of.
BETHEL: Just sitting on my very comfortable floor, eh? Lots of nice soft comfortable chairs, Reverend Mr Sloan.
GEORGE: [*Reconstituting himself*] I tripped—and fell rather heavily, Mrs Henry.
BETHEL: Oh, you should watch your feet in here, Reverend George Sloan. There are any number of low foot stools that could be the death of you. But what did you trip over away out there in the centre of the room?
GEORGE: A tree root.
BETHEL: What did you say?
GEORGE: My own feet. Yes, my great big own feet, Mrs Henry.

BETHEL *leaves. She is wearing an apron and carrying some plates.*
POLLY *enters in a different dress.*

POLLY: Did something happen, George? I thought I heard you call.
GEORGE: Nothing, Polly. I just got a little surprise, that's all. It was really my own fault. He understands! Serves me right.
POLLY: Who understands?

GEORGE: Oh—what an ugly surprise. I hope—

POLLY: Thank you for getting that old box opened, George.

GEORGE: Where did you find it?

POLLY: I dug it up in the lawn there.

GEORGE: The blacksmith had quite a time getting the lock sawed off. I—I took a look in the box. There was just that funny old glass Easter Egg all wrapped up in a yellow old piece of paper.

POLLY: Yes. I've been looking for the glass Easter Egg and the old piece of paper for a long time. Did you see the inscription on the Easter Egg?

GEORGE: Uh—no. I couldn't read it.

POLLY: I understand you had some good news today.

GEORGE: Yes. I've got an appointment. Archbishop Moosejaw is putting me in at Paradise, Manitoba.

POLLY: Paradise, Manitoba.

GEORGE: Paradise, Manitoba.

POLLY: George—George. Now that you have a job what were you thinking of saying next?

GEORGE: I don't know. I don't think I'd thought of saying anything. You're wearing the necklace I gave you. Mother's necklace.

POLLY: Yes. It's a lovely necklace.

GEORGE: What did you think I might think of saying next?

POLLY: Why, George Sloan. Very well. Two years ago you said you were in love with me. And I said I was with you. Right? Well—Right?

GEORGE: [Strangled] Yes.

POLLY: You then bought an old car and learned how to drive so we could court and I went along with that, didn't I? Right! Now—what has happened?

GEORGE: Oh—I still love you all right.

POLLY: I'm sure you do, but it can't just go on and on like this. Do you see what I mean?

GEORGE: Yes. Polly, I thought perhaps—I'd stay a year out there and see what it's like at Paradise, Manitoba, and then we might announce our engagement.

POLLY: George, that's already been announced.

GEORGE: Uh—has it?

POLLY: That was the old car. Everyone saw us driving about in it. That meant we were engaged.

GEORGE: I thought it had to be a ring.

POLLY: So did I. But times have changed. It's an old car. And instead of putting it on your sweetheart you put her inside and drive her around so everyone in the village can say: Why, that George Sloan. I'd never thought he had such get up and go. He's going out with the Henry girl and later on she'll be in his arms in the back of the car underneath the old willows by the Big Pond.

GEORGE: Polly!

POLLY: George! Now. Frankly I don't feel quite the way I did when it all started. Why should I? And neither do you. Why should you? One can't live with a fever for very long. You're supposed to break the fever with a marriage.

GEORGE: I suppose.

POLLY: Some of my friends have actually succeeded in getting married and it's not, they say, that you fall out of love, it's just that you don't have to reiterate the fact. Just like—why, when I was an older girl I imagined that people actually made love all night from eleven until the crack of dawn.

GEORGE: You did, eh?

POLLY: Yes, like in ballads. Now my friends tell me that that just isn't so. Neither do people sleep in each other's arms either. The pressure on somebody's arms would finally cause them to drop off. So we didn't adopt the cure for the fever soon enough and now we've got the cure we wonder where the disease has got to.

GEORGE: I suppose we do. Yes. The difficulty is—I can't quite fall in love. And I don't really quite know what love is. There ought to be a book that tells you.

POLLY: George, I don't quite know what it's like either. But perhaps it's me— awkwardly coming nearer and nearer to the point where I am going to have to propose—a solution. I'm beginning to see that a lot of marriages must have been like this to start with. Shucks, all the ads and stories give you the idea the young man is crazy to do something to you, even marry you. But he's not. Not around here at least. He isn't even particularly interested in the act of love when it's a distinct possibility, that is. Do you remember I offered out of sheer desperation and you said there wasn't time? You, a great big boy of twenty-two, had promised your father to be home by half past eleven.

GEORGE: You didn't know father. And you don't understand—it's an entangling thing. If you've got a conscience—and I have. Why—if I had, I'd have had to— I'd be entangled for life all because of one moment's madness.

POLLY: Of course it's entangling. It's good to be entangled! George, as for one moment's madness there's another kind of madness called cautiousness. George. George, I can see my whole life, my children—all in that salt-shaker of a body of yours. I could shake you until they tumbled out. George, answer me! Marriage— good idea or bad idea!

GEORGE: Good idea! Polly, the trouble is—I'm so shy *at times*. I can never make a decision.

POLLY: You're not shy, George. It would take a very bold person to torture yourself and myself as much as you have with this indecision. George—yes yes! or no no!

GEORGE: Oh my dear—yes. Yes, that would be a very good idea. To get married.

POLLY: Good! Now we announce it at Bethel's party tonight.

GEORGE: I suppose. Yes. I'd rather like that.

POLLY: Now. I was going to ask you something else, but you poor boy, I've really asked you enough for one lifetime.

GEORGE: You mean Kenneth, don't you? Sure, Polly. If you want to bring him along. We can fit him in somewhere.

POLLY: Would there be anywhere in Paradise we could board him out? It's too much for you, poor dear, to have him in the house all the time.

GEORGE: Actually they've got one idiot boy in the village already. We'll see. You've no idea of what Paradise, Manitoba, is like, have you? First of all—the Jehovah's Witnesses have made huge inroads into what used to be a sizeable flock.

POLLY: [*Holding her hand up like a Jehovah's Witness on the street with their Kingdom Hall* Watchtower *publications*] I'll reconvert them to the old Church of England faith.

GEORGE: And sometimes there isn't too much water. There's a small old mountain nearby. In the springtime everyone goes up, in April, and collects every bit of snow they can. You store it in your cistern so you'll have something to drink in July.

POLLY: Oh, I'll collect so much snow—we'll never be thirsty.

GEORGE: Sometimes their crops really fail. Here—I've got this little snuffbox. Do you see what's inside there?

POLLY: Snuff? I didn't know you took—it's wheat.

GEORGE: That's all one farmer got off about five hundred acres he'd sowed. He gave it to me—for a joke.

POLLY: Just that much?

GEORGE: [*Laughing*] Actually about two bushels but it all looked like that and might just as well have been that much.

POLLY: Poor shrivelled burnt little seeds.

GEORGE: I have something to live down there too.

POLLY: Good heavens, what!?

GEORGE: I was the student minister there you know—for a couple of summers. One week—one Sunday they asked me to pray for rain. The Jehovah's Witnesses had prayed and not a drop did Jehovah vouchsafe. So I prayed for rain. Polly, there was a regular cloudburst.

POLLY: Don't tell me they complained.

GEORGE: Farmers always do. Anyhow I think they had good cause. All their crops were washed out and one old man who lived in a gully was—drowned.

POLLY: Well. They should have asked you to pray for a medium rain. What do they think God is—a mind reader?

GEORGE: I don't know what they think He is, but a whole bunch joined the United Church.

POLLY: Why?

GEORGE: Half way between, you see. Jehovah's Witnesses—no rain. Anglicans—too much, so try half way between.

POLLY: Oh, the sillies. George, tell me the truth—you're not engaged to anybody out there, are you?

GEORGE: No, no. Several girls and ladies did make a fling—I even made a few converts that way—but I just let them fling. [*Slyly*] I let one of them fling herself rather far—but I didn't give her anything to catch hold of.

POLLY: Heavens! The less I hear about you the better. But you're going to be my husband now and I don't care.

GEORGE: There's just one thing, Polly. I'll have to ask Mrs Henry for your hand in marriage.

POLLY: You'll have to ask Bethel for what?

GEORGE: For your hand in marriage. She's your stepmother and your father and mother are both dead.

POLLY: George—don't you dare ask her if you can marry me. Oh, have pity on me!

GEORGE: But I have to ask her permission to marry you. She's your guardian, isn't she? It's only proper etiquette.

POLLY: Bethel was my guardian. But not now I'm of age. For Heaven's sake, I'm her godmother. She's my god-daughter.

GEORGE: Oh, it's just a form. If she says no, I can't marry you, never you fear, Polly, I will marry you. I wouldn't let a bit of etiquette stand in the way of love. But I do have to ask her.

POLLY: Why?

GEORGE: It says so in all the books I've read.

POLLY: George, no! No!

GEORGE: Polly, yes! You've had your way. Now I want my way. I happen to be a stickler for rules and etiquette. They're the invisible skeleton of society.

POLLY: And invisible is what they should be.

GEORGE: Well, I'm not going to have it said that I didn't do the right thing. If I didn't ask for your hand in marriage from some surviving parental figure, why, I'd feel I'd eloped.

POLLY: Fine. Golly, George. Let's elope right now. You're a minister. You can marry us right now. Off we go.

GEORGE: But then we can't go to Bethel's dinner party. And I was rather looking forward to a good meal. You know what the college cooking is like.

POLLY: But we could go to the Traveller's Hotel and have a good meal there—right now.

GEORGE: Uh-uh Polly. Their mashed potatoes are too watery.

POLLY: Well—there's the restaurant over at Regentsville.

GEORGE: Yes. Their pies are good. Homemade so I'm told. But that's twenty miles away and by the time we got there I'd be so hungry I'd have lost my appetite again. So—I have to eat soon and I'm expecting to eat one of Mrs Henry's famous dinners cooked by that harelip Ada.

POLLY: Did you ever try eating grass? Oh I know—a good meal is important.

GEORGE: It's not just the good meal, Polly. Unless I ask for your hand in marriage from our hostess we can't announce our marriage at the dinner party.

POLLY: By your reckoning—no. I guess not.

GEORGE: You see, I do want to announce it at the dinner party. Because I want to see the look on old Dr Ewell's face. Do you know what he had the utter gall to say once to me? I had complained that I thought the poetry of Catullus really was rather obscene. You know—the one about the man, the boy and the girl.[8]

POLLY: Yes, yes. Dr Ewell's favourite Latin poem. We all know it off by heart. It is one of the few Latin poems one doesn't need a crib for.

GEORGE: Polly, there is no crib. Not even Coles Book Market would dare translate it. So Dr Ewell laughed at me and called me a eunuch. So I just want to see the look on his face when I announce that we're getting married.

POLLY: It'll be worth watching—the old monster.

GEORGE: So.

POLLY: Oh George. Oh George. Very well. You've worn me down. I'll get Bethel for you.

[8]Poem 56 by the Roman poet Catullus (87-54? B.C.) describes the poet finding a boy and a girl making love and joining them.

GEORGE: But I can't ask her if I can marry you in front of you, Polly. You must avoid the scene.

POLLY: [*Leaving*] Yes. I'll avoid the scene. Oh dear, oh dear. I'm going out to the stable and stuff my ears with hay.

After a few moments BETHEL *enters by stages as if she is really not sure why* GEORGE *must see her. She, of course, has retrieved the necklace from* POLLY. *But* GEORGE, *taking his stand by the fireplace with one foot on something, waits for her with every appearance of supreme confidence.*

SCENE NINE

GEORGE: Mrs Henry, I have a very important question to ask you.

BETHEL *gives him a blank stare.*

Perhaps she didn't hear me the first time. [*Clearing his throat*] Mrs Henry, I have a very important question to ask you.

BETHEL: Aw, George.

GEORGE: Yes.

BETHEL: A very important question to ask me? Let me ask you an unimportant question first. How do you like my dress?

GEORGE: It's very beautiful.

BETHEL: More beautiful than Polly's?

GEORGE: They're both beautiful. Where—where did you get that necklace? Wasn't Polly just wearing it?

BETHEL: This necklace? Yes—it's a silly old thing Polly wears. But she promised it to me for the rest of the evening. Lord knows where she got it. Some pawnshop in Montreal more than likely. She haunts such places looking for bargains.

GEORGE: But she was just wearing it.

BETHEL: I know. But she'd promised I could have it for the dinner party so I tore it off her neck when she came into the kitchen so strangely just now. Say, I wondered what you and Polly were conspiring about in here. I guess she was getting your courage up for asking me.

GEORGE: Asking you—what?

BETHEL: Why—don't you know? Asking me this very important question you speak of. Yes. Yes, I'd say this necklace was straight out of Woolworth's about 1910. It must have been pawned for a penny. But it just goes with this dress. You know? Sometimes with a really swish rich dress you need a silly cheap ornament. Like with a sable wrap you might take a little pig straight from the sow and pin it upside down by its tail over the sable—just as a mad but utterly beautiful— effect. Or—

GEORGE: Mrs Henry—that happens to be a necklace I once gave Polly. It belonged to my mother. It's really an heirloom piece and I believe Papa had it shipped in from Birks in Montreal.

BETHEL: Aw, aw, I've offended him. Here. Aw. The poor boy. Here I am making a big *faux pas* about his mother's necklace. I was only teasing, George. Why it's a wonderful necklace. Here—kiss and make up. [*Kisses him*] And so— you've come to ask this question which is so important.

GEORGE: Yes.

BETHEL: Yes.

GEORGE: Yes.

BETHEL: Yes.

GEORGE: It's the question of—

BETHEL: I saw it all in my teacup this afternoon, but don't you think I'm just a bit old?

GEORGE: Too old? Too old for what?

BETHEL: How old are you for instance?

GEORGE: Twenty-four.

BETHEL: Twenty-four! Good Lord, you're too old. How come you're twenty-four?!

GEORGE: I got in the wrong course at college. First I was in Business Administration and then I flunked out so there seemed nothing left but—theology, after my other courses were pasted into a Pass Arts degree, and so—theology it was. By the time it was all over I was twenty-four.

BETHEL: So I'm not too old for you. I'm almost forty, but then you're almost thirty and besides I have a very baby-like and playful disposition. You might even call it mischievous.

GEORGE: Mrs Henry—you're making a dreadful mistake. I don't know—I can't bear to—

BETHEL: Maybe. But I love making mistakes. What would life be without mistakes?

Sit down over here. Tell me more about this mistake I'm making. Stand up! You sit here and I'll sit there. I want you in the good light so I can get a good look at you, George Sloan. What an adorable thumb you have. It has a wee pinched-in waist. Oh, you're so lucky. See my thumb has no waist at all. Just a straight line up and down. Men are so lucky. They have beautiful thumbs, long eyelashes and—beautiful thumbs.

George Sloan.

George Sloan. Why I remember you. Oh, I've certainly seen promise in you. I think I even watched you being born.

Just a red boiled little thing when you were born and to think, to *think* that mere blob of nothingness has expanded and pushed out and developed until it sits in front of me once more and asks me—important questions.

GEORGE: Mrs Henry before this goes any further—would you please stop talking. *Stop talking!*

BETHEL: Of course I'll stop. Very well. I'll stop talking. I won't say a word until you say a word.

GEORGE *clears his throat but says nothing.*

Well, I'm awfully sorry to break my promise, but have you been struck dumb or something? Do you want a glass of water or—wine? What's your name?

GEORGE: George. I sometimes have difficulty in speaking when I'm nervous.

BETHEL: Now, why should you be nervous at a joyful time like this? Yes. I can remember you bawling the whole grove down at a Sunday School picnic when you didn't get the prize in a race. A yellow ball. As a matter of fact it was our idiot boy-wonder who got that yellow ball and you fought and carried on something dreadful because we wouldn't give you the prize. And then when he did give it to you, you acted even worse. He showed up so nice opposite to you.

GEORGE: Don't talk about it, please.

BETHEL: Well, George, you've had your revenge on Kenneth by now, haven't you?

GEORGE: [Brightening] Have I ever. He's no longer adored by all the girls and boys and mammas and papas.

BETHEL: You felt rejected at the picnic, didn't you? Tell me the whole story of your twisted life, Georgie. Is it as twisted as mine? Let me see—your father was the Old English professor here, wasn't he?

GEORGE: I detested my father. He begat me after a stirring book on old Gothic verb tenses in a cold library.

BETHEL: I'm sure very few ever saw him with his pants down.

GEORGE: He always wormed things out of you. He'd lie on the leather couch in the study and make you stand there and tell him things. Not only done, but thought. He killed all the love in me and paralyzed all the will—like a glow-worm and a snail.

BETHEL: Poor little snail. And—mother?

GEORGE: She'd never wait till I could start my meal. She'd pitch in and feed it to me like a baby till I was twelve. She just shovelled it into my mouth.

BETHEL: You poor dear. Do you remember Kenneth's white kitten?

GEORGE: [Pause] I remember who you are!

BETHEL: Yes. Do you remember I leaned over the fence—I leaned over and handed you the white kitten and I said: 'Here's Kenneth's kitty. He's sick right now and he won't be able to touch you. He's feeling pretty low. Here—you play with his kitty.' And you hit it with a stick and threw it back over the fence. And I buried Kenneth's kitten after you were through playing with it.

GEORGE: I don't remember that.

BETHEL: But I do, you see.

GEORGE: All right. I do. And I've tried to tell Polly about it and I hate that within myself, the cruel streak. But I can't hate it enough. I give in to it. When I was a child I used to have dreadful fantasies that little men fell down from the sky and were completely in my power. And I cut them up with my penknife. Little pearl-handled knife.

BETHEL: What would Polly say to that, I wonder?

GEORGE: She'd say it didn't matter. That evil is accidental, love is permanent.

BETHEL: Cheerful old Polly.

GEORGE: What do you say?

BETHEL: I say good and evil's like two hands, mister. [She claps hers on his shoulder.] One left. One right. Both last forever.

GEORGE: [Struggling to get free] Polly says when we get to Heaven . . . she read me from a poet, a poet who says our two hands become one hand. Our two eyes—one eye.[9]

[9]Not an account of an actual poem, but suggested by Anne Hébert's 'Les deux mains' (1942), translated by F.R. Scott as 'The Two Hands' (The Tamarack Review, No. 7, 1958).

BETHEL: I wonder. We have much more in common than you thought, haven't we?

GEORGE: Yes. Don't tell Polly about the white kitten.

BETHEL: When that kitten disappeared Kenneth really went crazy. It most made for his breakdown.

GEORGE: Yes.

BETHEL: So—don't you ever dare talk to me about my swearing and me being the first bishop's widow you ever heard swear, eh?

GEORGE: I'm sorry.

BETHEL: And now—the important question. The marriage question. Have you really thought it out?

GEORGE: Mrs Henry, it was really about Polly I came.

BETHEL: Tell me. What is the difference between a man and a woman?

GEORGE: Well, I know that.

BETHEL: You know there's a difference, do you? Well—there is no difference between a man and a woman. It will come out later, the reason I stress this.

GEORGE: Come out later! Oh my God!

BETHEL: George, I'm just another man. A woman is a man outside in and a man is a woman inside out.

GEORGE: Oh, if you'd just stop talking my mind would clear.

BETHEL: During the act of love what the man really meets—do you know what the man really meets? He meets another man with even breasts like his only what he meets is simply inside where he is outside. What the woman meets is another woman who just happens to have got her/his womb displaced somewhat. You ever been at an autopsy? Well, I have. So there's no difference between us. It's just a convention.

GEORGE: Ugh! I'm going to be ill. The white kitten! Polly! Kenneth! Oh far better to be Kenneth than to be like this. I've tried to love and I can't. I've tried to have a nervous breakdown and I can't . . . there is a difference!

BETHEL: Then why male breasts? If men are really different then why nipples on their chests?

GEORGE: Who has the babies—men or women?

BETHEL: Men have microscopic babies. Women have larger ones, I'll admit. But who put the little microscopic babies into the man if not his mother?

GEORGE: Oh no—his father.

BETHEL: The mother.

GEORGE: The father.

BETHEL: How dare you contradict me, you young puppy! The mother! Isn't it wonderful to have a big mirror in a room? [*Waving at their reflections*] Hello you dear people up there.

GEORGE: Mrs Henry—it's about Polly I came.

BETHEL: Since there's no real difference between the sexes I can ask you the important question. I'll be the man and you the woman seeing you can't seem to bring yourself to ask it.

GEORGE: It's about Polly I'm asking.

BETHEL: The bat! The bat! He just flew out from the folds of those curtains over there. He haunts this parlour. George—go out into the vestibule and you'll find a couple of long brooms I've had specially made to get him with. Hurry. *[He pauses. Then darts out and gets the brooms. They do have long handles!]* It's these old-fashioned high ceilinged rooms. You need a long broom to swat a high bat in a tall old room. Here's your broom. Now—get him. Get him. Get that bat!

GEORGE, *at first reluctantly, but then with ever increasing zeal, joins in the dance. They pursue the bat with their brooms and the bat—a clever opponent— flies low across the floor as well as high up. They play badminton with the bat, they curl, they slap each other on the buttocks, they ride cock-a-horse, they narrowly miss each other's heads and eventually* GEORGE *does kill the bat. Dialogue here is mostly inarticulate but the various implications of the brooms might give rise to such ad libs as: 'Look at me!' or 'Look at me, I'm a witch.'*

Oh George, thank you. Throw it in the fireplace. You're the first person I've ever met who's been able to get that bat. Why it's kept me from my own parlour evening after evening. And think what it could have done to my guests tonight.

And so, George, in gratitude the answer to your important question is—yes, I'll marry you. It will be a wonderful experiment. You'll be the only man who's—that dreadful bat. Oh—now I can wear my hair girlishly long again and I'll marry you, George Sloan, I'll marry you!

GEORGE *looks blank.*

SCENE TEN

POLLY: *[Enters.]* Well, George, did you ask her?
GEORGE: She got mixed up and—*[Screams hoarsely.]*
BETHEL: Polly, I find it marvellous I'm still attractive to men. To know the old firefly in the swamp is still wink-wink-winking away. Why Polly, you're so white in the face. Did you think he wanted to marry you? If he did make overtures to you—it was only to come at me. I suppose you're going to come at me and tell me that he came in here to ask for your hand in marriage. Eh?
POLLY: Yes.
BETHEL: But if a man really loved you—he'd never ask your stepmother for permission. It was all simply an excuse on George's part to come at me. Oh, I haven't been so thrilled since I don't know when.
POLLY: George! Is this true? Are you going to marry her?
GEORGE: *[Pause]* Yes, Polly. I can't think—what else to say since I—killed the bat.
BETHEL: George understands. George understands.
IRA: *[Enters.]* I know I'm early for your party, Bethel. But after I had my swim and shower there was simply nothing else to do but drop in early.
POLLY: George Sloan. Say that again: 'I'm going to marry Bethel.'
GEORGE: I'm going to marry Bethel.
POLLY: Well, you're *not* going to marry her.
BETHEL: Oh ho! Isn't he though!

POLLY: He is not.

She goes over to the piano and plays the cadenza signal for KENNETH *to come.*

CURTAIN

ACT III

SCENE ELEVEN

They are all sitting as before. Everyone but POLLY *is sipping a drink. She sits apart, tense and miserable looking.*

BETHEL: Oh Polly—my dear Polly. You haven't congratulated me yet on my engagement to George.
IRA: Are you engaged to George, Bethel?! I thought Polly—
BETHEL: Polly herself hasn't said a word these last ten minutes while I've been rattling on to you men except go over to the piano and play that silly little cadenza now and again. [POLLY *goes to the piano and plays this again.*] That makes the third time you've played that, Polly.
POLLY: And the last time.
BETHEL: Are you by any chance signalling to somebody? If you're trying to get Kenneth to come down, why don't you ring my little bell I use for him?
POLLY: Because I detest ringing for him as if he's a pet dog.
BETHEL: You'd rather be Frederic Chopin playing for his George Sand.[1]
IRA: You've got the sexes mixed up, Bethel.
BETHEL: Didn't Frederic Chopin wear a dress and George Sand wear pants—I don't know, I always get history so mixed up.
GEORGE: Sometimes when they know it's their feeding time carp fish in ponds come to the sound of a bell. [*Hoarsely*] Swans are often trained to do the same. When Papa and Mamma took me to England when I was twelve the keeper let me ring the bell and the old swan came up. Followed by the pen and her cygnets.
BETHEL: Is that so, George? George, what is a pen?
GEORGE: It's, when used of swans, it's a female swan. The male swan is known as a cob. Sometimes it's so arranged that the carp or the swans can ring the bell themselves when it gets to be feeding time.
BETHEL: Is that so! What a lot George knows. Ira, doesn't George know a lot?
IRA: Don't kick me, please.
BETHEL: Surely that wouldn't be such a good idea though? Heavens, the old swan would be up there ringing the bell all the time.
IRA: This old swan isn't like you, Bethel.
BETHEL: Polly. Polly, if you really want Kenneth to join us—I do hope it's not your intention to have him to the party though—and if you won't use my bell sys-

---

[1] French novelist Aurore Dupin (1832-76) took the name George Sand and dressed in men's clothes; the composer Chopin was one of her several famous lovers.

tem, a system that's worked so far—then why don't you go up to his room and get him?

POLLY: Because I don't want to leave George alone with you ever again.

IRA: Oh! What has Bethel been up to? Bethel, you are indeed King of the Castle. Why that last speech of yours is one of the longest sentences and the most highly articulated—I've ever heard you use. Could you possibly say it over again?

BETHEL: Of course, I have a phonographic memory. Polly, if you really want Kenneth to join us—I do hope it's not your intention to have him to the party though—and if you won't use my bell system, a system that's worked so far— then why don't you go up to his room and get him?

POLLY: [Bursts into tears. IRA moves swiftly over to comfort her.] Ira, Ira, why doesn't Kenneth come? He's supposed to come when I play the piano like that.

IRA: Polly. There. There, there. Why are you crying? I don't understand.

BETHEL: Kenneth is eating his supper. He loves his supper and he's simply not going to come till he's finished his supper. Let the poor boy finish his sup sup.

POLLY: You're very likely right. I have no power. Even Kenneth betrays me. And George. Oh George—you sold me away for some etiquette and the fact that the Traveller's Hotel serves watery mashed potatoes.

IRA: But, Polly, I came to you. You have power over me.

POLLY: George!

GEORGE makes a very strangled sound indeed.

IRA: George, are you really engaged to Bethel?

GEORGE makes the strangled sound again.

What does [Strangled sound] mean?

GEORGE makes the sound again.

POLLY: I'll tell you what it means, Ira. That sound George is making means that I've been made a fool of. It means I'm a swan and I'm caught in the wire. My foot's caught in the barbed wire. I saw a wild duck caught like that once in some wire on the way to school. By the small pond. And every year you went by it—on the shortcut to school—and there was less and less of it left. Finally just some feathers and bones. Finally—not even that. Just—a thick spot on the wire.

IRA: But I've just been away for a swim at the college. And all this has happened?

BETHEL: All this has happened.

IRA: Sh! Did you hear that? Something breaking. A crash of glass?

We do hear this and it is a formidable, magic sound that should fill the whole theatre.

GEORGE: No one hurt, I hope!

POLLY: Something's frightened the pigeons. They're wheeling about again.

BETHEL: It's only Ada in the kitchen. She always breaks at least one dish before a dinner party.

IRA: Sh! [Pause] What a splashing sound. I know, Bethel, Ada always drowns

herself in your lily pond at least once before every dinner party.
BETHEL: It sounded heavier than Ada. Perhaps a tree fell over or—
POLLY: Ada's having an argument with someone in the kitchen!
BETHEL: Oh no!
POLLY: It's Kenneth!

SCENE TWELVE

KENNETH: [*Staggering in much bedraggled*] Polly! Do you want me? My door was locked. Somebody locked my door. [*Pause*] I heard you play the third time, so I ran at the window! Don't whip me, Bethy, and I fell—I rolled down the woodshed roof onto the hot-bed windows—mossy soft on the woodshed roof and my pet pigeons all flew up but crack, tinkle bang bang in the hot-beds. I'm sorry, Bethy, I squashed the watermelons. Ouch. Cut myself here. Ran round in the kitchen door—I fell kerspack into the wet pond lilies. Harelip Ada she chased me with a wooden spoon when I tried to get into the kitchen. I said: 'You harelip!' and she started to bawl. Did you hear her? She said: 'I'll not cook in this house any longer,' and I got out of there fast. Polly, did you think I was ever coming?
IRA: [*Pause*] Lots of new words there. Who said you knew anything about long sentences, Bethel? Polly, that's the most I've ever heard Kenneth say at a stretch.
POLLY: Ira. Have you a pencil?
IRA: Here, Polly.
POLLY: Don't go away. [*She prints something on a piece of paper.*]
BETHEL: Kenny, after this when I lock you in your room that means you stay there.
GEORGE: Kenny, you're a bad boy to smash up Bethel's house so.
BETHEL: I'll say he's a bad boy.
GEORGE: What are you doing, Polly?
BETHEL: Kenny, if you've not only smashed a window and the hot-bed glass but also driven Ada, my cook, away—I shall run away with you tonight—on a train, or a boat, to some place where Ira and Polly will never find you. I'm your legal mother, Kenny, never forget that. Until you can figure out things for yourself I figure them out, see?
KENNETH: I'm not afraid of you, Bethy. I can get out of the room. I can get out now no matter how you lock the door.
BETHEL: What did you say?!
POLLY: Bethel, you're not feeling well. Why don't you step into the kitchen and give Ada a helping word or hand. After all—just twenty minutes and your guests will be coming.
BETHEL: Oh no. I'm never going to leave you alone with Kenneth or with George ever again.
IRA: Much sought after young men. Popular types.
BETHEL: Polly—what is it you're writing—or printing?
POLLY: Kenneth, can you read this?
KENNETH: Yes, Polly.
POLLY: Then read it aloud to me in front of them.
KENNETH: 'I want to merry you, Polly. Please merry me.'

POLLY: So Bethel. Did you hear that?

BETHEL: Yeah. I never thought you'd do it though. Yeah, I heard it. Kenny, what does 'marry' mean?

KENNETH *mimes the word 'merry'*

IRA: There's a boy knows what love and marriage mean. I drink to him.

POLLY: Now, Bethel. I shall marry Kenneth if you insist on marrying George.

BETHEL: It's against the law.

IRA: It is not. He's not a minor and I'll vouch for his sanity.

GEORGE: Well I won't, and I'll certainly not marry them.

KENNETH: Who says you'll be asked? [*Pause*] Polly, I want to marry you. I want to marry you. [*He says the word correctly this time—or almost so.*]

BETHEL: We heard you. All right, Polly, go ahead and marry him. Incidentally if that performance was what he thinks marriage is all about you're going to have quite a time.

POLLY: Now. Bethel. You know the terms of his father's will, don't you?

BETHEL: But how did you know about them? It's odd the way he pronounces the word 'marry'. I didn't think he knew the word.

IRA: That's another new word, isn't it, Polly? [*She hushes him.*]

BETHEL: Let me see the piece of paper, Kenneth. Kenny! Here—give it to Bethy.

KENNETH: [*Grins at her as he tears the paper up into tiny pieces which he throws up into the air.*] Kenny's not going to give it to Bethy.

BETHEL: Oh Polly—George! What a terrible mistake I've been making all this time. George—do forgive and forget, you poor chap. I thought you were proposing marriage to me when all along—the important question—it was really about Polly. You wanted to ask permission to marry Polly!

GEORGE: Yes.

KENNETH: [*Looking out*] There's the little girl tied to the picket fence.

POLLY: Oh, Ira. That's the first time he's used the word 'fence'. He's always just said 'picket' before. Doesn't it frighten you, Bethel? Words. The more words Kenneth knows . . .

BETHEL: Didn't you hear me? You can have George back, Polly.

POLLY: I know. And for a moment I was wondering if—I really wanted you back, George. I guess I do.

IRA: Why doesn't she want Kenneth to marry you?

POLLY: I checked the will yesterday. Bethel, according to it you get power of attorney and quite a nice income until and up to the time that Kenneth marries. After that your guardianship is over and you get whatever reward Kenneth decides upon.

IRA: Kenneth will let you live up above the woodshed, Bethel.

BETHEL: Yes, yes.

POLLY: By the way, you're nowhere mentioned as Kenneth's stepmother although there is some talk about a debt owed to you and giving you Kenneth in return for your innocence.

BETHEL: Kenny's father made that will the day before he killed himself. He left out things.

POLLY: Well, it's a wonderful document.

IRA: I must say Bethel you didn't try marrying Kenneth off very hard.

BETHEL: If the girls wanted him they could come and get him. He used to be out on the front porch tied to the railing for all to see. A healthy male young animal.

POLLY: So—I can have George back, Bethel?

BETHEL: Yes.

GEORGE: Polly it's—

POLLY: Not yet, George. Just stay there. Kenneth. What do you see out of this window?

KENNETH: She's tied to the fence.

POLLY: What's on this side of the fence, Kenneth?

KENNETH: Garden. Flowers. [*Pause*] A butterfly.

POLLY: [*Leads him to an opposite window.*] What do you see out of this window?

KENNETH: [*Pause*] Grass. Shadows. Trees. And it's wet.

GEORGE: But it's just the other way around. Bethel's right about him, Polly.

BETHEL: Yes, Ira. If he's so much better and so very sane—you heard what he just said—how come he doesn't see what we can see?

POLLY: Because, Bethel, someone a long time ago took this house as if it were a doll's house and he was inside it and they turned it around on him. They turned it around on you, didn't they Kenneth? You woke up one morning to find—it wouldn't take very long—you could never be sure of where and here and there ever again.

BETHEL: While you're at it why not have me move the chimneys into the cellar?

POLLY: Kenneth. I can't accept the kind offer of your hand. Believe me, I would like to—but it can't be. What can I do for you though? You've helped me with her. Bethel.

KENNETH: [*Pause*] I would like to go to the party.

POLLY: Bethel, what about that? He could sit between me and Ira.

BETHEL: Never. Too embarrassing.

POLLY: And he knows how to use a knife and fork now.

BETHEL: He's just eaten one big dinner. D'you want him to die of fat?

KENNETH: I didn't touch any of it. He laughed at me. [*Points to* GEORGE.]

GEORGE: But he has no proper clothes, Polly. For Heaven's sake—

POLLY: We've found a suit he can wear. The shoes are a—

BETHEL: Never! It would make thirteen at table.

KENNETH: [*In a flash*] Ask Ada to come! [BETHEL *turns pale.*]

IRA: Well, of course, Bethel. The person who cooks the dinner must never sit down and eat it? You're quite right. No, they must never. That would ruin the taste of it for most of those invited. Dinner with a—

POLLY: What can I give you then, Kenneth? I know—go up to my room and bring down—it's a rusty metal box. Bring it down here and I'll show you what's inside. [*He darts off.*]

BETHEL: Now that you've let him out of his room there isn't time to fix the window. Ira, where can we put him?

IRA: I say—invite him to the feast. No more of this exclusiveness, Bethel. Everyone who lives in this house gets to come to your dinner party.

GEORGE: Mrs Henry is now paying for her earlier victory about the bat.

IRA: Whom are you engaged to now, George?

GEORGE: [*After a silence*] Polly?

POLLY: Yes. And in just fifteen minutes they'll all be here and we can tell them. Should we tell them? My heart is beating so fast I can hardly—

BETHEL: [*Coming up near her*] Polly, what's this you're giving him?

POLLY: Something I found that his godmother gave him once for Easter. It's a glass egg.

KENNETH *enters with the box.*

Yesterday you ordered Kenneth to dig in the garden. He went out into the centre of the lawn and started to dig near this. What he really dug up was the skeleton of a cat. Then you ran out and made him re-bury that. Then you made him dig in where the garden is today—on the other side of the house.

KENNETH: Cocoanut is my White Persian cat I have. He is half as old as I am and his hair is like shredded cocoanut you know and when he is scared—by a dog or a ghost—it was the most beautiful sight in the world. Like a huge icy white teazle or porcupine or thistle but all silver glitters sticking out. Where is Cocoanut? Cocoanut! Here Pussy! I had to slap him because he had the Archangel baby in his mouth and I was nearly not in time. And the garden has gone. Cocoa! Cocoanut!

BETHEL: You folks wanted him to talk.

POLLY: Oh, Kenneth. I saw from an upstairs window your mistake and last night I went out with a lantern when you were all asleep. And I dug where you had dug. I found Cocoanut's skeleton and then underneath it—this box. The blacksmith broke the lock today—did you bury them, Bethel?

BETHEL: Why would I bury anything?

GEORGE: Bethel, after I killed his white cat you know very well I watched you bury it.

BETHEL: Shut up, you idiot.

IRA: You two have met before, eh? Hunting, killing and burying.

POLLY: What was that, George?

GEORGE: I've tried to tell you, Polly. When I was about seven she held his pet cat over the fence and I killed it because I hated him and then she buried it.

BETHEL: Give me that! [*She makes a desperate grab at the box.* IRA *holds her back.*]

POLLY: It's a glass Easter Egg, Kenneth. The inscription says: 'To Kenneth—from his loving godmother. Happy Easter.' Here Kenneth—I found it back for you.

He steps forward, looks at it, darts out his hand to take it and then there is a blinding flash and he falls to the floor, rolling over as if he had been struck down by a great invisible boxer. POLLY *sets down the egg and kneels down by him, loosening his collar. The sound here should repeat the effect of his leaping through the window earlier.*

Kenneth!!

BETHEL: I knew you'd be at him till he had a fit. A real fit. She's more than likely killed him, Ira. Get him away from her.

IRA: [*Kneeling down*] Bethel, he's only fainted. It's only if he gets married you lose your job. Hmh! He's all right. I thought maybe it was his cut. It's—he's asleep.

GEORGE: That's a form mental derangement often takes. They sleep and sleep for years and you have to tend them like a baby. They're just a great big vegetable and you have to open up their belly buttons and feed them through there. [*Then changing*] I really think that during my whole existence I've never—Polly, lying about on the floor with an idiot. Really.

We can see them in the raked mirror. POLLY *has put her face close to* KEN-NETH's. *Occasionally we hear them murmuring to each other. Nothing is said up above them. We all watch them. Nothing happens. Then the telephone rings but in a way no earthly telephone rings—but as if silver hollow currants, goose-berries and cherries were being poured into a thin glass cup.* BETHEL *leaves the room.*

IRA: Where's she gone?

GEORGE: To answer the telephone.

IRA: Was that the telephone? It sounded—like an angel playing with sleighbells or something.

GEORGE: Just an ordinary telephone to me.

IRA: Oh. Who are you engaged to now, George?

GEORGE: For a—just a few moments there I was rather wondering if it might not be Bethel—again.

BETHEL *returns.*

IRA: Has Ada flown, by the way, Bethel?

BETHEL: No. She's crying and stirring the soup. I think she's at least going to stay until she's salted the soup.

IRA: Who was that on the phone?

BETHEL: The Principal himself. He's come back unexpectedly early from the conference so he expects to be fed at my dinner party. [*Shouting*] Ada, stop blub-bering and put all the extra leaves in the dining room table. I should have served whale rather than turbot there's that many coming. Yes, a great big whale. Leviathan himself. And a side order of frozen hairy mammoth.

And by the way, somebody either sitting or lying in this room put little black notebooks on all the dinner plates. Now who might that be? [KENNETH *laughs.*] I see. Brother Big-eyes down there, eh? For God's sweet sake, Polly. For his sake so he's alive. Get up so we can cart him off upstairs. He's had an epileptic fit or a brain tumour or lesion or seizure, something like that, and you can forget about his marrying you, and George too. You can't handle either George or Kenneth. One you let slip through your fingers and the other you give a knockout object.

IRA: By the way, Bethel, there's a rumour afloat in the village that your old mother's going to gate-crash your party.

BETHEL: My nerves! My nerves!

I didn't know I had any until an hour ago. All I asked was for him to dig the garden and polish the silver. I had a cup of tea. Then—pow! everything crumbled.

IRA: She's coming down in her old truck all tied up with wire and she's wearing a red petticoat.

GEORGE: I've always wanted to meet Bethel's mother.

BETHEL: Look Polly, look Ira, in exactly fourteen minutes my guests will be arriving. Think of it! The Principal, the Principal's wife, Dr Ewell and the Dean of Women. I show them in here—George and I got rid of the bat and now we've got a floorshow on our hands. Polly!

GEORGE: Polly, you are making a spectacle of yourself!

IRA: By the way, at this very present moment to whom are you engaged?

GEORGE: No one I think. When I get hungry, and I'm really hungry, I can't think. I can't think who even I am. Who am I? I'm just an oblong blur.

BETHEL: Thirteen minutes and my guests arrive. Saint Julian—pray for me now in my need.

IRA: Why Saint Julian?

BETHEL: When I was married to her father I learned all about the saints. Saint Julian's the patron saint of dinner parties.

GEORGE: You really mean hospitality, don't you? Saint Julian occurs in Chaucer's portrait of the Franklin.[2] Father read it to me in Middle English. Saint Julian is the patron saint of hospitality.

BETHEL: You're quite right. The connection between this dinner party and hospitality is going to be remote. Oh—at long last we assume the vertical.

POLLY *sits up, raises* KENNETH *to a sitting position, he hides his face on her shoulder and she pulls him to a stand. Slowly he turns and faces* IRA *who has stood up.* KENNETH *moves towards* IRA *and hugs him. Then he moves towards* POLLY.

KENNETH: Polly and Ira. What do you see out of this window?

POLLY: I see a garden. Flowers. A butterfly.

KENNETH: And here. [*At the other window*]

POLLY: Sometimes I can see the ghost. She's always tied to the fence. Towards evening—now you see her. But on this side of the fence, I see shadows and trees—dark green.

KENNETH: Ira, do you see that too?

IRA: I can't see your ghost. I gather that comes with residence here. But all the rest that Polly sees is also what I see.

KENNETH: [*Rest*] I see it too. I see what you see. Bethel. [*He picks up the Easter Egg.*] Someone has turned the house back again.

BETHEL: [*Yawning*] All talk as if my house were a merry-go-round or a ferris wheel. Twelve minutes and they're at my door.

KENNETH: . . . back again to where it was, Bethel, when you first noticed [*Pause*] that there were only two things between you and me.

BETHEL: Eleven and a half.

KENNETH: Cocoanut. And this. [*He holds up the egg. Places the egg on a chair*

[2] In the *General Prologue* to the *Canterbury Tales* at line 340.

rather as if it were an alter ego and then directly addresses us as if we had leapt ahead about two or three years. These flashfronts should be emphasized with lighting and there should be overlapping of speeches to suggest several layers of time.] **I remember then I wanted to say that between her and me there had also once been more than just a white kitten and a glass egg. There had also been my father.** [*He starts removing his shirt and using the place behind the couch from which he sprang out at* GEORGE *he slowly changes into clothes for the party.* IRA *and* POLLY *help him.*] **How was I to know you aren't supposed to change your clothes in front of everybody in the parlour? I can still hear her shrieking and saying:**

BETHEL: Ira! Ira, it's a new floorshow. A strip-tease. A male one. The worst kind. Surely, tell me—you are humouring him? You're not dressing him for my party! Oh Bethel, Bethel, you have done a very foolish thing. You sent him out to dig in the garden and naturally he went straight for that stupid glass egg he was always mooning about with one of the first signs, George and Ira and Polly, that he was going crazy. Why, when I hid it away from him he was immediately better.

KENNETH: **No, she's wrong, she's wrong, I had to have something if I was going to keep my head above water. No father, there was the kitten; no kitten there was this. No this, there was immediately a skin over everything. Bethel's skin. When Polly gave me back this, this** [*He walks about holding the egg above his head.*] **it was being circumcised of a tight fold of skin that held you back from ever quite touching anything or being a father or seeing—oh God, it hurt when she gave it to me, more than when I saw the window and the pigeons came flocking at me as I threw myself out—it hurt like a rabbi with a sharp bright silver knife, it cut away Bethel's skin over my eyes and I saw. Remember then I asked Ira: A young man. I am young then, am I?**

IRA: You're just over twenty-one, Kenneth.

KENNETH: That seems very old to me. [*He brings out the box of silver, sets up a polishing situation for* BETHEL *who will obey his gesture to get at the polishing.*] Ira, you're holding a tumbler. A tumbler. Polly, I know that word now. If I'm over twenty-one, Bethel, I'm old enough for the party. All the words I knew and did not know.

GEORGE: What is he doing, Bethel?

BETHEL: Going to set himself a place at my table.

GEORGE: Did you hear him? 'All the words I knew and did not know'. [KENNETH *gestures at* BETHEL. *She slowly gets busy at the silver.*] Tender buttons[3] and toasted Susie and other pieces by Gertrude Stein. He's not better. It's all a freakish splash in the fan—uh, flash in the pan—soon he'll have a verbal haemorrhage and then relapse into—

KENNETH: **I remember that it was then I thought—why not pretend in a few moments for a few moments that I'm not better, that I have had a relapse—it will keep Ira and Polly on their toes and what fun to see what Bethel and George will do.**

[3]*Tender Buttons* (1914) was Gertrude Stein's first experiment in using the sounds of words for effects that were separate from their meanings. 'Toasted Susie is my ice-cream' is a line from 'Precioscilla', a prose-poem in Stein's *Composition as Explanation* (1926).

POLLY: George, in one minute he's said more than you do in a month of sermons.

GEORGE: Polly, listen carefully to him. There are no subordinate clauses, no absolute phrases—it's all baby grammar and it does not quite make sense.

KENNETH: Abyssal nothingness.

IRA: How's that for an absolute phrase, George.

GEORGE: What does it mean though? He's heard it somewhere.

BETHEL: Abyssal nothingness. Sure. I used to sing it all the time in the kitchen.

KENNETH: [*Coldly*] Better re-do that fork again, Bethel. Small, small stain spot you missed. I missed it too, mind you, but you're supposed to be good at this. I'm not. And also **I remember I told them all then that indeed it was not Bethel who had said 'abyssal nothingness' to me or at me, but it was the last thing my father said just before he killed himself. I was sitting in a rocking chair looking at him. He said**

BETHEL: Seven minutes.

KENNETH: **Well, yes, there wasn't much time before that first party to find out things I didn't know. Why did my father—what was his name? I remember asking Polly what my last name was.**

POLLY: Ralph. Your last name. Ralph, Kenneth.

KENNETH: But isn't that a first name?

POLLY: You have a first name for a last name. Some folks have a last name for a first name. I have. Pollex Henry. My first name is my mother's last name.

GEORGE: Oh—you talk like him.

POLLY: Don't you two people see that he's changed?

BETHEL: Not in the least.

GEORGE: Oh, he's more voluble. But more sensible?

KENNETH: [*Looking out*] Untie that little girl from the fence.

POLLY: One can't, Kenneth. She's an apparition. Lots of people can't see her at all.

GEORGE: People whose common denominator is sanity.

KENNETH: Must she always be tied? Who tied her?

POLLY: It was your great-uncle who did it to punish her for stealing his currants.

KENNETH: What a wicked old man he was. She's gone! She's got away. Perhaps I'll never see her again.

BETHEL: Let's keep hoping. Six minutes.

KENNETH: What's she counting time backwards for?

POLLY: Her party. It's going to start in five minutes. You polished the silver for it.

KENNETH: You men are all wearing ties.

GEORGE: I repeat: *you're* not coming to Bethel's dinner party. She's having some such distinguished guests. The Principal—now. His wife. The Dean of Women. And Professor Ewell, world authority on—

KENNETH: These are people I should meet in my house.

He walks freely about now; almost dressed except for bare feet. He juggles with some cufflinks.

POLLY: I've got a tie. It's my Girl Guide tie, I'll dash upstairs and get it though it may take some finding.

IRA: Bring the cufflinks over here, Kenneth. Let's have a look at them. [*He helps* KENNETH *put them on.*]

KENNETH: Whose are they, Ira? They've got a double R written on them.

IRA: Well, like the suit, they must be your father's.

KENNETH: What was his first name?

IRA: George, you're not going to like this. Bethel, wasn't his first name exactly the same as his last name?

BETHEL: Ralph Ralph.

GEORGE: Ralph Ralph. Repetition runs in both their families. How much better to have a name like mine: first name George; second and last name—Sloan. And it sounds like a last name.

BETHEL: [*Grimacing into a silver tray*] And a doctor was in attendance.

KENNETH: Ira, [*Touching him*] you were hunting butterflies with your brother and you looked up at me. Suddenly. Father and Mother were having a nap. Bethel was making a salad in the kitchen. I got away out of the house—not a stitch on except . . .

IRA: I was telling Bethel about that earlier this afternoon.

KENNETH: I turned and ran away then. Today I came right up to you and stay and say . . . . What was the matter with my father?

IRA: Kenneth, I understand that he felt he had been responsible for your mother's death. There was a mix-up about her medicine and an inquest. Bethel, you were working here at the time, you must remember.

BETHEL: Ira, must I remember at this very moment? Stop talking.

IRA: Kenneth, it was an accident but it upset him dreadfully.

KENNETH: Bethy, do you remember? You were in bed with Father and I heard him say: 'Bethel, I'm not so old a man as you think, am I?' It was late morning. I came in and you said to him: 'You old monster, you killed her. You wanted her to die.'

BETHEL: [*Rising*] And then it was after breakfast, you devil, that he told you to come into his study and sit down in your birthday rocking chair.

KENNETH: [*Nervously*] Yes.

BETHEL: You were rocking away when—

KENNETH: I know. He took the gun and did away with himself.

BETHEL: I can hear your heart beating, Kenneth.

KENNETH: But you're so close to it, you see. Bethel, where is that rocking chair? [IRA *shakes his head.*]

BETHEL: I know exactly where I threw it.

KENNETH: Since you're through your polishing, bring it to me. I'd like to have a look at it. [*Going over to the ghost window*]

BETHEL: Ira and George. He asked me to bring it to him. So I did. Well, I will. [*Exit. Perhaps we hear her climbing stairs up to the attic, then down again.*]

IRA: Kenneth . . .

KENNETH: Where's her scissors? [*Finds them.*] That girl is tied to the fence again. [*He climbs right out the window and out of view.*]

GEORGE: Ira, we're alone together and I take the opportunity to remark that you are one of the strangest doctors I have ever met.

IRA: Well, since you're one of the strangest clergymen I've ever met it naturally follows, doesn't it, that—[*They are walking about nervously.*]

GEORGE: Yes, yes. Ira, please help me. We men have got to get hold of him when he comes in the window again, tie him up.

IRA: Why is Polly away so long? Why is it that it always takes longer to find a Girl Guide tie than a blood-stained rocking chair? [*Grabbing hold of* GEORGE] Yes, I am a strange doctor. I'm going to throw you on the floor George, and when Kenneth comes back with the scissors we'll cut you open to see whatever happened to your heart. [*Hoarse scream from* GEORGE. BETHEL *enters.*]

BETHEL: At last, Ira, you've seen the light. Hold him down while I phone for a straitjacket—[*Scream*] it's George. Ira! [KENNETH *has come in the window again and sets down the scissors.* BETHEL *sets the chair rocking; it is musical and plays a tune.*]

KENNETH: That's not my rocking chair. It's too small. Far too small and it never played that—

BETHEL: [*Picking it up*] Do you see here on the cushion? And on one of the arms, not where your hand was clenched so tightly we had to pry it off, but on either side soaked deep because I took the goddam filthy spattered thing and threw it as far back in the attic as I could [*Red light;* KENNETH *stumbles into the silver glitter of the cutlery and begins to collapse.*] Say it, Kenny. Don't be afraid. 'Pretty knives, forks and spoons.' My dear one. I've been a harsh mother but am I not gentleness itself compared with what she has given you this afternoon? [POLLY *appears with the tie. Both she and* IRA *watch helplessly.*] I locked you in a room whose walls were covered with just the words you knew. Your words. Polly lets you into a room whose walls are covered with so many fierce bad words you can never understand. Like 'His father hated them both. The cruelest thing that man ever did was to leave the boy alive. It would have been a kindness to take the boy with him and he knew it.'' [*She begins to back away from him towards the door in which* POLLY *is standing.*]

GEORGE: Kenneth, I just looked out the window and I saw the Principal and the Principal's wife just come out of their house. They're walking over here and what kind of evening do you want them to spend here? Hmh? Bethel's right. After all, it's a bit late in the day to come back into life. Your story just doesn't end that way. You see what's happened. Can you talk now? No. Just Mumbo Jumbo. Now I'm older than you and, why, I can barely get along as it is. Get all mixed up unless a strong hand guides me. So—go over to Bethel, now. Bethel's by the door. [*She rings a small bell. Slowly* KENNETH *shambles over to* BETHEL.]

BETHEL: That's a dear. We'll go away now. Somewhere restful. Away from all these meddlers. A room somewhere, Kenny.

GEORGE: They've gone back into their house. The Principal forgot his cane. Here comes the Dean of Women. [*But* KENNETH *walks past* BETHEL *to* POLLY *and receives the tie. She and* IRA *help him put it on.*] She's wearing one of her famous hats. All covered with violets and dozens of stuffed white mice.

BETHEL: I won't. I won't stay here a moment longer. I'm leaving. [*She circles. They say nothing.*]

POLLY: That's Dr Ewell. He's just opening the gate.

KENNETH: What a wise-looking old man. Is he a minister? He might marry us after supper.

IRA: No, he's not a minister, Kenneth. He's—

GEORGE: The Dean of Women.

BETHEL: Silly old fusspot. [*She is lighting candles.*]

KENNETH: They come chatting and talking of nothing. What is that marvellous thing she has about her neck? A crown?

IRA: I made it for her. It's a neck support, Kenneth.

POLLY: After a sherry party last March she fell down some stairs and strained her neck. So. [*She puts her hand around her own neck.*]

KENNETH: The neck lady is stopping.

GEORGE: The Principal's wife. I'm so hungry—

POLLY: She's straightening that ladder that leans so crookedly by the walnut tree.

BETHEL: A ring, a box and a ladder. Ada! Put on yet one more plate. Another guest!

As KENNETH *looks down at his bare feet,* BETHEL *exits with candles into the dining room. He advances now to greet the guests who ring the doorbell—one of those rusty pull ones—just as, or almost just as, the clock strikes the half hour.*

CURTAIN

Phyllis Webb

b. 1927

Phyllis Webb was born in Victoria, B.C., and grew up there and in Vancouver. In 1949 she received a B.A. in English and philosophy from the University of British Columbia. After an unsuccessful campaign as a CCF candidate, Webb moved to Montreal, where she worked as a secretary and attended graduate school at McGill for one year. In 1960 she returned to Vancouver and taught at UBC for four years. She then accepted a job with the CBC in Toronto as a program organizer and broadcaster (she had been freelancing for the CBC since 1955). From 1966 to 1969 she was executive producer of the radio program 'Ideas', which she had brought into being. Aided largely by government bursaries and awards, Webb was able to spend extended periods during the fifties and sixties in London, Paris, and San Francisco. Since 1969, when she left full-time radio work and returned to British Columbia, she has lived on Salt Spring Island and has taught at the Universities of British Columbia, Victoria, and Alberta.

Webb's first book, *Trio* (1954), was a showcase for her work and that of two other new writers, Gael Turnbull and Eli Mandel. In the next eleven years she produced three poetry collections: *Even Your Right Eye* (1956), *The Sea Is Also a Garden* (1962), and *Naked Poems* (1965). There followed a period of virtual silence—*Selected Poems 1954-1965* was published in 1971—until *Wilson's Bowl* appeared in 1980. Since then two more works have been published: *Talking: Selected Radio Talks and Other Essays* (1981) and *Selected Poems: The Vision Tree* (1982), a Governor General's Award winner that includes some new work.

Though Webb's poetry tends to be pessimistic, it is rarely morbid because it is always leavened with wit. Her concern with despair, suicide, and death is linked to a conscious existentialism (unusual in Canadian poetry), which is similar to that of Kierkegaard and Gide. While investigating what she sees as a sterile, even meaningless, world she presents her readers with strategies for survival. The topics of break-up and break-down—of major importance since the Second World War to writers as diverse as John Berryman, Doris Lessing, Adrienne Rich, and Margaret Atwood—have led her to suggest in her poetry that the individual must seek protective isolation and silence. In her own life she has found these in the silence of her native region: the beaches, water, and gardens of the Gulf Islands.

Webb's poetry, however, is not entirely introspective. Many of her poems allude to a wide range of interests in the world around her. The body of her work has been influenced on the one hand by the intricacies of metaphysical poetry techniques (as in 'Marvell's Garden' and 'The Glass Castle') and on the other by the stylistic simplicity of the Black Mountain and San Francisco poetry movements (as in *Naked Poems*). The complex structuring of much of her poetry resembles the work of contemporary scientists building new chromosomes and atoms: she strives to obey what she calls

the physics of the poem. Energy/Mass.
Waxy splendour, the massive quiet of the
fallen tulip petals. So much depends upon:
the wit of the syntax, the rhythm and speed
of the fall, the drop, the assumption of a
specific light, curved. (Talking)

Lear[1] on the Beach at Break of Day

Down on the beach at break of day
observe Lear calmly observing the sea:
he tosses the buttons of his sanity
like aged pebbles into the bay;

cold, as his sexless daughters were,
the pebbles are round by a joyless war,
worn down on a troubled, courtly ground,
they drop in the sea without a sound;

and the sea repeats their logical sin,
shedding ring after ring of watery thin   10
wheels of misfortune of crises shorn
which spin to no end—and never turn.

And there Lear stands, alone.
The sun is rising 'and the cliffs aspire,
and there Lear stands, with dark small stones
in his crazed old hands. But farther and higher

he hurls them now, as if to free
himself with them. But only stones drop
sullenly, a hardened crop,
into the soft, irrational sea.   20

1954

[1] In *King Lear*, Lear, having given over his throne to his daughters Goneril and Regan in exchange for their looking after him, is driven mad by their cruel and unfeeling treatment as they struggle against one another for complete power.

Marvell's Garden[1]

Marvell's garden, that place of solitude,[2]
is not where I'd choose to live
yet is the fixed sundial[3]
that turns me round
unwillingly
in a hot glade
as closer, closer I come to contradiction

[1] This poem contains many responses and allusions to 'The Garden' by the British poet Andrew Marvell (1621-78).
[2] Marvell chooses to be solitary in the garden, declaring: 'Society is all but rude/To this delicious solitude'.
[3] The sundial in Marvell's poem is equated with the garden itself; in the seventeenth century the sundial was often a symbol of a stable point against which to measure the illusions of experience.

to the shade green within the green shade.[4]

The garden where Marvell scorned love's solicitude[5]—
that dream—and played instead an arcane solitaire,   10
shuffling his thoughts like shadowy chance
across the shrubs of ecstasy,
and cast the myths away to flowering hours
as yes, his mind, that sea, caught at green
thoughts shadowing a green infinity.

And yet Marvell's garden was not Plato's
garden[6]—and yet—he *did* care more for the form
of things than for the thing itself—
ideas and visions,
resemblances and echoes,   20
things seeming and being
not quite what they were.

That was his garden, a kind of attitude
struck out of an earth too carefully attended,
wanting to be left alone.
And I don't blame him for that.
God knows, too many fences fence us out
and his garden closed in on Paradise.[7]

On Paradise! When I think of his hymning
Puritans in the Bermudas,[8] the bright oranges   30
lighting up that night! When I recall
his rustling tinsel hopes
beneath the cold decree of steel.[9]
Oh, I have wept for some new convulsion
to tear together this world and his.

[4]In this stanza and the next, Webb refers to lines in Marvell's poem:
  The mind, that ocean where each kind
  Does straight its own resemblance find;
  Yet it creates, transcending these,
  Far other worlds, and other seas;
  Annihilating all that's made
  To a green thought in a green shade.
[5]Marvell rejects physical love, approving of the mythical stories in which young women escape
seduction when they are transformed into flora.
[6]Marvell, while affirming the Platonic concept of ideal forms, departed from most of his contemporary Neo-Platonists in his belief that man's mind (equated in 'The Garden' with the ocean, which
was said to contain a parallel to every external thing) was superior to nature, and thus to the ideal reality, because it not only had a pre-existent knowledge of all the 'forms' of reality but also could
imaginatively create new 'forms' that have never before existed. In this stanza Webb plays with the
contradictory meanings suggested by the word 'form'.
[7]Marvell equates his garden to Eden before the creation of Eve and the fall of man.
[8]In the poem 'Bermudas', Marvell depicts religious dissenters rowing ashore to the Bermudas (long
celebrated as a kind of earthly paradise), singing a hymn of praise to God that includes the lines: 'He
hangs in shades the orange bright,/Like golden lamps in a green night.'
[9]Marvell himself was twice exiled to the Bermudas as a result of ecclesiastical persecution. Throughout his life he sought a middle ground in the political strife of England, which was being torn by civil
war.

But then I saw his luminous plumèd Wings[1]
prepared for flight,
and then I heard him singing glory
in a green tree,
and then I caught the vest he'd laid aside   40
all blest with fire.

And I have gone walking slowly in
his garden of necessity
leaving brothers, lovers, Christ
outside my walls
where they have wept without
and I within.

1956

[1] In 'The Garden' the poet undergoes a spiritual transformation:
Casting the body's vest aside,
My soul into the boughs does glide:
There like a bird it sits, and sings,
Then whets and combs its silver wings.

The Glass Castle

The glass castle is my image for the mind
that if outmoded has its public beauty.
It can contain both talisman and leaf,
and private action, homely disbelief.
And I have lived there as you must
and scratched with diamond and gathered diamond dust,
have signed the castle's tense and fragile glass
and heard the antique whores and stoned Cassandras[1]
call me, and I answered in the one voice I knew,
'I am here. I do not know . . .'   10
but moved the symbols and polished up the view.
For who can refrain from action—
there is always a princely kiss for the Sleeping Beauty—
when even to put out the light takes a steady hand,
for the reward of darkness in a glass castle
is starry and full of glory.

I do not mean I shall not crack the pane.
I merely make a statement, judicious and polite,
that in this poise of crystal space
I balance and I claim the five gods of reality[2]   20
to bless and keep me sane.

1962

[1] Cassandra was a Trojan soothsayer whose curse it was to have her prophecies ignored.
[2] That is, the five senses.

To Friends Who Have Also Considered Suicide

It's still a good idea.
Its exercise is discipline:
to remember to cross the street without looking,
to remember not to jump when the cars side-swipe,
to remember not to bother to have clothes cleaned,
to remember not to eat or want to eat,
to consider the numerous methods of killing oneself,
that is surely the finest exercise of the imagination:
death by drowning, sleeping pills, slashed wrists,
kitchen fumes, bullets through the brain or through   10
the stomach, hanging by the neck in attic or basement,
a clean frozen death—the ways are endless.
And consider the drama! It's better than a whole season
at Stratford when you think of the emotion of your
family on hearing the news and when you imagine
how embarrassed some will be when the body is found.
One could furnish a whole chorus in a Greek play
with expletives and feel sneaky and omniscient
at the same time. But there's no shame
in this concept of suicide.   20
It has concerned our best philosophers
and inspired some of the most popular
of our politicians and financiers.
Some people swim lakes, others climb flagpoles,
some join monasteries, but we, my friends,
who have considered suicide take our daily walk
with death and are not lonely.
In the end it brings more honesty and care
than all the democratic parliaments of tricks.
It is the 'sickness unto death'[1] it is death;   30
it is not death; it is the sand from the beaches
of a hundred civilizations, the sand in the teeth
of death and barnacles our singing tongue:
and this is 'life' and we owe at least this much
contemplation to our western fact: to Rise,
Decline, Fall, to futility and larks,
to the bright crustaceans of the oversky.

1962

---

[1]Phrase taken from *The Sickness Unto Death* (1849) by Danish philosopher and theologian Sören Kierkegaard (1813-55); for Kierkegaard, the 'sickness unto death' is despair.

From *Naked Poems*

Suite I

MOVING
to establish distance
between our houses.

It seems
I welcome you in.

Your mouth blesses me
all over.

There is room.

          AND
          here
          and here and
          here
          and over   and
          over   your mouth

TONIGHT
quietness.   In me
and the room.

I am enclosed
by a thought

and some walls.

          THE BRUISE

          Again you have left
          your mark.

          Or we
          have.

          Skins shuddered
          secretly.

FLIES

tonight
in this room

two flies
on the ceiling
are making
love
quietly.   Or

so it seems
down here.

YOUR BLOUSE

I people
this room
with things, a
chair,   a lamp,   a
fly,   two books by
Marianne Moore.

I have thrown my
blouse on the floor.

Was it only
last night?

YOU
took

with so much
gentleness

my dark

Suite II

While you were away

I held you like this
in my mind.

It is a good mind
that can embody
perfection   with exactitude.

The sun comes through
plum curtains.

I said
the sun is gold

in your eyes.

It isn't the sun
you said.

On the floor your blouse.
The plum light
falls more golden

going down.

Tonight
quietness
in the room.

We knew.

Then you must go.
I sat cross-legged
on the bed.
There is no room
for self-pity
I said.

I lied.

In the gold darkening
light

you dressed.

I hid my face
in my hair.

The room that held you

is still here.

You brought me clarity.

Gift after gift
I wear.

Poems   naked
in the sunlight

on the floor.

1965

234 | Phyllis Webb

For Fyodor[1]

I am a beetle in the cabbage soup they serve up for geniuses
in the House of the Dead.[2]

I am a black beetle and loll seductively at the bottom of the
warm slop.

Someday, Fyodor, by mistake you'll swallow me down and I'll become
a part of your valuable gutworks.

In the next incarnation I hope to imitate that idiot and saint,
Prince Myshkin,[3] drop off my wings for his moronic glory.

Or, if I miss out on the Prince, Sonya or Dunya might do.

I'm not joking. I am not the result of bad sanitation in the
kitchen, as you think.

Up here in Omsk in Siberia beetles are not accidents but destinies.

I'm drowning fast, but even in this condition I realize your bad
tempered haughtiness is part of your strategy.

You are about to turn this freezing hell into an ecstatic emblem.   10
A ferocious shrine.

Ah, what delicious revenge. But take care! A fit is coming![4]
Now, now I'll leap into your foaming mouth and jump your tongue.
Now I stamp on this not quite famous tongue

shouting: Remember Fyodor, you may hate men but it's here in
Omsk you came to love mankind.

But you don't hear, do you: there you are writhing in epileptic visions.

Hold your tongue! You can't speak yet. You are mine, Dostoevsky.

I am to slip down your gullet and improve myself.

[1]Fyodor Dostoevski (1821-81), Russian novelist. This 'portrait' poem is part of Webb's unfinished
sequence 'The Kropotkin Poems', which examines the ramifications of the Russian Revolution upon
modern society. Webb has commented: 'In "For Fyodor" the beetle is aggressive, enraged, mono-
loguing dramatically along the extended line. Poor Fyodor, foaming at the mouth, harangued by this
Trickster . . . Big-mouthed, proletarian, revolting beetle. The balance of power unbalanced . . .
Notes from the Insect Underground. Spider Webb' (*Talking*).
[2]The prison in Omsk, Siberia, that is the setting for Dostoevski's 1862 novel, *The House of the Dead*;
this novel is based on his experiences while serving four years' hard labour in this prison.
[3]Central character of *The Idiot* (1868); Sonya and Dunya are two characters from *Crime and Punishment* (1866).
[4]Dostoevski suffered from epilepsy.

I can almost hear what you'll say: 20

    Crime and Punishment
    Suffering and Grace

and of the dying

    pass by and forgive
    us our happiness

1980

Spots of Blood

I am wearing absent-minded red
slippers and a red vest—
spots of blood
to match the broken English
of Count Dracula being interviewed
on the radio in the morning sun.
I touch the holes in my throat
where the poppies bud—spots of blood
spots of womantime. '14,000 rats,'[1]
Dracula is saying, and the interviewer   10
echoes, '14,000 rats! So beautiful,'
he sighs, 'The Carpathian Mountains—
the photography, so seductive!' The Count
also loves the film; he has already seen it
several times. He tells in his dreamy voice
how he didn't need direction, didn't want
makeup, how he could have done it with his own
teeth. He glided in and out of this role
believing in reincarnation, in metamorphosis.
Yet 14,000 rats and the beleaguered   20
citizens of the Dutch town where those scenes
were shot (without him) are of no interest.
'And Hollywood?' the interviewer asks, himself
an actor, 'Hollywood next?' Who knows?
Who knows?

The blood pounds at my temples.
The women of the world parade before me
in red slippers and red vests, back and
forth, back and forth, fists clenched.
My heart emerges from my breast for   30
14,000 rats and the citizens of Delft,

[1] In *Nosferatu* (Germany, 1922), a film based on Bram Stoker's novel *Dracula* (1897), the vampire
sets a plague of rats upon a city. The heroine, sacrificing her own life in an effort to save mankind,
entices the vampire to her bed, where he remains until destroyed by the first rays of the morning
sun.

for the women of the world in their menses.
Yet I too imitate a crime of passion:
Look at these hands. Look at the hectic
red painting my cheekbones as I metamorphose
in and out of the Buddha's eye,[2] the *animus
mundi*.

In the morning sun Count Dracula leans
against my throat with his own teeth.
Breathing poppies. Thinking.   40

1980

[2]Buddha is said to be the Eye of the World, the All-Seeing Eye in which all existence rests. *'Animus
mundi'*: the world soul or mind; usually in the feminine form, *anima mundi*; here Webb refers to
(i) the Buddhist notion of an Absolute Mind out of which the world emanates, and (ii) the Jungian
principle of one's idealized sexual opposite. (Since the speaker is female, her ideal is male,
animus.)

Eschatology[1] of Spring

Death, Judgement, Heaven, Hell,
and Spring. The Five Last Things,
the least of which I am, being in
the azaleas and dog-toothed violets
of the South of Canada. Do not tell me
this is a cold country. I am also in
the camellias and camas of early, of
abrupt birth.
We are shooting up for the bloody
judgement of the six o'clock news.   10
Quick, cut us out from the deadlines
of rotting newspapers, quick, for the
tiny skeletons and bulbs will tell you
how death grows and grows in Chile and
Chad. Quick, for the small bones pinch
me and insects divulge occult excrement
in the service of my hyacinth, my trailing
begonia. And if you catch me resting
beside the stream, sighing against
the headlines of this pastoral, take   20
up your gun, the flowers blossoming
from its barrel, and join this grief, this
grief: that there are lambs, elegant black-
footed lambs in this island's eschatology,
Beloved.

1981

[1]The branch of theology that is concerned with the ultimate or last things. Webb has added Spring to
the traditional Four Last Things.

Robert Kroetsch

(b. 1927)

Growing up in Heisler, Alta., Robert Kroetsch saw first-hand the hardships that drought and depression brought to the Prairies in the thirties. Despite that sombre background, he is best known as a comic novelist whose fiction often recalls the wild and bawdy tall tales of the western beer-hall. More than simply tall tales, his novels move towards the retelling of some of the great myths. But while drawing on classical mythology and North American Indian tales, Kroetsch provides his reader with parodies as much as with parallels, creating a blend of comedy and fantasy that marked a new departure in Canadian fiction.

After earning an undergraduate degree at the University of Alberta in 1948, Kroetsch, a would-be writer in search of experience, journeyed north to the Slave River. He spent some time as a labourer on the Fort Smith Portage, two seasons sailing on Mackenzie riverboats, and several years in Labrador. He then travelled east to study at McGill University under Hugh MacLennan. During his summers he attended the Bread Loaf School of English at Middlebury College, Vermont, where he eventually completed an M.A. In 1965 he entered the Writers' Workshop program at the University of Iowa, earning his Ph.D. in 1961 with the draft of a novel (an early version of *The Studhorse Man*). He remained in the U.S. for the next fourteen years, teaching at the State University of New York at Binghamton, before returning to Canada in 1975. He has taught at the Universities of Lethbridge and Calgary and is now Professor of English at the University of Manitoba.

In 1965 Kroetsch published *But We Are Exiles*, a novel about the crew of a riverboat on the Mackenzie. In the fiction that followed he undertook what he felt to be the chief task of the western-Canadian novelist: to write his environment into existence and to discover the myths appropriate to the place. In a conversation with Margaret Laurence recorded in *Creation* (1970), Kroetsch remarked: 'In a sense we haven't got an identity until somebody tells our story. The fiction makes us real.' Kroetsch's most extended attempt to tell that story is in his Out West trilogy (he calls it a 'triptych') of novels: *The Words of My Roaring* (1966), *The Studhorse Man* (1969), for which he won a Governor General's Award, and *Gone Indian* (1973). These books, forming an extended investigation of an imagined Alberta landscape through four decades, playfully consider the political movements of the Depression thirties, the social dislocations following the Second World War, and the naive pastoralism of the sixties and early seventies. (Kroetsch's travel book, *Alberta*, 1968, by providing a more personal and objective response to his native province, serves as an interesting counterpoint to his triptych.) In 1975 Kroetsch published his fifth novel, *Badlands*, a surreal work about river-rafting through the Alberta Badlands in search of dinosaur bones. The densely layered composition of Kroetsch's fiction is made apparent in *The Crow Journals* (1980), a history of the construction of his most recent novel, *What the Crow Said* (1978).

During the seventies he turned much of his creative energy to poetry, collecting in *The Stone Hammer Poems* (1975) the short poems he had written in the previous decade. The title poem movingly documents the writer's struggle to elicit meaning from the objects of the past. Very interested in questions about form and structure in the modern long poem, Kroetsch also published in 1975 *The Ledger*, the beginning of an ongoing long poem that is continued by *Seed Catalogue* (1977), *The Sad Phoenician* (1979), and *The Criminal Intensities of Love as Paradise* (1981). This loosely unified work—which Kroetsch regards as still in progress—has been collected in *Field Notes* (1981). In his preface to that book, Eli Mandel wrote:

We have not had such an endeavour before, at least not in this country; for this is the long *poem, not just the narrative, of which Northrop Frye has written, not the documentary, of which Dorothy Livesay has much to say, but something big enough to hold the world and time, a space for the vast geography, a time for hidden history.*

Through his teaching, lecturing, and critical essays, and as co-founder in 1972 of the American critical journal *Boundary 2: A Journal of Post-Modern Literature*, Kroetsch has worked both to locate Canadian literature in an international context and to make the Canadian academic and literary communities more aware of recent international developments in literary theory. The critical and theoretical depths that emerge when he discusses his own writing are particularly evident in *Labyrinths of Voice* (1981), a book of conversations with Shirley Neuman and Robert Wilson. Among his many critical essays —collected in *Open Letter*, Series 5, No. 4 (1983)—'Unhiding the Hidden' has had special impact. An essay about the way Canadian writers are burdened by their cultural inheritance, it expresses Kroetsch's belief that writers must 'un-name' themselves and their environment. This act is dramatized in Albert Johnson's becoming the 'poet of our survival' through his refusal to give his name or even to speak (in 'Poem of Albert Johnson'), and in Kroetsch's vision of Grove's creating an identity after 'exfoliating' back to blankness (in the companion poem, 'F.P. Grove: The Finding'). For prairie writers in particular, such 'uncreating' carries them back to the essential elements of landscape or—as in 'Stone Hammer Poem'—to those objects associated with the earliest history of the place, and prepares them for the task of creating narratives and myths appropriate to their own experience.

Stone Hammer Poem

I

This stone
become a hammer
of stone, this maul

is the colour
of bone (no,
bone is the colour
of this stone maul).

The rawhide loops
are gone, the
hand is gone, the   10
buffalo's skull
is gone;

the stone is
shaped like the skull
of a child.

2

This paperweight on my desk

where I begin
this poem   was

found in a wheatfield
lost (this hammer,   20
this poem).

Cut to a function,
this stone was
(the hand is   gone—

3

Grey, two-headed,
the pemmican maul[1]

fell from the travois or
a boy playing   lost it in
the prairie wool or
a squaw   left it in   30
the brain of a buffalo or

It is a million
years older than
the hand that
chipped stone or
raised slough
water (or blood) or

4

This stone maul
was found.

In the field   40
my grandfather
thought
was his

my father
thought was his

---

[1]i.e. the hammer was used in the preparation of pemmican (preserved buffalo or caribou meat). 'Travois': Indian sledge made of a platform stretched between two shafts and pulled behind a horse.

5

It is a stone
old as the last
Ice Age, the
retreating/the
recreating ice,   50
the retreating
buffalo, the
retreating Indians

(the saskatoons bloom
white (infrequently
the chokecherries the
highbush cranberries the
pincherries bloom
white along the barbed
wire fence (the   60
pemmican   winter

6

This stone maul
stopped a plow
long enough for one
Gott im Himmel.

The Blackfoot (the
Cree?) not

finding the maul
cursed.

? did he curse   70
? did he try to
go back
? what happened
I have to/I want
to know (not know)
? WHAT HAPPENED

7

The poem
is the stone
chipped and hammered
until it is shaped   80
like the stone
hammer, the maul.

8

Now the field is
mine because
I gave it
(for a price)

to a young man
(with a growing son)
who did not

notice that the land   90
did not belong

to the Indian who
gave it to the Queen
(for a price) who
gave it to the CPR
(for a price) which
gave it to my grandfather
(for a price) who
gave it to my father
(50 bucks an acre
Gott im Himmel I cut
down all the trees I   100
picked up all the stones) who

gave it to his son
(who sold it)

9

This won't
surprise you.

My grandfather
lost the stone maul.

10

My father (retired)
grew raspberries.
He dug in his potato patch.   110
He drank one glass of wine
each morning.
He was lonesome
for death.

He was lonesome for the
hot wind on his face, the smell
of horses, the distant

hum of a threshing machine,
the oilcan he carried, the weight
of a crescent wrench in his hind pocket.   120

He was lonesome for his absent
son and his daughters,
for his wife, for his own
brothers and sisters and
his own mother and father.

He found the stone maul
on a rockpile in the
northwest corner of what
he thought of
as his wheatfield.   130

He kept it (the
stone maul) on the railing
of the back porch in
a raspberry basket.

11

I keep it
on my desk
(the stone).

Sometimes I use it
in the (hot) wind
(to hold down paper)   140

smelling a little of cut
grass or maybe even of
ripening wheat or of
buffalo blood hot
in the dying sun.

Sometimes I write
my poems for that

stone hammer.

1975

Poem of Albert Johnson[1]

It is his silence   they cannot allow
offended into a blood reason   the hunters
surround his cabin   with their loud law

he will give no name   to hate or love
neither forgive nor blame   the righteous
fusillade   no word of hurt or mercy

no word   only his rivalling guns
confide his awareness   of their assault
confuse the hunters   into the bomb-blast

unhousing the harried trapper   bare   10
to the Arctic night   the brave running
by which he will become   poet of survival

to our suburban pain   the silent man
circling back   to watch them coming
giving new tracks   to the blizzard-white trail

leaving the faint sleigh dogs   scent
of their lost game   (police and Indians
together at last   punished by dark

and wind   neglect the weather
of their intent)   he will give no name   20
only the cold camp   where he almost slept

letting gunshot   into his best pursuer
his self's shadow   dressed in red authority[2]
and after the quick exchanging   unspeakably dead

and gone beyond all living   the silent man
made the impossible crossing   the snowshoe pattern
over the closed pass   into the caribou herd

[1]Dubbed the 'Mad Trapper of Rat River' (little is known about his real identity), Albert Johnson appeared in the Peel River area of the Northwest Territories—above the Arctic Circle, just south of the Beaufort Sea—in the summer of 1931. In December he refused to open the door of his cabin on the Rat River or make any reply to RCMP constables who wanted to question him about a trap-line; when the constables returned three days later, Johnson fired through the door, seriously wounding one man. Nine days after this the Mounties returned with reinforcements, beginning a siege during which they used dynamite to force him from his cabin. Johnson finally abandoned his position in mid-January and fled westward, eluding pursuit for over a month before being shot down. He became the only man ever known to have travelled by foot across the mountains into the Yukon during the winter, and his survival during the harshest of northern winter conditions (daytime temperatures of around $-50°F$ were recorded during the pursuit), combined with his extraordinary skill in throwing off his pursuers—circling around behind them and walking backwards in his own tracks to confuse his trail—brought him his fame. This manhunt was the first ever to make use of radio and aircraft. For a prose version of the manhunt, see Rudy Wiebe's 'The Naming of Albert Johnson', p. 366.
[2]When the police overtook Johnson at his camp in the Richardson Mountains on 29 January 1932, he killed a constable and escaped once more.

that gave him a gap   out of the closing frame
the trap   forged by the roaring bush plane
out of six weeks' hunting   the silent man   30

having leapt their ring   walked back
and baited their pride   with his spent body
bought them the cry they sought   and only kept

his silence   (we stand at his grave in Aklavik
mosquitoes swarming at our heads   like the posse
that slammed him   out of his last loading)

the poet of our survival   his hands and feet
frozen   no name on his dead mouth
no words betraying   either love or hate

1975

F. P. Grove: The Finding[1]

I

Dreaming the well-born   hobo of yourself
against the bourgeois father[2]   dreaming Europe
if only to find   a place to be from

the hobo tragedian   pitching bundles
riding a freight   to the impossible city
the fallen archangel   of Brandon or Winnipeg

in all your harvesting   real
or imagined   did you really find
four aged stallions[3]   neigh

in your cold undertaking   on those trails north   10
in all the (dreamed) nights   in stooks
in haystacks   dreaming the purified dreamer

who lured you   to a new man (back
to the fatal earth)   inventing (beyond
America) a new world   did you find

[1] This poem is constructed around references to three of Grove's books, *Over Prairie Trails* (1922), *A Search for America* (1927), and *In Search of Myself* (1946). See Vol. I, pp. 257-8.
[2] In *In Search of Myself*, Grove describes his father as a wealthy Swedish landowner. In *A Seach for American* he recounts twenty years of wandering across North America as a tramp and a hobo. Both books were long thought of as autobiographical accounts but later discovered to be highly dramatized fictions.
[3] In Chapter Five of *In Search of Myself*, Grove says, 'I was hired as a teamster, and I owed the job to one single fact, namely, that of not being afraid of handling any kind of horse, not even the team I was offered which consisted of four aged stallions.'

did you dream   the French priest who hauled you
out of your *fleurs du mal*[4]   and headlong
into a hundred drafts   real

or imagined   of the sought form
(there are no models)   and always   20
(there are only models)   alone

2

alone in the cutter   in the blizzard[5]
two horses   hauling you into the snow
that buries the road   burying the forest

the layered mind   exfoliating[6]
back to the barren sea   (Greek to us,
Grove)   back to the blank sun

and musing snow to yourself   new
to the old rite of burial   the snow
lifting the taught man   into the coyote self   30

the silence of sight   'as if I were not myself
who yet am I'   riding the drifted snow
to your own plummeting   alone and alone

the *wirklichkeit*[7]   of the word itself
the name under the name   the sought
and calamitous edge   of the white earth

the horses   pawing the empty fall
the hot breath on the zero day   the man
seeing the new man so vainly   alone

we say with your waiting wife   (but she   40
was the world   before you invented it
old liar)   'You had a hard trip?'

1975

[4] According to Chapter Six of *In Search of Myself* Grove was persuaded to begin his teaching career by a chance encounter with a French priest who saw him reading Baudelaire's *Fleurs du mal* in a North Dakota train station.
[5] From here to the conclusion, the poem is based on the sketch 'Snow' from *Over Prairie Trails* (reprinted in Vol. I, pp. 259-76), which describes a particularly harrowing winter journey.
[6] Grove says that the snow-drifts he was crossing 'showed that curious appearance that we also find in the glaciated surfaces of granite rock and which, in them, geologists call exfoliation' (Vol. I, p. 264). Later Grove writes that as he looked at 'the infertile waste' around him: 'Unaccountably two Greek words formed on my lips: Homer's Pontos atrygetos—the barren sea' (I, 267).
[7] Reality; actual fact (German).

Unhiding the Hidden:
Recent Canadian Fiction

'Now we're on my home ground, foreign territory.'
—MARGARET ATWOOD, *Surfacing*

Survival itself is the Canadian apocalypse. The Canadian cannot die and therefore writes fiction. He longs to be destroyed by America; in his wrath at America's failure he sets out to be the destroyer. It is his only hope.

At one time I considered it the task of the Canadian writer to give names to his experience, to be the namer. I now suspect that, on the contrary, it is his task to un-name.

This necessity did not originate with Canadian writers. Heidegger says in his *Poetry, Language, Thought: 'Roman thought takes over the Greek words without a corresponding, equally authentic experience of what they say, without the Greek word.* The rootlessness of Western thought begins with this translation'.[1]

The Canadian writer's particular predicament is that he works with a language, within a literature, that appears to be authentically his own, and not a borrowing. But just as there was in the Latin word a concealed Greek experience, so there is in the Canadian word a concealed other experience, sometimes British, sometimes American.

In recent years the tension between his appearance of being just like someone else and the demands of authenticity has become intolerable—both to individuals and to the society. In recent Canadian fiction the major writers resolve the paradox—the painful tension between appearance and authenticity—by the radical process of demythologizing the systems that threaten to define them. Or, more comprehensively, they uninvent the world.

The most conspicuous example is the novel, *Surfacing,* by Margaret Atwood. In that novel the three *named* characters, Joe, Davie and Anna, live constantly in danger of becoming American. Waiting for the barbarians, they begin to become, in terms of the essential American paradox, the awaited barbarians. But the Canadian who borrows this posture as an account of his condition is metamorphosed into the inauthentic fool that David makes of himself with his speech and his camera, that Anna makes of herself with her mirror and her compact and her cunt.

Atwood's heroine must remove the false names that adhere to her experience. The terror of her journey is not that she, like her drowned father, like her drowned and revived antipodal brother, almost drowns; it is rather that she surfaces. The terror resides not in her going insane but in her going sane.

Atwood signals this very Canadian predicament when she has the narrator say early in the novel, 'Now we're on my home ground, foreign territory.' The truth is disguised, hidden. Camouflage, the narrator says, 'was one of my father's policies.' And she too is good at varieties of camouflage: she says of herself as commercial artist. 'I can imitate anything: fake Walt Disney, Victorian etchings in sepia, Bavarian cookies, ersatz Eskimo for the home market.

---

[1]Martin Heidegger (1889-1976), *Poetry, Language, Thought* (1971), edited and translated by Albert Hofstadter.

Though what they like best [her Canadian publishers] is something they hope will interest the English and American publishers too.' And as she is able to imitate art, so she imitates marriage, imitates friendship. She can fake, has been taught to and forced to fake, not only a personal identity, but adherence to a social order: looking at school pictures she sees herself 'in the stiff dresses, crinolines and tulle, layered like store birthday cakes; I was civilized at last, the finished product.'

But underneath this layering, this concealing, is a woman who still recognizes that something doesn't fit. Joe says, 'Do you love me, that's all,' and she thinks: 'It was the language again, I couldn't use it because it wasn't mine.'

The Roman writer borrowed a Greek word into a Latin context. The Canadian writer borrows an English word into an English-language context, a French word into a French-language context. The process of rooting that borrowed word, that totally exact homonym, in authentic experience, is then, must be, a radical one.

Atwood's heroine burns the drawings and the typescript from which she works. She takes off the ring that signifies her sham marriage, drops it into the fire. But even that is only the beginning:

Everything from history must be eliminated, the circles and the arrogant square pegs. I rummage under the mattress and bring out the scrapbooks, ripping them up, the ladies, dress forms with decorated china heads, the suns and the moons, the rabbits and their archaic eggs, my false peace, his [her brother's] wars, aeroplanes and tanks and the helmeted explorers . . . Even the guides, the miraculous double woman and the god with horns, they must be translated. The ladies on the wall too with their watermelon breasts and lampshade skirts, all my artifacts. . . . the map torn from the wall . . . When the paper things are burned I smash the glasses and plates and the chimney of the lamp. I rip one page from each of the books . . . When nothing is left intact and the fire is only smouldering I leave, carrying one of the wounded blankets with me. I will need it until the fur grows. The house shuts with a click behind me.

In the marvellous extravagance of this surfacing, this uninventing of the world, the narrator must finally deliver herself of the notion that she is a human being. Bare-assed she can become bear-assed—in accordance with the outrageous, seductive, fabulated contemporary female vision of what total freedom must be. At the end of *Surfacing* the narrator has achieved a state wherein she might—with minimal help from Joe, who has in him still a bit of the buffalo, a bit of the bear—give birth to her true identity. 'The word games, the winning and losing games are finished; at the moment there are no others but they will have to be invented, withdrawing is no longer possible and the alternative is death.'

Atwood's heroine will not die; rather, she will give birth to herself. And, curiously, a similar version of parthenogenesis marks the end of another fine recent novel.

David Staunton, the hero of Robertson Davies' *The Manticore,* like Atwood's heroine must begin by confronting death and the father. For eastern Canadian writers, this matter of literal ancestors is paramount. And David, named after his father's hero, the Prince of Wales, compared to Absalom,[2] must not so much learn as unlearn family history: be it in the form of a borrowed coat of arms, a family fortune, or the English origins of the family name. His father, like the father in Atwood's novel, must literally be brought back to the surface from death by water. And, quite literally, Boy Staunton (the father) is unmasked: the dentist-artist who would make a death-mask succeeds instead in removing the corpse's face.

Where the larger process of uninventing, in Atwood, becomes a journey into the wilderness, in Davies it is a journey to the old civilization, the sum of our ancestry. And yet, for both these novelists, the condition of prehistory is necessary to valid and authentic birth.

I cannot here examine Davies' skill in taking us on that journey: his use of theatrical devices of unmasking, his exploration of the theme of illusion, his concept of the role of the fool in the unhiding of the hidden, in the speaking of the unspeakable. Davies, the sophisticated novelist, works back to notebooks, to diaries, to confession, to psychoanalytic method, to Jungian archetypes.

What is central is that his hero, David Staunton, criminal lawyer, alcoholic, Oxford graduate, archetypal Canadian fucked virgin, literally goes back into the earth. High up in the mountains of Switzerland he crawls with a mysterious woman down into a cave. He goes back to the darkness, extinguishes the last light. He finds in that darkness, in that womb-like cave, the necessary connection between Felix, the stuffed bear that was his consolation at age four, and his bear-worshipping ancestors. The world has been uninvented: by this man, for this man who earlier was told, 'You think the world is your idea.' And now, reunited with his infancy, with his animal nature, with his emotions— gone back beyond thinking—he finds himself so close to death that in terror he shits himself.

At that 'lowest ebb,' the woman tells him: 'Go on, you dirty brute, go on.' And Staunton, his anima recognized, his whole ancestry acknowledged, is able at last to give birth to himself. He crawls out into the cold sunshine. It is Christmas eve. He is the new-born stranger ready to return to his 'home ground, foreign territory'. Like Atwood's heroine on her island, Davies' Staunton is ready to begin. Atwood's narrator hopes she is pregnant. Staunton is ready to look for a wife. Having uninvented the world, each is prepared—in the manner of the newly-wed couple at the end of the traditional comic novel—to invent a new one.

Atwood and Davies, using the established conventions of the novel, act out this process of decomposing the world in terms of individuals. Curiously, it has been left to western Canadian writers to act it out in a larger social context.

Grove is the paradigm of this larger mode. Felix Paul Greve he departed Europe; in mid-Atlantic he uninvented himself, unwrote his history, arrived in Canada a new self, Frederick Philip Grove, about to invent new ancestors. He is the true trickster in our prose tradition, as Layton and Birney are of the poetic. He is the fool-sage, the holy nut so pompously wise he could unlearn

---

[2]The favourite of King David, killed after he rebelled against his father (2 Samuel: 18).

not just himself but a literary tradition, a civilization; he could dis-cover the new form of *Over Prairie Trails*, the fictional reality of *In Search of Myself*. . . . And of his descendants, some of whom might not recognize their mysterious father, Rudy Wiebe is the most central to my thesis. But Robert Harlow's *Scann* is a reckless demolition of inauthenticity towards an Easter of recognition. And Dave Godfrey, that exiled westerner, has written a novel quite literally called *The New Ancestors*.

I choose to comment on Wiebe's *The Temptations of Big Bear* because here a bear-inspired man acts out, not only mythologically, but historically as well, the uninvention of the world. By an act of imagination that approaches the complexity of Grove's own, Wiebe makes of a tribe of Crees the epitome of our Canadian selves being extinguished into existence by the British and American cultures. Hounded, tricked, robbed, cheated, shot at, starved—we prove they cannot capture us: and then voluntarily we reveal ourselves to the destroying elements. Big Bear is the poet-creator who must himself be un-created in order to represent our necessary fate. He must resist temptations to be anything—farmer, politician, trading-post white man, Christian—other than his fated self. He must *talk* his way into his decreated and valid self; he must, dying, become the source and creator of the unimaginable new.

In his talking—in the language of the novel—he and Wiebe decreate the literary tradition that binds us into not speaking the truth. Wiebe and Harlow and Godfrey, like Grove before them, have a marvellous ability to keep the language clumsy, brutal, unbeautiful, vital, charged. Atwood makes a fine Canadian prose style of the run-on sentence. Davies distrusts any sentence that loses its connection with his newspaperman's background. But Wiebe is determined to destroy the sentence itself back to sense, back to its ground. He says in his dedication that he 'unearthed' the story. He recognizes the problem of language: we learn that Corporal Sleigh 'never read a book because people in them never walked in mud. . . . You never got the sense of anyone being downright dirty the way Territories' mud stuck to you in globs . . .' He demonstrates how the problem of language becomes one of culture, society, identity: Peter Houri attempts to translate, to speak of the crime against, Queen Victoria's 'crown and dignity'. Big Bear responds:

> . . . there is nothing true when they say I tried to steal her hat. How could I do that? Or knock it off, as Poundmaker said they told him, by throwing sticks at it. . . . I didn't know she had a hat and I never wear hats, what would I want it for to make me steal it, women's hats are nice but a man would be drunk—

Where Davies invented documents, Wiebe quotes from existing sources, lets government records and legal debate and newspapers and memoirs and journals speak for themselves. The sheer failure of that language to confront reality is both comic and appalling. We discover, finally, why Wiebe is driven into complicity with the so-called renegade Indians. Like them, he must experience the de-composition of the world. He must, whatever the cost, go Indian himself.

It is possible that the old obsessive notion of identity, of ego, is itself a spent fiction, that these new writers are discovering something essentially new, something essential not only to Canadians but to the world they would un-create. Whatever the case, they dare that ultimate *contra-diction:* they uncreate themselves into existence. Like Heidegger they will accept that the root meaning of the word truth is un-concealing, dis-closing, dis-covering, un-hiding. Or, to put it in prairie terms, they will, like Rudy Wiebe's Big Bear, even when locked up in the Stony Mountain pen, with the Archbishop generously in attendance—even then they will be loyal to their own first visions. Offered the consolation and pride of the old names, they will 'decline to be christened'.

1974, 1983

Hugh Hood

b. 1928

Hugh Hood was the second of three children born to Roman Catholic parents living in Toronto. He attended parochial school and in 1947 entered St Michael's College, University of Toronto. After completing his B.A., Hood remained at Toronto, earning a Ph.D. in 1955 with a thesis on theories of imagination. He then accepted a teaching position at Saint Joseph College in Hartford, Connecticut. In 1961 he joined the English faculty of the Université de Montréal, where he still teaches. The son of a French-Canadian mother, he is bilingual.

Hood began writing fiction while still an undergraduate and published his first story in the *Tamarack Review* in 1958. The 1962 publication of *Flying a Red Kite* made him the first major writer in Canada to begin his career with a book of short stories. This volume and the five collections published since—*Around the Mountain: Scenes from Montreal Life* (1967), *The Fruit Man, the Meat Man, and the Manager* (1971), *Dark Glasses* (1976), *Selected Stories* (1978), and *None Genuine Without This Signature* (1980)—have established him as one of Canada's foremost story writers. In this fiction Hood departs from conventions of

realism that had largely dominated the Canadian short story since the advent of Morley Callaghan. The publication of *Flying a Red Kite* in 1962—coming between Ethel Wilson's book of stories, *Mrs. Golightly* (1961), and Margaret Laurence's *The Tomorrow-Tamer* (1963)—helped announce the beginning of a new period of contemporary storytelling that has since seen the discovery in Canada of Mavis Gallant and Norman Levine and the emergence of such important new writers as Alice Munro, Clark Blaise, Alastair MacLeod, W. P. Kinsella, and W. D. Valgardson, among others who have done their most important work in the form of the short story.

Since the publication of the novel *White Figure, White Ground* (1965), Hood has also given his attention to longer fiction. In that book—about the difficulties besetting a Canadian painter—and in *The Camera Always Lies* (1967) and *A Game of Touch* (1970), Hood's fondness for social commentary, evident in most of his stories, carries him close to satire. This aspect of his writing is most dominant in *You Can't Get There from Here* (1972), a political allegory about the vulnerability of a bicultural country (an imaginary African nation) struggling for identity in the modern world.

In 1975 Hood published *The Swing in the Garden*, the first volume in a projected twelve-novel sequence collectively titled *The New Age*. He has since added three more novels to the series: *A New Athens* (1977)—the title alludes to Frances Brooke's suggestion that Canada will not prove 'a new Athens rising near the pole'; *Reservoir Ravine* (1979); and *Black and White Keys* (1982). Endeavouring to create a scrupulously detailed record of the manners and milieu of eastern Canada in the twentieth century, Hood plans to continue publishing a volume every two years until the year 2000. However daunting and ambitious this project may seem, it is one that coincides with Hood's sense of his stature. In an interview with J. R. (Tim) Struthers, he remarked:

I think it would be marvellous for Canada if we had one artist who could move easily and in a familiar converse with Joyce, and Tolstoy, and Proust; and I intend to be that artist if I possibly can; and I am willing to give the rest of my life to it . . . I really want to endow the country with a great imperishable work of art.
(Before the Flood, *1979)*

Hood's close attention in all his fiction to the details and even minutiae of work, politics, sports, and social life makes these works a blend of fiction and memoir; Hood refers to them as 'documentary fantasies'.

In *The Swing in the Garden*, his protagonist reflects: 'Does anybody care about that now? Does anybody know that the transfers for the Glen Road/Summerhill bus line were a rich buff colour with red lettering, that the King Street car line had chastely simple black-and-white transfers? I care so passionately about these matters that I am sometimes shaken by the power of the feeling.' Such 'feeling' about the past is not merely a reverence for history; it is an emotion like that found in Wordsworth's poetry, an almost ecstatic response to intensely perceived moments in time. Indeed, Hood's documentary impulse is really an aspect of a deeply held religious outlook. His complex version of Christianity leads him to find hidden meanings in his universe: in consequence he packs many of his stories—which are often associated with festal occasions—with symbolic events and places. Even the most mundane objects can become icons or take on allegorical significance—as in 'Flying a Red Kite':

He had noticed that people treated kites and kite-flying as somehow holy. They were a natural symbol, thought Fred, and he felt uneasily sure that he would have trouble getting this one to fly.

In later stories, such as 'The Woodcutter's Third Son', the question of the symbolism that man finds in his world is expanded to touch on the larger topic of the way man uses language and all its structures to give meaning to his universe.

Flying a Red Kite

The ride home began badly. Still almost a stranger to the city, tired, hot, and dirty, and inattentive to his surroundings, Fred stood for ten minutes, shifting his parcels from arm to arm and his weight from one leg to the other, in a sweaty bath of shimmering glare from the sidewalk, next to a grimy yellow-and-black bus stop. To his left a line of murmuring would-be passengers lengthened until there were enough to fill any vehicle that might come for them. Finally an obese brown bus waddled up like an indecent old cow and stopped with an expiring moo at the head of the line. Fred was glad to be first in line, as there didn't seem to be room for more than a few to embus.

But as he stepped up he noticed a sign in the window which said *Côte des Neiges—Boulevard* and he recoiled as though bitten, trampling the toes of the woman behind him and making her squeal. It was a Sixty-six bus, not the Sixty-five that he wanted. The woman pushed furiously past him while the remainder of the line clamoured in the rear. He stared at the number on the bus stop: Sixty-six, not his stop at all. Out of the corner of his eye he saw another coach pulling away from the stop on the northeast corner, the right stop, the Sixty-five, and the one he should have been standing under all this time. Giving his characteristic weary put-upon sigh, which he used before breakfast to annoy Naomi, he adjusted his parcels in both arms, feeling sweat run down his neck and down his collar between his shoulders, and crossed Saint Catherine against the light, drawing a Gallic sneer from a policeman, to stand for several more minutes at the head of a new queue, under the right sign. It was nearly four-thirty and the Saturday shopping crowds wanted to get home, out of the summer dust and heat, out of the jitter of the big July holiday weekend. They would all go home and sit on their balconies. All over the suburbs in duplexes and fourplexes, families would be enjoying cold suppers in the open air on their balconies; but the Calverts' apartment had none. Fred and Naomi had been ignorant of the meaning of the custom when they went apartment hunting. They had thought of Montreal as a city of the Sub-Arctic and in the summers they would have leisure to repent the misjudgement.

He had been shopping along the length of Saint Catherine between Peel and Guy, feeling guilty because he had heard for years that this was where all those pretty Montreal women made their promenade; he had wanted to watch without familial encumbrances. There had been girls enough but nothing outrageously special so he had beguiled the scorching afternoon making a great many small idle purchases, of the kind one does when trapped in a Woolworth's. A ball-point pen and a notepad for Naomi, who was always stealing his and leaving it in the kitchen with long, wildly-optimistic grocery lists scribbled in it. Six packages of cigarettes, some legal-size envelopes, two Dinky-toys, a long-playing record, two parcels of second-hand books, and the lightest of his burdens and the unhandiest, the kite he had bought for Deedee, two flimsy wooden sticks rolled up in red plastic film, and a ball of cheap thin string—not enough, by the look of it, if he should ever get the thing into the air.

When he'd gone fishing, as a boy, he'd never caught any fish; when playing hockey he had never been able to put the puck in the net. One by one the wholesome outdoor sports and games had defeated him. But he had gone on believing in them, in their curative moral values, and now he hoped that Deedee, though a girl, might sometime catch a fish; and though she obviously wouldn't play hockey, she might ski, or toboggan on the mountain. He had noticed that people treated kites and kite-flying as somehow holy. They were a natural symbol, thought Fred, and he felt uneasily sure that he would have trouble getting this one to fly.

The inside of the bus was shaped like a box-car with windows, but the windows were useless. You might have peeled off the bus as you'd peel the paper off a pound of butter, leaving an oblong yellow lump of thick solid heat, with the passengers embedded in it like hopeless bread-crumbs.

He elbowed and wriggled his way along the aisle, feeling a momentary sliver of pleasure as his palm rubbed accidentally along the back of a girl's skirt—once, a philosopher[1]—the sort of thing you couldn't be charged with. But you couldn't get away with it twice and anyway the girl either didn't feel it, or had no idea who had caressed her. There were vacant seats towards the rear, which was odd because the bus was otherwise full, and he struggled towards them, trying not to break the wooden struts which might be persuaded to fly. The bus lurched forward and his feet moved with the floor, causing him to pop suddenly out of the crowd by the exit, into a square well of space next to the heat and stink of the engine. He swayed around and aimed himself at a narrow vacant seat, nearly dropping a parcel of books as he lowered himself precipitately into it.

The bus crossed Sherbrooke Street and began, intolerably slowly, to crawl up Côte des Neiges and around the western spur of the mountain. His ears began to pick up the usual *mélange* of French and English and to sort it out; he was proud of his French and pleased that most of the people on the streets spoke a less correct, though more fluent, version than his own. He had found that he could make his customers understand him perfectly—he was a book salesman—but that people on the street were happier when he addressed them in English.

The chatter in the bus grew clearer and more interesting and he began to listen, grasping all at once why he had found a seat back here. He was sitting next to a couple of drunks who emitted an almost overpowering smell of beer. They were cheerfully exchanging indecencies and obscure jokes and in a minute they would speak to him. They always did, drunks and panhandlers, finding some soft fearfulness in his face which exposed him as a shrinking easy mark. Once in a railroad station he had been approached three times in twenty minutes by the same panhandler on his rounds. Each time he had given the man something, despising himself with each new weakness.

The cheerful pair sitting at right-angles to him grew louder and more blunt and the women within earshot grew glum. There was no harm in it; there never is. But you avoid your neighbour's eye, afraid of smiling awkwardly, or of looking offended and a prude.

'Now this Pearson,' said one of the revellers, 'he's just a little short-ass. He's just a little fellow without any brains. Why, some of the speeches he makes . . . I could make them myself. I'm an old Tory myself, an old Tory.'

'I'm an old Blue,' said the other.

'Is that so, now? That's fine, a fine thing.' Fred was sure he didn't know what a Blue was.[2]

'I'm a Balliol man. Whoops!' They began to make monkey-like noises to annoy the passengers and amuse themselves. 'Whoops,' said the Oxford man again, 'hoo, hoo, there's one now, there's one for you.' He was talking about a girl on the sidewalk.

'She's a one, now, isn't she? Look at the legs on her, oh, look at them now,

---

[1] 'There's an old joke about a young student who told Goethe that he was visiting a brothel that night for philosophical reasons. Next day Goethe asked him what he had thought. The young man replied that he found it very interesting and was going back on the very next night to pursue his researches. ''Aha,'' said Goethe, ''once, a philosopher; twice, a pervert'' ' (Hood, in a letter).

[2] 'Blue' refers to the speaker's having earned his colours at Oxford. (He reveals in his next speech that he attended Balliol College.) His respondent, the priest, who has identified himself above as a Tory, thinks that the Balliol man is referring to the political meaning of the word in Canada, particularly Quebec, where a 'Blue' means a Conservative.

isn't that something?' There was a noisy clearing of throats and the same voice said something that sounded like 'Shaoil-na-baig'.[3]

'Oh, good, good!' said the Balliol man.

'Shaoil-na-baig,' said the other loudly, 'I've not forgotten my Gaelic, do you see, shaoil-na-baig,' he said it loudly, and a woman up the aisle reddened and looked away. It sounded like a dirty phrase to Fred, delivered as though the speaker had forgotten all his Gaelic but the words for sexual intercourse.

'And how is your French, Father?' asked the Balliol man, and the title made Fred start in his seat. He pretended to drop a parcel and craned his neck quickly sideways. The older of the two drunks, the one sitting by the window, examining the passing legs and skirts with the same impulse that Fred had felt on Saint Catherine Street, was indeed a priest, and couldn't possibly be an imposter. His clerical suit was too well-worn, eggstained and blemished with candle-droppings, and fit its wearer too well, for it to be an assumed costume. The face was unmistakably a southern Irishman's. The priest darted a quick peek into Fred's eyes before he could turn them away, giving a monkey-like grimace that might have been a mixture of embarrassment and shame but probably wasn't.

He was a little grey-haired bucko of close to sixty, with a triangular sly mottled crimson face and uneven yellow teeth. His hands moved jerkily and expressively in his lap, in counterpoint to the lively intelligent movements of his face.

The other chap, the Balliol man, was a perfect type of English-speaking Montrealer, perhaps a bond salesman or minor functionary in a brokerage house on Saint James Street. He was about fifty with a round domed head, red hair beginning to go slightly white at the neck and ears, pink porcine skin, very neatly barbered and combed. He wore an expensive white shirt with a fine blue stripe and there was some sort of ring around his tie. He had his hands folded flatly on the knob of a stick, round face with deep laugh-lines in the cheeks, and a pair of cheerfully darting little blue-bloodshot eyes. Where could the pair have run into each other?

'I've forgotten my French years ago,' said the priest carelessly. 'I was down in New Brunswick for many years and I'd no use for it, the work I was doing, I'm Irish, you know.'

'I'm an old Blue.'

'That's right,' said the priest. 'John's the boy. Oh, he's a sharp lad is John. He'll let them all get off, do you see, to Manitoba for the summer, and bang, BANG!' All the bus jumped. 'He'll call an election on them and then they'll run.' Something caught his eye and he turned to gaze out the window. The bus was moving slowly past the cemetery of Notre Dame des Neiges and the priest stared, half-sober, at the graves stretched up the mountainside in the sun.

'I'm not in there,' he said involuntarily.

'Indeed you're not,' said his companion, 'lot's of life in you yet, eh, Father?'

'Oh,' he said, 'oh, I don't think I'd know what to do with a girl if I fell over one.' He looked out at the cemetery for several moments. 'It's all a sham,' he said, half under his breath, 'they're in there for good.' He swung around and

[3]'These are nonsense syllables in fake Gaelic which I made up, purely for fun . . .' (Hood, in a letter).

looked innocently at Fred. 'Are you going fishing, lad?'

'It's a kite I bought for my little girl,' said Fred, more cheerfully than he felt.

'She'll enjoy that, she will,' said the priest, 'for it's grand sport.'

'Go fly a kite!' said the Oxford man hilariously. It amused him and he said it again, 'Go fly a kite!' He and the priest began to chant together, 'Hoo, hoo, whoops,' and they laughed and in a moment, clearly, would begin to sing.

The bus turned lumberingly onto Queen Mary Road. Fred stood up confusedly and began to push his way towards the rear door. As he turned away, the priest grinned impudently at him, stammering a jolly goodbye. Fred was too embarrassed to answer, but he smiled uncertainly and fled. He heard them take up their chant anew.

'Hoo, there's a one for you, hoo. Shaoil-na-baig. Whoops!' Their laughter died out as the bus rolled heavily away.

He had heard about such men, naturally, and knew that they existed; but it was the first time in Fred's life that he had ever seen a priest misbehave himself publicly. There are so many priests in the city, he thought, that the number of bum ones must be in proportion. The explanation satisfied him but the incident left a disagreeable impression in his mind.

Safely home he took his shirt off and poured himself a Coke. Then he allowed Deedee, who was dancing around him with her terrible energy, to open the parcels.

'Give your Mummy the pad and pencil, sweetie,' he directed. She crossed obediently to Naomi's chair and handed her the cheap plastic case.

'Let me see you make a note in it,' he said, 'make a list of something, for God's sake, so you'll remember it's yours. And the one on the desk is mine. Got that?' He spoke without rancour or much interest; it was a rather overworked joke between them.

'What's this?' said Deedee, holding up the kite and allowing the ball of string to roll down the hall. He resisted a compulsive wish to get up and rewind the string.

'It's for you. Don't you know what it is?'

'It's a red kite,' she said. She had wanted one for weeks but spoke now as if she weren't interested. Then all at once she grew very excited and eager. 'Can you put it together right now?' she begged.

'I think we'll wait till after supper, sweetheart,' he said, feeling mean. You raised their hopes and then dashed them; there was no real reason why they shouldn't put it together now, except his fatigue. He looked pleadingly at Naomi.

'Daddy's tired, Deedee,' she said obligingly, 'he's had a long hot afternoon.'

'But I want to see it,' said Deedee, fiddling with the flimsy red film and nearly puncturing it.

Fred was sorry he'd drunk a Coke; it bloated him and upset his stomach and had no true cooling effect.

'We'll have something to eat,' he said cajolingly, 'and then Mummy can put it together for you.' He turned to his wife. 'You don't mind, do you? I'd only spoil the thing.' Threading a needle or hanging a picture made the normal slight tremor of his hands accentuate itself almost embarrassingly.

'Of course not,' she said, smiling wryly. They had long ago worked out their areas of uselessness.

'There's a picture on it, and directions.'

'Yes. Well, we'll get it together somehow. Flying it . . . that's something else again.' She got up, holding the note-pad, and went into the kitchen to put the supper on.

It was a good hot-weather supper, tossed greens with the correct proportions of vinegar and oil, croissants and butter, and cold sliced ham. As he ate, his spirits began to percolate a bit, and he gave Naomi a graphic sketch of the incident on the bus. 'It depressed me,' he told her. This came as no surprise to her; almost anything unusual, which he couldn't do anything to alter or relieve, depressed Fred nowadays. 'He must have been sixty. Oh, quite sixty, I should think, and you could tell that everything had come to pieces for him.'

'It's a standard story,' she said, 'and aren't you sentimentalizing it?'

'In what way?'

'The "spoiled priest" business, the empty man, the man without a calling. They all write about that. Graham Greene made his whole career out of that.'

'That isn't what the phrase means,' said Fred laboriously. 'It doesn't refer to a man who actually *is* a priest, though without a vocation.'

'No?' She lifted an eyebrow; she was better educated than he.

'No, it doesn't. It means somebody who never became a priest at all. The point is that you *had* a vocation but ignored it. That's what a spoiled priest is. It's an Irish phrase, and usually refers to somebody who is a failure and who drinks too much.' He laughed shortly. 'I don't qualify on the second count.'

'You're not a failure.'

'No, I'm too young. Give me time!' There was no reason for him to talk like this; he was a very productive salesman.

'You certainly never wanted to be a priest,' she said positively, looking down at her breasts and laughing, thinking of some secret. 'I'll bet you never considered it, not with your habits.' She meant his bedroom habits, which were ardent, and in which she ardently acquiesced. She was an adept and enthusiastic partner, her greatest gift as a wife.

'Let's put that kite together,' said Deedee, getting up from her little table, with such adult decision that her parents chuckled. 'Come on,' she said, going to the sofa and bouncing up and down.

Naomi put a tear in the fabric right away, on account of the ambiguity of the directions. There should have been two holes in the kite, through which a lugging-string passed; but the holes hadn't been provided and when she put them there with the point of an ice pick they immediately began to grow.

'Scotch tape,' she said, like a surgeon asking for sutures.

'There's a picture on the front,' said Fred, secretly cross but ostensibly helpful.

'I see it,' she said.

'Mummy put holes in the kite,' said Deedee with alarm. 'Is she going to break it?'

'No,' said Fred. The directions were certainly ambiguous.

Naomi tied the struts at right-angles, using so much string that Fred was sure the kite would be too heavy. Then she strung the fabric on the notched ends of the struts and the thing began to take shape.

'It doesn't look quite right,' she said, puzzled and irritated.

'The surface has to be curved so there's a difference of air pressure.' He remembered this, rather unfairly, from high-school physics classes.

She bent the cross-piece and tied it in a bowed arc, and the red film pulled taut. 'There now,' she said.

'You've forgotten the lugging-string on the front,' said Fred critically, 'that's what you made the holes for, remember?'

'Why is Daddy mad?' said Deedee.

'I'M NOT MAD!'

It had begun to shower, great pear-shaped drops of rain falling with a plop on the sidewalk.

'That's as close as I can come,' said Naomi, staring at Fred, 'we aren't going to try it tonight, are we?'

'We promised her,' he said, 'and it's only a light rain.'

'Will we all go?'

'I wish you'd take her,' he said, 'because my stomach feels upset. I should never drink Coca-Cola.'

'It always bothers you. You should know that by now.'

'I'm not running out on you,' he said anxiously, 'and if you can't make it work, I'll take her up tomorrow afternoon.'

'I know,' she said, 'come on, Deedee, we're going to take the kite up the hill.' They left the house and crossed the street. Fred watched them through the window as they started up the steep path hand in hand. He felt left out, and slightly nauseated.

They were back in half an hour, their spirits not at all dampened, which surprised him.

'No go, eh?'

'Much too wet, and not enough breeze. The rain knocks it flat.'

'OK!' he exclaimed with fervour. 'I'll try tomorrow.'

'We'll try again tomorrow,' said Deedee with equal determination—her parents musn't forget their obligations.

Sunday afternoon the weather was nearly perfect, hot, clear, a firm steady breeze but not too much of it, and a cloudless sky. At two o'clock Fred took his daughter by the hand and they started up the mountain together, taking the path through the woods that led up to the University parking lots.

'We won't come down until we make it fly,' Fred swore, 'that's a promise.'

'Good,' she said, hanging on to his hand and letting him drag her up the steep path, 'there are lots of bugs in here, aren't there?' ·

'Yes,' he said briefly—he was being liberally bitten.

When they came to the end of the path, they saw that the campus was deserted and still, and there was all kinds of running room. Fred gave Deedee careful instructions about where to sit, and what to do if a car should come along, and then he paid out a little string and began to run across the parking lot towards the main building of the University. He felt a tug at the string and throwing a glance over his shoulder he saw the kite bobbing in the air, about twenty feet off the ground. He let out more string, trying to keep it filled with air, but he couldn't run quite fast enough, and in a moment it fell back to the ground.

'Nearly had it!' he shouted to Deedee, whom he'd left fifty yards behind.

'Daddy, Daddy, come back,' she hollered apprehensively. Rolling up the string as he went, he retraced his steps and prepared to try it again. It was important to catch a gust of wind and run into it. On the second try the kite went higher than before but as he ran past the entrance to the University he felt the air pressure lapse and saw the kite waver and fall. He walked slowly back, realizing that the bulk of the main building was cutting off the air currents.

'We'll go up higher,' he told her, and she seized his hand and climbed obediently up the road beside him, around behind the main building, past ash barrels and trash heaps; they climbed a flight of wooden steps, crossed a parking lot next to L'Ecole Polytechnique and a slanting field further up, and at last came to a pebbly dirt road that ran along the top ridge of the mountain beside the cemetery. Fred remembered the priest as he looked across the fence and along the broad stretch of cemetery land rolling away down the slope of the mountain to the west. They were about six hundred feet above the river, he judged. He'd never been up this far before.

'My sturdy little brown legs are tired,' Deedee remarked, and he burst out laughing.

'Where did you hear that,' he said, 'who has sturdy little brown legs?'

She screwed her face up in a grin. 'The gingerbread man,' she said, beginning to sing, 'I can run away from you, I can, 'cause I'm the little gingerbread man.'

The air was dry and clear and without a trace of humidity and the sunshine was dazzling. On either side of the dirt road grew great clumps of wild flowers, yellow and blue, buttercups, daisies and goldenrod, and cornflowers and clover. Deedee disappeared into the flowers—picking bouquets was her favourite game. He could see the shrubs and grasses heave and sway as she moved around. The scent of clover and of dry sweet grass was very keen here, and from the east, over the curved top of the mountain, the wind blew in a steady uneddying stream. Five or six miles off to the southwest he spied the wide intensely grey-white stripe of the river. He heard Deedee cry: 'Daddy, Daddy, come and look.' He pushed through the coarse grass and found her.

'Berries,' she cried rapturously, 'look at all the berries? Can I eat them?' She had found a wild raspberry bush, a thing he hadn't seen since he was six years old. He'd never expected to find one growing in the middle of Montreal.

'Wild raspberries,' he said wonderingly, 'sure you can pick them dear; but be careful of the prickles.' They were all shades and degrees of ripeness from black to vermilion.

'Ouch,' said Deedee, pricking her fingers as she pulled off the berries. She put a handful in her mouth and looked wry.

'Are they bitter?'

'Juicy,' she mumbled with her mouth full. A trickle of dark juice ran down her chin.

'Eat some more,' he said, 'while I try the kite again.' She bent absorbedly to the task of hunting them out, and he walked down the road for some distance and then turned to run up towards her. This time he gave the kite plenty of string before he began to move; he ran as hard as he could, panting and handing the string out over his shoulders, burning his fingers as it slid through them. All at once he felt the line pull and pulse as if there were a living thing on the other end and he turned on his heel and watched while the kite danced into the upper air-currents above the treetops and began to soar up and up. He gave it more line and in an instant it pulled high up away from him across the fence, two hundred feet and more above him up over the cemetery where it steadied and hung, bright red in the sunshine. He thought flashingly of the priest saying 'It's all a sham,' and he knew all at once that the priest was wrong. Deedee came running down to him, laughing with excitement and pleasure and singing joyfully about the gingerbread man, and he knelt in the dusty roadway and put his arms around her, placing her hands on the line between his. They gazed, squinting in the sun, at the flying red thing, and he turned away and saw in the shadow of her cheek and on her lips and chin the dark rich red of the pulp and juice of the crushed raspberries.

1962

The Woodcutter's Third Son

John Flamborough went to a dinner party in his green middle-age and found himself seated next to a young woman whom he remembered vaguely as the bearer of one of those childish pet names which a certain breed of person never outgrows. What 'breed of person'? The phrase intimated an adversary's view of the state of being which folds one's baby-name about one's shoulders into adulthood. The woman was perhaps twenty-three, he calculated, almost without awareness of his reckoning. Betsy? Mamie? She was some sort of student; that much was clear from her plain, ardent wish to rehearse before him her present mental enthusiasm. After a single small measure of the delicate Moselle which arrived with the salmon, she turned her glasses down. The first of them made the faintest of stains on the cloth, a pale circle the colour of a saint's nimbus in Victorian stained glass. Flamborough caught her troubled glance at the snowy expanse of stiff linen, now just that least peccant golden-ringed diameter removed from immaculate innocence. He said, 'It will come clean.'

His host's aunt, seated at his left, claimed his attention briefly with a tale, well-worn from many recitations, of the rudenesses of taxi-drivers. '. . . and then he said, "Thank you, Ma'am. You're one of the great native Canadians and you'll live in my memory," and slammed the door and drove off. He was so sarcastic that I almost wept, and all I'd done was offer him too small a tip, ten percent of the fare. He was unquestionably an immigrant. In the last generation I'd have taken his number and had his permit revoked, but in these days we have no recourse. They speak to us as they please. For thirty years, when I shopped in the department stores I used the same clerks. They had little business cards with their names on them, almost as if they had an interest in the firm. There was a woman who sold shoes at Eaton's whom I used to go and see annually as if she were my niece. She had a little girl who was blind, I believe.'

Flamborough recollected with a sense of the waters closing over his head that of all persons known to him this Aunt Frances was the one who most perfectly embodied a literary conception: the disappointed single lady with a grievance and a powerful family connection. Non-appearance at the starting gate of lover or husband had not lessened the urgency of Frances Stratton's bill of demand upon fortune, for replenishment of the springs of her self-conception. She had neither lowered her guard and invited the knockout blow of elderly isolation, nor in any way compromised herself in venturesome proposals or excursions: Caribbean cruises, service on arts committees, a postgraduate degree. Her hair was the same faintly blue grey that he remembered from times when he had come to this house as an undergraduate, an almost colourless hue which suggested further bottles of Moselle. Aunt Frances's close coiffure concealed nothing but pale bone, he reflected, and no exquisite flowery intoxicant. He saw with relief that Mary de Savigny, perhaps over-familiar with the taxicab saga, was about to cut across her husband's mother's sister's complaint with a soothing initiative.

His duty done, he turned to the girl at his right. Not Mamie, he was almost certain. He had positively not dandled this person on his knee, though she was surely young enough to have been so encouraged by someone not much older than he. Thoughts of decisive gaps in age-spans appeared at the back of his mind and he wondered, as he had begun increasingly to do nowadays, where the line between is drawn. When does it become a gulf which cannot be traversed, too deep, too absolutely unfathomable? He imagined that he could still just stay within hailing distance of this remote woman, who stared at the stained table-cloth as if her virginal life somehow depended on it. She was a small girl with affectingly narrow shoulders and slender neck; at his side in her chair she had to twist her head sidewise and upwards to gaze at him, which lent her the attitude of a supplicant, someone who had favours to request. He now saw that he could at no time have dandled her on either knee; there was the possibility of conversation. She was indeed a year or two older than he had imagined at first, perhaps twenty-seven. Not Mamie. Emmy? 'Breed of person'?

Why had he felt impelled to dismiss the elegantly rigged and outfitted figure, the snug dove-grey bodice and long narrow waist, the dim pattern of small forms moving in obscurity round and round her quietly rustling silk skirt? These forms seemed on hasty covert inspection like an army of tiny walking figures descending in spiralling rows to an invisible hem. There was somewhere a suggestion of lace. He reconsidered the dismissive phrase, 'breed of person,' and charged himself with loss of moral points. Very often on first inspection some person not quite a stranger, for whom we may perhaps have inherited or otherwise acceded to an unwelcome responsibility, seems to require classification in general terms, as if the generality of conception may mitigate too distinct accuracy of imagining, the lurking fear of a further call on slender resources be exorcised in succinct abstraction. He understood that she was not simply a girl with a charming but infantine Christian name, a Susie, Ellie, Mamie, least of all a Rosie. Here was nothing of the comic sweet young girl confronted by certainties whose granite foundations seemed to her too cold to provide an engaging perch.

'Those vines have very tender grapes,' he offered, 'even when *goldbeerenauslese*,[1] which these certainly were not. The colour is in the skin and pulp, in the weakest concentration imaginable, certainly incapable of resisting the agent your contemporary laundress might employ, bleach, detergent, fabric softener.' He started to laugh uncomfortably. 'See how our vocabularies have evolved?' He glanced along the table. 'I doubt that Aunt Frances would permit the words "fabric softener" to cross her lips, even if she were able to conceive of the existence of such subversion of mere dirt.'

'Oh I do my own laundry,' said the girl, a trifle morosely, thought Flamborough. 'Everybody does nowadays. And at home I simply used to put my things out. They disappeared, and came back three days later, starched, ironed. They never required bleach.'

'But we're better off,' asserted Flamborough, not sure of this ground. He had had pervasively in these last years an obscure awareness that his life was turning in some new direction, an important earlier stage terminated, a group of piers and underpinnings shifting deep within under rearrangements of stress.

'That is a political observation,' said the girl, 'and an exceedingly incautious one, considering its source. Nobody takes John Flamborough for a democrat, a friend of the masses, an egalitarian.'

There seemed no direct way to identify her. 'How many people make a mass?' he inquired, hoping to draw her out.

'Of course there is no such thing as a mass or "the masses", since things are always singular. But we can imagine mass behaviour, and our conception of it has some use in both psychiatry and political analysis.'

He had her now. 'You must realise, Cecy, that conceptual fictions have no bearing whatsoever on what you or I may do.'

'Oh but they do!' she exclaimed.

Cecy Howard, daughter of the late chief justice of the provincial supreme court, of which his own father, the redoubtable Jesse Flamborough, continued a member. Cecy, he thought, recollecting his first hearing of the name when he was fifteen, one summer at the lake.

'Ifounda Newbaby,' his mother had ejaculated. 'It sounds like the name of a character in a Marx brothers' movie.' He had laughed without paying attention.

'That Naomi Howard,' said his mother censoriously, 'she should know better than to attempt delivery at her age. Ifounda Newbaby.'

This was one of his mother's many playful tricks of mentality, the seizing of an ordinary form of words and compressing it by a change in stress and pitch into fewer words which meant something quite different from the original form, usually an exotic name. People named Wanda Gotobed, Ifounda Newbaby, Siobhan Stoborrow-Macombe, Anne O'Rexia Nervosa (always identified as

---

[1]The highest of the four grades of grapes used for Rhine wine.

'exotic, tempestuous Irish-Spanish danseuse') crowded her verbal imagination. He had in some degree caught this habit from her, a habit of which his father had always disapproved.

'What are they calling the child?' his father had asked mildly, lifting his eyes from contemptuous scrutiny of the editorial page of the morning newspaper.

'Cecy.'

John's ears had wrung with pleasure.

'Short for Cecilia,' said mother.

He had read a Yankee children's book called *What Katy Did* when he was eight and in this work there had been a girl next door called Cecy, a bit of a minx, slightly morally questionable, not as sweet as Katy, sweet in a different risky way. He had always preferred Cecy to Katy; the faint tang of what was nowadays called, with great unsubtlety, bitchiness, had first unnerved and then enchanted him.

He said slowly, 'Most persons on the bench prefer to work from case law and precedent rather than from code, or interpretation of the arbitrary regulations of administrative boards.'

'You are repeating what your father has taught you,' said the young woman, tracing a circle on the tablecloth with her fish fork.

'Not at all.'

'I think so. I remember that my own father always used to say . . . ,' she paused and he saw with alarm that her eyes glistened. She was still mourning for her father, he realised with compassion, and why should she not? Chief Justice Howard had been the most admired of his father's colleagues, a jurist with much that was heroic in his nature and his professional attainments, a man willing to risk parenthood of this clearly exceptional young woman when almost fifty. Middle-age, thought Flamborough, quivering. He felt an impulse to take Cecy by the hand, and placed his open palm on the table, knocking over a wine glass and calling attention to himself from across the board.

Char said, 'Don't torment poor Cecy, John, she has worries of her own.'

'My dear Charlotte,' said their host reprovingly.

Flamborough covered Cecy's hand with his. He said, 'There seems a greater distance between the rubrics which are evolved to control conduct and those actions which in fact come to pass. It is just here that the notion of law, and that of legality, break on the rock of the singular. Every crime is singular just as every thing—insofar as it is a thing—is singular. The law never bears fully and wholly on what has been done, nor does any psychiatric criticism prove adequate to my mental lack of ease, or yours.'

'Precisely,' said Cecy, looking at her left hand and gently uncovering it. 'It is as Bettelheim[2] rightly says. We rule our lives by our inheritance from folklore, by spell, by conjuration.'

John hadn't read the book but had read the reviews, and felt himself able to guess its tendency. He had no faith whatsoever in any analysis of motivation

---

[2]Bruno Bettelheim, Austrian-born American psychiatrist and child psychologist; in *The Uses of Enchantment* (1976) he argues that fairy tales function on a subconscious level to help children understand the world and cope with their anxieties.

proffered by professional 'scientific' psychiatry. 'What are the uses of enchantment?' he asked Cecy, and at the chiming of this first, serious inquiry they fell deeply into conversation.

'More than we are able to conceive—and I choose the word with care—we rule our lives by, well, not quite supersitition, but by the invention, so to speak, of spirits. We have not left behind the animistic universe of the cave-dwellers or the nomadic huntsmen. Each of us attributes spirit to his dearest possessions, his little snug apartment, his bed, his books . . .'

'Her bed, her books?'

'His or her. I am speaking without personal reference at this point. I might say "we". We all populate our lives with invisible agents who live in things. I know a woman who has taken her automobile as her patron saint. She speaks of her snow tires as her guardian angels. What are we to make of this?'

'What indeed?'

'The jolly green giant,' said Cecy, breaking into laughter. 'A vegetation god in a tin, with a little green sprout as his messenger sprite.'

'Has Bettelheim put all this into your head? This seems an entirely new folklore.'

'He has and he hasn't and yes, I'm afraid it is.'

'Would a new folklore of this kind be desirable, as a crutch for the mentally disabled or the fatally alienated person?'

'That remains to be seen,' said the girl, twisting round to look at him more closely. He heard Char teasing, as from a great distance.

'I'm not certain of the bearings of your argument,' he said.

'It isn't formally an argument at all, as we reject the scientific principle in making any such series of observations. Bettelheim tells us, for example, as he might tell children a bedtime story—precisely in that soothing way—that each one of us, whether consciously aware of the corpus of legend, fairy story, and folktale or not, carries far within himself an identification of his spirit with that of some principal, major, or say simply famous character in these narratives.'

'Say that again, more simply still.'

'It's merely that we all see ourselves as one particular recurring character in fairy story. So, now, tell me, without pausing for an instant to think about it, quick, quick, QUICK. Which are you?'

'I'm the woodcutter's third son,' said Flamborough without the smallest pause.

This sentence fled from his lips like an escaping prisoner and afterwards he marvelled at its readiness to depart.

'You see?' said Cecy, and she laughed cruelly, the minx.

Having extorted this spontaneity, she lowered her head modestly, twisting her lips. She was wearing a necklace of cranberry-coloured crystals, very tiny, certainly precious, glinting. Her head swayed on the slender neck, whose nape invited a passionate salute. He did not intend to allow her to evade responsibility for this discovery. Already a painful comprehension, more exactly an imaged and felt physical grab or clutch at what he had revealed to her and to himself, was agitating him. He knew that he would spend much time working through that sentence.

'Let me tell you about myself,' he begged in an undertone, as she turned to him with a faint smile. 'I won't ask you to identify yourself as any but the youngest and least wicked of witches.'

'I'm not a fully-qualified witch, actually.'

'More of an enchantress?'

'I have been known, from time to time, to cast a very unobtrusive spell, nothing too intoxicating.'

'That's what I mean,' he said, 'that's what I'm menaced by, not what you've said about yourself but the idea, which I find terrifying, entirely novel. It tells me more about myself than I want to know.'

'That may be what Doctor Bettleheim intended.'

'People ought not to write such books; they're as unnerving as the Gospel; they incite to riot—of emotion at least. I only mean this: I've never in my life until this moment identified myself as any character in fairytale, as the citizen of a magical world. But when I think about it . . .'

'You see the application?'

'. . . I see the application, and the perception strips away a veil of rationalism from my view of myself, revealing a world of spell and enchantment. I was obviously born in the forest, the youngest son of a poor woodcutter whose spouse, worn out with hardship and toil, had yielded up her soul to the care of the Almighty at my birth. My father, labouring in the heart of the forest from sunrise till dusk, found himself unable to raise his three boys, the apples of his eye, without the aid of a motherly partner. He accordingly invited into his home as a second wife a rosy-cheeked lass who nurtured his sons in his absence, preparing their frugal meals and darning their worn clothes while the good woodcutter sang happily at his tasks in one or another arboreal dell.'

'Is any of this founded on fact?'

'I have a father.'

'Not a woodcutter, an eminent jurist. Had you a stepmother?'

'As it happens, no. But the facts aren't the important element. The imaginative drift—that's the important element. The stepmother found that she could command no place in the affections of the elder brothers. The oldest son, an upright sturdy lad, already half-grown at the time of his mother's death, would inherit his father's craft and his love of the forest life. In time he took his turn with the father at the handle of the great saw, felled the tall trees with energy and enthusiasm, and lived out a happy and useful life as his father's heir.'

'I know that boy,' said Cecy, 'and I rather like him.'

'The second son was a wayward youth who brooked no interference with his own conduct or his ready acceptance of his fate. The death of his mother affected him more than his brothers, somehow disturbing the foundations of his being. At the earliest opportunity he vanished from the little cottage deep in the shadows of the giant oaks and beeches, and was never seen there again. Long after, the stepmother learned that he had repaired to the great port city several days' journey from their home, and there succumbed to evil courses, wicked companions, luxurious living, drink, gaming, meeting at last an ignominious and early death.'

'You only have one brother, that I'm aware of.'

'But the third son, the youngest, the darling, for whose existence the mother had lain down her life, the child whom the father and his second wife had cared for most tenderly, this lad grew to young manhood as the spoiled favoured child of fortune. The eldest son might labour, his father regarded him little, but the youngest had only to whisper a wish in his sleep for it to be granted at once, often so as to allow the gift, or permission, or sum of money required, to greet him on his pillow as he opened his eyes next morning. And the eldest son took no offence; he smilingly encouraged his brother and wished him well.'

'Isn't your brother a year or two younger than you?'

'Miles? Two years. But he was born an eldest brother and he'll be an eldest brother till he dies. There are no favoured golden children in the distinguished law partnerships of Toronto.'

'I expect not.'

'Indeed no.'

'That seems a pity.'

'There you perceive some of the limitations of the way we live now. It isn't that we can do nothing for ourselves—an unredeemed colonialism—but that we can only do certain things for ourselves. The ably eccentric, the wickedly luna-tic, all that is attractive or spellbinding, these elements of life are not found here; our law disallows them; prudence casts no enchantment.'

'Alas,' cried Cecy, and he took her up and echoed her; they lamented chorally, as it were, 'alas, alas, *hélas, eheu*.'

'*Oi weh*,' said Cecy.

'*Ist mir*,'[3] finished John, and they chortled together; matters were going well, he saw. 'I too went into the world to seek my fortune,' he continued, 'bringing with me only my father's blessing, my dear brother's hearty good wishes, cheeks burning with my stepmother's farewell kisses. Soon I found myself in perils: dragons in dark caves, malevolent elves, witches speaking me fair but concealing fell purposes.'

'Oh, come on!'

'Visions, dreams, miraculous fountains.'

'There isn't a single miraculous fountain in Canada,' said Cecy.

'That's all you know! Mirrors in which the face of the beloved might be descried on certain special midnights. Who was it told me how to beguile Ata-lanta[4] from her pursuit of rule?'

Cecy glanced at Charlotte, now explaining to Bill de Savigny with great ani-mation that her husband would not return to the federal cabinet at any future time. Flamborough followed the glance and frowned.

---

[3]'Oh woe is me' (German).

[4]In classical mythology Atalanta was raised by a bear and by hunters after her father, the king, aban-doned her in a forest. As an adult she swore to remain a virgin because of an oracle predicting disaster if she married. Her accomplishments as a huntress led her father to take her back into the royal house-hold but with the proviso that she marry. She consented on condition that prospective suitors would first wager their lives against their ability to defeat her in a footrace. Many young men died before she was beaten by Melanion, who was aided by three golden apples plucked by Aphrodite from her sacred grove. As they ran he tossed one ahead of her; when she stopped to pick it up, he overtook her, dropped the others in her path, and crossed the finish line first. After their marriage Melanion and Atalanta angered Zeus by yielding to their passions while visiting a sacred shrine. For their sacrilege they were changed into lions—a doubly cruel punishment since, according to legend, lions mate only with leopards, not with each other.

He heard Charlotte say, 'After a certain point, there are limits to the uses of money.'

'What point is that?' asked Bill

'Golden apples, wasn't that how you did it?' asked Cecy.

'Precisely. I stole the three golden apples from the tree which grew in the sacred glade. I had been warned of the risk, but judged the reward worthy of any risk. I snatched the apples from the tree and advanced to the palace where the race was to be run. "Atalanta the swift", people called her; they said she had never been overtaken by a suitor and never would be. Those who failed in the race underwent strange metamorphoses—they put on weight, had to give up smoking and rich food, joined health clubs, took up jogging—became what they were. The king's golden daughter remained inviolate, high in the palace, lodged in the tallest tower, clad in the lightest of silks. No Adidas for her! I resolved to run against her, concealing the golden apples in my cloak. The race began; the fleet girl distanced me. I laboured far behind, then cast the first apple a long distance through the air. It rolled past the princess and was lost to her view in the grass. As she searched for it, beguiled like a child from her purpose, I sped past, building up a long lead against her resumption of the course. It was not long, however, before I heard her footsteps. This time I didn't wait. I launched the second golden sphere, a ring of light like the ring you've left on the tablecloth, a halo, spinning in the sunlight along a beguiling arc. Atalanta left the track at once, to the cheers of the crowd, and sought the apple in the tall grass. I didn't linger, I ran on ahead, hearing the encouragement of the fellows in the cheap seats who badly wanted me to win and give the princess, as they thought a well-deserved comeuppance. As I ran, I wondered what form her punishment might take. Having me for a consort would, I decided, be no true chastisement, no matter how royal she might be. She now had two apples folded into her blouse. She might not chase a third, I thought, and when she caught up to me the finish line was drawing near. Then I had to calculate carefully how long to retain the last of the three, and when to throw it. She might ignore it, having been lured from the path twice before, or she might not. I had to trust my luck, and it held. It has always held. Fifty yards from the tape, I hurled the last prize past her, throwing her a curve, making the apple bounce at her feet, then rebound crazily to one side. She paused, half-started, turned aside, looked for the tempting gleam, located it, and left the race as I sprinted past.'

'How well you do the play-by-play!'

'Yes, don't I?' The whole table was listening in silence, even Char, who had never heard their courtship recounted in these terms.

'Then I had an inspiration. I saw that I could not win by a stratagem, for such a triumph would be no triumph at all. I stood drinking in the cheers and the urgings, feeling the backslappings of wellwishers who wanted to see Atalanta done down good and proper, and I chose not to finish the race unless we could saunter to the line together. As she approached me, actually juggling the three apples, if you can imagine it, she smiled submissively, threw the apples to me, one, two, three, and held out her arm for me to lead her captive to her father. But I stepped aside, bowed, motioned her past me and followed her across the finish line. She won the race. She took me willingly as her consort, and encouraged me to ripen into kingship.'

The whole assembly applauded as Flamborough finished, a soft hand-clapping, muted but emphatic, and Aunt Frances exclaimed with happy inspiration, 'What magnanimity! And how much we need it in our politics!' The guests looked from Charlotte to John, expecting some more or less public declaration and receiving only a disclaimer. 'There's no place for magnanimity in Canadian public life,' said Flamborough. His wife smiled at him and nodded; the guests sighed; the dinner party dispersed. At his back, he heard Cecy Howard muttering, 'What became of the prodigal son, after he came home?'

A mistake to confuse folklore with divine revelation, thought Flamborough much later. The tales of the golden boy, the favoured youngest on whose behalf fountains speak and sorcerers lend tricky rings, have nothing in common with that one great emblem of thoughtlessness and subsequent enlightenment, the tale of the boy who took his patrimony and went into a far country, spent all he had and was reduced to begging for the husks rejected by the swine.[5] Biblical analogies had always held a supreme importance in his life. He had tried to live out their implications, had held fiercely in his mind the story of the Samaritan, the descent of the archangel Raphael to the well, the exile into Egypt, into Babylon, and the exile's God-bidden, God-aided return.[6] These forms of narrative had made him, he thought, the forty-one year old perplexed, confused, seeking man that he now was. He didn't believe that the categories of romance or folklore really obtained. He had been fortunate—much more than merely fortunate—all his life. The sentence which proposes that much will be demanded of him who has received much had seemed both merciful and just. He stood ready, as he thought, to cope with the exactions of justice. That he had arrived where he was in a state of unqualified contentment, unadulterated by feelings of guilt or fear of retribution, had seemed to him the fruit of special grace. A cloudlessly happy marriage, a spouse who continued marvellously beautiful and wonderfully loving, freedom from any want or the necessity of the least hope deferred, a promising and extravagantly healthy pair of children, girl and boy, almost every blessing, all this had come unearned. He knew that such a fate could not be earned, that in some final sense nothing was wholly earned, neither bliss nor despair. He couldn't guess why all this had been given to him, when it might perfectly easily have been withheld, bestowed upon some other. He had nobody to envy, that sin was denied him. He had to trust, but in whom should he trust? Trust in God was not the same exercise as walking a tightrope. When he felt—as he sometimes felt, for humanity will quail as much in the face of blessedness as desolation—that an axe was somewhere slowly, quietly, determinedly, unavoidably being sharpened against some fearful grindstone, he knew that the apprehension was base, groundless. His luck would surely hold.

Dinner at the de Savignys' with Aunt Frances, Cecy Howard, the airy banter

---

[5]This parable, told by Jesus, can be found in Luke 15:11-32. The prodigal son was welcomed back by his father, to the consternation of his jealous older brother.

[6]For the story of the good Samaritan, see Luke 10:37. Raphael is traditionally associated with the angel who troubles the pool of Bethesda (John 5). The Bible not only recounts the periods of the Jews' exile in Egypt before being led to Canaan by Moses, and during their captivity in Babylon in the sixth century B.C., but also contains stories of many individual exiles, including those of Joseph, Ishmael, and the prodigal son.

of his dear Char, the inquiries about his fated, angel-protected, career, anxieties about the future of the nation, urgings to take up this or that banner, began to coalesce in his thoughts into a significant pattern, proposing a fundamental personal dilemma. He put the matter to himself in this way: most of us, probably all of us, rule our lives not according to what is actually happening out there in the air around us where physical beings come and go, the world of determinable social and historical fact, where the battle of Waterloo took place and the historical Jesus was in fact executed on such-and-such a day. We do not form our expectations of ourselves or others according to the rule of historical causality. Instead we act out our stories: we are the woodcutter's third son, or his first, or the pitiable wastrel second. He knew six men who seemed to him to qualify at first inspection as the bad son who went to the big city and got into trouble. Legal practice was full of people who were finding themselves at one or another stage of that sad story. They misappropriated funds from their imagining that the action was what must be found in the next-to-last chapter. In the last chapter they would either be transported to Australia or hanged. Social reality never broke into these automatic fantasies.

Bettelheim's book was dangerous precisely because it substituted the world of folklore and fairy tale for the world of religious revelation. In one setting action is compulsive, engineered, in the other illuminated and free. The imitation of Christ is not the aping of a fixed model, but a dizzying exercise in spontaneous perfection, whereas conjuration and spell depend upon mechanical cause-and-effect. Speak the formula and the three wishes will arbitrarily be granted. He began to dread the presence of the arbitrary and magical in his life. He wondered: what part of my conduct is virtuous, graceful, and truly spontaneous, and what part is acted out in the terms of fairy story, where things happen to me merely because I've been cast in a part? Sanctity was more gratuitous than unearned good fortune. The difficulty was to distinguish the two courses of life in their effect upon the soul.

He had been briefly in the cabinet as Secretary of State, and for some time before that Member of Parliament for a comfortable constituency in midtown Toronto. The newspapers called him 'the member for Varsity', and were not slow to predict that his tenure in cabinet would not be long, and they were right. He had found the daily routine of house attendance, constant contact with the news media, the conduct of his ministry, cabinet meetings, an intolerable burden. You could not exist in that medium and attempt to draw the breath of thought, as fish extract oxygen from water. The thick soup, in which he and his cabinet colleagues swam perforce, contained many gases in its structure, some noxious, some nourishing, none food for thought.

He had been elected because of his book, a famous book, even for some an entertaining book, though read from first page to last by none who professed to find it entertaining. Long acquaintance with readers and long meditation on the fruits of authorship—even amateur and unpremeditated authorship—had made Flamborough aware that he must never press a reader who claimed a knowledge of his book to display that knowledge circumstantially. People remembered very little of what they read, and it seemed graceless to cross-question them upon their claims.

'I enjoyed it so much!'

'I'm so glad. Which parts did you like best?'

This question was always unspoken. Flamborough had a nice care for the feelings of the folks who were kind enough to admit to having heard of *Legality and Society*, a work sometimes described as 'a seminal Canadian book', though never by its author—with a straight face. Fifteen years of teaching jurisprudence at the university law school, and meditation for the whole of the time on the public notion of law as it exists in Canada, had caused him to review in a disinterested spirit some of the features of Canadian life whose legal underpinnings seemed to him particularly obscure, especially noteworthy from the point of view of the consenting governed: the use of injunctions to terminate labour disputes, the rules proposed by federally appointed administrative boards for their own conduct, the concealment of various forms of police activity from the officers of the state charged with the maintenance of legality. These and many less significant shapings of the legal by government authorities had struck him, not so much because of the naively greedy behaviour of governments—which is a human constant—but chiefly because of what the governed would put up with. Canadians, he had concluded, possessed no personal sense of private right, or public right, or of the limitations of the authority of government. The authority extended as far as ignorance and the attitudes of the petty crook—shared by most of the citizenry—allowed. The government could do what it could successfully conceal from inspection.

He saw that there had never existed amongst Canadians, from the nation's beginnings, a clear, formal, understanding of what the law was, what its ethical derivate, legality, might be. In the conduct of human affairs and in the perilous defense of human liberty, what matters is not so much what the constitution of the state, the positive enactments on the books, allow, but rather what the people conceive to be allowed and disallowed by their shared, profound, implicit agreement about the nature of law, and the constitution of legality in psychological fact. The Canadian notion of criminality was highly peculiar, having almost nothing to do with precedent, statute, enactment, constitutionality. Few or no Canadians had any notion of what might constitute a treasonable act under the existing rule of law. No Canadian knew or cared what a constitution was, or how it might function.

Jewish law, Roman law, British common law, the code of Hammurabi,[7] all partake in some measure of the essential nature of law and jurisprudence, and all address themselves to questions of testament, property, contract, the nature of corporations, criminality, the state of being a legal process. But each compendium of law has its own distinct political, ethical, and social character. A man will conceive his personal freedoms precisely depending upon the legal climate in which he has been nurtured. Under one notion of legality he will view himself as the favoured darling of magical fortune, under another as the prodigal son, under a third as the stone rejected by the builders, under a fourth as, say, the great Gatsby.

In *Legality and Society* Flamborough had denounced Canadians and their soci-

---

[7]One of the first legal codes in history, developed by the king of Babylon c. 1700 B.C.

ety, never mind superficial differences of language and culture which were always local and positive in nature and easily resolved in the long run, for ignorance and uncaringness about the law itself, its nature, its constitutive place in their values, their hearts, their collective and their individual consciences. They were a people without thought for the law, who had taken their positive enactments from hither and yon without a care for contradictions.

A Canadian, he had concluded, is a man who will do anything he can get away with, as private citizen or prime minister. He didn't want to be such a man himself, and he sought some deeper source of what we may and may not do in himself, in the nature of a consenting people, and finally of course in the divine nature.

And so he was led in the end to wonder why he, alone among Canadians, was impelled to write a book so much in the stance and attitude of Jeremiah,[8] his favourite Old Testament author. From whence did he derive the moral authority to write such a book? Wasn't he simply a man who had been endowed with every gift and found them all without salt or savour? What was the matter with him anyway, who had been given so much and continued to want everything?

Here, exactly here, lay the danger of sin. In the current phrase, he had it all. Voices sang to him from television commercials about a popular make of car which 'had it all', and he knew that the commercial was inaccurate. Nothing has it all: nobody has it all. There rang in his imagining ears a loftier advertisement, 'Praise God from Whom all blessings flow'. There could be no reconciliation of the conflicting assertions of magical folklore and sacred scripture. Such a reconciliation had been the characteristic undertaking of every great imaginative writer from the age of Dante and Chaucer until the present decline of religious assent had begun, and then poetry had resigned the task and sunk into magic. And it simply wouldn't do!

What he seemed to require was one hell of a temptation, some situation in which he absolutely must forbear. Hence Cecy Howard. He had to see and know and yet abstain, endure. Nothing had tested him; how should he presume to take the stance of Jeremiah? He waited weeks, then without either concealing his action or calling attention to it, he went to the telephone in his study one evening after dinner and invited Cecy to lunch later in the week. He would court temptation. The still small voice whispered, 'Don't do it!' But he did after all feel so strongly impelled . . .

Theological dialectic has been over this ground for two millenia. Can one, should one go looking for temptation, if one leads an effortlessly sinless life? Might one in fact turn out to be that fated person, the hero to whom nothing whatsoever happened?

He said to Char, 'I'm taking Cecy Howard to lunch at the club tomorrow. Would you like to come along? It might be fun. It might be an act of kindness.'

Char studied him expressionlessly. 'You don't want me.'

'I always want you. Everywhere, all the time. No question.'

'Oh God, you're so smug.'

'How do you mean?'

[8]One of the major Hebrew prophets, best known for his lamentations about the decline in public morality.

'You've got it all arranged just the way you want it, haven't you, with the grand public image, the distinguished career, the loving wife, the good children. The darling of the gods.'

Flamborough looked at his wife in amazement; he couldn't remember ever hearing her take this line, speak in this tone. I don't understand, he thought. I'm not smug. I'm deeply concerned. How can that be smug? He felt his face growing warm. He thought of his brother Miles, at this time of day most likely half-reclining in an enormous leather chair, studying the profit-and-loss statement of a Québec corporation and drafting representations to the ministry about tax protection. Miles had no personal responsibilities. He simply sat on boards and saw that payrolls were met, drew up contracts with loopholes, refused to talk to journalists, exercised the grand Canadian prudence and got away with it.

'Well say something, for goodness' sake and take that hurt-little-boy look off your face. I hate that look. My God, the nerve of you. "I'm taking Cecy Howard to lunch tomorrow." Do you imagine that my presence would provide an air of legitimacy for your sordid goings-on? Keep it all out in the open, eh? Let the world know that there's nothing going on.'

'What are you talking about, Lottie? I can't understand you.'

'He can't understand me,' she echoed. 'Don't "Lottie" me!'

'Lottie' had been an early pet name, long abandoned. She was not the sort of person who would accept childish endearment in maturity.

'It slipped out,' said Flamborough, genuinely confused.

'Oh, go and entertain your mistress, see if I care.'

'Mistress? Charlotte, you must be joking.'

'Do you think I wasn't watching you the other night at the de Savignys? I've never been so humiliated . . . you didn't address a civil word to me the whole time. You were absorbed in that child, and mighty ridiculous you looked, I'll tell you. Why she's twenty years younger than you are.'

'Fourteen,' said John.

'The whole thing's absurd.'

'If you'd heard what we were saying . . .'

'I don't want to hear what you were saying. Your whole trouble, John, is that bloody verbal facility. You think because you can explain yourself so perfectly that anything goes. I've heard you a hundred times explaining how everything's permitted you because you're so obviously mother's spoiled darling.'

This was accurate but unlooked-for.

'Perhaps we'd better not say any more,' he said stiffly.

His wife danced up and down in rage. 'That's it, that's it, that's so perfectly you. Get the thing going good and proper and then back out in the middle, leaving me like this.'

'I didn't start it,' he said defensively, and as the words crossed his lips he felt about twelve years old and laughter overtook him just when he least wanted to laugh.

'Oh you,' said Char, 'oh you . . .'

Flamborough left his house in confusion and distress. The last thing in the world he wanted to admit to was smugness. Anything but that. He began, and saw that he began, to defend himself by thinking about what he had said, wrapping the fresh, violent feelings in a cocoon of moral pronouncement, 'Smug.' 'Mother's spoiled darling.' 'Mistress.' Where had he been while all this was brewing up?

He wondered whether he could risk communicating some of his bewilderment to Cecy, when he encountered her at lunch next day. I will ply her with food and drink, he thought, trying to put the matter in a humorous light. They sat in a restaurant known for seafood and picked at sole, salad, the remnants of their earlier conversation.

'. . . whatever can have induced you to say anything to your wife? A child of ten would know better.'

'I'm incapable of deception,' he said gloomily. There was no way to disentangle the threads of truth and falsehood in this statement, he thought. 'I've said two things spontaneously in the last month, and both utterances have caused me immense trouble.'

'What are they?'

' "I'm the woodcutter's third son," and "I'm taking Cecy Howard to lunch tomorrow. Would you care to come along?" '

'Those were very foolish things to say. You may think in that way perhaps, but you must never say so.'

He looked directly at her, taking her in from the discreet sleekness of her crown to the modest concealment of her legs beneath the table. How attractive she was, and how absolutely unapproachable!

'One of the most remarkable things that's ever happened to me, our encounter at the de Savignys.'

'In what way?'

'Oh, I've no intention of making any kind of irregular avowal to you, Cecy. Be calm. Relax! I can see—how I can see—that you are an attractive woman. But you don't attract me, you've made me see that I'm trying to operate under two contradictory notions of character. Not just my character, which isn't very important, but character as we all enact it. I've been role-playing, as they say nowadays, and I've been autonomous at the same time, been myself. And it doesn't seem to work out.'

'It's unthinkable.'

'Oh it's thinkable, all too thinkable, but it's ruinous to think in that way. It divides the soul. It turns me against myself. I'm neither a fairy prince nor a pilgrim.'

'There must be some alternative,' said Cecy.

'The uses of enchantment,' said Flamborough, with considerable bitterness. 'Does your mentor propose a future for these illusions? This . . . this . . . psychiatrist!' He spoke the word like a curse.

'He seems to feel that sleepers ought not, on the whole, to wake. Keep your illusions, cherish your glories, live in your fairy tale.'

'I won't be able to do that,' said Flamborough.

Cecy observed him closely. 'I didn't think so,' she said gravely. She covered his palm with hers and said, 'Smugness is the homage hypocrisy pays to virtue.' The observation did not materially help matters, so she rose and left him sitting there.

He drank more coffee, paid his bill, then sat for a quarter of an hour, leaning his elbows on the narrow table and trying to dispel the mists of romance. He began to see that as they cleared away they would reveal him to himself naked, shivering in the blast, alone on a withered plain which at its verge began to slope downhill.

1980

D.G. Jones

b. 1929

Douglas Gordon Jones is one of the few Canadian writers at home in both English- and French-Canadian cultures. Born in Bancroft, Ont., he was educated at McGill University (B.A., 1952) and Queen's University (M.A., 1954). He has taught literature at the Royal Military College, Guelph Agricultural College (now the University of Guelph), Bishop's University, and, since 1963, at the Université de Sherbrooke. After moving to Quebec in the early sixties he became one of the founding editors of *Ellipse* (1969-), a literary journal in which poems by French- and English-Canadian poets appear in their original language and in translation.

Spare and strongly visual, Jones's poetry is concerned with man's relationship to a landscape that is both inviting and frightening. One can see his perspective on landscape changing, however, in the five collections he has published since 1957: *Frost on the Sun* (1957); *The Sun is Axeman* (1961); *Phrases from Orpheus* (1967); *Under the Thunder the Flowers Light Up the Earth* (1977), winner of a Governor General's Award; and *A Throw of Particles: The New and Selected Poetry of D.G. Jones* (1983). While in early poems such as 'Beautiful Creatures Brief as These' the voice is that of an observer detached from his surroundings, in later poems such as

'For Eve' it tends to be more personal and to suggest that man can achieve union with the land. In recent poetry (for example, 'A Garland for Milne'), Jones depicts man as both a product of his landscape and a creator of it through his imaginative abilities.

Many of Jones's poems (like those of Jay Macpherson) are written from the perspective of archetypal personae, such as Orpheus, Orestes, and the archangel Michael. Other poems focus on historical figures such as Archibald Lampman, David Milne, and Alex Colville. For Jones, however, they are all avatars of Adam, his most important archetype (as in 'For Eve').

An important feature of the Eden myth in this poetry is that Adam, the namer of all created things, cannot define his own nature without losing his place in Eden. The various speakers in Jones's poetry face the same situation as Adam, who must either designate himself superior to the landscape and remain obediently in the garden, or leave the garden for the wilderness and replace divine judgement with his own. Those who, in Jones's later work, elect the wilderness discover, amid its death and violence, their own true identity.

In *Butterfly on Rock* (1970), the first important thematic study of Canadian literature, Jones uses the Adam archetype to extend Northrop Frye's notion that Canadian identity is based on a garrison mentality: a way of thinking in which psychic walls have been erected against the reality of a frightening, alien wilderness. Jones suggests that

the world of Canadian literature is an Old Testament world, it is a world of Adam separated from his Creator and cast out of Eden to wander in the wilderness. It is a world of the scattered tribes of Israel, in exile from the Old Kingdom and not yet restored to the New, in bondage to foreign powers, aliens in their own land, tied to the law of the fathers from which their hearts tend nonetheless continually to turn away. It is a world of angry patriarchs and rebellious children, and of the prophets of the wrath of God. It is a world in which life in all its fullness remains distinctly a promise rather than an actuality. Its prophets go into the desert to listen to the still small voice, to wrestle with the angel, or to discover the mountain of God, the Sinai, Ararat, or Eden from which a Moses, Noah, or New Adam shall bring down the word and reveal the new order of the world. It is an Old Testament world which implies, sometimes without much hope, sometimes with great confidence, its completion in the New . . . Canadian literature exhibits not only a sense of exile, or alienation from a vital community, but also a sense of expectation, or restoration to that community. Here we find the exiled Old Adam. Here we also find the sleeping Adam or dreaming Adam, who is a somewhat different figure. He is the sleeping giant, the major man, or, if you like, the personification of a world order, lost or as yet undiscovered . . . Here we are placed in exile. Our pivot-picture is that of Adam, once the major man at home in Eden but now cast out in the wilderness.

Jones sees in Canadian writing a development from the image of the colonist as Adam, vainly trying to keep his walled Eden intact, to that of the Canadian as A.M. Klein's 'nth Adam', out of whom the garden springs as he 'names' himself part of the wilderness. Canadians, expelled from the Old World garden, first suffered as outcasts in their own land; believing that there ought to be a benevolent universe, a divinely created garrison, they found instead a hostile landscape. Finally recognizing all garrisons to be false Edens, Canadians now, according to Jones, have the potential to become a new kind of Adam who can accept the wilderness itself as home and garden. In a 1973 article that in many ways serves as an epilogue to *Butterfly on Rock*, Jones expands on this new possibility: he sees a Canadian who is now ready to live 'in his own imagination . . . in his own myth larger than life'. He and his surroundings are finally real, not abstract ideals or models of a lost way of life: 'He is Adam in Eden, unused to the place but nevertheless making himself at home' ('Myth, Frye and the Canadian Writer', *Canadian Literature*, 55, 1973).

While associated with the Canadian mythopoeic writers such as Frye and Macpherson, Jones is in many ways a modern Romantic, attempting to come to terms with the dehumanizing aspects of a technological world. This can be seen not only in his writing, with its focus on man's need to recreate the garden, but in his choice of rural life in North Hatley, Que.

Beautiful Creatures Brief as These

For Jay Macpherson

Like butterflies but lately come
From long cocoons of summer
These little girls start back to school
To swarm the sidewalks, playing-fields,
And litter air with colour.

So slight they look within their clothes,
Their dresses looser than the Sulphur's wings,[1]
It seems that even if the wind alone
Were not to break them in the lofty trees,
They could not bear the weight of *things*.   10

And yet they cry into the morning air
And hang from railings upside down
And laugh, as though the world were theirs
And all its buildings, trees, and stones
Were toys, were gifts of a benignant sun.

1961

[1]That is, the sulphur butterfly's wings.

I Thought There Were Limits

I thought there were limits, Newtonian
Laws of emotion—

I thought there were limits to this falling away,
This emptiness. I was wrong.

The apples, falling, never hit the ground.

So much for grass, and animals—
Nothing remains,
No sure foundation on the rock. The cat

Drifts, or simply dissolves.

L'homme moyen sensuel[1]   10
Had better look out: complete
Deprivation brings

Dreams, hallucinations which reveal

[1]The average sensual man, i.e. the average man, more sensual than intellectual.

The sound and fury of machines
Working on nothing—which explains

God's creation: *ex nihilo fecit.*[2]

Wrong again. I now suspect
The limit is the sea itself,
The limitless.

So, neither swim nor float. Relax.   20
The void is not so bleak.

Conclude: desire is but an ache,
An absence. It creates
A dream of limits

And it grows in gravity as that takes shape.

1967

[2]Out of nothing, he made [it].

For Eve

It is the reverberations of silence,
The sound of the waves, washing,
Washing, washing in on the stones.

And the one stone, emerging
Wet in the sunlight, gone
Wet in the silence, emerging

In the curtseying world. The days
Are full of clouds without design.
The steadying wind. And

I love you for the fear in your eyes   10
And your beauty like a generous stone
Washing away, in sleep, in the sun!

Because you are beautiful, dying,
And because there is nothing—
On the certain ground that is no

Ground—nothing to fear.
I would laugh, cry, kiss you all over,
Hold you away, in my arms.

For there is nothing like this
Except everything, and they do not know it,   20
The stones, diving, emerging.

And our noises are certainly silence,
Our permanent waves the dream.
Our delight is the wind

As we know it is, never believe it,
Know it is, deep in the silence
Which is continuous sound.

1967

From 'Kate, These Flowers . . . (The Lampman Poems)'[1]

ii
Kisses are knowledge, Kate
aphasia[2] confounds us with a new
   tongue
        too Pentecostal,[3] too
Eleusinian,[4] perhaps, for us
moderate Anglicans

You blush and the immoderate blood
riots like a rose
        we are both
exposed   10
       I who hate Sundays
dream how I will boldly
rush out and overnight paint
Ottawa crimson
         I come
secretly to the fold, would find
election[5] in your mouth

iii
Wild carrot, daisy, buttercup
I scatter words in the air
like your bouquet
          petal, sepal, leaf
delicate explosions

[1]Written in response to Archibald Lampman's suppressed sonnet sequence to Katherine Waddell; see Vol. I, p. 177 and p. 189.
[2]Partial or total loss of the ability to articulate ideas, resulting from brain damage; here used figuratively with regard to the dysfunction.
[3]Here an allusion to 'speaking in tongues'; Pentecostal Christians, when they believe themselves to be possessed by the Holy Ghost, can speak in obscure and unknown languages (of which they have no previous knowledge), in emulation of the disciples' being 'filled with the Holy Ghost' on Pentecost, the seventh Sunday after Easter (Acts 2).
[4]Of the mysteries of Eleusis, rites celebrated by ancient Greeks, the secrets of which were so well kept that little about them has ever been discovered.
[5]Salvation.

        prestidigitations, Kate
        rabbits from hats, from atoms
        instant nebulae

                    thus fields
        mimic your grace, thus words   10
        rearticulate the trace
        of outcast energy

                        All day the wind
        sun took tresses, ribbons, dress
        Enna's vale[6] remembered less
        stripped of its flowering text

        v
        Puritan or paradox? this land
        arctic, temperate
                        white
        like your small breasts, yet
        explosive to the sun

        slim margins underwrite the flowers
        nudging through snow
        ours too
                    our kind of spare
        wordless joy   10

                        this country where
        desire becomes restraint
        refractory, silence
        our orator
                        and thus apparent
        paradox
                    until the petalled flesh
        speak as to the deaf and blind

        x
        Gone, love's body, like a field
        reclaimed by winter
        all its flowers, exhausted
        sick of passion, flesh itself
        surrendered to the uniform
        Euclidian space: blank wall
        shut door, blind discreetly drawn

        illusory propriety: beneath the surface
        nothing is dissolved

[6]'. . . the place where the god of Hades presumably carried off Persephone, while, according to Milton, she was gathering flowers, "herself a fairer flower" ' (Jones, in a letter). Previously printed as 'Etna's vale'; here emended.

stones in the wet weather   10
nudge through snow, and the black
orphaned boughs, and grass
whispering of the humpy world

xi
Loneliness becomes us, we
advance through separations, learning
to love cold skies, empty
even to the last high
hail and farewell of birds
arrowing south
                    wilderness
waste fields become us

thistles matted with their own seed
haggard thorn trees   10
originals
                    ourselves, or mere
reticulations[7] of the wind
nameless
                    bright precipitates of our desire
scattered in grass

xiii
Milkweed unpacks itself
riddling the wind with packaged
roots, parachutes, poems
ordnance for a spring offensive

Winter, then, and wars

                          and memory
lays cut flowers in
empty carpels[8]
                    absurd
yet from absurdity our love   10
fits out an underground
resistance

                Who foresaw?
increasing violence accompanies
technique, the empty self

heaven is a mortal flower

1977

---

[7]Networks.
[8]The female organs of the flower; each is composed of a modified leaf forming one or more sections
of the pistil.

The Diamond Sutra[1]

For Reina and Nick Troobiscoff

Just because you don't know
anything about this island[2] (red roofs and
fishermen's huts between mountains
or what it means to be dining out
at Diamond House, the walls
flapping in the Caribbean night, is no reason
to be not there

the problem is to keep the air
clear
      to keep the lungs clear   10
especially in the morning (the bowels
are another matter
             to keep the mind
empty, no glass
            and why not precisely
here where the night with a cool
counterpoint of tree frogs washes
through the whole house, old boards
white-painted lintels and rafters, a
coming and going, the mind   20
free now from the menacing click
of the picture window
               anyway, dancing
it was good, it was not
necessary to remind yourself
the price of oil is international
the Pitons[3] plunging into the sea-bed
rise again slowly in North America
the world being one, seamless, and also
a placenta of islands   30
            it was good
to see drawings, the paintings, someone
actively pulling together
burlap, the baggy swatches of Michigan
Columbia, Saskatoon, fibers and letters
fixed in the pigments, discovering
a new spectrum
          even as we
with our various fibers, word-strands

[1]The oldest extant printed book (China, 11 May A.D. 868); the Diamond Sutra belongs to a class of sacred Buddhist texts that are intended to present the concentrated 'Perfection of Transcendental Wisdom'; this sutra is a very compressed scripture in which spiritual intuition takes precedence over conventional logic.
[2]'. . . the island in question is the West Indian island of St. Lucia, where many of the old plantations or plantation houses were given the names of jewels—this old remnant, in the poem, being Diamond House, which suggested the title' (Jones, in a letter).
[3]Two cone-like peaks at the entrance to the harbour of the town of Soufrière in St Lucia; they are among the most photographed landmarks in the Caribbean.

curious fragments, improvise   40
an island canvas, drinking
of the night

it is not knowledge, no, but a constant
reintegration

it is, Ross[4] gone, his and also the existing
open architecture, which someone
keeps changing
                    or the gently unravelling
music of the Steel Band that drifts
each morning up from the black and white   50
fake frigate rounding the cape
(the diminished excursionists peering
through the bright sounds to beach
buildings, the palm trees half-hiding
the oil-tanks of the harbour

                    air now
and light surf breaking, wash
round the rocks below
                    the world keeps
dismantling the syntax, escaping   60
a final sentence
                    Penelope weaving
and unweaving, night, day,[5] to
avoid closure

            the sudden gust
rattling the banana leaves

the glint, remembered, of Nick's glasses
gold in the lamplight
                    or the little, running
dance he does   70
when the gravity of the situation
is suddenly lifted

1977

[4] "Ross" is Ross Kembar, a Canadian architect, whose family had a house in Soufrière and who worked in St. Lucia for a number of years before returning to Canada. He had spoken of the idea of "open architecture", where one can re-arrange walls and inner space according to changing needs.'
' "Nick" [mentioned in line 67] is Nick Troobitscoff . . . a manager/owner of the main hotel just outside Soufrière. At the time he was wearing gold-rimmed glasses' (Jones, in a letter).
[5] Penelope, whose husband Odysseus was absent for twenty years, wove a shroud by day and unwove it by night in order to fend off her suitors.

Introduction to *Butterfly on Rock*

Having reached the Pacific, Canadians have begun to turn back on themselves, to create that added dimension Teilhard de Chardin calls the noosphere[1] or, to put it more simply, Canadian culture. Of course, we have been at this for some time, but to use the words of Robert Frost quoted elsewhere in this study, more than ever before we have arrived at a point where we recognize, not only that the land is ours, but that we are the land's.[2]

The north remains, and the cultural implications of that future settlement have hardly been felt. But our westward expansion is complete, and in the pause to reflect upon ourselves we become increasingly aware that our identity and our view of the world are no longer determined by our experience of Europe, but by our experience of life as it is lived between two oceans in a stretch of land that has been referred to as a few acres of snow and, more recently, as America's attic.[3] It is apparent that we must now move into our own cultural house, for we are no longer at home in the houses of others. As John Newlove says in his poem 'The Pride':[4]

> we stand alone,
> we are no longer lonely
> but we have roots,
> and the rooted words
> recur in the mind, mirror, so that
> we dwell on nothing else, in nothing else,
> touched, repeating them,
> at home freely
> at last, in amazement.

This book dwells deliberately on some of the words that have taken root in Canadian poetry and fiction during the past three generations. It is not primarily a survey, nor does it attempt to deal fully with any single author or work. Rather, by isolating certain themes and images it attempts to define more clearly some of the features that recur in the mind, the mirror of our imaginative life.

Undoubtedly there are other important themes and images to be studied in Canadian literature, but those explored here have been singled out by virtue of their recurrence in a wide variety of authors and often over a period of several generations. The study touches on most of the principal poets writing between 1880 and the present as well as on many of the novels that have provoked serious discussion. Still others might have been cited. Thus, though there may be indi-

[1]Literally the globe of the mind; Pierre Teilhard de Chardin (1881-1955), Jesuit theologian, scientist, and philosopher, introduced this neologism into theoretical thinking in 1949, borrowing from the philosophical term 'noölogy', which distinguished a mental or spiritual life as separate from a physical one, and from the old Ptolemaic universe of a succession of spheres enclosing one another; Teilhard's 'noösphere' was the newest step of evolution in which the realm of man's collective mind encompasses the physical reality of the world, or the 'biosphere', and thus can manipulate the 'laws of nature', to create a better world.
[2]Frost's line in 'The Gift Outright' is 'The land was ours before we were the land's'.
[3]A phrase from 'Poem on Canada' in *The White Centre* (1946) by Patrick Anderson; this is also the inspiration for Robertson Davies' title to his collection of essays, *A Voice from the Attic* (1960); 'a few acres of snow' was Voltaire's dismissive description of Canada.
[4](1968); this poem about the Indians of western Canada ends, 'we/are their people, come/back to life again.'

vidual writers who ignore these themes or who treat them quite differently, there can be little doubt that they are central and characteristic themes in Canadian literature. To study them closely should reveal essential features of both individual writers and the literature generally. It may also reveal something of the Canadian temper.

As the last remarks suggest, the approach here is cultural and psychological rather than purely aesthetic or literary. It parallels that of such critics as Northrop Frye[5] and Warren Tallman, and the present discussion can only hope to confirm and amplify many of their observations. Such an approach has its dangers, too. It can lead into a discussion of general ideas that may blur the distinctions between individual authors or grossly simplify the complex perceptions of an individual work. It assumes a relationship between literature and life that can never be defined with precision and that invariably involves one in a maze of circular arguments. One can never be sure that, as one reader suggested, the result is not simply another poem. If so, it is a possible poem, and one that is well worth writing. In other words, it seems worth the risks. And whatever we call the result, it must be judged on the basis of the evidence it presents and the experience of readers over a period of time.

Meanwhile, the persistent concern of widely different authors with similar themes and images certainly suggests that the individual writers share a common cultural predicament. It may also suggest that they participate in and help to articulate a larger imaginative world, a supreme fiction of the kind that embodies the dreams and nightmares of a people, shapes their imaginative vision of the world, and defines, as it evolves, their cultural identity.

Louis Dudek does not go that far. In his article 'Nationalism in Canadian Poetry',[6] he argues that many Canadian poets, both French and English, share a common cultural predicament, but that it is one defined almost exclusively by an inherited literary tradition. Their preoccupation with the theme of a national identity is simply a reflection of the nineteenth-century Romanticism within which Canadian poetry first developed. Undoubtedly there is some truth in this argument, but it strikes me as superficial and as involving a rather narrow conception of what is meant by a national identity. Quite apart from the fact that the spirit of nineteenth-century nationalism is by no means dead, in Canada as in other parts of the world, the question of a national identity is not to be equated with simple national pride, political independence, or some inevitably chauvinistic self-assertion. For Canadians, as for others, it is a question of recognizing and articulating a view of life within which they can live with some assurance, or at least with some conviction. That is, it is less a question of nationalism than of an imaginative stance towards the world, towards nature and culture, past and present, the life of the body and the life of the mind, the fact of death. It is a question of finding a satisfying interpretation of these fundamental elements in human life so that one can take a stand, act with definitive convictions, have an identity. As John Newlove puts it, it is a question of feeling at home.

---

[5] See Vol. 1, pp. 533-65 and also *The Bush Garden* (1971). Tallman's essay, 'The Wolf in the Snow' (*Canadian Literature* 5 & 6, 1960), was an early and influential thematic analysis of Canadian fiction.

[6] *Queen's Quarterly*, 75 (1968), 557-67.

Such are some of the questions explored in the work we shall study. Their treatment there should make it evident that the cultural predicament prompting different writers to take up the same themes is not defined simply by a literary tradition, but by the actual experience of many Canadians. It suggests to begin with that we have not always felt freely at home here, partly because of the influence of such traditions.

The first part of this study is devoted to the expression, in prose and in poetry, of a sense of exile, of being estranged from the land and divided within oneself. A number of voices have made the point that the conventional culture, largely inherited from Europe, fails to reflect the sometimes crude but authentic experience of our lives and that this experience is in urgent need of expression in native terms. There is something that grows in us, says John Newlove:

> and idles about and hides
> until the moment is due—
>
> the knowledge
> of our origins, and where
> we are in truth,
> whose land this is
> and is to be.

Though Newlove asserts that this knowledge will spring upon us out of our own mouths when the moment is due, many have felt the moment to be long overdue. They attest to a failure to give voice to this knowledge, and they dramatize the sense of frustration that attends such a failure.

The knowledge of our origins to which Newlove's poem refers is a knowledge of our American rather than our European roots. 'The Pride' centres upon the life of the North American Indians, and it is our North American inheritance embodied here in the Indians that idles about and hides, waiting to be given a voice. On that point many of the writers we are to study agree: the voice that demands to be heard is the voice of the land.

Chapters 2 and 3 might well have been called the mirror of landscape. The analysis of various novels and poems in which the land plays a prominent role reveals that the land is associated with the most vital elements in the lives of the characters and that these vital elements are frequently suppressed by the conventional life of the community. Frustrated, they remain inarticulate or unconscious. The drama then centres upon the division or, more seriously, the antagonism between culture and nature. Society and its official representatives are pitted against the land; men are divided against each other and against themselves.

In his 'Conclusion' to *Literary History of Canada,*[7] Northrop Frye offered an explanation for the antagonism between culture and nature that informs a good deal of our literature. It is, he suggested, a literary reflection of the colonial mentality, which is, practically by definition, a garrison mentality. Again and again we are confronted by a garrison culture confronting a hostile wilderness. The present study confirms and illustrates this point. But it would also suggest that Frye's metaphor may be extended.

[7]See Vol. I, pp. 536-65.

The division between culture and nature dramatized in some of the literature goes far beyond any purely Canadian colonialism; it can only be considered to reflect an antagonism towards nature characteristic of western culture generally. It will not disappear with the disappearance of the colonial mentality in Canada. A book like Leonard Cohen's *Beautiful Losers* implies that western culture is itself a garrison culture confronting a hostile wilderness.

Given the tendency to discriminate the whole range of our experience into light and dark, western man has shown a marked inclination to ally himself wholly with the so-called forces of light in an all-out attack on the so-called forces of darkness. In the name of various spiritual or intellectual ideals he has embarked on a kind of holy war against the material world, the world of the flesh and the devil. Whether his ideal has been secular or divine, he has set himself against all that is mortal and seemingly irrational in nature, human and non-human. It is in this perspective that the hostile wilderness becomes, not just a Canadian wilderness but the whole natural universe. Only within such a perspective can the antagonism between culture and nature evident in the work of Leonard Cohen[8] or Frederick Philip Grove, E.J. Pratt or Archibald Lampman, be fully appreciated.

Here Canadian writers take up themes common to western literature. It is interesting to note how such themes are developed in native terms, to see the great flour mill in Grove's *The Master of the Mill* performing the same symbolic function as the coal mine in Lawrence's *Women in Love,* to see the Indian or the half-breed in various poems and stories playing something of the same role as the Congolese native in Conrad's *Heart of Darkness*. For it becomes clear that the world symbolized by D.C. Scott's Powassan,[9] by Newlove's Indians, as by the half-breed in a novel such as Howard O'Hagan's *Tay John,* is not only the undigested raw material of Canadian experience but all that is primitive in nature and man.

The need to make a transition from a garrison culture to one in which the Canadian will feel at home in his world makes itself felt at a time when western man generally feels compelled to make a similar transition. In this perspective the search for a Canadian identity cannot be divorced from that larger search for identity that provides a common theme in so much contemporary writing. Modern literature is filled with images of the exile, the outsider, the alienated man. The same man appears in Douglas LePan's *The Deserter* and, indeed, in Jay Macpherson's image of Adam wandering in the waste wood while Eve lies abandoned on the barren shore.[1]

The weakness of the colonial mentality is that it regards as a threat what it should regard as its salvation; it walls out or exploits what it should welcome and cultivate. The same weakness is inherent in the assumptions of western culture that lead man to view the universe as an enemy. Though he may be less inclined to view it, in a religious sense, as the playground of the devil, he is still inclined to regard it with a wary eye.

---

[8]See pp. 346-53; for Grove, Vol. I, pp. 257-83; for Pratt, Vol. I, pp. 283-335; for Lampman, Vol. I, pp. 177-94.
[9]Indian character in Scott's poetry ('Powassan's Drum').
[1]In the poem 'Eve in Reflection' from *The Boatman* (1959).

Not infrequently modern man stands like Job before a creation that, however magnificent, appears violent, irrational, and without justice. For no apparent reason it has given him birth and at the same time sentenced him to death. The Old Testament Job may be said to face two problems: he must contend with his comforters, each of whom is the mouthpiece of a conventional wisdom that is no longer convincing, and he must contend with Jehovah, with a universe that evinces an awesome creative exuberance and an almost equally awesome disregard for the creatures it has produced. More precisely, it lacks any human sense of justice and fails to discriminate between the lion and the lamb. The problems are as alive as ever and occupy the imagination of a good many Canadian writers. The chapter entitled 'The Problem of Job' focusses particularly on the paralysis that results from a failure to resolve one or the other or both of these problems. Actually they cannot be divorced, for the conventional wisdom of an inherited culture is itself an answer to the question of how to take the universe. When it has become unconvincing, it tends on the one hand to stifle life through the perpetuation of moribund attitudes and purely ineffectual gestures and on the other to increase the difficulty of life through the often more desperate assertion of inappropriate but materially effective attitudes and gestures. Grove and Cohen, Lampman and Pratt, Douglas LePan[2] and Jay Macpherson, all point out that the more completely man sets himself against nature and her imperfections the more completely he alienates himself from his world. And when he turns his theological or his technological weapons upon nature in the hope of completely walling out or annihilating the threats of disorder, suffering and death, he only adds to life's violence and pain. He quickly reaches a point where the supposed instruments of his salvation become rather the instruments of his death.

In a recent poem called 'Progressive Insanities of a Pioneer',[3] Margaret Atwood writes:

> If he had known unstructured
> space is a deluge
> and stocked his log house-
> boat with all the animals
>
> even the wolves,
>
> he might have floated.

The only effective defence for a garrison culture is to abandon defence, to let down the walls and let the wilderness in, even to the wolves. This is the advice that Miss Macpherson's Ark gives to an apprehensive Noah in the midst of the deluge.[4] If he would but accept rather than defy the engulfing sea, his exile would end and he would discover instead his community with an apparently hostile universe. He would become Miss Macpherson's 'Anagogic Man', discovering that he was not contained by, but himself contained the whole of creation.

---

[2]See Vol. I, pp. 652-64; for Macpherson, see pp. 288-300.
[3]For the complete poem, see pp. 459-61.
[4]This advice is given in a sequence of poems in *The Boatman*. For the text of the poem 'Anagogic Man', see pp. 292-3.

The majority of writers examined in the later chapters of the book appear to move towards a similar resolution of the problem of man's alienation from his world. Again and again these writers dramatize the difficulty of affirming life in a world constantly threatened by absurdity, suffering, and death. Again and again they end by emphasizing the necessity of affirming life despite these threats. Particularly they emphasize the necessity of courage, not the courage to resist so much as the courage to accept, not the courage to defy but the courage to affirm, to love, and celebrate a world that sooner or later demands of them the sacrifice of their lives. Only within such an affirmation can man discover his identity and community with the rest of nature. . . .

* * *

The present vitality of Canadian literature in both languages, particularly of Canadian poetry, may be partly ascribed to a growing conviction as to the power of language in the recovery and definition of our experience, in the re-creation of our cultural vision, and in the articulation of a more profound and inclusive communion between man and the universe he lives in. In recent work we may detect something of the excitement of contributing to the full culture of occupation, an excitement that springs from a sense, as Irving Layton describes it in 'The Birth of Tragedy',[5] that someone from afar off blows birthday candles for the world. For Irving Layton as for Gabrielle Roy, the whole inarticulate creation cries out for expression. To give it expression is the job of the poet, the artist, the makers of human culture. And it must find that expression in a cultural vision that grows out of the rock, whether the rock is the Laurentian Shield or the globe itself. As Layton says in his poem 'Butterfly on Rock':

> . . . the rock has borne this;
> this butterfly is the rock's grace,
> its most obstinate and secret desire
> to be a thing alive made manifest.[6]

1970

---

[5]See Vol. I, p. 570. 'Gabrielle Roy': French-Canadian writer (b. 1909) from Manitoba whose novel, *Bonheur d'occasion (The Tin Flute)* won international acclaim.
[6]For the complete poem, see Vol. I, p. 577. Jones concludes the penultimate chapter of *Butterfly on Rock*, 'The Sacrificial Embrace' (originally intended as the book's final chapter), with an allusion to this poem: 'It is the butterfly that emerges from the rock, sprung like Yeats' fountain out of life's own self-delight, despite the hand that will crush it, the rock beneath the hand'.

Jay Macpherson

b. 1931

Born in England, Jay Macpherson moved with her mother and brother to Newfoundland in 1940, and in 1944 to Ottawa, where she later attended Carleton College (now Carleton University), receiving her B.A. in 1951. After a year in London and a subsequent year in Montreal (completing library school at McGill University), Macpherson entered graduate school at the University of Toronto (M.A., 1955; Ph.D., 1964). She has remained at Toronto where she has been a member of the English department of Victoria College since 1954.

Macpherson's poems first appeared at the end of the forties in Alan Crawley's magazine, *Contemporary Verse*. She produced two chapbooks, *Nineteen Poems* (1952), published on the occasion of her twenty-first birthday by Robert Graves' Seizin Press, and *O Earth Return* (1954), printed by her own small press. From 1954 to 1963 Macpherson's Emblem Books published poets such as Daryl Hine, Dorothy Livesay, Alden Nowlan, and Al Purdy. In 1957 Oxford University Press published *The Boatman*, her best-known book and winner of a Governor General's Award, which incorporated new poems and much of her earlier poetry into a complex, unified work. For the next decade Macpherson wrote little new poetry, although she published a textbook for young readers on Greek mythology, *Four Ages of Man* (1962), and added sixteen new poems to be included with her earlier book when it was republished as *The Boatman and Other Poems* (1968). In 1974 she completed and published privately a new sequence of poems, *Welcoming Disaster*, which is simpler and more colloquial in style than *The Boatman*. *Poems Twice Told* (1981) reprints *The Boatman and Other Poems*

and *Welcoming Disaster* in one volume. In 1982 she published a scholarly work, *The Spirit of Solitude: Conventions and Continuities in Late Romance*.

Macpherson, who has been strongly influenced by Northrop Frye, is one of several poets of the fifties who began an extensive exploration of myth. Her poetry is central to that of the 'mythopoeic school', which includes the writing of James Reaney and the early work of Irving Layton and Eli Mandel. Like the poems of Yeats and of A.J.M. Smith, it exists at the pole of modernism opposite to that in which realism, documentation, and reportorial accuracy are valued. *The Boatman* in particular represents the antithesis of the experiential poetics exemplified by Raymond Souster and Louis Dudek. In James Reaney's words, 'The situations, the beings, the speakers are all gloriously artificial like the themes of Bach, which no "real" bird, no "real" train whistle could imitate or has ever imitated. Artifice is a theme as well as a feature of Macpherson's poetry' (*Canadian Literature*, 2, 1959). *The Boatman* is constructed around the myth of Noah and his ark: Noah, builder and preserver, is an allegorical representation of the artist (the creative aspect of man) and the ark is his work of art. Art is presented as not simply an imitation of the world but a reflection of the ideal as well as the real, epitomizing an eternity that contains both Eden and Sodom, the serpent and the seraph. In *The Boatman*, Macpherson is making both a philosophical and theological statement: man, by creating a microcosm within himself, can hold the macrocosm of the universe.

The sequence of poems in *Welcoming Disaster* was written after Macpherson experienced a writer's block, a long period during which she lost touch with her inner imaginative life and could no longer recall even her own dreams. To provide herself with imaginative sustenance she began to attend old horror films and found that the experience freed her to descend into her unconscious, confront its repressed material, and write once again; this is the 'disaster' that she welcomes in these poems. *Welcoming Disaster* is also structured around another descent: the universal myth of a descent into hell. Like Dante in his journey into the Inferno, the narrator of *Welcoming Disaster* is guided through the darker side of knowledge. A relic of childhood, Tedward (or Tadwit), a stuffed bear, conducts Macpherson's narrator not through a literal hell, as Virgil does Dante, but through the inner realms of the psyche. As the narrator is forced to examine her own nature, she comes to recognize familiar things and situations that have been rearranged and dislocated as they are in horror stories and dreams: they have been transformed by the individual subconscious into a personal symbolism that encom-

passes all aspects of self. The reader sees in the sequence a mythology of personality in which creativity gives—as it did in *The Boatman*—substance to life's emptiness.

Although these two books are complex, the individual poems of which they are composed are simple in form and diction. At the same time the poems contain resonant echoes—recalling a line or the style of a writer (such as Milton, Blake, Yeats, or Eliot) or suggesting a source (such as myth, the Bible, or nursery rhymes)—that give them great richness. The effect, as Northrop Frye observes, is that 'one has a sense of rereading as well as reading, of meeting new poems with a recognition that is integrally and specifically linked with the rest of one's poetic experience.' (*The Bush Garden*, 1971).

While the quantity of Macpherson's poetry is small, its quality is exceptional and its influence widespread. Following in the wake of Macpherson's ark are such writers as Gwendolyn MacEwen and Margaret Atwood, D.G. Jones and Robert Kroetsch.

From *The Boatman*[1]

The Thread

Each night I do retrace
My heavy steps and am compelled to pass
To earlier places, but take up again
The journey's turning skein.[2]

The thread Night's daughters[3] spin
Runs from birth's dark to death's, a shining line.
The snipping Fate attends its end and mine,
Ends what the two begin.

[1]The sequence of seventy-nine poems that makes up *The Boatman* is divided into six parts (I. Poor Child, II. O Earth Return, III. The Plowman in Darkness, IV. The Sleepers, V. The Boatman, VI. The Fisherman). 'The Thread' and 'The Third Eye' come from Part I; 'Eurynome [I]' from Part II; 'Eurynome [II]' from Part III; 'The Old Enchanter' from Part IV; 'The Boatman' and 'The Anagogic Man' from Part V; and 'The Fisherman'—which concludes the sequence—from Part VI.
[2]Although the principal myth used in this poem is that of Theseus, who followed a magic ball of thread into the labyrinth to kill the Minotaur and retraced his steps with the thread as a guide to escape from the maze, this stanza is also reminiscent of another escape: Aeneas's from Hades after he entered the underworld via the cave next to the lake, Avernus. In relating the Theseus myth in *Four Ages of Man*, Macpherson translates from Virgil:
The descent to Avernus is easy: but to retrace your way and escape to the upper world, that is the difficulty. (Aeneid, *VI, 126*)
[3]The Fates—Clotho, Lachesis, and Atropos; the thread of life is spun on Clotho's spindle, measured on Lachesis' rod, and snipped by Atropos' shears.

My mother gave to lead
My blind steps through the maze a daedal thread[4]   10
Who slept, who wept on Naxos now star-crowned
Reigns she whom I disowned.

The ceaseless to and from
Hushes the cry of the insatiate womb
That I wind up the journey I have come
And follow it back home.

[4]Theseus was given the magic ball of thread by Ariadne, who had received it from Daedalus. Ariadne, the daughter of King Minos and half-sister of the Minotaur, goes against her family when she helps Theseus in exchange for his pledge of marriage. Theseus, however, escapes from Crete with Ariadne, only to abandon her on the island of Naxos where she is found weeping by Dionysus, who marries her and gives her a crown that becomes the constellation Corona Borealis.

The Third Eye[1]

Of three eyes, I would still give two for one.
The third eye clouds: its light is nearly gone.
The two saw green, saw sky, saw people pass:
The third eye saw through order like a glass
To concentrate, refine and rarefy
And make a Cosmos of miscellany.
Sight, world and all to save alive that one
Fading so fast! Ah love, its light is done.

[1]Traditionally associated with mystical vision, the figurative portal through which man can see the numinous dimensions of the universe. Usually located in the forehead above the bridge of the nose, the third eye in some cultures (particularly that of Hindu India) is an invisible link between a mortal and the Universal Soul; in others it is a metaphor for a range of abilities and gifts, from imaginative thought to second sight.

Eurynome I[1]

In the snake's embrace mortal she lies,
Dies, but lives to renew her torment,
Under her, rock, night on her eyes.
In the wall around her was set by One
Upright, staring, to watch for morning
With bread and candle, her little son.

[1]The Boatman has a number of paired poems that approach the same subject from different perspectives. 'Eurynome': the goddess of all things, a First Cause in early Greek myths. Predating even the Titans, Eurynome emerged from Chaos to create first the sea and the sky, and then, because she was lonely, a companion, Boreas, or the North Wind. Rubbing Boreas between her hands she rolled the wind into the great serpent Ophion, with whom she mated, producing the beginning of the universe and her son Eros, or Love. In most versions of the myth Eurynome, becoming angry with Ophion for boasting that he was the real creator of the universe, bruises his head with her heel, blinds him, and banishes him to the caves beneath the earth. Macpherson here shows how martriarchal myths are altered by subsequent patriarchal cultures, with the universal progenitrix displaced by a male creator and becoming simply the bearer of his progeny.

Eurynome II

Come all old maids that are squeamish
And afraid to make mistakes,
Don't clutter your lives up with boyfriends:
The nicest girls marry snakes.

If you don't mind slime on your pillow
And caresses as gliding as ice
—Cold skin, warm heart, remember,
And besides, they keep down the mice—

If you're really serious-minded,
It's the best advice you can take: 10
No rumpling, no sweating, no nonsense,
Oh who would not sleep with a snake?

The Old Enchanter[1]

The old enchanter who laid down his head
In woman's mazeful lap was not betrayed
By love or doting, though he gave a maid
His rod and book and lies now like the dead.

The world's old age is on us. Long ago,
Shaken by dragons, swamped with sea-waves, fell
The island fortress, drowned like any shell.
This dreamer hears no tales of overthrow,

In childish sleep brass-walled[2] by his own charms.
In Merlin's bosom Arthur and the rest   10
Sleep their long night; and Arthur's dragon crest
Seems pacified, though in a witch's arms.

[1]Merlin, the sorcerer who guided King Arthur and his round table, became enchanted himself by the witch Nimue and, forfeiting his magic powers, slept away eternity trapped inside a rock.
[2]Impregnable; a wall of brass was traditionally a magician's enchantment to protect those within it from attack (see the plays *Doctor Faustus*, c. 1588, and *Friar Bacon and Friar Bungay,* 1592).

The Boatman

You might suppose it easy
For a maker not too lazy
To convert the gentle reader to an Ark:
But it takes a willing pupil
To admit both gnat and camel
—Quite an eyeful, all the crew that must embark.

After me when comes the deluge
And you're looking round for refuge
From God's anger pouring down in gush and spout,
Then you take the tender creature   10
—You remember, that's the reader—
And you pull him through his navel inside out.

That's to get his beasts outside him,
For they've got to come aboard him,
As the best directions have it, two by two.
When you've taken all their tickets
And you've marched them through his sockets,
Let the tempest bust Creation: heed not you.

For you're riding high and mighty
In a gale that's pushing ninety   20
With a solid bottom under you—that's his.
Fellow flesh affords a rampart,
And you've got along for comfort
All the world there ever shall be, was, and is.[1]

[1]A recasting of the second line of the response *Gloria Patri:*
Glory be to the Father, and to the Son: and to the Holy Ghost.
As it was in the beginning, is now, and ever shall be world without end. Amen.

The Anagogic[1] Man

Noah walks with head bent down;
For between his nape and crown
He carries, balancing with care,
A golden bubble round and rare.

Its gently shimmering sides surround
All us and our worlds, and bound
Art and life, and wit and sense,
Innocence and experience.

Forbear to startle him, lest some
Poor soul to its destruction come,   10
Slipped out of mind and past recall
As if it never was at all.

[1]Literally spiritual or uplifted; in *Anatomy of Criticism* (1957) Frye writes 'On the anagogic level, man is the container of nature . . . Nature is now inside the mind of an infinite man . . .'; in the interpretation of allegory, the universal level.

O you that pass, if still he seems
One absent-minded or in dreams,
Consider that your senses keep
A death far deeper than his sleep.

Angel, declare: what sways when Noah nods?
The sun, the stars, the figures of the gods.

The Fisherman

The world was first a private park
Until the angel,[1] after dark,
Scattered afar to wests and easts
The lovers and the friendly beasts.

And later still a home-made boat
Contained Creation set afloat,
No rift nor leak that might betray
The creatures to a hostile day.

But now beside the midnight lake
One single fisher[2] sits awake   10
And casts and fights and hauls to land
A myriad forms upon the sand.

Old Adam on the naming-day
Blessed each and let it slip away:
The fisher of the fallen mind
Sees no occasion to be kind,

But on his catch proceeds to sup;
Then bends, and at one slurp sucks up
The lake and all that therein is
To slake that hungry gut of his,   20

Then whistling makes for home and bed
As the last morning breaks in red;
But God the Lord with patient grin
Lets down his hook and hoicks[3] him in.

1957

[1]Traditionally it is believed that the archangel Michael drove Adam and Eve from the Garden of Eden.
[2]See Matthew 4:18-20 and Mark 1:16-17 for Christ's description of the apostles as fishers of men. The fisherman in Macpherson's poetry is also associated with the Fisher King, the sacred mythic ruler who fishes to sustain the life of his kingdom. Usually the fish provide wisdom as well as sustenance. The myth's most familiar manifestation is in the Grail legend contained in the King Arthur narratives. For further information, see Jessie L. Weston's *From Ritual to Romance* (1920).
[3]Yanks up.

From *Welcoming Disaster*[1]

Substitutions

Tedward was a
Woolworth's bear,
Filling in for
One not there
(Parents' attic?
Thrown away?
Long-dulled need re-
vived one day):
Lost the arche-
typal ted,   10
Friendly Tedward
Did instead.

Tedward, friend to
—Let's say—He,
Came in tow to
Visit Me:
Quaint arrangement,
I away
When this pair ar-
rived to stay.   20
I, returning,
Hoped to find,
Briefly, Him: no—
Left behind,
Though, was Tedward
In a chair,
Filling in for
Him not there.

Tedward, whelmed with
Spite and blame—   30
Lo! My Tadwit
He became:
Nose though hard and
Look though dim,
Friendly substi-
tute for Him.
Is love haunted?
To receive

---

[1]The sequence of forty-two poems that makes up *Welcoming Disaster* is divided into five parts (I. Invocations, II. The Way Down, III. The Dark Side, IV. Recognitions, V. Shadows Flee), plus an Epilogue. 'Substitutions' is from Part I; 'A Lost Soul' and 'After the Explosion' from Part II; 'Orion' from Part III; 'Surrogate' from Part IV; and 'Visiting' from Part V. 'Old Age of the Teddy-Bear' is in the Epilogue.

What another
Needs to give   40
Always, somewhat,
Looked at square,
Filling in for
Those not there?

A Lost Soul

Some are plain lucky—we ourselves among them:
Houses with books, with gardens, all we wanted,
Work we enjoy, with colleagues we feel close to—
        Love we have, even:

True love and candid, faithful, strong as gospel,
Patient, untiring, fond when we are fretful.
Having so much, how is it that we ache for
        Those darker others?

Some days for them we could let slip the whole damn
Soft bed we've made ourselves, our friends in Heaven   10
Let slip away, buy back with blood our ancient
        Vampires and demons.

First loves and oldest, what names shall I call you?
Older to me than language, old as breathing,
Born with me, in this flesh: by now I know you're
        Greed, pride and envy.

Too long I've shut you out, denied acquaintance,
Favoured less barefaced vices, hoped to pass for
Reasonable, rate with those who are more inclined to
        Self-hurt than murder.   20

You were my soul: in arrogance I banned you.
Now I recant—return, possess me, take my
Hands, bind my eyes, infallibly restore my
        Share in perdition.

After the Explosion

Now we're alone at length, my tadsome witsome,
All lids blown off, all old companions frighted,
Back to the basics—sobbing in my bed, and
    Clutching my dolly.

No-one at the window—even Nosferatu,[1]
Weary of blood, has gone off picking daisies;
Nor at the door pleads, dank with night, the lover.
    Empty, unhaunted

Stands now my house, though cleared and swept for devils.
Meantime my garden sprouts, unhelped, unhindered.   10
No need to ask, death and its host departed,
    What we do after.

Let's make a grave, my ted, and put you in it,
Under the compost heap, where all things quicken.
Take with you silence—secrets: I commit us to
    Earth with her courses.

[1]See Macpherson's poem 'Notes & Acknowledgements' (p. 299).

Orion

Orion is the winter-king
Among heaven's bright designs.[1]
His up is down: his height is set
In Hell, and yet he shines.

Those stars of night the fiend[2] drew down,
That followed in his train,
At midnight stand above the town:
They glitter in their pain.

My foolstar hero, stretched at length,
The sky's pins through his head,[3]   10
Basks at those fires his dreary strength
That's slanted to the dead.

Come, darkness, fill my heart and eyes:
I'll sink below the light,
And, buried with Orion, rise
To winter and to night.

[1]Orion, named for the hero of Greek myth, is a brilliant winter constellation that descends below the southern horizon except for two months of the year.
[2]Lucifer, who fell from heaven for leading a rebellion against God and took with him other rebel angels.
[3]In Greek myth Artemis, virgin goddess of fertility, shot the handsome giant Orion through the head with her arrow because of his amorous transgressions.

Surrogate

Not common wormfood, quick to rot—
An alien in the earth—
A simple ted, with nylon thread,
What should he know of birth?

Shaped from another stock than me,
Digged from a different pit,
He went before to find a door,
And he can open it.

He is the Tammuz[1] of my song,
Of death and hell the key,   10
And gone to mend the primal wrong,
That rift in Being, Me.

To with my flesh explore the fire,
Or in the springs to drown,
Or seek, this late, the earthward stair
Where Tadwit hurried down,

No need: poor changeling, never born,
Stuffed brain and glassy eye,
Is planted by the spring of tears,
The first of me to die.   20

[1]Babylonian demi-god, the spirit of annual vegetation and lover of Ishtar, the great earth-mother goddess; the occasion of Tammuz's death and its annual remembrance was a time of mourning and weeping. Ishtar, in quest of Tammuz, followed him into the underworld, and during her absence the earth lay infertile, without sexual passion. Tammuz is linked to other fertility gods—such as Adonis and Osiris—who, after death, journey to the underworld before being resurrected.

Visiting

Like me, you're expert in
Those upper rooms
—Intimate places,
Both lights and glooms—
Where, before cockcrow, the
Revenant[1] comes—

Buried bride, demon king,
Treacherous guest
(Cold, and you warmed him;
Tired, you let rest: 10
Now there's a leaden pain
Rankling your breast).

There was that other one
You couldn't see:

[1]Ghost who returns after death; one who returns after an absence.

Takes one to know one: he
Never fooled me,
Even without the
Blood on the key.

Likely we've both of us
Been here before,   20
Maybe too often: I
Can't any more
Tell you to what, love, you've
Opened your door.

Old Age of the Teddy-Bear

Ted getting shabby—
skull beneath skin?[1]
No, but as matting,
bare patches, begin,
nameless maimed baby
peers out from within.

Once it was Tadwit,
now merely It:
old links with You and Him
no longer fit: 10
the melting snowman's slide,
leaving just grit?

Poor ted? no—frightening,
way it seems now:
angel that shielded me
gone soft like dough:
now to that damaged thing
what do I owe?

Something in both of us
never got born: 20
too late to hack it out,
or to unlearn
needed, familiar pain.
Come, little thorn.

1974

[1]In his poem 'Whispers of Immortality', T.S. Eliot wrote that Jacobean playwright John Webster 'saw the skull beneath the skin'.

Notes & Acknowledgements[1]

Reader, if the names appall,
Panic's needless, after all.
'Nosferatu' is a movie,
Murnau,[2] '22 (yes, groovy)—
Dracula without permission,
Hence the names received revision.
Homer's[3] here, but in the light
Of A.B. Lord and Jackson Knight:
Sapphics[4] likewise impure, stemming
From the hymn-tune known as Flemming.   10
Tammuz, Dumuzi,[5] are the same
(Sorry, that's the way they came),
Babylon & Sumer versions
(Always were elusive persons—
Still, for details see J.B.
Pritchard, ed., *A N E T*).

Twenty some-odd years ago
Oxford took an ark in tow,
And thereafter never quite
Chose to let it slip from sight.   20
Heartfelt thanks I here express,
Bill Toye, alias Oxford Press!

This, though now in Oxford's book,
First came forth on private hook.
Friends assisted, not a few—
Bear up, Muse, we'll list just two
In a thanks-again review
(Pausing, though, to not pass over
Picture sourcebooks pub. by Dover):
Best of readers, Northrop Frye   30
Cast a sure arranging eye;

[1]This appears as the last poem in *Poems Twice Told*; a shorter version concluded *Welcoming Disaster*.
[2]F.W. Murnau (1888-1931) was the director of *Nosferatu, A Symphony of Terror* (1922)—a pirated German version of Bram Stoker's novel *Dracula* (1897).
[3]That is, references to Greek myths and the tale of the fall of Troy, including the adventures of the survivors of the Trojan war, are alluded to in many of the *Welcoming Disaster* poems. See 'Orion'. Albert B. Lord and W.F. Jackson Knight are classical scholars who have worked extensively with the Trojan stories.
[4]A verse form, named for the Greek poet Sappho (b. 612 B.C.), that consists of a four-line stanza; the first three lines are composed of eleven syllables, the fourth contains five syllables. Friedrick Ferdinand Flemming (1778-1813) composed a popular hymn tune (used for many different lyrics) that follows the Sapphic structure, diverging in its own pattern of accented beats within the eleven-syllable lines. See 'After the Explosion' and 'A Lost Soul' for Macpherson's use of Sapphics. Macpherson also uses another popular hymn stanza composed of four alternating lines of eight and six syllables. See 'Orion' and 'Surrogate'.
[5]See p. 297, n. 1 for Tammuz. The two names for the same god reflect the blend of Assyro-Babylonian mythology arising from the two ancient regions of the middle east, Sumer and Akkad. *ANET* is *Ancient Near Eastern Texts Relating to the Old Testament*.

David Blostein,[6] craftsman fine,
Caught, with steadier hand than mine,
Ted, glum chum, in subtle line.
Major debts thus once more noted,
Muse, let's jump: our boat's re-floated.

1974, rev. 1981

[6]A colleague at Victoria College, University of Toronto, who drew an illustration of Tedward that first appeared in *Welcoming Disaster* and is reprinted on the back of *Poems Twice Told*.

Alice Munro

b. 1931

Alice Munro has divided her life between two regions of Canada. Born Alice Laidlaw, she grew up in Wingham, Ont., and at nineteen moved to nearby London to attend the University of Western Ontario. After two years there she married Bill Munro and with him settled in British Columbia. She lived in Vancouver and Victoria for more than twenty years, writing, helping her husband manage a bookstore, and raising three daughters. In 1972 she returned to western Ontario; she now lives in Clinton, not far from Wingham, with her second husband.

Munro began writing early—her first published work appeared in UWO's undergraduate literary magazine in 1950—but it was only in 1961, when she wrote 'The Red Dress, 1946', that she found her real voice. A slow and meticulous craftsman, she did not publish her first collection of stories, *Dance of the Happy Shades*, until 1968. This book signalled the advent of a major new short-story writer and won her a Governor General's Award for fiction. (She received a second in 1978.) As well as two more collections of short fiction, *Something I've Been Meaning to Tell You*

(1974) and *The Moons of Jupiter* (1982), Munro has published two linked story-sequences that have sometimes been described as novels: *Lives of Girls and Women* (1971) and *Who Do You Think You Are?* (1978). Most of Munro's new stories—like those of Mavis Gallant—appear first in *The New Yorker*.

Munro's narrative structures are frequently developed through the use of oppositions, which may take the form of contrasting characters (such as Et and Char in 'Something I've Been Meaning to Tell You'), the balancing of the 'female' world against the 'male', or the playing off of *then* against *now*. This last opposition, one of the most prominent features of Munro's writing, gives her stories a complex movement back and forth across time that reproduces the movement of the mind in its act of recovering and reassessing the past. Indeed, Munro sees fiction as something to move around in, even to live in. She says that her conception of the story can be explained by how she reads stories written by other people:

I can start reading anywhere; from beginning to end, from end to beginning, from any point in between in either direction. So obviously I don't take up a story and follow it as if it were a road, taking me somewhere, with views and neat diversions along the way. I go into it, and move back and forth and settle here and there, and stay in it for a while. It's more like a house. (Making It New: Contemporary Canadian Stories, *edited by John Metcalf, 1982*)

Munro furnishes her fictional 'houses' meticulously. A regionalist, she usually sets her stories in small-town Ontario, working with material she knows personally and evoking fully realized milieus. At the same time, beneath the ordinariness of the world she creates, disaster often lurks (or is longed for) and many secrets are glimpsed but remain untold. Munro once remarked in an interview with Jill Gardiner:

. . . the whole act of writing is more an attempt at recognition than of understanding, because I don't understand many things. I feel a kind of satisfaction in just approaching something that is mysterious and important. . . . I believe that we don't solve these things—in fact our explanations take us further away. (M.A. thesis, University of New Brunswick).

In the title story of Munro's most recent collection, the 'moons of Jupiter'—distant, enigmatic, yet somehow important—serve as an emblem for this sense of the inexplicable that is central to Munro's fiction. Because her stories refuse to yield up all their meaning, and are sometimes more puzzling than illuminating, they haunt the imagination long after they have been read.

Something I've Been Meaning To Tell You

'Anyway he knows how to fascinate the women,' said Et to Char. She could not tell if Char went paler, hearing this, because Char was pale in the first place as anybody could get. She was like a ghost now, with her hair gone white. But still beautiful, she couldn't lose it.

'No matter to him the age or the size,' Et pressed on. 'It's natural to him as breathing, I guess. I only hope the poor things aren't taken in by it.'

'I wouldn't worry,' Char said.

The day before, Et had taken Blaikie Noble up on his invitation to go along on one of his tours and listen to his spiel. Char was asked too, but of course she didn't go. Blaikie Noble ran a bus. The bottom part of it was painted red and the top part was striped, to give the effect of an awning. On the side was painted: LAKESHORE TOURS, INDIAN GRAVES, LIMESTONE GARDENS, MILLIONAIRE'S MANSION, BLAIKIE NOBLE, DRIVER, GUIDE. Blaikie had a room at the hotel, and he also worked on the grounds, with one helper, cutting grass and clipping hedges and digging the borders. What a comedown, Et had said at the beginning of the summer when they first found out he was back. She and Char had known him in the old days.

So Et found herself squeezed into his bus with a lot of strangers, though before the afternoon was over she had made friends with a number of them and had a couple of promises of jackets needing letting out, as if she didn't have enough to do already. That was beside the point, the thing on her mind was watching Blaikie.

And what did he have to show? A few mounds with grass growing on them, covering dead Indians, a plot full of odd-shaped, grayish-white, dismal-looking limestone things—far-fetched imitations of plants (there could be the cemetery, if that was what you wanted)—and an old monstrosity of a house built with liquor money. He made the most of it. A historical discourse on the Indians, then a scientific discourse on the Limestone. Et had no way of knowing how much of it was true. Arthur would know. But Arthur wasn't there; there was nobody there but silly women, hoping to walk beside Blaikie to and from the sights, chat with him over their tea in the Limestone Pavilion, looking forward to having his strong hand under their elbows, the other hand brushing somewhere around the waist, when he helped them down off the bus ('I'm not a tourist,' Et whispered sharply when he tried it on her).

He told them the house was haunted. The first Et had ever heard of it, living ten miles away all her life. A woman had killed her husband, the son of the millionaire, at least it was believed she had killed him.

'How?' cried some lady, thrilled out of her wits.

'Ah, the ladies are always anxious to know the means,' said Blaikie, in a voice like cream, scornful and loving. 'It was a slow—poison. Or that's what they said. This is all hearsay, all local gossip.' (*Local my foot*, said Et to herself.) 'She didn't appreciate his lady friends. The wife didn't. No.'

He told them the ghost walked up and down in the garden, between two rows of blue spruce. It was not the murdered man who walked, but the wife, regretting. Blaikie smiled ruefully at the busload. At first Et had thought his attentions were all false, an ordinary commercial flirtation, to give them their money's worth. But gradually she was getting a different notion. He bent to each woman he talked to—it didn't matter how fat or scrawny or silly she was—as if there was one thing in her he would like to find. He had a gentle and laughing but ultimately serious, narrowing look (was that the look men finally had when they made love, that Et would never see?) that made him seem to want to be a deepsea diver diving down, down through all the emptiness and cold and wreckage to discover the one thing he had set his heart on, something small and precious, hard to locate, as a ruby maybe on the ocean floor. That was a look she would like to have described to Char. No doubt Char had seen it. But did she know how freely it was being distributed?

Char and Arthur had been planning a trip that summer to see Yellowstone Park and the Grand Canyon, but they did not go. Arthur suffered a series of dizzy spells just at the end of school, and the doctor put him to bed. Several things were the matter with him. He was anemic, he had an irregular heartbeat, there was trouble with his kidneys. Et worried about leukemia. She woke at night, worrying.

'Don't be silly,' said Char serenely, 'He's overtired.'

Arthur got up in the evenings and sat in his dressing gown. Blaikie Noble came to visit. He said his room at the hotel was a hole above the kitchen, they were trying to steam-cook him. It made him appreciate the cool of the porch. They played the games that Arthur loved, schoolteacher's games. They played a geography game, and they tried to see who could make the most words out of the name Beethoven. Arthur won. He got thirty-four. He was immensely delighted.

'You'd think you'd found the Holy Grail,' Char said.

They played 'Who Am I?' Each of them had to choose somebody to be—real or imaginary, living or dead, human or animal—and the others had to try to guess it in twenty questions. Et got who Arthur was on the thirteenth question. Sir Galahad.

'I never thought you'd get it so soon.'

'I thought back to Char saying about the Holy Grail.'

'*My strength is as the strength of ten,*' said Blaikie Noble, '*Because my heart is pure.*[1] I didn't know I remembered that.'

'You should have been King Arthur,' Et said. 'King Arthur is your namesake.'

'I should have. King Arthur was married to the most beautiful woman in the world.'

'Ha,' said Et. 'We all know the end of that story.'

Char went into the living room and played the piano in the dark.

> *The flowers that bloom in the spring, tra-la,*
> *Have nothing to do with the case. . . .*[2]

When Et arrived, out of breath, that past June, and said, 'Guess who I saw downtown on the street?' Char, who was on her knees picking strawberries, said, 'Blaikie Noble.'

'You've seen him.'

'No,' said Char. 'I just knew. I think I knew by your voice.'

A name that had not been mentioned between them for thirty years. Et was too amazed then to think of the explanation that came to her later. Why did it need to be a surprise to Char? There was a postal service in this country, there had been all along.

'I asked him about his wife,' she said. 'The one with the dolls.' (As if Char wouldn't remember.) 'He says she died a long time ago. Not only that. He married another one and she's dead. Neither could have been rich. And where is all the Nobles' money, from the hotel?'

'We'll never know,' said Char, and ate a strawberry.

The hotel had just recently been opened up again. The Nobles had given it up in the twenties and the town had operated it for a while as a hospital. Now some people from Toronto had bought it, renovated the dining room, put in a cocktail lounge, reclaimed the lawns and garden, though the tennis court seemed to be beyond repair. There was a croquet set put out again. People came to stay in the summers, but they were not the sort of people who used to come. Retired couples. Many widows and single ladies. Nobody would have walked a block to see them get off the boat, Et thought. Not that there was a boat any more.

That first time she met Blaikie Noble on the street she had made a point of not being taken aback. He was wearing a creamy suit and his hair, that had always been bleached by the sun, was bleached for good now, white.

---

[1]Tennyson, 'Sir Galahad'. The whole poem is about Galahad's being faithful to the quest for the Grail rather than seeking the favour of ladies. Galahad's behaviour contrasts with that of Sir Lancelot, the knight who betrays King Arthur by committing adultery with Queen Guinevere—'the end of that story' to which Et refers.

[2]From a song in Gilbert and Sullivan's *The Mikado*. The lines quoted refer to the 'case' of Nanki-Poo who, in love with Yum-Yum, is forced into an engagement with Katisha, 'a most unattractive old thing, tra-la, with a caricature of a face'.

'Blaikie. I knew either it was you or a vanilla ice-cream cone. I bet you don't know who I am.'

'You're Et Desmond and the only thing different about you is you cut off your braids.' He kissed her forehead, nervy as always.

'So you're back visiting old haunts,' said Et, wondering who had seen that.

'Not visiting. Haunting.' He told her then how he had got wind of the hotel opening up again, and how he had been doing this sort of thing, driving tour buses, in various places, in Florida and Banff. And when she asked he told her about his two wives. He never asked was she married, taking for granted she wasn't. He never asked if Char was, till she told him.

Et remembered the first time she understood that Char was beautiful. She was looking at a picture taken of them, of Char and herself and their brother who was drowned. Et was ten in the picture, Char fourteen and Sandy seven, just a couple of weeks short of all he would ever be. Et was sitting in an armless chair and Char was behind her, arms folded on the chair-back, with Sandy in his sailor suit cross-legged on the floor—or marble terrace, you would think, with the effect made by what had been nothing but a dusty, yellowing screen, but came out in the picture a pillar and draped curtain, a scene of receding poplars and fountains. Char had pinned her front hair up for the picture and was wearing a bright blue, ankle-length silk dress—of course the color did not show—with complicated black velvet piping. She was smiling slightly, with great composure. She could have been eighteen, she could have been twenty-two. Her beauty was not of the fleshy timid sort most often featured on calendars and cigar boxes of the period, but was sharp and delicate, intolerant, challenging.

Et took a long look at this picture and then went and looked at Char, who was in the kitchen. It was washday. The woman who came to help was pulling clothes through the wringer, and their mother was sitting down resting and staring through the screen door (she never got over Sandy, nobody expected her to). Char was starching their father's collars. He had a tobacco and candy store on the Square and wore a fresh collar every day. Et was prepared to find that some metamorphosis had taken place, as in the background, but it was not so. Char, bending over the starch basin, silent and bad-humored (she hated washday, the heat and steam and flapping sheets and chugging commotion of the machine—in fact, she was not fond of any kind of housework), showed in her real face the same almost disdainful harmony as in the photograph. This made Et understand, in some not entirely welcome way, that the qualities of legend were real, that they surfaced where and when you least expected. She had almost thought beautiful women were a fictional invention. She and Char would go down to watch the people get off the excursion boat, on Sundays, walking up to the Hotel. So much white it hurt your eyes, the ladies' dresses and parasols and the men's summer suits and Panama hats, not to speak of the sun dazzling on the water and the band playing. But looking closely at those ladies, Et found fault. Coarse skin or fat behind or chicken necks or dull nests of hair, probably ratted. Et did not let anything get by her, young as she was. At school she was respected for her self-possession and her sharp tongue. She was the one to tell you if you had been at the blackboard with a hole in your stocking or a ripped hem. She was the one who imitated (but in a safe corner of the schoolyard, out of earshot, always) the teacher reading 'The Burial of Sir John Moore.'[3]

All the same it would have suited her better to have found one of those ladies beautiful, not Char. It would have been more appropriate. More suitable than Char in her wet apron with her cross expression, bent over the starch basin. Et was a person who didn't like contradictions, didn't like things out of place, didn't like mysteries or extremes.

She didn't like the bleak notoriety of having Sandy's drowning attached to her, didn't like the memory people kept of her father carrying the body up from the beach. She could be seen at twilight, in her gym bloomers, turning cartwheels on the lawn of the stricken house. She made a wry mouth, which nobody saw, one day in the park when Char said, 'That was my little brother who was drowned.'

The park overlooked the beach. They were standing there with Blaikie Noble, the hotel owner's son, who said, 'Those waves can be dangerous. Three or four years ago there was a kid drowned.'

And Char said—to give her credit, she didn't say it tragically, but almost with amusement, that he should know so little about Mock Hill people—'That was my little brother who was drowned.'

Blaikie Noble was not any older than Char—if he had been, he would have been fighting in France—but he had not had to live all his life in Mock Hill. He did not know the real people there as well as he knew the regular guests at his father's hotel. Every winter he went with his parents to California, on the train. He had seen the Pacific surf. He had pledged allegiance to their flag. His manners were democratic, his skin was tanned. This was at a time when people were not usually tanned as a result of leisure, only work. His hair was bleached by the sun. His good looks were almost as notable as Char's but his were corrupted by charm, as hers were not.

It was the heyday of Mock Hill and all the other towns around the lakes, of all the hotels which in later years would become Sunshine Camps for city children, T.B. sanatoriums, barracks for R.A.F. training pilots in World War II. The white paint on the hotel was renewed every spring, hollowed-out logs filled with flowers were set on the railings, pots of flowers swung on chains above them. Croquet sets and wooden swings were set out on the lawns, the tennis court rolled. People who could not afford the hotel, young workingmen, shop clerks and factory girls from the city, stayed in a row of tiny cottages, joined by lattice-work that hid their garbage pails and communal outhouses, stretching far up the beach. Girls from Mock Hill, if they had mothers to tell them what to do, were told not to walk out there. Nobody told Char what to do, so she walked along the boardwalk in front of them in the glaring afternoon, taking Et with her for company. The cottages had no glass in their windows, they had only propped-up wooden shutters that were closed at night. From the dark holes came one or two indistinct, sad or drunk invitations, that was all. Char's looks and style did not attract men, perhaps intimidated them. All through high school in Mock Hill she

[3]'The Burial of Sir John Moore at Corunna', written in 1816 by Charles Wolfe on an English general who died fighting the French.

had not one boy friend. Blaikie Noble was her first, if that was what he was.

What did this affair of Char's and Blaikie Noble's amount to in the summer of 1918? Et was never sure. He did not call at the house, at least not more than once or twice. He was kept busy, working at the hotel. Every afternoon he drove an open excursion wagon, with an awning on top of it, up the lakeshore road, taking people to look at the Indian graves and the limestone garden and to glimpse through the trees the Gothic stone mansion, built by a Toronto distiller and known locally as Grog Castle. He was also in charge of the variety show the hotel put on once a week, with a mixture of local talent, recruited guests, and singers and comedians brought in especially for the performance.

Late mornings seemed to be the time he and Char had. 'Come on,' Char would say, 'I have to go downtown,' and she would in fact pick up the mail and walk part way round the Square before veering off into the park. Soon Blaikie Noble would appear from the side door of the hotel and come bounding up the steep path. Sometimes he would not even bother with the path but jump over the back fence, to amaze them. None of this, the bounding or jumping, was done the way some boy from Mock Hill High School might have done it, awkwardly yet naturally. Blaikie Noble behaved like a man imitating a boy; he mocked himself but was graceful, like an actor.

'Isn't he stuck on himself?' said Et to Char, watching. The position she had taken up right away on Blaikie was that she didn't like him.

'Of course he is,' said Char.

She told Blaikie. 'Et says you're stuck on yourself.'

'What did you say?'

'I told her you had to be, nobody else is.'

Blaikie didn't mind. He had taken the position that he liked Et. He would with a quick tug loosen and destroy the arrangement of looped-up braids she wore. He told them things about the concert artists. He told them the Scottish ballad singer was a drunk and wore corsets, that the female impersonator even in his hotel room donned a blue nightgown with feathers, that the lady ventriloquist talked to her dolls—they were named Alphonse and Alicia—as if they were real people, and had them sitting up in bed one on each side of her.

'How would you know that?' Char said.

'I took her up her breakfast.'

'I thought you had maids to do that.'

'The morning after the show I do it. That's when I hand them their pay envelope and give them their walking papers. Some of them would stay all week if you didn't inform them. She sits up in bed trying to feed them bits of bacon and talking to them and doing them answering back, you'd have a fit if you could see.'

'She's cracked I guess,' Char said peacefully.

One night that summer Et woke up and remembered she had left her pink organdy dress on the line, after handwashing it. She thought she heard rain, just the first few drops. She didn't, it was just leaves rustling, but she was confused, waking up like that. She thought it was far on in the night, too, but thinking about it later she decided it might have been only around midnight. She got up and went downstairs, turned on the back kitchen light, and let herself out the back door, and standing on the stoop pulled the clothesline towards her. Then almost under her feet, from the grass right beside the stoop, where there was a big lilac bush that had grown and spread, untended, to the size of a tree, two figures lifted themselves, didn't stand or even sit up, just roused their heads as if from bed, still tangled together some way. The back kitchen light didn't shine directly out but lit the yard enough for her to see their faces. Blaikie and Char.

She never did get a look at what state their clothes were in, to see how far they had gone or were going. She wouldn't have wanted to. To see their faces was enough for her. Their mouths were big and swollen, their cheeks flattened, coarsened, their eyes holes. Et left her dress, she fled into the house and into her bed where she surprised herself by falling asleep. Char never said a word about it to her next day. All she said was, 'I brought your dress in, Et. I thought it might rain.' As if she had never seen Et out there pulling on the clothesline. Et wondered. She knew if she said, 'You saw me,' Char would probably tell her it had been a dream. She let Char think she had been fooled into believing that, if that was what Char was thinking. That way, Et was left knowing more; she was left knowing what Char looked like when she lost her powers, abdicated. Sandy drowned, with green stuff clogging his nostrils, couldn't look more lost than that.

Before Christmas the news came to Mock Hill that Blaikie Noble was married. He had married the lady ventriloquist, the one with Alphonse and Alicia. Those dolls, who wore evening dress and had sleek hairdos in the style of Vernon and Irene Castle,[4] were more clearly remembered than the lady herself. The only thing people recalled for sure about her was that she could not have been under forty. A nineteen-year-old boy. It was because he had not been brought up like other boys, had been allowed the run of the hotel, taken to California, let mix with all sorts of people. The result was depravity, and could have been predicted.

Char swallowed poison. Or what she thought was poison. It was laundry blueing. The first thing she could reach down from the shelf in the back kitchen. Et came home after school—she had heard the news at noon, from Char herself in fact, who had laughed and said, 'Wouldn't that kill you?'—and she found Char vomiting into the toilet. 'Go get the Medical Book,' Char said to her. A terrible involuntary groan came out of her. 'Read what it says about poison.' Et went instead to phone the doctor. Char came staggering out of the bathroom holding the bottle of bleach they kept behind the tub. 'If you don't put up the phone I'll drink the whole bottle,' she said in a harsh whisper. Their mother was presumably asleep behind her closed door.

Et had to hang up the phone and look in the ugly old book where she had read long ago about childbirth and signs of death, and had learned about holding a mirror to the mouth. She was under the mistaken impression that Char had been drinking from the bleach bottle already, so she read all about that. Then she found it was the blueing. Blueing was not in the book, but it seemed the best

[4]An American ballroom dance team, popular in 1912-17.

thing to do would be to induce vomiting, as the book advised for most poisons—
Char was at it already, didn't need to have it induced—and then drink a quart of
milk. When Char got the milk down she was sick again.

'I didn't do this on account of Blaikie Noble,' she said between spasms.
'Don't you ever think that. I wouldn't be such a fool. A pervert like him. I did it
because I'm sick of living.'

'What are you sick of about living?' said Et sensibly when Char had wiped her
face.

'I'm sick of this town and all the stupid people in it and Mother and her dropsy
and keeping house and washing sheets every day. I don't think I'm going to
vomit any more. I think I could drink some coffee. It says coffee.'

Et made a pot and Char got out two of the best cups. They began to giggle as
they drank.

'I'm sick of Latin,' Et said. 'I'm sick of Algebra. I think I'll take blueing.'

'Life is a burden,' Char said. 'O Life, where is thy sting?'

'O Death. O Death, where is thy sting?'[5]

'Did I say Life? I meant Death. O Death, where is thy sting? Pardon me.'

One afternoon Et was staying with Arthur while Char shopped and changed
books at the Library. She wanted to make him an eggnog, and she went searching in Char's cupboard for the nutmeg. In with the vanilla and the almond extract
and the artificial rum she found a small bottle of a strange liquid. *Zinc phosphide*.
She read the label and turned it around in her hands. A rodenticide. Rat poison,
that must mean. She had not known Char and Arthur were troubled with rats.
They kept a cat, old Tom, asleep now around Arthur's feet. She unscrewed the
top and sniffed at it, to know what it smelled like. Like nothing. Of course. It
must taste like nothing too, or it wouldn't fool the rats.

She put it back where she had found it. She made Arthur his eggnog and took
it in and watched him drink it. A slow poison. She remembered that from Blaikie's foolish story. Arthur drank with an eager noise, like a child, more to please
her, she thought, than because he was so pleased himself. He would drink anything you handed him. Naturally.

'How are you these days, Arthur?'

'Oh, Et. Some days a bit stronger, and then I seem to slip back. It takes
time.'

But there was none gone, the bottle seemed full. What awful nonsense. Like
something you read about, Agatha Christie. She would mention it to Char and
Char would tell her the reason.

'Do you want me to read to you?' she asked Arthur, and he said yes. She sat
by the bed and read to him from a book about the Duke of Wellington. He had
been reading it by himself but his arms got tired holding it. All those battles, and
wars, and terrible things, what did Arthur know about such affairs, why was he
so interested? He knew nothing. He did not know why things happened, why
people could not behave sensibly. He was too good. He knew about history but
not about what went on, in front of his eyes, in his house, anywhere. Et differed

---

[5] 1 Corinthians 5:55: 'O death, where is thy sting? O grave, where is thy victory?'

from Arthur in knowing that something went on, even if she could not understand why; she differed from him in knowing there were those you could not
trust.

She did not say anything to Char after all. Every time she was in the house she
tried to make some excuse to be alone in the kitchen, so that she could open the
cupboard and stand on tiptoe and look in, to see it over the tops of the other bottles, to see that the level had not gone down. She did think maybe she was going
a little strange, as old maids did; this fear of hers was like the absurd and
harmless fears young girls sometimes have, that they will jump out a window, or
strangle a baby, sitting in its buggy. Though it was not her own acts she was
frightened of.

Et looked at Char and Blaikie and Arthur, sitting on the porch, trying to decide if
they wanted to go in and put the light on and play cards. She wanted to convince
herself of her silliness. Char's hair, and Blaikie's too, shone in the dark. Arthur
was almost bald now and Et's own hair was thin and dark. Char and Blaikie
seemed to her the same kind of animal—tall, light, powerful, with a dangerous
luxuriance. They sat apart but shone out together. *Lovers.* Not a soft word, as
people thought, but cruel and tearing. There was Arthur in the rocker with a quilt
over his knees, foolish as something that hasn't grown its final, most necessary,
skin. Yet in a way the people like Arthur were the most trouble-making of all.

'I love my love with an R, because he is ruthless. His name is Rex, and he
lives in a—restaurant.'

'I love my love with an A, because he is absent-minded. His name is Arthur,
and he lives in an ashcan.'

'Why Et,' Arthur said. 'I never suspected. But I don't know if I like about the
ashcan.'

'You would think we were all twelve years old,' said Char.

After the blueing episode Char became popular. She became involved in the productions of the Amateur Dramatic Society and the Oratorio Society, although she
was never much of an actress or a singer. She was always the cold and beautiful
heroine in the plays, or the brittle exquisite young society woman. She learned to
smoke, because of having to do it onstage. In one play Et never forgot, she was a
statue. Or rather, she played a girl who had to pretend to be a statue, so that a
young man fell in love with her and later discovered, to his confusion and perhaps disappointment, that she was only human. Char had to stand for eight minutes perfectly still on stage, draped in white crepe and showing the audience her
fine indifferent profile. Everybody marvelled at how she did it.

The moving spirit behind the Amateur Dramatic Society and the Oratorio Society was a high school teacher new to Mock Hill, Arthur Comber. He taught Et
history in her last year. Everybody said he gave her A's because he was in love
with her sister, but Et knew it was because she worked harder than she ever had
before; she learned the History of North America as she had never learned anything in her life. Missouri Compromise. Mackenzie to the Pacific, 1793. She
never forgot.

Arthur Comber was thirty or so, with a high bald forehead, a red face in spite of not drinking (that later paled) and a clumsy, excited manner. He knocked a bottle of ink off his desk and permanently stained the History Room floor. 'Oh dear, oh dear,' he said, crouching down to the spreading ink, flapping at it with his handkerchief. Et imitated that. 'Oh dear, oh dear!' 'Oh good heavens!' All his flustery exclamations and miscalculated gestures. Then, when he took her essay at the door, his red face shining with eagerness, giving her work and herself such a welcome, she felt sorry. That was why she worked so hard, she thought, to make up for mocking him.

He had a black scholar's gown he wore over his suit, to teach in. Even when he wasn't wearing it, Et could see it on him. Hurrying along the street to one of his innumerable, joyfully undertaken obligations, flapping away at the Oratorio singers, jumping on stage—so the whole floor trembled—to demonstrate something to the actors in a play, he seemed to her to have those long ridiculous crow's wings flapping after him, to be as different from other men, as absurd yet intriguing, as the priest from Holy Cross. Char made him give up the gown altogether, after they were married. She had heard that he tripped in it, running up the steps of the school. He had gone sprawling. That finished it, she ripped it up.

'I was afraid one of these days you'd really get hurt.'

But Arthur said, 'Ah. You thought I looked like a fool.'

Char didn't deny it, though his eyes on her, his wide smile, were begging her to. Her mouth twitched at the corners, in spite of herself. Contempt. Fury. Et saw, they both saw, a great wave of that go over her before she could smile at him and say, 'Don't be silly.' Then her smile and her eyes were trying to hold on to him, trying to clutch onto his goodness (which she saw, as much as anybody else did, but which finally only enraged her, Et believed, like everything else about him, like his sweaty forehead and his galloping optimism), before that boiling wave could come back again, altogether carry her away.

Char had a miscarriage during the first year of her marriage and was sick for a long time afterwards. She was never pregnant again. Et by this time was not living in the house; she had her own place on the Square, but she was there one time on washday, helping Char haul the sheets off the line. Their parents were both dead by that time—their mother had died before and their father after the wedding—but it looked to Et like sheets for two beds.

'It gives you plenty of wash.'

'What does?'

'Changing sheets like you do.'

Et was often there in the evening, playing rummy with Arthur while Char, in the other room, picked at the piano in the dark. Or talking and reading library books with Char, while Arthur marked his papers. Arthur walked her home. 'Why do you have to go off and live by yourself anyway?' he scolded her. 'You ought to come back and live with us.'

'Three's a crowd.'

'It wouldn't be for long. Some man is going to come along some day and fall hard.'

'If he was such a fool as to do that I'd never fall for him, so we'd be back where we started.'

'I was a fool that fell for Char, and she ended up having me.'

Just the way he said her name indicated that Char was above, outside, all ordinary considerations—a marvel, a mystery. No one could hope to solve her, they were lucky just being allowed to contemplate her. Et was on the verge of saying, 'She swallowed blueing once over a man that wouldn't have her,' but she thought what would be the good of it, Char would only seem more splendid to him, like a heroine out of Shakespeare. He squeezed Et's waist as if to stress their companionable puzzlement, involuntary obeisance, before her sister. She felt afterwards the bumpy pressure of his fingers as if they had left dents just above where her skirt fastened. It had felt like somebody absent-mindedly trying out the keys of a piano.

Et had set up in the dressmaking business. She had a long narrow room on the Square, once a shop, where she did all her fitting, sewing, cutting, pressing and, behind a curtain, her sleeping and cooking. She could lie in bed and look at the squares of pressed tin on her ceiling, their flower pattern, all her own. Arthur had not liked her taking up dressmaking because he thought she was too smart for it. All the hard work she had done in History had given him an exaggerated idea of her brains. 'Besides,' she told him, 'it takes more brains to cut and fit, if you do it right, than to teach people about the War of 1812. Because, once you learn that, it's learned and isn't going to change you. Whereas every article of clothing you make is an entirely new proposition.'

'Still it's a surprise,' said Arthur, 'to see the way you settle down.'

It surprised everybody, but not Et herself. She made the change easily, from a girl turning cartwheels to a town fixture. She drove the other dressmakers out of business. They had been meek, unimportant creatures anyway, going around to people's houses, sewing in back rooms and being grateful for meals. Only one serious rival appeared in all Et's years, and that was a Finnish woman who called herself a designer. Some people gave her a try, because people are never satisfied, but it soon came out she was all style and no fit. Et never mentioned her, she let people find out for themselves; but afterwards, when this woman had left town and gone to Toronto—where, from what Et had seen on the streets, nobody knew a good fit from a bad—Et did not restrain herself. She would say to a customer she was fitting, 'I see you're still wearing that herringbone my foreigner friend tacked together for you. I saw you on the street.'

'Oh, I know,' the woman would say. 'But I do have to wear it out.'

'You can't see yourself from behind anyway, what's the difference.'

Customers took this kind of thing from Et, came to expect it, even. She's a terror, they said about her, Et's a terror. She had them at a disadvantage, she had them in their slips and corsets. Ladies who looked quite firm and powerful, outside, were here immobilized, apologetic, exposing such trembly, meek-looking thighs squeezed together by corsets, such long sad breast creases, bellies blown up and torn by children and operations.

Et always closed her front curtains tight, pinning the crack.

'That's to keep the men from peeking.'

Ladies laughed nervously.

'That's to keep Jimmy Saunders from stumping over to get an eyeful.'

Jimmy Saunders was a World War I veteran who had a little shop next to Et's, harness and leather goods.

'Oh, Et. Jimmy Saunders has a wooden leg.'

'He hasn't got wooden eyes. Or anything else that I know of.'

'Et you're terrible.'

Et kept Char beautifully dressed. The two steadiest criticisms of Char, in Mock Hill, were that she dressed too elegantly, and that she smoked. It was because she was a teacher's wife that she should have refrained from doing either of these things, but Arthur of course let her do anything she liked, even buying her a cigarette holder so she could look like a lady in a magazine. She smoked at a high school dance, and wore a backless satin evening dress, and danced with a boy who had got a high school girl pregnant, and it was all the same to Arthur. He did not get to be Principal. Twice the school board passed him over and brought in somebody from outside, and when they finally gave him the job, in 1942, it was only temporarily and because so many teachers were away at war.

Char fought hard all these years to keep her figure. Nobody but Et and Arthur knew what effort that cost her. Nobody but Et knew it all. Both of their parents had been heavy, and Char had inherited the tendency, though Et was always as thin as a stick. Char did exercises and drank a glass of warm water before every meal. But sometimes she went on eating binges. Et had known her to eat a dozen cream puffs one after the other, a pound of peanut brittle, or a whole lemon meringue pie. Then pale and horrified she took down Epsom salts, three or four or five times the prescribed amount. For two or three days she would be sick, dehydrated, purging her sins, as Et said. During these periods she could not look at food. Et would have to come and cook Arthur's supper. Arthur did not know about the pie or the peanut brittle or whatever it was, or about the Epsom salts. He thought she had gained a pound or two and was going through a fanatical phase of dieting. He worried about her.

'What is the difference, what does it matter?' he would say to Et. 'She would still be beautiful.'

'She won't do herself any harm,' said Et, enjoying her food, and glad to see that worry hadn't put him off his. She always made him good suppers.

It was the week before the Labor Day weekend. Blaikie had gone to Toronto, for a day or two he said.

'It's quiet without him,' said Arthur.

'I never noticed he was such a conversationalist,' Et said.

'I only mean in the way that you get used to somebody.'

'Maybe we ought to get unused to him,' said Et.

Arthur was unhappy. He was not going back to the school; he had obtained a leave of absence until after Christmas. Nobody believed he would go back then.

'I suppose he has his own plans for the winter,' he said.

'He may have his own plans for right now. You know I have my customers from the hotel. I have my friends. Ever since I went on that excursion, I hear things.'

She never knew where she got the inspiration to say what she said, where it came from. She had not planned it at all, yet it came so easily, believably.

'I hear he's taken up with a well-to-do woman down at the hotel.'

Arthur was the one to take an interest, not Char.

'A widow?'

'Twice, I believe. The same as he is. And she has the money from both. It's been suspected for some time and she was talking about it openly. He never said anything, though. He never said anything to you, did he, Char?'

'No,' said Char.

'I heard this afternoon that now he's gone, and she's gone. It wouldn't be the first time he pulled something like this. Char and I remember.'

Then Arthur wanted to know what she meant and she told him the story of the lady ventriloquist, remembering even the names of the dolls, though of course she left out all about Char. Char sat through this, even contributing a bit.

'They might come back but my guess is they'd be embarrassed. He'd be embarrassed. He'd be embarrassed to come here, anyway.'

'Why?' said Arthur, who had cheered up a little through the ventriloquist story. 'We never set down any rule against a man getting married.'

Char got up and went into the house. After a while they heard the sound of the piano.

The question often crossed Et's mind in later years—what did she mean to do about this story when Blaikie got back? For she had no reason to believe he would not come back. The answer was that she had not made any plans at all. She had not planned anything. She supposed she might have wanted to make trouble between him and Char—make Char pick a fight with him, her suspicions roused even if rumors had not been borne out, make Char read what he might do again in the light of what he had done before. She did not know what she wanted. Only to throw things into confusion, for she believed then that somebody had to, before it was too late.

Arthur made as good a recovery as could be expected at his age, he went back to teaching history to the senior classes, working half-days until it was time for him to retire. Et kept up her own place on the Square and tried to get up and do some cooking and cleaning for Arthur, as well. Finally, after he retired, she moved back into the house, keeping the other place only for business purposes. 'Let people jaw all they like,' she said. 'At our age.'

Arthur lived on and on, though he was frail and slow. He walked down to the Square once a day, dropped in on Et, went and sat in the park. The hotel closed down and was sold again. There was a story that it was going to be opened up and used as a rehabilitation center for drug addicts, but the town got up a petition and that fell through. Eventually it was torn down.

Et's eyesight was not as good as it used to be, she had to slow down. She had to turn people away. Still she worked, every day. In the evenings Arthur watched television or read, but she sat out on the porch, in the warm weather, or in the dining room in winter, rocking and resting her eyes. She came and watched the news with him, and made him his hot drink, cocoa or tea.

There was no trace of the bottle. Et went and looked in the cupboard as soon as she could—having run to the house in response to Arthur's early morning call, and found the doctor, old McClain, coming in at the same time. She ran out and looked in the garbage, but she never found it. Could Char have found the time to bury it? She was lying on the bed, fully and nicely dressed, her hair piled up. There was no fuss about the cause of death as there is in stories. She had complained of weakness to Arthur the night before, after Et had gone, she had said she thought she was getting the flu. So the old doctor said heart, and let it go. Nor could Et ever know. Would what was in that bottle leave a body undisfigured, as Char's was? Perhaps what was in the bottle was not what it said. She was not even sure that it had been there that last evening, she had been too carried away with what she was saying to go and look, as she usually did. Perhaps it had been thrown out earlier and Char had taken something else, pills maybe. Perhaps it really was her heart. All that purging would have weakened anybody's heart.

Her funeral was on Labor Day and Blaikie Noble came, cutting out his bus tour. Arthur in his grief had forgotten about Et's story, was not surprised to see Blaikie there. He had come back to Mock Hill on the day Char was found. A few hours too late, like some story. Et in her natural confusion could not remember what it was. Romeo and Juliet, she thought later. But Blaikie of course did not do away with himself afterwards, he went back to Toronto. For a year or two he sent Christmas cards, then was not heard of any more. Et would not be surprised if her story of his marrying had not come true in the end. Only her timing was mistaken.

Sometimes Et had it on the tip of her tongue to say to Arthur, 'There's something I've been meaning to tell you.' She didn't believe she was going to let him die without knowing. He shouldn't be allowed. He kept a picture of Char on his bureau. It was the one taken of her in her costume for that play, where she played the statue-girl. But Et let it go, day to day. She and Arthur still played rummy and kept up a bit of garden, along with raspberry canes. If they had been married, people would have said they were very happy.

1974

The Moons of Jupiter

I found my father in the heart wing, on the eighth floor of Toronto General Hospital. He was in a semi-private room. The other bed was empty. He said that his hospital insurance covered only a bed in the ward, and he was worried that he might be charged extra.

'I never asked for a semi-private,' he said.

I said the wards were probably full.

'No. I saw some empty beds when they were wheeling me by.'

'Then it was because you had to be hooked up to that thing,' I said. 'Don't worry. If they're going to charge you extra, they tell you about it.'

'That's likely it,' he said. 'They wouldn't want those doohickeys set up in the wards. I guess I'm covered for that kind of thing.'

I said I was sure he was.

He had wires taped to his chest. A small screen hung over his head. On the screen a bright jagged line was continually being written. The writing was accompanied by a nervous electronic beeping. The behavior of his heart was on display. I tried to ignore it. It seemed to me that paying such close attention—in fact, dramatizing what ought to be a most secret activity—was asking for trouble. Anything exposed that way was apt to flare up and go crazy.

My father did not seem to mind. He said they had him on tranquillizers. You know, he said, the happy pills. He did seem calm and optimistic.

It had been a different story the night before. When I brought him into the hospital, to the emergency room, he had been pale and closemouthed. He had opened the car door and stood up and said quietly, 'Maybe you better get me one of those wheelchairs.' He used the voice he always used in a crisis. Once, our chimney caught on fire; it was on a Sunday afternoon and I was in the dining room pinning together a dress I was making. He came in and said in that same matter-of-fact, warning voice, 'Janet. Do you know where there's some baking powder?' He wanted it to throw on the fire. Afterwards he said, 'I guess it was your fault—sewing on Sunday.'

I had to wait for over an hour in the emergency waiting room. They summoned a heart specialist who was in the hospital, a young man. He called me out into the hall and explained to me that one of the valves of my father's heart had deteriorated so badly that there ought to be an immediate operation.

I asked him what would happen otherwise.

'He'd have to stay in bed,' the doctor said.

'How long?'

'Maybe three months.'

'I meant, how long would he live?'

'That's what I meant, too,' the doctor said.

I went to see my father. He was sitting up in bed in a curtained-off corner. 'It's bad, isn't it?' he said. 'Did he tell you about the valve?'

'It's not as bad as it could be,' I said. Then I repeated, even exaggerated, anything hopeful the doctor had said. 'You're not in any immediate danger. Your physical condition is good, otherwise.'

'Otherwise,' said my father, gloomily.

I was tired from the drive—all the way up to Dalgleish, to get him, and back to Toronto since noon—and worried about getting the rented car back on time, and irritated by an article I had been reading in a magazine in the waiting room. It was about another writer, a woman younger, better-looking, probably more talented than I am. I had been in England for two months and so I had not seen this article before, but it crossed my mind while I was reading that my father would have. I could hear him saying, Well, I didn't see anything about you in *Maclean's*. And if he had read something about me he would say, Well, I didn't think too much of that writeup. His tone would be humorous and indulgent but would produce in me a familiar dreariness of spirit. The message I got from him was simple: Fame must be striven for, then apologized for. Getting or not getting it, you will be to blame.

I was not surprised by the doctor's news. I was prepared to hear something of the sort and was pleased with myself for taking it calmly, just as I would be pleased with myself for dressing a wound or looking down from the frail balcony of a high building. I thought, Yes, it's time; there has to be something, here it is. I did not feel any of the protest I would have felt twenty, even ten, years before. When I saw from my father's face that he felt it—that refusal leapt up in him as readily as if he had been thirty or forty years younger—my heart hardened, and I spoke with a kind of badgering cheerfulness. 'Otherwise is plenty,' I said.

The next day he was himself again.

That was how I would have put it. He said it appeared to him now that the young fellow, the doctor, might have been a bit too eager to operate. 'A bit knife-happy,' he said. He was both mocking and showing off the hospital slang. He said that another doctor had examined him, an older man, and had given it as his opinion that rest and medication might do the trick.

I didn't ask what trick.

'He says I've got a defective valve, all right. There's certainly some damage. They wanted to know if I had rheumatic fever when I was a kid. I said I didn't think so. But half the time then you weren't diagnosed what you had. My father was not one for getting the doctor.'

The thought of my father's childhood, which I always pictured as bleak and dangerous—the poor farm, the scared sisters, the harsh father—made me less resigned to his dying. I thought of him running away to work on the lake boats, running along the railway tracks, toward Goderich, in the evening light. He used to tell about that trip. Somewhere along the track he found a quince tree. Quince trees are rare in our part of the country; in fact, I have never seen one. Not even the one my father found, though he once took us on an expedition to look for it. He thought he knew the crossroad it was near, but we could not find it. He had not been able to eat the fruit, of course, but he had been impressed by its existence. It made him think he had got into a new part of the world.

The escaped child, the survivor, an old man trapped here by his leaky heart. I didn't pursue these thoughts. I didn't care to think of his younger selves. Even his bare torso, thick and white—he had the body of a workingman of his generation, seldom exposed to the sun—was a danger to me; it looked so strong and young. The wrinkled neck, the age-freckled hands and arms, the narrow, courteous head, with its thin gray hair and mustache, were more what I was used to.

'Now, why would I want to get myself operated on?' said my father reasonably. 'Think of the risk at my age, and what for? A few years at the outside. I think the best thing for me to do is go home and take it easy. Give in gracefully. That's all you can do, at my age. Your attitude changes, you know. You go through some mental changes. It seems more natural.'

'What does?' I said.

'Well, death does. You can't get more natural than that. No, what I mean, specifically, is not having the operation.'

'That seems more natural?'

'Yes.'

'It's up to you,' I said, but I did approve. This was what I would have expected of him. Whenever I told people about my father I stressed his independence, his self-sufficiency, his forbearance. He worked in a factory, he worked in his garden, he read history books. He could tell you about the Roman emperors or the Balkan wars. He never made a fuss.

Judith, my younger daughter, had come to meet me at Toronto Airport two days before. She had brought the boy she was living with, whose name was Don. They were driving to Mexico in the morning, and while I was in Toronto I was to stay in their apartment. For the time being, I live in Vancouver. I sometimes say I have my headquarters in Vancouver.

'Where's Nichola?' I said, thinking at once of an accident or an overdose. Nichola is my older daughter. She used to be a student at the Conservatory, then she became a cocktail waitress, then she was out of work. If she had been at the airport, I would probably have said something wrong. I would have asked her what her plans were, and she would have gracefully brushed back her hair and said, 'Plans?'—as if that was a word I had invented.

'I knew the first thing you'd say would be about Nichola,' Judith said.

'It wasn't. I said hello and I—'

'We'll get your bag,' Don said neutrally.

'Is she all right?'

'I'm sure she is,' said Judith, with a fabricated air of amusement. 'You wouldn't look like that if I was the one who wasn't here.'

'Of course I would.'

'You wouldn't. Nichola is the baby of the family. You know, she's four years older than I am.'

'I ought to know.'

Judith said she did not know where Nichola was exactly. She said Nichola had moved out of her apartment (that dump!) and had actually telephoned (which is quite a deal, you might say, Nichola phoning) to say she wanted to be incommunicado for a while but she was fine.

'I told her you would worry,' said Judith more kindly on the way to their van. Don walked ahead carrying my suitcase. 'But don't. She's all right, believe me.'

Don's presence made me uncomfortable. I did not like him to hear these things. I thought of the conversations they must have had, Don and Judith. Or Don and Judith and Nichola, for Nichola and Judith were sometimes on good terms. Or Don and Judith and Nichola and others whose names I did not even know. They would have talked about me. Judith and Nichola comparing notes, relating anecdotes; analyzing, regretting, blaming, forgiving. I wished I'd had a boy and a girl. Or two boys. They wouldn't have done that. Boys couldn't possibly know so much about you.

I did the same thing at that age. When I was the age Judith is now I talked with my friends in the college cafeteria or, late at night, over coffee in our cheap rooms. When I was the age Nichola is now I had Nichola herself in a carry-cot or squirming in my lap, and I was drinking coffee again all the rainy Vancouver afternoons with my one neighborhood friend, Ruth Boudreau, who read a lot and was bewildered by her situation, as I was. We talked about our parents, our childhoods, though for some time we kept clear of our marriages. How thoroughly we dealt with our fathers and mothers, deplored their marriages, their mistaken ambitions or fear of ambition, how competently we filed them away, defined them beyond any possibility of change. What presumption.

I looked at Don walking ahead. A tall ascetic-looking boy, with a St Francis cap of black hair, a precise fringe of beard. What right did he have to hear about me, to know things I myself had probably forgotten? I decided that his beard and hairstyle were affected.

Once, when my children were little, my father said to me, 'You know those years you were growing up—well, that's all just a kind of a blur to me. I can't sort out one year from another.' I was offended. I remembered each separate year with pain and clarity. I could have told how old I was when I went to look at the evening dresses in the window of Benbow's Ladies' Wear. Every week through the winter a new dress, spotlit—the sequins and tulle, the rose and lilac, sapphire, daffodil—and me a cold worshipper on the slushy sidewalk. I could have told how old I was when I forged my mother's signature on a bad report card, when I had measles, when we papered the front room. But the years when Judith and Nichola were little, when I lived with their father—yes, blur is the word for it. I remember hanging out diapers, bringing in and folding diapers; I can recall the kitchen counters of two houses and where the clothesbasket sat. I remember the television programs—*Popeye the Sailor, The Three Stooges, Funorama.* When *Funorama* came on it was time to turn on the lights and cook supper. But I couldn't tell the years apart. We lived outside Vancouver in a dormitory suburb: Dormir, Dormer, Dormouse—something like that. I was sleepy all the time then; pregnancy made me sleepy, and the night feedings, and the West Coast rain falling. Dark dripping cedars, shiny dripping laurel; wives yawning, napping, visiting, drinking coffee, and folding diapers; husbands coming home at night from the city across the water. Every night I kissed my homecoming husband in his wet Burberry and hoped he might wake me up; I served up meat and potatoes and one of the four vegetables he permitted. He ate with a violent appetite, then fell asleep on the living-room sofa. We had become a cartoon couple, more middle-aged in our twenties than we would be in middle age.

Those bumbling years are the years our children will remember all their lives. Corners of the yards I never visited will stay in their heads.

'Did Nichola not want to see me?' I said to Judith.

'She doesn't want to see anybody, half the time,' she said. Judith moved ahead and touched Don's arm. I knew that touch—an apology, an anxious reassurance. You touch a man that way to remind him that you are grateful, that you realize he is doing for your sake something that bores him or slightly endangers his dignity. It made me feel older than grandchildren would to see my daughter touch a man—a boy—this way. I felt her sad jitters, could predict her supple attentions. My blunt and stocky, blonde and candid child. Why should I think she wouldn't be susceptible, that she would always be straightforward, heavy-footed, self-reliant? Just as I go around saying that Nichola is sly and solitary, cold, seductive. Many people must know things that would contradict what I say.

In the morning Don and Judith left for Mexico. I decided I wanted to see somebody who wasn't related to me, and who didn't expect anything in particular from me. I called an old lover of mine, but his phone was answered by a machine: 'This is Tom Shepherd speaking. I will be out of town for the month of September. Please record your message, name, and phone number.'

Tom's voice sounded so pleasant and familiar that I opened my mouth to ask him the meaning of this foolishness. Then I hung up. I felt as if he had deliberately let me down, as if we had planned to meet in a public place and then he hadn't shown up. Once, he had done that, I remembered.

I got myself a glass of vermouth, though it was not yet noon, and I phoned my father.

'Well, of all things,' he said. 'Fifteen more minutes and you would have missed me.'

'Were you going downtown?'

'Downtown Toronto.'

He explained that he was going to the hospital. His doctor in Dalgleish wanted the doctors in Toronto to take a look at him, and had given him a letter to show them in the emergency room.

''Emergency room?' I said.

'It's not an emergency. He just seems to think this is the best way to handle it. He knows the name of a fellow there. If he was to make me an appointment, it might take weeks.'

'Does your doctor know you're driving to Toronto?' I said.

'Well, he didn't say I couldn't.'

The upshot of this was that I rented a car, drove to Dalgleish, brought my father back to Toronto, and had him in the emergency room by seven o'clock that evening.

Before Judith left I said to her, 'You're sure Nichola knows I'm staying here?'

'Well, I told her,' she said.

Sometimes the phone rang, but it was always a friend of Judith's.

'Well, it looks like I'm going to have it,' my father said. This was on the fourth day. He had done a complete turnaround overnight. 'It looks like I might as well.'

I didn't know what he wanted me to say. I thought perhaps he looked to me for a protest, an attempt to dissuade him.

'When will they do it?' I said.

'Day after tomorrow.'

I said I was going to the washroom. I went to the nurses' station and found a woman there who I thought was the head nurse. At any rate, she was gray-haired, kind, and serious-looking.

'My father's having an operation the day after tomorrow?' I said.

'Oh, yes.'

'I just wanted to talk to somebody about it. I thought there'd been a sort of decision reached that he'd be better not to. I thought because of his age.'

'Well, it's his decision and the doctor's.' She smiled at me without condescension. 'It's hard to make these decisions.'

'How were his tests?'

'Well, I haven't seen them all.'

I was sure she had. After a moment she said, 'We have to be realistic. But the doctors here are very good.'

When I went back into the room my father said, in a surprised voice, *'Shoreless seas.'*

'What?' I said. I wondered if he had found out how much, or how little, time he could hope for. I wondered if the pills had brought on an untrustworthy euphoria. Or if he had wanted to gamble. Once, when he was talking to me about his life, he said, 'The trouble was I was always afraid to take chances.'

I used to tell people that he never spoke regretfully about his life, but that was not true. It was just that I didn't listen to it. He said that he should have gone into the Army as a tradesman—he would have been better off. He said he should have gone on his own, as a carpenter, after the war. He should have got out of Dalgleish. Once, he said, 'A wasted life, eh?' But he was making fun of himself, saying that, because it was such a dramatic thing to say. When he quoted poetry, too, he always had a scoffing note in his voice, to excuse the showing-off and the pleasure.

'Shoreless seas,' he said again. ' "Behind him lay the gray Azores,/Behind the Gates of Hercules;/Before him not the ghost of shores,/Before him only shoreless seas." '[1] That's what was going through my head last night. But do you think I could remember what kind of seas? I could not. Lonely seas? Empty seas? I was on the right track but I couldn't get it. But there now when you came into the room and I wasn't thinking about it at all, the word popped into my head. That's always the way, isn't it? It's not all that surprising. I ask my mind a question. The answer's there, but I can't see all the connections my mind's making to get it. Like a computer. Nothing out of the way. You know, in my situation the thing is, if there's anything you can't explain right away, there's a great temptation to—well, to make a mystery out of it. There's a great temptation to believe in—You know.'

'The soul?' I said, speaking lightly, feeling an appalling rush of love and recognition.

'Oh, I guess you could call it that. You know, when I first came into this room there was a pile of papers here by the bed. Somebody had left them here—one of those tabloid sort of things I never looked at. I started reading them. I'll read anything handy. There was a series running in them on personal experiences of people who had died, medically speaking—heart arrest, mostly—and had been brought back to life. It was what they remembered of the time when they were dead. Their experiences.'

'Pleasant or un-?' I said.

'Oh, pleasant. Oh yes. They'd float up to the ceiling and look down on themselves and see the doctors working on them, on their bodies. Then float on further and recognize some people they knew who had died before them. Not see them exactly but sort of sense them. Sometimes there would be a humming and sometimes a sort of—what's that light that there is or color around a person?'

[1] From 'Columbus', by the American poet 'Joaquin' Miller (1841-1913).

'Aura?'

'Yes. But without the person. That's about all they'd get time for; then they found themselves back in the body and feeling all the mortal pain and so on— brought back to life.'

'Did it seem—convincing?'

'Oh, I don't know. It's all in whether you want to believe that kind of thing or not. And if you are going to believe it, take it seriously, I figure you've got to take everything else seriously that they print in those papers.'

'What else do they?'

'Rubbish—cancer cures, baldness cures, bellyaching about the younger generation and the welfare bums. Tripe about movie stars.'

'Oh, yes. I know.'

'In my situation you have to keep a watch,' he said, 'or you'll start playing tricks on yourself.' Then he said, 'There's a few practical details we ought to get straight on,' and he told me about his will, the house, the cemetery plot. Everything was simple.

'Do you want me to phone Peggy?' I said. Peggy is my sister. She is married to an astronomer and lives in Victoria.

He thought about it. 'I guess we ought to tell them,' he said finally. 'But tell them not to get alarmed.'

'All right.'

'No, wait a minute. Sam is supposed to be going to a conference the end of this week, and Peggy was planning to go along with him. I don't want them wondering about changing their plans.'

'Where is the conference?'

'Amsterdam,' he said proudly. He did take pride in Sam, and kept track of his books and articles. He would pick one up and say, 'Look at that, will you? And I can't understand a word of it!' in a marvelling voice that managed nevertheless to have a trace of ridicule.

'Professor Sam,' he would say. 'And the three little Sams.' This is what he called his grandsons, who did resemble their father in braininess and in an almost endearing pushiness—an innocent energetic showing-off. They went to a private school that favored old-fashioned discipline and started calculus in Grade Five. 'And the dogs,' he might enumerate further, 'who have been to obedience school. And Peggy . . . '

But if I said, 'Do you suppose she has been to obedience school, too?' he would play the game no further. I imagine that when he was with Sam and Peggy he spoke of me in the same way—hinted at my flightiness just as he hinted at their stodginess, made mild jokes at my expense, did not quite conceal his amazement (or pretended not to conceal his amazement) that people paid money for things I had written. He had to do this so that he might never seem to brag, but he would put up the gates when the joking got too rough. And of course I found later, in the house, things of mine he had kept—a few magazines, clippings, things I had never bothered about.

Now his thoughts travelled from Peggy's family to mine. 'Have you heard from Judith?' he said.

'Not yet.'

'Well, it's pretty soon. Were they going to sleep in the van?'

'Yes.'

'I guess it's safe enough, if they stop in the right places.'

I knew he would have to say something more and I knew it would come as a joke.

'I guess they put a board down the middle, like the pioneers?'

I smiled but did not answer.

'I take it you have no objections?'

'No,' I said.

'Well, I always believed that, too. Keep out of your children's business. I tried not to say anything. I never said anything when you left Richard.'

'What do you mean, "said anything"? Criticize?'

'It wasn't any of my business.'

'No.'

'But that doesn't mean I was pleased.'

I was surprised—not just at what he said but at his feeling that he had any right, even now, to say it. I had to look out the window and down at the traffic to control myself.

'I just wanted you to know,' he added.

A long time ago, he said to me in his mild way, 'It's funny. Richard when I first saw him reminded me of what my father used to say. He'd say if that fellow was half as smart as he thinks he is, he'd be twice as smart as he really is.'

I turned to remind him of this, but found myself looking at the line his heart was writing. Not that there seemed to be anything wrong, any difference in the beeps and points. But it was there.

He saw where I was looking. 'Unfair advantage,' he said.

'It is,' I said. 'I'm going to have to get hooked up, too.'

We laughed, we kissed formally; I left. At least he hadn't asked me about Nichola, I thought.

The next afternoon I didn't go to the hospital, because my father was having some more tests done, to prepare for the operation. I was to see him in the evening instead. I found myself wandering through the Bloor Street dress shops, trying on clothes. A preoccupation with fashion and my own appearance had descended on me like a raging headache. I looked at the women in the street, at the clothes in the shops, trying to discover how a transformation might be made, what I would have to buy. I recognized this obsession for what it was but had trouble shaking it. I've had people tell me that waiting for life-or-death news they've stood in front of an open refrigerator eating anything in sight—cold boiled potatoes, chili sauce, bowls of whipped cream. Or have been unable to stop doing crossword puzzles. Attention narrows in on something—some distraction—grabs on, becomes fanatically serious. I shuffled clothes on the racks, pulled them on in hot little changing rooms in front of cruel mirrors. I was sweating; once or twice I thought I might faint. Out on the street again, I thought I must remove myself from Bloor Street, and decided to go to the museum.

I remembered another time, in Vancouver. It was when Nichola was going to kindergarten and Judith was a baby. Nichola had been to the doctor about a cold, or maybe for a routine examination, and the blood test revealed something about her white blood cells—either that there were too many of them or that they were enlarged. The doctor ordered further tests, and I took Nichola to the hospital for them. Nobody mentioned leukemia but I knew, of course, what they were looking for. When I took Nichola home I asked the babysitter who had been with Judith to stay for the afternoon and I went shopping. I bought the most daring dress I ever owned, a black silk sheath with some laced-up arrangement in front. I remember that bright spring afternoon, the spike-heeled shoes in the department store, the underwear printed with leopard spots.

I also remembered going home from St Paul's Hospital over the Lions Gate Bridge on the crowded bus and holding Nichola on my knee. She suddenly recalled her baby name for bridge and whispered to me, 'Whee—over the whee.' I did not avoid touching my child—Nichola was slender and graceful even then, with a pretty back and fine dark hair—but realized I was touching her with a difference, though I did not think it could ever be detected. There was a care—not a withdrawal exactly but a care—not to feel anything much. I saw how the forms of love might be maintained with a condemned person but with the love in fact measured and disciplined, because you have to survive. It could be done so discreetly that the object of such care would not suspect, any more than she would suspect the sentence of death itself. Nichola did not know, would not know. Toys and kisses and jokes would come tumbling over her; she would never know, though I worried that she would feel the wind between the cracks of the manufactured holidays, the manufactured normal days. But all was well. Nichola did not have leukemia. She grew up—was still alive, and possibly happy. Incommunicado.

I could not think of anything in the museum I really wanted to see, so I walked past it to the planetarium. I had never been to a planetarium. The show was due to start in ten minutes. I went inside, bought a ticket, got in line. There was a whole class of schoolchildren, maybe a couple of classes, with teachers and volunteer mothers riding herd on them. I looked around to see if there were any other unattached adults. Only one—a man with a red face and puffy eyes, who looked as if he might be here to keep himself from going to a bar.

Inside, we sat on wonderfully comfortable seats that were tilted back so that you lay in a sort of hammock, attention directed to the bowl of the ceiling, which soon turned dark blue, with a faint rim of light all around the edge. There was some splendid, commanding music. The adults all around were shushing the children, trying to make them stop crackling their potato-chip bags. Then a man's voice, an eloquent professional voice, began to speak slowly, out of the walls. The voice reminded me a little of the way radio announcers used to introduce a piece of classical music or describe the progress of the Royal Family to Westminster Abbey on one of their royal occasions. There was a faint echo-chamber effect.

The dark ceiling was filling with stars. They came out not all at once but one after another, the way the stars really do come out at night, though more quickly. The Milky Way appeared, was moving closer; stars swam into brilliance and kept on going, disappearing beyond the edges of the sky-screen or behind my head. While the flow of light continued, the voice presented the stunning facts. A few light-years away, it announced, the sun appears as a bright star, and the planets are not visible. A few dozen light-years away, the sun is not visible, either, to the naked eye. And that distance—a few dozen light-years—is only about a thousandth part of the distance from the sun to the center of our galaxy, one galaxy, which itself contains about two hundred billion suns. And is, in turn, one of millions, perhaps billions, of galaxies. Innumerable repetitions, innumerable variations. All this rolled past my head, too, like balls of lightning.

Now realism was abandoned, for familiar artifice. A model of the solar system was spinning away in its elegant style. A bright bug took off from the earth, heading for Jupiter. I set my dodging and shrinking mind sternly to recording facts. The mass of Jupiter two and a half times that of all the other planets put together. The Great Red Spot.[2] The thirteen moons. Past Jupiter, a glance at the eccentric orbit of Pluto, the icy rings of Saturn. Back to Earth and moving in to hot and dazzling Venus. Atmospheric pressure ninety times ours. Moonless Mercury rotating three times while circling the sun twice; an odd arrangement, not as satisfying as what they used to tell us—that it rotated once as it circled the sun. No perpetual darkness after all. Why did they give out such confident information, only to announce later that it was quite wrong? Finally, the picture already familiar from magazines: the red soil of Mars, the blooming pink sky.

When the show was over I sat in my seat while the children clambered across me, making no comments on anything they had just seen or heard. They were pestering their keepers for eatables and further entertainments. An effort had been made to get their attention, to take it away from canned pop and potato chips and fix it on various knowns and unknowns and horrible immensities, and it seemed to have failed. A good thing, too, I thought. Children have a natural immunity, most of them, and it shouldn't be tampered with. As for the adults who would deplore it, the ones who promoted this show, weren't they immune themselves to the extent that they could put in the echo-chamber effects, the music, the churchlike solemnity, simulating the awe that they supposed they ought to feel? Awe—what was that supposed to be? A fit of the shivers when you looked out the window? Once you knew what it was, you wouldn't be courting it.

Two men came with brooms to sweep up the debris the audience had left behind. They told me that the next show would start in forty minutes. In the meantime, I had to get out.

'I went to the show at the planetarium,' I said to my father. 'It was very exciting—about the solar system.' I thought what a silly word I had used: 'exciting.' 'It's like a slightly phony temple,' I added.

He was already talking. 'I remember when they found Pluto. Right where they thought it had to be. Mercury, Venus, Earth, Mars,' he recited. 'Jupiter, Saturn, Nept—no, Uranus, Neptune, Pluto. Is that right?'

'Yes,' I said. I was just as glad he hadn't heard what I said about the phony

[2]A large red area of turbulence in Jupiter's upper atmosphere.

temple. I had meant that to be truthful, but it sounded slick and superior. 'Tell me the moons of Jupiter.'

'Well, I don't know the new ones. There's a bunch of new ones, isn't there?'

'Two. But they're not new.'

'New to us,' said my father. 'You've turned pretty cheeky now I'm going under the knife.'

' "Under the knife." What an expression.'

He was not in bed tonight, his last night. He had been detached from his apparatus, and was sitting in a chair by the window. He was bare-legged, wearing a hospital dressing gown, but he did not look self-conscious or out of place. He looked thoughtful but good-humored, an affable host.

'You haven't even named the old ones,' I said.

Give me time. Galileo named them. Io.'

'That's a start.'

'The moons of Jupiter were the first heavenly bodies discovered with the telescope.'[3] He said this gravely, as if he could see the sentence in an old book. 'It wasn't Galileo named them, either; it was some German. Io, Europa, Ganymede, Callisto. There you are.'

'Yes.'

'Io and Europa, they were girlfriends of Jupiter's, weren't they? Ganymede was a boy. A shepherd? I don't know who Callisto was.'

'I think she was a girlfriend, too,' I said. 'Jupiter's wife—Jove's wife— changed her into a bear and stuck her up in the sky. Great Bear and Little Bear. Little Bear was her baby.'

The loudspeaker said that it was time for visitors to go.

'I'll see you when you come out of the anesthetic,' I said.

'Yes.'

When I was at the door, he called to me, 'Ganymede wasn't any shepherd. He was Jove's cupbearer.'

When I left the planetarium that afternoon, I had walked through the museum to the Chinese garden. I saw the stone camels again, the warriors, the tomb. I sat on a bench looking toward Bloor Street. Through the evergreen bushes and the high grilled iron fence I watched people going by in the late-afternoon sunlight. The planetarium show had done what I wanted it to after all—calmed me down, drained me. I saw a girl who reminded me of Nichola. She wore a trenchcoat and carried a bag of groceries. She was shorter than Nichola—not really much like her at all—but I thought that I might see Nichola. She would be walking along some street maybe not far from here—burdened, preoccupied, alone. She was one of the grownup people in the world now, one of the shoppers going home.

If I did see her, I might just sit and watch, I decided. I felt like one of those people who have floated up to the ceiling, enjoying a brief death. A relief, while it lasts. My father had chosen and Nichola had chosen. Someday, probably soon, I would hear from her, but it came to the same thing.

---

[3]The four major satellites of Jupiter were discovered in 1610 by Galileo, who called them the Medicean moons; they were given their present names by Simon Marius (1573-1624).

I meant to get up and go over to the tomb, to look at the relief carvings, the stone pictures, that go all the way around it. I always mean to look at them and I never do. Not this time, either. It was getting cold out, so I went inside to have coffee and something to eat before I went back to the hospital.

1982

Mordecai Richler

b. 1931

Mordecai Richler was born in Montreal at the beginning of the Depression. His experience of growing up in the working-class neighbourhood around St Urbain Street, and of attending Baron Byng, the predominantly Jewish high school nearby, is recorded in both his fiction and in sketches such as 'The Summer My Grandmother Was Supposed to Die'. Richler's childhood and adolescence were dominated by the conflicts provoked by Fascism—the Spanish Civil War and the Second World War—and in his writing he has often expressed regret that his generation was too young to take part in those heroic events. As a student at Sir George Williams College (now part of Concordia University), Richler made friends with the veterans returned from Europe; after they graduated he dropped out and, using savings from a life-insurance policy, left Canada. He spent the next two years in Europe, chiefly in Paris—of which he has said, '. . . it was, in the truest sense, my university. St Germain des Prés was my campus, Montparnasse my frat house'—and became part of a group of young and aspiring expatriate writers who would gather in the cafés to try out their wit and irony on each other.

Returning to Canada in 1952, Richler worked briefly for the CBC. In 1954 *The Acrobats*—about Spain after the Civil War and written while Richler was in Europe—was published in England. This first novel, which shows its author beginning his ca-

reer under the influence of Hemingway, Sartre, and Malraux, seems seriously marred by its disjointed construction and occasionally overblown writing; however, it was surprisingly successful and was reprinted in an American paperback edition and translated into Danish, Norse, and German.

Convinced that he had to return to Europe to fulfil his literary ambitions, Richler moved to England soon after *The Acrobats* appeared. The novel he published the following year, *Son of a Smaller Hero* (1955), gives an account of a young Jew's struggle to free himself from the restrictions of family, ghetto, and North American society in general, and ends with a similar decision to leave Canada. His treatment of Montreal Jewry in that novel, and his later ironic portrayal of the London expatriate writers and film-makers who had taken refuge from American McCarthyism (in *A Choice of Enemies*, 1957), revealed Richler's willingness to expose for critical examination those communities of which he was a member.

Although remaining abroad, Richler continued to write about his Montreal past, and in 1959 he published the novel that established his reputation, *The Apprenticeship of Duddy Kravitz*, a morally complex story of a bumptious young hustler who will go to any lengths to achieve his goals. In this novel, and in *Saint Urbain's Horseman* (1971), in which Duddy briefly reappears, as well as in *Joshua Then and Now* (1980), Richler shows the particular qualities that have most attracted his readers: an impressive ability to create fully developed characters and to locate them in authentic and densely textured milieus. The two novels that Richler published in the sixties—*The Incomparable Atuk* (1963) and *Cocksure* (1968)—are works of a very different sort: mordant and surreal fables that marked him as the most vitriolic satirist of his generation. The savage and frequently bawdy humour of *Cocksure* (one of Richler's own favourites) made it an object of controversy when it was chosen for a Governor General's Award. Richler won a second award for *Saint Urbain's Horseman*, which portrays a rootless expatriate who, all but overwhelmed by the 'competing mythologies' of the modern world, creates a new mythic figure to suit his own needs.

Richler has helped to finance his career as a novelist, and filled the time between novels, by working as a script-writer for radio, television, and films (including *Life at the Top*, 1965; *The Apprenticeship of Duddy Kravitz*, 1973; and *Fun with Dick and Jane*, 1977) and as a freelance journalist. Some of his journalism has been collected in *Hunting Tigers under Glass* (1968), *Shovelling Trouble* (1972), and *The Great Comic Book Heroes and Other Essays* (1978), a selection from the two earlier volumes. In 1969 his various autobiographical sketches about his youth were collected in *The Street*. Richler is also the author of a successful children's book, *Jacob Two-Two Meets the Hooded Fang* and of the text of a travel book, *Images of Spain* (1977); and he is the editor of the anthology *Canadian Writing Today* (1970). In 1972 Richler returned permanently to Montreal, ending his long period of expatriation.

The Summer My Grandmother Was Supposed to Die

Dr Katzman discovered the gangrene on one of his monthly visits. 'She won't last a month,' he said.

He said the same the second month, the third and the fourth, and now she lay dying in the heat of the back bedroom.

'God in heaven,' my mother said, 'what's she holding on for?'

The summer my grandmother was supposed to die we did not chip in with the Greenbaums to take a cottage in the Laurentians. My grandmother, already bedridden for seven years, could not be moved again. The doctor came twice a week. The only thing was to stay in the city and wait for her to die or, as my mother said, pass away. It was a hot summer, her bedroom was just behind the kitchen, and when we sat down to eat we could smell her. The dressings on my grandmother's left leg had to be changed several times a day and, according to Dr Katzman, any day might be her last in this world. 'It's in the hands of the Almighty,' he said.

'It won't be long now,' my father said, 'and she'll be better off, if you know what I mean?'

A nurse came every day from the Royal Victorian Order. She arrived punctually at noon and at five to twelve I'd join the rest of the boys under the outside staircase to peek up her dress as she climbed our second-storey flat. Miss Bailey favoured absolutely beguiling pink panties, edged with lace, and that was better than waiting under the stairs for Cousin Bessie, for instance, who wore enormous cotton bloomers, rain or shine.

I was sent out to play as often as possible, because my mother felt it was not good for me to see somebody dying. Usually, I would just roam the scorched streets. There was Duddy, Gas sometimes, Hershey, Stan, Arty and me.

'Before your grandmaw kicks off,' Duddy said, 'she's going to roll her eyes and gurgle. That's what they call the death-rattle.'

'Aw, you know everything. *Putz.*'

'I read it, you jerk,' Duddy said, whacking me one, 'in Perry Mason.'

Home again I would usually find my mother sour and spent. Sometimes she wept.

'She's dying by inches,' she said to my father one stifling night, 'and none of them ever come to see her. Oh, such children,' she added, going on to curse them vehemently in Yiddish.

'They're not behaving right. It's certainly not according to Hoyle,' my father said.

Dr Katzman continued to be astonished. 'It must be will-power alone that keeps her going,' he said. 'That, and your excellent care.'

'It's not my mother any more in the back room, Doctor. It's an animal. I want her to die.'

'Hush. You don't mean it. You're tired.' Dr Katzman dug into his black bag and produced pills for her to take. 'Your wife's a remarkable woman,' he told my father.

'You don't so say,' my father replied, embarrassed.

'A born nurse.'

My sister and I used to lie awake talking about our grandmother. 'After she dies,' I said, 'her hair will go on growing for another twenty-four hours.'

'Says who?'

'Duddy Kravitz. Do you think Uncle Lou will come from New York for the funeral?'

'I suppose so.'

'Boy, that means another fiver for me. Even more for you.'

'You shouldn't say things like that or her ghost will come back to haunt you.'

'Well, I'll be able to go to her funeral anyway. I'm not too young any more.'

I was only six years old when my grandfather died, and so I wasn't allowed to go to his funeral.

I have one imperishable memory of my grandfather. Once he called me into his study, set me down on his lap, and made a drawing of a horse for me. On the horse he drew a rider. While I watched and giggled he gave the rider a beard and the fur-trimmed round hat of a rabbi, a *straimel*, just like he wore.

My grandfather had been a Zaddik,[1] one of the Righteous, and I've been assured that to study Talmud with him had been an illuminating experience. I wasn't allowed to go to his funeral, but years later I was shown the telegrams of condolence that had come from Eire and Poland and even Japan. My grandfather

---

[1] Holy man (Hebrew); the Talmud is an extensive set of commentaries on the Torah (the first five books of the Bible).

had written many books: a translation of the Book of Splendour (the Zohar)[2] into modern Hebrew, some twenty years' work, and lots of slender volumes of sermons, hasidic tales, and rabbinical commentaries. His books had been published in Warsaw and later in New York.

'At the funeral,' my mother said, 'they had to have six motorcycle policemen to control the crowds. It was such a heat that twelve women fainted—and I'm *not* counting Mrs Waxman from upstairs. With her, you know, *anything* to fall into a man's arms. Even Pinsky's. And did I tell you that there was even a French Canadian priest there?'

'Aw, you're kidding me.'

'The priest was some *knacker*.[3] A bishop maybe. He used to study with the *zeyda*. The *zeyda* was a real personality, you know. Spiritual and worldly-wise at the same time. Such personalities they don't make any more. Today rabbis and peanuts come in the same size.'

But, according to my father, the *zeyda* (his father-in-law) hadn't been as celebrated as all that. 'There are things I could say,' he told me. 'There was another side to him.'

My grandfather had sprung from generations and generations of rabbis, his youngest son was a rabbi, but none of his grandchildren would be one. My Cousin Jerry was already a militant socialist. I once heard him say, 'When the men at the kosher bakeries went out on strike the *zeyda* spoke up against them on the streets and in the *shuls*.[4] It was of no consequence to him that the men were grossly underpaid. His superstitious followers had to have bread. Grandpappy,' Jerry said, 'was a prize reactionary.'

A week after my grandfather died my grandmother suffered a stroke. Her right side was completely paralysed. She couldn't speak. At first it's true, she could manage a coherent word or two and move her right hand enough to write her name in Hebrew. Her name was Malka. But her condition soon began to deteriorate.

My grandmother had six children and seven step-children, for my grandfather had been married before. His first wife had died in the old country. Two years later he had married my grandmother, the only daughter of the most affluent man in the *shtetl*,[5] and their marriage had been a singularly happy one. My grandmother had been a beautiful girl. She had also been a shrewd, resourceful and patient wife. Qualities, I fear, indispensible to life with a Zaddik. For the synagogue paid my grandfather no stipulated salary and much of the money he picked up here and there he had habitually distributed among rabbinical students, needy immigrants and widows. A vice, for such it was to his impecunious family, which made him as unreliable a provider as a drinker. To carry the analogy fur-

---

[2]The most influential work of the cabalistic or mystical tradition of Judaism and therefore of especial importance to Chassidic (or Hasidic) Jews; the Zohar is an eclectic mixture of tales, secret wisdom, folklore, dream interpretation, numerology, spiritual commentary, and mysticism dating from the thirteenth century. Because of the amount of superstitious lore it contained, the laity were sometimes warned against studying it.
[3]Big shot (Yiddish; the initial 'k' is sounded); '*zeyda*': grandfather (Yiddish).
[4]Synagogues (Yiddish).
[5]Literally 'village' (Yiddish): any of the ghettos to which Jews were once confined in Eastern Europe.

ther, my grandmother had to make hurried, surreptitious trips to the pawnbroker with her jewellery. Not all of it to be redeemed, either. But her children had been looked after. The youngest, her favourite, was a rabbi in Boston, the oldest was the actor-manager of a Yiddish theatre in New York, and another was a lawyer. One daughter lived in Montreal, two in Toronto. My mother was the youngest daughter and when my grandmother had her stroke there was a family conclave and it was decided that my mother would take care of her. This was my father's fault. All the other husbands spoke up—they protested hotly that their wives had too much work—they could never manage it—but my father detested quarrels and so he was silent. And my grandmother came to stay with us.

Her bedroom, the back bedroom, had actually been promised to me for my seventh birthday, but now I had to go on sharing a room with my sister. So naturally I was resentful when each morning before I left for school my mother insisted that I go in and kiss my grandmother goodbye.

'Bouyo-bouyo,' was the only sound my grandmother could make.

During those first hopeful months—'Twenty years ago who would have thought there'd be a cure for diabetes?' my father asked. 'Where there's life, you know.'—my grandmother would smile and try to speak, her eyes charged with effort; and I wondered if she knew that I was waiting for her room.

Even later there were times when she pressed my hand urgently to her bosom with her surprisingly strong left arm. But as her illness dragged on and on she became a condition in the house, something beyond hope or reproach, like the leaky ice-box, there was less recognition and more ritual in those kisses. I came to dread her room. A clutter of sticky medicine bottles and the cracked toilet chair beside the bed; glazed but imploring eyes and a feeble smile, the wet smack of her crooked lips against my cheeks. I flinched from her touch. And after two years, I protested to my mother, 'What's the use of telling her I'm going here or I'm going there? She doesn't even recognize me any more.'

'Don't be fresh. She's your grandmother.'

My uncle who was in the theatre in New York sent money regularly to help support my grandmother and, for the first few months, so did the other children. But once the initial and sustaining excitement had passed the children seldom came to our house any more. Anxious weekly visits—'And how is she today, poor lamb?'—quickly dwindled to a dutiful monthly looking in, and then a semi-annual visit, and these always on the way to somewhere.

When the children did come my mother was severe with them. 'I have to lift her on that chair three times a day maybe. And what makes you think I always catch her in time? Sometimes I have to change her linen twice a day. That's a job I'd like to see your wife do,' she said to my uncle, the rabbi.

'We could send her to the Old People's Home.'

'Now there's an idea,' my father said.

'Not so long as I'm alive.' My mother shot my father a scalding look, 'Say something, Sam.'

'Quarreling will get us nowhere. It only creates bad feelings.'

Meanwhile, Dr Katzman came once a month. 'It's astonishing,' he would say each time. 'She's as strong as a horse.'

'Some life for a person,' my father said. 'She can't speak—she doesn't recognize anybody—what is there for her?'

The doctor was a cultivated man; he spoke often for women's clubs, sometimes on Yiddish literature and other times, his rubicund face hot with menace, the voice taking on a doomsday tone, on the cancer threat. 'Who are we to judge?' he asked.

Every evening, during the first few months of my grandmother's illness, my mother would read her a story by Sholem Aleichem.[6] 'Tonight she smiled,' my mother would report defiantly. 'She understood. I can tell.'

Bright afternoons my mother would lift the old lady into a wheelchair and put her out in the sun and once a week she gave her a manicure. Somebody always had to stay in the house in case my grandmother called. Often, during the night, she would begin to wail unaccountably and my mother would get up and rock her mother in her arms for hours. But in the fourth year of my grandmother's illness the strain began to tell. Besides looking after my grandmother, my mother had to keep house for a husband and two children. She became scornful of my father and began to find fault with my sister and me. My father started to spend his evenings playing pinochle at Tansky's Cigar & Soda. Weekends he took me to visit his brothers and sisters. Wherever my father went people had little snippets of advice for him.

'Sam, you might as well be a bachelor. One of the other children should take the old lady for a while. You're just going to have to put your foot down for once.'

'Yeah, in your face maybe.'

My Cousin Libby, who was at McGill, said, 'This could have a very damaging effect on the development of your children. These are their formative years, Uncle Samuel, and the omnipresence of death in the house . . .'

'What you need is a boy friend,' my father said. '*And how.*'

After supper my mother took to falling asleep in her chair, even in the middle of Lux Radio Theatre. One minute she would be sewing a patch on my breeches or making a list of girls to call for a bingo party, proceeds for the Talmud Torah,[7] and the next she would be snoring. Then, inevitably, there came the morning she just couldn't get out of bed and Dr Katzman had to come round a week before his regular visit. 'Well, well, this won't do, will it?'

Dr Katzman led my father into the kitchen. 'Your wife's got a gallstone condition,' he said.

My grandmother's children met again, this time without my mother, and decided to put the old lady in the Jewish Old People's Home on Esplanade Street. While my mother slept an ambulance came to take my grandmother away.

'It's for the best,' Dr Katzman said, but my father was in the back room when my grandmother held on tenaciously to the bedpost, not wanting to be moved by the two men in white.

'Easy does it, granny,' the younger man said.

Afterwards my father did not go to see my mother. He went out for a walk.

[6] The pen-name of Sholom Rabinowitz (1859-1916), a Russian-born American Jewish writer famous for his folktale-like comic stories written in Yiddish.
[7] Hebrew school.

When my mother got out of bed two weeks later her cheeks had regained their normal pinkish hue; for the first time in months, she actually joked with me. She became increasingly curious about how I was doing in school and whether or not I shined my shoes regularly. She began to cook special dishes for my father again and resumed old friendships with the girls on the parochial school board. Not only did my father's temper improve, but he stopped going to Tansky's every night and began to come home early from work. But my grandmother's name was seldom mentioned. Until one evening, after I'd had a fight with my sister, I said, 'Why can't I move into the back bedroom now?'

My father glared at me. 'Big-mouth.'

'It's empty, isn't it?'

The next afternoon my mother put on her best dress and coat and new spring hat.

'Don't go looking for trouble,' my father said.

'It's been a month. Maybe they're not treating her right.'

'They're experts.'

'Did you think I was never going to visit her? I'm not inhuman, you know.'

'Alright, go.' But after she had gone my father stood by the window and said, 'I was born lucky, and that's it.'

I sat on the outside stoop watching the cars go by. My father waited on the balcony above, cracking peanuts. It was six o'clock, maybe later, when the ambulance slowed down and rocked to a stop right in front of our house. 'I knew it,' my father said. 'I was born with all the luck.'

My mother got out first, her eyes red and swollen, and hurried upstairs to make my grandmother's bed.

'You'll get sick again,' my father said.

'I'm sorry, Sam, but what could I do? From the moment she saw me she cried and cried. It was terrible.'

'They're recognized experts there. They know how to take care of her better than you do.'

'Experts? Expert murderers you mean. She's got bedsores, Sam. Those dirty little Irish nurses they don't change her linen often enough, they hate her. She must have lost twenty pounds in there.'

'Another month and you'll be flat on your back again. I'll write you a guarantee, if you want.'

My father became a regular at Tansky's again and, once more, I had to go in and kiss my grandmother in the morning. Amazingly, she had begun to look like a man. Little hairs had sprouted on her chin, she had grown a spiky grey moustache, and she was practically bald.

Yet again my uncles and aunts sent five dollar bills, though erratically, to help pay for my grandmother's support. Elderly people, former followers of my grandfather, came to inquire about the old lady's health. They sat in the back bedroom with her, leaning on their canes, talking to themselves and rocking to and fro. 'The Holy Shakers,' my father called them. I avoided the seamed, shrunken old men because they always wanted to pinch my cheeks or trick me with a dash of snuff and laugh when I sneezed. When the visit with my grandmother was over the old people would unfailingly sit in the kitchen with my mother for another hour, watching her make *lokshen,*[8] slurping lemon tea out of a saucer. They would recall the sayings and books and charitable deeds of the late Zaddik.

'At the funeral,' my mother never wearied of telling them, 'they had to have six motorcycle policemen to control the crowds.'

In the next two years there was no significant change in my grandmother's condition, though fatigue, ill-temper, and even morbidity enveloped my mother again. She fought with her brothers and sisters and once, after a particularly bitter quarrel, I found her sitting with her head in her hands. 'If, God forbid, I had a stroke,' she said, 'would you send me to the Old People's Home?'

'Of course not.'

'I hope that never in my life do I have to count on my children for anything.'

The seventh summer of my grandmother's illness she was supposed to die and we did not know from day to day when it would happen. I was often sent out to eat at an aunt's or at my other grandmother's house. I was hardly ever at home. In those days they let boys into the left-field bleachers of Delormier Downs free during the week and Duddy, Gas sometimes, Hershey, Stan, Arty and me spent many an afternoon at the ball park. The Montreal Royals, kingpin of the Dodger farm system, had a marvellous club at the time. There was Jackie Robinson, Roy Campanella, Lou Ortiz, Red Durrett, Honest John Gabbard, and Kermit Kitman. Kitman was our hero. It used to give us a charge to watch the crafty little Jew, one of ours, running around out there with all those tall dumb southern crackers. 'Hey, Kitman,' we would yell, 'Hey, shmo-head, if your father knew you played ball on *shabus*—'[9] Kitman, alas, was all field and no hit. He never made the majors. 'There goes Kermit Kitman,' we would holler, after he had gone down swinging again, 'the first Jewish strike-out king of the International League.' This we promptly followed up by bellowing choice imprecations in Yiddish.

It was after one of these games, on a Friday afternoon, that I came home to find a crowd gathered in front of our house.

'That's the grandson,' somebody said.

A knot of old people stood staring at our front door from across the street. A taxi pulled up and my aunt hurried out, hiding her face in her hands.

'After so many years,' a woman said.

'And probably next year they'll discover a cure. Isn't that always the case?'

The flat was clotted. Uncles and aunts from my father's side of the family, strangers, Dr Katzman, neighbours, were all milling around and talking in hushed voices. My father was in the kitchen, getting out the apricot brandy. 'Your grandmother's dead,' he said.

'Where's Maw?'

'In the bedroom with . . . You'd better not go in.'

'I want to see her.'

My mother wore a black shawl and glared down at a knot of handkerchief clutched in a fist that had been cracked by washing soda. 'Don't come in here,' she said.

[8]Noodles (Yiddish).
[9]The Sabbath (Yiddish).

Several bearded round-shouldered men in shiny black coats surrounded the bed. I couldn't see my grandmother.

'Your grandmother's dead.'

'Daddy told me.'

'Go wash your face and comb your hair.'

'Yes.'

'You'll have to get your own supper.'

'Sure.'

'One minute. The *baba*[1] left some jewellery. The necklace is for Rifka and the ring is for your wife.'

'Who's getting married?'

'Better go and wash your face. Remember behind the ears, please.'

Telegrams were sent, the obligatory long distance calls were made, and all through the evening relatives and neighbours and old followers of the Zaddik poured into the house. Finally, the man from the funeral parlour arrived.

'There goes the only Jewish businessman in town,' Segal said, 'who wishes all his customers were German.'

'This is no time for jokes.'

'Listen, life goes on.'

My Cousin Jerry had begun to affect a cigarette holder. 'Soon the religious mumbo-jumbo starts,' he said to me.

'Wha'?'

'Everybody is going to be sickeningly sentimental.'

The next day was the sabbath and so, according to law, my grandmother couldn't be buried until Sunday. She would have to lie on the floor all night. Two grizzly women in white came to move and wash the body and a professional mourner arrived to sit up and pray for her. 'I don't trust his face,' my mother said. 'He'll fall asleep.'

'He won't fall asleep.'

'You watch him, Sam.'

'A fat lot of good prayers will do her now. Alright! Okay! I'll watch him.'

My father was in a fury with Segal.

'The way he goes after the apricot brandy you'd think he never saw a bottle in his life before.'

Rifka and I were sent to bed, but we couldn't sleep. My aunt was sobbing over the body in the living room; there was the old man praying, coughing and spitting into his handkerchief whenever he woke; and the hushed voices and whimpering from the kitchen, where my father and mother sat. Rifka allowed me a few drags off her cigarette.

'Well, *pisherke*,[2] this is our last night together. Tomorrow you can take over the back room.'

'Are you crazy?'

'You always wanted it for yourself, didn't you?'

'She died in there, but.'

'So?'

[1] Old woman; grandmother (Russian/Yiddish).
[2] A mild Yiddish vulgarity; idiomatically 'a little squirt', a nobody.

'I couldn't sleep in there now.'

'Good night and happy dreams.'

'Hey, let's talk some more.'

'Did you know,' Rifka said, 'that when they hang a man the last thing that happens is that he has an orgasm?'

'A wha'?'

'Skip it. I forgot you were still in kindergarten.'

'Kiss my Royal Canadian—'

'At the funeral, they're going to open the coffin and throw dirt in her face. It's supposed to be earth from Eretz.[3] They open it and you're going to have to look.'

'Says you.'

A little while after the lights had been turned out Rifka approached my bed, her head covered with a sheet and her arms raised high. 'Bouyo-bouyo. Who's that sleeping in my bed? Woo-woo.'

My uncle who was in the theatre and my aunt from Toronto came to the funeral. My uncle, the rabbi, was there too.

'As long as she was alive,' my mother said, 'he couldn't even send her five dollars a month. I don't want him in the house, Sam. I can't bear the sight of him.'

'You're upset,' Dr Katzman said, 'and you don't know what you're saying.'

'Maybe you'd better give her a sedative,' the rabbi said.

'Sam will you speak up for once, please.'

Flushed, eyes heated, my father stepped up to the rabbi. 'I'll tell you this straight to your face, Israel,' he said. 'You've gone down in my estimation.'

The rabbi smiled a little.

'Year by year,' my father continued, his face burning a brighter red, 'your stock has gone down with me.'

My mother began to weep and she was led unwillingly to a bed. While my father tried his utmost to comfort her, as he muttered consoling things, Dr Katzman plunged a needle into her arm. 'There we are,' he said.

I went to sit on the stoop outside with Duddy. My uncle, the rabbi, and Dr Katzman stepped into the sun to light cigarettes.

'I know exactly how you feel,' Dr Katzman said. 'There's been a death in the family and the world seems indifferent to your loss. Your heart is broken and yet it's a splendid summer day . . . a day made for love and laughter . . . and that must seem very cruel to you.'

The rabbi nodded; he sighed.

'Actually,' Dr Katzman said, 'it's remarkable that she held out for so long.'

'Remarkable?' the rabbi said. 'It's written that if a man has been married twice he will spend as much time with his first wife in heaven as he did on earth. My father, may he rest in peace, was married to his first wife for seven years and my mother, may she rest in peace, has managed to keep alive for seven years. Today in heaven she will be able to join my father, may he rest in peace.'

Dr Katzman shook his head. 'It's amazing,' he said. He told my uncle that he

[3]The land (of Jerusalem); the Promised Land.

was writing a book based on his experiences as a healer. 'The mysteries of the human heart.'

'Yes.'

'Astonishing.'

My father hurried outside. 'Dr Katzman, please. It's my wife. Maybe the injection wasn't strong enough. She just doesn't stop crying. It's like a tap. Can you come in, please?'

'Excuse me,' Dr Katzman said to my uncle.

'Of course.' My uncle turned to Duddy and me. 'Well, boys,' he said, 'what would you like to be when you grow up?'

1969

Alden Nowlan

1933-1983

The sympathy for victims of emotional and economic poverty that is often expressed in the writing of Alden Nowlan derives in part from personal experience. Nowlan grew up near Nova Scotia's Annapolis Valley, in a small 'thin-soil' settlement that he describes as little touched by the Depression because it was already impoverished. Although he quit school in Grade 5, eventually going to work in nearby lumber mills and on farms, he continued his education by reading whatever he could find. At nineteen he took a position on the Hartland *Observer* in New Brunswick. During his ten years as a journalist and editor at the *Observer*, and later at the Saint John *Telegraph-Journal*, he developed a simple, direct style that may be seen in the poetry and short fiction he began writing in the mid-1950s. In 1957 he met Maritime poet and educator Fred Cogswell, whose encouragement led to the publication of Nowlan's first collection of poems, *The Rose and the Puritan* (1958). Since then Nowlan has published eleven more volumes of poetry, including *Bread, Wine and*

Salt (1967), which won a Governor General's Award; *The Mysterious Naked Man* (1969); *Playing the Jesus Game: Selected Poems* (1970); *Smoked Glass* (1977); and *I Might Not Tell Everybody This* (1982). He has also written short stories—collected in *Miracle at Indian River* (1968)—that deal with the brutal cultural trap in which his fellow Maritimers are caught. His novel, *Various Persons Named Kevin O'Brien* (1973), is an essentially autobiographical account of his difficult boyhood. *Double Exposure*, a collection of his journalistic pieces, was published in 1978.

From 1969 on, Nowlan was associated with the University of Brunswick, while working as a writer and freelance journalist. In the 1970s he collaborated with Walter Learning in writing plays; two of them focus on popular figures—Frankenstein (in *Frankenstein: The Man Who Became God*, 1974), and Sherlock Holmes (in *The Incredible Murder of Cardinal Tosca*, 1978).

In his poetry, as in his stories, Nowlan is a chronicler—he called himself a 'witness'—of a rural Maritime way of life that has remained virtually unchanged for centuries. He has observed that when he moved to small-town New Brunswick, he also moved from the eighteenth century into the twentieth, leaving behind a boyhood home that had 'no furnace, no plumbing, no electricity, no refrigerator, no telephone . . . [a home, where] we used kerosene lamps and on the coldest winter nights water froze in the bucket in the kitchen'. Nowlan pictures a Maritimes landscape (as in 'On the Barrens' and 'Canadian January Night') that seems primitive in comparison with those seen in such famous nineteenth-century poems as Roberts' 'Tantramar Revisited' and Carman's 'Low Tide on Grand Pré'. The perspective of Nowlan's poems is notably different from that of his predecessors: he captures not the picturesque but the commonplace. Unlike Roberts or Carman, Nowlan is not a detached observer telling his audience about a region but is both a part of a milieu and a reporter of it—a dual role that he often found uncomfortable. A harsh, uncompromising realism in his poetry prevents it from becoming mundane or naive. The sentimentality implicit in focusing on the crippling effects of the guilt and repression that Nowlan saw as his cultural heritage ('I am a product of a culture that fears any display of emotion and attempts to repress any true communication') is regularly undercut by an ironic humour that suggests imagination is man's only real escape from adversity and deprivation.

Dancer

The sun is horizontal, so the flesh
of the near-naked girl bouncing a ball
is netted in its light, an orange mesh
weaving between her and the shadowed wall.

Her body glistening and snake-crescendoes
electric in her lighted muscles, she
pauses before each pitch, then rears and throws
the ball against the darkness, venomously.

The interlocking stones cry out and hurl
the black globe back, all human purpose stript 10
from its wild passage, and the bounding girl
bolts in and out of darkness, after it.

Stumbling in the shadows, scalded blind
each time she whirls to face the sunlight, she
at last restores the pattern of her mind.
But every ball's more difficult to see.

1962

Canadian Love Song

Your body's a small word with many meanings.
Love. If. Yes. But. Death.
Surely I will love you a little while,
perhaps as long as I have breath.

December is thirteen months long,
July's one afternoon; therefore,
lovers must outwit wool,
learn how to puncture fur.

To my love's bed, to keep her warm,
I'll carry wrapped and heated stones.   10
That which is comfort to the flesh
is sometimes torture to the bones.

1962

The Sleepwalker

Zeno of Elea[1] said an arrow doesn't move:
it is always at rest
at one of a series
of points: so it is with a sleepwalker

who always seems to know where he's going
without knowing where he is,
the body saying
'no' to its own
movements, and the eyes
focussed on something so far away   10
nobody can see it
without going blind
to everything between;

and when he wakes up
in his own house
in the world
where he's lived
all his life,
he says:
where am I?   20
how did I get here?

[1]Greek philosopher (about 490-430 B.C.), who defended Parmenides' doctrine that 'being' is real by demonstrating the logical absurdities in the opposing view, which held that plurality and change are real. His arguments against the reality of motion ('Zeno's Paradox') are his best known.

while the vision
darts like a fish,
signet of Christ,
cymbal of wisdom,
into the swirling
depths of his eyes.

1967

Temptation

The boy is
badgering the man
to lower him down the
face of the cliff
to a narrow shelf
about eight feet
below:
'Your hands are strong,
and I'm not afraid.
The ledge is wide enough,   10
I won't hurt myself
even if you let go.'

'Don't be a fool.
You'd break every bone
in your body.
Where in God's name
do you get such ideas?
It's time we went home.'

But there is no
conviction in the   20
man's voice and
the boy persists;
nagging his wrists,
dragging him nearer.
Their summer shirts
balloon in the wind.

While devils whisper
what god-like sport
it would be
to cling to the   30
edge of the world
and gamble
one's only son
against the wind
and rocks
and sea.

1967

The First Stirring of the Beasts

The first stirring of the beasts
is heard at two or three or four
in the morning, depending on the season.

You lie, warm and drowsy, listening,
wondering how there is so much difference
between the sounds
cattle and horses make,
moving in their stanchions[1] or halters,
so much difference that you can't explain,
so that if someone asked you   10
which of them is moving now?
you couldn't answer
but lying there, not quite awake,
you know, although it doesn't matter,
and then a rooster crows
and it sounds, or maybe you imagine this,
unsure and a little afraid,
                              and after a little
there are only the sounds of night
that we call silence.   20

The second stirring of the beasts
is the one everybody understands.
You hear it at dawn
and if you belong here
you get up.
Anyway, there is no mystery
in it, it is the other stirring,
the first brief restlessness
which seems to come for no reason
that makes you ask yourself   30
what are they awake for?

1969

___
[1]Two vertical posts between which a cow's head is placed to keep the animal in its stall.

Country Full of Christmas

Country full of Christmas,
the stripped, suspicious elms
groping for the dun sky—
what can I give my love?

The remembrance—mouse hawks
scudding on the dykes, above
the wild roses; horses and cattle
separate in the same field.
It is not for my love.

Do you know that foxes   10
believe in nothing
but themselves—everything
is a fox disguised: men, dogs and rabbits.

1969

Hymn to Dionysus[1]

The trick is to loose
    the wild bear
        but hold tight
to the chain,
    woe
        when the bear
snatches up
    the links
        and the man dances.

1969

---

[1]Greek god of vegetation, wine, and pleasure; often seen as the god of frenzied creativity.

Canadian January Night

Ice storm: the hill
a pyramid of black crystal
down which the cars
slide like phosphorescent beetles
while I, walking backwards in obedience
to the wind, am possessed
of the fearful knowledge
my compatriots share
but almost never utter:
this is a country   10
where a man can die
                    simply from being
caught outside.

1971

Survival

The first man who ever stepped on a lion and survived
was Og
who afterwards attributed
his good fortune to his poor eyesight,
he having been unable
to see anything but claws,
teeth and a monstrous body
while his companion
stood transfixed by the indescribably beautiful
visions that he saw with his third good eye.[1]   10

1971

---

[1]See note to'The Third Eye', p. 290.

The Broadcaster's Poem

I used to broadcast at night
alone in a radio station
but I was never good at it,
partly because my voice wasn't right
but mostly because my peculiar
metaphysical stupidity
made it impossible
for me to keep believing
there was somebody listening
when it seemed I was talking   10
only to myself in a room no bigger
than an ordinary bathroom.
I could believe it for a while
and then I'd get somewhat
the same feeling as when you
start to suspect you're the victim
of a practical joke.
                So one part of me
was afraid another part
might blurt out something   20
about myself so terrible
that even I had never until
that moment suspected it.
                This was like the fear
of bridges and other
high places: Will I take off my glasses
and throw them
into the water, although I'm
half-blind without them?
Will I sneak up behind   30
myself and push?
                Another thing:
as a reporter
I covered an accident in which a train
ran into a car, killing
three young men, one of whom
was beheaded. The bodies looked
boneless, as such bodies do.
More like mounds of rags.
And inside the wreckage   40
where nobody could get at it
the car radio
was still playing.
                I thought about places
the disc jockey's voice goes
and the things that happen there
and of how impossible it would be for him
to continue if he really knew.

1974

On the Barrens

'Once when we were hunting cattle
    on the barrens,'
so began many of the stories they told,
gathered in the kitchen, a fire still
    the focus of life then,
the teapot on the stove as long as
    anyone was awake,
mittens and socks left to thaw on
    the open oven door,
chunks of pine and birch piled   10
    halfway to the ceiling,
and always a faint smell of smoke
    like spice in the air,
the lamps making their peace with
    the darkness,
the world not entirely answerable
    to man.

They took turns talking, the listeners
    puffed their pipes,
he whose turn it was to speak used his   20
    as an instrument,
took his leather pouch from a pocket
    of his overalls,
gracefully, rubbed tobacco between
    his rough palms
as he set the mood, tamped it into
    the bowl
at a moment carefully chosen, scratched
    a match when it was necessary
to prolong the suspense. If his pipe   30
    went out it was no accident,
if he spat in the stove it was done
    for a purpose.
When he finished he might lean back
    in his chair so that it stood
on two legs; there'd be a short silence.

The barrens were flat clay fields,
    twenty miles from the sea
and separated from it by dense woods
    and farmlands.   40
They smelled of salt and the wind
    blew there
constantly as it does on the shore
    of the North Atlantic.

There had been a time, the older men
    said, when someone had owned

the barrens but something had happened
long ago and now anyone who wanted to
    could pasture there.
The cattle ran wild all summer,   50
sinewy little beasts, ginger-coloured
    with off-white patches,
grazed there on the windswept barrens
    and never saw a human
until fall when the men came to round
    them up,
sinewy men in rubber boots and tweed caps
    with their dogs beside them.

Some of the cattle would by now have
    forgotten   60
there'd been a time before they'd
    lived on the barrens.
They'd be truly wild, dangerous, the
    men would loose the dogs on them,
mongrel collies, barn dogs with the
    dispositions of convicts
who are set over their fellows,
    the dogs would go for the nose,
sink their teeth in the tender flesh,
    toss the cow on its side,   70
bleating, hooves flying, but shortly
    tractable.
There were a few escaped,
    it was said, and in a little while
they were like no other cattle—
    the dogs feared them,
they roared at night and the men
    lying by their camp-fires
heard them and moaned in their sleep,
    the next day tracking them   80
found where they'd pawed the moss,
    where their horns had scraped
bark from the trees—all the stories
    agreed
in this: now there was nothing to do
    but kill them.

1977

Leonard Cohen

b. 1934

Born and raised in Montreal, Leonard Norman Cohen graduated from McGill (B.A., 1955) and briefly attended graduate school at Columbia University before returning to Montreal and becoming a professional writer. Over the next twenty years he not only began to publish the poetry he had been writing since his teens, but saw two novels through the press by the time he was thirty-two and expanded his career to become a successful songwriter and singer. Cohen left Canada in 1963, spending ten years as an expatriate, largely on the Greek island of Hydra and in a California Zen monastery. Since the early seventies he has divided his time between Montreal and abroad.

Cohen is the Canadian artist whose career has most closely parallelled the trends in world literature during the last twenty-five years. His first book of poetry, *Let Us Compare Mythologies* (1956), shows what Sandra Dwja calls Cohen's 'Black Romantic' viewpoint. It was influenced by the American Beat movement, which rejected the structures of society for the ideal of personal freedom and embraced, in romantic fascination with self-destruction, a bohemian way of life largely associated with drugs, sexual permissiveness, and other forms of social experimentation. In *Let Us Compare Mythologies* Cohen not only assumed the Beat position of social outsider, but also took on the role of mythmaker. Finding that the myths and legends he grew up with were no longer adequate, he began a search for a new myth that could provide meaning, a synthesis of different, often hostile, traditions—particularly those of his Jewish, Westmount childhood and the working-class Catholic values that he experienced in French Montreal. Out of

Cohen's mythmaking came a central theme: the necessity of achieving sainthood, which received its fullest expression in his second novel, *Beautiful Losers* (1966). (His most idealized figure of the modern secular saint appears in the poem 'Suzanne Takes You Down'.) Although other Canadian writers, such as Robertson Davies, have also been concerned with sainthood, few share the notion that occupies Cohen in much of his later work: that the individual must actively seek his own martyrdom at the hands of an inherently hostile society.

In Cohen's second collection, *The Spice-Box of Earth* (1961), a preoccupation with eroticism emerged that has continued to be central to his later work. While the poems in *Spice-Box* are often read for their sensual surfaces, they are rarely valentines. In Cohen's writing, erotic experience is linked to death and violence and is thus not so much a union between two people as a means of saintly purification. *Flowers for Hitler* (1964) gives further prominence to death, violence, and eroticism and employs rhetoric that allies it with the protest poetry of the mid-sixties; the first of Cohen's books intended to alienate the reader, it is also his most explicit piece of social criticism. The perversely dark visions of these and later poems, however, are frequently countered by Cohen's use of traditional styles and conventions that recall the work of Renaissance poets and of Yeats and Eliot, or else by the excessively lush surfaces that Cohen—much like the nineteenth-century Decadents—sometimes gives to his writing.

In the sixties, his most prolific period, Cohen wrote his two novels, *The Favorite Game* (1963) and *Beautiful Losers*. While the earlier novel is the more conventional in form, both books are not so much narrative works as exercises in introspection and perspective. *The Favorite Game*, indebted to Joyce's *Portrait of the Artist as a Young Man* as well as to the tradition of the American-Jewish novel and to contemporary film, gives the reader Cohen's first important treatment of madness, a topic extensively developed in *Beautiful Losers*. More than any other work *Beautiful Losers* ties together all the important elements in Cohen's writing. A pornographic, self-indulgent book, it is nevertheless a dazzling tour-de-force, the novel as stylistic exhibition: myths and images embellish one another as Cohen builds what he calls 'a model of sainthood'—the achievement of a self-destructive Dionysiac madness.

In the late sixties, as a result of his success as a songwriter and performer, Cohen became a media personality—the artist-hero who was his own creation, playing out the role of sacrificial victim. Like Norman Mailer and Alan Ginsberg, Cohen was given to grand gestures (such as refusing a Governor General's Award in 1969), and assumed the pose of ageless, wandering rebel whose public and personal identities are one and whose task is to exhibit his own martyrdom. In this he continued his project of presenting, as Michael Ondaatje has observed, 'Cohen's dreamworlds, Cohen and death, Cohen and love, the legend of Cohen—no matter what the topic is, Cohen is at the centre of the story' (*Leonard Cohen*, 1967). Cohen toured North America and Europe and produced seven records. His songs not only gained him international fame ('Suzanne' became -

one of the most recorded popular songs of the decade) but they also contain some of his best writing.

As early as 1966, however, there were signs of Cohen's having reached a point of stasis as a poet. The collection *Parasites of Heaven* (1966) seemed to be largely culled from the rejects of his earlier books. The small group of new poems in *Selected Poems: 1956-1968* (1968) were more closely related to his songs, in their simplicity and subdued style, than to his other poetry; and even the writing of new songs almost ceased in the early seventies. In 1972 he published *The Energy of Slaves*, a nihilistic and grim collection based on the themes of suicide and artistic burnout. He produced no new books until *Death of a Lady's Man* (1978)—although he did put out two records: *New Skin for the Old Ceremony* (1974), a return to his old forms and stances, and *Death of a Ladies' Man* (1977), a recording (over which he had little control) produced by Phil Spector. The book *Death of a Lady's Man* is a mixture of poetry, prose-poems, and prose that is presented in the form of excerpts from a longer work, 'My Life in Art', accompanied by running commentaries and extensive quotations from notebook sources. In the tradition of Nabokov's *Pale Fire* and Doris Lessing's *The Golden Notebook*, it continues Cohen's examination of multiple perspectives and madness. The struggle between sexuality and asceticism remains important as Cohen elaborates more of his myth—his ongoing attempt to face the despair that follows a loss of faith in all authority, and the subsequent erosion of belief in one's self.

For Anne

With Annie gone,
Whose eyes to compare
With the morning sun?

Not that I did compare,
But I do compare
Now that she's gone.

1961

You Have the Lovers

You have the lovers,
they are nameless, their histories only for each other,
and you have the room, the bed and the windows.
Pretend it is a ritual.
Unfurl the bed, bury the lovers, blacken the windows,
let them live in that house for a generation or two.
No one dares disturb them.
Visitors in the corridor tip-toe past the long closed door,
they listen for sounds, for a moan, for a song:
nothing is heard, not even breathing.   10
You know they are not dead,
you can feel the presence of their intense love.
Your children grow up, they leave you,
they have become soldiers and riders.
Your mate dies after a life of service.
Who knows you? Who remembers you?
But in your house a ritual is in progress:
it is not finished: it needs more people.
One day the door is opened to the lover's chamber.
The room has become a dense garden,   20
full of colours, smells, sounds you have never known.
The bed is smooth as a wafer of sunlight,
in the midst of the garden it stands alone.
In the bed the lovers, slowly and deliberately and silently,
perform the act of love.
Their eyes are closed,
as tightly as if heavy coins of flesh lay on them.
Their lips are bruised with new and old bruises.
Her hair and his beard are hopelessly tangled.
When he puts his mouth against her shoulder   30
she is uncertain whether her shoulder
has given or received the kiss.
All her flesh is like a mouth.
He carries his fingers along her waist
and feels his own waist caressed.
She holds him closer and his own arms tighten around her.
She kisses the hand beside her mouth.

It is his hand or her hand, it hardly matters,
there are so many more kisses.
You stand beside the bed, weeping with happiness,   40
you carefully peel away the sheets
from the slow-moving bodies.
Your eyes are filled with tears, you barely make out the lovers.
As you undress you sing out, and your voice is magnificent
because now you believe it is the first human voice
heard in that room.
The garments you let fall grow into vines.
You climb into bed and recover the flesh.
You close your eyes and allow them to be sewn shut.
You create an embrace and fall into it.   50
There is only one moment of pain or doubt
as you wonder how many multitudes are lying beside your body,
but a mouth kisses and a hand soothes the moment away.

1961

A Kite Is a Victim

A kite is a victim you are sure of.
You love it because it pulls
gentle enough to call you master,
strong enough to call you fool;
because it lives
like a desperate trained falcon
in the high sweet air,
and you can always haul it down
to tame it in your drawer.

A kite is a fish you have already caught   10
in a pool where no fish come,
so you play him carefully and long,
and hope he won't give up,
or the wind die down.

A kite is the last poem you've written,
so you give it to the wind,
but you don't let it go
until someone finds you
something else to do.

A kite is a contract of glory   20
that must be made with the sun,
so you make friends with the field
the river and the wind,
then you pray the whole cold night before,
under the travelling cordless moon,
to make you worthy and lyric and pure.

1961

Another Night with Telescope

Come back to me
            brutal empty room
Thin Byzantine face[1]
            preside over this new fast
I am broken with easy grace
Let me be neither
            father nor child
but one who spins
on an eternal unimportant loom
            patterns of wars and grass   10
which do not last the night
            I know the stars
are wild as dust
and wait for no man's discipline
            but as they wheel
from sky to sky they rake
            our lives with pins of light

1964

[1] i.e. an elongated face like the stylized ones of Byzantine icons.

In the Bible Generations Pass . . .

In the Bible generations pass in a paragraph, a betrayal is
disposed of in a phrase, the creation of the world consumes a
page. I could never pick the important dynasty out of a
multitude, you must have your forehead shining to do that, or to
choose out of the snarled network of daily evidence the denials
and the loyalties. Who can choose what olive tree the story will
need to shade its lovers, what tree out of the huge orchard will
give them the particular view of branches and sky which will
unleash their kisses. Only two shining people know, they go
directly to the roots they lie between. For my part I describe the
whole orchard.

1966

Suzanne Takes You Down

Suzanne takes you down
to her place near the river,
you can hear the boats go by
you can stay the night beside her.
And you know that she's half crazy
but that's why you want to be there
and she feeds you tea and oranges
that come all the way from China.
Just when you mean to tell her

that you have no gifts to give her,   10
she gets you on her wave-length
and she lets the river answer
that you've always been her lover.
    And you want to travel with her,
    you want to travel blind
    and you know that she can trust you
    because you've touched her perfect body
    with your mind.

Jesus was a sailor
when he walked upon the water[1]   20
and he spent a long time watching
from a lonely wooden tower
and when he knew for certain
only drowning men could see him
he said All men will be sailors then
until the sea shall free them,
but he himself was broken
long before the sky would open,
forsaken, almost human,
he sank beneath your wisdom like a stone.   30
    And you want to travel with him,
    you want to travel blind
    and you think maybe you'll trust him
    because he touched your perfect body
    with his mind.

Suzanne takes your hand
and she leads you to the river,
she is wearing rags and feathers
from Salvation Army counters.
The sun pours down like honey   40
on our lady of the harbour
as she shows you where to look
among the garbage and the flowers,
there are heroes in the seaweed
there are children in the morning,
they are leaning out for love
they will lean that way forever
while Suzanne she holds the mirror.
    And you want to travel with her
    and you want to travel blind   50
    and you're sure that she can find you
    because she's touched her perfect body
    with her mind.

1966

---

[1]The account of Jesus' walking on the wave-tossed sea to his desciples on a ship can be found in Matthew 14:22-33. Peter tried to emulate him, but lost faith and began to sink.

Priests

And who will write love songs for you
When I am lord at last
And your body is some little highway shrine
That all my priests have passed
That all my priests have passed.

My priests they will put flowers there
They will stand before the glass
But they'll wear away your little window, love
They will trample on the grass
They will trample on the grass.   10

And who will aim the arrow
That men will follow through your grace
When I am lord of memory
And all of your armour has turned to lace
And all your armour has turned to lace?

The simple life of heroes
And the twisted life of saints
They just confuse the sunny calendar
With their red and golden paints[1]
With their red and golden paints.   20

And all of you have seen the dance
That God has kept from me
But He has seen me watching you
When all your minds were free
When all your minds were free.

1969[2]

---

[1]Red and gold are associated with festivals in the church calendar and the colour of vestments worn for them; they also appear often in religious art.
[2]Published in *Songs of Leonard Cohen*; Cohen has never recorded 'Priests', though Judy Collins has on her *Wildflowers* album.

From *The Energy of Slaves*

Welcome to these lines . . .

Welcome to these lines
There is a war on
but I'll try to make you comfortable
Don't follow my conversation
it's just nervousness
Didn't I make love to you
when we were students of the East
Yes the house is different

the village will be taken soon
I've removed whatever   10
might give comfort to the enemy
We are alone
until the times change
and those who have been betrayed
come back like pilgrims to this moment
when we did not yield
and call the darkness poetry

1972

From *Death of a Lady's Man*

I Decided

I decided to jump literature ahead a few years. Because you are angry, I decided to infuriate you. I am infected with the delirious poison of contempt when I rub my huge nose into your lives and your works. I learned contempt from you. Philistine implies a vigour which you do not have. This paragraph cannot be seized by an iron fist. It is understood immediately. It recoils from your love. It has enjoyed your company. My work is alive.

I Decided

Did he "jump literature ahead a few years"? Certainly, this phase of his work constitutes one of the fiercest attacks ever launched against both the "psychological" and "irrationalist" modes of expression. There is a new freedom here which invites, at the very least, a new scheme of determinism. There is also a willing sense of responsibility and manliness such as we do not find among the current and endless repetitions of stale dada-ist re-discovery. There are guidelines here that will take us well into the two-thousands. He has indicated a process, perhaps even sketched out the handbook, by which we may go to "the end of love." I love this boy, not yet out of his middle-age. He taught me how to breathe and he gave me a dungeon to roast my heart in and a view of the noble cartoon. But listen to him now, in the Notebooks, as he approaches his own doubt in the matter:

So it ends, my conversation with the song. Not so sweetly as it began, but still pleasantly unimportant. I almost tried to make a living with it. Deep down the genius plots his crooked revenge. Change all taste around and make this page an anthem of the change. I'd rather listen to something else. . . . Consign this all to eccentricity. Affirm the mainstream, everyone.

1978

Leon Rooke

b. 1934

Leon Rooke immigrated to Canada in 1969 and settled in Victoria, B.C. Born and educated in North Carolina, he began writing short stories in high school—though his initial recognition came as a dramatist while attending Mars Hill College (1953-5). He continued to write both stories and plays as a student at the University of North Carolina (B.A. 1957). From 1957 to 1964 he travelled extensively in the United States, picking up temporary jobs and serving eighteen months in the army. He was writer-in-residence at UNC in 1965 and then remained in the area as a journalist on a weekly Durham newspaper. He is now a full-time writer who occasionally teaches creative writing at the University of Victoria.

Rooke has had several of his plays produced, including *Ms. America* and *Krokodile* in Toronto and *Sword/Play* in New York; three have been published: *Krokodile* (1973), *Sword/Play* (1974), and *Cakewalk* (1980). In the late fifties his fiction began to appear in journals, and his first collection of short stories, *Last One Home Sleeps in the Yellow Bed*, was published in 1968. His other collections are *The Love Parlour* (1977), *The Broad Back of the Angel* (1977), *Cry Evil* (1980), *Death Suite* (1981), and *The Birth Control King of the Upper Volta* (1982). He has also published four short novels: *Vault* (1973), *Fat Woman* (1980), *The Magician in Love* (1981), and *Shakespeare's Dog* (1983). In 1981 he won the Canada-Australia Literary Award, which is given for an author's overall work.

Because for Rooke life takes place as much in the mind as outside it, his fiction focuses on the validity of imaginative and emotional experience. The most striking feature of Rooke's work, which is mainly told from the viewpoint of first-person narrators, is its use of dramatic voices that present the reader not so much with plots as with the inner workings of the mind. His stories therefore often take the form of monologues—recastings of the narrators' experience, illusions, and fantasies—that are most effective when read aloud. (Rooke himself is well known for his flamboyant public readings of his work.) These narrators speak in the present, about a past whose locale and time are relatively unimportant. Susan March, for example, moves between past and future without regard for sequential time as she drifts between telling us what happened and what she wished to have happen. Close to drama, especially the absurdist plays of Ionesco, these stories have dramatic immediacy: they seem to occur as we read them. Unlike many contemporary writers, Rooke does not seek to alienate or disconnect his readers from the text, but rather emphasizes their dependence on the voice of the speaker as the only stable point of reference in his fiction. These densely woven dramatic monologues—similar in intensity to those in the novels of William Faulkner and Virginia Woolf and in the stories of Dylan Thomas—thus become the whole of the story.

For Rooke, as Stephen Scobie has suggested, form *is* story: 'the wildness, the exuberance, the grotesqueness, and the sudden tonal shifts from fantasy to the catching and placing of realistic detail in the context of humdrum existence, are all as relevant thematically as they are dazzling technically' (*Books in Canada*, Nov. 1981). This formal extravagance gives Rooke's fiction a humorous tone. Constantly undercutting pain with irony and absurdity, Rooke balances the serious (Susan March's agonized search for life in the midst of death) against the frivolous (her frantic and erotic dip in the pool with Mr Reeves). Form in Rooke's stories develops not so much out of the conventional balance between setting, event, and character as out of the elements that make up character itself—memory, fantasy, self-image and, most important, language. Words, syntax, cadence, dialect are the means by which Rooke brings his characters and their narratives into existence. Speaking a language filled with comic incongruities, and with clichés that regain their original vitality in a resurrected logic of slang, his narrators convey to us both the wealth of words and the poverty of speech.

Sixteen-year-old Susan March Confesses to the Innocent Murder of All the Devious Strangers Who Would Drive Her Down

O Love, Daddy,

the first day the first hour the first lovely moment I met him O that first afternoon in my mother's lonely home I said to myself O God Susan March you're going to lose your wits and your heart over this man for look at him he is beautiful isn't he the most beautiful gentle charming exciting man you ever saw and why of course Daddy he was and even as he sat in my mother's chair primly inspecting the room and judging its contents for value and taste and ourselves my mother and me for the way we fitted or did not fit in with it and wondering probably where you were Daddy or even if I had a father or what he would think if *he* were our father/husband/lover even then I was murmuring in my heart THIS is the man I would lay down for THIS is the man I would have for no Daddy I did not think I could bear to let him perish as those others had and I knew he was aware of my thoughts and was listening to my secret words as I said them over and over

O! O! O! O! O! Oh I said

Mr Reeves I know it's crazy and absurd and out of the question even but I declare myself I yearn I ache I love you Mr Reeves for god's sake don't let me keep sitting here too fragile in this instance even to remove my eyes from your face O tell me what I should do how I might give myself help me Mr Reeves because this has never happened to me with those others I shall show you in our lake for I am my father's virgin and have waited here for you but of course it probably happens to you all the time because you're so perfect women can't help themselves O say something Mr Reeves I said and

Lovely tea he said Daddy

though how did I hear for I was dancing all around the room even as I sat brittle and moist with sweat and apprehension in my mother's Queen Elizabeth chair without a hair out of place or a smudge any place and nothing to do with him Daddy until we could circumvent mother's stern presence across the room and advance towards each other over the Persian floor and take each other in our arms

O crumple me Mr Reeves I said almost a scream I wanted this so much O melt me within your

but wait Daddy what were they saying my mother and Mr Reeves that day that hour in our quiet house O what a wasting of time and cruel that time was

I would love to he said I would adore sailing on your daughter's boat out on this beautiful lake but no I've never sailed haven't the knack but yes I can see your daughter is/would be the ideal yachtslady you're all so tanned and beautiful here I can see you love to get out and get your share of

Oh we get our share of pleasures Mr Reeves my poor mother said and already I saw myself out on the lake with him Daddy with you Daddy and hungry for the breeze to quit the lake to lie calm that we might drift under the sun and our eyes closed his arms around me Daddy his lips on my lips his fingers in my hair his

and we would not come back oh would not come back at all until the sun dropped down and mother stood on the shore in the darkness screaming her fear of waves   wind   the night that hid all danger in that greedy spread of water and knowing all the while that the nice Mr Reeves would love me and leave me and break my heart so that I might never again look into the eyes of any man and every man thereafter would look on me with soulful pathetic eyes

O sad Daddy sad sad

and pity that I had given up my heart to someone not worthy of my heart and now no heart left Daddy for anyone.

Mr Reeves my mother said would you like tea? cream with your tea and sugar here's the sugar if sugar is to your taste she said and he said No thank you don't use the stuff bad for the complexion or so I hear and nervously laughed and I did too I touched my burning cheeks and watched him spin the silver spoon inside mother's fine china cup and balance the cup on his knees and oh I spun I spun myself watching him sip and sip and pat his lips and nod his thanks and all the while curling his lashes at me his looks secretive his gaze furtive oh furtively on mine because that day Daddy that first hour the first moment I set eyes on him I/we/he declared our love oh I was not missing even his heartbeat I was attuned to his every breath and on him like a leech and waiting oh waiting pining to be alone with him holding him yielding and giving Daddy although there was not even the need for that because we were together and joined from that first lovely second our eyes met our paths linking and forging a thing massive and insoluble and bound for all eternity and all created out of that first instant when I opened the door   said you must be Mr Reeves   here to see about the Queen Charlotte house here to   oh please do come in mother is   why yes we have both been expecting you

and I seated him in the drawing room and scurried away to catch my breath

O! O! O! to catch my breath!

My daughter is worried Mr Reeves my mother said to him the child can't decide whether to return to school or to stay here with me by the lake this year what do you think she should do Mr Reeves can you advise this troubled girl advise me I am afraid I am of such little use to her in these affairs I've always held that people should make up their own minds don't you think so too but of course life now is so unpredictable and plans hard to keep the roof is always falling in and advice is the last thing I care to give especially where my own flesh and blood are concerned and perhaps you think so as well my own life you see is so untenable and masked I should say so deceptive and riddled with mistake and misdirection and misuse and broken vows at every turn oh I admit it Mr Reeves I am at the mercy of whatever forces at any moment stir yes I think I could say that but as for Susan well my pretty Susan does have her own secret life you know her own curious way of seeing things come to that I suppose we all do wouldn't you say? So what do you think Mr Reeves should my daughter return to school plot her path up through the indifferent world or has she got all the good out of that of course I realize that all these difficulties will end once she leaves me once she meets and marries the man she loves and has children you see a life of her own and all that that involves all my other daughters are quite well-placed in marriage and in the home they are away and settled you see and I know it's difficult for poor Susan who is the youngest child and our prize and was always my favourite and yes her father's too he pampered her gave in to her every whim oh they were very close inseparable which is why it was so cruel what he did Mr Reeves cruel and there was no excuse for it whatever he might say or you might think

and OH OH Daddy I could have gone through the floor could have hung my head in shame for my eyes were suddenly wet and you were beside me Daddy leading me down to shore explaining this explaining that and *going* Daddy *going* while I cried *You can't You can't* and held on to you Daddy held you tightly my arms around your legs crying *You can't You can't* and my mother running berserk at us and away from us through the trees tearing up the earth and finally flinging herself down and calling helplessly to me *Don't let him Susan Stop him Susan* while you walked steadily away

oh vicious Daddy vicious you were

So how do you see it Mr Reeves my mother said don't you think our Susan will have a nice and normal life whatever advice we may or may not choose to give her now can't she expect the same as any other girl with her advantages might expect a home a family a man to look after who will look after her

Oh Mr Reeves I saw it saw his heart leap his eyes shroud over saw gloom walk over him at mention of any man other than himself in my life his tea cup clattering down his shoulders drooping at the thought of my body bearing children not his own at the vision of the cold hands of these men bewitching me

I wanted to stroke his face to bring his face up close to mine and calm him saying Oh don't listen to her Mr Reeves ignore her Mr Reeves only listen to me

I have no one

have had no one

want no one

want only you Mr Reeves and will offer you my proof the minute we are alone I will be yours Mr Reeves and you will never again be made to feel these hot splashes of jealousy this false treachery this pitiful acrimony my mother would inflict on us she is only worried Mr Reeves vengeful and remembering because the truth is she knows how we feel can remember what it was like to know desire and love like ours she's nervous and frightened Mr Reeves and certain that you will murder my soul and mangle my heart and take my pride and whatever beauty I might have whatever innocence and hope and trample me humiliate me leave me at last alone and miserable and waiting out my life as she is waiting hers but oh Mr Reeves Daddy may I describe him now?

His eyes lovely his shoulders lovely his face smooth oh smooth Daddy as a tailor's dummy his nose straight as a postman's and his hands I loved the way he kept lifting his hands and letting them fall with nothing said the palms turning and settling soundlessly down his long fingers fluttering through air and then descending like something that had forgotten why and all the time fidgeting uncomfortably in his chair so anxious that the moment of this meeting would pass and moment would be all there was and this all so unnecessary I thought for how could a thing so grand as how we felt ever perish so soon but

ah, ah Daddy

his tweedy suit his fine shirt his hand-loomed narrow tie worn how many years now past its rightful hour like the wing-collars of my ancestors in their oval frames his trousers with their wide cuffs and pleats his baggy knees and shiny shoes I wanted to get him out of those clothes knew he had only dressed up for us wanting to be proper and distinguished when he called around for the keys to our summer Queen Charlotte place and I wondered if he knew I had had to do the same my mother instructing me to change out of my levis and the sleeveless yellow blouse

because we don't want Mr Reeves to think we don't care   must make ourselves presentable mustn't we   can't have Mr Reeves thinking the worst of us can we   we should all be ladies shouldn't we   so change my darling make yourself beautiful for Mr Reeves

my mother had said and she had proved right again I was glad I had made myself beautiful for him I couldn't wait for him to put down his tea for mother to go away the two of us to rush upstairs into my room and throw off our clothes and close the door oh

close the door Daddy and

O! O! O! the clock would spin and at last we would bound back down the stairs leap into my boat glide and sail

sail on past darkness

darkness towards dawn and it would be too late for him to leave on his long drive home and my mother would say Oh stay the night Mr Reeves

more than enough room

glad to have you and he would come to my room once silence settled over the house and enter my bed slide warm beside me on the sheets and enter me and joined oh like that joined Daddy we would meet the dawn and of course at breakfast mother would give him withering looks accuse him of taking advantage of her hospitality of my innocence and youth and Mr Reeves would leave steal away and I would never see him again poor Susan would pine away become embittered and HURT Daddy HURT with nothing now ever to take the place of that stolen love

of your betrayal Mr Reeves

and nothing ever again to keep my breathing firm my cheeks flushed my eyes without the look of painted death

and yet even with this knowledge I ached to give myself and this although I knew nothing of him except his name and what he wore how he looked at me how he wanted me and this despite the wife he had the poor woman waiting somewhere for him to return with our keys to the Queen Charlotte place so that she might go there with him

which hurt Daddy it did

for I should be there with him I love that place it's a thousand miles from here and in a place so beautiful I ever have it inside of me and all just the way I had him inside me that first day that first hour as we sat in our swoop-backed chairs in my mother's spotless sitting room my mother politely describing the tea

It's jasmine Mr Reeves

Lovely lovely he said it's lovely tea

So sorry your wife couldn't come Mr Reeves my daughter and I were so looking forward to meeting both of you

Ah yes well

he said and oh how my eyes bored into him I would wrench her from his skin and slice her with razor blades slice her for all those parts of him I couldn't have and slice her my mother too so much I wanted to be alone with him

So hot in here my mother said so mercilessly hot whyever are we sitting in here when outside there's the lake the breeze oh but you'll find the island weather perfect this time of the year

You don't like jasmine Mr Reeves

and closed her bodice demurely desperate hands quietly raking the air above the pot of tea which we were all too nervous for perhaps she said you'd like to go for a swim while you're here   in the lake   or in   I'm sure my daughter could

we could find   a suit for you the lake you see well the lake well yes better perhaps the pool and O Daddy I thought it had all been given away that he was lost to me would turn and run but no she was saying the pool you see because the lake water is so cold   so deep and cold Mr Reeves and O Oh Daddy he was satisfied he suspected nothing at all he was even amused for mother was saying it seemed to her it seems to me she said that death is afloat out there accident and suicide and well I never go in myself although of course Susan goes in all the time lake or pool it makes no difference to her she says she likes the lake all lurking snares and slimy silken skin over submerged logs booby traps and

O Daddy she was laughing she was teasing me

but

in the next second her mood changed she fell silent she sat with closed eyes her body rigid her lap napkin twisted taut between her hands while Mr Reeves contemplated the air above his cup and cleared his throat a dozen times and squirming until at last my mother stood   said

if you will excuse me Mr Reeves

and he and I were instantly on our feet

headache she sighed so tired oh always something

and then going oh going she was actually going and Oh God I was suddenly alone with Mr Reeves alone and trembling with Mr Reeves.

So you're Susan he said and Daddy I laughed I truly did for of course I was Susan and I took his hand I said this way please and led him through the dining room set for twelve and out through the archway into the sunroom so dazzling green with its potted monstrous plants hulking against the glass walls like evil persons placed there to breed and out we came onto the green tiles of the enclosed pool and looked the two of us at the placid queer chlorine-scented water and at the translucent green-fluted walls and he murmured O Love Daddy yes he did

pretty pretty Susan

he said my Susan Oh Susan he said and I thought how perfectly he stands how tall and iron-trapped and what a hush there was too with mother gone he took my breath away into his eyes into his very hands as he stripped off my clothes and stepped out of his own and ran naked diving head-first into the pool and I followed fast and swam abreast of him midway the pool and in the water beneath the diving board our arms closed around each other closed Daddy and I knew I could not would never get enough oh god of him.

And afterwards he scooped the water up in his hands and said this is your water the water in which you swim I love this water because it held you before I came and because it will hold you after I have gone and thus I drink this water Lady Susan and he did

but you'll be sick I said and he said

oh no I'll drink some more he said and I said why then I will drink it too and did and afterwards we made love on the sobbing diving board mindless of whether my mother might return for I was determined to love him until there was no love left in me once he walked away.

Thus we entered the afternoon had lunch and walked downhill with my mother between tall evergreens to the shore and stood by the waters' slushing edge looking out across the glistening surface to where perhaps a dozen boats sailed in vivid solitude and the sky that day was absolutely clear and

I heard him say to her

Such a pity that you and your daughter must ever leave this lake this house these trees how can your Queen Charlotte house compare and

My mother sighed and sighed for what answer could she give could she say Mr Reeves I have buried my husband here and it is sordid with all the reminders his death bequeathed to me oh Mr Reeves how stupid and cruel men are and how stupid I was myself ever to put my trust in him never once imagining that the vows of a lifetime could be broken easily as I break this twig or that she was herself now flotsam or floating half-submerged log coated by the green algae his memory gave

that stupid man

I thought oh stupid Daddy stupid all of you and stood myself in that instance forlorn and perishable and hating everyone my head bent low and now on my knees that the grass might fold up and cover me and I might lie forever only with myself in the cold cold ground all the fragments of the past stitching and binding me to that bed and that final grave whose surface was even and unmarked and less disrupted even than the waters of the lake under the hidden wind but

Deep he asked deep is it deep is the water deep this lake how deep is it in its deepest parts

and oh my Christ my mother and I stood like dull burdens cast to shore by some long-forgotten storm and unable in that moment to comprehend even the most simple question put to us

My mother there holding herself oh holding herself within her own arms and trembling while I stood transplanted within her skin single bereaved and haunted image of what is left after flesh has emptied itself of soul has yielded to time and pain and abandoned love oh the stark winter trees that cloak the Queen Charlotte place how like them we are but

Deep Deep he asked is it deep and

at last I cleared her skin heard her reply

we have had drownings here the latest no more than one week ago a young woman my daughter's age it's said she swam out too far committed suicide committed but oh men Mr Reeves you know how extraordinary and despicable how ruthless and faithless men are Mr Reeves the lengths they will drive us to and

I shuddered thinking yes wanting to tell him of my father that my father was there now and abandoned too but we started to walk the beach instead the three of us my mother saying the real she was saying is only what we see through these lampshade torches we call eyes the tree falls Mr Reeves in the empty forest and makes no sound and those people out there on the lake in their boats when I turn my back to them they also are no longer there the real is only what stands here in front of me this these trees this landscaped earth the two of you here beside me and this hand I place in front of me all the rest is as nothing and no concern of ours if indeed we accept the notion that the falling tree makes no sound

and oh I wanted to take him in my arms and love him insisting that our lives could not be so arbitrary so much accident without design that the tree the sound the tree makes in its silent forest is what compels it to stand in the first place Daddy like you once stood and that when the tree falls the earth goes on shuddering for a million years that what we are seeing now in front of us is not nearly so real as what we saw yesterday or the day before or will see again past this ambush of years this trap of fateful circumstance that finds us here now Daddy looking to find you O look look I wanted to say O Love Daddy let us celebrate this life by pointing our eyes directly at the sun for in its flash and fire do we become transmogrified and replenished and ever in the end purified for no ghosts live outside that fiery centre we swim Mr Reeves in fields of unremitting heat and our lives extend only into its pull but

Ah Mr Reeves my mother was saying so you're interested in suicide and her voice was raised and pinned him Daddy to where he stood so much as if she had enclosed him within a vault or tomb

why yes he said in the vague conventional way I suppose I am

and of course I thought *liar liar* why does he lie and saw my mother smile place a light placating hand over his arm and guide him back along the beach and into the shadowed coil of trees

while for my part she said I am more interested in murder

in murder he said

and my mother told him yes Mr Reeves murder is so much more interesting than suicide for the simple reason that what others would do to us is ever so much more desperate than what we could do to ourselves although I see what you mean

for instance only a month ago a woman I know went out alone in her boat a small
runabout I forget was it a Brampian a Rawson I can't be sure though she called it
her Sundance boat was that the name Susan

    and I trembled whispering yes

    nice name he said and

I slid my hand in his and walked a little behind that my mother wouldn't see and
closed my eyes to hear her say

    at night it was so dark oh very dark the boat rammed at high speed into a float-
ing deck that some of the young people here had constructed out of abandoned
logs and twigs and

    Look

she said

    Look

and I turned with him to follow her floating hand for sight of that speck far out
over the lake's surface near the shore on the other side where the boat

    Can you see it

she asked him and said my daughter Mr Reeves goes there sometimes to dive
she takes off her bathing suit and the people whose houses share this beach put
binoculars to their eyes and watch her dive nor can I blame them she's so beautiful wouldn't you say so Mr Reeves and

    I hung my head thinking oh all the trees are falling tonight oh every one of
them but

    he said why I think I see it is that it he said way over there but my mother and I
walked on because we knew he could not see it at all and very likely it was no
longer there not a scrap of it because the boat had exploded into it and even the
splinters now had washed ashore

    even so he went on studying whatever speck his mind had fixed there and see-
ing in his mind's eye as I saw it in mine the boat surging powerfully over the
black skin of water with a blind berserk woman at its wheel and smashing into
the platform and then in the darkness the sudden meliorative burst of flames and
noise and shattered fragments rising in the smooth darkness looping into sky and
falling in thinnest silence with no more mark on the water's roof than the summer
rain and then the darkness expanding to hold it there Daddy the way my mother
and I held it when you said *I'm going going* and walked steadily away from us

    vicious Daddy vicious

just as my mother that moment was as she lunged past Mr Reeves crying Oh take
her Mr Reeves take this foolish girl why not have your fun with her and struck off
then to disappear into her own private ambush of trees and

    Oh Mr Reeves I whispered hold me Mr Reeves I need you now

    and he did

our twin bodies struggled against ground and the earth yielded explosions shook
my flesh my parts burst into the air shot high outside of me and cascaded weightlessly back down again inside of me without a sound my parts looping up and
looping back and cascading weightlessly down as the sun spun and hovered
above us near enough to be lust itself my mother shrieking from her ambush of
trees

    Leeches Leeches

she shrieked you have only to look around this lake Mr Reeves it's awful awful
and weeping I leaned my head past his and stared out over the water its face a
shelter of warm eiderdown and far away up there the thin mist rising where the
lake's mouth opened out to sea

where warm water met the cold

and all to obscure defeat and deny this pirate's cove with my body pressed
against his body and my mother shrieking

Leeches Leeches

why can't we build houses to live with the lake the way our trees live with the sky
the way I was meant to live with him and I knew what she meant I felt it myself
the fierce clutch we have on love like the clutch these houses have the hooked
claws these houses have upon the lake

and you Daddy gone

and so I rolled from beneath him I stood and let my dress fall and shook down my
hair and stood erect as Eve hearing him say I don't want to go to the island now
no never I would stay here with you always with you and I smiled and took his
hand and we took the path down through the trees coming upon my mother there
kneeling in an ancient garden plot holding in her hands a wanton delicate green
new shoot and rolling its tender nub between her fingers quietly moaning

Diseased diseased

and now crawling on her knees to search the rampaging grass while behind us he
stalked out of impatience and need to have me forever with him and whispering

Let's go out in your boat now

and so I took his hand and said I would and mother stood with her dirty knees and
dirty hands and smudged cheeks and rolling tufts of grass between her palms and
flinging the rubbed grass aside so that now her hands smelled of grass and her
sleeves which she wiped them on and finally now reaching into her pocket and
producing our key to the Queen Charlotte place saying Mr Reeves we know you
and your wife will be happy there but

And then we got the boat my mother and I and him and rigged it up for sail and
went slow out onto the lake guiding for the centre which yet was free and pointing out to him as we drifted by all the imprisoned bodies chained to our submerged rotting logs our lake floor thick with the rocking corpses of those who
had entered our lives and now swaying beneath the surface of our green and
slimy mould growing everywhere but over their eyes the water that day perfectly
clear and littered to its furthermost depths with all the naked strangers we had
known and you there in my ear to steer us Daddy whispering

O Mr Reeves

O Mr Reeves

Ohhhhhhhhhhhhhhhhh . . .

1981

Rudy Wiebe

b. 1934

Born in a Mennonite farming community in northern Saskatchewan, near Fairholm, Rudy Wiebe grew up in a polyglot environment in which the Low German dialect was the language of everyday life, English that of school, and High German that of religion. After receiving his primary and secondary education in Saskatchewan and Alberta, where his family moved in 1947, Wiebe graduated from the University of Alberta in 1966. He then continued his studies at the University of Tübingen, West Germany, and completed his M.A. back at the University of Alberta. (His thesis was the manuscript of his first novel.) After earning a teaching certificate at the University of Manitoba and a Bachelor of Theology from the Mennonite Brethren Bible College, Wiebe worked for a year and a half for the *Mennonite Brethren Herald*, a weekly church publication. He resigned following a controversy over the details about Mennonite life revealed in *Peace Shall Destroy Many* (1962), a novel about the crisis a young man faces when he must choose between Mennonite pacifism and aligning himself with the general social atmosphere of Canada during the Second World War. He took a job teaching English at a Mennonite liberal arts college in Indiana, where he remained until 1967, when he accepted his present position in the English department of the University of Alberta.

Wiebe's second novel, *First and Vital Candle* (1966), describes a crisis of faith for a young man who, displaced from modern society, cannot find a satisfactory alternative among the native peoples in the North. Wiebe's next three books—*The Blue Mountains of China* (1970), a complex, panoramic history of the Mennonites; *The Temptations of Big Bear* (1973, Governor General's Award), an account of the disintegration of Indian culture that resulted from the growth of the Canadian nation; and *The Scorched-Wood People* (1977), the related story of Louis Riel's struggle to establish recognition for the Métis—are all epic stories of minority peoples who fight to maintain the integrity of their communities. In 1983 Wiebe published *My Lovely Enemy*, a contemporary love story that marks a departure from his previous subject matter. Wiebe's short fiction was collected in *Where is the Voice Coming From?* (1974); he later provided stories for *Alberta/A Celebration* (1979). Stories selected from both books were republished in *The Angel of the Tar Sands and Other Stories* (1982). Wiebe has also written a play, *Far as the Eye Can See* (1977), and edited a number of anthologies, some focusing on the western-Canadian short story, and others, such as *The Storymakers* (1970), placing the Canadian short story in an international context.

The single most important feature of Wiebe's writing is the moral vision that derives from his religious background. Central to Mennonite belief is the rejection of worldly loyalties and values, particularly those associated with the state, in favour of commitment to a Christian community. (Revolutionary pacifists, Mennonites fled Germany and the Netherlands in the eighteenth and nineteenth centuries, going to Russia and the Americas, as much in an effort to preserve their community as to avoid the persecution and violence they had frequently encountered.) Wiebe believes that today this close, nonconformist community is no longer functioning as it should: he sees the Mennonites in North America as having accepted middle-class values and goals and become part of the modern, urban culture. Still, even though much of the original vitality of the community has been replaced by a reverence for heritage—which offers no free choices for the individual—and the once revolutionary new ways have become rituals, Wiebe considers these eroded communities better than none at all: in 'The Naming of Albert Johnson', the isolation of the individual yields only violence and self-destruction. Wiebe does not see the loss of community and the alienation of the individual as unique to the Mennonites, and his fiction confronts these problems in other and larger contexts as well. In his three major novels he outlines what he sees as the obligatory human action: remaining true to one's beliefs while attempting to build, maintain, or re-establish a community—a spiritual collective that gains its identity from the antagonism of the outside world and from the martyrdom its leaders freely seek. His heroes are men who speak not for themselves or for man-made systems but for a spiritual ideal.

While Wiebe's interest in uniting present with historical events is not uncommon in Canadian writing, his faith in the redemptive value of revitalized history is. His method of reclaiming the forgotten past by adding imagined details of daily life and individual perceptions to material available in documents is an attempt to provide readers with the texture of a spiritual community that is missing from their own experience. (Wiebe's interest in the complex relationship of document, history, and fiction is dramatized in one of his best-known stories, 'Where is the Voice Coming From?') In a way that is parallel to his belief that communities must be almost inaccessible to those outside them, Wiebe makes entry into his fictional worlds difficult, through the use of unfamiliar dialects, a sometimes opaque style, complex time shifts, and meticulous detail. It is as if he writes his novels for an audience that shares his views, or is at least willing to be converted or tested.

In his novels Wiebe's central characters are men of spiritual insight—often saintly—with whom the reader is asked to identify. In his stories, however, Wiebe often writes about people who are much less ideal. In 'The Naming of Albert Johnson' Wiebe's interest in his title character lies in Johnson's romantic role of western outlaw rather than in the injustice of his actual deeds. The bravado of Johnson's struggle against an intruding authority, however, is undone by his horrific loneliness: without community, he condemns himself in his isolation to a subhuman damnation of violence and death. Within this story Wiebe replaces results with their causes by having time unwind in reverse, only gradually supplying the reader with the 'history' that lies behind Johnson's death, a history that began with his loss of belonging. In contrast, Wiebe's treatment of the same event in his short novel, *The Mad Trapper* (1980), focuses on another character who supports the ideal of community. The short story, however, is much closer to Wiebe's other writing than to *The Mad Trapper* (which resembles a film scenario) in its density of language and complexity of technique.

The Naming of Albert Johnson[1]

1. *The Eagle River, Yukon:* Wednesday, February 17, 1932
   Tuesday, February 16

There is arctic silence at last, after the long snarl of rifles. As if all the stubby trees within earshot had finished splitting in the cold. Then the sound of the airplane almost around the river's bend begins to return, turning as tight a spiral as it may up over bank and trees and back down, over the man crumpled on the bedroll, over the frantic staked dogteams, spluttering, down, glancing down off the wind-ridged river. Tail leaping, almost cart-wheeling over its desperate roar for skis, immense sound rocketing from that bouncing black dot on the level glare but stopped finally, its prop whirl staggering out motionless just behind the man moving inevitably forward on snowshoes, not looking back, step by step up the river with his rifle ready. Hesitates, lifts one foot, then the other, stops, and moves forward again to the splotch in the vast whiteness before him.

The pack is too huge, and apparently worried by rats with very long, fine teeth. Behind it a twisted body. Unbelievably small. One outflung hand still clutching a rifle, but no motion, nothing, the airplane dead and only the distant sounds of dogs somewhere, of men moving at the banks of the river. The police rifle points down, steadily extending the police arm until it can lever the body, already stiffening, up. A red crater for hip. As if one small part of that incredible toughness had rebelled at last, exploded red out of itself, splattering itself with itself when everything but itself was at last unreachable. But the face is turning up. Rime, and clots of snow ground into whiskers, the fur hat hurled somewhere by bullets perhaps and the whipped cowlick already a mat frozen above half-open eyes showing only white, nostrils flared, the concrete face wiped clean of everything but snarl. Freezing snarl and teeth. As if the long clenched jaws had tightened down beyond some ultimate cog and openly locked their teeth into their own torn lips in one final wordlessly silent scream.

The pilot blunders up, gasping. 'By god, we got the son of a bitch!' stumbles across the back of the snowshoes and recovers beside the policeman. Gagging a little, 'My g—' All that sudden colour propped up by the rifle barrel on the otherwise white snow. And the terrible face.

The one necessary bullet, in the spine where its small entry cannot be seen at this moment, and was never felt as six others were, knocked the man face down

---

[1]For an account of the Albert Johnson manhunt, see n. 1, p. 243. Wiebe has also published an essay, 'The Death and Life of Albert Johnson: Collected Notes on a Possible Legend' (in *Figures in a Ground: Canadian Essays on Modern Literature Collected in Honor of Sheila Watson*, 1978), which outlines the facts in the case and also cites the available documentary and literary sources about the Johnson story. There Wiebe comments:

My own fascination with Johnson gradually settled in two areas: first; that during the incredible trek he largely walked backwards in an attempt to mislead his pursuit (then, after laying several false trails, he would circle around, behind his pursuers, but several times they were still so far behind him that he came back on his own trail ahead of them); second; that the man floating down the Peel River never called himself Johnson until a Loucheux Indian asked him 'Are you Albert Johnson,' and he said 'Yes'—though a day later it was obvious that he was not the Albert Johnson then being expected at Fort McPherson. Considering these two aspects of the Johnson mystery, it came to me that structurally the true story of Albert Johnson cannot be approached in chronological fashion; it must go from the death battle on the Eagle River in February 1932 back to its true climax: his naming on the Peel in July, 1931. Once I understood that, the question of my fiction's structure was resolved.

in the snow. Though that would never loosen his grip on his rifle. The man had been working himself over on his side, not concerned as it seemed for the bullets singing to him from the level drifts in front of him or the trees on either bank. With his left hand he was reaching into his coat pocket to reload his Savage .30-.30, almost warm on the inside of his other bare hand, and he knew as every good hunter must that he had exactly thirty-nine bullets left besides the one hidden under the rifle's butt plate. If they moved in any closer he also had the Winchester .22 with sixty-four bullets, and closer still there will be the sawed-off shotgun, though he had only a few shells left, he could not now be certain exactly how many. He had stuffed snow tight into the hole where one or perhaps even two shells had exploded in his opposite hip pocket. A man could lose his blood in a minute from a hole that size but the snow was still white and icy the instant he had to glance at it, packing it in. If they had hit him there before forcing him down behind his pack in the middle of the river, he could not have moved enough to pull out of the pack straps, leave alone get behind it for protection. Bullets twitch it, whine about his tea tin like his axe handle snapping once at his legs as he ran from the eastern river bank too steep to clamber up, a very bad mistake to have to discover after spending several minutes and a hundred yards of strength running his snowshoes towards it. Not a single rock, steep and bare like polished planks. But he had gained a little on them, he saw that as he curved without stopping towards the centre of the river and the line of trees beyond it. That bank is easily climbed, he knows because he climbed it that morning, but all the dogs and men so suddenly around the hairpin turn surprised him toward the nearest bank, and he sees the teams spreading to outflank him, three towards the low west bank. And two of them bending over the one army radio-man he got.

Instantly the man knew it was the river that had betrayed him. He had outlegged their dogs and lost the plane time and again on glare-ice and in fog and brush and between the endless trails of caribou herds, but the sluggish loops of this river doubling back on itself have betrayed him. It is his own best move, forward and then back, circle forward and further back, backwards, so the ones following his separate tracks will suddenly confront each other in cursing bewilderment. But this river, it cannot be named the Porcupine, has out-doubled him. For the dogs leaping towards him around the bend, the roaring radioman heaving at his sled, scrabbling for his rifle, this is clearly what he saw when he climbed the tree on the far bank, one of the teams he saw then across a wide tongue of land already ahead of him, as it seemed, and he started back to get further behind them before he followed and picked them off singly in whatever tracks of his they thought they were following. These dogs and this driver rounding to face him as he walks so carefully backwards in his snowshoes on the curve of his own tracks.

Whatever this river is spiralling back into the Yukon hills, his rifle will not betray him. Words are bellowing out of the racket of teams hurtling around the bend. His rifle speaks easily, wordlessly to the army radioman kneeling, sharpshooter position, left elbow propped on left knee. The sights glided together certain and deadly, and long before the sound had returned that one kneeling was already flung back clean as frozen wood bursting at his axe.

He has not eaten, he believes it must be two days, and the rabbit tracks are so old they give no hope for his snares. The squirrel burrow may be better. He is scraping curls from tiny spruce twigs, watching them tighten against the lard pail, watching the flames as it seems there licking the tin blacker with their gold tongues. The fire lives with him, and he will soon examine the tinfoil of matches in his pocket, and the tinfoil bundle in his pack and also the other two paper-wrapped packages. That must be done daily, if possible. The pack, unopened, with the .22 laced to its side is between his left shoulder and the snow hollow; the moose hides spread under and behind him; the snowshoes stuck erect into the snow on the right, the long axe lying there and the rifle also, in its cloth cover but on the moosehide pouch. He has already worked carefully on his feet, kneading as much of the frost out of one and then the other as he can before the fire though two toes on the left are black and the heel of the right is rubbed raw. Bad lacing when he walked backwards, and too numb for him to notice. The one toe can only be kept another day, perhaps, but he has only a gun-oily rag for his heel. Gunoil? Spruce gum? Wait. His feet are wrapped and ready to move instantly and he sits watching warmth curl around the pail. Leans his face down into it. Then he puts the knife away in his clothes and pulls out a tiny paper. His hard fingers unfold it carefully, he studies the crystals a moment, and then as the flames tighten the blackened spirals of spruce he pours that into the steaming pail. He studies the paper, the brownness of it; the suggestion of a word beginning, or perhaps ending, that shines through its substance. He lowers it steadily then until it darkens, smiling as a spot of deep brown breaks through the possible name and curls back a black empty circle towards his fingers. He lets it go, feeling warmth like a massage in its final flare and dying. There is nothing left but a smaller fold of pepper and a bag of salt so when he drinks it is very slowly, letting each mouthful move for every part of his tongue to hold a moment this last faint sweetness.

He sits in the small yellow globe created by fire. Drinking. The wind breathes through the small spruce, his body rests motionlessly; knowing that dug into the snow with drifts and spruce tips above him they could see his smokeless fire only if they flew directly over him. And the plane cannot fly at night. They are somewhere very close now, and their plane less than a few minutes behind. It has flown straight in an hour, again and again, all he had overlaid with tangled tracks in five weeks, but the silent land is what it is. He is now resting motionlessly. And waiting.

And the whisky-jacks are suddenly there. He had not known them before to come after dark, but grey and white tipped with black they fluffed themselves at the grey edge of his light, watching, and then one hopped two hops. Sideways. The first living thing he had seen since the caribou. But he reaches for the bits of babiche[2] he had cut and rubbed in salt, laid ready on the cloth of the riflebutt. He throws, the draggle-tail is gone but the other watches, head cocked, then jumps so easily the long space his stiff throw had managed, and the bit is gone. He does not move his body, tosses another bit, and another, closer, closer, and then draggle-tail is there scrabbling for the bit, and he twitches the white string lying beside the bits of babiche left by the rifle, sees the bigger piece tug from the snow and draggle-tail leap to it. Gulp. He tugs, feels the slight weight as the thread lifts

[2]Strips of leather, usually made from caribou or moose hide, used for laces or strings.

from the snow in the firelight, and now the other is gone while draggle-tail comes towards him inevitably, string pulling the beak soundlessly agape, wings desperate in snow, dragged between rifle and fire into the waiting claw of his hand. He felt the bird's blood beat against his palm, the legs and tail and wings thud an instant, shuddering and then limp between his relentless fingers.

Wings. Noiselessly he felt the beautiful muscles shift, slip over bones delicate as twigs. He could lope circles around any dogs they set on his trail but that beast labelled in letters combing the clouds, staring everywhere until its roar suddenly blundered up out of a canyon or over a ridge, laying its relentless shadow like words on the world: he would have dragged every tree in the Yukon together to build a fire and boil that. Steel pipes and canvas and wires and name, that stinking noise. In the silence under the spruce he skims the tiny fat bubbles from the darkening soup; watches them coagulate yellow on the shavings. Better than gunoil, or gum. He began to unwrap his feet again but listening, always listening. The delicate furrow of the bird pointed toward him in the snow.

2. *The Richardson Mountains,* N.W.T.: Tuesday, February 9, 1932
Saturday, January 30

Though it means moving two and three miles to their one, the best trail to confuse them in the foothill ravines was a spiral zig-zag. West of the mountains he has not seen them; he has outrun them so far in crossing the Richardson Mountains during the blizzard that when he reaches a river he thought it must be the Porcupine because he seems at last to be inside something that is completely alone. But the creeks draining east lay in seemingly parallel but eventually converging canyons with tundra plateaus glazed under wind between them, and when he paused on one leg of his zag he sometimes saw them, across one plateau or in a canyon, labouring with their dogs and sleds as it seems ahead of him. In the white scream of the mountain pass where no human being has ever ventured in winter he does not dare pause to sleep for two days and the long night between them, one toe and perhaps another frozen beyond saving and parts of his face dead, but in the east he had seen the trackers up close, once been above them and watched them coming along his trails towards each other unawares out of two converging canyons with their sleds and drivers trailing, and suddenly round the cliff to face each other in cursing amazement. He was far enough not to hear their words as they heated water for tea, wasting daylight minutes, beating their hands to keep warm.

The police drive the dog teams now, and the Indians sometimes; the ones who best track him on the glazed snow, through zags and bends, always wary of ambush, are the two army radiomen. One of the sleds is loaded with batteries when it should be food, but they sniff silently along his tracks, loping giant circles ahead of the heaving dogs and winging arms like semaphores when they find a trail leading as it seems directly back towards the sleds they have just left. He would not have thought them so relentless at unravelling his trails, these two who every morning tried to raise the police on their frozen radio, and when he was convinced they would follow him as certainly as Millen and the plane roared up, dropping supplies, it was time to accept the rising blizzard over the mountains and find at last, for certain, the Porcupine River.

It is certainly Millen who brought the plane north just before the blizzard, and it was Millen who saw his smoke and heard him coughing, whistling in that canyon camp hidden in trees under a cliff so steep he has to chop handholds in the frozen rock to get out of there. Without dynamite again, or bombs, they could not dig him out; even in his unending alert his heart jerks at the sound of what was a foot slipping against a frozen tree up the ridge facing him. His rifle is out of its sheath, the shell racking home in the cold like precise steel biting. There is nothing more; an animal? A tree bursting? He crouches motionless, for if they are there they should be all around him, perhaps above on the cliff, and he will not move until he knows. Only the wind worrying spruce and snow, whining wordlessly. There, twenty yards away a shadow moves, Millen certainly, and his shot snaps as his rifle swings up, as he drops. Bullets snick from everywhere, their sound booming back and forth along the canyon. He has only fired once and is down, completely aware, on the wrong side of his fire and he shoots carefully again to draw their shots and they come, four harmlessly high and nicely spaced out: there are two—Millen and another—below him in the canyon and two a bit higher on the right ridge, one of them that slipped. Nothing up the canyon or above on the cliff. With that knowledge he gathered himself and leaped over the fire against the cliff and one on the ridge made a good shot that cut his jacket and he could fall as if gut-shot in the hollow of deadfall. Until the fire died, he was almost comfortable.

In the growing dusk he watches the big Swede, who drove dogs very well, crawl toward Millen stretched out, face down. He watches him tie Millen's legs together with the laces of his mukluks and drag him backwards, plowing a long furrow and leaving the rifle sunk in the snow. He wastes no shot at their steady firing, and when they stop there are Millen's words still

You're surrounded. King isn't dead. Will you give

waiting, frozen in the canyon. He lay absolutely motionless behind the deadfall against the cliff, as if he were dead, knowing they would have to move finally. He flexed his feet continuously, and his fingers as he shifted the rifle no more quickly than a clock hand, moving into the position it would have to be when they charged him. They almost outwait him; it is really a question between the coming darkness and his freezing despite his invisible motions, but before darkness Millen had to move. Two of them were coming and he shifted his rifle slightly on the log to cover the left one—it must have been the long cold that made him mistake that for Millen—who dived out of sight, his shot thundering along the canyon, but Millen did not drop behind anything. Simply down on one knee, firing. Once, twice bullets tore the log and then he had his head up with those eyes staring straight down his sights and he fired two shots so fast the roar in the canyon sounded as one and Millen stood up, the whole length over him, whirled in that silent unmistakable way and crashed face down in the snow. He hears them dragging and chopping trees for a stage cache[3] to keep the body, and in the darkness he chops handholds up the face of the cliff, step by step as he hoists himself and his pack out of another good shelter. As he has had to leave others.

[3]Platform.

3. *The Rat River*, N.W.T.: Saturday, January 10, 1932
Thursday, December 31, 1931
Tuesday, July 28

In his regular round of each loophole he peers down the promontory toward their fires glaring up from behind the riverbank. They surround him on three sides, nine of them with no more than forty dogs, which in this cold means they already need more supplies than they can have brought with them. They will be making plans for something, suddenly, beyond bullets against his logs and guns and it will have to come soon. In the long darkness, and he can wait far easier than they. Dynamite. If they have any more to thaw out very carefully after blowing open the roof and stovepipe as darkness settled, a hole hardly big enough for one of them—a Norwegian, they were everywhere with their long noses—to fill it an instant, staring down at him gathering himself from the corner out of roof-sod and pipes and snow: the cabin barely stuck above the drifts but that one was gigantic to lean in like that, staring until he lifted his rifle and the long face vanished an instant before his bullet passed through that space. But the hole was large enough for the cold to slide down along the wall and work itself into his trench, which would be all that saved him when they used the last of their dynamite. He began to feel what they had stalked him with all day: cold tightening steadily as steel around toes, face, around fingers.

In the clearing still nothing stirs. There is only the penumbra of light along the circle of the bank as if they had laid a trench-fire to thaw the entire promontory and were soundlessly burrowing in under him. Their flares were long dead, the sky across the river flickering with orange lights to vanish down into spruce and willows again, like the shadow blotting a notch in the eastern bank and he thrust his rifle through the chink and had almost got a shot away when a projectile arced against the sky and he jerked the gun out, diving, into the trench deep under the wall among the moose hides that could not protect him from the roof and walls tearing apart so loud it seemed most of himself had been blasted to the farthest granules of sweet, silent, earth. The sods and foot-thick logs he had built together where the river curled were gone and he would climb out and walk away as he always had, but first he pulled himself up and out between the splinters, still holding the rifle, just in time to see yellow light humpling through the snow toward him and he fired three times so fast it sounded in his ears as though his cabin was continuing to explode. The shadows around the light dance in one spot an instant but come on in a straight black line, lengthening down, faster, and the light cuts straight across his eyes and he gets away the fourth shot and the light tears itself into bits. He might have been lying on his back staring up into night and had the stars explode into existence above him. And whatever darkness is left before him then blunders away, desperately plowing away from him through the snow like the first one who came twice with a voice repeating at his door

I am Constable Alfred King, are you in there?

fist thudding the door the second time with a paper creaking louder than his voice so thin in the cold silence

I have a search warrant now, we have had complaints and if you don't open and then plowing away in a long desperate scrabble through the sun-shot snow while the three others at the riverbank thumped their bullets hopelessly high into the logs but shattering the window again and again until they dragged King and each other head first over the edge while he placed lead carefully over them, snapping willow bits on top of them and still seeing, strangely, the tiny hole that had materialized up into his door when he flexed the trigger, still hearing the grunt that had wormed in through the slivers of the board he had whipsawn himself. Legs and feet wrapped in moose hide lay a moment across his window, level in the snow, jerking as if barely attached to a body knocked over helpless, a face somewhere twisted in gradually developing pain that had first leaned against his door, fist banging while that other one held the dogs at the edge of the clearing, waiting

Hallo? Hallo? This is Constable Alfred King of the Royal Canadian Mounted Police. I want to talk to you. Constable Millen

and they looked into each other's eyes, once, through his tiny window. The eyes peering down into his—could he be seen from out of the blinding sun?—squinted blue from a boy's round face with a bulging nose bridged over pale with cold. King, of the Royal Mounted. Like a silly book title, or the funny papers. He didn't look it as much as Spike Millen, main snooper and tracker at Arctic Red River who baked pies and danced, everybody said, better than any man in the north. Let them dance hipped in snow, get themselves dragged away under spruce and dangling traps, asking, laying words on him, naming things

You come across from the Yukon? You got a trapper's licence? The Loucheaux[4] trap the Rat, up towards the Richardson Mountains. You'll need a licence, why not

Words. Dropping out of nothing into advice. Maybe he wanted a kicker[5] to move that new canoe against the Rat River? Loaded down as it is. The Rat drops fast, you have to hand-line the portage anyway to get past Destruction City[6] where those would-be Klondikers wintered in '98. He looked up at the trader above him on the wedge of gravel. He had expected at least silence. From a trader standing with the bulge of seven hundred dollars in his pocket; in the south a man could feed himself with that for two years. Mouths always full of words, pushing, every mouth falling open and dropping words from nothing into meaning. The trader's eyes shifted finally, perhaps to the junction of the rivers behind them, south and west, the united river clicking under the canoe. As he raised his paddle. The new rifle oiled and ready with its butt almost touching his knees as he kneels, ready to pull the canoe around.

4. *Above Fort McPherson*, N.W.T.: Tuesday, July 7, 1931

The Porcupine River, as he thought it was then, chuckled between the three logs

---

[4]Indians of the Peel River region who have rights to trap the Rat River. Johnson was accused of stealing from a Loucheux trap line.
[5]Outboard motor.
[6]Name given to the debris-covered spot in the Richardson Mountains where gold-seekers, travelling from Edmonton to the Klondike via the Mackenzie Valley, were forced by the difficult rapids on the Rat River to winter over in 1898-9. Many were severely frost-bitten and some died.

of his raft. He could hear that below him, under the mosquitoes probing the mesh about his head, and see the gold lengthen up the river like the canoe that would come toward him from the north where the sun just refused to open the spiky horizon. Gilded, hammered out slowly, soundlessly toward him the thick gold. He sat almost without breathing, watching it come like silence. And then imperceptibly the black spired riverbend grew pointed, stretched itself in a thin straight line double-bumped, gradually spreading a straight wedge below the sun through the golden river. When he had gathered that slowly into anger it was already too late to choke his fire; the vee had abruptly bent toward him, the bow man already raised his paddle; hailed. Almost it seemed as if a name had been blundered into the silence, but he did not move in his fury. The river chuckled again.

'. . . o-o-o-o . . .' the point of the wedge almost under him now. And the sound of a name, that was so clear he could almost distinguish it. Perhaps he already knew what it was, had long since lived this in that endlessly enraged chamber of himself, even to the strange Indian accent mounded below him in the canoe bow where the black hump of the stern partner moved them straight toward him out of the fanned ripples, crumpling gold. To the humps of his raft below on the gravel waiting to anchor them.

'What d'ya want.'

'You Albert Johnson?'

It could have been the sternman who named him. The sun like hatchet-strokes across slanted eyes, the gaunt noses below him there holding the canoe against the current, their paddles hooked in the logs of his raft. Two Loucheaux half-faces, black and red kneeling in the roiled gold of the river, the words thudding softly in his ears.

You Albert Johnson?

One midnight above the Arctic Circle to hear again the inevitability of name. He has not heard it in four years, it could be to the very day since that Vancouver garden, staring into the evening sun and hearing this quiet sound from these motionless—perhaps they are men kneeling there, perhaps waiting for him to accept again what has now been laid inevitably upon him, the name come to meet him in his journey north, come out of north around the bend and against the current of the Peel River, as they name that too, to confront him on a river he thought another and aloud where he would have found after all his years, at long last, only nameless silence.

You Albert Johnson?

'Yes,' he said finally.

And out of his rage he begins to gather words together. Slowly, every word he can locate, as heavily as he would gather stones on a Saskatchewan field, to hold them for one violent moment against himself between his two hands before he heaves them up and hurls them—but they are gone. The ripples of their passing may have been smoothing out as he stares at where they should have been had they been there. Only the briefly golden river lies before him, whatever its name may be since it must have one, bending back somewhere beyond that land, curling back upon itself in its giant, relentless spirals down to the implacable, and ice-choked, arctic sea.

1974

George Bowering

b. 1935

A playful sense of humour has led George Bowering to add to the substantial body of work under his own name so many poems and reviews under various pseudonyms that his bibliographers may never straighten out all the questions of authorship. He has similarly confused his biographers by giving at least three different towns as his birthplace: Osoyoos, Penticton, and Oliver. ('A very slow birth in a fast-moving car' is the way he once explained this). In any case, these towns are all near one another in the Okanagan Valley of British Columbia where he grew up. He left to become an aerial photographer for the RCAF (1954-7) and then enrolled at the University of British Columbia, where he earned a B.A. in history (1960) and an M.A. in English (1963).

At UBC Bowering studied creative writing under Earle Birney and visiting professor Robert Creeley (who was Bowering's M.A. thesis adviser). Along with Frank Davey, Fred Wah, and Lionel Kearns, he also became part of a group of aspiring writers who collected around Warren Tallman, a teacher of contemporary poetry at the university. Tallman put these students in touch with the aesthetic theories and poetic practices current on the American west coast, especially those derived from William Carlos Williams and the Black Mountain movement (a school of poetry begun at Black Mountain College in North Carolina by Charles Olson, Robert Duncan, and Creeley), and from other *avant-garde* writers including Jack Spicer and Beat poet Allen Ginsberg. Following a 1961 visit to Vancouver by Duncan—who discussed Black Mountain theories and also talked about the importance of 'little magazines' in new poetry movements—these young

B.C. poets decided to launch their own literary periodical. The anagramatically-named *Tish* became a monthly poetry 'newsletter' that patterned itself in part after such magazines as *Origin* in the U.S. and Louis Dudek's *Delta* in Canada.

The writers associated with the magazine, who came to be called the '*Tish* group', were greatly influenced by the Black Mountain movement's spare style (derived from the imagist tradition), its use of a loose poetic line based on the rhythms and pauses of colloquial speech, its emphasis on local and regional aspects of experience, and its belief in the communal nature of writing. Especially interested in the long poem (in the tradition of Williams's *Paterson*) and in the serial poem (as developed by Spicer), they rejected the lyric mode associated with what they decried as the 'humanism' and 'romanticism' of poetry from eastern Canada and the eastern U.S. Following Olson, they called for a poetry of essentials, accurate and objective, written by poets who, as Bowering later said, 'turned their attention upon the factual things that make up the world, men included among them' (*Tish*, No. 20, 1963).

Although *Tish* lasted for eight years (forty-five issues), its founders left after issue No. 19 to pursue other interests. Bowering accepted a teaching position at the University of Calgary, and went from there to the University of Western Ontario for further graduate studies before becoming writer-in-residence, and subsequently professor, at Sir George Williams University (now part of Condordia). In 1971 he returned to British Columbia to teach English and creative writing at Simon Fraser University. After leaving *Tish*, Bowering remained committed to little-magazine publishing in Canada, first founding and editing *Imago* (1964-74) and then becoming contributing editor for Frank Davey's influential literary journal, *Open Letter* (1965-).

The most prolific of the *Tish* group, Bowering has published some twenty-six books of poetry, most of them with small presses. His first book, *Sticks & Stones* (with a preface by Creeley), appeared in 1963 as a Tishbook. A second collection, *Points on the Grid*, was published the following year by Contact Press, and a third, *The Man in Yellow Boots*, appeared in 1965 as a special issue of the English-language Mexican literary magazine *El Corno Emplumado*. Bowering received a Governor General's Award in 1969 for two of his books of poetry: *Rocky Mountain Foot* and *The Gangs of Kosmos*. In 1971 *Touch: Selected Poems 1960-70* was published, and in 1980 *Selected Poems: Particular Accidents*. Since 1970 Bowering's most important work has taken the form of loosely unified long poems; 'Desert Elm', reprinted below, is a somewhat shorter example of these. A number of book-length poems have been reprinted in *The Catch* (1976) and in *West Window* (1982). Like other poets of the *Tish*-group, Bowering avoids rhetorical devices as well as myth and metaphor, preferring a language and style close to common speech. (Indeed, two of his long works—*Autobiology*, 1972, and *A Short Sad Book*, 1977—seem to straddle the borderline between prose and poetry.) His poetry is saved from prosiness, however, by a subtle musical quality in the diction and rhythms, and from slackness by its sharply etched observations.

Although best known for his poetry, Bowering has also written a number of prose works, including short stories (collected in *Flycatcher & Other Stories*, 1974; *Protective Footwear: Stories and Fables*, 1978; and *A Place to Die*, 1983); critical essays (collected in *A Way With Words*, 1982; and *The Mask in Place: Essays on Fiction in North America*, 1983); a monograph on Al Purdy; and two novels: *A Mirror on the Floor* (1967) and *Burning Water* (1980). *Burning Water*, about George Vancouver's search for the Northwest Passage (a subject Bowering approached earlier in his long poem *George, Vancouver*, 1970), won Bowering his second Governor General's Award.

All of Bowering's writing—like that of other members of the *Tish* group—strives to communicate a sense of *process*, a sense of the writer contained in his writing and of the work as only one part of his life. Such writing is post-modern in its rejection of the modernist doctrine of the artist as a detached maker of impersonal and permanent artifacts. Bowering is not, however, a 'confessional' poet, simply mining his biography; the poem is always more important to him than the poet, and his allegiance is to the raw material of poetry—the language itself. When asked in a 1976 interview if he believed in himself, he responded:

I believe in the language. When it's coming over all right, I can tell . . . I think the language speaks. The language knows how to talk. It's been around a lot longer than I have. I'm the one who had to learn how to talk, the language knows how to talk already. (Out-Posts, 1978, edited by Jack David and Caroline Bayard).

It is no wonder that Bowering earlier wrote in his long poem *Allophanes* (1976): 'If you don't understand the story you'd better tell it.'

Harbour Beginnings & That Other Gleam

She has it in her power
(continually or not)
                    to give me back my face
when she will.

But this world (I constructed it
from whole cloth)
                    is a world of bargain.
That is, I have my part to do,
continual tailor, to ply this needle

(yes, relentless metaphor)   10
or this manly implement, to seek
its well-known place. It is often in
the dark.

          Then a halo of her excitement
settles around my neck, & there by her
term magic,
                    my face, shining. She has told me
it does, then.

1969

Thru

She says it makes her mad
I wake her up
laughing in my sleep.

I dont remember that happiness
wrapt with her & the sheets,
& if it is the edge of

what? where is that place,
maybe for ease we call it eternity,
what was funny there?

Dont wake the sleep-   10
walker they say, how about
the man giggling with his eyes closed?

He may be left in the place
we court so solemnly
in our poems—he may

have been laughing
to enrich his courage, faced
with unspeakable horror.

Or one time I will
catch myself laughing among friends,   20
& a glimpse of it,

in the moment their faces
melt away, that instant's
springtime, the monster

under the grass, that I return to,
the mystery best forgotten
in the springtime of waking

to the alarm, the alarm.

1969

From *Autobiology*

CHAPTER I: THE RASPBERRIES

    When I was thirty I had free raspberries in
the back yard & I loved them. In the back yard &
I ate them. & I ate them in the kitchen out of
an aluminum pot. When I was thirty I loved raspberries, I loved to eat them. I loved the way
they were made of many pieces in my mouth, & they
came from the outside of the bush & the inside.
They came from the outside in the sunshine & from
the inside in the darkness, & that is where they
went again. But inside in the darkness is where   10
we are told the subconscious is & that is why I
could not eat raspberries. I could not eat raspberries when I was three years old when we had
free raspberries in the front yard. In Peachland,
where the free raspberries grow, & they grew outside in the sunshine where I could reach them
when I was three & a half. I could reach one & I
ate it & I thought there was a bug on it. But I
ate it too fast to know for certain. Years later
I saw a face at a girl's window & I thought it   20
was a man named Russell, but I went away too
soon & so I never knew. I never knew whether I
ate a bug on a raspberry. I had never eaten a
bug before so I didn't know what they taste like.
I could not eat raspberries for years after that
day in our front yard when I was over three years
old, even though the raspberries always look so
good with all their round pieces in a cone or
bunch. But there is a hole inside the raspberry
& it could always have a bug in it.   30

1972

Desert Elm

I

I woke, & woke again, to see her smiling
at me, & turned to find soft sleep in the
green pillow.

Later in the day she said what were you
dreaming, you were smiling in your sleep,
but again it was my sleep, though I have
never said that.

Later I felt the pain three times inside
my left arm, driving the red car, & I remembered, I had dreamt that I too had had   10
my heart attack.

Attack, I didn't mean that when I told her,
sitting now on my lap, it was simply all
I could remember of my dream & thinking,
of course, but I am nearly thirty years
younger than him.

He finally had his on the green grass of
the golf course, how mundane, how it
filled my mother's voice with unwonted
fear, to be telling this to *me*.   20

I thought of a rock, not quite round, tonight, reading H.D.[1] on the old age of the
professor, a rock, not quite round, beginning to crack, it will crumble, will
I know this earth.

II

The earth he made me on, we dug into
side by side, has not long been there,
has been carried there by the glacier,
all rocks & all round rocks, all stones
rolled together.   30

We toiled among the stones, that rattling
sound is my earth, where I grew up looking like him. There was some light falling always into the valley, always blue,
the blue that hovers over heat, a blue
I saw cooling the Adriatic shore.

[1]Hilda Doolittle (1886-1961), one of the early and influential American imagist poets; the remarks on
'the old age of the professor', here alluded to, are in her *Tribute to Freud* (1956).

It is the blue fading in his eyes, they
are not startling blue, it is the family
colour I never got, they are not bright
blue but fading to a transparency you   40
will notice only if you are watching
closely, I mean within a few feet.

They found a desert & made it bloom, made
it green, but even the fairways seen from
across the valley are under a blue haze,
the smoke of space it seemed on high summer days, not a cloud in the sky, no mote
in that eye.

The earth is not brown but grey, grey of
stones, the flat stones round to the eye   50
looking straight down.

III
I never saw him attack anything but a
baseball, a golf ball, his own records,
to be beaten despite his getting older,
to compete satisfactorily with himself.
That is why he never rebuked her, he is
more pure than I.

He said hold the hammer at the handle's
end, for leverage, not because he was a
science teacher, because he knew how to   60
do it, full out, not thinking or rather
thinking wide open, down the lines of
energy.

He had those muscles you can see under
the skin, the large vein down the middle
of his bicep I never had, I didnt get
the blue eyes or that, & not the straight
nose, I would perhaps never have broken
it then.

He is associated with no colour, no colour   70
clothes or car or house, he would as soon
eat a peach as an apple. I think of the
apple splitting in half as some can make
it between their hands, as he could likely
do that, & it is white.

In the last two years his hair is thin
& one may see between them, & they are
white. His slacks were white below the
purple blazer, & worn twice a month.

IV
Rounding the bases his neck became red as   80
a turkey's but it was a home run, every
one like me has to see his father do that
once, fearing his father is like him, not
as good.

Red as a turkey neck, his eyes bulging,
his heart already something to frighten
the young boy, was it something she said
as this other says now to me playing my
guerrilla ball, I dont want you collapsing
& dying on the field. It is a playing field,   90
I say, I can feel my blood running red
under the skin.

I tell him about it whenever I can, my
average, joking as if I am my team & he is
his, & sometime we must come together,
clasp & both of us, win. He was his mother's
first child, I was my mother's first child,
& after us came just all the rest, the
bases cleared already.

But he didn't get it done till a quarter   100
century later, he lay they say on the fresh
cut grass, all the red gone from under the
skin of his face, pale, these pale blue
eyes looking for her?

In my dream I thought of course, I too,
what will I take up when too old to round
the bases, what crimson driver.

V
I thought of a rock, not quite round
sticking half out of the earth where I
would put the ladder's foot. In a hurry,   110
without patience to place it safely, to
be up that tree & working.

& working. Never half as fast as he could
do it, but in some ways inheriting his
quiet efficiency & turning it to grace.
He said he could never play second base
& I found it the easiest position, bending
over occasionally to pick stones off the
ground.

Even this summer, a month before his fall,   120
he pickt twenty pounds while I pickt

eleven, just more than half & I am more
than half at last, thirty-seven, moving
around to the other half of the tree,
but someone guesst, that is under the
ground, the root system.

A tree, growing downward as I dreamed I
would or desperately hoped I would, to
become this child again, never having the
nerve or wit, age four, to follow that to   130
its home, from one hundred back to the
seed, & then what. A new lease on life?
For him?

The earthly tree grows downward, we do it
after all, bypassing the womb, back where
we came from, down the rabbit hole on the
golf course, above the shade of the old
cherry tree.

VI
General knowledges are those knowledges
that idiots possess. What words would you   140
use to characterize your relationship with
your parents. Scratchy tweed pants they
provided for sunday school. I remember because of my legs. They look now like his
legs, shorts he wears at the golf course,
no embarrassment, he has come this far,
what are they to him?

Prophecy is finally simple & simply more
interesting than characterization. We are
not characters, we devise characters. I   150
sat as still as possible, the backs of my
knees held forward from the hard curved
wood. Those pants were never worn out,
though they belonged unused to some uncle
first.

His white slacks hung for two weeks in the
closet we'd built some years earlier, he
took them out two Tuesdays each month. A
lifetime uses few such garments. Who wears
the pants in this family is no sociological   160
question. Prophecy is no answer. If you
need an answer go make up a question &
leave me alone without it.

He has those muscles you can see under the
skin, the calf muscle like mine tending to-

ward the other, inside the line of shin
bone. I see his lines every morning in the
mirror.

VII

I woke & again I woke, to find her smiling
at me, & turned to return to soft sleep
in the green pillow. A tree, growing downward as I dreamed we all would or hoped
we would, against my god or what they
gave me as my god, their god, given them
against their will, we punish the generation that succeeds us.

Did I mean to say he did that. No, he
never tried to bend my life, never stood
between me & the sun, this tree grew where
the seed fell. A new lease on life? For
him? In the thick dark forest the trees
grow tall before they extend wings. Tall
green pillow.

They found a desert & made it bloom, made
it green, but even the trees feel blue
smoke curling among their branches, the
smoke that holds away the frost, the early
message that fills our hearts with ice,
lovely to taste fresh from the branch,
but it doesn't travel well. All stones
rolled together, long enough & they will
all be dust, hanging in the air over our
blue lakes.

Prophecy is finally simple, & simply a
pair of eyes thru which the blue of the
sky travels, an observation thru a lens.

VIII

Staring straight into his eyes for the
first time, I see the blue, a sky with
some puffy clouds many miles away.
Step into the nearby field, over the sill,
into footprints that disappear as I step
into them, into the blue sky that is not
above but straight in front of me. Straight
eyes, in all the photographs, & in one old
brown kodak print of the family assembled
I look into his oval eyes & see inside
them a man walking backward, out of his
footsteps.

My eyes are brown, walking inside them

170

180

190

200

would be moving over burned grass on low   210
hills. They found a desert & made it bloom.
I move closer, zooming into his eyes &
find the first aperture completely filled
with one petal of a blue flower, a closeup of a star weeping in surrender to the
earth, a tear, Aurora[2] weeping helplessly
on the edge of the Blue Nile.

He's no sun of mine, I never stood between
him & the brightness, the mistakes I make
will live as long as these ovals stay open.   220
I walkt into his open eye, over the sill
& saw two enormous black holes in the sky.
A voice came thru a nose & reduced them
to personality. I had never said the word
poetry without a funny accent.

IX
Men who love wisdom should acquaint themselves with a great many particulars.[3]
Cutting the crisp apple with a French knife
I saw that the worm had lived in the core
& chewed his way out, something I've seen   230
a thousand times & never understood & while
I'm looking he's on the other side of the
green tree picking. One two one two, the
wisdom of the tree filling his picking bag,
its weight strapt over his shoulders. He
showed me, you cross the straps like this
& keep it high. Get above the apples & look
down at them.

& I still do it wrong, reaching up, pick-
ing with sore arms, strain rather than wis-   240
dom filling me not the bag. He said the
safest step on the ladder is the top, he
was trying to get me up, & always right,
this one I have learned & Saturday I was
on the top step picking apples, wanting
someone to advise. That is how one becomes
acquainted, working to gather.

It could be a woman but is it a woman. Is
it a woman you can work together with, is
it a woman you know doesnt feel the part-   250
iculars as you do, they are apples, not the
picking of them, the filling. She has been

---

[2]Goddess of the dawn who wept each morning for her dead son, Memnon, King of Ethiopia; her tears become the dew.
[3]These two lines are from Fragment 35 by the pre-Socratic philosopher Heraclitus (*fl.* 500 B.C.).

without a man for years, she offers ladders,
tools, bags for the apples. You want someone to advise to be him, but do it silently
knowing your expertise is somehow, known.

X
I did not see him lying on the grass, I
may as well have been under the ground,
perhaps entangled in the tree growing down-   260
ward, an earth. His earth, our particular
earth, as it sifts back & forth, composing
like dust on a piano. The piano is black
but where it has been rubbed it is brown.
He never sat at a piano, only an old black
typewriter with round keys, making faint
words.

So faint they barely heard him. It was August & the grass dry, the thin words rose
like a tree into the air, lightly, as blue   270
as the thin smoke hanging over the green
fairway. It has nothing to do with justice.
He spent thousands of hours in those trees
picking pennies for me, this day he was
knocking them into a hole, I'm glad to hear
that.

In the ocean light of the ward window his
eyes are barely blue & deep in his head
like my daughter's. He woke again to see
me smiling at him, his head straight in   280
the pillow, a rock nearly round. In the
desert the rocks simply lie upon each other
on the ground, a tree is overturned out
of the ground, its shallow widespread roots
coiled around small rocks. By these fruits
we measure our weight & days.

1976

W.P. Kinsella

b. 1935

Born in Edmonton and raised on a farm in the Alberta bush, William Patrick Kinsella was educated by correspondence until he was ten. After finishing high school in Edmonton in 1954, he worked as a government clerk and as a businessman before moving to Victoria, B.C., in 1967. He operated a restaurant there until 1972, when he began to work as a cabdriver to put himself through the University of Victoria, earning a B.A. in creative writing (1974). After working as a part-time instructor for a year, Kinsella spent two years at the University of Iowa Writer's Workshop and received an M.F.A. in 1978. He now teaches creative writing and English at the University of Calgary.

Kinsella has published five collections of short fiction, drawn from the large number of stories that, in the last decade, have appeared in Canadian and American literary journals. *Dance Me Outside* (1977), *Scars* (1978), *Born Indian* (1981), and *The Moccasin Telegraph* (1983) all contain stories dealing with Indians, while a collection of non-Indian stories, *Shoeless Joe Jackson Comes to Iowa* (1980), is made up mainly of modern fantasies. From the title story of this volume, he developed the novel *Shoeless Joe* (1982), which won the Houghton Mifflin Literary Fellowship.

Kinsella has achieved great popular success with the stories about Indians, which deal—often comically—with the rescue of humane values from the absurdity of everyday life, particularly a life that is largely controlled from outside by bureaucratic authorities. Told mostly from the perspective of an eighteen-year-old Cree named Silas Ermineskin, in his own dialect, they have the quality of anecdotal storytelling. Each

story exists independently of the others, but they all return to the same characters and place, so that together they build up a fully realized picture of life in and near Hobbema, Alta.

When writing about his own culture, Kinsella is also interested in exposing the dehumanizing aspects of modern society. However, like many western writers in Canada and the United States he chooses to blur the boundaries between the fantastic reality of our contemporary technological world, with its airports and Disneylands, and the realistic fantasy of his characters, with their magic baseball fields and dreams of Janis Joplin. This technique—sometimes referred to as 'magic realism'—raises the question of whether our sense of reality comes from external perceptions or an internal truth. It receives Kinsella's most extended use in the novel *Shoeless Joe*, in which an ordinary farmer who can 'feel the magic building like a gathering storm' brings together baseball players from the distant past (one of them his dead father) and J.D. Salinger, the reclusive author of *Catcher in the Rye*. Baseball—an important subject for Kinsella—serves as a metaphor for a lost ordered world in which individual excellence and heroism are still admired, a world that can be recovered through the magic of the game itself. In 'First Names and Empty Pockets', which develops through parallels between the narrator's real life and his nightmarish vision of Janis Joplin's world, the concern with the restoration of a lost order manifests itself as the need to rescue those whom a media-dominated society has discarded.

The kind of complex fantasy in 'First Names and Empty Pockets' and *Shoeless*

Joe has been used by many recent writers, including Richard Brautigan (whom Kinsella acknowledges as an influence). Such fiction suggests that the imperfections of the modern world can be remedied only by the imagination. The narrator of 'First Names and Empty Pockets', who runs a doll hospital in the American midwest, repeatedly constructs versions of a story in which, while on holiday from Iowa, he meets and saves Joplin from self-destruction. In 'saving' her he also rescues himself from the emptiness of a life with friends who watch soap operas and collect marching-band records. By 'recalling' his wild years with Joplin, he is able to do what Kinsella himself wants to do in all his writing: 'insert a little humanity into situations which are inherently lacking in humanity'.

First Names and Empty Pockets

A doll is a witness
who cannot die,
with a doll you are never alone.
—Margaret Atwood[1]

Fact, fiction, fantasy, folklore, swirl in a haze of colour, like a hammer-thrower tossing a rainbow. And always, I am haunted by images of broken dolls. Old dolls, lying, arms and legs askew, as if dropped from a great height; dolls with painted, staring eyes, faces full of egg-shell cracks, powdered with dust, smelling of abandonment.

JOPLIN TOPS CHARTS!
SPLASHERS MAKES A SPLASH!

The headlines are from *Billboard* and *Cashbox*, publications which have become my main reading fare over the past two decades. We've been married for nearly fifteen years, Janis and I. *Splashers* is her seventeenth album.

The idea for the album cover was mine: Janis seated sidesaddle on a chromed Harley. Two views: one, she is facing the camera, her carrot-coloured hair below her shoulders, less frizzed, but wild and wind-blown as always; she is wearing jeans, pale-blue platform shoes, rhinestones imbedded in the criss-cross straps that disappear under her cuffs, a denim jacket, open, showing a white tee-shirt with SPLASHERS! in bold red capitals. She looks scarcely a day older than when I met her. The cosmetics of the years, the lines around the corners of her mouth, eyes, and at the bridge of her nose, have been air-brushed away and she grins, eyes flashing. She is smoking a cigarette, looking tough and sexy.

The flip side of the album features Janis' back and spotlights the cycle-gang colours: a golden patch on the faded denim in the shape of a guitar, again with the word *Splashers* only this time in black script.

Before I met Janis my life was peopled by antiseptic women with short hair and cool dresses, sexless as dolls. Always they lurk like ghosts just out of my vision. I smell their coolness, hear their measured voices, see their shapes when I close my eyes. I shudder them away and think of Janis crooning her love for me alone, our bodies tangled and wet. I think of her and of our mouths overflowing with the taste of each other, and I recall the San Francisco street where I first told her my name. My whole name.

[1]From 'Five Poems for Dolls', in *Two-Headed Poems* (1978).

'Man, you got something nobody else on the street has.'

'Huh?'

'A last name, man. Around here it's all first names and empty pockets. Beer and hard times. Watching the streets turn blue at 4 a.m. while you cadge quarters at a bus stop or outside a bar. Do they have freaky chicks like me where you come from?'

Also, on the back of the album, there is an inset photo of the band, Saturday Night Swindle. *Splashers* is their sixth album with us. It was my idea to change bands—Big Brother and The Holding Company were never much—but Janis started with them and we stuck with them for eleven albums.

'This is what I do instead of having kids,' Janis jokes. And it is true that she has averaged an album every nine months for nearly ten years.

I know little about music, even after all these years. *Janis* is my job, my life. 'Like holding a lid on a pressure cooker with bare hands,' is how I described my life with Janis to *Time* magazine, the last time they did a cover story. Generally, I trust the judgment of record producers when it comes to music, although recording the Tanya Tucker song, 'What's Your Mama's Name?' was my idea. The album, our unlucky thirteenth, has sold nearly two million. I chose the musicians for Saturday Night Swindle. I had an agent I trusted send me resumés of five musicians for each position. Musically there was little to choose, but I had their backgrounds investigated and chose with endurance in mind. There are no heavy drinkers and no hard drug users in this band. The less temptation available the better.

While they were photographing Janis for the album cover, redoing the front scene for the twentieth time, I crossed the set to her, knelt down and turned up the left cuff of her jeans about three one-inch turns: the way you see it on the album cover.

'What the fuck are you doing?' Janis demanded.

'It's just a touch. It's the way you were when we first met. Do you remember?'

'Nah. My memory don't go that far back. That's all ancient fucking history.'

I raise my head and look at her. She grins and her eyes tell me that she does indeed remember.

I straighten up. 'I'd kiss you, but the make-up man would hemmorhage.'

'Later, Sugar,' and she purses her lips in an imitation kiss.

One of the photographers looks quizzically at the rolled-up denim and then at me.

'Trust me,' I say.

She sidled up to me, plump, wide-waisted, a sunset of hair in a frizzy rainbow around her face. Her hand hooked at the sleeve of my jacket.

'Looking for a girl?'

'How much?' There was a long pause as though she was genuinely surprised that I was interested. Her eyes flashed on my face, instantly retreated to the sidewalk. Then she uttered a single, almost inaudible word, like a solitary note of music that hung in the silence of the soft San Francisco night.

'Five.'

I almost laughed it was so pitiful. Would have if she had resembled the whores I'd seen downtown: booted, bra-less, hard as bullets, whores who asked for $30, sometimes $40, plus the room. I took a quick look at her, a husky, big-boned girl, with a wide face and squarish jaw, anything but pretty, but I found her appealing, vulnerable, in need.

There was another long pause before I said, 'Okay.' Her fingers still gripped the sleeve of my jacket. We were on a dark street a mile or more from downtown San Francisco, a street full of ghostly old houses and occasional small shops. The houses were three-storey, some with balconies, all with latticework, and cast eerie shadows over the street. It was my first of three days in San Francisco. I had never been there before.

'Where do we go?' she said and looked around the deserted street as though hoping that a hotel might suddenly materialize.

'I'm a stranger here,' I said. 'I thought you'd know of a place.'

'Yeah, well I'm kind of lost myself. Just got to walking. I don't usually leave the downtown. Business hasn't been very good tonight,' and she made an effort at a smile. She was wearing faded jeans, one cuff rolled up about four inches as if she had recently ridden a bicycle.

The Iowa town where I come from, where I've lived all my life is a white-siding and veranda town of 20,000 souls, of old but newly painted houses on tree-lined streets, lilacs, American flags, one-pump service stations, and good neighbours.

I work framing buildings, sawing, pounding nails, bare to the waist in the humid summers, bronzed as maple, sweat blinding my eyes, my hands scarred. I will likely never leave this town except for a brief holiday to San Francisco, and possibly a honeymoon trip; later, we will take our daughters to Disneyland.

The house where I live with my parents is square and white, so perfect it might have been built with a child's blocks. There are marigolds, asters, and bachelor buttons growing in a kaleidoscope of color between the sidewalk and the soft, manicured lawn. On a porch pillar, just above the black metal mailbox, is a sign, black on white, about a foot square that reads: DOLL HOSPITAL.

In my workshop I make dolls as well as repair them. I show them to no-one for they are always incomplete. Broken dolls: fat pink arms that end at shredded wrists, sightless eyes, a twisted leg, a scar on a maligned cheek like an apple cut by a thumbnail. There is a balance to be kept. I make the unwhole whole, but . . .

The dolls are my way of being different. A delicate rebellion. They are my way of handling energies that I don't understand, electric energies which course like wine and neon through me, wailing like trains in my arms and chest.

'There are hotels,' she said, and laughed, a stuttering sound like a bird trapped in a box. 'Maybe if we walk down to . . .' she named a street unfamiliar to me. She wore a man's blue-and-red-checkered work shirt with the cuffs open, jeans, and unisex loafers worn down at the sides.

We walked for a couple of blocks. She scuffed one of her feet, a sound that magnified and made the late evening silence almost ominous. We both, I'm certain, felt ridiculous in the company of the other. I was wearing brown slacks, freshly cleaned and creased, a pastel shirt and a brown corduroy jacket. Nondescript, straight, I have always felt that pastels provided me with anonymity, a privacy that I craved as much as Janis feasted on spotlights and crowds. We fought about my image. Slowly I have let go. I have let my hair grow; had it styled. I wear faded jeans and a Pierre Cardin shirt, and hand-tooled boots and belt of leather, soft and warm as sundrenched moss.

'Do you think we're getting closer to downtown or farther away?' I asked.

'I don't know.' There was an ice-cream store across the street, closed of course, a pink neon cone blinked in the window.

'I have a room.'

'Where?'

I named the hotel.

'I don't know it.' I fished the key out of my jacket pocket. We checked the address on the oxblood tag, our heads together under a streetlight. Neither of us knew where it was. It was there that we exchanged names. Close to her, I discovered about her the odour of peaches ripe in the sun. I remembered visiting my grandmother in summer, walking in a peach orchard near Wenatchee in the Willamette Valley in Washington where the peaches lay like copper coins on the grass, where the distant-engine drone of wasps filled the air as they sucked away the flesh from the fallen fruit. As they did, the peach scent thickened making the air soft and sweet as a first kiss. Walking in San Francisco that night was like stepping among peach petals.

'Perhaps if I get a taxi,' I said, looking around. The street was dark in all directions.

'I've never done this before,' Janis said, and leaned against me, taking my hand, hers rough and dry as cardboard.

'I believe you,' I said. We both laughed then. Hers less nervous now, coarse and throaty, full of barrooms, and stale beer.

'I mean, I've propositioned guys before, but no-one ever took me up on it. They practically walked right through me like I was fucking invisible.'

'Everyone has to start someplace,' I said inanely.

'When we get to the top of the hill we'll be able to tell by the lights where downtown is,' Janis said.

'Or we could look for moss on the north side of the utility poles?'

'You're weird,' she said, and I could see, as the golden tines of streetlight touched her face that she had thousands of freckles. 'Gimme a cigarette.'

'I don't have any . . . I don't smoke.'

'I don't suppose you'd have a drink on you either?'

'No.'

'You're sure you want a girl?' and her mouth widened into a beautiful grin as she held my hand tighter and we both laughed. 'Where you from?'

'Iowa.'

'They grow corn there don't they? A state full of corn farmers. Are you a corn farmer?'

'No, I repair dolls.' I looked quizically at her to see how she'd react.

'No shit? That's weird, man. You're funny. I don't mean queer funny. Well, maybe I do. No, I think funny, funny. You are, aren't you?'

'And you,' I said, 'where do you come from?'

'About fifteen miles from Louisiana,' she said, and it was her turn to look at me with lifted eyebrows.

'I don't understand,' I said.

'You don't need to. It's a private joke,' and she paused. 'I sing a little.' We had reached the top of the hill. 'Hey, we are going in the right direction. When we get down to the lights we can ask somebody how to get to that hotel of yours.'

But before we went to the hotel she wanted to go to a bar. 'There's this joint I know. It's downstairs and there isn't a window in the place. I love it. It's always the same there . . . no night or day . . . it's like being closed up in a bottle of water . . . time just stands still . . .'

I looked at her, scruffy as a tomcat, but radiating the same kind of pride.

It was a forlorn bar, a dozen stools and a few wooden tables. A place that looked as if it had endured a century of continuous Monday nights. There was a red exit sign above a bandstand where a lonely guitar leaned against a yellowed set of drums.

Old men dozed at the tables, a woman with straight grey hair, dressed in a man's tweed topcoat, glared angrily into a beer. A black man, looking like a failed basketball player, drunk or drugged, lolled crazily on a bar stool. A sampling of Janis' favourite people.

'I understand them,' she says.

She has infinite patience with drunks. She'll listen to their stupid convoluted ramblings as they whine about how badly the world has treated them.

'I've been there. I'd be there now if I hadn't met you.'

Janis, when she was drunk, had her own sad story. 'The Famous Story of the Saturday Night Swindle,' she called it, and depending upon her mood the story could take up to an hour to tell. Condensed, it was simply that all our lives we are conditioned to expect a good time Saturday night, we look forward to and plan for it. And almost always we are disappointed. Yet we keep on trying for there will always be another Saturday night.

In the winter, her freckles become pale, seem to sink just below the surface of her skin like trout in a shallow stream. In summer they multiply: dandelions on a spring lawn. 'Fuck, look at me; I look like I've been dipped in Rice Krispies.'

'I love your freckles,' I say. 'Each and every one of them. I am turned on by freckles,' and I hold her, kissing slowly across her cheeks and nose.

I love to watch the light in the eyes of little girls as they retrieve their dolls from me. In my workroom I have a row of shoe-box hospital beds. I have painted brown bed-ends on the apple-green wall above each box. On the front of each box is a make believe medical chart. The wall glows with flowered decals and sunny happy-faces. Sometimes, if I have to order parts all the way from Baltimore, I let the children visit their dolls for a while on Saturday afternoons.

My own children are like dolls, girls, all angel eyes and soft little kisses. Cory, my wife, makes their clothes. We walk to church each Sunday down the heavily treed streets of white houses. Our home is surrounded and overpowered by lilacs.

There is a groaning porch swing where we sit in the liquid summer dusk. Even in the humid summers Cory always wears a sweater, usually a pale pink or blue, pulled tight across her shoulders as if it were a shield that might protect her.

'What'll it be?' the bartender asked as we settled on the stools.

'Kentucky Red,' said Janis.

'The same,' I shrugged. I had no idea what I was ordering. The bartender had a flat face with a permanent case of razor burn, and short hair that he might have cut himself with a bowl and a mirror.

'I'm afraid I'm gonna turn out like that,' Janis said, inching closer to me by shifting her weight on the bar stool. She nodded toward the shaggy old woman sitting alone and hostile, a cigarette burning toward her fingers. 'I'm afraid I'm gonna be one of them loud old women who wear heavy stockings all year and slop from bar to bar getting drunker and more cantankerous by the minute. I don't want to, but the writing's on the fucking wall,' she said, hefting her glass.

I moved myself closer to her. I have an abiding fear of old men who sit in bars and hotel lobbies, brittle and dry as insects mounted under glass. I thought of my hotel, decaying on a sidehill, an ancient facade decorated like a fancy wedding cake, a brown linoleum floor in a lobby full of old men and dying ferns.

Janis tossed back her second drink. I pushed mine toward her, barely touched.

'You ain't a juicer?' she said and grinned.

'Should we go look for the hotel?' I said. I was feeling edgy. Perhaps she only wanted a mark to buy her drinks and cigarettes.

'You mean you still want to?' she said, surprised. She eyed me warily, like a dog that had been kicked too many times. 'I mean, man, you seen me in some light, and you've been with me long enough to make up your mind . . .'

'I still want to.'

Deep in the night I turned over, away from Janis, but with no intention of leaving the bed. She grasped at my arm, much the same as she had grasped at my sleeve earlier in the evening.

'Don't fucking leave me, man.' I moved back closer to her. 'You any idea what it's like to wake up in the middle of the night alone and know that there ain't a person in the whole fucking world who cares if you live or die? You feel so useless. . . .' And she held me fiercely, crying, kissing, trying to pull me close enough to heal her wounds—fuse me to her—store my presence for the lonely nights she anticipated.

Years later, Janis at Woodstock, blue her favourite colour, blue her chosen mood—anxiety nibbling at her like rats, before she went on stage. But the magical change in her as she did: like throwing an electric switch in her back; she pranced on stage stoned in mind and body by whatever evil she could stab into her veins or gulp into her stomach. Footwork like a boxer, waving the microphone phallicly in front of her mouth—blue shades, blue jacket, blue toreador pants, sweating booze, blind, barefoot, she spun like an airplane. She made his-

tory on stage. She collapsed into my arms as she came off.
'Sweet Jesus, but I was awful.'
'You were a wonder.'
'I'll never be able to appear in public again.' She holds me like the end of the
world. She is wet with sweat and pants into my shoulder while I tell her again
and again how great she was. Finally she relaxes. I have done my job.

'Yeah? You really want to? How about that,' and she smiled like a kid. 'Harry?'
she said to the bartender, 'is it okay?' and she nodded toward the tiny, dark
stage.
'Sure, Janis' he replied. 'You know you're welcome any time.'
Her music: like a woman making a declaration of love with a fishbone caught
in her throat. All the eerie beauty and loneliness of the Northern Lights. Like getting laid, lovingly and well. That is what the critics said about her.
How to explain her success? Voyeurism? Vicarious living? The world likes to
watch people bleed, suffer, and die. Janis stands up on stage and metaphorically
slits her wrists while the audience says, 'Yeah! Man, that's the way I feel. That's
what I want to do, but don't have the nerve.'
She opens her chest and exposes her heartbeat like a bloody strobe light, and
they watch and they scream and they stomp and have wet dreams and climax as
they stand on their chairs and say, 'Man, that was wonderful. But I'm glad it's
her and not me.'

'Why on earth do you want to go to San Francisco?' my mother said to me when
I told her of my decision to holiday on the west coast. 'Why go way out there?
California is full of strange people.' She was wearing a grey-hen-colored house-
dress, a kerchief on her hair, her gold-rimmed glasses sparking in the bright
kitchen light.
'I'd like to see some strange people.'
'Well, your daddy and I went to St Louis on our honeymoon. Saw the sight of
the World's Fair and your daddy went to see the St Louis Browns play baseball,
though I'll never understand why. Goodness knows that team never won a game
to my recollection.'

In the bar again the next evening, Janis a little drunk. 'Jesus, don't keep looking
at me like that.'
'I'm sorry.'
'You're a gawker. They're the worst kind. You must spend your life looking
over fences and through windows. What's the matter with me? You look like the
creeps I went to school with. What the fuck are you doing with a sleazy chick
like me?'
'I like you,' I said lamely.
'Cheap thrills . . . you can go back to . . . wherever, and tell your fucking
dolls about the weird chick you balled in San Francisco. Everybody who looks
weird gets fucked over . . . did you know that? I been fucked over so many
times. Mostly by guys I don't want. But by the ones I want too. Shit, I been
turned down more times than the bedspread in a short-time room.'

And on and on, and I listen and shrug it off, for I understand her, and I sense that when she goes after me with words sharp as a gutting knife, that she is really slashing at herself. If she can make me hate her, then I'll leave her and she'll be alone, the way she feels she deserves to be.

She is so unlike Cory. Janis protects herself with loud words, loud music, loud colours, clouds of feathers and jangling bracelets, but they could be twins, each of their bodies is riddled with fear.

Cory: tiny and gentle. Afraid of the world. Cory loves me. I love her as carefully as if she were flower petals or fine china. Our loving is silent, unlike with Janis who screams and moans and thrashes and tries to absorb my very body into hers. Cory is a broken doll, an abused child, battered, raped, bartered, reviled. She clings to me in her silence. Her climax is barely a shiver. That first night in the hotel Janis shrieked as if she were on stage, a note, clear and sharp as a tuning fork, hung in the air of that sad hotel room as her body fairly exploded beneath me.

The only place Janis is not afraid is on the stage. Bracelets splashing lights like diamonds, she high-steps to the microphone and begins her cooing, growling, gutteral delivery. She is the spirit of Bessie Smith, Billie Holiday, and every gritty, gutsy blues singer who ever wailed. There is a sensuality, a sexuality, in the primeval sounds she emits. There is terror, love, sex, passion, pain, but mainly sex.

'I sound like I'm in heat,' she said to an interviewer once, 'and baby, I am. Sometimes I go right from the stage and I pick up my honey here,' she said referring to me, 'and we go right to the hotel and ball, and ball, and ball.'

'I sing right from my pussy,' she said another time, then pulled her blue sunglasses down on her nose so she could peek over them to get the full shocked reaction.

'Why did you choose to sing?' an interviewer once asked her.

'It was a way out,' she replied. 'Where I come from a girl works at catching a man—then has a lot of kids and keeps her mouth shut. I'm hyper . . . I've always been like a pan of boiling water.'

'Do you know what the difference is?' I asked Janis as she clung to me after a concert, sobbing, repeating over and over how awful she had been . . . *awful*, after 15,000 people had danced in the aisles and screamed out their love for her. 'The difference between what you do and what I used to do is that mine, and almost everyone else's work, is tangible. I'd build a house or a garage, or even repair a doll and when I was finished I could say, ''There is the house I built or the doll I've repainted.'' You have to wait to be evaluated. You sing a song or record an album but it means nothing until the fans buy or the critics say, ''Yes, this is good.'' '

It takes very special people to bare their souls for mere humans to evaluate. Not many can stand up to it. I have always tried to remember that when I find Janis drunk or stoned—when she rages and accuses and smashes, and vomits, and lies in a fitful sleep, sweat on her upper lip and forehead, her mouth agape.

My assignment, as I sometimes look upon it, has been to protect Janis from herself and from people: those who would tap her veins and draw the life from her like so many vampires with straws. I am known as the most protective manager in the business. We hardly ever tour anymore. There are the albums and Janis plays Vegas for twelve weeks a year.

Has it been worth it? Has what I've gone through been worth it to prolong a career for a few more years? In just a month or two it's going to happen. I will go home to Iowa, alone, 'for a holiday', I'll say. But I'll know differently. Janis will be left alone in the house near Las Vegas: that desert house, arid and dry as Janis' hands the night we met. A $20,000 boat stands like the mythical, mystical ark, on a trailer in the back driveway. The nearest lake is sixty miles away and artifically created. Janis bought the boat like anyone else would buy a Tonka Toy as a gift for a child. We have never used it. I stare at it and shudder.

While I am away, the mouse will play, and play, and play. And she will finish doing what I interrupted in San Francisco, what she has been trying to do all her life, not maliciously, or viciously, or violently, but with that lack of care, of restraint, that has always characterized her.

Fog is heavy in my life, dimensions of time telescope—I have been called. I have given nearly twenty years of my life for ten of hers. But no-one knows. Really knows. There are other dimensions where Janis no longer exists, where I never left Iowa, where I sit tonight on a white front porch in the humid dusk and string my dolls.

'Nobody ever stays with me,' Janis said in the grey morning light of my creaking hotel room.

'I'll stay as long as I can,' I said.

'How long is that?' And I couldn't bring myself to answer. My flight home was booked for the next afternoon.

'You know, just the sound of your voice, even if you're talking about dolls, is more to me than solid food. I just get so fucking lonely.'

'Nobody likes to be alone.'

'Was I crying last night?'

'A little.'

'More than that wasn't it? I do that when I get drunk. I cried on your shoulder, right?'

'You weren't any trouble.'

'Thanks for staying with me. I mean, really.'

We walked the warm morning streets for a while, small clouds were low enough to touch, still as the foggy gulls perched on posts along the piers. We breakfasted at a squalid café. Again we sat on stools at the counter. An oriental, wrapped tight as a mummy in a filthy white apron was cook and waiter. I ordered bacon and eggs. Good, solid, nutritious North American food. Janis had pecan pie, ice cream, and a Coke. Junkie food I was to learn later as my education progressed. She grinned at me through the haze of her Marlboro.

'I'm sorry you're not staying.'

'So am I.'

'Well, I'll move on,' she said, sliding off the stool. 'Maybe I'll see you around . . .'

'You're not going to leave,' I said. 'I don't have to go until tomorrow.'
'You mean you *want* to stay with me? I'm grateful you stayed last night . . .
you don't have to put yourself out.'
  'I want to stay with you.'
  'But you have to go back to . . . Iowa.'
  'I have a job to get back to . . . and my dolls.'
  'F'crissakes.'
  'I have to . . . I'm sorry.'
  'Still, it's weird though, a big man like you messing with dolls.'

An eight-inch steel implement that looks like a large crochet hook is the main tool of my trade; accessories consist of a supply of sturdy elastics, glue, a tea kettle, a set of pastel paints. Exposure to a steaming tea kettle allows me to soften joints and remove arms, legs and heads. Like Dr Christiaan Barnard I perform transplants. Like the good Dr Frankenstein, I have a box of leftover parts from which I often extract a leg or an eye to make a broken doll good as new.

When we reached the room, we were both perilously shy, Janis even slightly reluctant. The exchange of money was forgotten. 'Are you sure?' Janis asked several times, still expecting to be rejected.
  'I am,' I reassured, though I wondered why. She was so opposite to the girls I knew at home. I couldn't explain my excitement, my desire for this plain, shoddily dressed, rather vulgar girl. Perhaps even then I felt the charisma. I never confused her with her singing. I wanted her before she ever sang to me. But there was the power about her. She has the ability to stand on stage and hold the audience as if she were whispering in the ear of a lover, or lead them to dance in the aisles, or stand on the tables and stomp out her rhythms like a biker putting boots to a cop.

'You know what they did to me? At the university I was voted "Ugliest Man On Campus". You any idea what that did to me? Those straight chicks in angora sweaters and skirts, lipstick, and about a ton of hairspray, and the guys in cords and sweaters, or even shirts and ties . . . and just because I was different . . .'
  I had asked about her former life. Sometimes I try to learn the why of her, but gently, like unwinding gauze from a wound. Years have passed and she trusts me now, as much as she ever trusts anyone. I never made my flight back to Iowa. Have never left her. I paid for my parents to visit us once. Only once.
  'Your workshop's just as you left it,' my mother said. 'I just closed up the door. Had to take the sign down eventually . . . Little girls kept coming to the house.'

'Oh, they thought they were so fucking righteous. But I'll show them. I can buy and sell them all now. I showed them once. I'm gonna show them for the rest of my life. They all married each other and live in the city and have split-level plastic houses, and plastic kids, and cars, and cocks, and cunts . . .' and she broke off amid a mixture of laughter and tears. 'I suppose I should be happy just not to be part of them anymore . . . be happy being different . . . shit, it was only fifteen miles to Louisiana, and that was where the real people were, and real music. That was where I did my first gigs, and learned how to drink, and yeah, that too. God, did I ever tell you about high school? What they did to me? You don't want to hear, Sugar. It was too awful to even talk about.'

'Are you sorry?' Janis once asked me, in a strange soft voice, as if she had suddenly had a glimpse through the veil at what could have been: at what life would have been like if we hadn't met.
　'I miss handling nails in the sunshine—the raw strength in my arms. My hands would blister now if I really worked.'
　'And your dolls.'
　'I miss them too.'
　'You know, I've never seen you fix a doll. I bet you were good. I've told you you could . . .'
　'It wouldn't be the same.'
　'Maybe when we're old?'
　'Maybe.'

The third morning. The same café. Our going there a fragile attempt at ritual.
　'Do you need anything?' I was reaching for my wallet.
　'Hell, no. I'll get by. I always do. I'm just as tough as I look. Tougher.' We walked out of the café hand in hand.
　She turned to me then to be kissed. A shy, hurried brushing of lips, our bodies barely touching. About us, the beautiful scent of peaches.
　'Be cool. Maybe I'll see you around,' and she gave me the peace sign, something I'd never seen before, and shambled away among the moving crowd.

Here, on the lazy verandah in the Iowa dusk, as my children sleep, as my dolls sleep, as my wife waits with her delicate love, I dream. Am haunted by the spirit of a dead girl. A dead singer who died a broken doll, pitched face-first into a blondwood night table in a Los Angeles motel. Nose broken, spewing blood, she wedged between the table and the bed, her life ebbing while the needle grinned silver in the darkness. I remember her in my arms in that sad hotel in San Francisco, wild, enveloping, raucous as her songs, her tongue like a wet, sweet butterfly in my mouth. I am haunted by her death and by what might have been. And what I might have done to prevent her rendezvous with the needle: surrogate cock. Evil little silver dildo. A sexual partner she didn't have to fear. The needle never left her alone in the middle of the night. I sometimes look at my hands, marvelling that there are no wounds, so many times have I pushed the needle away.
　'If you can't get love one way—in the physical way—then you get it in another,' she said to me during those fine days we spent together before it all began. During the few gigs she'd done she had discovered that the applause, screams, cheers, wails, were enough for then. 'I'm only somebody when I sing, but God, the gigs are so few and far between.' Of course, that was to change, and soon.

Friends were visiting Cory and me the night that Janis' death was announced. It was an afterthought item at the end of the news, between weed killer and fertilizer commercials.

'Oh,' was all Cory said.

'Who?' said my parents.

'Who?' said our friends, noting my consternation. *She* watches the soap operas in the afternoons. *He* collects records of marching bands.

After our first breakfast we walked all day, looked at the ocean, the terraced houses frosty white as splashes of tropic sun. The day was full of spring—all San Francisco tasted and smelled of peaches.

The magic of her—whirling onto the stage—a white girl singing black music—the trills, the shrieks, the croaks, the moans, as she made love through her music. 'The only love I know is with the audience—that's my whole life,' she told an interviewer once, as I shrank into the shadows. But the gods of music would have been pleased with her, 'a whirling dervish with blue nail polish, a wall of hair closing over her face like drapes,' is how *Rolling Stone Magazine* described her recently. 'The biggest, wildest, roughest, most flawed diamond in show business.' We have sold more records than anyone but Elvis.

The picture-taking session over, Janis, exhausted, rests her head on my shoulder. 'Sweet Jesus, but I need a drink.'

'Just one,' I say, and she makes a face at me, shaking her head.

'Aw, Sugar, after a session like that Mama needs to cut loose.'

'We'll see,' I say as we walk off the set.

I think of all the people that her life touched in the sixties and until her death: all those people whose lives are different in countless tiny and not so tiny ways because I appeared to Janis on a dark San Francisco street on a spring night.

I can't help but wonder how much of history I have personally changed. I know what is going to happen soon but am powerless to stop it, not even sure that I would if I could. In my workshop a few swatches of blue satin, a dozen lion-coloured hairs, a few feathers and rhinestones . . .

1980

Audrey Thomas

b. 1935

Born in Binghamton, New York, Audrey Grace Callahan was educated at Smith College, with a year abroad at St Andrews University, Scotland. After completing her B.A. at Smith in 1955, she returned to Britain, taking employment as a teacher in Birmingham. There she met her husband, Ian Thomas, and immigrated with him to British Columbia in 1959. She completed an M.A. at the University of British Columbia in 1963, writing a thesis on Henry James, and—after spending two years in Ghana—returned to UBC for further graduate studies. In 1972, following a divorce, she and her three daughters settled on Galiano Island off the B.C. coast. Although she has left Galiano from time to time to travel or teach creative writing—at UBC (1975-6), Concordia University (1978), and the University of Victoria 1978-9)—she continues to make her home there.

Thomas published her first short story, 'If One Green Bottle', in the *Atlantic Monthly* in 1965; two years later it and nine other stories were collected in *Ten Green Bottles*. She has since published *Ladies and Escorts* (1977) and *Real Mothers* (1981), as well as *Two in the Bush and Other Stories* (1981), which draws from her first two collections. In addition to her short fiction, Thomas has written several longer works, beginning with the novel *Mrs. Blood* (1970) and the paired novellas published as *Munchmeyer and Prospero on the Island* (1971). In *Songs My Mother Taught Me* (1973) she provides a fictional account of her childhood and adolescence. *Blown Figures* (1975), an experimental novel based on her African experience, was followed by *Latakia* (1979), a short novel about a failed romance.

This fiction is usually about a woman—often called Isobel in the early work—whose life resembles the author's. (Like Thomas, she had an unhappy childhood and a traumatic miscarriage in Ghana.) However, Thomas does not simply recreate experience, for although she breaks down the barrier that divides fiction from life, she does so without attempting either the kind of documentary narrative practised by Hugh Hood or the confessional writing of John Glassco. Her narratives are not so much about what occurred as about what *seemed* to have happened. For Thomas event is less important than perception: using oblique perspectives and detailed examinations of internal thought processes that suggest the influence of Henry James, she can view an event from a variety of angles. Thomas moves away from simple realism in other ways as well. For example, in stories such as 'Green Stakes for the Garden' she stretches out the duration of the action so that the reader is given enough time to understand its psychological consequences.

Thomas calls herself a woman's writer who, in dealing with the questions women confront in today's society, usually focuses on conflict between men and women. Her stories are of two types: those that treat the physical aspect—and its effects on women's bodies—of relationships between the sexes, and those that deal with intellectual dynamics, especially when the protagonist is an artist. The central female character in her fiction is often fragmented, either because she verges on schizophrenia or because she and the external narrator of the story share one consciousness. Such divisions—which not only allow Thomas to dramatize the individual's capacity for a variety of responses to a single event but call attention to the split between Thomas's own life and the fiction she makes of it—have led her to make intricate use of complementary perspectives. For example, the paired novellas *Munchmeyer and Prospero on the Island* take the form of the diary of a woman writing (on an island resembling Galiano) a novel called 'Munchmeyer', which takes the form of a male writer's diary. In such fiction male and female are shown to be as much aspects of one another as they are separate forces. Such doubling and mirroring appears elsewhere in Thomas's fiction, as in *Latakia*, where the protagonist—in love with another writer—finds herself competing with the man's wife in a way that suggests that neither of the conventional or independent roles available to contemporary women proves satisfactory.

In the paired stories reprinted below, Thomas carefully establishes the appearance of reality, only to expose it as a fiction while creating a new reality in its place. By doing this she forces her reader to realize that fiction is arbitrary, unreal, and partial. She throws the reader off balance and thereby conveys some sense of the confusion and alienation felt by her characters. Thomas's fiction is not, however, despairing: although recording the failure of personal quests, it urges a continued search.

Green Stakes for the Garden

His voice came first, by itself, propelled by the lazy afternoon which twitched like a sleeping dog and made a quick, spasmodic statement of how it felt about having the summer stillness interrupted; irritated, it flung his words out of the deserted street and over her garden gate—'Lady, can I cut the grass?'

Long before, or what seemed long before, his head and neck declared themselves over the top, tense and with as-yet-unexplained desperation, as owners or desperate keepers of the runaway voice which was saying again, perhaps had not paused at all except to take a breath—'Lady, can I cut the grass?' Faded red-plaid flannel shirt (and some part of her mind thinking flannel on an afternoon like this!) and faded skin, too, grey-, sidewalk-, city-coloured, but the eyes quite different, gas blue, flaming as the gate swung forward under his weight and a part of her mind thinking, even then, we really ought to have a latch, as he shot, stumbled, flung himself across the grass as if he, the keeper of the runaway voice, needed no apology or warrant or by-your-leave in his precipitous rush to recapture such a desperate and dangerous thing. 'Lady, can I cut the grass?'

She was startled and not startled, said automatically, 'Mind the teacups,' without raising her voice, and hardly her eyes after that first, automatic, glance—behaved much as she would if one of the children had rushed in slightly off-balance with excitement, explosive with news of a dog fight, a dead bird or the imminent possibility of an ice-cream cone, 'Mind the teacups,' in her professional mother's voice. So that for—how long?—five, ten, fifteen seconds they remained silent, their bodies confronting one another, but she not yet acknowledging his existence as stranger and intrusion, holding determinedly to the scene in the garden before his abrupt and apocalyptic entrance, thinking to herself, if I don't look maybe he'll go away, while her companion, who had been stretched out lazily in the other deck chair, sat up with a 'What the hell?' And at the sound of *that* voice, slurred, rough, as if wakened abruptly from a sleep, she became aware, really aware, of the stranger's presence and regarded him dismayed, not because she was really afraid, but because his precipitous entrance had indeed smashed something as delicate as her grandmother's flowered cups and saucers; and the thread she had been spinning so carefully between herself and the young man sprawled beside her dangled now forlornly from her fingers (and a part of her mind said isn't that just my luck!).

She adjusted the chair two notches forward so that she could sit up straight and with one hand reached forward, palm outward, toward the stranger, warning him that he had come (gone) quite far enough. With the other she unconsciously pulled her skirt below her knees.

'Are you accustomed to come barging into other people's gardens uninvited?' (Yet even as she said it she knew she had adopted the wrong tone, could sense rather than see the young man look at her, puzzled, as if she had picked up, somehow, the wrong script. This made her even more resentful; why should *she* be in the wrong! While the strange man simply stared at her as if she had replied to him with gibberish.)

'Listen,' he said, 'I gotta have work. This grass here,' he made a wide proprietorial sweep with his arm, taking in the tiny garden. She noticed his nails had been bitten down so low the tips of his fingers extended, naked and greyish, a quarter of an inch; so that he looked deformed, spatulate—with those naked pinky-grey pads at the ends of his fingers instead of nails. Horrible. 'This here grass, I could cut it real nice for a coupala dollars.' He swayed back and forth a few feet from the end of her chair while she gave him another long, careful look, still taking him in as a visual fact—a drastic rearrangement of the landscape of her afternoon. (And why should she feel bothered when *he* said what the hell in that funny tone of voice? Because that too was out of place.) The back yard seemed to have contracted so that they were practically on top of one another— she, the young man and the stranger—were eyeing each other, panting, and would soon leap forward with a snarl, the three of them rolling over and over in the hot dry grass. Over and over, crashing into the border and crushing the flowers underneath them in their terrible animal-like resentment. Even the temperature seemed to have shot suddenly upward ten degrees, although she and the young man had been saying to each other (only five minutes ago?) that this must be some kind of record.

The two chairs underneath the apple tree, the teacups, the plate of little cakes, the sprinkler moving slowly, gently across the border—it had all been so carefully thought out; had given her such *aesthetic* satisfaction. No-one, she thought miserably, would ever understand that aspect of it. How, for instance, she had carefully selected just those little cakes and no others—and just that number—to go on just that plate. And even remembered to buy three over so there wouldn't be any trouble at lunch. And how the whole day had seemed (until now) inspired, each little detail working itself out so beautifully that it was only natural to think in terms of plays and paintings. Even the green stakes had been a stroke of genius.

Yet now it was all animal-like, smouldering; she could smell the stranger's sweat from where she sat. What was she supposed to do? Get up and offer him a cup of tea? (She thought of those queer spatulate fingers curled around one of her grandmother's teacups and for the first time felt afraid.)

'There's no work for you here. Please go.' He never moved, never changed his movement, stood swaying back and forth and back as if he had a pain, or was still recovering from his incredible journey through the garden gate.

Her companion spoke. 'You heard the lady, didn't you?' He swung one lean brown leg over onto the grass, but she motioned him back.

'No,' she said softly. 'It will be all right.' (And a part of her mind thinking it's all very well for you to play Sir Galahad now! And again that slow smouldering resentment flickered between them.) She arranged her face in a smile.

'I'm afraid this isn't a very good neighbourhood for yard work. We all do our own. Why don't you try the church two blocks over? They might have something you could do.' The smile hurt and she put her hand to her face in an effort to keep it in place. What time was it?

The children would be back soon; the afternoon was nearly over. And it had all been so perfect after the first awkward moments, hers not his, for she had never seen him awkward, had thought of him to herself as somehow lacquered or varnished—always shining, always 'ready for company' as it were. And there she was, her voice fluttering around him as if he were some lacquered brass lamp and she a moth impatient to embrace her doom. But the green stakes had saved her.

'How would you like to lend me a hand with the garden?' And he amused, skeptical: 'I'm not much of a gardener.'

He had held out his lean brown hands and she had marvelled at the nails, so regular, a faint pencil line of white above the smooth shell-pink. But strong hands, a golden brown of a colour that made her think of chickens roasting slowly on a spit. She had a sudden impulse to reach over and bite into one of his hands, was quite dizzy with the desire to simply take one up and bite it; they looked delicious.

'Oh, neither am I,' she cried. 'But I bought some stakes to prop up the snapdragons this morning. I feel terribly guilty about them, poor things. The children said they'd help but I really hate putting it off another minute.' She had literally run into the garage for the stakes and garden shears and twine, cried gaily, busily, 'I'll hold them if you'll tie,' thrusting the ball of twine into his skeptical golden hands.

They had moved slowly up the narrow border, careful not to step on the other plants and flowers. The snapdragons were bent over or lying flat. They appealed to her: strange little puffs of colour, lemon, mauve, raspberry pink, like summer sweets or summer dresses. Cool. Reminiscent of childhood. And yet their paradoxical shape, labial, curiously exciting, swollen and stretched. She lifted the stalks carefully, holding them tight against the stakes as he snipped and tied, snipped and tied, the sun strong on his golden arms and hands.

'Look how twisted they are,' she mourned, caressing the tip of a blossom with her finger. 'I've been promising for weeks—and now I'm afraid they're crippled for life.'

She really meant it, bent over her poor, pastel invalids, felt genuinely guilty about the thing. What was so beautiful was that he had understood, had kept silent and snipped and tied, looking quietly into her eyes as they reached the end and she took the garden things from his firm, brown, polished hands. 'I'll get the tea.'

'I'll wait under that nice apple tree of yours.' Then it had all been understood between them, just like that; so that she had run up the back stairs like a girl and giggled when she nearly dropped the sugar bowl.

And she had lain back gracefully in the long chair, sipping lemon tea, surveying the border through half-shut eyes, her heart reaching out to those brave, brave snapdragons, so desperately erect—like old and wounded warriors on parade. While his firm brown fingers moved lazily up and down her leg and she had felt at any minute she might begin to purr.

So that she was actually smiling at him, lips parted, when the stranger started in again, holding onto the picnic table now, bent over as if over a basin and she became quite terrified as she used to be as a child in the midst of a nightmare knowing she was dreaming, straining to wake herself up. He spewed forth words and cries, not looking at her—looking instead, if looking at all, down through the slats of the table at the grass below as if it were personally responsible for his fate.

'You never give a guy a chance you bastards think you're all so goddamn smart she said and don't come back until you pay at last for what I've given out for free I must have been a nut and them in the corner laughin to beat hell you gotta give me what's a coupala dollars. I'll trim the hedge real nice for free your hedge needs trimmin too and she just layin there with nothin underneath saying where'd you think the money came from? Why don't you listen to me lady why . . .'

So that the silence was even worse when for a brief moment sound was shut off and all she could hear was a dull thud as if something overripe had fallen, quite near her, off the tree; and all she could see was a blur and thought my God I'm going even deeper. When her vision cleared and the stranger gave her one last pleading look out of the blood grotesquely red against his face, unreal, outrageous as if some spiteful child had scrawled a crayoned obscenity across her pastel world.

And then her would-be lover's hands reached out and caught the stranger once, grasping his shoulders hard, the knuckles white, so that all she saw was the back of his head as he went back out the way he burst in, muttering and sobbing to himself out of the garden gate and up the outraged street.

And she, 'My God, my God,' giving the flowers one last despairing glance as she picked up the tray and headed for the stairs. All along a part of her saying isn't that just my luck!

1977

Initram

Writers are terrible liars. There are nicer names for it, of course, but liars will do. They take a small incident and blow it up, like a balloon—puff puff—and the out-of-work man who comes to ask if he can cut the grass ends up in their story as an out-of-control grey-faced, desperate creature who hurls himself through the garden gate and by his sheer presence wrecks a carefully arranged afternoon between a married woman and her intended lover.

The truth is I was reading an old friend's manuscript. The truth is I thought the man hadn't gone but was lurking in the back lane just beyond the blackberry bushes.

The truth is I only thought I saw him there—flashes of a red-plaid shirt beyond the green. (Writers also lie to themselves.)

The truth is that when the police came and I was asked to describe this man I was overcome with shame and embarrassment to suddenly notice him, half a block away, moving a neighbour's lawn mower up and down in regular and practical stripes.

The truth is I still insisted (to myself, after the grinning policeman had gone) that the man had been sinister, menacing, unpleasant. And of course he is, in my story.

But what do writers do with the big events in life—births and broken hearts and deaths—the great archetypal situations that need no real enhancement or 'touching up?' Surely they simply *tell* these, acting as mediums through which the great truths filter. Not at all—or not usually or maybe sometimes when they happen to other people.

That is why I decided to call Lydia when my marriage broke up. I was living on an island—felt I needed a wider audience, an audience that would understand and accept my exaggerations for what they were. It had to be a fellow writer, preferably a woman. I called her up long-distance. One of her daughters answered and said she wasn't there could I leave my number? I put the phone down, already planning the ferry trip, the excitement of the telling of my terrible news. Lydia was perfect. Yes. I couldn't wait for her to call me back.

I didn't, in fact, know her very well. I had done a review of her first published book and then later, when I went to visit her city, had on a sudden whim called from a phone booth and identified myself. She had told me to come right over. I had my husband and three kids with me. That seemed too much of an imposition on anyone we didn't know so I took the littlest and he agreed to take the others to the Wax Museum. We drove up a very classy road, with huge houses—some were really what we used to call mansions—on either side. I began to get cold feet.

I had visions of a patrician face and perfect fingernails—drinking tea from her grandmother's bone china cups. We would talk about Proust and Virginia Woolf with a few casual remarks about *Nightwood*[1] and the diaries of Anais Nin.

As we drove up to the front door of a big, imposing, mock-tudor residence I thought of 'Our Gal Sunday', a soap-opera I had loved when I was a kid. It always began with a question as to whether a beautiful young girl from a small mining town in the West could find happiness as the wife of England's wealthiest and most titled lord, Lord Henry Brinthrop.

It was her stories, you see. They were about life on the prairies—about farms and poverty (both spiritual and material) and, very often, a young girl's struggle against those things. Yet here was this house, on this road and a statue in the garden.

'Wait for me,' I said to my husband. 'If a butler or maid answers, I'm not going in.'

[1] (1936); an experimental novel by Djuna Barnes.

But Lydia answered—in black slacks and an old black sweater and no shoes. She gave me a hug and I went in with my littlest child and didn't look back.

Through the hall into the sitting-room, then the dining-room (an impression of a piano and lots of books, of a big antique dining table covered with clutter generally, now that I think back on it. Somewhere upstairs a small child was screaming), through another narrow hall and into a big kitchen. She asked if my little girl wanted some orange juice. She wouldn't answer so I answered for her as mothers do on such occasions.

'Yes please.'

When Lydia opened the refrigerator a great pile of things fell out on the kitchen floor. Frozen pizzas, a dish of leftover mashed potatoes, the bottle of juice, something unidentifiable in a glass jar. We looked at each other and began to laugh.

'The house,' I said. 'I was terrified.'

'I *hate* this house,' she said. 'I hate it.'

Then talked and talked while our two little girls (we each had three, extraordinary! We each had the same dinner set bought on special at the Hudson's Bay Company years before, 'Cherry Thieves' it was called—she used one of the saucers for an ash tray) played something or other upstairs.

She was older than I was (but not much) and very beautiful with dark curly chaotic hair and the kind of white skin that gives off the radiance a candle does when it has burnt down at the core and the sides are still intact. Her book had brought her fame (if not fortune) but she was having trouble with her second one, a novel.

She hated the house and couldn't keep it up. Her husband was a professor—he loved it. It was miserably cold in the winter—sometimes the furnace stopped altogether. What did I think of Doris Lessing, of Joyce Carol Oates, of *The Edible Woman*? Her daughter had made a scene in the supermarket and called her a 'fucking bitch'. Did that kind of thing happen to me? Her neighbour was a perfect housewife, perfect. She was always sending over cakes and preserves. One day she took one of her neighbour's cheesecakes and stamped all over it with her bare feet, she said. An aging Canadian writer (male) had told her drunkenly, 'Well, I might read ya, but I'd never fuck ya.' Did I think it was all right to send a kid to day care when she was only three?

And even while I was talking with her, marvelling at her, helping her mop up the floor, I kept wondering why she didn't write about all this, why she had stopped at twenty years ago and written nothing about her marriage or this house or her child who had been still-born and how the doctor (male) and her husband couldn't understand why it took her so long to get over it. I wondered about her husband but he was off somewhere practicing with a chamber-music group. He liked old instruments, old houses, things with a patina of history and culture. His family accepted her now that she'd won awards.

I only saw her a few times after that—we lived in different cities and there was a boat ride between us. But we wrote (occasionally); she had large round handwriting, like a child's.

Her novel was not going well—it kept turning itself into stories—she was going to Ireland with her husband for a holiday. How was I? Not literary letters:

we were both too busy, too involved in our own affairs. Just little notes, like little squeezes or hugs which said, 'Sister, I am here.'

We read once, at a Women's Week, or rather I read, with two others, while Lydia sat on the blue-carpeted floor with a Spanish cape over her head and let somebody else read for her. She and I were both scared and had gotten drunk before we went—by not reading she had somehow let me down. We four ladies all had dinner together and talked about what it was like to be woman and writer and egged each other on to new witticisms and maybe a few new insights but I did not feel close to Lydia that evening. I was still sore about the way she'd plonked herself down on the carpet and pulled her shawl over her head and let somebody else read for her. It was very clever, I thought to myself, and very dramatic. For there was Lydia's story, unrolling out of the mouth of another woman (whose story it was not), and there was the author herself sitting like an abandoned doll, on the floor beside the reader. The audience loved it and sent out sympathetic vibrations to her. I thought it was a con. And almost said to her, 'Lydia, I think that was a very clever con,' but didn't because I realized that maybe I wished I had thought of it first and why not store it away for some future date—it was a nice piece of dramatic business.

And once we had lunch in her city—at a medieval place where we swept in in our capes (I had a cape too by then) and ate and drank our way through a rainy West Coast afternoon. I wasn't staying overnight so I still hadn't met her husband. Her novel was out and she was winning more awards. I was a little jealous. My books came out and vanished into the well of oblivion. She just went up and up and up. 'I've been writing for twenty years,' she said, 'don't forget that. Two books in twenty years.'

She had pretended she was making the sitting-room curtains when her neighbours invited her over for coffee. She always worked in a basement room. Now her secret was well and truly out.

'How does your husband feel about it all?'

'Oh, I never write about *him*,' she said. She lit a cigarette. 'He's probably my biggest fan.'

Now I waited for her to call me back. My husband (correction, my ex-husband) was coming over to be with his children. I had a whole day and a night off. Whether I wanted to or not, I had to leave this place. And I wanted to, I really wanted to. What was the point in hanging around while he was here, in crying over spilt milk, in locking empty, horseless barn doors, in trying to pick up nine stitches, or in mopping up all the water under the goddamn bridge. I baked bread and cleaned the cabin and got supper for the kids and still she hadn't called. My ex-husband called, however, and said in his new strained, estranged voice, was it all set for tomorrow and I said sure but began to feel sorry for myself because there was really no place I wanted to go except this one place— Lydia's—and I'd got it into my head that if I couldn't go there I couldn't go anywhere and would have to end up going back to the city I had left behind and getting a room in some cheap hotel down near Hastings street, and drinking myself into oblivion with cheap red wine. Or going back and forth all day on the ferry, ending up at midnight on one of the neighbouring islands, getting a room at the inn. A stranger in a brown wool cape. Going into the public room and ordering a drink. Did they have a public room? Would there be local characters sitting around and playing darts—a handsome stranger whose sailing boat was tied up because of the storm? There was not even a small craft warning out but never mind—the weather was almost as fickle as friendship—it was not inconceivable that a sailboat-disabling storm could blow up by tomorrow night—

'I'll always care what happens to you,' he said.

We were teasing wool on the floor in front of the potbelly stove, the three of us—the youngest child was asleep. There was only the oil lamp on and the CBC was broadcasting a documentary about Casals.[2] 'The quality of a man's life is as important as the quality of his art,' the old man said. Our hands were soft and oily from the lanolin in the wool. We touched each other's faces with our new, soft hands. Yes, I thought, yes. And maybe I'll be all right after all. The fleece had been bought by my husband's lover, my ex-best friend. It was from New Zealand, the finest wool in the world. I paid for it, the wool. I had left a cheque on the table the last time I was in town. On the phone my ex-husband mentioned it wasn't enough, she'd mistaken the price or the price had been incorrectly quoted. But it was all right, he'd make up the difference.

'I bet you will,' I said.

I was seeing everything symbolically. Lydia phoned and I said, 'Just a minute I have to light a candle.' The room with the phone in it was in darkness. I stuck the candle in the window and picked up the phone again with my soft lanolin-soaked hands.

'Hello,' I said. 'Can I come and visit you tomorrow and stay overnight?' Her voice sounded a bit funny but that could be the line, which was notoriously bad.

'Sure,' she said. 'Of course. But I'll be out until suppertime. Can you find something to do until suppertime?'

'Can I come a little before? I want to talk to you.'

'Come around four,' she said. She sounded as though she had a cold.

'I'll bring a bottle,' I said.

'Fine.'

I had to be away on the first ferry—what would I do all day? I rubbed lanolin into my face. Sheep shed their old coats and went on living. Snakes too. I could hear Casals' child laughing in the background. Someone had lent us a spinner and it stood in the corner of the front room. Not a fairytale spinner which would turn straw into gold. Very solid and unromantic—an Indian spinner without even the big wheel. Nothing for a Sleeping Beauty to prick her finger on. It worked like an old treadle sewing machine but I didn't have the hang of it yet—my wool always broke. Whirr whirr. There was something nice about just pressing down on the treadle.

I took the candle into the kitchen and wrapped my bread in clean tea towels. I put out a jar of blackberry jam and two poems folded underneath the jar. That would have to do.

When I got to Lydia's house she was frying chicken in the kitchen. Same black slacks and old black sweater. Same bare feet and clutter. There were two enor-

[2]Pablo Casals (1876-1973), famous Spanish cellist.

mous frying pans full of chicken wings both hissing and spitting away and Lydia had a long two-prong kitchen fork in her hand.

I took off my cape and sat down, unwrapping the bottle.

'Good,' she said, 'pour us a glass.' Her voice didn't sound as if she had a cold any more; it sounded harsh and a little loud, as if she were talking to someone slightly deaf. She was jabbing the chicken wings as if they were sausages in need of pricking. She couldn't leave those chicken wings alone and after my second glass I began.

'Listen,' I said, 'I've got something I want to tell you.'

'I've got something I want to tell you too,' she said, and then, rather absent-mindedly, 'did you buy only one bottle?'

'Sorry. But have some more, it doesn't matter.'

'It's all right,' she said, 'we'll drink the dinner wine. Tony will just have to bring some more.'

I was anxious to begin. I wanted to make it funny and witty and brave—to get rid of the pain or to immortalize it and fix it—which? I don't know, I never know. I took another drink of my sherry and wished she'd stop poking at those chicken wings.

'I don't actually live here any more,' she said, waving the long-handled fork. 'I only come back to cook the dinners.'

'You what?'

Turning all the chicken wings over one more time, she lowered the heat under the pans and came to sit down next to me. She kept her fork with her, however, and laid it on the tablecloth where it left a greasy two-pronged stain.

'I've left him,' she said, 'the bastard.' Her voice was very harsh, very tough. I felt she'd put something over on me, just as I'd felt the day of the reading when she sat on the floor and pulled her cape over her head.

'I wish you'd told me over the phone.'

'I couldn't. It's too complicated. Besides, I come back here every day in any case.'

It was both moving and bizarre. He had been supposed to move out, she had even found him an apartment only a few minutes away. But at the last minute he panicked, said he couldn't live in an apartment, talked about his piano, his collection of old instruments, the upheaval. He suggested she move out instead.

'But what about the children?'

'That's the trouble. I have to pick Ellen up from school—he can't do it of course and so I just stay on and make the dinners. The other two are all right, it's only the little one who still needs to be looked after.'

'But that's crazy.'

'Is it? What would you do?'

I admitted that I didn't know.

'But how can you all eat together—how can you stand it?'

'I can't,' she admitted, 'but he won't move out, and finding a house big enough for me and the girls is going to take time.' She got up and rummaged in the pantry. Came back with a bottle of wine.

'I think we'd better start on this,' she said. I undid the cork while she got up to turn the chicken wings.

'He brought her right to the house,' she said. 'When I was on that reading tour. Brought her right here and the children were here too.'

The name of the wine was Sangré de Toro.

'At least she wasn't your best friend,' I said.

'I knew her, I knew her, she's one of his students. I used to think she was mousey. I encouraged her to do something with herself. Ha. And I think the lady next door too,' she said.

'The one who bakes cakes.'

'That's the one. The perfect mother.'

'Maybe you're just being paranoid.'

'Maybe.'

We began the Sangré de Toro.

'What's your big news?' she said.

The two older girls were out somewhere for the evening so there was just the youngest child, who must have been six or seven, Lydia, her husband and myself. She and I were pretty drunk by the time we finished the Sangré de Toro but she had insisted I call her husband at the University and ask him to bring home another bottle.

'Tell him specifically what you want,' she yelled at me from the kitchen. 'Otherwise he'll bring home Calona Red.'

I told him. Now he sat opposite me with two huge plates of chicken wings between us. I didn't want to look at his baffled eyes, his embarrassed smile.

'He still wears a white handkerchief in his breast pocket,' she had said. 'Irons them himself.'

The vegetable was frozen peas and there was bread on the table because Lydia had forgotten all about potatoes. The child was raucous and unpleasant. I wondered what happened when she woke up in the night with a bad dream and whether he went in to her or whether her teenage sisters did. I wondered if she had been the one to tell about the student. Kids will do things like that and not always out of innocence.

Lydia ate one chicken wing after another. We were all going out as soon as the dishes were done and the babysitter came. My real self didn't want to go but my drunken self thought what the hell it's better than staying here with these three miserable people.

While Tony was doing the dishes Lydia hauled me upstairs, pulled me up after her like an older sister a younger, or a mother a reluctant child. I understood the fierce energy of her anger. It was like someone who is hurt during an exciting game. While the excitement is there the pain is simply not felt. She hurled me into their bedroom.

'Look,' she said.

I don't know what I expected to see. Stained sheets piled up in a corner or the student stark naked and manacled to the bed or what. But everything seemed all right. No shattered mirrors or blood-stained bedspreads, just an ordinary pleasant-looking bedroom.

'I don't see.'

'Look,' she was pointing to the walk-in closet.

'I've left all my shoes here except one pair. Crazy isn't it? I just can't seem to take my shoes away.'

'Maybe you don't really want to go.'

'Oh no, I want to go. I have to go. Or he does. One of us anyway. It isn't just the girl.'

'It never is.'

On his side of the closet the tweed jackets and neatly pressed trousers were hung with military precision. On her side there were only empty hangers and a large heap of shoes piled any which way. Was that significant, the order/disorder? Was it an attempt to break through this orderly self that made him bring his student to this bed? Or had he just been lonely? I didn't want to think about that for after all, wasn't he the enemy?

We went back downstairs.

The babysitter came and we went out. Lydia had put on a filthy white crocheted wool poncho. Tony objected mildly. 'Are you going out in that? It's dirty.'

'That's tough,' Lydia said.

They were playing to me, an audience of one. Maybe that's why we were going out—to gain a larger audience. I panicked—what if I had too much to drink and began to cry? Lydia looked witchy and wicked with her uncombed hair and dirty poncho. I felt she was quite capable of doing something terrible to her husband—mocking him or humiliating him in some way, and I was to be her accomplice. He had a heavy projector in his hand.

'We had arranged to show some slides,' he said, 'before we knew you were coming.'

'Slides of our European trip,' Lydia said. 'One of Tony's colleagues is going this summer—he wanted to see them.'

I thought it was strange they didn't invite him over here, but maybe Lydia had refused to actually entertain. I found the whole thing strange—sitting between them in the car, following them up the steps of their friend's house, saying hello and taking off my cape, patting my face to keep the smile in place, the way some women pat their hair before they go into a room. Our host was shy and pale and had a club foot. There didn't seem to be any hostess. But there were two other people in the sitting-room, a tall, lean man, in a bright blue shirt, string tie and cowboy boots, and a plump woman in a black crêpe dress, black pointy fifties shoes and a rhinestone brooch. Both the man and the woman had nice faces, expectant faces, as if they expected that whoever walked through the next door was bound to be cheerful and interesting and good. Innocent faces, almost the faces of small children. We were introduced and asked what we would like to drink and Tony began to set up the projector.

Lydia was talking to Tony's colleague in her strange new brassy tough-gal voice, flirting with him, making him smile. 'Does he know?' I wondered. He had introduced her as Tony's wife. I sat down next to the man in the blue shirt.

'What do you do?' I asked.

'I'm a bee-keeper,' he said.

'You might say he's a bee-baron,' said his brother. I could see they were brothers in their smiles and something to do with their ears, a strange extra little fold where the ear joined the head. Other than that they didn't really look alike, the one small and dark and with the pallor of the academic, the other tall and fair and with what we call a 'weathered' skin.

'A swarm of bees in May,' said Lydia, 'is worth a load of hay. I remember hearing farmers say that when I was a kid. I grew up on a farm,' she said and flashed a smile at the bee-keeper's wife.

'Do you like it,' I asked, 'keeping bees?' I had thought of buying one or two hives for the island. I already had hens and a fleece for spinning and would have my nine bean rows in the spring. Lydia had laughed when I told her my real dream was to have a little farm.

'Ha. Only city people yearn to live on a farm. I hated it.'

'Why?'

'I'm not even sure why any more. The constant work—the catastrophes—the exhaustion—the women always in the kitchen—something always being butchered, beheaded or skinned or pickled or preserved.'

'Maybe it doesn't have to be that way?'

'It has to be that way. If you really live off the land you live off the land. Nothing can be put off or wasted or ignored. I always felt the kitchen smelled of blood or sugar or vinegar or manure or all of these. I felt I went to school stinking of all of it.'

'Those are good smells. Honest smells. I worked in an asylum once—I got that smell on me. I used carbolic soap and tried to get it off.'

She shook her head and changed the subject, only adding, 'They weren't good smells when I was going to school.'

Had she been teased, then? Had the boys pulled chicken feathers out of her dark curly hair—had her dresses been too long—were her hands all wrinkled from washwater? I realized how little I actually knew about her except through her stories. I guess this conversation took place before her novel came out.

Tony asked in his apologetic manner if we were ready to see the slides. Lydia and the bee-keeper's wife were sitting in easy chairs on the other side of the room, where the screen had been set up, so they had to move. Lydia came and sat cross-legged on the floor by my feet. The bee-keeper and I were on the couch and we shoved over to make room for the bee-keeper's wife. Tony was next to me, behind the projector and his friend was next to him on a kitchen chair. He got up and after offering us another drink (only Lydia and I accepted) turned out all the lights.

I don't remember much about the slide show. Tony projected and Lydia commented. Ireland, England, Scotland, Wales and then across the Channel into France and down through Spain. They were all 'views'—that is to say they told me nothing about the two people who had taken that trip. Alone. Without the children. Was that when they first suspected they had nothing to say to one another? Had they set off with high hopes and become more and more disenchanted? What had finally driven that orderly controlled man to introduce that student into his bedroom? Not secretly but openly, 'in front of the children.' From where I was sitting I could see that his hands shook every time he put in another slide.

'You've got that one in backwards,' Lydia said. We all came to attention and studied the screen—it was a bull fight scene and looked perfectly all right to me.

'I don't think—' Tony began.

'Look for yourself. Look at it. Can't you see it's back to front?'

'I sure don't see anything funny,' said the bee-keeper.

' "Initram",' Lydia said in her bold brassy voice. 'Look at the advertisements and tell me what kind of a drink is Initram.'

'Oh,' he said, 'Sorry.'

'Ha.'

His hands shook a little more as he carefully pried out the offending slide and turned it around.

'There,' he said. 'Is that better?'

'Oh God,' said Lydia. 'You've done it again.' And sure enough he had. There was 'Initram' being advertised again.

'I'd like another drink,' said Lydia, 'Initram on the rocks.'

Tony switched the projector off and for a minute we were in a complete and tension-filled darkness before his friend had enough presence of mind to reach up and switch on the lights.

'That's all folks,' he said, trying to sound like Woody Woodpecker, trying to be funny.

'Don't you want to show the rest of the slides?' Lydia said.

'No, I think that's enough.'

'Well, tell us about bees then,' she said, turning around and facing the sofa, backing away a little bit so she could gaze up at the bee-keeper, her pretty head cocked on one side.

'What do you want to know?' he said, smiling. But uncomfortable too for he was not so dumb or naïve that he didn't see what she was doing to her husband.

'Oh. Everything. Everything.' She waved her hand. 'Their mating habits for instance. Do they really only mate once? The queens, I mean.'

'No, they can mate more than once, maybe two, three times. But usually only once. It's funny,' he said, 'when you stop to think of it. From a human point of view the drone that wins is the loser really.'

'I don't follow you,' I said. I really knew nothing about bees. Whereas I had a funny feeling about Lydia. Would a kid who had a grandfather who kept bees—? Or maybe she never did have such a grandfather. Maybe her grandfather just said that whenever he saw a swarm—the way my father used to say, 'Red sky at night, sailor's delight' when he'd never been near the ocean.

'Fun, frolic and death,' he said, 'fun, frolic and death. Those drones are the laziest devils you'd like to see. Waited on hand and foot by their sisters—don't have to do nothing except eat and lie around and take the occasional look-see outside. Then one day the queen just zooms up into the blue with hundreds of those drones dashin' after her. A fantastic sight—fantastic.'

'And the race is to the swift,' said Lydia, taking a long sip of her drink as if it were some strange nectar, then parting her lips and looking up at the bee-keeper with her new bold look.

'The strongest and swiftest catches her,' he said. 'Sometimes she even zooms back toward 'em, because she wants to be caught you know. That's all part of it.'

'She wants to be caught,' repeated Lydia. 'She has to be caught.' She took another long sip of her drink. The bee-keeper's wife just sat back against the cushions and smiled.

'She has to be caught.'

'So she is caught.'

'And then?'

'And then he clasps her to him, face to face—there's a little explosion as all his male organs pop out and they fly together like that face to face, while he fertilizes her.'

'Then he dies?' I asked.

'Then he dies. You see, they fall to the ground together, outside the home hive of the queen, and when she tries to pull away, he's stuck so fast to her she pulls most of his abdomen away.'

'Ab-*do*-men,' said Lydia, lightly mocking him. But not in the way she said, 'Initram.'

'My brother probably knows more about bees than any man in North America,' said the man with the club foot. 'He could write a book about them.'

'It's my job,' he said simply.

'Oh don't,' cried Lydia. 'Don't ever write a book about them.' She gave a mock shudder. 'I wonder what it feels like,' she said. 'To fly out like that after the darkness of the hive into the blue sky and the green trees and to feel the sunshine on her back. To know that her destiny is about to be fulfilled.' Then she turned toward the bee-keeper's wife. 'And you. Is it your life too? Bees?'

She nodded her head, serene in her black dress and rhinestones. She had a strong Southern accent.

'It's my life too.'

Then the bee-keeper did a beautiful thing. He just reached over and put his lean brown hand over hers.

'We try to study the bees,' he said. 'We try to do what they do.'

'Fun, frolic and death?' said Lydia, flirting, slyly mocking.

'No,' he said, but not angrily. He didn't swat at her any more than he might swat at a bee who flew a little too close to his ear.

'They are true communists—the bees. No-one works for any profit to himself. Everything is done only for the good of the colony. If we could live like that—'

'Ah yes, Utopia.' Lydia sighed. 'Perhaps if we all ate more honey?' She was mocking him again, circling back. She smiled at the three men in the room. All she needed was a yellow sweater.

'Who knows? That's where our word honeymoon comes from, you know— the old belief in the magical powers of honey. Germany I think it was, or Austria. The newly-married couple would drink mead for a month after the wedding.'

'What was it supposed to do for them?'

'Now that I'm not sure of. Make 'em happy and industrious I guess.'

'Is it true,' said Lydia, 'that the queen can sting over and over—that she doesn't die when she stings? I read that somewhere I think. Tony, do you remember reading that somewhere or somebody telling us that the queen could sting over and over?'

'I don't remember.'

'Well, it's true, isn't it?' She appealed to the bee-keeper.

'It's true. She has to defend herself. It's her nature.'

'There, you see Tony, I was right. It's her nature.'

'There is usually only one queen,' said the bee-keeper, 'she kills off all the others.'

'Why not?' Lydia said, 'it's natural.'

Then we were all leaving—I can't remember who stood up first. We said goodbye to the bee-keeper and his wife. I wrote down the name of a supply house where I could get supers[2] and bee suits. I wrote down the names of two books. He (the bee-keeper) went out to his van and came back with a little jar of honey for each of us. Alfalfa honey, clear and thick and golden.

'Jim Ritchie and Sons,' it said. 'Abbotsford, BC,' and 'Unpasteurized' underneath. 'Mary Beth designed the labels,' he said proudly.

I slept downstairs in a little parlour with a fireplace. They had coal and started a fire for me. Made up the Hide-A-Bed and went off upstairs together. I lay in the darkness under Lydia's grandmother's Star of Bethlehem quilt and smelled the smell of the coal fire and was back fourteen years under a quilt in a big double bed in Scotland. On my honeymoon. The maid had come in with a stone hot water bottle but we were already warm from drinking a strange mixture in the public bar—something called Athol Bross and now that I thought of it, I seemed to remember that it was made of porridge and honey. Or maybe I just had honey on the brain.

What had happened to us? What had happened to us all? I began to cry while Lydia made noisy love upstairs. I heard her—she wanted me to hear her. It was the last line in the last paragraph of the story she'd been writing all evening. I wondered if she'd come down the next morning with Tony's abdomen irrevocably stuck to her front.

We don't see each other very much any more. She lives in a distant city. But once a year we meet—at the Writers Union annual general meeting—and compare children and lovers and ideas for stories, usually in that order. We flirt, we get drunk, we congratulate ourselves that somehow miraculously we have survived another year, that we each have money and a room of one's own and are writing fiction. This year I told her (lying) that I was thinking of writing a story about her.

'I'm calling it ''Chicken Wings'',' I said.

'Chicken Wings?'

'The night I came to see you, and you and Tony had just split up.'

'And you wanted to tell me about your break-up.'

'*Sangré de Toro*,' I said. We began to laugh.

'Do you remember the bee-keeper and his wife?'

'Of course, they're in the story.'

'Fun, frolic and death—oh God.'

We laughed until we cried.

[2]Boxes used by beekeepers for storing honey.

'What name d'you want?' I said. 'You can choose your own name.'
'Lydia,' she said. 'I always wanted to be called Lydia.'
'All right,' I said. 'You can be Lydia.'
'But I don't like your title,' she said. 'I think you'll have to change it.'

1977

Alistair MacLeod

b. 1936

Born in North Battleford, Sask., Alistair MacLeod grew up in various small prairie settlements in Saskatchewan and Alberta until 1946, when his parents moved back to the family farm in Cape Breton. He graduated from high-school there and worked to support himself in a variety of jobs (salesman, editor, logger, truck driver, public-relations man, miner, and teacher), put himself through Nova Scotia Teachers' College, and during the sixties earned degrees at St Francis Xavier University (B.A., B.Ed.), the University of New Brunswick (M.A.), and the University of Notre Dame (Ph.D., 1968). He taught at the University of Indiana for three years before taking his present position at the University of Windsor in 1969. He teaches English and creative writing and is fiction editor for the *University of Windsor Review*.

MacLeod's fiction began to appear in journals in Canada and the United States while he was still a graduate student. Although his output is small—MacLeod has published only one collection of short stories, *The Lost Salt Gift of Blood* (1976)—he has received international recognition. In these stories Cape Breton Island, with its beauty and simplicity as well as its austerity and ugliness, stands in contrast to the urban complexities that often tempt yet never satisfy the Cape's young. Opposed to the urban life of the mainland, which provides neither history nor identity, life on Cape Breton is rich with memory and its extended families are drawn together by the sea, the land, and the underground mines on which they base their livelihood. Neither island nor mainland is ideal, but Cape Breton remains the region of the heart.

The Lost Salt Gift of Blood

Now in the early evening the sun is flashing everything in gold. It bathes the blunt grey rocks that loom yearningly out toward Europe and it touches upon the stunted spruce and the low-lying lichens and the delicate hardy ferns and the ganglia-rooted moss and the tiny tough rock cranberries. The grey and slanting rain squalls have swept in from the sea and then departed with all the suddenness of surprise marauders. Everything before them and beneath them has been rapidly, briefly, and thoroughly drenched and now the clear droplets catch and hold the sun's infusion in a myriad of rainbow colours. Far beyond the harbour's mouth more tiny squalls seem to be forming, moving rapidly across the surface of the sea out there beyond land's end where the blue ocean turns to grey in rain and distance and the strain of eyes. Even farther out, somewhere beyond Cape Spear lies Dublin and the Irish coast; far away but still the nearest land and closer now than is Toronto or Detroit to say nothing of North America's more western cities; seeming almost hazily visible now in imagination's mist.

Overhead the ivory white gulls wheel and cry, flashing also in the purity of the sun and the clean, freshly washed air. Sometimes they glide to the blue-green surface of the harbour, squawking and garbling; at times almost standing on their pink webbed feet as if they would walk on water, flapping their wings pompously against their breasts like over-conditioned he-men who have successfully passed their body-building courses. At other times they gather in lazy groups on the rocks above the harbour's entrance murmuring softly to themselves or looking also quietly out toward what must be Ireland and the vastness of the sea.

The harbour itself is very small and softly curving, seeming like a tiny, peaceful womb nurturing the life that now lies within it but which originated from without; came from without and through the narrow, rock-tight channel that admits the entering and withdrawing sea. That sea is entering again now, forcing itself gently but inevitably through the tightness of the opening and laving the rocky walls and rising and rolling into the harbour's inner cove. The dories rise at their moorings and the tide laps higher on the piles and advances upward toward the high-water marks upon the land; the running moon-drawn tides of spring.

Around the edges of the harbour brightly coloured houses dot the wet and glistening rocks. In some ways they seem almost like defiantly optimistic horseshoe nails: yellow and scarlet and green and pink; buoyantly yet firmly permanent in the grey unsundered rock.

At the harbour's entrance the small boys are jigging for the beautifully speckled salmon-pink sea trout. Barefootedly they stand on the tide-wet rocks flicking their wrists and sending their glistening lines in shimmering golden arcs out into the rising tide. Their voices mount excitedly as they shout to one another encouragement, advice, consolation. The trout fleck dazzlingly on their sides as they are drawn toward the rocks, turning to seeming silver as they flash within the sea.

It is all of this that I see now, standing at the final road's end of my twenty-five-hundred-mile journey. The road ends here—quite literally ends at the door of a now abandoned fishing shanty some six brief yards in front of where I stand. The shanty is grey and weatherbeaten with two boarded-up windows, vanishing wind-whipped shingles and a heavy rusted padlock chained fast to a twisted door. Piled before the twisted door and its equally twisted frame are some marker buoys, a small pile of rotted rope, a broken oar and an old and rust-flaked anchor.

The option of driving my small rented Volkswagen the remaining six yards and then negotiating a tight many-twists-of-the-steering-wheel turn still exists. I would be then facing toward the west and could simply retrace the manner of my coming. I could easily drive away before anything might begin.

Instead I walk beyond the road's end and the fishing shanty and begin to descend the rocky path that winds tortuously and narrowly along and down the cliff's edge to the sea. The small stones roll and turn and scrape beside and beneath my shoes and after only a few steps the leather is nicked and scratched. My toes press hard against its straining surface.

As I approach the actual water's edge four small boys are jumping excitedly upon the glistening rocks. One of them has made a strike and is attempting to reel in his silver-turning prize. The other three have laid down their rods in their enthusiasm and are shouting encouragement and giving almost physical moral support: 'Don't let him get away, John,' they say. 'Keep the line steady.' 'Hold the end of the rod up.' 'Reel in the slack.' 'Good.' 'What a dandy!'

Across the harbour's clear water another six or seven shout the same delirious messages. The silver-turning fish is drawn toward the rock. In the shallows he flips and arcs, his flashing body breaking the water's surface as he walks upon his tail. The small fisherman has now his rod almost completely vertical. Its tip sings and vibrates high above his head while at his feet the trout spins and curves. Both of his hands are clenched around the rod and his knuckles strain white through the water-roughened redness of small-boy hands. He does not know whether he should relinquish the rod and grasp at the lurching trout or merely heave the rod backward and flip the fish behind him. Suddenly he decides upon the latter but even as he heaves his bare feet slide out from beneath him on the smooth wetness of the rock and he slips down into the water. With a pirouetting leap the trout turns glisteningly and tears itself free. In a darting flash of darkened greenness it rights itself with the regained water and is gone. 'Oh damn!' says the small fisherman, struggling upright onto his rock. He bites his lower lip to hold back the tears welling within his eyes. There is a small trickle of blood coursing down from a tiny scratch on the inside of his wrist and he is wet up to his knees. I reach down to retrieve the rod and return it to him.

Suddenly a shout rises from the opposite shore. Another line zings tautly through the water throwing off fine showers of iridescent droplets. The shouts and contagious excitement spread anew. 'Don't let him get away!' 'Good for you.' 'Hang on!' 'Hang on!'

I am caught up in it myself and wish also to shout some enthusiastic advice but I do not know what to say. The trout curves up from the water in a wriggling arch and lands behind the boys in the moss and lichen that grow down to the sea-washed rocks. They race to free it from the line and proclaim about its size.

On our side of the harbour the boys begin to talk. 'Where do you live?' they ask me and is it far away and is it bigger than St John's? Awkwardly I try to tell them the nature of the North American midwest. In turn I ask them if they go to school. 'Yes,' they say. Some of them go to St Bonaventure's which is the Catholic school and others go to Twilling Memorial. They are all in either grade four or grade five. All of them say that they like school and that they like their teachers.

The fishing is good they say and they come here almost every evening. 'Yesterday I caught me a nine-pounder,' says John. Eagerly they show me all of their simple equipment. The rods are of all varieties as are the lines. At the lines' ends the leaders are thin transparencies terminating in grotesque three-clustered hooks. A foot or so from each hook there is a silver spike knotted into the leader. Some of the boys say the trout are attracted by the flashing of the spike; others say that it acts only as a weight or sinker. No line is without one.

'Here, sir,' says John, 'have a go. Don't get your shoes wet.' Standing on the slippery rocks in my smooth-soled shoes I twice attempt awkward casts. Both times the line loops up too high and the spike splashes down far short of the running, rising life of the channel.

'Just a flick of the wrist, sir,' he says, 'just a flick of the wrist. You'll soon get the hang of it.' His hair is red and curly and his face is splashed with freckles and his eyes are clear and blue. I attempt three or four more casts and then pass the rod back to the hands where it belongs.

And now it is time for supper. The calls float down from the women standing in the doorways of the multi-coloured houses and obediently the small fishermen gather up their equipment and their catches and prepare to ascend the narrow upward-winding paths. The sun has descended deeper into the sea and the evening has become quite cool. I recognize this with surprise and a slight shiver. In spite of the advice given to me and my own precautions my feet are wet and chilled within my shoes. No place to be unless barefooted or in rubber boots. Perhaps for me no place at all.

As we lean into the steepness of the path my young companions continue to talk, their accents broad and Irish. One of them used to have a tame sea gull at his house, had it for seven years. His older brother found it on the rocks and brought it home. His grandfather called it Joey.[1] 'Because it talked so much,' explains John. It died last week and they held a funeral about a mile away from the shore where there was enough soil to dig a grave. Along the shore itself it is almost solid rock and there is no ground for a grave. It's the same with people they say. All week they have been hopefully looking along the base of the cliffs for another sea gull but have not found one. You cannot kill a sea gull they say, the government protects them because they are scavengers and keep the harbours clean.

The path is narrow and we walk in single file. By the time we reach the shanty and my rented car I am wheezing and badly out of breath. So badly out of shape for a man of thirty-three; sauna baths do nothing for your wind. The boys walk easily, laughing and talking beside me. With polite enthusiasm they comment upon my car. Again there exists the possibility of restarting the car's engine and driving back the road that I have come. After all, I have not seen a single adult except for the women calling down the news of supper. I stand and fiddle with my keys.

The appearance of the man and the dog is sudden and unexpected. We have been so casual and unaware in front of the small automobile that we have neither seen nor heard their approach along the rock-worn road. The dog is short, stocky and black and white. White hair floats and feathers freely from his sturdy legs and paws as he trots along the rock looking expectantly out into the harbour. He takes no notice of me. The man is short and stocky as well and he also appears as black and white. His rubber boots are black and his dark heavy worsted trousers are supported by a broadly scarred and blackened belt. The buckle is shaped like a dory with a fisherman standing in the bow. Above the belt there is a dark navy woollen jersey and upon his head a toque of the same material. His hair beneath the toque is white as is the three-or-four-day stubble on his face. His eyes are blue and his hands heavy, gnarled, and misshapen. It is hard to tell from looking at him whether he is in his sixties, seventies, or eighties.

'Well, it is a nice evening tonight,' he says, looking first at John and then to me. 'The barometer has not dropped so perhaps fair weather will continue for a day or two. It will be good for the fishing.'

[1]That is, after Joey Smallwood (b. 1900), former premier of Newfoundland.

He picks a piece of gnarled grey driftwood from the roadside and swings it slowly back and forth in his right hand. With desperate anticipation the dog dances back and forth before him, his intense eyes glittering at the stick. When it is thrown into the harbour he barks joyously and disappears, hurling himself down the bank in a scrambling avalanche of small stones. In seconds he reappears with only his head visible, cutting a silent but rapidly advancing *V* through the quiet serenity of the harbour. The boys run to the bank's edge and shout encouragement to him—much as they had been doing earlier for one another. 'It's farther out,' they cry, 'to the right, to the right.' Almost totally submerged, he cannot see the stick he swims to find. The boys toss stones in its general direction and he raises himself out of the water to see their landing splashdowns and to change his wide-waked course.

'How have you been?' asks the old man, reaching for a pipe and a pouch of tobacco and then without waiting for an answer, 'perhaps you'll stay for supper. There are just the three of us now.'

We begin to walk along the road in the direction that he has come. Before long the boys rejoin us accompanied by the dripping dog with the recovered stick. He waits for the old man to take it from him and then showers us all with a spray of water from his shaggy coat. The man pats and scratches the damp head and the dripping ears. He keeps the returned stick and thwacks it against his rubber boots as we continue to walk along the rocky road I have so recently travelled in my Volkswagen.

Within a few yards the houses begin to appear upon our left. Frame and flat-roofed, they cling to the rocks looking down into the harbour. In storms their windows are splashed by the sea but now their bright colours are buoyantly brave in the shadows of the descending dusk. At the third gate, John, the man, and the dog turn in. I follow them. The remaining boys continue on; they wave and say, 'So long.'

The path that leads through the narrow whitewashed gate has had its stone worn smooth by the passing of countless feet. On either side there is a row of small, smooth stones, also neatly whitewashed, and seeming like a procession of large white eggs or tiny unbaked loaves of bread. Beyond these stones and also on either side, there are some cast-off tires also whitewashed and serving as flower beds. Within each whitened circumference the colourful low-lying flowers nod; some hardy strain of pansies or perhaps marigolds. The path leads on to the square green house, with its white borders and shutters. On one side of the wooden doorstep a skate blade has been nailed, for the wiping off of feet, and beyond the swinging screen door there is a porch which smells saltily of the sea. A variety of sou'westers and rubber boots and mitts and caps hang from the driven nails or lie at the base of the wooden walls.

Beyond the porch there is the kitchen where the woman is at work. All of us enter. The dog walks across the linoleum-covered floor, his nails clacking, and flings himself with a contented sigh beneath the wooden table. Almost instantly he is asleep, his coat still wet from his swim within the sea.

The kitchen is small. It has an iron cookstove, a table against one wall and three or four handmade chairs of wood. There is also a wooden rocking-chair covered by a cushion. The rockers are so thin from years of use that it is hard to believe they still function. Close by the table there is a wash-stand with two pails of water upon it. A wash-basin hangs from a driven nail in its side and above it is an old-fashioned mirrored medicine cabinet. There is also a large cupboard, a low-lying couch, and a window facing upon the sea. On the walls a barometer hangs as well as two pictures, one of a rather jaunty young couple taken many years ago. It is yellowed and rather indistinct; the woman in a long dress with her hair done up in ringlets, the man in a serge suit that is slightly too large for him and with a tweed cap pulled rakishly over his right eye. He has an accordion strapped over his shoulders and his hands are fanned out on the buttons and keys. The other picture is of the Christ-child. Beneath it is written, 'Sweet Heart of Jesus Pray for Us'.

The woman at the stove is tall and fine featured. Her grey hair is combed briskly back from her forehead and neatly coiled with a large pin at the base of her neck. Her eyes are as grey as the storm scud[2] of the sea. Her age, like her husband's, is difficult to guess. She wears a blue print dress, a plain blue apron and low-heeled brown shoes. She is turning fish within a frying pan when we enter.

Her eyes contain only mild surprise as she first regards me. Then with recognition they glow in open hostility which in turn subsides and yields to self-control. She continues at the stove while the rest of us sit upon the chairs.

During the meal that follows we are reserved and shy in our lonely adult ways; groping for and protecting what perhaps may be the only awful dignity we possess. John, unheedingly, talks on and on. He is in the fifth grade and is doing well. They are learning percentages and the mysteries of decimals; to change a percent to a decimal fraction you move the decimal point two places to the left and drop the percent sign. You always, always do so. They are learning the different breeds of domestic animals: the four main breeds of dairy cattle are Holstein, Ayrshire, Guernsey, and Jersey. He can play the mouth organ and will demonstrate after supper. He has twelve lobster traps of his own. They were originally broken ones thrown up on the rocky shore by storms. Ira, he says nodding toward the old man, helped him fix them, nailing on new lathes and knitting new headings. Now they are set along the rocks near the harbour's entrance. He is averaging a pound a trap and the 'big' fishermen say that that is better than some of them are doing. He is saving his money in a little imitation keg that was also washed up on the shore. He would like to buy an outboard motor for the small reconditioned skiff he now uses to visit his traps. At present he has only oars.

'John here has the makings of a good fisherman,' says the old man. 'He's up at five most every morning when I am putting on the fire. He and the dog are already out along the shore and back before I've made tea.'

'When I was in Toronto,' says John, 'no one was ever up before seven. I would make my own tea and wait. It was wonderful sad. There were gulls there though, flying over Toronto harbour. We went to see them on two Sundays.'

After the supper we move the chairs back from the table. The woman clears away the dishes and the old man turns on the radio. First he listens to the weather forecast and then turns to short wave where he picks up the conversations from

[2]Clouds.

the offshore fishing boats. They are conversations of catches and winds and tides and of the women left behind on the rocky shores. John appears with his mouth organ, standing at a respectful distance. The old man notices him, nods, and shuts off the radio. Rising, he goes upstairs, the sound of his feet echoing down to us. Returning he carries an old and battered accordion. 'My fingers have so much rheumatism,' he says, 'that I find it hard to play anymore.'

Seated, he slips his arms through the straps and begins the squeezing accordion motions. His wife takes off her apron and stands behind him with one hand upon his shoulder. For a moment they take on the essence of the once young people in the photograph. They began to sing:

> Come all ye fair and tender ladies
> Take warning how you court your men
> They're like the stars on a summer's morning
> First they'll appear and then they're gone.

> I wish I were a tiny sparrow
> And I had wings and I could fly
> I'd fly away to my own true lover
> And all he'd ask I would deny.

> Alas I'm not a tiny sparrow
> I have not wings nor can I fly
> And on this earth in grief and sorrow
> I am bound until I die.

John sits on one of the home-made chairs playing his mouth organ. He seems as all mouth-organ players the world over: his right foot tapping out the measures and his small shoulders now round and hunched above the cupped hand instrument.

'Come now and sing with us, John,' says the old man.

Obediently he takes the mouth organ from his mouth and shakes the moisture drops upon his sleeve. All three of them begin to sing, spanning easily the half century of time that touches their extremes. The old and the young singing now their songs of loss in different comprehensions. Stranded here, alien of my middle generation, I tap my leather foot self-consciously upon the linoleum. The words sweep up and swirl about my head. Fog does not touch like snow yet it is more heavy and more dense. Oh moisture comes in many forms!

> All alone as I strayed by the banks of the river
> Watching the moonbeams at evening of day
> All alone as I wandered I spied a young stranger
> Weeping and wailing with many a sigh.

> Weeping for one who is now lying lonely
> Weeping for one who no mortal can save
> As the foaming dark waters flow silently past him
> Onward they flow over young Jenny's grave.

> Oh Jenny my darling come tarry here with me
> Don't leave me alone, love, distracted in pain

For as death is the dagger that plied us asunder
Wide is the gulf, love, between you and I.

After the singing stops we all sit rather uncomfortably for a moment. The mood seeming to hang heavily upon our shoulders. Then with my single exception all come suddenly to action. John gets up and takes his battered school books to the kitchen table. The dog jumps up on a chair beside him and watches solemnly in a supervisory manner. The woman takes some navy yarn the colour of her husband's jersey and begins to knit. She is making another jersey and is working on the sleeve. The old man rises and beckons me to follow him into the tiny parlour. The stuffed furniture is old and worn. There is a tiny wood-burning heater in the centre of the room. It stands on a square of galvanized metal which protects the floor from falling, burning coals. The stovepipe rises and vanishes into the wall on its way to the upstairs. There is an old-fashioned mantelpiece on the wall behind the stove. It is covered with odd shapes of driftwood from the shore and a variety of exotically shaped bottles, blue and green and red, which are from the shore as well. There are pictures here too: of the couple in the other picture; and one of them with their five daughters; and one of the five daughters by themselves. In that far-off picture time all of the daughters seem roughly between the ages of ten and eighteen. The youngest has the reddest hair of all. So red that it seems to triumph over the non-photographic colours of lonely black and white. The pictures are in standard wooden frames.

From behind the ancient chesterfield the old man pulls a collapsible card table and pulls down its warped and shaky legs. Also from behind the chesterfield he takes a faded checkerboard and a large old-fashioned matchbox of rattling wooden checkers. The spine of the board is almost cracked through and is strengthened by layers of adhesive tape. The checkers are circumferences of wood sawed from a length of broom handle. They are about three quarters of an inch thick. Half of them are painted a very bright blue and the other half an equally eyecatching red. 'John made these,' said the old man, 'all of them are not really the same thickness but they are good enough. He gave it a good try.'

We begin to play checkers. He takes the blue and I the red. The house is silent with only the click-clack of the knitting needles sounding through the quiet rooms. From time to time the old man lights his pipe, digging out the old ashes with a flattened nail and tamping in the fresh tobacco with the same nail's head. The blue smoke winds lazily and haphazardly toward the low-beamed ceiling. The game is solemn as is the next and then the next. Neither of us loses all of the time.

'It is time for some of us to be in bed,' says the old woman after a while. She gathers up her knitting and rises from her chair. In the kitchen John neatly stacks his school books on one corner of the table in anticipation of the morning. He goes outside for a moment and then returns. Saying good-night very formally he goes up the stairs to bed. In a short while the old woman follows, her footsteps travelling the same route.

We continue to play our checkers, wreathed in smoke and only partially aware of the muffled footfalls sounding softly above our heads.

When the old man gets up to go outside I am not really surprised, any more than I am when he returns with the brown, ostensible vinegar jug. Poking at the declining kitchen fire, he moves the kettle about seeking the warmest spot on the cooling stove. He takes two glasses from the cupboard, a sugar bowl and two spoons. The kettle begins to boil.

Even before tasting it, I know the rum to be strong and overproof. It comes at night and in fog from the French islands of St Pierre and Miquelon. Coming over in the low-throttled fishing boats, riding in imitation gas cans. He mixes the rum and the sugar first, watching them marry and dissolve. Then to prevent the breakage of the glasses he places a teaspoon in each and adds the boiling water. The odour rises richly, its sweetness hung in steam. He brings the glasses to the table, holding them by their tops so that his fingers will not burn.

We do not say anything for some time, sitting upon the chairs, while the sweetened, heated richness moves warmly through and from our stomachs and spreads upward to our brains. Outside the wind begins to blow, moaning and faintly rattling the window's whitened shutters. He rises and brings refills. We are warm within the dark and still within the wind. A clock strikes regularly the strokes of ten.

It is difficult to talk at times with or without liquor; difficult to achieve the actual act of saying. Sitting still we listen further to the rattle of the wind; not knowing where nor how we should begin. Again the glasses are refilled.

'When she married in Toronto,' he says at last, 'we figured that maybe John should be with her and with her husband. That maybe he would be having more of a chance there in the city. But we would be putting it off and it weren't until nigh on two years that he went. Went with a woman from down the cove going to visit her daughter. Well, what was wrong was that we missed him wonderful awful. More fearful than we ever thought. Even the dog. Just pacing the floor and looking out the window and walking along the rocks of the shore. Like us had no moorings, lost in the fog or on the ice-floes in a snow squall. Nigh sick unto our hearts we was. Even the grandmother who before that was maybe thinking small to herself that he was trouble in her old age. Ourselves having never had no sons only daughters.'

He pauses, then rising goes upstairs and returns with an envelope. From it he takes a picture which shows two young people standing self-consciously before a half-ton pickup with a wooden extension ladder fastened to its side. They appear to be in their middle twenties. The door of the truck has the information: 'Jim Farrell, Toronto: Housepainting, Eavestroughing, Aluminum Siding, Phone 535-3484,' lettered on its surface.

'This was in the last letter,' he says. 'That Farrell I guess was a nice enough fellow, from Heartsick Bay he was.

'Anyway they could have no more peace with John than we could without him. Like I says he was here too long before his going and it all took ahold of us the way it will. They sent word that he was coming on the plane to St John's with a woman they'd met through a Newfoundland club. I was to go to St John's to meet him. Well, it was all wrong the night before the going. The signs all bad; the grandmother knocked off the lampshade and it broke in a hunnerd pieces— the sign of death; and the window blind fell and clattered there on the floor and then lied still. And the dog runned around like he was crazy, moanen and cryen worse than the swiles[3] does out on the ice, and throwen hisself against the walls and jumpen on the table and at the window where the blind fell until we would have to be letten him out. But it be no better for he runned and throwed hisself in the sea and then come back and howled outside the same window and jumped against the wall, splashen the water from his coat all over it. Then he be runnen back to the sea again. All the neighbours heard him and said I should bide at home and not go to St John's at all. We be all wonderful scared and not know what to do and the next mornen, first thing I drops me knife.

'But still I feels I has to go. It be foggy all the day and everyone be thinken the plane won't come or be able to land. And I says, small to myself, now here in the fog be the bad luck and the death but then there the plane be, almost like a ghost ship comen out the fog with all its lights shinen. I think maybe he won't be on it but soon he comen through the fog, first with the woman and then see'n me and starten to run, closer and closer till I can feel him in me arms and the tears on both our cheeks. Powerful strange how things will take one. That night they be killed.'

From the envelope that contained the picture he draws forth a tattered clipping:

Jennifer Farrell of Roncesvalles Avenue was instantly killed early this morning and her husband James died later in emergency at St Joseph's Hospital. The accident occurred about 2 A.M. when the pickup truck in which they were travelling went out of control on Queen St W. and struck a utility pole. It is thought that bad visibility caused by a heavy fog may have contributed to the accident. The Farrells were originally from Newfoundland.

Again he moves to refill the glasses. 'We be all alone,' he says. 'All our other daughters married and far away in Montreal, Toronto, or the States. Hard for them to come back here, even to visit; they comes only every three years or so for perhaps a week. So we be hav'n only him.'

And now my head begins to reel even as I move to the filling of my own glass. Not waiting this time for the courtesy of his offer. Making myself perhaps too much at home with this man's glass and this man's rum and this man's house and all the feelings of his love. Even as I did before. Still locked again for words.

Outside we stand and urinate, turning our backs to the seeming gale so as not to splash our wind-snapped trousers. We are almost driven forward to rock upon our toes and settle on our heels, so blow the gusts. Yet in spite of all, the stars shine clearly down. It will indeed be a good day for the fishing and this wind eventually will calm. The salt hangs heavy in the air and the water booms against the rugged rocks. I take a stone and throw it against the wind into the sea.

Going up the stairs we clutch the wooden bannister unsteadily and say goodnight.

The room has changed very little. The window rattles in the wind and the unfinished beams sway and creak. The room is full of sound. Like a foolish Lockwood[4] I approach the window although I hear no voice. There is no Catherine who cries to be let in. Standing unsteadily on one foot when required I man-

---

[3]Seals.

[4]The narrator of *Wuthering Heights*; in a dream, Lockwood turns away the ghost of the heroine, Catherine, as it pleads for entry at the window of her childhood bedroom.

age to undress, draping my trousers across the wooden chair. The bed is clean. It makes no sound. It is plain and wooden, its mattress stuffed with hay or kelp. I feel it with my hand and pull back the heavy patchwork quilts. Still I do not go into it. Instead I go back to the door which has no knob but only an ingenious latch formed from a twisted nail. Turning it, I go out into the hallway. All is dark and the house seems even more inclined to creak where there is no window. Feeling along the wall with my outstretched hand I find the door quite easily. It is closed with the same kind of latch and not difficult to open. But no one waits on the other side. I stand and bend my ear to hear the even sound of my one son's sleeping. He does not beckon any more than the nonexistent voice in the outside wind. I hesitate to touch the latch for fear that I may waken him and disturb his dreams. And if I did what would I say? Yet I would like to see him in his sleep this once and see the room with the quiet bed once more and the wooden chair beside it from off an old wrecked trawler. There is no boiled egg or shaker of salt or glass of water waiting on the chair within this closed room's darkness.

Once though there was a belief held in the outports, that if a girl would see her own true lover she should boil an egg and scoop out half the shell and fill it with salt. Then she should take it to bed with her and eat it, leaving a glass of water by her bedside. In the night her future husband or a vision of him would appear and offer her the glass. But she must only do it once.

It is the type of belief that bright young graduate students were collecting eleven years ago for the theses and archives of North America and also, they hoped, for their own fame. Even as they sought the near-Elizabethan songs and ballads that had sailed from County Kerry and from Devon and Cornwall. All about the wild, wide sea and the flashing silver dagger and the lost and faithless lover. Echoes to and from the lovely, lonely hills and glens of West Virginia and the standing stones of Tennessee.

Across the hall the old people are asleep. The old man's snoring rattles as do the windows; except that now and then there are catching gasps within his breath. In three or four short hours he will be awake and will go down to light his fire. I turn and walk back softly to my room.

Within the bed the warm sweetness of the rum is heavy and intense. The darkness presses down upon me but still it brings no sleep. There are no voices and no shadows that are real. There are only walls of memory touched restlessly by flickers of imagination.

Oh I would like to see my way more clearly. I, who have never understood the mystery of fog. I would perhaps like to capture it in a jar like the beautiful childhood butterflies that always die in spite of the airholes punched with nails in the covers of their captivity—leaving behind the vapours of their lives and deaths; or perhaps as the unknowing child who collects the grey moist condoms from the lovers' lanes only to have them taken from him and to be told to wash his hands. Oh I have collected many things I did not understand.

And perhaps now I should go and say, oh son of my *summa cum laude* loins, come away from the lonely gulls and the silver trout and I will take you to the land of the Tastee Freeze where you may sleep till ten of nine. And I will show you the elevator to the apartment on the sixteenth floor and introduce you to the buzzer system and the yards of the wrought-iron fences where the Doberman pinscher runs silently at night. Or may I offer you the money that is the fruit of my collecting and my most successful life? Or shall I wait to meet you in some known or unknown bitterness like Yeats's Cuchulain[5] by the wind-whipped sea or as Sohrab and Rustum by the future flowing river?

Again I collect dreams. For I do not know enough of the fog on Toronto's Queen St West and the grinding crash of the pickup and of lost and misplaced love.

I am up early in the morning as the man kindles the fire from the driftwood splinters. The outside light is breaking and the wind is calm. John tumbles down the stairs. Scarcely stopping to splash his face and pull on his jacket, he is gone, accompanied by the dog. The old man smokes his pipe and waits for the water to boil. When it does he pours some into the teapot then passes the kettle to me. I take it to the wash-stand and fill the small tin basin in readiness for my shaving. My face looks back from the mirrored cabinet. The woman softly descends the stairs.

'I think I will go back today,' I say while looking into the mirror at my face and at those in the room behind me. I try to emphasize the 'I'. 'I just thought I would like to make this trip—again. I think I can leave the car in St John's and fly back directly.' the woman begins to move about the table, setting out the round white plates. The man quietly tamps his pipe.

The door opens and John and the dog return. They have been down along the shore to see what has happened throughout the night. 'Well, John,' says the old man, 'what did you find?'

He opens his hand to reveal a smooth round stone. It is of the deepest green inlaid with veins of darkest ebony. It has been worn and polished by the unrelenting restlessness of the sea and buffed and burnished by the gravelled sand. All of its inadequacies have been removed and it glows with the lustre of near perfection.

'It is very beautiful,' I say.

'Yes,' he says, 'I like to collect them.' Suddenly he looks up to my eyes and thrusts the stone toward me. 'Here,' he says, 'would you like to have it?'

Even as I reach out my hand I turn my head to the others in the room. They are both looking out through the window to the sea.

'Why, thank you,' I say. 'Thank you very much. Yes, I would. Thank you. Thanks.' I take it from his outstretched hand and place it in my pocket.

We eat our breakfast in near silence. After it is finished the boy and dog go out once more. I prepare to leave.

'Well, I must go,' I say, hesitating at the door. 'It will take me a while to get to

---

[5] A hero from Celtic myth who is driven mad because he has killed his son, Colaoch, in a battle while each was ignorant of the other's identity. In Yeats's poem 'Cuchulain's Fight with the Sea', Cuchulain is doomed eternally to battle the tide as he stands at the ocean's edge. A parallel story of the Persian hero Rustum, who slays his son in ignorance, is told in Matthew Arnold's poem 'Sohrab and Rustum'. In the conclusion of that poem the river Oxus flows on (like the river of Time in Arnold's poem 'The Future'), moving forward in time and space, beyond the point where the story has occurred and where the main characters remain.

St John's.' I offer my hand to the man. He takes it in his strong fingers and shakes it firmly.

'Thank you,' says the woman. 'I don't know if you know what I mean but thank you.'

'I think I do,' I say. I stand and fiddle with the keys. 'I would somehow like to help or keep in touch but . . .'

'But there is no phone,' he says, 'and both of us can hardly write. Perhaps that's why we never told you. John is getting to be a pretty good hand at it though.'

'Good-bye,' we say again, 'good-bye, good-bye.'

The sun is shining clearly now and the small boats are putt-putting about the harbour. I enter my unlocked car and start its engine. The gravel turns beneath the wheels. I pass the house and wave to the man and woman standing in the yard.

On a distant cliff the children are shouting. Their voices carol down through the sun-washed air and the dogs are curving and dancing about them in excited circles. They are carrying something that looks like a crippled gull. Perhaps they will make it well. I toot the horn. 'Good-bye,' they shout and wave, 'good-bye, good-bye.'

The airport terminal is strangely familiar. A symbol of impermanence, it is itself glisteningly permanent. Its formica surfaces have been designed to stay. At the counter a middle-aged man in mock exasperation is explaining to the girl that it is Newark he wishes to go to, *not* New York.

There are not many of us and soon we are ticketed and lifting through and above the sun-shot fog. The meals are served in tinfoil and in plastic. We eat above the clouds looking at the tips of wings.

The man beside me is a heavy-equipment salesman who has been trying to make a sale to the developers of Labrador's resources. He has been away a week and is returning to his wife and children.

Later in the day we land in the middle of the continent. Because of the changing time zones the distance we have come seems eerily unreal. The heat shimmers in little waves upon the runway. This is the equipment salesman's final destination while for me it is but the place where I must change flights to continue even farther into the heartland. Still we go down the wheeled-up stairs together, donning our sunglasses, and stepping across the heated concrete and through the terminal's electronic doors. The salesman's wife stands waiting along with two small children who are the first to see him. They race toward him with their arms outstretched. 'Daddy, Daddy,' they cry, 'what did you bring me? What did you bring me?'

1976

John Newlove

b. 1938

On the move since childhood, John Herbert Newlove grew up in a number of farming communities in his native Saskatchewan before leaving the Prairies in 1960. Since then he has lived in California, British Columbia, Ontario, Quebec, and the Maritimes. In 1979 he returned to Regina, his birthplace, where he remained until 1983 when he moved to Nelson, B.C. A writer of poetry since his late teens, he has supported himself primarily as an editor and writer-in-residence. Since the appearance of his first book, *Grave Sirs* (1962), he has published ten collections, among which are *Moving in Alone* (1965); *Black Night Window* (1968); *The Cave* (1970); *Lies* (1972), winner of a Governor General's Award; and *The Fat Man: Selected Poems 1962-1972* (1977).

Early in his career Newlove developed the distinctive prairie voice—spare, and free of complex imagery and metaphor—later heard in the poetry of other western writers (including Robert Kroetsch and Eli Mandel). This voice is particularly well suited to Newlove's harsh vision of the world. His clipped syntax and austere diction give an ironic tone to his natural lyricism and create a dissonant style that expresses the psychic dissonance resulting from the combination of his wonder at the prairie landscape and the restless malaise that denies him complete union with his environment. In Newlove's work mankind, lacking control over its fate, searches fruitlessly for some pattern to give meaning to life but repeatedly fails to recognize such order as exists. (In 'The Prairie', for example, the individual is doomed to 'never be at ease' as he migrates 'from city to city/seeking some almost seen/god or food or earth or word'.) The dominant tone of Newlove's writing is therefore pessimistic, sometimes even nihilistic. The personal poetry of his early books, in which his youthful *esprit* leavened his natural cynicism, gives way in later works to depictions of a joyless death amid universal alienation. In this work only occasional figures from the past—Riel, Hearne, and the nomadic Indians that peopled the West—achieve a necessary, if harrowing, integration with the landscape. In contrast to these heroic types are the many defeated personae who dwell in a world marred by man's corrupt nature.

Newlove's latest book, *The Green Plain* (1981), marks a change from this view. In the Preface, Newlove writes that, although his alienation has always made him identify with 'Cain the spoiler [who] disrupted a second Arcadia', he can now affirm not just 'the real knowledge of the tiny monster, the ogre, lurking like a shadow in the greenness' but also 'the real knowledge of a veritable paradise' ('An Accidental Life'). In *The Green Plain* Newlove no longer takes on the role of a fallen puritan looking back on an unrealized life with nostalgic regret. Now he finds it possible to perceive directly a universe that, if indifferent, nevertheless offers a profound experience of beauty.

Four Small Scars

This scar beneath my lip
is symbol of a friend's rough love
though some would call it anger,
mistakenly. This scar

crescent on my wrist
is symbol of a woman's delicate anger
though some would call it love,
mistakenly. My belly's scar

is symbol of a surgical precision:
no anger, no love. The small   10
fading mark on my hand

is token of my imprecision,
of my own carving, my anger and my love.

1965

Crazy Riel[1]

Time to write a poem
or something.
Fill up a page.
The creature noise.
Huge massed forces of men
hating each other.
What young men do not know.
To keep quiet,
contemporaneously.
Contempt. The robin diligently   10
on the lawn sucks up worms,
hopping from one to another.
Youthfully. Sixteen miles
from my boyhood home
the frogs sit in the grassy marsh
that looks like a golf course
by the lake. Green frogs.
Boys catch them for bait or sale.
Or caught them. Time.
To fill up a page.   20
To fill up a hole.
To make things feel better. Noise.

[1]As a result of leading the Métis in the Red River Rebellion of 1870, Louis Riel (1844-85) was banished to the U.S. An excitable man who suffered a mental breakdown characterized by irrational behaviour and a belief in himself as divinely inspired, he was later confined to mental institutions in Quebec in 1876-8 (legends persist that Riel feigned his madness, or that the Canadian government trumped it up). Following the North West Rebellion of 1885, he was tried for treason and hanged. During the trial Riel affirmed his sanity and was also pronounced by doctors to be of sound mind.

The noise of the images
that are people I will never understand.
Admire them though I may.
Poundmaker.[2] Big Bear. Wandering Spirit,
those miserable men.
Riel. Crazy Riel. Riel hanged.
Politics must have its way.
The way of noise. To fill up.   30
The definitions bullets make,
and field guns.
The noise your dying makes,
to which you are the only listener.
The noise the frogs hesitate
to make as the metal hook
breaks through the skin
and slides smoothly into place
in the jaw. The noise
the fish makes caught in the jaw,   40
which is only an operation
of the body and the element,
which a stone would make
thrown in the same water, thrashing,
not its voice.
The lake is not displaced
with one less jackfish body.
In the slough that looks like a golf course
the family of frogs sings. Metal throats.
The images of death hang upside-down.   50
Grey music.
It is only the listening for death,
fingering the paraphernalia,
the noise of the men you admire.
And cannot understand.
Knowing little enough about them.
The knowledge waxing.
The wax that paves hell's road,
slippery as the road to heaven.
So that as a man slips   60
he might as easily slide
into being a saint as destroyer.
In his ears the noise magnifies.
He forgets men.

1968

---

[2](1838-86), Cree chief who attacked Battleford and shortly afterwards won a battle at Cut Knife Hill during the North West Rebellion; after the capture of Riel he surrendered, was tried, and sentenced to a three-year prison term, of which he served one year. 'Big Bear': Chief of the Plains Cree (d. 1888) who, having given the Indians leadership before the North West Rebellion, was unable to stop the massacre at Frog Lake and the burning of Fort Pitt; Big Bear surrendered, was tried, and sentenced to two years' imprisonment. 'Wandering Spirit': leader of Big Bear's Cree at the Frog Lake massacre of April 1885 in which several whites were killed.

The Double-Headed Snake

Not to lose the feel of the mountains
while still retaining the prairies
is a difficult thing. What's lovely
is whatever makes the adrenalin run;
therefore I count terror and fear among
the greatest beauty. The greatest
beauty is to be alive, forgetting nothing,
although remembrance hurts
like a foolish act, is a foolish act.

Beauty's whatever   10
makes the adrenalin run. Fear
in the mountains at night-time's
not tenuous, it is not the cold
that makes me shiver, civilized man,
white, I remember
the stories of the Indians,
Sis-i-utl, the double-headed snake.[1]

Beauty's what makes
the adrenalin run. Fear at night
on the level plains, with no horizon   20
and the stars too bright, wind bitter
even in June, in winter
the snow harsh and blowing,
is what makes me
shiver, not the cold air alone.

And one beauty cancels another. The plains
seem secure and comfortable
at Crow's Nest Pass;[2] in Saskatchewan
the mountains are comforting
to think of; among
the eastwardly diminishing hills   30
both the flatland and the ridge
seem easy to endure.

As one beauty
cancels another, remembrance
is a foolish act, a double-headed snake
striking in both directions, but I
remember plains and mountains, places
I come from, places I adhere and live in.

1968

[1]According to Newlove, a figure from west-coast Indian tales; the sight of either end of the snake
turns one to stone.
[2]Pass in the Rocky Mountains between Alberta and British Columbia through which a branch CPR
line was built in 1898.

Samuel Hearne[1] in Wintertime

I

In this cold room
I remember the smell of manure
on men's heavy clothes as good,
the smell of horses.

It is a romantic world
to readers of journeys
to the Northern Ocean—

especially if their houses are heated
to some degree, Samuel.

Hearne, your camp must have smelled   10
like hell whenever you settled down
for a few days of rest and journal-work:

hell smeared with human manure,
hell half-full of raw hides,
hell of sweat, Indians, stale fat,
meat-hell, fear-hell, hell of cold.

2

One child is back from the doctor's while
the other one wanders about in dirty pants
and I think of Samuel Hearne and the land—

puffy children coughing as I think,   20
crying, sick-faced,
vomit stirring in grey blankets
from room to room.

It is Christmastime—
the cold flesh shines.
No praise in merely enduring.

3

Samuel Hearne did more
in the land (like all the rest

full of rocks and hilly country,
many very extensive tracts of land,   30

[1](1745-92), early Canadian explorer and author of a classic travel narrative, *A Journey from Prince of Wales's Fort in Hudson's Bay to the Northern Ocean* (1795), about his explorations in the North (see Volume I, pp. 23-4). The conclusion of Newlove's poem alludes to a famous passage in that book recounting Hearne's accompanying a band of Indians in their massacre of an Eskimo village; in it Hearne describes the death of an eighteen-year-old girl who, when struck by a spear, twisted herself about his legs and—as Hearne pleaded for mercy for her—was dispatched by two more Indians, her body 'twining round their spears like an eel!' (The full account is reprinted in Volume I, pp. 29-32.)

tittimeg, pike and barble,[2]

and the islands:
the islands, many
of them abound

as well as the main
land does
with dwarf woods,

chiefly pine
in some parts intermixed
with larch and birch) than endure.   40

The Indians killed twelve deer.
It was impossible to describe
the intenseness of the cold.

4
And, Samuel Hearne,
I have almost begun to talk

as if you wanted to be
gallant, as if you went
through that land for a book—

as if you were not SAM, wanting
to know, to do a job.   50

5
There was that Eskimo girl
at Bloody Falls, at your feet,

Samuel Hearne, with two spears in her,
you helpless before your helpers,

and she twisted about them like
an eel, dying, never to know.

1968

---

[2]Three types of fish that Hearne found in the north.

Ride Off Any Horizon

Ride off any horizon
and let the measure fall
where it may—

on the hot wheat,
on the dark yellow fields
of wild mustard, the fields

of bad farmers, on the river,
on the dirty river full
of boys and on the throbbing

powerhouse and the low dam   10
of cheap cement and rocks
boiling with white water,

and on the cows and their powerful
bulls, the heavy tracks
filling with liquid at the edge

of the narrow prairie
river running steadily away.

      *

Ride off any horizon
and let the measure fall
where it may—   20

among the piles of bones
that dot the prairie

in vision and history
(the buffalo and deer,

dead indians, dead settlers
the frames of lost houses

left behind in the dust
of the depression,

dry and profound, that
will come again in the land   30

and in the spirit, the land
shifting and the minds

blown dry and empty—
I have not seen it! except

in pictures and talk—
but there is the fence

covered with dust, laden,
the wrecked house stupidly empty)—

here is a picture for your wallet,
of the beaten farmer and his wife   40
leaning toward each other—

sadly smiling, and emptied of desire.

*

Ride off any horizon
and let the measure fall
where it may—

off the edge
of the black prairie

as you thought you could fall,
a boy at sunset

not watching the sun   50
set but watching the black earth,

never-ending they said in school,
round: but you saw it ending,

finished, definite, precise—
visible only miles away.

*

Ride off any horizon
and let the measure fall
where it may—

on a hot night the town
is in the streets—   60

the boys and girls
are practising against

each other, the men
talk and eye the girls—

the women talk and

eye each other, the indians
play pool: eye on the ball.

*

Ride off any horizon
and let the measure fall
where it may—   70

and damn the troops, the horsemen
are wheeling in the sunshine,
the cree, practising

for their deaths: mr poundmaker,[1]
gentle sweet mr bigbear,
it is not unfortunately

quite enough to be innocent,
it is not enough merely
not to offend—

at times to be born   80
is enough, to be
in the way is too much—

some colonel otter[2], some
major-general middleton will
get you, you—

indian. It is no good to say,
I would rather die
at once than be in that place—

though you love that land more,
you will go where they take you.   90

*

Ride off any horizon
and let the measure fall—

where it may;
it doesn't have to be

the prairie. It could be
the cold soul of the cities

---

[1]See p. 429, n. 2.
[2]Sir William Dillon Otter (1843-1929), Canadian colonel in command to the militia that relieved the
settlers under attack at Fort Battleford and who was defeated by Poundmaker at Cut Knife Hill.
'Major-General Middleton': Sir Frederick Dobson Middleton (1825-98), British commander of the
Canadian militia during the suppression of the North West Rebellion.

blown empty by commerce
and desiring commerce
to fill up emptiness.

The streets are full of people. 100

It is night, the lights
are on; the wind

blows as far as it may. The streets
are dark and full of people.

Their eyes are fixed as far as
they can see beyond each other—

to the concrete horizon, definite,
tall against the mountains,
stopping vision visibly.

1968

The Prairie

One compiles, piles, plies
these masses of words, verbs,
massifs, mastiffs barking meaning,
dried chips
of buffalo dung, excreta from beasts

the prairie fed, foddered,
food for generations: men roaming
as beasts seen through dips
in history, fostered by legend,
invented remembrance. Scenes shake, 10

the words do not suffice. One bred
on the same earth wishes himself
something different, the other's
twin, impossible thing, twining
both memories, a double meaning,

but cannot be—never
to be at ease, but always migrating
from city to city
seeking some almost seen
god or food or earth or word. 20

1970

The Green Plain

Small human figures and fanciful monsters
abound. Dreams surround us,
preserve us. We praise constancy as brave,
but variation's lovelier.

Rain surrounds us, arguments and dreams, there are
forests between us, there are
too many of us for comfort, always were.

                                                 Is civilization
only lack of room, only
an ant-heap at last?—the strutting cities   10
of the East, battered gold,
the crammed walls of India,
humanity swarming, indistinguishable
                           from the earth?

Even the nomads roaming the green plain, for them
at last no land was ever enough.

Spreading—but now we can go anywhere
                          and we are afraid
and talk of small farms instead of the stars
                                and all the places we go   20
space is distorted.

How shall we save the symmetry of the universe?—
or our own symmetry, which is the same.

                                        Which myths
should capture us, since we do not wish
to be opened, to be complete?—
or are they the same, all of them?

Now a dream involves me, of a giant sprawled among stars,
face to the dark, his eyes closed.

         Common.   30

Only he is not breathing, he does not heave.
Is it Gulliver?—huge, image of us, tied, webbed in,
and never learning anything,

            always ignorant,
always amazed, always capable of delight,
and giving it, though ending in hatred, but
an image only. Of disaster. But there is no disaster.
It is just that we lose joy and die.

But is there a symmetry?
          Is there reason   40
in the galaxies—Or is this all glass,
a block bubbled in a fire, accident only,
prettiness fused without care, pettiness,
though some logic, alien but understandable,
in the ruined crystal?

      The forests, the forests, swaying,
there is no reason why they should be beautiful.
They live for their own reasons, not ours.
But they are.

It is not time that flows but the world.   50

And the world flows,
still flows. Even in these worn-out days,
worn-out terms,
once in a while our poets
must
speak

of Spring! Of all things! The flowers

blow in their faces too, and they smell perfumes,
and they are seduced
by colour—rural as the hairy crocus or urban as a waxy   60
    tulip.

                             But confusion. The world
flows past. It is hard to remember age. Does
this always world flow? Does it? Please say it does,
not time.
              Do not say time flows.
Say: We do. Say: We live.

Fly-speck, fly-speck. In this ever island Earth
we are the tiny giants, swaggering
behind the dinosaurs, lovely,   70
tame brontosaurus, sweet cows lumbering
among the coal trees, fronds offering
shade and future fuel.

And the land around us green and happy,
waiting as you wait for a killer to spring,
a full-sized blur,
waiting like a tree in southern Saskatchewan,
remarked on, lonely and famous as a saint.

The mechanisms by which the stars generate invention
live all over and around us   80
and yet we refine machines, defer
to tricks as discovery. Everything is always here,
and burning.

There are no surprises, there is only
what is left. We live
inside the stars,

                            burning, burning,
the mechanisms.

Stars, rain, forests.
Stars rain forests.   90
Sew up the lives together. There is
this only world. Thank God: this World
and its wrapped variations
spreading around and happy, flowing,
flowing through the climate of intelligence,
beautiful confusion looking around,
seeing the mechanics and the clouds
and marvelling, O Memory . . .
1981

Jack Hodgins

b. 1938

Jack Hodgins published his first collection of short stories, *Spit Delaney's Island* in 1976. Since then he has produced two novels, *The Invention of the World* (1977) and *The Resurrection of Joseph Bourne* (1979), which won a Governor General's Award, as well as a second collection of short fiction, *The Barclay Family Theatre* (1981). Most of Hodgins' narratives centre on the community life of northern Vancouver Island, where he was born and has spent much of his adult life. Raised in the small farming and logging town of Merville, B.C.—in which, according to Hodgins, everyone was either a relative or a friend—he attended the University of British Columbia, receiving a B.Ed. in 1961. He then took a job teaching high-school English in Nanaimo, where he remained until 1979. Since that time he has been writer-in-residence and visiting professor at the University of Ottawa, while retaining a home near Lantzville on Vancouver Island.

Hodgins' form of storytelling combines the exaggeration of the tall tale with the anecdotal quality of a back-country yarn. His fiction is almost always humorous and tends to point to parallels—often more grotesque than heroic—between ordinary life and a world of myth. His novels are flamboyant epics with a sense of the marvellous that recalls the fiction of such Latin American writers as Jorge-Luis Borges and Gabriel García Márquez. The fantasy that characterizes much of Hodgins' writing seems to arise naturally from the innocently corrupt island communities that are his settings. Unlike the planned settlements of the mainland, these Edens gone to seed have evolved haphazardly—founded by a madman in *The Invention of the World* and restored by a dead man in *The Resurrection of Joseph Bourne*—and in their ingrown state, normality and eccentricity exist in comfortable symbiosis. In such a world Hodgins does not need to create new mythologies; rather he selects from those abundantly available to him.

While Hodgins' extravagant vision is characteristically western, it differs from that of many western novelists because it develops from a Vancouver Island environment that—in contrast to the empty Prairie landscapes of Sinclair Ross, W.O. Mitchell, and even Robert Kroetsch—seems plentiful and even idyllic. This island way of life shapes the characters in *The Barclay Family Theatre*, Hodgins' collection of tales about the Barclay sisters (who first appeared in *Spit Delaney's Island*) and their relatives. Even when abroad—as Philip Desmond is in 'The Leper's Squint'—they carry their island point of view with them and, perceiving the absurdity of the world, remain islanded from it.

The Lepers' Squint

Today, while Mary Brennan may be waiting for him on that tiny island high in the mountain lake called Gougane Barra,[1] Philip Desmond is holed up in the back room of this house at Bantry Bay, trying to write his novel. A perfect stack of white paper, three black nylon-tipped pens, and a battered portable typewriter are set out before him on the wooden table. He knows the first paragraph already, has already set it down, and trusts that the rest of the story will run off the end of it like a fishing line pulled by a salmon. But it is cold, it is so cold in this house, even now in August, that he presses both hands down between his thighs to warm them up. It is so cold in this room that he finds it almost impossible to sit still, so damp that he has put on the same clothes he would wear if he were walking out along the edge of that lagoon, in the spitting rain and the wind. Through the small water-specked panes of the window he can see his children playing on the lumpy slabs of rock at the shore, beyond the bobbing branches of the fuchsia hedge. Three children; three red quilted jackets; three faces flushed up by the steady force of the cold wind; they drag tangled clots of stinking seaweed up the slope and, crouching, watch a family of swans explore the edges of a small weedy island not far out in the lagoon.

A high clear voice in his head all the while insists on singing to him of some girl so fair that the ferns uncurl to look at her. The voice of an old man in a mountain pub, singing without accompaniment, stretched and stiff as a rooster singing to the ceiling and to the crowd at the bar and to the neighbours who sit around him. *The ferns uncurled to look at her, so very fair was she, with her hair as bright as the seaweed that floats in from the sea.* But here at Ballylickey the seaweed is brown as mud and smells so strong your eyes water.

Mrs O'Sullivan is in the next room, Desmond knows, in her own room, listening. If he coughs she will hear. If he sings. She will know exactly the moment he sets down his next word on that top sheet of paper. Mrs O'Sullivan is the owner of this house, which Desmond rented from home through the Borde Failte[2] people before he discovered that she would live in it with them, in the centre of the house, in her two rooms, and silently listen to the life of his family going on around her. She is a tall dry-skinned old woman with grey finger-waves caged in blue hair net, whose thick fingers dig into the sides of her face in an agony of desire to sympathize with everything that is said to her. 'Oh I know I know I know,' she groans. Last night when Desmond's wife mentioned how tired she was after the long drive down from Dublin, her fingers plucked at her face, her dull eyes rolled up to search for help along the ceiling: 'Oh I know I know I know.' There is no end to her sympathy, there is nothing she doesn't already know. But she will be quiet as a mouse, she promised, they won't know she is here.

'Maybe she's a writer,' Desmond's wife whispered to him, later in bed. 'Maybe she's making notes on us. Maybe she's writing a book called *North Americans I Have Eaves-dropped On.*'

'I can't live with someone listening to me breathe,' Desmond said. 'And I

---

[1] In a park just north of Bantry Bay, Ireland, on the road to Killarney.   [2] Tourist board (Irish).

can't write with someone sitting waiting.'

'Adjust,' his wife said, and flicked at his nose. She who could adjust to anything, or absorb it.

On this first day of his novel Desmond has been abandoned by his wife, Carrie, who early this morning drove the car in to Cork. There are still, apparently, a few Seamus Murphy[3] statues she hasn't seen, or touched. 'Keep half an eye on the kids,' she said before she left. Then she came back and kissed him and whispered, 'Though if you get busy it won't matter. I'm sure Mrs O'Sullivan won't miss anything.' To be fair, to be really fair, he knows that his annoyance is unjustified. He didn't tell her he intended to work today, the first day in this house. She probably thinks that after travelling for six weeks through the country he'll rest a few more days before beginning; she may even believe that he is glad to be rid of her for the day, after all those weeks of unavoidable closeness. She certainly knows that with Mrs O'Sullivan in the house no emergency will be overlooked, no crisis ignored.

Desmond, now that his hands have warmed a little, lifts one of the pens to write, though silently as possible, as if what he is about to do is a secret perversion from which the ears of Mrs O'Sullivan must be protected. But he cannot, now, put down any new words. Because if the novel, which has been roaring around in his head all summer and much longer, looking for a chance to get out, should not recognize in the opening words the crack through which it is to spring forth, transformed into a string of words like a whirring fish line, then he will be left with all that paper to stare at, and an unmoving pen, and he is not ready to face that. Of course he knows the story, has seen it all in his mind a hundred times as if someone else had gone to the trouble of writing it and producing it as a movie just for him. But he has never been one for plunging into things, oceans or stories, and prefers to work his way in gently. That opening paragraph, though, is only a paragraph after all and has no magic, only a few black lifeless lines at the top of the paper. So he writes his title again, and under it his name: Barclay Philip Desmond. Then he writes the opening paragraph a second time, and again under that, and again, hoping that the pen will go on by itself to write the next words and surprise him. But it does not happen, not now. Instead, he discovers he is seeing two other words which are not there at all, as if perhaps they are embedded, somehow, just beneath the surface of the paper.

Mary Brennan.

Desmond knows he must keep the name from becoming anything more than that, from becoming a face too, or the pale scent of fear. He writes his paragraph again, over and over until he has filled up three or four pages. Then, crumpling the papers in his hand, he wonders if this will be one of those stories that remain forever in their authors' heads, driving them mad, refusing to suffer conversion into words.

It's the cold, he thinks. Blame it on the bloody weather. His children outside on the rocky slope have pulled the hoods of their jackets up over their heads. Leaves torn from the beech tree lie soaked and heavy on the grass. At the far side of the lagoon the family of swans is following the choppy retreating tide out through the gap to the open bay; perhaps they know of a calmer inlet somewhere.

[3](1907-75), a sculptor from Cork.

The white stone house with red window frames in its nest of bushes across the water has blurred behind the rain, and looks more than ever like the romantic pictures he has seen on postcards. A thin line of smoke rises from the yellowish house and the gate sign *Carrigdhoun*.[4]

But it is easier than writing, far easier, to allow the persistent daydreams in, and memory. That old rooster-stiff man, standing in the cleared-away centre of the bar in Ballyvourney to pump his song out to the ceiling, his hands clasping and unclasping at his sides as if they are responsible for squeezing those words into life. The ferns uncurled to see her, he sings, so very fair was she. Neighbours clap rhythm, or stamp their feet. Men six-deep at the bar-counter continue to shout at each other about sheep, and the weather. With hair as bright as the seaweed that floats in from the sea.

''Tis an island of singers sure!' someone yells in Desmond's ear. 'An island of saints and paupers and bloody singers!'

But Desmond thinks of Mary Brennan's hot apple-smelling breath against his face: 'Islands do not exist until you have loved on them.' The words are a Caribbean poet's,[5] she explains, and not her own. But the sentiment is adaptable. The ferns may not uncurl to see the dark brown beauty of her eyes, but Desmond has seen men turn at her flash of hair the reddish-brown of gleaming kelp. Turn, and smile to themselves. This day while he sits behind the wooden table, hunched over his pile of paper, he knows that she is waiting for him on a tiny hermitage island in a mountain lake not far away, beneath the branches of the crowded trees. Islands, she had told him, do not exist until you've loved on them.

Yesterday, driving south from Dublin across the Tipperary farmland, they stopped again at the Rock of Cashel so that Carrie could prowl a second time through that big roofless cathedral high up on the sudden limestone knoll and run her hands over the strange broken form of St Patrick's Cross. The kings of Munster lived there once, she told him, and later turned it over to the church. St Patrick himself came to baptize the king there, and accidentally pierced the poor man's foot with the point of his heavy staff.

'There's all of history here, huddled together,' she said, and catalogued it for him. 'A tenth-century round tower, a twelfth-century chapel, a thirteenth-century cathedral, a fourteenth-century tower, a fifteenth-century castle, and . . .' she rolled her eyes, 'a twentieth-century tourist shop.'

But it was the cross itself that drew her. Originally a cross within a frame, it was only the central figure of a man now, with one arm of the cross and a thin upright stem that held that arm in place. Rather like a tall narrow pitcher. There was a guide this second time, and a tour, and she pouted when he insisted they stick to the crowd and hear the official truths instead of making guesses or relying on the brief explanations on the backs of postcards. She threw him a black scowl when the guide explained the superstition about the cross: that if you can touch hand to hand around it you'll never have another toothache as long as you live. Ridiculous, she muttered; she'd spent an hour the last time looking at that

[4]Brown rock (Irish). (This is also the name of the Irish village in *The Invention of the World*.)
[5]Derek Walcott; from the poem 'Islands' in *In a Green Night* (1962); the original lines are: 'But islands can only exist / If we have loved in them'.

thing, marvelling at the beautiful piece of scuplture nature or time or perhaps vandals had accidentally made of it, running her hands over the figures on the coronation stone at its base and up the narrow stem that supported the remaining arm of the cross.

He was more curious, though, about the round swell of land which could be seen out across the flat Tipperary farms, a perfect green hill crowned with a circle of leafy trees. The guide told him that after one of the crusades a number of people returned to Ireland with a skin disease which was mistaken for leprosy and were confined to that hill, inside that circle, and forbidden to leave it. They were brought across to Mass here on Sundays, she said, before leading him back inside the cathedral to show a small gap in the stones far up one grey wall of the empty Choir. 'The poor lepers, a miserable lot altogether as you can imagine, were crowded into a little room behind that wall,' she said, 'and were forced to see and hear through that single narrow slit of a window. It's called the Lepers' Squint, for obvious reasons.'

Afterwards, when the crowd of nuns and priests and yellow-slickered tourists had broken up to walk amongst the graves and the Celtic crosses or to climb the stone steps to the round tower, Desmond would like to have spoken to one of the priests, perhaps the short red-faced one, to say, 'What do you make of all this?' or 'Is it true what she told us about that fat archbishop with all his wives and children?' But he was intimidated by the black suit, that collar, and by the way the priest seemed always to be surrounded by nuns who giggled like schoolgirls at the silly jokes he told, full of words Desmond couldn't understand. He would go home without ever speaking to a single member of the one aristocracy this country still permitted itself.

But while he stood tempted in the sharp wind that howled across the high hump of rock the guide came over the grass to him. ''Tis certain that you're not American as I thought at first,' she said, 'for you speak too soft for that. Would you be from England then?'

'No,' he said. And without thinking: 'We're from Vancouver Island.'

'Yes?' she said, her eyes blank. 'And where would that be now?'

'A long way from here,' he said. 'An island, too, like this one, with its own brand of ruins.

'There's a tiny island off our coast,' he said, 'where they used to send the lepers once, but the last of them died a few years ago. It's a bare and empty place they say now, except for the wind. There are even people who believe that ghosts inhabit it.'

But then there were people, too, who said he was crazy to take the children to this uneasy country. It's smaller than you think, they said. You'll hear the bombs from above the border when you get there. What if war breaks out? What if the IRA decides that foreign hostages might help their cause? What about that bomb in the Dublin department store?

Choose another country, they said. A warmer safer one. Choose an island where you can lie in the sun and be waited on by smiling blacks. Why pick Ireland?

Jealousy, he'd told them. Everyone else he knew seemed to have inherited an 'old country', an accent, a religion, a set of customs, from parents. His family fled the potato famine in 1849 and had had five generations in which to fade out into Canadians. 'I don't know what I've inherited from them,' he said, 'but whatever it is has gone too deep to be visible.'

They'd spent the summer travelling; he would spend the fall and winter writing.

His search for family roots, however, had ended down a narrow hedged-in lane: a half-tumbled stone cabin, stony fields, a view of misty hills, and distant neighbours who turned their damp hay with a two-tined fork and knew nothing at all of the cabin's past.

'Fled the famine did they?' the old woman said. ''Twas many a man did that and was never heard from since.'

The summer was intended as a literary pilgrimage too, and much of it was a disappointment. Yeats's castle tower near Coole had been turned into a tourist trap as artificial as a wax museum, with cassette recorders to listen to as you walk through from room to room, and a souvenir shop to sell you books and postcards; Oliver Goldsmith's village was not only deserted, it had disappeared, the site of the little schoolhouse nothing more than a potato patch and the parsonage just half a vine-covered wall; the James Joyce museum only made him feel guilty that he'd never been able to finish *Ulysses*, though there'd been a little excitement that day when a group of women's libbers crashed the male nude-bathing beach just behind the tower.

A man in Dublin told him there weren't any live writers in this country. 'You'll find more of our novelists and poets in America than you'll find here,' he said. 'You're wasting your time on that.'

With a sense almost of relief, as though delivered from a responsibility (dead writers, though disappointing, do not confront you with flesh, as living writers could, or with demands), he took the news along with a handful of hot dogs to Carrie and the kids, who had got out of the car to admire a statue. Watching her eat that onion and pork sausage 'hot dog' he realized that she had become invisible to him, or nearly invisible. He hadn't even noticed until now that she'd changed her hair, that she was pinning it back; probably because of the wind. In the weeks of travel, in constant too-close confinement, she had all but disappeared, had faded out of his notice the way his own limbs must have done, oh, thirty years ago.

If someone had asked, 'What does your wife look like?' he would have forgotten to mention short. He might have said dainty but that was no longer entirely true; sitting like that she appeared to have rounded out, like a copper Oriental idol: dark and squat and yet fine, perhaps elegant. He could not have forgotten her loud, almost masculine laugh of course, but he had long ago ceased to notice the quality of her speaking voice. Carrie, his Carrie, was busy having her own separate holiday, almost untouched by his, though they wore each other like old comfortable unnoticed and unchanged clothes.

'A movie would be nice,' he said. 'If we could find a babysitter.'

But she shook her head. 'We can see movies at home. And besides, by the evenings I'm tired out from all we've done, I'd never be able to keep my eyes open.'

After Cashel, on their way to the Bantry house, they stopped a while in the city of Cork. And here, he discovered, here after all the disappointments, was a dead literary hero[6] the tourist board hadn't yet got ahold of. He forgot again that she even existed as he tracked down the settings of the stories he loved: butcher shops and smelly quays and dark crowded pubs and parks.

The first house, the little house where the famous writer was born, had been torn down by a sports club which had put a high steel fence around the property, but a neighbour took him across the road and through a building to the back balcony to show him the Good Shepherd Convent where the writer's mother had grown up, and where she returned often with the little boy to visit the nuns. 'If he were still alive,' Desmond said, 'if he still lived here, I suppose I would be scared to come, I'd be afraid to speak to him.' The little man, the neighbour, took off his glasses to shine them on a white handkerchief. 'Ah, he was a shy man himself. He was back here a few years before he died, with a big crew of American fillum people, and he was a friendly man, friendly enough. But you could see he was a shy man too, yes. 'Tis the shy ones sometimes that take to the book writing.'

Carie wasn't interested in find the second house. She had never read the man's books, she never read anything at all except art histories and museum catalogues. She said she would go to the park, where there were statues, if he'd let her off there. She said if the kids didn't get out of the car soon to run off some of their energy they would drive her crazy, or kill each other. You could hardly expect children to be interested in old dead writers they'd never heard of, she said. It was no fun for them.

He knew as well as she did that if they were not soon released from the backseat prison they would do each other damage. 'I'll go alone,' he said.

'But don't be long. We've got a good ways to do yet if we're going to make it to that house today.'

So he went in search of the second house, the house the writer had lived in for most of his childhood and youth and had mentioned in dozens of his stories. He found it high up the sloping streets on the north side of the river. Two rows of identical homes, cement-grey, faced each other across a bare sloping square of dirt, each row like a set of steps down the slope, each home just a gate in a cement waist-high wall, a door, a window. Somewhere in this square was where the barefoot grandmother had lived, and where the lady lived whose daughter refused to sleep lying down because people died that way, and where the toothless woman lived who between her sessions in the insane asylum loved animals and people with a saintly passion.

The house he was after was half-way up the left hand slope and barely distinguishable from the others, except that there was a woman in the tiny front yard, opening the gate to come out.

'There's no home,' she said when she saw his intentions. 'They weren't expecting me this time, and presumably, they weren't expecting you either.'

'Then it *is* the right house?' Desmond said. Stupidly, he thought. Right house for what?

[6]Frank O'Connor (1903-66), pseudonym of Michael O'Donovan; born in Cork, O'Connor was involved with the Irish revolution and later became director of the Abbey Theatre; he emigrated and lived the rest of his life in America, where he became famous as a writer of short stories with Irish settings.

But she seemed to understand. 'Oh yes. It's the right house. Some day the city will get around to putting a plaque on the wall but for the time being I prefer it the way it is. My name, by the way,' she added, 'is Mary Brennan. I don't live here but I stop by often enough. The old man, you see, was one of my teachers years ago.'

She might have been an official guide, she said it all so smoothly. Almost whispering. And there was barely a trace of the musical tipped-up accent of the southern counties in her voice. Perhaps Dublin, or educated. Her name meant nothing to him at first, coming like that without warning. 'There would be little point in your going inside anyway, even if they were home,' she said. 'There's a lovely young couple living there now but they've redone the whole thing over into a perfectly charming but very modern apartment. There's nothing at all to remind you of him. I stop by for reasons I don't begin to understand, respect perhaps, or inspiration, but certainly not to find anything of him here.'

In a careless, uneven way, she was pretty. Even beautiful. She wore clothes— a yellow skirt, a sweater—as if they'd been pulled on as she'd hurried out the door. Her coat was draped over her arm, for the momentary blessing of sun. But she was tall enough to get away with the sloppiness and had brown eyes which were calm, calming. And hands that tended to behave as if they were helping deliver her words to him, stirring up the pale scent of her perfume. He would guess she was thirty, she was a little younger than he was.

'Desmond,' he said. 'Uh, Philip Desmond.'

She squinted at him, as if she had her doubts. Then she nodded, consenting. 'You're an American,' she said. 'And probably a writer. But I must warn you. I've been to your part of the world and you just can't do for it what he did for this. It isn't the same. You don't have the history, the sense that everything that happens is happening on top of layers of things which have already happened. Now I saw you drive up in a motor car and I arrived on a bus so if you're going back down to the city centre I'll thank you for a ride.'

Mary Brennan, of course. Why hadn't he known? There were two of her books in the trunk of his car. Paperbacks. Desmond felt his throat closing. Before he'd known who she was she hadn't let him say a word, and now that she seemed to be waiting to hear what he had to offer, he was speechless. His mind was a blank. All he could think of was *Mary Brennan* and wish that she'd turned out to be only a colourful eccentric old lady, something he could handle. He was comfortable with young women only until they turned out to be better than he was at something important to him. Then his throat closed. His mind pulled down the shades and hid.

All Desmond could think to say, driving down the hill towards the River Lee, was: 'A man in Dublin told me there was no literature happening in this country.' He could have bitten off his tongue. This woman *was* what was happening. A country that had someone like her needed no one else.

She would not accept that, she said, not even from a man in Dublin. And she insisted that he drive her out to the limestone castle restaurant at the mouth of the river so she could buy him a drink there and convince him Dublin was wrong. Inside the castle, though, while they watched the white ferry to Swansea slide out past their window, she discovered she would rather talk about her divorce, a messy thing which had been a strain on everyone concerned and had convinced her if she needed convincing that marriage was an absurd arrangement. She touched Desmond, twice, with one hand, for emphasis.

Oh, she was a charming woman, there was no question. She could be famous for those eyes alone, which never missed a detail in that room (a setting she would use, perhaps, in her next novel of Irish infidelity and rebellion?) and at the same time somehow returned to him often enough and long enough to keep him frozen, afraid to sneak his own glances at the items she was cataloguing for herself. 'Some day,' she said, 'they will have converted all our history into restaurants and bars like this one, just as I will have converted it all to fiction. Then what will we have?'

And when, finally, he said he must go, he really must go, the park was pretty but didn't have all that much in it for kids to do, she said, 'Listen, if you want to find out what is happening here, if you really do love that old man's work, then join us tomorrow. There'll be more than a dozen of us, some of the most exciting talent in the country, all meeting up at Gougane Barra . . . you know the place, the lake in the mountains where this river rises . . . it was a spot he loved.'

'Tomorrow,' he said. 'We'll have moved in by then, to the house we've rented for the winter.'

'There's a park there now,' she said. 'And of course the tiny hermitage island. It will begin as a picnic but who knows how it will end.' The hand, a white hand with unpainted nails, touched him again.

'Yes,' he said. 'Yes. We've been there. There's a tiny church on the island, he wrote a story[7] about it, the burial of a priest. And it's only an hour or so from the house, I'd guess. Maybe. Maybe I will.'

'Oh you must,'she said, and leaned forward. 'You knew, of course, that they call it Deep-Valleyed Desmond[8] in the songs.' She drew back, biting on a smile.

But when he'd driven her back to the downtown area, to wide St Patrick's Street, she discovered she was not quite ready yet to let him go. 'Walk with me,' she said, 'for just a while,' and found him a parking spot in front of the Munster Arcade where dummies dressed as monks and Vikings and Celtic warriors glowered at him from behind the glass.

'This place exists,' she said, 'because he made it real for me. He and others, in their stories. I could never write about a place where I was the first, it would panic me. I couldn't be sure it really existed or if I were inventing it.'

She led him down past the statue of sober Father Matthew[9] and the parked double-decker buses to the bridge across the Lee. A wind, coming down the river, brought a smell like an open sewer with it. He put his head down and tried to hurry across.

'If I were a North American, like you,' she said, 'I'd have to move away or become a shop girl. I couldn't write.'

He was tempted to say something about plastering over someone else's old

[7]'The Moss Island' in *A Set of Variations* (1969).
[8]'Desmond' is the ancient name for the south of Munster province, in which Cork and Gougane Barra are located.
[9](1790-1838), a famous leader of the Irish Temperance movement.

buildings, but thought better of it. He hadn't even read her books yet, he knew them only by reputation, he had no right to comment. He stopped, instead, to lean over the stone wall and look at the river. It was like sticking his head into a septic tank. The water was dark, nearly black, and low. Along the edges rats moved over humps of dark shiny muck and half-buried cans and bottles. Holes in the stone wall dumped a steady stream of new sewage into the river. The stories, as far as he could remember, had never mentioned this. These quays were romantic places where young people met and teased each other, or church goers gathered to gossip after Mass, or old people strolled. None of them, apparently, had noses.

Wind in the row of trees. Leaves rustling. Desmond looked at her hands. The perfect slim white fingers lay motionless along her skirt, then moved suddenly up to her throat, to touch the neck of her sweater. Then the nearer one moved again, and touched his arm. Those eyes, busy recording the street, paused to look at him; she smiled. Cataloguing me too? he thought. Recording me for future reference? But she didn't know a thing about him.

'I've moved here to work on a book,' he said.

Her gaze rested for a moment on the front of his jacket, then flickered away. 'Not about *here*,' she said. 'You're not writing about *this* place?' She looked as if she would protect it from him, if necessary, or whisk it away.

'I have my own place,' he said. 'I don't need to borrow his.'

She stopped, to buy them each an apple from an old black-shawled woman who sat up against the wall by her table of fruit. Ancient, gypsy-faced, with huge earrings hanging from those heavy lobes. Black Spanish eyes. Mary Brennan flashed a smile, counted out some silver pieces, and picked over the apples for two that were red and clear. The hands that offered change were thick and wrinkled, with crescents of black beneath the nails. They disappeared again beneath the shawl. Desmond felt a momentary twinge about biting into the apple; vague memories of parental warnings. You never know whose hands have touched it, they said, in a voice to make you shudder in horror at the possibilities and scrub at the skin of fruit until it was bruised and raw.

Mary Brennan, apparently, had not been subjected to the same warnings. She bit hugely. 'Here,' she said, at the bridge, 'here is where I'm most aware of him. All his favourite streets converge here, from up the hill. Sunday's Well, over there where his wealthy people lived. And of course Blarney Lane. If you had the time we could walk up there, I could show you. Where his first house was, and the pub he dragged his father home from.'

'I've seen it,' Desmond said, and started across the bridge. She would spoil it all for him if he let her.

But she won him again on the way back down the other side with her talk of castles and churches. Did he know, she asked, the reason there was no roof on the cathedral at Cashel? Did he know why Blackrock Castle where they'd been a half hour before was a different style altogether than most of the castles of Ireland? Did he know the origin of the word 'blarney'?

No he did not, but he knew that his wife would be furious if he didn't hurry back to the park. They passed the noise of voices haggling over second-hand clothes and old books at the Coal Market, they passed the opera house, a tiny yellow book store. She could walk, he saw, the way so many women had forgotten how to walk after high-heeled shoes went out, with long legs and long strides, with some spring in her steps as if there were pleasure in it.

'Now you'll not forget,' she said at his car, in his window. 'Tomorrow, in Deep-Valleyed Desmond where the Lee rises.' There was the scent of apple on her breath. Islands, she leaned in to say, do not exist until you've loved on them.

But today, while Mary Brennan waits on that tiny island for him, Philip Desmond is holed up in the back room of this house at Bantry Bay, trying to write his novel. His wife has taken the car to Cork. When she returns, he doesn't know what he will do. Perhaps he'll get into the car and drive up the snaking road past the crumbling O'Sullivan castle into the mountains, and throw himself into the middle of that crowd of writers as if he belongs there. Maybe he will make them think that he is important, that back home he is noticed in the way Mary Brennan is noticed here, that his work matters. And perhaps late at night, when everyone is drunk, he will lead Mary Brennan out onto the hermitage island to visit the oratory, to speak in whispers of the stories which had happened there, and to lie on the grass beneath the trees, by the quiet edge of the lake. It is not, Desmond knows, too unthinkable. At a distance.

The piece of paper in front of him is still blank. Mrs O'Sullivan will advertise the laziness of writers, who only pretend they are working when they are actually dreaming. Or sleeping. She will likely be able to tell exactly how many words he has written, though if he at the end of this day complains of how tired he is, she will undoubtedly go into her practised agony. He wonders if she too, from her window, has noticed that the tide had gone out, that the lagoon is empty of everything except brown shiny mud and seaweed, and that the nostril-burning smell of it is penetrating even to the inside of the house, even in here where the window hasn't been opened, likely, in years. He wonders, too, if she minds that the children, who have tired of their sea-edge exploring, are building a castle of pebbles and fuchsia branches in the middle of her back lawn. The youngest, Michael, dances like an Indian around it; maybe he has to go to the bathroom and can't remember where it is. While his father, who could tell him, who could take him there, sits and stares at a piece of paper.

For a moment Desmond wonders how the medieval masses in the cathedral at Cashel must have appeared to the lepers crowded behind that narrow hole. Of course he has never seen a Mass of any kind himself, but still he can imagine the glimpses of fine robes, the bright colours, the voices of a choir singing those high eerie Latin songs, the voice of a chanting priest, the faces of a few worshippers. It was a lean world from behind that stone wall, through that narrow hole. Like looking through the eye of a needle. The Mass, as close as they were permitted to get to the world, would be only timidly glimpsed past other pressed straining heads. For of course Desmond imagines himself far at the back of the crowd.

('Yes?' the guide said. 'And where would that be now?'

'A long way from here,' he said. 'An island, too, like this one, with its own brand of ruins. You've never heard of it though it's nearly the size of Ireland?'

'I have, yes. And it's a long way you've come from home.'

'There's a tiny island just off our coast where they used to send the lepers, but the last of them died there a few years ago. It's a bare and empty place they say now, except for the wind. There are even people who believe that ghosts inhabit it.')

What does the world look like to a leper, squinting through that narrow hole? What does it feel like to be confined to the interior of a circle of trees, at the top of a hill, from which everything else can be seen but not approached? Desmond likes to think that he would prefer the life of that famous fat archbishop, celebrating Mass in the cathedral and thinking of his hundred children.

Somewhere in the house a telephone rings. Desmond hasn't been here long enough to notice where the telephone is, whether it is in her part of the house or theirs. But he hears, beyond the wall, the sudden rustling of clothes, the snap of bones, the sound of feet walking across the carpet. Why should Mrs O'Sullivan have a phone? There are so few telephones in this country that they are all listed in the one book. But her footsteps return, and he hears behind him the turning of his door handle, the squeal of a hinge. Then her voice whispering: 'Mr Desmond? Is it a bad time to interrupt?'

'Is it my wife?'

No it is not. And of course Desmond knows who it is. Before he left the castle-restaurant she asked for his address, for Mrs O'Sullivan's name, for the name of this village.

'I'm sorry, Mrs O'Sullivan,' he said. 'Tell her, tell them I'm working, they'll understand. Tell them I don't want to be disturbed, not just now anyway.'

He doesn't turn to see how high her eyebrows lift. He can imagine. Working, she's thinking. If that's working. But when she has closed the door something in him relaxes a little—or at least suspends its tension for a while—and he writes the paragraph again at the top of the page and then adds new words after it until he discovers he has completed a second. It is not very good; he decides when he reads it over that it is not very good at all, but at least it is something. A beginning. Perhaps the dam has been broken.

But there is a commotion, suddenly, in the front yard. A car horn beeping. The children run up the slope past the house. He can hear Carrie's voice calling them. There is a flurry of excited voices and then one of the children is at the door, calling, 'Daddy, Daddy, come and see what Mommy has!'

What Mommy has, he discovers soon enough, is something that seems to be taking up the whole back seat, a grey lumpy bulk. And she, standing at the open door, is beaming at him. 'Come help me get this thing out!' she says. There is colour in her face, excitement. She has made another one of her finds.

It is, naturally, a piece of sculpture. There is no way Desmond can tell what it is supposed to be and he has given up trying to understand such things long ago. He pulls the figure out, staggers across to the front door, and puts it down in the hall.

'I met the artist who did it,' she says. 'He was in the little shop delivering something. We talked, it seemed, for hours. This is inspired by the St Patrick's Cross, he told me, but he abstracted it even more to represent the way art has taken the place of religion in the modern world.'

'Whatever it represents,' Desmond says, 'we'll never get it home.'

Nothing, to Carrie, is a problem. 'We'll enjoy it here, in this house. Then before we leave we'll crate it up and ship it home.' She walks around the sculpture, delighted with it, delighted with herself.

'I could have talked to him for hours,' she says, 'we got along beautifully. But I remembered you asked me to have the car home early.' She kisses him, pushes a finger on his nose. 'See how obedient I am?'

'I said that?'

'Yes,' she says. 'Right after breakfast. Some other place you said you wanted to go prowling around in by yourself. I rushed home down all that long winding bloody road for you. On the wrong side, I'll never get used to it. Watching for radar traps, for heaven's sake. Do you think the gardai[1] have radar traps here?'

But Desmond is watching Mrs O'Sullivan, who has come out into the hall to stare at the piece of scuplture. Why does he have this urge to show her his two paragraphs? Desmond doesn't even show Carrie anything until it is finished. Why, he wonders, should he feel just because she sits there listening through the wall that she's also waiting for him to produce something? She probably doesn't even read. Still, he wants to say, 'Look. Read this, isn't it good? And I wrote it in your house, only today.'

Mrs O'Sullivan's hand is knotting at her throat. The sculpture has drawn a frown, a heavy sulk. ''Tis a queer lot of objects they've been making for the tourists, and none of them what you could put a name to.'

'But oh,' Carrie says, 'he must be nearly the best in the country! Surely. And this is no tourist souvenir. I got it from an art shop in Cork.'

Mrs O'Sullivan's hand opens and closes, creeps closer to her mouth. 'Oh,' she says. 'Cork.' As if a lot has been explained. 'You can expect anything at all from a city. Anything at all. There was people here staying in this house, 'twas last year yes, came back from Cork as pleased as the Pope with an old box of turf they had bought. They wanted to smell it burning in my fire if you don't mind. What you spend your money on is your own business, I told them, but I left the bogs behind years ago, thank you, and heat my house with electricity. Keep the turf in your car so.'

Carrie is plainly insulted. Words struggle at her lips. But she dismisses them, apparently, and chooses diversion. 'I'll make a pot of tea. Would you like a cup with us, Mrs O'Sullivan? The long drive's made me thirsty.'

And Mrs O'Sullivan, whose role is apparently varied and will shift for any occasion, lets her fingers pluck at her face. 'Oh I know I know I know!' Her long brown-stockinged legs move slowly across the patterned carpet. 'And Mr Desmond, too, after his work. I was tempted to take him a cup but he shouldn't be disturbed I know.'

'Work?' Carrie says. 'Working at what?'

'I started the novel,' Desmond says.

'You have? Then that's something we should celebrate. Before you go off wherever it is you think you're going.'

'It's only a page,' Desmond says. 'And it's not very good at all, but it's a start. It's better than the blank paper.'

[1]Police (Irish).

Like some children, he thinks, he's learned to make a virtue out of anything. Even a page of scribble. When he'd be glad to give a thousand pages of scribble for the gift of honesty. Or change. Or even blindness of a sort. What good is vision after all if it refuses to ignore the dark?

Because hasn't he heard, somewhere, that artists—painters—deliberately create frames for themselves to look through, to sharpen their vision by cutting off all the details which have no importance to their work?

He follows the women into the kitchen, where cups already clatter onto saucers. 'Maybe after tea,' he says, 'I'll get a bit more done.'

Pretending, perhaps, that the rest of the world sits waiting, like Mrs O'Sullivan, for the words he will produce. Because his tongue, his voice, has made the decision for him. Desmond knows that he may only sit in front of that paper for the rest of that day, that he may only play with his pen—frustrated—until enough time has gone by to justify his coming out of the room. To read one of the books he's bought. To talk with Carrie about her shopping in Cork, about her sculptor. To play with the children perhaps, or take them for a walk along the road to look for donkeys, for ruins. Desmond knows that the evening may be passed in front of the television set, where they will see American movies with Irish commercials, and will later try to guess what *an naught*² is telling them about the day's events, and that he will try very hard not to think of Mary Brennan or of the dozen Irish writers at Gougane Barra or of the tiny hermitage island which the famous writer loved. Deep-Valleyed Desmond. He knows that he could be there with them, through this day and this night, celebrating something he'd come here to find; but he acknowledges, too, the other. That words, too, were invented perhaps to do the things that stones can do. And he has come here, after all, to build his walls.

1981

---

²The news (Irish).

Margaret Atwood

b. 1939

Since winning a Governor General's Award at twenty-seven (for *The Circle Game*, her first full-length book), Margaret Atwood has created a substantial body of writing—poetry, fiction, and criticism—which has gained her an international reputation. She has also been active in the publishing and writing community—she was an editor for the House of Anansi and a member of its board in the early seventies, the president of the Writers' Union in 1982-3, and the editor of *The New Oxford Book of Canadian Verse* in 1982—and has lectured and read from her work in Canada, the U.S., Europe, Russia, and Australia.

Born in Ottawa, Atwood grew up there, in Sault Ste Marie, and in Toronto. As a result of her father's entomological research she spent extended periods of her childhood with her family in the northern Ontario and Quebec bush, and did not attend a full year of formal school until grade eight. In 1957 she entered Victoria College, University of Toronto (where her teachers included Northrop Frye), completing her B.A. in 1961 and publishing a slim book of poems, *Double Persephone*, the same year. She then enrolled in graduate studies at Harvard, taking a master's degree (1962) and beginning a doctoral thesis on 'the English metaphysical romances' of George MacDonald and H. Rider Haggard. She returned to Toronto to work briefly as a market researcher; then, between 1964 and 1973, she taught English—at the University of British Columbia, Sir George Williams (now Concordia University), the University of Alberta, and York University—and spent a year at the University of Toronto as writer-in-residence.

Atwood's writing can be separated into two main periods. The poems collected in

The Circle Game (1966), *The Animals in That Country* (1968), *Procedures for Underground* (1970), and *You Are Happy* (1974)—as well as those in the book-length sequences *The Journals of Susanna Moodie* (1970) and *Power Politics* (1973)—have a stylistic and thematic unity that is also evident in her novels of the period: *The Edible Woman* (1969), *Surfacing* (1972), and *Lady Oracle* (1976). Utilizing a stark and unemotional style, this writing can startle readers out of conventional expectations and into new ways of perceiving—as in the short poem that opens *Power Politics*:

> *You fit into me*
> *like a hook into an eye*
>
> *a fish hook*
> *an open eye.*

Frequently written from the point of view of alienated individuals (sometimes on the verge of nervous breakdowns), this poetry and fiction express a distrust of the everyday world, finding it a place of deceptive appearances and emotional shallowness. To this world Atwood opposes the claims made on us by dreams, hallucinations, and visions, showing her readers the necessity of making a 'journey to the interior' and suggesting that it is only through descents into the psyche and the rediscovery of the primitive and mythic dimensions of both mind and world that one can experience wholeness.

For Atwood the problem of inauthenticity—a central theme for many contemporary writers—is especially associated with women (in *Power Politics* and *The Edible Woman*) and with Canadians (in *Surfacing* and *The Journals of Susanna*

Moodie). She has written on the dangers of a colonial mentality, and the consequent lack of Canadian identity, not only in her poetry and fiction, but also in *Survival: A Thematic Guide to Canadian Literature* (1972). In this popular work of literary criticism—which came out of and fuelled the cultural nationalism of its time—she builds on Northrop Frye's 'garrison' thesis, arguing that Canadians are not only alienated from their environment but, having existed in a colonial relationship first to England and then to America, are obsessed with a sense of themselves as victims. Although her reading of the literature has been criticized as one-sided and subjective, this study revealed to many a previously unrecognized coherence in Canadian culture and stimulated valuable debate about Canadian literature and criticism. *Survival* also sheds light on Atwood's own work: her fiction and poetry develop out of the tradition she describes and are intended as a corrective to it. ('This above all, to refuse to be a victim' is the final lesson learned by the protagonist of *Surfacing*.)

In moving towards the post-colonial society that Atwood desires, the writer has a special function—that of helping to claim a psychic space. In 'Northrop Frye Observed' she writes:

*Frye's push towards naming, towards an interconnected system, seems to me a Canadian reaction to a Canadian situation. Stranded in the midst of a vast space which nobody has made sense out of for you, you settle down to map-making, charting the territory, the discovery of where things are in relation to each other, the extraction of meaning. (*Second Words, 1982)

Although Atwood's ideas are often visible in her writing, one should not overlook her craftsmanship. For example, in an interview with Joyce Carol Oates on the occasion of the American publication of her *Selected Poems*, Atwood emphasized the way 'a texture of sound . . . is at least as important to me as the "argument"' ', explaining:

My poems usually begin with words or phrases which appeal more because of their sound than their meaning, and the movement and phrasing of a poem are very important to me. But like many modern poets I tend to conceal rhymes by placing

them in the middle of lines, and to avoid immediate alliteration and assonance in favour of echoes placed later in the poems. (The New York Times Book Review, *21 May 1978*)

The publication in 1976 and 1977 of two compilations of earlier work, *Selected Poems* and *Dancing Girls* (a collection of short stories), marked the end of a phase in Atwood's writing career. In her work of the late seventies and the eighties—the poetry of *Two-Headed Poems* (1978) and *True Stories* (1981) and the novels *Life Before Man* (1979) and *Bodily Harm* (1981)—Atwood does not abandon the concerns of her earlier writing, but she does employ a greater range of style and topics. She is by turns more lyrical, more personal, and more political. She treats domestic subjects in some of her poems, and even gives the reader glimpses of members of her own family. The characters in her novels are more fully drawn and more varied (in *Life Before Man* she uses a male viewpoint for the first time) and in a poem such as 'Variation on the Word *Sleep*' she can write without irony of a woman's love for a man. At the same time politics assumes a new importance. *Two-Headed Poems* takes its title from a sequence of poems about Canada's division between two cultures. (The title also suggests a preoccupation with doubleness and duality that has always been present in Atwood's work.) Elsewhere in that book, as well as the sequence in *True Stories* called 'Notes Towards a Poem That Cannot Be Written', protesting against torture as an instrument of political repression, Atwood adopts a global perspective reflecting association with Amnesty International. The sense that Canada must now look beyond its own border is also evident in *Bodily Harm*, with its tale of a Canadian travel-writer's naive involvement in a political coup in the Caribbean.

In 1982 Atwood published a large selection of reviews, lectures, and essays (some of which complement or comment on *Survival*) in *Second Words*; in 1983 she ventured into a new form—brief prose pieces that resemble poetic meditations—in *Murder in the Dark: Short Fictions and Prose Poems*. In all her work—whether fiction, non-fiction, or poetry—Atwood takes very seriously both the power of the

written word and the writer's duty to society. As a passage in *Murder in the Dark* suggests, writing is an act of great consequence, and so, therefore, is reading:
. . . *Beneath the page is a story. Beneath the page is everything that has ever happened, most of which you would rather not hear about.*

Touch the page at your peril: it is you who are blank and innocent, not the page. Nevertheless you want to know, nothing will stop you. You touch the page, it's as if you've drawn a knife across it, the page has been hurt now, a sinuous wound opens, a thin incision. Darkness wells through. ('The Page'*)*

This is a Photograph of Me

It was taken some time ago.
At first it seems to be
a smeared
print: blurred lines and grey flecks
blended with the paper;

then, as you scan
it, you see in the left-hand corner
a thing that is like a branch: part of a tree
(balsam or spruce) emerging
and, to the right, halfway up   10
what ought to be a gentle
slope, a small frame house.

In the background there is a lake,
and beyond that, some low hills.

(The photograph was taken
the day after I drowned.

I am in the lake, in the center
of the picture, just under the surface.

It is difficult to say where
precisely, or to say   20
how large or small I am:
the effect of water
on light is a distortion

but if you look long enough,
eventually
you will be able to see me.)

1966

Pre-Amphibian

Again so I subside
nudged by the softening
driftwood of your body,
tangle on you like a water-
weed caught
on a submerged treelimb

with sleep like a swamp
growing, closing around me
sending its tendrils through the brown
sediments of darkness   10
where we   transmuted   are
part of this warm rotting
of vegetable flesh
this quiet spawning of roots

released
from the lucidities of day
when you are something I can
trace a line around, with eyes
cut shapes
from air, the element   20
where we
must calculate according to
solidities

but here I blur
into you   our breathing sinking
to green milleniums
and   sluggish   in our blood
all ancestors
are warm fish moving

The earth   30
shifts, bringing
the moment before focus, when
these tides recede; and we
see each other through the
hardening scales of waking

stranded, astounded
in a drying world

we flounder, the air
ungainly in our new lungs
with sunlight streaming merciless on the shores of morning

1966

The Reincarnation
of Captain Cook[1]

Earlier than I could learn
the maps had been coloured in.
When I pleaded, the kings told me
nothing was left to explore.

I set out anyway, but
everywhere I went
there were historians, wearing
wreaths and fake teeth
belts; or in the deserts, cairns
and tourists. Even the caves had   10
candle stubs, inscriptions quickly
scribbled in darkness. I could

never arrive. Always
the names got there before.

Now I am old I know my
mistake was my acknowledging
of maps. The eyes raise
tired monuments.

Burn down
the atlases, I shout   20
to the park benches; and go

past the cenotaph
waving a blank banner
across the street, beyond
the corner

into a new land cleaned of geographies,
its beach gleaming with arrows.

1968

---

[1]Captain James Cook (1728-79), English explorer and mapmaker who mapped the St Lawrence River and the Newfoundland coast; later he explored the northwest Pacific coast, claiming Vancouver Island for England, and went as far north as the Bering Strait in search of a northwest passage.

Progressive Insanities of a Pioneer

i

He stood, a point
on a sheet of green paper
proclaiming himself the centre,

with no walls, no borders
anywhere; the sky no height
above him, totally un-
enclosed
and shouted:

Let me out!

ii

He dug the soil in rows,   10
imposed himself with shovels.
He asserted
into the furrows, I
am not random.

The ground
replied with aphorisms:

a tree-sprout, a nameless
weed, words
he couldn't understand.

iii

The house pitched   20
the plot staked
in the middle of nowhere

At night the mind
inside, in the middle
of nowhere.

The idea of an animal
patters across the roof.

In the darkness the fields
defend themselves with fences
in vain: 30
        everything
        is getting in.

iv

By daylight he resisted.
He said, disgusted
with the swamp's clamourings and the outbursts
of rocks.
       This is not order
       but the absence
       of order

He was wrong, the unanswering   40
forest implied:

       It was
       an ordered absence

v

For many years
he fished for a great vision,
dangling the hooks of sown
roots under the surface
of the shallow earth.

It was like
enticing whales with a bent   50
pin. Besides he thought

in that country
only the worms were biting.

vi

If he had known unstructured
space is a deluge
and stocked his log house-
boat with all the animals

even the wolves,

he might have floated.

But obstinate he   60
stated, The land is solid
and stamped,

watching his foot sink
down through stone
up to the knee.

vii

Things
refused to name themselves; refused
to let him name them.

The wolves hunted
outside.   70

On his beaches, his clearings,
by the surf of under-
growth breaking
at his feet, he foresaw
disintegration
            and in the end
through eyes
made ragged by his
effort, the tension
between subject and object,   80

the green
vision, the unnamed
whale invaded.

1968

From *The Journals of Susanna Moodie*[1]

From JOURNAL I, 1832-1840

Disembarking at Quebec

Is it my clothes, my way of walking,
the things I carry in my hand
—a book, a bag with knitting—
the incongruous pink of my shawl

this space cannot hear

or is it my own lack
of conviction which makes
these vistas of desolation,
long hills, the swamps, the barren sand, the glare
of sun on the bone-white   10
driftlogs, omens of winter,
the moon alien in day-
time a thin refusal

[1]In this book Atwood uses the historical Susanna Moodie (1803-85) as the speaker in poems inspired by her two narratives of settlement, *Roughing It in the Bush* (1852) and *Life in the Clearings* (1853). Most of the people and events alluded to in the poems reprinted here may be found in the selections from *Roughing It in the Bush* in Vol. I, pp. 77-126.

The others leap, shout

Freedom![2]

The moving water will not show me
my reflection.

The rocks ignore.

I am a word
in a foreign language.   20

[2]In Chapter 2 of *Roughing It*, Moodie says she was 'not a little amused at the extravagant expectations entertained by some of our steerage passengers. . . . In spite of the remonstrances of the captain
and the dread of the cholera, they all rushed on shore to inspect the land of Goshen, and to endeavour
to realize their absurd anticipations.'

Further Arrivals

After we had crossed the long illness
that was the ocean, we sailed up-river

On the first island
the immigrants threw off their clothes
and danced like sandflies[1]

We left behind one by one
the cities rotting with cholera,
one by one our civilized
distinctions

and entered a large darkness.   10

It was our own
ignorance we entered.

I have not come out yet

My brain gropes nervous
tentacles in the night, sends out

[1]In the first chapter of *Roughing It* the Moodies visited Grosse Isle for an afternoon while their ship
stood off shore following an inspection by health officers (Quebec was then experiencing a cholera
epidemic): 'Never shall I forget the extraordinary spectacle that met our sight . . . A crowd of many
hundred Irish emigrants had been landed . . . and all this motley crew—men, women, and children
. . . —were employed in washing clothes. . . . The men and boys were *in* the water, while the
women, with their scanty garments tucked above their knees, were tramping their bedding in tubs or
in holes in the rocks. Those [not washing] were running to and fro, screaming and scolding in no
measured terms . . . all accompanying their vociferations with violent and extraordinary gestures,
quite incomprehensible to the uninitiated.'

fears hairy as bears,
demands lamps; or waiting

for my shadowy husband, hears
malice in the trees' whispers.

I need wolf's eyes to see   20
the truth.

I refuse to look in a mirror.

Whether the wilderness is
real or not
depends on who lives there.

First Neighbours

The people I live among, unforgivingly
previous to me, grudging
the way I breathe their
property, the air,
speaking a twisted dialect to my differently-
shaped ears

though I tried to adapt

(the girl in a red tattered
petticoat, who jeered at me for my burned bread

Go back where you came from   10

I tightened my lips; knew that England
was now unreachable, had sunk down into the sea
without ever teaching me about washtubs)

got used to being
a minor invalid, expected to make
inept remarks,
futile and spastic gestures

(asked the Indian
about the squat thing on a stick
drying by the fire: Is that a toad?   20
Annoyed, he said No no,
deer liver, very good)

Finally I grew a chapped tarpaulin
skin; I negotiated the drizzle
of strange meaning, set it
down to just the latitude:

something to be endured
but not surprised by.

Inaccurate. The forest can still trick me:
one afternoon while I was drawing   30
birds, a malignant face
flickered over my shoulder;
the branches quivered.

    Resolve: to be both tentative and hard to startle
    (though clumsiness and
    fright are inevitable)

    in this area where my damaged
    knowing of the language means
    prediction is forever impossible

The Planters

They move between the jagged edge
of the forest and the jagged river
on a stumpy patch of cleared land

my husband, a neighbour, another man
weeding the few rows
of string beans and dusty potatoes.

They bend, straighten; the sun
lights up their faces and hands, candles
flickering in the wind against the

unbright earth. I see them; I know   10
none of them believe they are here.
They deny the ground they stand on,

pretend this dirt is the future.
And they are right. If they let go
of that illusion solid to them as a shovel,

open their eyes even for a moment
to these trees, to this particular sun
they would be surrounded, stormed, broken

in upon by branches, roots, tendrils, the dark
side of light   20
as I am.

The Wereman

My husband walks in the frosted field
an X, a concept
defined against a blank;
he swerves, enters the forest
and is blotted out.

Unheld by my sight
what does he change into
what other shape
blends with the under-
growth, wavers across the pools   10
is camouflaged from the listening
swamp animals

At noon he will
return; or it may be
only my idea of him
I will find returning
with him hiding behind it.

He may change me also
with the fox eye, the owl
eye, the eightfold   20
eye of the spider

I can't think
what he will see
when he opens the door

Paths and Thingscape

Those who went ahead
of us in the forest
bent the early trees
so that they grew to signals:

the trail was not
among the trees but
the trees

and there are some who have dreams
of birds flying in the shapes
of letters; the sky's   10
codes;
            and dream also
the significance of numbers (count
petals of certain flowers)

            In the morning I advance

through the doorway: the sun
on the bark, the inter-
twisted branches, here
a blue movement in the leaves, dispersed
calls/no trails; rocks   20
and grey tufts of moss

The petals of the fire-
weed fall where they fall

I am watched like an invader
who knows hostility but
not where

The day shrinks back from me

When will be
that union and each
thing (bits   30
of surface broken by my foot
step) will without moving move
around me
into its place

The Two Fires[1]

One, the summer fire
outside: the trees melting, returning
to their first red elements
on all sides, cutting me off
from escape or the saving
lake

I sat in the house, raised up
between that shapeless raging
and my sleeping children
a charm: concentrate on   10
form, geometry, the human
architecture of the house, square
closed doors, proved roofbeams,
the logic of windows

(the children could not be wakened:
in their calm dreaming
the trees were straight and still
had branches and were green)

[1]In Chapter 20 of *Roughing It* Moodie tells of fighting the fire (with the help of a girl she had just hired) that destroyed their second house; it started because the servant was incautious with the Franklin stove during a severe winter chill.

The other, the winter
fire inside: the protective roof   20
shrivelling overhead, the rafters
incandescent, all those corners
and straight lines flaming, the carefully-
made structure
prisoning us in a cage of blazing
bars
      the children
were awake and crying;

I wrapped them, carried them
outside into the snow.   30
Then I tried to rescue
what was left of their scorched dream
about the house: blankets,
warm clothes, the singed furniture
of safety cast away with them
in a white chaos

Two fires in-
formed me,

(each refuge fails
us; each danger   40
becomes a haven)

left charred marks
now around which I
try to grow

Departure from the Bush

I, who had been erased
by fire, was crept in
upon by green
         (how
lucid a season)

        In time the animals
arrived to inhabit me,

first one
  by one, stealthily
(their habitual traces   10
burnt); then
having marked new boundaries
returning, more

confident, year
by year, two
by two

but restless: I was not ready
altogether to be moved into

They could tell I was
too heavy: I might   20
capsize;

I was frightened
by their eyes (green or
amber) glowing out from inside me

I was not completed; at night
I could not see without lanterns.

He wrote, We are leaving. I said
I have no clothes
left I can wear

The snow came. The sleigh was a relief;[1]   30
its track lengthened behind,
pushing me towards the city

and rounding the first hill, I was
(instantaneous)
unlived in: they had gone.

There was something they almost taught me
I came away not having learned.

---

[1]In the final chapter of *Roughing It* ('Adieu to the Woods') Moodie describes how, after her husband had been appointed Sheriff of Victoria District, she passed 'the last night I ever spent in the bush—in the dear forest home which I had loved in spite of all hardships', and then departed for Belleville, with her household, by sleigh.

From JOURNAL II, 1840-1871

Dream 2: Brian the Still-Hunter[1]

The man I saw in the forest
used to come to our house
every morning, never said anything;
I learned from the neighbours later
he once tried to cut his throat.

I found him at the end of the path
sitting on a fallen tree
cleaning his gun.

There was no wind;
around us the leaves rustled.   10

He said to me:
I kill because I have to

but every time I aim, I feel
my skin grow fur
my head heavy with antlers
and during the stretched instant
the bullet glides on its thread of speed
my soul runs innocent as hooves.

Is God just to his creatures?

I die more often than many.   20

He looked up and I saw
the white scar made by the hunting knife
around his neck.

When I woke
I remembered: he has been gone
twenty years and not heard from.

[1] A 'still-hunter' is one who hunts stealthily on foot. In Chapter 10 of *Roughing It* Moodie describes her friendship with Brian, a man once subject to such fits of depression that he had tried to commit suicide. Brian tells her a vivid story of watching a 'noble deer' pulled down by a pack of wolves, concluding:
'At that moment he seemed more unfortunate even than myself, for I could not see in what manner he had deserved his fate. All his speed and energy, his courage and fortitude, had been exerted in vain. I had tried to destroy myself; but he, with every effort vigorously made for self-preservation, was doomed to meet the fate he dreaded! Is God just to his creatures?'
Moodie ends the chapter by saying:
We parted with the hunter as an old friend; and we never met again. His fate was a sad one. After we left that part of the country, he fell into a moping melancholy, which ended in self-destruction.

From JOURNAL III, 1871-1969

Thoughts from Underground[1]

When I first reached this country
I hated it
and I hated it more each year:

in summer the light a
violent blur, the heat
thick as a swamp,
the green things fiercely
shoving themselves upwards, the
eyelids bitten by insects

In winter our teeth were brittle   10
with cold. We fed on squirrels.
At night the house cracked.
In the mornings, we thawed
the bad bread over the stove.

Then we were made successful
and I felt I ought to love
this country.
            I said I loved it
and my mind saw double.

I began to forget myself   20
in the middle
of sentences. Events
were split apart

I fought. I constructed
desperate paragraphs of praise, everyone
ought to love it because

and set them up at intervals

        due to natural resources, native industry, superior
        penitentiaries
        we will all be rich and powerful   30

flat as highway billboards

        who can doubt it, look how
        fast Belleville is growing

(though it is still no place for an english gentleman)

[1] This poem is spoken by Moodie after her death.

Afterword to
The Journals of Susanna Moodie

These poems were generated by a dream. I dreamt I was watching an opera I had written about Susanna Moodie. I was alone in the theatre; on the empty white stage, a single figure was singing.

Although I had heard of Susanna Moodie I had never read her two books about Canada, *Roughing It in the Bush* and *Life in the Clearings*. When I did read them I was disappointed. The prose was discursive and ornamental and the books had little shape: they were collections of disconnected anecdotes. The only thing that held them together was the personality of Mrs Moodie, and what struck me most about this personality was the way in which it reflects many of the obsessions still with us.

If the national mental illness of the United States is megalomania, that of Canada is paranoid schizophrenia. Mrs Moodie is divided down the middle: she praises the Canadian landscape but accuses it of destroying her; she dislikes the people already in Canada but finds in people her only refuge from the land itself; she preaches progress and the march of civilization while brooding elegiacally upon the destruction of the wilderness; she delivers optimistic sermons while showing herself to be fascinated with deaths, murders, the criminals in Kingston Penitentiary and the incurably insane in the Toronto lunatic asylum. She claims to be an ardent Canadian patriot while all the time she is standing back from the country and criticizing it as though she were a detached observer, a stranger. Perhaps that is the way we still live. We are all immigrants to this place even if we were born here: the country is too big for anyone to inhabit completely, and in the parts unknown to us we move in fear, exiles and invaders. This country is something that must be chosen—it is so easy to leave—and if we do choose it we are still choosing a violent duality.

Once I had read the books I forgot about them. The poems occurred later, over a period of a year and a half. I suppose many of them were suggested by Mrs Moodie's books, though it was not her conscious voice but the other voice running like a counterpoint through her work that made the most impression on me. Although the poems can be read in connection with Mrs Moodie's books, they don't have to be: they have detached themselves from the books in the same way that other poems detach themselves from the events that give rise to them.

The arrangement of the poems follows, more or less, the course of Mrs Moodie's life. Journal I begins with her arrival in Canada and her voyage up the St Lawrence, past Quebec and Montreal where a cholera epidemic is raging. In Upper Canada she encounters earlier settlers who despise the Moodies as greenhorns and cheat them whenever possible. Later, on a remote bush farm, she can neither hold on to her English past nor renounce it for a belief in her Canadian future. After seven years of struggle and near starvation, and just as she is beginning to come to terms with her environment, the family moves away.

After 1840 the Moodies lived in Belleville, where Susanna's husband had been made sheriff as a result of his helping to suppress the rebellion of 1837. (Ironically, Susanna later admitted that the rebellion was probably a good thing for Canada.) Journal II contains reflections about the society Mrs Moodie finds herself in, as well as memories of the years spent in the bush. At the beginning of this section Mrs Moodie finally accepts the reality of the country she is in, and at its end she accepts also the inescapable doubleness of her own vision.

Most of Journal III was written after I had come across a little-known photograph of Susanna Moodie as a mad-looking and very elderly lady. The poems take her through an estranged old age, into death and beyond. After her death she can hear the twentieth century above her, bulldozing away her past, but she refuses to be ploughed under completely. She makes her final appearance in the present, as an old woman on a Toronto bus who reveals the city as an unexplored, threatening wilderness. Susanna Moodie has finally turned herself inside out, and has become the spirit of the land she once hated.

1970

Procedures for Underground

(Northwest Coast)

The country beneath
the earth has a green sun
and the rivers flow backwards;

the trees and rocks are the same
as they are here, but shifted.
Those who live there are always hungry;

from them you can learn
wisdom and great power,
if you can descend and return safely.

You must look for tunnels, animal   10
burrows or the cave in the sea
guarded by the stone man;

when you are down you will find
those who were once your friends
but they will be changed and dangerous.

Resist them, be careful
never to eat their food.
Afterwards, if you live, you will be able

to see them when they prowl as winds,
as thin sounds in our village. You will   20
tell us their names, what they want, who

has made them angry by forgetting them.
For this gift, as for all gifts, you must
suffer: those from the underland

will be always with you, whispering their
complaints, beckoning you
back down; while among us here

you will walk wrapped in an invisible
cloak. Few will seek your help
with love, none without fear.   30

1970

Dream: Bluejay
or Archeopteryx[1]

kneeling on rock
by lakeside, sun
in the sky and also in
the water, that other
self of mine also
kneeling on rock

on the seared bushes the hard
berries squeezed out from
stem ends in spite of

the red needles crackling   10
on the ground, the sand, among
the roots, firedry

my four hands gathering
in either world, the berries
in the dish glowed blue
embers

         a bird
lit on both branches

his beak split/his tin
scream forked in the air   20

warning. above me
against the sun I saw
his lizard eye
         looked
down.   gone

in the water

[1]Literally 'ancient wing', a tree-climbing crow-like bird that lived during the age of the dinosaurs and
was a primitive evolutionary link between birds and reptiles.

under my shadow
there was an outline, man
surfacing, his body sheathed
in feathers, his teeth   30
glinting like nails, fierce god
head crested with blue flame

1970

Tricks with Mirrors

i

It's no coincidence
this is a used
furniture warehouse.

I enter with you
and become a mirror.

Mirrors
are the perfect lovers,

that's it, carry me up the stairs
by the edges, don't drop me,

that would be bad luck,   10
throw me on the bed

reflecting side up,
fall into me,

it will be your own
mouth you hit, firm and glassy,

your own eyes you find you
are up against   closed   closed

ii

There is more to a mirror
than you looking at

your full-length body   20
flawless but reversed,

there is more than this dead blue
oblong eye turned outwards to you.

Think about the frame.
The frame is carved, it is important,

it exists, it does not reflect you,
it does not recede and recede, it has limits

and reflections of its own.
There's a nail in the back

to hang it with; there are several nails,　　　　　30
think about the nails,

pay attention to the nail
marks in the wood,

they are important too.

iii
Don't assume it is passive
or easy, this clarity

with which I give you yourself.
Consider what restraint it

takes: breath withheld, no anger
or joy disturbing the surface　　　　　40

of the ice.
You are suspended in me

beautiful and frozen, I
preserve you, in me you are safe.

It is not a trick either,
it is a craft:

mirrors are crafty.

iv
I wanted to stop this,
this life flattened against the wall,

mute and devoid of colour,　　　　　50
built of pure light,

this life of vision only, split
and remote, a lucid impasse.

I confess: this is not a mirror,
it is a door

I am trapped behind.

I wanted you to see me here,

say the releasing word, whatever
that may be, open the wall.

Instead you stand in front of me   60
combing your hair.

v

You don't like these metaphors.
All right:

Perhaps I am not a mirror.
Perhaps I am a pool.

Think about pools.

1974

Siren Song[1]

This is the one song everyone
would like to learn: the song
that is irresistible:

the song that forces men
to leap overboard in squadrons
even though they see the beached skulls

the song nobody knows
because anyone who has heard it
is dead, and the others can't remember.

Shall I tell you the secret   10
and if I do, will you get me
out of this bird suit?

I don't enjoy it here
squatting on this island
looking picturesque and mythical

with these two feathery maniacs,
I don't enjoy singing
this trio, fatal and valuable.

[1]In Greek mythology the sirens were beautiful young women (usually three in number) who had been changed into creatures that were half-women and half-birds; their enchanting songs lured sailors to their deaths on dangerous rocks. This poem is one of a sequence called 'Songs of the Transformed'. (In speaking to Joyce Carol Oates of her childhood love for Grimm's fairytales, Atwood said, 'It was not the gore . . . that caught my attention, but the transformations.')

I will tell the secret to you,
to you, only to you.   20
Come closer. This song

is a cry for help: Help me!
Only you, only you can,
you are unique

at last. Alas
it is a boring song
but it works every time.

1974

Marrying the Hangman[1]

She has been condemned to death by hanging. A man may
escape this death by becoming the hangman, a woman by
marrying the hangman. But at the present time there is no
hangman; thus there is no escape. There is only a death,
indefinitely postponed. This is not fantasy, it is history.

*

To live in prison is to live without mirrors. To live without
mirrors is to live without the self. She is living selflessly, she
finds a hole in the stone wall and on the other side of the wall, a
voice. The voice comes through darknesss and has no face. This
voice becomes her mirror.

*

In order to avoid her death, her particular death, with wrung
neck and swollen tongue, she must marry the hangman. But
there is no hangman, first she must create him, she must
persuade this man at the end of the voice, this voice she has
never seen and which has never seen her, this darkness, she
must persuade him to renounce his face, exchange it for the
impersonal mask of death, of official death which has eyes but
no mouth, this mask of a dark leper. She must transform his

[1]'Jean Corolère, a drummer in the colonial troops at Québec, was imprisoned for duelling in 1751. In
the cell next to his was Françoise Laurent, who had been sentenced to hang for stealing. Except for
letters of pardon, the only way at the time for someone under sentence of death to escape hanging
was, for a man, to become a hangman, or, for a woman, to marry one. Françoise persuaded Corolère
to apply for the vacant (and undesirable) post of executioner, and also to marry her.—Condensed
from the *Dictionary of Canadian Biography*, Volume III, 1741-1770' (Atwood's note).

hands so they will be willing to twist the rope around throats that have been singled out as hers was, throats other than hers. She must marry the hangman or no one, but that is not so bad. Who else is there to marry?

*

You wonder about her crime. She was condemned to death for stealing clothes from her employer, from the wife of her employer. She wished to make herself more beautiful. This desire in servants was not legal.

*

She uses her voice like a hand, her voice reaches through the wall, stroking and touching. What could she possibly have said that would have convinced him? He was not condemned to death, freedom awaited him. What was the temptation, the one that worked? Perhaps he wanted to live with a woman whose life he had saved, who had seen down into the earth but had nevertheless followed him back up to life. It was his only chance to be a hero, to one person at least, for if he became the hangman the others would despise him. He was in prison for wounding another man, on one finger of the right hand, with a sword. This too is history.

*

My friends, who are both women, tell me their stories, which cannot be believed and which are true. They are horror stories and they have not happened to me, they have not yet happened to me, they have happened to me but we are detached, we watch our unbelief with horror. Such things cannot happen to us, it is afternoon and these things do not happen in the afternoon. The trouble was, she said, I didn't have time to put my glasses on and without them I'm blind as a bat, I couldn't even see who it was. These things happen and we sit at a table and tell stories about them so we can finally believe. This is not fantasy, it is history, there is more than one hangman and because of this some of them are unemployed.

*

He said: the end of walls, the end of ropes, the opening of doors, a field, the wind, a house, the sun, a table, an apple.

She said: nipple, arms, lips, wine, belly, hair, bread, thighs, eyes, eyes.

They both kept their promises.

*

The hangman is not such a bad fellow. Afterwards he goes to the refrigerator and cleans up the leftovers, though he does not wipe up what he accidentally spills. He wants only the simple things: a chair, someone to pull off his shoes, someone to watch him while he talks, with admiration and fear, gratitude if possible, someone in whom to plunge himself for rest and renewal. These things can best be had by marrying a woman who has been condemned to death by other men for wishing to be beautiful. There is a wide choice.

*

Everyone said he was a fool.
Everyone said she was a clever woman.
They used the word *ensnare*.

*

What did they say the first time they were alone together in the same room? What did he say when she had removed her veil and he could see that she was not a voice but a body and therefore finite? What did she say when she discovered that she had left one locked room for another? They talked of love, naturally, though that did not keep them busy forever.

*

The fact is there are no stories I can tell my friends that will make them feel better. History cannot be erased, although we can soothe ourselves by speculating about it. At that time there were no female hangmen. Perhaps there have never been any, and thus no man could save his life by marriage. Though a woman could, according to the law.

*

He said: foot, boot, order, city, fist, roads, time, knife.

She said: water, night, willow, rope hair, earth belly, cave, meat, shroud, open, blood.

They both kept their promises.

1978

Variation on the Word *Sleep*

I would like to watch you sleeping,
which may not happen.
I would like to watch you,
sleeping. I would like to sleep
with you, to enter
your sleep as its smooth dark wave
slides over my head

and walk with you through that lucent
wavering forest of bluegreen leaves
with its watery sun & three moons   10
towards the cave where you must descend,
towards your worst fear

I would like to give you the silver
branch, the small white flower, the one
word that will protect you
from the grief at the center
of your dream, from the grief
at the center. I would like to follow
you up the long stairway
again & become   20
the boat that would row you back
carefully, a flame
in two cupped hands
to where your body lies
beside me, and you enter
it as easily as breathing in

I would like to be the air
that inhabits you for a moment
only. I would like to be that unnoticed
& that necessary.   30

1981

Last Poem

Tonight words fall away from me like shed clothing
thrown casually on the floor as if there's no
tomorrow, and there's no tomorrow.

One day halfway up the mountain or down the freeway,
air in any case whistling by,
you stop climbing or driving and you know you will never get there.

I lie on a blue sofa and suck icecubes
while my friends and the friends of my friends and women

I hardly know get cancer.
There's one a week, one a minute; we all discuss it.   10

I'm a plague worker, I brush finger to finger,
hoping it's not catching, wondering how to say
goodbye gracefully and not merely snivel.
There are small mercies, granted, but not many.

Meanwhile I sit here futureless with you:
in one second something will wrench like a string or a zipper
or time will slide on itself like the granite sides of a fissure
and houses, chairs, lovers collapse in a long tremor.

That's your hand sticking out of the rubble.
I touch it, you're still living;   20
to have this happen I would give anything,
to keep you alive with me despite the wreckage.

I hold this hand as if waiting for the rescue
and that one action shines like pure luck.
Because there's nothing more I can do I do nothing.

What we're talking about is a table and two glasses,
two hands, a candle, and outside the curtained window
a charred landscape with the buildings and trees still smouldering.
Each poem is my last and so is this one.

1981

From *Murder in the Dark*

Making Poison

When I was five my brother and I made poison. We were living in a city then, but we probably would have made the poison anyway. We kept it in a paint can under somebody else's house and we put all the poisonous things into it that we could think of: toadstools, dead mice, mountain ash berries which may not have been poisonous but looked it, piss which we saved up in order to add it to the paint can. By the time the can was full everything in it was very poisonous.

The problem was that once having made the poison we couldn't just leave it there. We had to do something with it. We didn't want to put it into anyone's food, but we wanted an object, a completion. There was no one we hated enough, that was the difficulty.

I can't remember what we did with the poison in the end. Did we leave it under the corner of the house, which was made of wood and brownish yellow? Did we throw it at someone, some innocuous child? We wouldn't have dared an adult. Is this a true image I have, a small face streaming with tears and red berries, the sudden knowledge that the poison was really poisonous after all? Or did we throw it out, do I remember those red berries floating down a gutter, into a culvert, am I innocent?

Why did we make the poison in the first place? I can remember the glee with which we stirred and added, the sense of magic and accomplishment. Making poison is as much fun as making a cake. People like to make poison. If you don't understand this you will never understand anything.

Strawberries

The strawberries when I first remember them are not red but blue, that blue flare, before the whitehot part of the wire, sun glancing from the points of waves. It was the heat that made things blue like that, rage, I went into the waste orchard because I did not want to talk to you or even see you, I wanted instead to do something small and useful that I was good at. It was June, there were mosquitoes, I stirred them up as I pushed aside the higher stems, but I didn't care, I was immune, all that adrenalin kept them away, and if not I was in the mood for minor lacerations. I don't get angry like that any more. I almost miss it.

I'd like to say I saw everything through a haze of red; which is not true. Nothing was hazy. Everything was very clear, clearer than usual, my hands with the stained nails, the sunlight falling on the ground through the apple-tree branches, each leaf, each white five petalled yellow centred flower and conical fine-haired dark red multi-seeded dwarf berry rendering itself in dry flat two dimensional detail, like background foliage by one of the crazier Victorian painters, just before the invention of the camera; and at some time during that hour, though not for the whole hour, I forgot what things were called and saw instead what they are.

1983

The Resplendent Quetzal

Sarah was sitting near the edge of the sacrificial well. She had imagined something smaller, more like a wishing well, but this was huge, and the water at the bottom wasn't clear at all. It was mud-brown; a few clumps of reeds were growing over to one side, and the trees at the top dangled their roots, or were they vines, down the limestone walls into the water. Sarah thought there might be some point to being a sacrificial victim if the well were nicer, but you would never get her to jump into a muddy hole like that. They were probably pushed, or knocked on the head and thrown in. According to the guidebook the water was deep but it looked more like a swamp to her.

Beside her a group of tourists was being rounded up by the guide, who obviously wanted to get the whole thing over with so he could cram them back onto their pink and purple striped *turismo* bus and relax. These were Mexican tourists, and Sarah found it reassuring that other people besides Canadians and Americans wore big hats and sunglasses and took pictures of everything. She wished she and Edward could make these excursions at a less crowded time of year, if they had to make them at all, but because of Edward's teaching job they were limited to school holidays. Christmas was the worst. It would be the same even if he had a different job and they had children, though; but they didn't have any.

The guide shooed his charges back along the gravel path as if they were chickens, which was what they sounded like. He himself lingered beside Sarah, finishing his cigarette, one foot on a stone block, like a conquistador. He was a small dark man with several gold teeth, which glinted when he smiled. He was smiling at Sarah now, sideways, and she smiled back serenely. She liked it when these men smiled at her or even when they made those juicy sucking noises with their mouths as they walked behind her on the street; so long as they didn't touch. Edward pretended not to hear them. Perhaps they did it so much because she was blonde: blondes were rare here. She didn't think of herself as beautiful, exactly; the word she had chosen for herself some time ago was 'comely'. Comely to look upon. You would never use that word for a thin woman.

The guide tossed his cigarette butt into the sacrificial well and turned to follow his flock. Sarah forgot about him immediately. She'd felt something crawling up her leg, but when she looked nothing was there. She tucked the full skirt of her cotton dress in under her thighs and clamped it between her knees. This was the kind of place you could get flea bites, places with dirt on the ground, where people sat. Parks and bus terminals. But she didn't care, her feet were tired and the sun was hot. She would rather sit in the shade and get bitten than rush around trying to see everything, which was what Edward wanted to do. Luckily the bites didn't swell up on her the way they did on Edward.

Edward was back along the path, out of sight among the bushes, peering around with his new Leitz binoculars. He didn't like sitting down, it made him restless. On these trips it was difficult for Sarah to sit by herself and just think. Her own binoculars, which were Edward's old ones, dangled around her neck; they weighed a ton. She took them off and put them into her purse.

His passion for birds had been one of the first things Edward had confided to her. Shyly, as if it had been some precious gift, he'd shown her the lined notebook he'd started keeping when he was nine, with its awkward, boyish printing—*Robin, Bluejay, Kingfisher*—and the day and the year recorded beside each name. She'd pretended to be touched and interested, and in fact she had been. She herself didn't have compulsions of this kind; whereas Edward plunged totally into things, as if they were oceans. For a while it was stamps; then he took up playing the flute and nearly drove her crazy with the practising. Now it was pre-Columbian ruins, and he was determined to climb up every heap of old stones he could get his hands on. A capacity for dedication, she guessed you would call it. At first Edward's obsessions had fascinated her, since she didn't understand them, but now they merely made her tired. Sooner or later he'd dropped them all anyway, just as he began to get really good or really knowledgeable; all but the birds. That had remained constant. She herself, she thought, had once been one of his obsessions.

It wouldn't be so bad if he didn't insist on dragging her into everything. Or rather, he had once insisted; he no longer did. And she had encouraged him, she'd let him think she shared or at least indulged his interests. She was becoming less indulgent as she grew older. The waste of energy bothered her, because it was a waste, he never stuck with anything, and what use was his encyclopaedic knowledge of birds? It would be different if they had enough money, but they were always running short. If only he would take all that energy and do something productive with it, in his job for instance. He could be a principal if he wanted to, she kept telling him that. But he wasn't interested, he was content to poke along doing the same thing year after year. His Grade Six children adored him, the boys especially. Perhaps it was because they sensed he was a lot like them.

He'd started asking her to go birding, as he called it, shortly after they'd met, and of course she had gone. It would have been an error to refuse. She hadn't complained, then, about her sore feet or standing in the rain under the dripping bushes trying to keep track of some nondescript sparrow, while Edward thumbed through his *Peterson's Field Guide* as if it were the Bible or the bird was the Holy Grail. She'd even become quite good at it. Edward was nearsighted, and she was quicker at spotting movement than he was. With his usual generosity he acknowledged this, and she'd fallen into the habit of using it when she wanted to get rid of him for a while. Just now, for instance.

'There's something over there.' She'd pointed across the well to the tangle of greenery on the other side.

'Where?' Edward had squinted eagerly and raised his binoculars. He looked a little like a bird himself, she thought, with his long nose and stilt legs.

'That thing there, sitting in that thing, the one with the tufts. The sort of bean tree. It's got orange on it.'

Edward focused. 'An oriole?'

'I can't tell from here. . . . Oh, it just flew.' She pointed over their heads while Edward swept the sky in vain.

'I think it lit back there, behind us.'

That was enough to send him off. She had to do this with enough real birds to keep him believing, however.

Edward sat down on the root of a tree and lit a cigarette. He had gone down the first side-path he'd come to; it smelled of piss, and he could see by the decomposing Kleenexes further along that this was one of the places people went when they couldn't make it back to the washroom behind the ticket counter.

He took off his glasses, then his hat, and wiped the sweat off his forehead. His face was red, he could feel it. Blushing, Sarah called it. She persisted in attributing it to shyness and boyish embarrassment; she hadn't yet deduced that it was simple rage. For someone so devious she was often incredibly stupid.

She didn't know, for instance, that he'd found out about her little trick with the birds at least three years ago. She'd pointed to a dead tree and said she saw a bird in it, but he himself had inspected that same tree only seconds earlier and there was nothing in it at all. And she was very careless: she described oriole-coloured birds behaving like kingbirds, woodpeckers where there would never be any woodpeckers, mute jays, neckless herons. She must have decided he was a total idiot and any slipshod invention would do.

But why not, since he appeared to fall for it every time. And why did he do it, why did he chase off after her imaginary birds, pretending he believed her? It was partly that although he knew what she was doing to him, he had no idea why. It couldn't be simple malice, she had enough outlets for that. He didn't want to know the real reason, which loomed in his mind as something formless, threatening and final. Her lie about the birds was one of the many lies that propped things up. He was afraid to confront her, that would be the end, all the pretences would come crashing down and they would be left standing in the rubble, staring at each other. There would be nothing left to say and Edward wasn't ready for that.

She would deny everything anyway. 'What do you mean? Of course I saw it. It flew right over there. Why would I make up such a thing?' With her level gaze, blonde and stolid and immovable as a rock.

Edward had a sudden image of himself, crashing out of the undergrowth like King Kong, picking Sarah up and hurling her over the edge, down into the sacrificial well. Anything to shatter that imperturbable expression, bland and pale and plump and smug, like a Flemish Madonna's. Self-righteous, that's what it was. Nothing was ever her fault. She hadn't been like that when he'd met her. But it wouldn't work: as she fell she would glance at him, not with fear but with maternal irritation, as if he'd spilled chocolate milk on a white tablecloth. And she'd pull her skirt down. She was concerned for appearances, always.

Though there would be something inappropriate about throwing Sarah into the sacrificial well, just as she was, with all her clothes on. He remembered snatches from the several books he'd read before they came down. (And that was another thing: Sarah didn't believe in reading up on places beforehand. 'Don't you want to understand what you're looking at?' he'd asked her. 'I'll see the same thing in any case, won't I?' she said. 'I mean, knowing all those facts doesn't change the actual statue or whatever.' Edward found this attitude infuriating; and now that they were here, she resisted his attempts to explain things to her by her usual passive method of pretending not to hear.

'That's a Chac-Mool,[1] see that? That round thing on the stomach held the bowl where they put the hearts, and the butterfly on the head means the soul flying up to the sun.'

'Could you get out the suntan lotion, Edward. I think it's in the tote bag, in the left-hand pocket.'

And he would hand her the suntan lotion, defeated once again.)

No, she wouldn't be a fit sacrifice, with or without lotion. They only threw people in—or perhaps they jumped in, of their own free will—for the water god, to make it rain and ensure fertility. The drowned were messengers, sent to carry requests to the god. Sarah would have to be purified first, in the stone sweathouse beside the well. Then, naked, she would kneel before him, one arm across her breast in the attitude of submission. He added some ornaments: a gold necklace with a jade medallion, a gold circlet adorned with feathers. Her hair, which she usually wore in a braid coiled at the back of her head, would be hanging down. He thought of her body, which he made slimmer and more taut, with an abstract desire which was as unrelated as he could make it to Sarah herself. This was the only kind of desire he could feel for her any more: he had to dress her up before he could make love to her at all. He thought about their earlier days, before they'd married. It was almost as if he'd had an affair with another woman,

---

[1] A statute of Toltec origin, a reclining figure with a shallow dish for offerings on its stomach. The various details of the setting suggest that the story takes place at Chichén-Itzá in Yucatan.

she had been so different. He'd treated her body then as something holy, a white and gold chalice, to be touched with care and tenderness. And she had liked this; even though she was two years older than he was and much more experienced she hadn't minded his awkwardness and reverence, she hadn't laughed at him. Why had she changed?

Sometimes he thought it was the baby, which had died at birth. At the time he'd urged her to have another right away, and she'd said yes, but nothing had happened. It wasn't something they talked about. 'Well, that's that,' she said in the hospital afterwards. A perfect child, the doctor said; a freak accident, one of those things that happen. She'd never gone back to university either and she wouldn't get a job. She sat at home, tidying the apartment, looking over his shoulder, towards the door, out the window, as if she was waiting for something.

Sarah bowed her head before him. He, in the feathered costume and long-nosed, toothed mask of the high priest, sprinkled her with blood drawn with thorns from his own tongue and penis. Now he was supposed to give her the message to take to the god. But he couldn't think of anything he wanted to ask for.

And at the same time he thought: what a terrific idea for a Grade Six special project! He'd have them build scale models of the temples, he'd show the slides he'd taken, he'd bring in canned tortillas and tamales for a Mexican lunch, he'd have them make little Chac-Mools out of papier-mâché . . . and the ball game where the captain of the losing team had his head cut off, that would appeal to them, they were blood-thirsty at that age. He could see himself up there in front of them, pouring out his own enthusiasm, gesturing, posturing, acting it out for them, and their response. . . . Yet afterwards he knew he would be depressed. What were his special projects anyway but a substitute for television, something to keep them entertained? They liked him because he danced for them, a funny puppet, inexhaustible and a little absurd. No wonder Sarah despised him.

Edward stepped on the remains of his cigarette. He put his hat back on, a wide-brimmed white hat Sarah had bought for him at the market. He had wanted one with a narrower brim, so he could look up through his binoculars without the hat getting in his way; but she'd told him he would look like an American golfer. It was always there, that gentle, patronizing mockery.

He would wait long enough to be plausible; then he would go back.

Sarah was speculating about how she would be doing this whole trip if Edward had conveniently died. It wasn't that she wished him dead, but she couldn't imagine any other way for him to disappear. He was omnipresent, he pervaded her life like a kind of smell; it was hard for her to think or act except in reference to him. So she found it harmless and pleasant to walk herself through the same itinerary they were following now, but with Edward removed, cut neatly out of the picture. Not that she would be here at all if it wasn't for him. She would prefer to lie in a deck chair in, say, Acapulco, and drink cooling drinks. She threw in a few dark young men in bathing suits, but took them out: that would be too complicated and not relaxing. She had often thought about cheating on Ed-ward—somehow it would serve him right, though she wasn't sure what for—but she had never actually done it. She didn't know anyone suitable, any more.

Suppose she was here, then, with no Edward. She would stay at a better hotel, for one thing. One that had a plug in the sink; they had not yet stayed in a hotel with a plug. Of course that would cost more money, but she thought of herself as having more money if Edward were dead: she would have all of his salary instead of just part of it. She knew there wouldn't be any salary if he really were dead, but it spoiled the fantasy to remember this. And she would travel on planes, if possible, or first-class buses, instead of the noisy, crowded second-class ones he insisted on taking. He said you saw more of the local colour that way and there was no point going to another country if you spent all your time with other tourists. In theory she agreed with this, but the buses gave her headaches and she could do without the closeup tour of squalor, the miserable thatched or tin-roofed huts, the turkeys and tethered pigs.

He applied the same logic to restaurants. There was a perfectly nice one in the village where they were staying, she'd seen it from the bus and it didn't look that expensive; but no, they had to eat in a seedy linoleum-tiled hutch, with plastic-covered tablecloths. They were the only customers in the place. Behind them four adolescent boys were playing dominoes and drinking beer, with a lot of annoying laughter, and some smaller children watched television, a program that Sarah realized was a re-run of *The Cisco Kid*,[2] with dubbed voices.

On the bar beside the television set there was a crêche, with three painted plaster Wise Men, one on an elephant, the others on camels. The first Wise Man was missing his head. Inside the stable a stunted Joseph and Mary adored an enormous Christ Child which was more than half as big as the elephant. Sarah wondered how the Mary could possibly have squeezed out this colossus; it made her uncomfortable to think about it. Beside the crêche was a Santa Claus haloed with flashing lights, and beside that a radio in the shape of Fred Flintstone, which was playing American popular songs, all of them ancient.

'*Oh someone help me, help me, plee-ee-ee-eeze . . .*'

'Isn't that Paul Anka?' Sarah asked.

But this wasn't the sort of thing Edward could be expected to know. He launched into a defence of the food, the best he'd had in Mexico, he said. Sarah refused to give him the consolation of her agreement. She found the restaurant even more depressing than it should have been, especially the crêche. It was painful, like a cripple trying to walk, one of the last spastic gestures of a religion no one, surely, could believe in much longer.

Another group of tourists was coming up the path behind her, Americans by the sound of them. The guide was Mexican, though. He scrambled up onto the altar, preparing to give his spiel.

'Don't go too near the edge, now.'

'Who me, I'm afraid of heights. What d'you see down there?'

'Water, what am I supposed to see?'

The guide clapped his hands for attention. Sarah only half-listened: she didn't really want to know anything more about it.

'Before, people said they threw nothing but virgins in here,' the guide began.

[2] An American western TV series (1951-6) that had the unusual feature of a cowboy hero and his companion who were Mexican-Americans, albeit stereotypes.

'How they could tell that, I do not know. It is always hard to tell.' He waited for the expected laughter, which came. 'But this is not true. Soon, I will tell you how we have found this out. Here we have the altar to the rain god Tlaloc . . .'

Two women sat down near Sarah. They were both wearing cotton slacks, high-heeled sandals and wide-brimmed straw hats.

'You go up the big one?'

'Not on your life. I made Alf go up, I took a picture of him at the top.'

'What beats me is why they built all those things in the first place.'

'It was their religion, that's what he said.'

'Well, at least it would keep people busy.'

'Solve the unemployment problem.' They both laughed.

'How many more of these ruins is he gonna make us walk around?'

'Beats me. I'm about ruined out. I'd rather go back and sit on the bus.'

'I'd rather go shopping. Not that there's much to buy.'

Sarah, listening, suddenly felt indignant. Did they have no respect? The sentiments weren't that far from her own of a moment ago, but to hear them from these women, one of whom had a handbag decorated with tasteless straw flowers, made her want to defend the well.

'Nature is very definitely calling,' said the woman with the handbag. 'I couldn't get in before, there was such a lineup.'

'Take a Kleenex,' the other woman said. 'There's no paper. Not only that, you just about have to wade in. There's water all over the floor.'

'Maybe I'll just duck into the bushes,' the first woman said.

Edward stood up and massaged his left leg, which had gone to sleep. It was time to go back. If he stayed away too long, Sarah would be querulous, despite the fact that it was she herself who had sent him off on this fool's expedition.

He started to walk back along the path. But then there was a flash of orange, at the corner of his eye. Edward swivelled and raised his binoculars. They were there when you least expected it. It was an oriole, partly hidden behind the leaves; he could see the breast, bright orange, and the dark barred wing. He wanted it to be a Hooded Oriole, he had not yet seen one. He talked to it silently, begging it to come out into the open. It was strange the way birds were completely magic for him the first time only, when he had never seen them before. But there were hundreds of kinds he would never see; no matter how many he saw there would always be one more. Perhaps this was why he kept looking. The bird was hopping further away from him, into the foliage. *Come back,* he called to it wordlessly, but it was gone.

Edward was suddenly happy. Maybe Sarah hadn't been lying to him after all, maybe she had really seen this bird. Even if she hadn't, it had come anyway, in answer to his need for it. Edward felt he was allowed to see birds only when they wanted him to, as if they had something to tell him, a secret, a message. The Aztecs thought hummingbirds were the souls of dead warriors, but why not all birds, why just warriors? Or perhaps they were the souls of the unborn, as some believed. 'A jewel, a precious feather,' they called an unborn baby, according to *The Daily Life of the Aztecs. Quetzal,* that was *feather*.

'This is the bird I want to see,' Sarah said when they were looking through *The*

Birds of Mexico before coming down.

'The Resplendent Quetzal,' Edward said. It was a green and red bird with spectacular iridescent blue tail plumes. He explained to her that Quetzal Bird meant Feather Bird. 'I don't think we're likely to see it,' he said. He looked up the habitat. ' *"Cloud forests."* I don't think we'll be in any cloud forests.'

'Well, that's the one I want,' Sarah said. 'That's the only one I want.'

Sarah was always very determined about what she wanted and what she didn't want. If there wasn't anything on a restaurant menu that appealed to her, she would refuse to order anything; or she would permit him to order for her and then pick around the edges, as she had last night. It was no use telling her that this was the best meal they'd had since coming. She never lost her temper or her self-possession, but she was stubborn. Who but Sarah for instance would have insisted on bringing a collapsible umbrella to Mexico in the dry season? He'd argued and argued, pointing out its uselessness and the extra weight, but she'd brought it anyway. And then yesterday afternoon it had rained, a real cloudburst. Everyone else had run for shelter, huddling against walls and inside the temple doorways, but Sarah had put up her umbrella and stood under it, smugly. This had infuriated him. Even when she was wrong, she always managed, somehow, to be right. If only just once she would admit . . . what? That she could make mistakes. This was what really disturbed him: her assumption of infallibility.

And he knew that when the baby had died she had blamed it on him. He still didn't know why. Perhaps it was because he'd gone out for cigarettes, not expecting it to be born so soon. He wasn't there when she was told; she'd had to take the news alone.

'It was nobody's fault,' he told her repeatedly. 'Not the doctor's, not yours. The cord was twisted.'

'I know,' she said, and she had never accused him; nevertheless he could feel the reproach, hanging around her like a fog. As if there was anything he could have done.

'I wanted it as much as you did,' he told her. And this was true. He hadn't thought of marrying Sarah at all, he'd never mentioned it because it had never occurred to him she would agree, until she told him she was pregnant. Up until that time, she had been the one in control; he was sure he was just an amusement for her. But the marriage hadn't been her suggestion, it had been his. He'd dropped out of Theology, he'd taken his public-school teaching certificate that summer in order to support them. Every evening he had massaged her belly, feeling the child move, touching it through her skin. To him it was a sacred thing, and he included her in his worship. In the sixth month, when she had taken to lying on her back, she had begun to snore, and he would lie awake at night listening to these gentle snores, white and silver they seemed to him, almost songs, mysterious talismans. . . . Unfortunately Sarah had retained this habit, but he no longer felt the same way about it.

When the child had died, he was the one who had cried, not Sarah. She had never cried. She got up and walked around almost immediately, she wanted to get out of the hospital as quickly as possible. The baby clothes she'd been buying disappeared from the apartment; he never found out what she'd done with them, he'd been afraid to ask.

Since that time he'd come to wonder why they were still married. It was illogical. If they'd married because of the child and there was no child, and there continued to be no child, why didn't they separate? But he wasn't sure he wanted this. Maybe he was still hoping something would happen, there would be another child. But there was no use demanding it. They came when they wanted to, not when you wanted them to. They came when you least expected it. A jewel, a precious feather.

'Now I will tell you,' said the guide. 'The archaeologists have dived down into the well. They have dredged up more than fifty skeletons, and they have found that some of them were not virgins at all but men. Also, most of them were children. So as you can see, that is the end of the popular legend.' He made an odd little movement from the top of the altar, almost like a bow, but there was no applause. 'They do not do these things to be cruel,' he continued. 'They believe these people will take a message to the rain god, and live forever in his paradise at the bottom of the well.'

The woman with the handbag got up. 'Some paradise,' she said to her friend. 'I'm starting back. You coming?'

In fact the whole group was moving off now, in the scattered way they had. Sarah waited until they had gone. Then she opened her purse and took out the plaster Christ Child she had stolen from the crèche the night before. It was inconceivable to her that she had done such a thing, but there it was, she really had.

She hadn't planned it beforehand. She'd been standing beside the crèche while Edward was paying the bill, he'd had to go into the kitchen to do it as they were very slow about bringing it to the table. No one was watching her: the domino-playing boys were absorbed in their game and the children were riveted to the television. She'd just suddenly reached out her hand, past the Wise Men and through the door of the stable, picked the child up and put it into her purse.

She turned it over in her hands. Separated from the dwarfish Virgin and Joseph, it didn't look quite so absurd. Its diaper was cast as part of it, more like a tunic, it had glass eyes and a sort of page-boy haircut, quite long for a newborn. A perfect child, except for the chip out of the back, luckily where it would not be noticed. Someone must have dropped it on the floor.

You could never be too careful. All the time she was pregnant, she'd taken meticulous care of herself, counting out the vitamin pills prescribed by the doctor and eating only what the books recommended. She had drunk four glass of milk a day, even though she hated milk. She had done the exercises and gone to the classes. No one would be able to say she had not done the right things. Yet she had been disturbed by the thought that the child would be born with something wrong, it would be a mongoloid or a cripple, or a hydrocephalic with a huge liquid head like the ones she'd seen taking the sun in their wheelchairs on the lawn of the hospital one day. But the child had been perfect.

She would never take that risk, go through all that work again. Let Edward strain his pelvis till he was blue in the face; 'trying again,' he called it. She took the pill every day, without telling him. She wasn't going to try again. It was too much for anyone to expect of her.

What had she done wrong? She hadn't done anything wrong, that was the trouble. There was nothing and no one to blame, except, obscurely, Edward; and he couldn't be blamed for the child's death, just for not being there. Increasingly since that time he had simply absented himself. When she no longer had the child inside her he had lost interest, he had deserted her. This, she realized, was what she resented most about him. He had left her alone with the corpse, a corpse for which there was no explanation.

'*Lost*' people called it. They spoke of her as having lost the child, as though it was wandering around looking for her, crying plaintively, as though she had neglected it or misplaced it somewhere. But where? What limbo had it gone to, what watery paradise? Sometimes she felt as if there had been some mistake, the child had not been born yet. She could still feel it moving, ever so slightly, holding on to her from the inside.

Sarah placed the baby on the rock beside her. She stood up, smoothing out the wrinkles in her skirt. She was sure there would be more flea bites when she got back to the hotel. She picked up the child and walked slowly towards the well, until she was standing at the very brink.

Edward, coming back up the path, saw Sarah at the well's edge, her arms raised above her head. *My God,* he thought, *she's going to jump.* He wanted to shout to her, tell her to stop, but he was afraid to startle her. He could run up behind her, grab her . . . but she would hear him. So he waited, paralyzed, while Sarah stood immobile. He expected her to hurtle downwards, and then what would he do? But she merely drew back her right arm and threw something into the well. Then she turned, half stumbling, towards the rock where he had left her and crouched down.

'Sarah,' he said. She had her hands over her face; she didn't lift them. He kneeled so he was level with her. 'What is it? Are you sick?'

She shook her head. She seemed to be crying, behind her hands, soundlessly and without moving. Edward was dismayed. The ordinary Sarah, with all her perversity, was something he could cope with, he'd invented ways of coping. But he was unprepared for this. She had always been the one in control.

'Come on,' he said, trying to disguise his desperation, 'you need some lunch, you'll feel better.' He realized as he said this how fatuous it must sound, but for once there was no patronizing smile, no indulgent answer.

'This isn't like you,' Edward said, pleading, as if that was a final argument which would snap her out of it, bring back the old calm Sarah.

Sarah took her hands away from her face, and as she did so Edward felt cold fear. Surely what he would see would be the face of someone else, someone entirely different, a woman he had never seen before in his life. Or there would be no face at all. But (and this was almost worse) it was only Sarah, looking much as she always did.

She took a Kleenex out of her purse and wiped her nose. *It is like me,* she thought. She stood up and smoothed her skirt once more, then collected her purse and her collapsible umbrella.

'I'd like an orange,' she said. 'They have them, across from the ticket office. I saw them when we came in. Did you find your bird?'

1977

Patrick Lane

b. 1939

Born in Nelson, B.C., Pat Lane grew up in the British Columbia interior, near Vernon, and has remained a resident of western Canada most of his life. After high school he began to travel extensively through North and South America, working at such manual jobs as logger and miner. (His time in Latin America provided him with material for many of his poems.) He began to write poetry in his early twenties, around the time of the death of his brother, the *Tish* poet Red Lane (whose collected work he later edited). In 1966 he helped found, with poets bill bissett and Seymour Mayne, Very Stone House, a small press that was later called Very Stone House in Transit (1971-80), an allusion to Lane's moving from place to place. This press brought out his first book, *Letters From the Savage Mind* (1966). Since then he has written a number of broadsheets, pamphlets, and books of poetry, among which are *Beware the Months of Fire* (1974); *Unborn Things* (1975); *Albino Pheasants* (1977); *Poems, New and Selected* (1978), which won a Governor General's Award; *No Longer Two People* (1979), written with Lorna Uher; *The Measure* (1980); and *Old Mother* (1982). Since 1976 he has taught creative writing, or been a writer-in-residence, at the University of Notre Dame at Nelson, and the Universities of Manitoba, Ottawa, and Alberta. He now lives in Regina.

Much of Pat Lane's poetry is anecdotal narrative, usually depicting the incidents in the life of the poor and the working class in western Canada and South America, a life in which cruelty and sadism are commonplace. Extremes of violence, Lane suggests, characterize man's behaviour as much as that of the lower animals, and animals in his poetry—whether predators or prey—are frequently emblematic of man. Birds, in particular, appear as objects of man's mindless aggression, as victims of a predatory universe, or as symbols of human vulnerability. Lane's is a vision of a capricious universe in which life and death are ceaselessly transformed into one another, and no one can long remain with hands unbloodied.

This view of linked creation and destruction (which recalls the Indian trickster *mythos* investigated by other western writers such as Robert Kroetsch and Sheila Watson) is developed by a violently beautiful lyricism, balanced precariously between the sensual and the sensational, that shocks the reader out of complacency. Lane, like the existentialists before him, sees the individual as living intensely only in the face of danger and death. Because of this his poetry is often an affirmation of destruction: by bringing such moments of intensity to his readers, he forces them to confront their own values and ways of life.

Poetry for Lane provides catharsis not only for the reader but for the poet himself, whom he sees as an outlaw, escaping the restraints of society for the bondage of art: *He is the outlaw surging beyond the only freedom he knows, beauty in bondage, and so spins towards the margins of his experience like a rotting apple at the end of a string being swung in the hands of a satyr, and the locus of that spinning is* the word surrounded and permeated with desire and feeling. ('To the Outlaw', *New: American and Canadian Poetry*, no. 15, 1971).

Because I Never Learned

For John

Because I never learned how
to be gentle and the country
I lived in was hard with dead
animals and men I didn't question
my father when he told me
to step on the kitten's head
after the bus had run over
its hind quarters.

Now, twenty years later,
I remember only: 10
the silence of the dying
when the fragile skull collapsed
under my hard bare heel,
the curved tongue in the dust
that would never cry again
and the small of my father's back
as he walked tall away.

1974

Unborn Things

After the dog drowns in the arroyo[1]
and the old people stumble into the jungle
muttering imprecations at the birds
and the child draws circles in the dust
for bits of glass to occupy
like eyes staring out of earth
and the woman lies on her hammock
dreaming of the lover who will save her
from the need to make bread again
I will go into the field   10
and be buried with corn.

Folding my hands on my chest
I will see the shadow of myself; the same
who watched a father when he moved
with hands on the dark side of a candle
create the birds and beasts of dreams.

One with unborn things
I will open my body to the earth

[1] Creek.

and watch worms reach like pink roots
as I turn slowly tongue to stone   20
and speak of the beginning of seeds
as they struggle in the earth;
pale things moving toward the sun
that feel the feet of men above,
the tread of their marching
thudding into my earth.

1975

The Hustler

In a rainbow bus we begin to descend
a gorge that gapes open like a wound.
The women, who chattered like black beans
in a dry gourd, cover their faces and moan
while the men, not wanting to admit the fear
that turns their knuckles white,
light cigarettes and squint their eyes.

The air fills with hands making crosses.
I make the sign of the cross
with a small grey woman   10
but she doesn't see me. She has no time
for a gringo when the manifold sins
of a lifetime must be confessed.
Her eyes are buried in the hole
three thousand feet below.

The driver stops the bus, adjusts
the plastic Jesus that obscures
half of his windshield and his eyes—
gets out and stands beside each tire
shaking his head. His face is a scowl   20
of despair. He kicks each tire in turn,
opens the hood and pounds the carburetor
then gets back on the bus
and crosses himself slowly as the women
begin to weep and children scream.

He mutters two *Pater Nosters*
and a dozen *Ave Marias* as he walks
through the bus with hat extended
to the people who fill it with coins.
He smiles then, bravely, as if the world   30
had been lifted from his shoulders
and like the thief that Christ forgave[1]

[1]On the cross Christ forgave one of the men, a thief, with whom he was being crucified (Luke 23:39-43).

walks out the broken doors to a roadside shrine
and empties his hat into the hands of a Mary
whose expression of humility
hasn't changed in a hundred years.

The people sigh and consign their souls to God
and I relax because I saw him as he knelt there
cross his hands on his crotch as if
he were imploring the Mother of God's help   40
in preserving his manhood on the road to Hell
and pour the collected sucres² in his pocket
the price of safety embodied in the vulture
who lifted off her beatific head,
the men shushing their children grandly
and me, peeling a banana and eating,
gazing into the endless abyss.

1975

²Coins; the basic monetary unit of Ecuador.

The Children of Bogota

The first thing to understand, Manuel says,
is that they're not children. Don't start feeling
sorry for them. There are five thousand
roaming the streets of this city

and just because they look innocent
doesn't make them human. Any one
would kill you for the price of a meal.
Children? See those two in the gutter

behind that stall? I saw them put out
the eyes of a dog with thorns because   10
it barked at them. Tomorrow it could be you.
No one knows where they come from

but you can be sure they're not going.
In five years they'll be men and tired of killing
dogs. And when that happens you'll be the first
to cheer when the carabineros¹ shoot them down.

1975

¹Riflemen; soldiers.

At the Edge of the Jungle

At the edge of the jungle
I watch a dog bury his head
in the mud of the Amazon
to drive away the hovering
mass of flies around his eyes.
The swarm expands like a lung
and settles again on the wound.

I turn to where orchids gape
like the vulvas of hanged women.
Everything is a madness: 10
a broken melon bleeds a pestilence
of bees; a woman squats and pees
balancing perfectly her basket
of meat; a gelding falls to its knees
under the goad of its driver.

Images catch at my skull like thorns.
I no longer believe
the sight I have been given
and live inside the eyes of a rooster
who walks around a pile of broken bones.   20
Children have cut away his beak
and with a string have staked him
where he sees but cannot eat.

Diseased clouds bloom in the sky.
They throw down roots of fire.
The bird drags sound from its skin.
I am grown older than I imagined:
the garden I dreamed does not exist
and compassion is only the beginning
of suffering. Everything deceives.   30

A man could walk into this jungle
and lying down be lost
among the green sucking of trees.
What reality there is resides
in the child who holds the string
and does not see
the bird as it beats its blunt head
again and again into the earth.

1975

Albino Pheasants

At the bottom of the field
where thistles throw their seeds
and poplars grow from cotton[1] into trees
in a single season I stand among the weeds.
Fenceposts hold each other up with sagging wire.
Here no man walks except in wasted time.
Men circle me with cattle, cars and wheat.
Machines rot on my margins.
They say the land is wasted when it's wild
and offer plows and apple trees to tame   10
but in the fall when I have driven them away
with their guns and dogs and dreams
I walk alone. While those who'd kill
lie sleeping in soft beds
huddled against the bodies of their wives
I go with speargrass and hooked burrs
and wait upon the ice alone.

Delicate across the mesh of snow
I watch the pale birds come
with beaks the colour of discarded flesh.   20
White, their feathers are white,
as if they had been born in caves
and only now have risen to the earth
to watch with pink and darting eyes
the slowly moving shadows of the moon.
There is no way to tell men what we do . . .
the dance they make in sleep
withholds its meaning from their dreams.
That which has been nursed in bone
rests easy upon frozen stone   30
and what is wild is lost behind closed eyes:
albino birds, pale sisters, succubi.[2]

1977

[1]i.e. the downy poplar seeds.
[2]Female demons who descend upon and have sexual intercourse with men while they sleep.

Stigmata[1]

For Irving Layton[2]

What if there wasn't a metaphor
and the bodies were only bodies
bones pushed out in awkward fingers?
Waves come to the seawall, fall away,
children bounce mouths against the stones
that man has carved to keep the sea at bay
and women walk with empty wombs
proclaiming freedom to the night.
Through barroom windows rotten with light
eyes of men open and close like fists.   10

I bend beside a tidal pool and take a crab from the sea.
His small green life twists helpless in my hand
the living bars of bone and flesh
a cage made by the animal I am.
This thing, the beat, the beat of life
now captured in the darkness of my flesh
struggling with claws as if it could tear its way
through my body back to the sea.
What do I know of the inexorable beauty,
the unrelenting turning of the wheel I am inside me?   20
Stigmata. I hold a web of blood.

I dream of the scrimshawed[3] teeth of endless whales,
the oceans it took to carve them. Drifting ships
echo in fog the wounds of Leviathan[4]
great grey voices giving cadence to their loss.
The men are gone
who scratched upon white bones their destiny.
Who will speak of the albatross in the shroud of the man,
the sailor who sinks forever in the Mindanao Deep?[5]
I open my hand. The life leaps out.   30

1977

---

[1]Marks corresponding to the crucifixion wounds of Christ.
[2]See Vol. I, pp. 566-82; compare particularly 'Butterfly on Rock' (where the poet crushes the butterfly under his hand) with the conclusion to this poem.
[3]Intricately carved; scrimshaw is usually made from whale ivory, bone, or shells.
[4]Biblical sea monster; a whale.
[5]Deepest point in the oceans.

The Witnesses

To know as the word is known, to know little
or less than little, nothing, to contemplate
the setting sun and sit for hours, the world
turning you into the sun as day begins again

To remember words, to remember nothing
but words and make out of nothing the past,
to remember my father, the McLeod Kid
carrying the beat, riding against time

On the rodeo circuit of fifty years ago
the prairie, stretched wet hide   10
scraped by a knife, disappearing everywhere
to know the McLeod Kid was defeated

To know these things
to climb into the confusions
which are only words, to climb into desire
to ride in the sun, to ride against time

The McLeod Kid raking his spurs on the mare
the cheers from the wagon-backs
where the people sit to watch the local
boy ride against the riders from Calgary   20

To spit melon seeds into the dust
to roll cigarettes, to leave them hanging
from the lip, to tip your hat back and grin
to laugh or not laugh, to climb into darkness

Below the stands and touch Erla's breast
to eat corn or melons, to roll cigarettes
to drink beer, bottles hidden in paper bags
to grin at the RCMP, horseless, dust on their boots

To watch or not watch, to surround the spectacle
horses asleep in their harness, tails switching   30
bees swarming on melon rinds, flys buzzing
and what if my words are their voices

What if I try to capture an ecstasy that is not
mine, what if these are only words saying
this was or this was not, a story told to me
until I now no longer believe it was told to me

The witnesses dead, what if I create a past
that never was, make out of nothing
a history of my people whether in pain
or ecstasy, my father riding in the McLeod Rodeo   40

The hours before dawn when in the last of darkness
I make out of nothing a man riding against time
and thus my agony, the mare twisted sideways
muscles bunched in knots beneath her hide

Her mane, black hair feathered in the wind
that I believe I see, caked mud in her eyes
the breath broken from her body and the McLeod Kid
in the air, falling, the clock stopped.

1978

Thinking on that Contest

Thinking on that contest women do
with clothespins in the country
having to hold all the pins in one hand
and they could do it
with hands trained by diapers
and blue workshirts in winter
hand-soaping in a steel tub

as if it was a measure of survival
like an axe falling in a far valley
where sound comes late to you   10
or not at all
they having learned it in harder times
cursing the cold
clothes hanging frozen to the line
for days going on days
bringing them in piecemeal
to hang over the fire
and let them melt there
reassuming the shape of a man
in time for him to shrug into   20
before going down to the graveyard
shift at the mines

thinking on that time of trouble
turned into a game
how struggle roots itself in ritual
hands full of clothespins
leaning into wind
never dropping a pin into the snow below

1978

A Murder[1] of Crows

It is night and somewhere
a tree has fallen across the lines.
There was a time when I would have slept
at the end of the sun and risen with light.
My body knows what I betray.
Even the candle fails, its guttering stub
spitting out the flame. I have struggled
tonight with the poem as never before
wanting to tell you what I know—
what can be said? Words are dark rainbows   10
without roots, a murder of crows,
a memory of music reduced to guile.
Innocence, old nightmare, drags behind
me like a shadow and today I killed again.

The body hanging down from its tripod.
My knife slid up and steaming ribbons of gut
fell to the ground. I broke the legs
and cut the anus out, stripped off the skin
and chopped the head away; maggots of fat
clinging to the pale red flesh. The death?   20
If I could tell you the silence
when the body refused to fall
until it seemed the ground reached up
and pulled it down. Then I could tell you
everything: what the grass said
to the crows as they passed over,
the eyes of moss, the histories of stone.

It is night and somewhere
a tree has fallen across the lines.
Everything I love has gone to sleep.   30
What can be said?
The flesh consumes while in the trees
black birds perch waiting first light.
It is night and mountains
and I cannot tell you what the grass said
to the crows as they passed over
can only say how when I looked
I lost their bodies in the sun.

1978

[1] A collective term for a group of crows.

CPR Station—Winnipeg

You sit and your hands are folded in
upon you. The coffee is bleak, black. This
catacomb is lighted with the pale death
our fathers called marble in their pride.
This is an old song. This country.

This country was still a hope.
It is the CPR Station in Winnipeg.
It is 11:30 and no one is leaving again.
The trains are late. The passengers wait
for the passing freight of the nation.   10

The people have turned to stone, cannot be
moved. The coffee is bleak. The night is far
above us. Steel passes over in the rumbling
called destinations. The gates are dark.
There is no passing here.

There is no desire to pass. Someone with
a lantern hesitates and moves on.
The river of white marble swirls cold
beneath us. It is worn, worn by the feet
of a nation. Your heavy hands. Your   20

fingers are huge, swollen with the
freight of years. This country has
travelled through you. The man with the
lantern sits in the far corner, waiting.
If you could lift your head I could go

out into the night with grace. O hell,
you are old. Winter is above us. Steel
wheels. If you could lift your head.
Bleak black. White marble.
And the trains, the trains pass over.   30

1980

The Long Coyote Line

For Andy Suknaski

The long coyote line crosses the pure
white and the prairie is divided
again by hunger. The snowshoe hare
thin as January creates a running
circle encompassing a moon of snow
as the lean lope of the coyote
cuts in a curving radius
bringing escape down to a single terror.
It is the long line, coyote, and the man
who stands in your small disturbance   10
counting the crystals of blood and bone:
three by three, coyote, hare and the howl
where the true prairie begins.

1980

Weasel

Thin as death,
the dark brown weasel slides
like smoke through night's hard silence.
The worlds of the small are still. He glides
beneath the chicken house. Bird life
above him sleeps in feathers as he creeps
among the stones, small nose testing every board
for opening, a hole small as an eye, a fallen knot,
a crack where time has broken through.
His sharp teeth chatter.   10
Again and again he quests the darkness
below the sleeping birds. A mouse freezes,
small mouth caught by silence in the wood.
His life is quick. He slips into his hole.
Thin as death, the dark brown weasel slides
like smoke. His needles worry wood.
The night is long.
Above him bird blood beats.

1982

Dennis Lee

b. 1939

Dennis Beynon Lee has been shaped by Toronto: born in that city, raised in suburban Etobicoke, educated at the University of Toronto Schools and at Victoria College, University of Toronto (B.A., 1962; M.A., 1965), he continues to make it his home. In 1967, with Dave Godfrey, Lee founded the House of Anansi Press, which became the nucleus of a group of young writers, including Margaret Atwood, Matt Cohen, Graeme Gibson, and Michael Ondaatje. Lee is an influential editor who, since leaving the directorship of Anansi in 1972, has continued to work with Canadian publishers, first Macmillan and now McClelland and Stewart. A teacher as well as an editor, Lee has been an instructor at Victoria College, Rochdale College (a short-lived educational collective that Lee helped found), and York University. He has also been writer-in-residence at Trent University, the University of Toronto, and, on a special exchange fellowship, at the University of Edinburgh.

Since Lee's rather conventional first collection, *Kingdom of Absence* (1967), his poetry has developed in two apparently divergent directions: on the one hand he has written complex, often difficult meditations and social commentaries; and on the other he has become a popular author of children's verse. His second book, *Civil Elegies* (1968), is a sequence of poems that reflects his intense feelings about the public responsibilities of the individual; it was revised for *Civil Elegies and Other Poems* (1972), which won a Governor General's Award. In this poetry Lee begins an exploration of the multiple voices, public and private, that an individual assumes in life. He continues to experiment with a complex blend of authorial and narrative voices in

his next three long poems: *Not Abstract Harmonies But* (1974), *The Death of Harold Ladoo* (1976), and *The Gods* (1978). In 1979 these poems (substantially revised) were published in a single volume entitled *The Gods*. 'Riffs', his most recent long poem (published as part of *Tasks of Passion*, 1982, a book of essays by and about Lee) represents a new experiment with poetic voice, one that attempts to produce a literary equivalent of jazz variations.

Believing that Canadian children needed an indigenous and living poetry, Lee undertook the writing of 'kids' stuff' in the mid-sixties. His whimsical and zany children's verse has grown in popularity since the appearance of *Wiggle to the Laundromat* (1970) and *Alligator Pie* (1974). They were followed by *Nicholas Knock and Other People* (1974), *Garbage Delight* (1977), and *The Ordinary Bath* (1979). In 1983 he began writing song lyrics for the children's television program *Fraggle Rock*.

At the centre of Lee's work—as poet, children's writer, lyricist, essayist, educator, and editor—is a struggle with modernism. Lee is concerned not just with the modernist literary movement but with cultural modernism in general: the philosophical and technological developments that have radically altered twentieth-century living. He sees the shift from an unselfconscious way of life (in which ethics and belief were indivisible, and one always had a sense of belonging) to our contemporary, compartmentalized existence (in which complete relativity is the only absolute) as resulting in an erosion of faith in oneself and in what one perceives to be reality. As Lee suggests in poems such as *The Death of Harold Ladoo*, the individual finds himself in a kind of double bind. He can either erroneously accept his milieu as real, or attempt to define what makes it inauthentic—but to do the latter is also to acquiesce to the modernist environment, since for Lee the act of naming falsifies a thing by restricting it to a limited idea. In the meditative ode on his friend Ladoo, the speaker discovers this dilemma. Stripping away the layers of Ladoo's actions, he confronts his own falsehoods and is finally left mute, awaiting the return of an authentic existence.

Lee's essay about his predicament as writer, 'Cadence, Country, Silence', is the beginning of his attempt to define these same issues in prose; in it Lee delineates the factors that fill contemporary Canadians with a sense of self-alienation and irrevocable loss. This essay speaks to the need for a Canadian identity—a need that particularly concerned writers around the end of the sixties, especially those associated with Anansi. In *Savage Fields* (1977), Lee's book of literary criticism and 'cosmology', he extends his discussion of a disenfranchised, colonized existence to include all those who have been affected by modernist values. For Lee, both literature and life must be restored to a mystical experience in which separate concepts such as form and content, or writer and reader, are replaced by an emerging, intuitive wholeness.

It follows that Lee's work cannot be easily analysed. In addition to being shaped by his continuing struggle with modernism, it is enriched by his interest in meditation and music; the influence of German philosophy and poetry; and the struggle to evolve a civil and personal *self* within his writing. Because Lee is a writer of process (he compulsively revises all his work, even long after its original publication), his poetry and essays do not form a stable corpus of discrete units but become a single work in progress, one that is always subject to further revision, always in development, always aspiring to a philosophy of life that lies beyond the written page. Deep within his work is a religious impulse that manifests itself as an urge to create cosmologically, to edit the messy stuff of life into a vision that is whole *and* all-inclusive because it contains comprehensively the very nature of *being*.

When I Went Up to Rosedale[1]

When I went up to Rosedale
I thought of kingdom come
Persistent in the city
Like a totem in a slum.

The ladies off across the lawns
Revolved like haughty birds.
They made an antique metaphor.
I didn't know the words.

Patrician diocese! the streets
Beguiled me as I went   10
Until the tory founders seemed
Immortal government—

---

[1]An old area of Toronto known for its concentration of wealthy and powerful residents.

For how could mediocrities
Have fashioned such repose?
And yet those men were pygmies,
As any schoolboy knows.

For Head[2] reduced the rule of law
To frippery and push.
Tradition-conscious Pellatt[3] built
A drawbridge in the bush.   20

And Bishop Strachan[4] gave witness, by
The death behind his eyes,
That all he knew of Eden
Was the property franchise.

And those were our conservatives!—
A claque[5] of little men
Who took the worst from history
And made it worse again.

The dream of tory origins
Is full of lies and blanks,   30
Though what remains when it is gone,
To prove that we're not Yanks?

Nothing but the elegant
For Sale signs on the lawn,
And roads that wind their stately way
To dead ends, and are gone.

When I came down from Rosedale
I could not school my mind
To the manic streets before me
Nor the courtly ones behind.   40

1979

---

[2]Sir Francis Bond Head (1793-1875), whose handling of the Rebellion of 1837 was so capricious and unreasoned that it led to his early resignation from public office.

[3]Sir Henry Mill Pellatt (1860-1939), financier and soldier, who built Casa Loma, a palatial residence that is now a public landmark.

[4]John Strachan (1778-1867), first Anglican bishop of Toronto and one of the leaders of the 'Family Compact'. Bishop Strachan argued that the Church of England should have exclusive rights to the revenues from the Clergy Reserves (Crown lands set aside for the maintenance of the Protestant clergy).

[5]Originally, an audience hired to applaud a performance; now also any group of fawning admirers. (Here, a self-admiring group.)

The Death of Harold Ladoo[1]

I

The backyards wait in the dusk. My neighbour's elm
      is down now, dismembered, the chainsaw finally
      muzzled, and the racket of kids has dwindled
to dreams of crying, Tim-ber! as it falls.
               Along the scrubby lane
      the air-conditioners hum, they
            blur small noises.
               Darkness rises through the leaves.
And here I am, Harold,
      held in the twitchy calm of the neighbourhood, remiss and   10
            nagged by an old compulsion, come at last
      to wrestle with your death—
               waiting on magisterial words
               of healing and salute,
      the mighty cadence poets summoned in their grief
      when one they cherished swerved from youth to dead,
           and every thing went numb until
their potent words resumed his life and I, though
           least of these and unendowed
               with Muse or Holy Ghost, still   20
lug your death inside me and it
           festers still, it
will not be placated till I speak the words of
           high release
         which flex and gather now,
      as though somehow the fences' silhouette, the
      linden tree, the bulk of the
             huddled garages—there but
      going fast in the fading light—
all, all have ripened here to ampler elegiac presence,   30
           and the dusk and
              the hush and the
         pressure of naked need
begin at last to coax your dying into words of wholeness and salute.

Five years ago this spring—
      remember how we met? We drank
      outside at the Lion, sun lathering us, the transport-trailers
         belting along on Jarvis, your manuscript
      between us on the table and
         what did I see then?   40
A skinny brown man in a suit—voice tense, eyes shifting, absurdly
      respectful . . . and none of it connected:
      that raucous, raging thing I'd read, and this

[1]'Harold Sonny Ladoo was born in Trinidad, in 1945 or earlier, of East Indian descent. In 1968 he came to Canada, where he published two novels with the House of Anansi Press. He was murdered in 1973 during a visit to Trinidad' [Lee's note]. Ladoo's literary executor, novelist Peter Such, found enough material among his papers for several more novels.

deferential man.
Then it began: your body
        didn't work   you had to learn it all
right now! it was part of one huge saga (*what* was?)
                Greek restaurants
till 3 a.m. after class   in the cane fields
           till eight and you learned to read   50
           in hospitals the professors here
all dunces   your vicious unlikely family and
          dead soon, you would be
              dead and nothing
          came right on the page, you went and
pitched the lot   was this guy for real?   then it hit, the
          lethal whirling saga
   the table going
        away, the drinks, the traffic   those liquid
eyes unhooding, a current like jolts of   60
          pain in the air—I'd
never seen the urge to write so badly
        founded; nor so quiet, deadly, and convincing—
and I was at home, relaxed.

      How it all floods back in a rush in my forearms: those
endless sessions together, the
        swagger & hard-edge glee. . . .
And as my nerve-ends flicker now they do they
       start up in the dark—
the words I've waited for: 70

'If any be rage,
   pure word, you:
not in the mouth   not in the brain, nor the blastoff ambition—
    yet pure word still, your
    lit up body of rage. As though . . .'

But Harold—Harold what bullshit! sitting here making up epitaphs.
        You're *dead.*
    Your look won't smoulder on Jarvis again, and
       what is hard
is when good men die in their rising prime, and the scumbags flourish,   80
       and the useless *Why?* that
    flails up cannot furnish even
the measure of such injustice,
       save by its uselessness.
And what am I doing, stirring the pot again
      when every riff I try, every pass at a high salute
        goes spastic in my mouth? . . .
    And suppose I come closer, come clean—what
happens? What's in it for me?

But the friendship came so fast—at the Lion, already   90
we were comrades.
That's how it seemed.
For I was drunk on the steady flood of talent,
the welter of manuscripts that kept
surfacing month after month and often
with lives attached: I'd seen
good sudden friends appear, two dozen savage hacks
descending like a tribe,
a shaggy new
community of rage where each had thought himself alone   100
and claimed our heritage, not
by choice but finding it laced from birth through our being,
denial of spirit and flesh,
and strove I hoped to open room to live in, enacting in words
the right to ache, roar, prattle, keen, adore—to be
child, shaggy animal, rapt
celebrant and all in the one skin,
flexing manic selves in the waste of the self's deprival. And I was
flesh at last and alive and I cherished those
taut, half-violent women and men   110
for their curious gentleness, and also the need
in extremis to be.
They made good books,
and the time was absolute. And often we flirted with chaos
although it was more than that, for mostly I cherished
the ones who wore their incandescent pain
like silent credentials, not flaunting it,
and who moved into their own abyss with a hard, intuitive grace.
And the breakdown quotient was high, but
we did what had to be done and   120
we were young, and sitting there
on the porch of the Lion in sunlight, drinking beside you
listening hour after hour,
I knew that you made one more among us, dragging old
generations of pain as perpetual fate and landscape, bound
to work it through in words,
and I relaxed.

Our talks all blur together. That soft voice pushing
deep, and deeper, then catching fire—thirty novels, fifty—
a lifetime of intricate fury, no, four   130
centuries of caste and death
come loose in your life, the murdered
slaves come loose, great cycles of race and blood, the feuds,
come loose the wreckage of mothers and sons
in Trinidad, white
daytime Christ and the voodoo darkness loose, your voice
hypnotic and I sat there
time and again in a dazzle—

then: quick change, the
      swagger of tricky humility—and then again, quick change and   140
          four days writing straight, no
      sleep say it *all,*
and then the phonecall—one more
         livid book in draft: from the Caribbean to
  Canada,
       the saga piecing together.

Driven, caring, proud: it was
community somehow. And your
dying, Harold your dying
diminished the thing on earth we longed to be, for   150
rampant with making we recognized
no origin but us. . . .
But my mind bangs back as I say that, jerks and
bangs backwards.
Why should I tell it like a poem? Why not speak the truth?
although it cancels
all those images of chiselled desolation,
the transcendental heroes I made up
and fastened to the contours of my friends.
But more & more it's a bore, dragging those   160
props around, arranging
my friends inside.
Piss on the abyss. And on hard intuitive grace.
We were a tiresome gang of honking egos:
graceless, brawling, greedy, each one in love with
style and his darling career. And images of liberation
danced in our fucked-up heads, we figured
aping those would somehow make us writers,
cock and a dash of the logos[2]
oh—and Canada,   170
but all it's done is make us life-and-blood cliches.
Media fodder. Performing rebels. The works.
Wack-a-doo!
For this I tied my life in knots?

And as for you, Ladoo!—you never missed a trick.
You soaked up love like a sponge, cajoling
hundreds of hours, and bread, and fine-tuned publication
and then accepted them all with a nice indifference,
as though they were barely enough. You had us taped, you knew white
liberals inside out: how to   180
guilt us; which buttons to push; how hard; how long.
Three different times, in close-mouthed confidence you spoke of
three horrific childhoods; it was *there* you first
gave blood, now you could use it

---

[2]Cosmic reason; the revealed thought and will of God; expression of reason in words and things (from *logos*, Greek for word, reason, or speech).

to write. And I was
lethally impressed, and only later realised
two of the childhoods had to be somebody else's,
and all those dues you paid were so much literature.
You couldn't tell which one of you was real.
But I can, now: you were   190
a routine megalomaniac, taking the short-cut
through living men and women to try and make it big.
It turns my stomach! Come on, did I live
that way too?
But leave me wallow in no more crap about the Anansi years.
Ladoo, you bastard, goodbye: you bled me dry.
You used me! and though the words are
not what I intended, they rankle but let me get them said:
goodbye, and good riddance.

         For eight straight years of crud in public places   200
           we worked to incite a country to belong to.
              But here, on this leafy street,
       I wince at those hectic unreal selves
         I made up year by year,
   and found I could not shed them when I tried to.
             Though how to be in the world?
     And leaving them behind
       I got here needing
    roots, renewals, dwelling space,
        not knowing how to live   210
       the plain shape of a day's necessities, nor how to heed
the funny rhythms generated by
      the woman I love, three kids, a difficult craft
that takes the measure of my life.
         Intricate rhythms of the commonplace:
         a friend, a sky, a walk through green ravines,
       and I am at home.
  Though not to die here, fat & marooned—like a curled-up
       slug in a dream of the suburbs. But for
     now I am   220
       here, Ladoo, here like
         this in the yard and tomorrow,
    and grief and joy rain down on me, and often I
  think of those headlong years with bafflement,
      good friends and deaths ago,
   when voice by voice we raged like a new noise in the orchestra
as though each deficit we harboured needed only to be named
          to take on public resonance
and every honest word on a page meant news of another comrade—
       like you, Harold.   230

      And the books kept
    pouring through your system like heart attacks,
       nine in three years,

and the manuscripts rose in your bedroom, uneditable for
    new ones would come and
  sabotage your life. And
        the life and the work wrenched farther apart:
you stabbed a man, berserk they had
    doped your drink and you
went on brooding on style, your ear emphatic with   240
    Faulkner, Milton, Achebe,[3]
    Naipaul, Gibson, Godfrey, García Márquez,
      Harris, Carrier: these men you meant to
  write into the ground.
No Pain Like This Body[4] came out, that spare and
    luminous nightmare and you
    went back to
dishwashing, writing all night and flexing new
    voices, possessed;
each time we met, your body was   250
    closer to skeletal fury,
    your eyes more
    deadly & on fire.
It was all too much, it was gorgeous, it was
    vanishing into your own myth,
and I watched bemused, and awed, as the circles grew
    tighter and tighter, those frenzied drafts more
    brilliant, and botched, and envious.

  For I needed you, Harold, as
    outlaw, rock-bottom   260
  loser, one more time that
perfect outsider forging his way through sheer raw talent & nerve.
    And I cherished that holy rage, I believe I
    sponged off it.
Me, a nice WASP kid from the suburbs—how could I
    live it on my own?
I could barely raise my voice if somebody stepped on my feet in a movie.
    But this, now! this had
  hair on it. It stank! It breathed like a ten-ton truck.
    It bled and it called for blood.   270
    I wanted some of that.
        And not just you: I mean
    the whole chaotic gospel.
There was something in me that craved the welter of sudden friendships,
    the unpurged intensity, booze, the all-night sessions,
    even the breakdowns, the trials & suicides, and underneath it all,

[3]Chinua Achebe (b. 1930), Nigerian novelist and short-story writer, best known for *Things Fall Apart* (1958); 'Naipaul': V.S. Naipaul (b. 1932), West Indian novelist, best known for *A House for Mr Biswas* (1961); 'García Márquez': Gabriel García Márquez (b. 1928), Colombian novelist and short-story writer, winner of the 1982 Nobel Prize for Literature; 'Harris': Wilson Harris (b. 1921), novelist and poet who was born in British Guiana (now Guyana), grew up in Demerara, and is best known for *Palace of the Peacock* (1960); 'Carrier': Roch Carrier (b. 1937), French-Canadian short-story writer and novelist, many of whose books have been published in translation by Anansi.
[4](1972) one of the two novels by Ladoo published by Anansi.

半 half crazed,
the pressure of unremitting talent
revved up and honing in through
marathons of drafts.   280
It was a power source, it validated words
and the dubious act of writing.
But make no mistake, Ladoo.
I was devouring you too, in the overall
carnage and we did feed off each other,
you gave your blood at last.
I needed you to be the thing of fantasy
I now detest, as also I detest
the shoddy yen in myself.
Jesus! that gentle editor   290
with his tame thesaurus & verse—
out for the kill, like
all the others
taking what he could get: salvation by proxy,
which meant raw energy, and the will to charge ahead
and live in words and not ask any questions,
no matter who got screwed.
Say it: I used you, Harold,
like a hypocrite voyeur.

The wide night drifts and soars.   300
From here to the luminous moon, this very instant,
how many burnt-out rocketships go stranded
in flawless orbit, whirling through the
stations of mechanical decay
in outer space, our dump though once sublime,
the pleasure ground of God while he was Lord?
But they preside up there. And here—down
here is jumble:
version by version I shuffle images of you
and cannot make them fit.   310
A man should not make of his friends a
blur of aesthetic alternatives:
nor of himself, though it feels good.
Yet I also remember your sideways grin, the way it slid like a
slow fuse.
And what was real was not the adrenalin highs,
the hype and ego-baths: not only that.
Men and women were real, for sometimes
they handled each other gently.
As one spun out in the frenzy of his number   320
another would be beside him, as if to say,
'I do not take this seriously
though you must. . . . Keep pushing. You can be
more than this.'
Beneath the pyrotechnics, beneath the endless
bellyful of ego, yes and even though

each one of us kept skittering through
the tyranny dance of his difficult compulsions,
what surfaced day after day was a
deep tough caring.   330
Quizzical. Easy. Frustrated. For real.
Allowing the clamour & jazz, yet
reaching past them, past
the very act of words
to the plain gestures of being human together.
And I value the books, but now what fastens me
is not the words but the lives.
And my heart spins out to hold each one, to
cherish them entire although
I could not say that face to face and finally   340
too little has come real for me, in the
casual blurt of day to day
the roots and resonance I crave too seldom cohere,
and it is only here that daily living half makes sense at all,
and I cannot relinquish a single one of those whose lives went
blundering through to love, albeit
ropily, and grew indelible.
And I unsay nothing, friend I must continue
locked with you for keeps in this tug of cherishing war,
but always now I return to the deep unscheduled ground of caring   350
in which we lived our lives
and the words arrive.

'Great raging maker, Ladoo: go dead and legendary
            in permanent regions of praise.
If any be end, or
                comely by excess of being
        if any be incandescent,
                on earth like me and gone . . .'

But still it is not enough!
I know words too, but when I hear your inflections on the   360
subway now I
turn and always you are dead,
nothing but dead.
What more is there to say?
I would rather spit on your grave than decorate this poem
                                            with your death.

            And yet to
                    die, Harold,
        that's hard. To die—
                    simply to die, and   370
            not to be:
                    no more to
        saunter by on the sidewalk, the
                way a human does,

                     sensing the prick of
                            renewal each spring
in small green leaves and also the used-up bodies of
       winos, for these come
                     mildly rife once more.
       To be finished.   380
Commotion between the legs: no more to
                     accede to its
              blurred supremacy, the way a
              human does.
              Nor to
       spend your last good
muscle or wit on something you
                     half believe in, half
       despise. Not even to know
              the wet sweet tangled   390
       stink of earth after rain;
                     a streetcar's
clatter; the grain of wood
              in a desk the way
       a human does. And not to feel
              exasperated pleasure any longer
as flesh you instigated shoulders
                     pell-mell past you, out to
              live it all from the start. It's hard.
              I cannot imagine—   400
                     to be under ground.
       And the press of another life on your own, no
              miracle but acts &
       patience that cohere: all that
                     sweet & cross-hatched bitter noble aching sold-out
       thrash of life, all
              gone as you reached it, Harold I cannot
              imagine, to be
                     dead the way to be
              not a   410
                     human does.

                            II
One drowsy bird, from another yard, and again
the neighbourhood is still;
the linden tree, the fence, the huddled garages, gone
anonymous in the dark. And though we
make our peace as man and man
the words haven't come to praise you—oh but friend,
you should not have gone to the island alone!
you should not be dead so soon!
But I'm floundering still, and every cell in my body   420
bridles, and tells me this is only beginning;
and I must brood against the grain again,
taking the long way round, interrogating

more than just the accident of who we were.
For often now at night
when the stillness begins to
tick, or if I take on too many meetings,
there is a question, not my own, which stymies my life:
'What good are poets in a time of dearth?'[5]
Hölderlin asked that, master of poets. Who knew.   430
But I just get embarrassed.
Alienation and Integration: The Role of the Artist in Modern Society.
Panel at 8, Discussion 8:30, Refreshments.
And mostly I believe the artists further
the systematic murder of the real, and if their work does have
the tang of authentic life
it is one more sign that they are in business to kill.
For a civilization cannot sustain
lobotomy, meaning the loss of awe,
the numbing of *tremendum*[6]—and its holy of holies   440
goes dead, even the
nearest things on earth
shrink down and lose their savour—
it cannot dispel the numinous, as we have done for
centuries without those exiled gods and demons rushing back
in subterranean concourse,
altered, mocking, bent on genocide.
For the gods are not dead; they stalk among us, grown murderous.
Gone from the kingdom of reason they surface
in hellish politics, in towering minds   450
entranced by pure technique, and in an art refined by
carnage and impotence, where only form is real.
And thus we re-enact
the fierce irrational presencing we denied them—only warped,
grown monstrous in our lives.

A world that denies
the gods, the gods
make mad. And they choose their
instruments with care.
Leaders, artists, rock stars are among their darlings. And   460
to the artist they promise
redemptive lunacy, and they do bestow the gift but what they deliver
is sauce for the nerve ends, bush-league paranoia,
fame as a usable freak, depression, and silence.
Yet nothing is wasted. The artist they favour
becomes a priest indeed, he mediates
the sacraments of limbo.
For a world without numinous being is
intolerable, and it is his gorgeous vocation

[5]From the poem *Brot und Wein (Bread and Wine)* by German poet Friedrich Hölderlin (1770-1843).
[6]*Mysterium tremendum*, the sense of awe inspired by the numinous, or supernatural, dimension of the universe; 'holy of holies': the innermost sanctuary of the Jewish temple; a most sacred shrine.

to bludgeon the corpse for signs of life, achieving   470
impossible feats of resuscitation, returning, pronouncing it
dead again. Opening new
fever paths in the death heaps of a civilization.
And he names the disease, again and again he makes great
art of it, squandering
what little heritage of health and meaning remains,
although his diagnoses are true, they are
truly part of the disease
and they worsen it, leaving
less of life than they found; yet in our time   480
an art that does not go that route
is deaf and blind, a coward's pastorale,
unless there be grace in words.

But the role comes down like lucid
catharsis:[7] *creator!* taking the poor old
world as
neuter space, as one more specimen, sanctioning
lunacy and rage, the gift of the mutant gods.
And the floating role is alive on its own and always
there now, it idles about & waits, it is after   490
a man—who knows? bank-clerk, dishwasher, writer, professor—
and when he appears, he is shanghaied.
So, Harold, your difficult life
was yanked into orbit, and kindled, and given coherence,
and blasted apart by the play of that living myth.
Almost you had no say.

Galvanic art! new carnal assertions! fresh nervous systems!
              adrenalin ascensions for the chosen!
It is the need to be
              one, to be taken whole & alive   500
     by that which is more than oneself, sensing
              the body,
                     the brain, the being
       absolved at last in a radiant therapy,
                     carried beyond themselves, resolved
              in single emphatic wholeness:
     to live on fire in words, heroic
              betrayal.
And I think of others we knew, comrades in Toronto
       who toppled headlong like you to the calm of their own myth   510
     accepting its violent poise like the fit of a new skeleton, all that
       great fury in focus now in its settled gestures of being,
their lives in shambles still but redeemed by mythic contours
       and it moves like fluid skin around them,
              holding the
                     breakable ego, titanic
              energies in place at last, no more

[7] A purging, specifically a cleansing or purifying of the emotions.

questions, or so it seems to one
with myths galore but no fixed will to inhabit them.
And our lives were single then, we were made   520
valid, though wasted, for I
know the thing I write and I would
gladly go back to that, gladly but I do not believe it.
But you, Harold: you
went and lived in words.
You pushed it past the limit, further than any of us
and also you died of it,
face down, no teeth in your head, at twenty-eight,
dead on a backroad in Trinidad—
though that I believe in. But not   530
the vanishing into words.

The night winds come and go
and linden drifts like snow around me:
paradise row, and somehow it is
permitted to live here.
But though things fit themselves now, graciously
easing into place and
are, as
though they had always known,
that too has its proper measure, and cannot stay on   540
beyond its own good time.
Yet in this blessed breathing space, I see that
every thing must serve too many selves.
And we, who thought by words to blitz
the carnal monuments of an old repression—
we were ourselves in hock, and acting out
possessive nightmares of a
straitened century.
Surprise! we weren't
God's hitmen, nor the   550
harbingers of raunchy absolutes; and nor is
any thing on earth.
For madness, violence, chaos, all that primitive hankering
was real necessity, yet
bound to the gods' revenge and to
prolong it would be death.

People, people I speak from
private space but all these
civil words keep coming and they
muddle me!   560
Salvations come & go, they
singe us by the root-hair—to live for
revolution, for the dear one, for chemical highlights
for power for history for art—
and each one turns demonic, for it too gets cherished as
absolute.

Even that glorious dream
of opening space to be in, of saying
the real words of that space—[8]
that too was false, for we cannot   570
idolize a thing without it going infernal,
and in this season of dearth
there are only idols.
Though how to live from that and still
resist real evil, how to keep from
quietist fadeouts, that I
scarcely know. But
epiphanies[9] will come when
they will come, will
go; they are not   580
trademarks of grace; they
do not matter, surprise.
'Everything matters, and
nothing matters.'[1]
It is harder to live by that on earth and stubborn than to
rise, full-fledged and abstract,
and snag apocalypse.

Harold, how shall I exorcize you?
This is not for blame.
I know that   590
it lived you, there was no
choice: some men do carry this century
malignant in their cells from birth
like the tick of genetic stigmata,[2]
and it is no longer
whether it brings them down, but only
when. You were a fresh explosion
of that lethal paradigm: the
Tragic Artist, yippee and
forgive me friend.   600
But you heard your own death singing, that much I know.
And went to meet it mesmerized—to get
the man that got your mother, yes—but also plain
wooing it, telling Peter you'd
never be back alive. And the jet's trajectory
a long sweet arc of dying, all the way down.
For the choice was death by writing, that
airless escape
from a world that would not work unless you wrote it
and could not work if you did—   610

[8]Lee here refers to the goals enunciated in *Civil Elegies*.
[9]Spiritual events in which the essence of an insight or manifestation is revealed in a sudden flash.
[1]Lee identifies this phrase as a Hindu commonplace.
[2]Marks figuratively corresponding to the crucifixion wounds of Jesus.

or death in the only place you cared to live in
except it christened men
with boots, machetes, bloodwash of birth and vengeance.
The choice was death, or death.
And whatever the lurid scuffle that
ended the thing—your body
jack-knifed, pitch dark, in the dirt—
it was after the fact. You had lived inside that gesture for years,
you were already one of the chosen.
Your final heritage   620
two minor early novels, one being nearly first-rate.

I read these words and flinch, for I had not meant
to quarrel with you, Harold.
Nor friends, good men, who also lived these things.
Nor with myself.
Though I feel nothing for you
I did not feel before your death,
I loved you, and I owed you words of my own.
But speaking the words out loud has brought me close to the bone.

Night inches through. It's cold. I wish I were sleeping,   630
or stronger, more rooted in something real
this endless night of the solstice, June, 1975.
Ten minutes more, then bed.
But I know one thing, though
barely how to live it.
We must withstand the gods awhile, the mutants.
And mostly the bearers of gifts, for they have
singled us out for unclean work; and supremely
those who give power, whether at words or
the world for it will bring   640
criminal prowess.
But to live with a measure, resisting their terrible inroads:
I hope this is enough.
And, to let the beings be.
And also to honour the gods in their former selves,
albeit obscurely, at a distance, unable
to speak the older tongue; and to wait
till their fury is spent and they call on us again
for passionate awe in our lives, and a high clean style.

1976 rev. 1979

From 'Cadence, Country, Silence: Writing in Colonial Space'

[The long essay 'Cadence, Country, Silence' is divided into three parts, suggested by the title, in which Lee attempts to define the three important factors that influence his writing. In the first section Lee does not directly define cadence but calls it a 'presence, both outside myself and inside my body opening out and trying to get into words'. A 'massive infinitely fragile polyphony', cadence is the medium of poetry as raw stone is that of sculpture:

Content is already there in the cadence. And writing a poem means cutting away everything in the cadence that isn't that poem. You can't 'write' a poem, in fact, you can only help it stand free in the torrent of cadence. Most of my time with a pen is spent giving words, images, bright ideas that are borne along in cadence their permission to stay off the paper. The poem is what remains, it is local cadence minus whatever is extraneous to its shapely articulation.

For Lee, 'local cadence' was prevented from expressing itself in his poetry because he lived in a colonized environment without an authentic language in which to express his Canadian actuality. The 'Country' section excerpted below examines this problem of the nature of Canada as a colony and its effects on the writer.]

2. COUNTRY

* * *

The prime fact about my country as a public space is that in the last twenty-five years it has become an American colony. But we speak the same tongue as our new masters; we are the same colour, the same stock. We know their history better than our own. Thus, while our civil inauthenticity has many tangible monuments, from TIME to Imperial Esso, the way it undercuts our writing is less easy to discern—precisely because there are so few symptomatic literary battle-grounds (comparable to the anglicized French of Quebec) in which the takeover is immediately visible. Nevertheless, many writers here know how the act of writing calls itself radically into question.

Though you may not be familiar with all their detail, I will take the external pressures for granted—the American tidal-wave that inundates us, in the cultural sphere as much as in the economic and political. How maybe two per cent of the books on our paperback racks are Canadian, because the American-owned distributors refuse to carry them; how Canadian film-makers have to go to the States to seek distribution arrangements for Canada—where they are commonly turned down, which means the film is not made; how almost all our prime TV time is filled with yankee programmes; how a number of Alberta schoolchildren are still being taught that Abraham Lincoln is their country's greatest president.

Every one of these idiocies must be changed. And we are such a supine people that every one of the changes requires a seemingly endless campaign of public education and lobbying—I mean in Canada, directed at *ourselves*—before we are prepared to treat our right to exist with the most elementary respect. It's no wonder that nationalists, in frustration, end up repeating the litany of our thrall-dom so obsessively, so mechanically even.

But I want to go further here, for there are dimensions of cultural colonialism which can't be reduced to a list of specific abuses, or even to the necessary cures: legislation and money and a spirit of common resolve. Those things are crucial, and my country will not survive unless we deal with them. But here I want to step back and explore how, in a colony, the simple exercise of the imagination becomes a problem to itself.

•

I shall be speaking of 'words,' but not merely those you find in a dictionary. I mean all the resources of the verbal imagination, from single words through verse forms, conventions about levels of style, characteristic versions of the hero, resonant structures of plot. And I use my own experience with words because I know it best. It tallies with things other writers of my generation have said, but I don't know how many would accept it fully.

I began writing about 1960, when I was twenty-one. My sense at the time— and this lasted five or six years—was that I had access to a great many words: those of the British, the American, and (so far as anyone took it seriously) the Canadian traditions. Yet at the same time those words seemed to lie in a great random heap, which glittered with promise so long as I considered it in the mass but within which each individual word went stiff, inert, was somehow clogged with sludge, the moment I tried to move it into place in a poem. I could stir words, prod at them, cram them into position; but there was no way I could speak them directly. They were completely external to me, though since I had never known the words of poetry in any other way I assumed that was natural.

Writers everywhere don't have to begin with a resistant, external language; something more was involved than just getting the hang of the medium during apprenticeship. In any case, after I had published one book of poems and finished another, a bizarre thing happened: I stopped being able to use words on paper at all.

Everywhere around me—in England, America, even in Canada—writers opened their mouths and words spilled out like crazy. But increasingly when I opened mine I simply gagged; finally, the words no longer came. For about four years at the end of the sixties I tore up everything I wrote; twenty words on a page were enough to set me boggling at their palpable inauthenticity. And looking back at my previous writing, I felt as if I had been fishing pretty beads out of a vat of crank-case oil and stringing them together. The words weren't limber or alive or even mine.

To discover that you are mute in the midst of all the riches of a language is a weird experience. I had no explanation for it; by 1968 it had happened to me, but I didn't know why. Today, as I go back and try to stylize the flux to understand it, I am suspicious of the cause-and-effect categories that assert themselves; half the effects, it seems, came before their causes. But this is a recent scruple. At that time I could barely take in *what* had happened; I had just begun to write, and now I was stopped. I would still sit down in my study with a pen and paper from time to time, and every time I ended up ripping the paper to pieces and pitching it out. The stiffness and falsity of the words appalled me; the reaction was more in my body than my mind, but it was very strong.

•

Those of us who stumbled into this kind of problem in the 1960s were suffering the recoil from something Canadians, certainly Upper Canadians, had learned very profoundly in the fifties. To want to see one's life, we had been taught, to see one's own most banal impulses and deeper currents made articulate on paper, in a film, on records—that was ridiculous, uppity. Canadians were by definition people who looked over the fence and through the windows at America, unself-consciously learning from its movies, comics, magazines and TV shows how to go about being alive. The disdainful amusement I and thousands like me felt for Canadian achievement in any field, especially those of the imagination, was a direct reflection of our self-hatred and sense of inferiority. And while we sneered at American mass culture, we could only separate ourselves from it by soaking up all the elite American culture we could get at. If anyone from another country was around we would outdo ourselves with our knowledge of Mailer and Fiedler and Baldwin, of the beatniks and the hipsters, of—if we were really showing our breadth of mind—the new plays from angry London.[1] And we fell all over ourselves putting down the Canadians. This was between 1955 and 1965.

We were shaping up to be perfect little Toms and vendus.[2] And like intellectual Toms in most places, we were prepared to sell out, not for a cut of the action or a position of second-level power, but simply on condition that we not be humiliated by being treated like the rest of the natives. We were desperate to make that clear: we weren't like the rest. The fact that we would never meet the Americans we admired from one end of the year to the next didn't cramp our style; we managed to feel inferior and put down anyway, and we compensated like mad. We kept up with *Paris Review* and *Partisan*,[3] shook our heads over how Senator McCarthy had perverted the traditions of our country; in some cases we went down to Selma or Washington[4] to confront our power structure, and in all cases we agreed that the greatest blot on our racial history was the way we had treated the Negroes. It boggles the imagination now, but that was really what we did—it was how we really *felt*. We weren't pretending, we were desperate. And the idea that these things confirmed our colonialism with a vengeance would have made us laugh our continentalized heads off. We weren't all that clear on colonialism to begin with, but if anybody had colonialism it was our poor countrymen, the Canadians, who in some unspecified way were still in fetters to England. But we weren't colonials; hell, *we* could have held our heads up in New York, if it had occurred to anyone to ask us down. Though it was a bit of a relief that no one ever did.

---

[1] That is, the work of the 'Angry Young Men' (such as John Osborne) who, in the fifties, played the same anti-establishment role in Britain as that of the Beat writers in the United States.

[2] Pejorative French term for those who have sold out; comparable to 'Uncle Tom' in American Black parlance.

[3] *The Paris Review* (1953-) and the left-wing *Partisan Review* (1934-) were important magazines for the American intellectual establishment in the fifties; 'Senator McCarthy': Joseph McCarthy (1909-57), an American politician who, on little or no evidence, blacklisted people he accused of being Communists or Communist sympathizers and created a climate of hysterical distrust in the fifties.

[4] Important marches in the sixties in support of the U.S. civil-rights movement.

My awakening from this astonishing condition was private and extremely confusing. It was touched off by the radical critique of America that originated in America, especially over Viet Nam; but it ended up going further. From that muddled process I remember one particularly disorienting couple of months in 1965, after a teach-in on Viet Nam held at the University of Toronto (in the fashion of American teach-ins) by a group of first-rate professors and students. It lasted a weekend, and as I read the background material and followed the long, dull speeches in the echoing cavern of Varsity Arena, two things dawned on me. The first was that the American government had been lying about Viet Nam. The second was that the Canadian media, from which I had learnt all I knew about the war, were helping to spread its lies.

I present these discoveries in all the crashing naiveté with which they struck me then. Interestingly, while the first revelation shocked me more at the time, it was the second that gnawed at me during the ensuing months. I couldn't get my mind around it. I did not believe that our newspapers or radio and TV stations had been bought off directly by Washington, of course. But if it was not a case of paid corruption, the only reason for co-operating in such a colossal deception—consciously or unconsciously—was that they were colonial media, serving the interests of the imperial rulers.

This language made me bridle—it conjured up images of mindless five-hour harangues in Havana or Peking, foreign frenzies of auto-hypnosis, numb rhetoric. I'd read about *that* in the papers too. But no matter; it was the only language that made sense of what had been happening, and though I did not accept the terminology for another five years, I accepted its substance almost at once.

Worse than that, however, was the recognition that the sphere of imperial influence was not confined to the pages of newspapers. It also included my head. And that shook me to the core, because I could not even restrict the brainwashing I began to recognize to the case of Viet Nam. More and more of the ideas I had, my assumptions, even the instinctive path of my feelings well before they jelled into notions, seemed to have come north from the States unexamined. That had once been what I strove for (though I wouldn't have put it that way). But now the whole thing began to turn around, and I was jarred loose. After ten years of continentalizing my ass, what had I accomplished? . . . I was a colonial.

It was during the period when my system began to rebel against our spineless existence in this colonial space—by 1967, say—that I began to find literary words impossible. I read far less, I stopped going to Stratford, I squirmed in front of TV. And nothing I wrote felt real. I didn't know why. I couldn't even say what was the problem, for any words I might use to articulate it were already deadened, numb, inert in the same peculiar way. So none of this got said, except by the revulsion of my nervous system; otherwise I was mute. Writing had become a full-fledged problem to itself; it had grown into a search for authenticity, but all it could manage to be was a symptom of inauthenticity. I couldn't put my finger on what was inauthentic, but I could feel it with every nerve-end in my body. And I only wanted to write, I said, if I could also convey the muteness that established—like a key in music—the particular inauthenticity of this word, and that word. (At the time I called it 'silence' but most of it—I think now—was simple muteness.) I couldn't write that way. So for four years I shut up.

•

Though I hope not to over-dramatize this, it was when I read a series of essays by the philosopher George Grant[5] that I started to comprehend what we had been living inside. Many people were turning to Marcuse[6] for such clarification, and through him to Marx; others found perspective in Leary[7] and Brown. I want to know more about Marx now. But at that time I found the most salutary toughness and depth in Grant's thought. And it felt like home. That mattered to me, because I never again wanted to spend time chasing somebody else's standards of what was good.

Grant's analysis of 'Canadian Fate and Imperialism,' which I read in *Canadian Dimension*, was the first that made any contact whatsoever with my tenuous sense of living here—the first that seemed to be speaking the words of our civil condition. My whole system had been coiling in on itself for want of them. As subsequent pieces appeared (they eventually came out as *Technology and Empire*), I realized that somehow it had happened: a man who knew this paralyzing condition first-hand was nevertheless using words authentically, from the very centre of everything that had tied my tongue. Grant's thought is still growing and changing, of course, so it could not be treated as a body of doctrine. Its subtlety, breadth and austerity can be conveyed only in a glancing way here.

One central perception was that, in refusing the American dream, our Loyalist forebears (the British Americans who came north after 1776) were groping to reaffirm a classical European tradition, one which embodies a very different sense of public space. By contrast with the liberal assumptions that gave birth to the United States, it taught that reverence for what is is more deeply human than conquest of what is. That men are subject to sterner civil necessities than liberty or the pursuit of happiness—that they must respond, as best they can, to the demands of the good. And that men's presence here is capable of an organic continuity which cannot be ruptured except at the risk of making their condition worse—that any such change should be undertaken in fear and trembling. (Grant would not claim that all Hellenic or Christian societies used to live by these ideals, only that they understood themselves to be acting well or badly in their light.) And while our ancestors were often mediocre or muddling, convictions like these demonstrably did underlie many of their attitudes to law, the land, indigenous peoples, and Europe. Their refusal of America issued, in part, from disagreement with the Americans about what it meant to be a human being.

What the Loyalists were refusing was the doctrine of essential human freedom, which in an argument of inspired simplicity Grant sees as the point of generation of technological civilization. That doctrine led to a view of everything but

[5](b. 1918), author of *Lament for a Nation: The Defeat of Canadian Nationalism* (1965), which was highly influential in the movement for Canadian economic nationalism. His later book, *Technology and Empire: Perspectives on North America* (1969), a more philosophical examination of the effects of liberalism and technology on Canadian culture, was edited by Lee for the House of Anansi.
[6]Herbert Marcuse (1898-1979), German-born neo-Marxist philosopher who, as a U.S. professor and author, was influential for his anti-technological and anti-establishment arguments in the fifties and sixties.
[7]Timothy Leary (b. 1920), anti-establishment figure of the sixties who promulgated the use of psychedelic drugs, particularly LSD, and coined the slogan 'Turn on. Tune in. Drop out.' 'Brown': Norman O. Brown (b. 1913), literary critic and social commentator whose books, *Life Against Death* (1959) and *Love's Body* (1966), were an examination of modern culture from a perspective of neo-Freudian mysticism.

one's own will—the new continent, native peoples, other nations, outer space, one's own body—as raw material, to be manipulated and remade according to the hungers of one's nervous system and the innate demands of one's technology. But not only did this view of an unlimited human freedom seem arrogant and suicidal; it also seemed inaccurate, wrong, a piece of self-deception. For we are not radically free, in simple fact, and to act as if we were is to behave with lethal naiveté. What is more, trying to force everything around us to conform to our own wills is not the best use of what freedom we do have.

This overstates what Grant finds in the Loyalists, in order to clarify the deep novelty of his perspective. In fact, he declares that the typical Loyalist was 'straight Locke with a dash of Anglicanism;'[8] the British tradition he held to had already broken with the classical understanding of the good which Grant cherishes. Loyalism was a gesture in the right direction, perhaps, but it never succeeded in being radically un-American; it did not have the resources.

This undercutting of a past he would have liked to make exemplary is a characteristic moment in Grant's thought, and it reveals the central strength and contradiction of his work. He withdraws from the contemporary world, and judges it with passionate lucidity, by standing on a 'fixed point' which he then reveals to be no longer there. To dismiss his thought for that reason is sheer self-indulgence, of course, for it is to shy back from recognizing the extremity of our impasse, to imply that we ourselves have access to more-than-liberal resources which stand up where Grant's crumble. Nevertheless, this strange way of proceeding makes Grant's thought difficult to live with—a fact which his own best work explores rigorously.

I found the account of being alive that Grant saw in the classic tradition far less self-indulgent than the liberal version that achieved its zenith in America—far closer to the way things are. And suddenly there were terms in which to recognize that, as we began to criticize our new masters during the sixties, we were not just wanting to be better Americans than the Americans, to dream their dream more humanely. Our dissent went as deep as it did because, obscurely, we did not want to be American at all. Their dream was wrong.

Before Grant, a person who grew up in as deeply colonized a Canadian decade as the fifties had no access to such a fundamental refusal of America, no matter how viscerally he felt it. Hence before Grant many of us had no way of entering our native space. Moreover our tiresome beginnings had always been a source of embarrassed amusement to us; they were hardly something we could have lapsed from or betrayed. As this was stood on its head, relatively at least, Grant gave us access to our past as well.

But Grant is scarcely an apostle of public joy. His next perception virtually cancels his reclamation of space to be in. By now, he says, we have replaced our forebears' tentative, dissenting space with a wholehearted and colonial American space. The sellout of Canada which has been consummated over the last few

---

[8]That is, an empiricist who believed in individual rights but who accepted the English precepts of duty and the common good; Grant opposes this to the Americans who 'had incorporated in their revolution a mixture of Locke with elements of Rousseau', which led to a more individualistic philosophy.

decades does not involve just real estate or corporate takeovers, nor who will put the marionettes in Ottawa through their dance. It replaces one human space with another.

For the political and military rule of the United States, and the economic rule of its corporations, are merely the surface expression of modernity in the West. That modernity is also inward. It shapes the expression of our bodies' impulses, the way we build cities, what we do in our spare time. Always we are totally free men, faced with a world which is raw material, a permanent incitement to technique. Any problem caused by our use of our freedom is merely accidental, and can be remedied by a greater application of the technology which expresses that freedom. There is simply no court of appeal outside that circuit. And even though we can observe the results of that world-view destroying the planet, the capacity for such gloomy perception does not give us access to another world-view.

Finally, Grant declares that to dissent from liberal modernity is necessarily to fall silent, for we now have no terms in which to speak that do not issue from the space we are trying to speak against. The conservative impulse, in which Grant sees the future we almost used to have, he judges finally to be mute as a contemplative stance and half impotent as a practical one. It can sense 'intimations of deprival' to which liberal men are not open, but it can sense them only in waiting and silence.

What is most implacable in this modern despair, Grant holds, is that it cannot get outside itself. Any statement of ideals by which we might bring our plight into perspective turns out to be either a hollow appeal to things we no longer have access to, or (more commonly) a restatement of the very liberal ideals that got us into the fix in the first place. And while this is not a problem that preoccupies most people in their day-to-day lives, it creates a Catch-22 situation at the levels from which any civilization draws its deepest resources. Grant explores that Catch-22 with a clarity which induces vertigo.

I recognize the bleakness for which Grant is often criticized. But only with my head; for months after I read his essays I felt a surge of release and exhilaration. To find one's tongue-tied sense of civil loss and bafflement given words at last, to hear one's own most inarticulate hunches out loud, because most immediate in the bloodstream—and not prettied up, and in prose like a fastidious ground-swell—was to stand erect at last in one's own space.

I do not expect to spend my life agreeing with George Grant. But, in my experience, the sombre Canadian has enabled us to say for the first time where we are, who we are—to become articulate. That first gift of speech is a staggering achievement. And in trying to comprehend the deeper ways in which writing is a problem to itself in Canada, I can start nowhere but with Grant.

•

Grant showed me that we have been colonized, not just by American corporations and governments but by the assumptions and reflexes of the liberalism they embody. And this inward colonization is an even more serious thing; it means that we are now ex-Canadians—or to put it at its most recklessly hopeful, that we are not-yet-Canadians. At our best, we have kept open a dissenting and constantly-about-to-vanish civil space, in which to explore an alternative version of being North American. That is an heroic fate. But what does it do to a writer who wants to work from his roots?

I think of the answer Margaret Atwood gave in *Survival*; much of our literature, she says, is an involuntary symptom or projection of colonial experience. The dominant themes of Canadian writing have been death, failure of nerve, and the experience of being victimized by forces beyond our control. Heroes lose, personal relations go awry, animals, Indians and immigrants are mowed down with such knee-jerk regularity that we seem to have moved past candour to compulsiveness.

Why do Canadian writers return to the lot of the victim with such dreary zest? Atwood's explanation is tempting: the species 'Canadian human' has felt itself to be powerless and threatened from the beginning, and as a result the collective author 'Canada' projects itself time and again as a victim.

This is hardly a full account of Canadian writing. But the one-sided truth it lays hold of is indispensable. I wonder, though, whether the explanation shouldn't be re-focussed. The colonial writer does not have words of his own. Is it not possible that he projects his own condition of voicelessness into whatever he creates? that he articulates his own powerlessness, in the face of alien words, by seeking out fresh tales of victims? Perhaps the colonial imagination is driven to recreate, again and again, the experience of writing in colonial space.

We are getting close to the centre of the tangle. Why did I stop being interested in Shakespeare at Stratford, when I had gone assiduously for ten summers? Why did I fidget and squirm in front of TV, and read so much less? And why did I dry?

The words I knew said Britain, and they said America, but they did not say my home. They were always and only about someone else's life. All the rich structures of language were present, but the currents that animated them were not home to the people who use the language here.

But the civil self seeks nourishment as much as the biological self; it too fuels the imagination. And if everything it lays hold of is alien, it may protect itself in a visceral spasm of refusal. To take an immediate example: the words I used above—'language', 'home', 'here'—have no native charge; they convey only meanings in whose face we have been unable to find ourselves since the eighteenth century. This is not a call for arbitrary new 'Canadian' definitions, of course. It is simply to point out that the texture, weight and connotation of almost every word we use comes from abroad. For a person whose medium is words, who wants to use words to recreate our being human here—and where else do we live?—that fact creates an absolute impasse.

Why did I dry for four years? The language was drenched with our non-belonging, and words—bizarre as it sounds, even to myself—words had become the enemy. To use them as a writer was to collaborate further in one's extinction as a rooted human being. And so, by a drastic and involuntary stratagem of self-preserval, words went dead.

The first necessity for the colonial writer—so runs the conventional wisdom—is to start writing of what he knows. His imagination must come home. But that first necessity is not enough. For if you are Canadian, home is a place that is not home to you—it is even less your home than the imperial centre you used to dream about. Or to say what I really know best, the *words* of home are silent. And to write a classical ode to the harvests of Saskatchewan, or set an American murder mystery in Newfoundland, is no answer at all. Try to speak the words of your home and you will discover—if you are a colonial—that you do not know them.

To speak unreflectingly in a colony, then, is to use words that speak only alien space. To reflect is to fall silent, discovering that your authentic space does not have words. And to reflect further is to recognize that you and your people do not in fact have a privileged authentic space just waiting for words; you are, among other things, the people who have made an alien inauthenticity their own. You are left chafing at the inarticulacy of a native space which may not exist. So you shut up.

•

But perhaps—and here was the breakthrough—perhaps our job was not to fake a space of our own and write it up, but rather to speak the words of our space-lessness. Perhaps that *was* home. This dawned on me gradually. Instead of pushing against the grain of an external, uncharged language, perhaps we should finally come to writing *with* that grain.

To do that was a homecoming—and a thoroughly edgy, uncertain homecoming it was. You began by giving up the idea of writing from inside the same continuum as Lowell,[9] Roethke, Ginsberg, Olson, Plath, Hughes. This was not a question of accepting lower standards than theirs; finding the standards of your own indigenous voice would be far chancier to begin with, and they would have to be every bit as exacting as other peoples' were for them. It was a question of starting from your own necessities—of assuming that what is for real, what is first rank by the toughest criteria in the world, can be claimed by a Canadian in the language of his own time and place. If he can learn to speak that language.

And so you began striving to hear what happened in words—in 'love', 'inhabit', 'fail', 'earth', 'house'—as you let them surface in your own mute and native land. It was a strange, visceral process; there was nothing as explicit as starting to write in *joual*, though the process was comparable. There was only the decision to let words be how they actually are for us. But I am distorting the experience again by writing it down. There was nothing conscious about this decision, initially at least—it was a direction one's inner ear took up. I know I fought it.

The first mark of words, as you began to re-appropriate them in this space-less civil space, was a kind of blur of unachieved meaning. I had already experienced that, though only as something oppressing and negative. But the oppressiveness started to change, for I began to sense something more.

Where I lived, a whole swarm of inarticulate meanings lunged, clawed, drifted, eddied, sprawled in half-grasped disarray beneath the tidy meaning which the simplest word had brought with it from England and the States. 'City':

---

[9]Robert Lowell (1917-77), Theodore Roethke (1908-63), Allen Ginsberg (b. 1926), Charles Olson (1910-70), and Sylvia Plath (1932-63) are poets representative of distinctive American voices early in Lee's career. English poet Ted Hughes (b. 1930), Plath's husband, was an important new poet who emerged in England around the same time.

once you learned to accept the blurry, featureless character of that word—responding to it as a Canadian word, with its absence of native connotation—you were dimly savaged by the live, inchoate meanings trying to surface through it. The whole tangle and Sisyphean[1] problematic of people's existing here, from the time of the *coureurs de bois* to the present day, came struggling to be included in the word 'city'. Cooped up beneath the familiar surface of the word as we use it ('city' as London, as New York, as Los Angeles)—and cooped up further down still, beneath the blank and blur you heard when you sought some received indigenous meaning for the word—listening all the way down, you began to overhear the strands and communal lives of millions of people who went their particular ways here, whose roots and lives and legacy come together in the cities we live in. Vancouver, Edmonton, Toronto, Montreal, Halifax: 'city' meant something still unspoken, but rampant with held-in energy. Hearing it was like watching the contours of an unexpected continent gradually declare themselves through the familiar lawns and faces of your block.

Though that again is hindsight: all of it. You heard an energy, and those lives were part of it. Under the surface alienation and the second-level blur of our words there was a living barrage of meaning: private, civil, religious—unclassifiable finally, but there, and seamless, and pressing to be spoken. And I *felt* that press of meaning; I had no idea what it was, but I could sense it teeming towards words. I called it cadence.

And hearing that cadence, I started to write again.

•

Why does this tale of writing, falling silent for four years, beginning to write again, seem slightly foreign to me?

Perhaps because I barely recognize the protagonist. The story implies a ten-year coherence of purpose, for example—which I admire as I read about it. But what I actually felt as a writer, during most of that decade, was a sense of beleaguered drifting. And while it was punctuated with flashes of clarity and direction, such epiphanies (I'm mortified to report) were often completely at odds with one another.

Moreover, the chronology which a reader is likely to fill in is wrong. The story implies a sequence that runs like this: poet writes artificial early work; in dissatisfaction with its stiffness, he stops writing; George Grant's essays furnish an explanation for his impasse; as a result something called 'cadence' happens to him, and he starts writing again.

That's edifying, and easy to follow, but it has little to do with what happened. In fact it went more like this: poet writes artificial early work, some of it a log-jammed attempt to write in Hölderlin's[2] cadences; eventually he does arrive at a stilted version of that voice, and writes a book-length poem (published as *Civil Elegies* in 1968); throughout this time, he has been reading George Grant in dribs and snatches; for no reason he can discern, he stops being able to write once the

[1]Like Sisyphus, who was condemned in Hades to the endless task of rolling a massive boulder up a hill only to have it roll down again; i.e. everlastingly laborious.
[2]Friedrich Hölderlin (1770-1843), German poet whose work was rediscovered in the early twentieth century; classically balanced in form and syntax, his poems contain a powerful language and a romantic longing for unity with nature and God.

book has come out; after four years, again for no apparent reason, he is able to write in cadence more effectively and revises the long poem (re-published in 1972).

There are so many loose ends there that I've given up looking for a sequential logic; none of the causes and effects are in the right place. But even a thematic account of the process, which is what I have tried to sketch, seems to dramatize and streamline things that were much more tangled, murky and banal as they occurred. So I find myself getting twitchy inside the stylized version of a life which this essay, willy-nilly, creates.

•

Those are scruples that need to be mentioned, but they are less important than the story that generates them.

Something I find now is that I can write only from the insistings of cadence. I can no more have an experience on the streetcar, come home, and write it up than I can fly to Mars. And as a colonial writer, I discover that cadence surfaces mainly through silence—through the silence that ensues when we try to hear words which bespeak ourselves, and learn that we do not possess them.

It will not do to ignore our halting tongues and simply write of other things; nor to spend all our energy castigating the external causes, as if the hateful condition were wholly outside ourselves; nor to invert that tongue-tied estate and fake a passionate cascade of words, as if we could will ourselves to be everything we are not. The impasse of writing that is problematic to itself is transcended only when the impasse becomes its own subject, when writing accepts and enters and names its own condition as it is naming the world. Any other course (except in deliberately minor work, though I do not put that down) leads to writing whose joints and musculature do not work together, which remains constantly out of synch with itself. We have had a lot of both in Canada.

Putting it differently: to be authentic, the voice of being alive here and now must include the inauthenticity of our lives here and now. We can expect no lightning or thunder to come down from heaven, to transform our past or our present. Part of the truth about us is that we have betrayed our own truths, by letting ourselves be robbed of them. To say that for real, the betrayal must be incorporated faithfully—in both grief and anger—in the saying. Just as the grief and anger must be incorporated, on a different front, in the struggle to reclaim our independent, interdependent communal lives.

To name your colonial condition is not necessarily to assign explicit terms to it. It may be, as in some of the poetry of bill bissett[3] or Gaston Miron. But the weight of the silence can also be conveyed by the sheer pressure behind the words that finally break it. Then to name one's own condition is to recreate the halt and stammer, the wry self-deprecation, the rush of celebratory elan and the

[3](b. 1939), concrete and sound poet, who has expressed anger both at Canadian society and at Canada's lack of independence. Gaston Miron (b. 1928), political and social activist as well as a poet, felt great personal distress at 'the semantic perversion of Québec's language' because of the encroachments of English; Caroline Bayard has written that he responded to his sense of predicament by rejecting both regionalism and universalism, and utilizing a 'language [that] articulated a specific territory as well as a unique moment in time, yet . . . also transcended these and reached for all alienated, dispossessed human beings' (*The Oxford Companion to Canadian Literature*, 1983).

vastness of the still unspoken surround, in which a colonial writer finally comes to know *his* house, *his* father, *his* city, *his* terrain—encounters them in their own unuttered terms and finds words being born to say them. I think of Al Purdy's poems. Or, in a different explosion, of bissett's barbaric tongue.

Beneath the words our absentee masters have given us, there is an undermining silence. It saps our nerve. And beneath that silence, there is a raw welter of cadence that tumbles and strains toward words and makes the silence a blessing, because it shushes easy speech. That cadence is home.

We do not own cadence. It is not in Canada—vice-versa—nor is it real only for colonials. But it has its own way of being here for us, if we are willing to be struck dumb first. And through us it seeks to issue in the articulate gestures of being human. Here.

[In the final section of the essay, 'Silence', Lee examines the need for the writer to encounter the reality of his own 'nonbeing':
And for some, at least, the cadence of what is abounds only when we meet it in its fullest grounding in nonbeing. Then each thing comes to resound in its own silence.
Because 'the inauthenticity of our civil space is one such grounding', the Canadian poet must see himself in terms of this void. He will then write a poem that: enacts in words the presence of what we live among . . . that moving cadence of being.

To be human is to live through such movements of being.

Quick in its own silence, cadence seeks to issue in the articulate gesture of being human here.]

1972; rev. 1973, 1983[4]

---

[4]'Cadence, Country, Silence: Writing in a Colonial Space' originated as a lecture given by Lee at the Third Annual Rencontre Québécoise Internationale des Ecrivains held in Montreal in Spring, 1972. It was expanded and published in *Liberté*, Vol. 14, No. 6 (1972); then revised and expanded for *Open Letter*, Ser. 2, No. 6 (1973); this selection is from Lee's newest revision, which will appear in a volume of selected essays.

W.D. Valgardson

b. 1939

William Dempsey Valgardson's stories take place in those Manitoba communities settled by Icelandic immigrants who, in the last quarter of the nineteenth century, exchanged one harsh northern environment for another. Born in Winnipeg, Valgardson grew up in one of these communities, Gimli, in the Interlake region where fishing and farming, often at a subsistence level, are still the primary means of livelihood. After high school Valgardson left Gimli for university, taking a B.A. from United College (1961) and a B.Ed. from the University of Manitoba (1965). He then attended the University of Iowa Writers' Workshop, where he received an M.F.A. in 1969. For the next four years he worked as professor and chairman in the English department of a small women's college in Nevada, Missouri, before accepting his present position as professor of creative writing at the University of Victoria. Although Valgardson's education and work have taken him away from Gimli, he returns there each summer, often selling his own books (as he frequently does elsewhere across Canada) to the townspeople from whom he fashions his fictional characters.

Valgardson's three collections of stories—*Bloodflowers* (1973), *God Is Not a Fish Inspector* (1975), and *Red Dust* (1978)—as well as his novel, *Gentle Sinners* (1980), and much of the poetry in his collection, *In the Gutting Shed* (1976)—grow directly out of the Icelandic literary tradition in which he was raised; their structure and world view recall the great Icelandic sagas. Though his stories are of flawed, even weak, mortal men rather than of mythic heroes, they chronicle the same unending struggle with an unrelenting, overwhelming environment. Valgardson is concerned not so much with good and evil as with fate itself, and his stories are about moral trials in which a character's mettle is tested. Like the sagas, they have an open-ended structure reflecting the continuing nature of this life-long struggle. Downfall and tragedy often result from the failure of Valgardson's characters to recognize their proper place in their community. This loss of perspective may come *either* from rejecting community for personal goals or from placing the need to belong to it above a necessity for heroic action.

Valgardson's stories often resemble documentaries: his omniscient point of view and stark style, combined with detailed descriptions of a bleak existence, give them reportorial verisimilitude. However, they also tend to have a mythic quality, which derives not only from Valgardson's familiarity with Norse sagas but from his interest in Jungian archetypes. Unlike those of many Canadian writers, his tales do not suggest a loss of Eden. Instead they depict a timeless, narrow world, without a point of origin, in which things have always been harsh and difficult. In this environment his characters gauge their worth by their ability to struggle against the forces of men and nature, and even against their own fate as it overtakes them. For Valgardson, the central issue in life is not survival; rather he asks, 'How can a man die better than facing fearful odds?'

God is Not a Fish Inspector

Although Emma made no noise as she descended, Fusi Bergman knew his daughter was watching him from the bottom of the stairs.

'God will punish you,' she promised in a low, intense voice.

'Render unto Caesar what is Caesar's,' he snapped. 'God's not a fish inspector. He doesn't work for the government.'

By the light of the front ring of the kitchen stove, he had been drinking a cup of coffee mixed half and half with whisky. Now, he shifted in his captain's chair so as to partly face the stairs. Though he was unable to make out more than the white blur of Emma's nightgown, after living with her for 48 years he knew exactly how she would look if he turned on the light.

She was tall and big boned with the square, pugnacious face of a bulldog. Every inch of her head would be crammed with metal curlers and her angular body hidden by a plain white cotton shift that hung from her broad shoulders like a tent. Whenever she was angry with him, she always stood rigid and white lipped, her hands clenched at her sides.

'You prevaricate,' she warned. 'You will not be able to prevaricate at the gates of Heaven.'

He drained his cup, sighed, and pulled on his jacket. As he opened the door, Fusi said, 'He made fish to catch. There is no place in the Bible where it says you can't catch fish when you are three score and ten.'

'You'll be the ruin of us,' she hissed as he closed the door on her.

She was aggressive and overbearing, but he knew her too well to be impressed. Behind her forcefulness, there was always that trace of self-pity nurtured in plain women who go unmarried until they think they have been passed by. Even if they eventually found a husband, the self-pity returned to change their determination into a whine. Still, he was glad to have the door between them.

This morning, as every morning, he had wakened at three. Years before, he had trained himself to get up at that time and now, in spite of his age, he never woke more than five minutes after the hour. He was proud of his early rising for he felt it showed he was not, like many of his contemporaries, relentlessly sliding into the endless blur of senility. Each morning, because he had become reconciled to the idea of dying, he felt, on the instant of his awakening, a spontaneous sense of amazement at being alive. The thought never lasted longer than the brief time between sleep and consciousness, but the good feeling lingered throughout the day.

When Fusi stepped outside, the air was cold and damp. The moon that hung low in the west was pale and fragile and very small. 50 feet from the house, the breakwater that ran along the rear of his property loomed like the purple spine of some great beast guarding the land from a lake which seemed, in the darkness, to go on forever.

Holding his breath to still the noise of his own breathing, Fusi listened for a cough or the scuff of gravel that would mean someone was close by, watching and waiting, but the only sound was the muted rubbing of his skiff against the piling to which it was moored. Half a mile away where the land was lower, rows of gas boats roped five abreast lined the docks. The short, stubby boats with their high cabins, the grey surface of the docks and the dark water were all tinged purple from the mercury lamps. At the harbour mouth, high on a thin spire, a red light burned like a distant star.

Behind him, he heard the door open and, for a moment, he was afraid Emma might begin to shout, or worse still, turn on the back-door light and alert his enemies, but she did neither. Above all things, Emma was afraid of scandal, and would do anything to avoid causing an unsavoury rumour to be attached to her own or her husband's name.

Her husband, John Smith, was as bland and inconsequential as his name. Moon faced with wide blue eyes and a small mouth above which sat a carefully trimmed moustache, he was a head shorter than Emma and a good 50 pounds lighter. Six years before, he had been transferred to the Eddyville branch of the Bank of Montreal. His transfer from Calgary to a small town in Manitoba was the bank's way of letting him know that there would be no more promotions. He would stay in Eddyville until he retired.

A year after he arrived, Emma had married him and instead of her moving out, he had moved in. For the last two years, under Emma's prodding, John had been taking a correspondence course in theology so that when he no longer worked at the bank he could be a full-time preacher.

On the evenings when he wasn't balancing the bank's books, he laboured over the multiple-choice questions in the Famous Preacher's course that he received each month from the One True and Only Word of God Church in Mobile, Alabama. Because of a freak in the atmosphere one night while she had been fiddling with the radio, Emma had heard a gospel hour advertising the course and, although neither she nor John had ever been south of Minneapolis and had never heard of the One True and Only Word of God Church before, she took it as a sign and immediately enrolled her husband in it. It cost $500.

John's notes urged him not to wait to answer His Call but to begin ministering to the needy at once for the Judgment Day was always imminent. In anticipation of the end of the world and his need for a congregation once he retired, he and Emma had become zealous missionaries, cramming their Volkswagen with a movie projector, a record-player, films, trays of slides, religious records for every occasion, posters and pamphlets, all bought or rented from the One True and Only Word of God Church. Since the townspeople were obstinately Lutheran, and since John did not want to give offence to any of his bank's customers, he and Emma hunted converts along the grey dirt roads that led past tumble-down farmhouses, the inhabitants of which were never likely to enter a bank.

Fusi did not turn to face his daughter but hurried away because he knew he had no more than an hour and a half until dawn. His legs were fine as he crossed the yard, but by the time he had mounted the steps that led over the breakwater, then climbed down fifteen feet to the shore, his left knee had begun to throb.

Holding his leg rigid to ease the pain, he waded out, loosened the ropes and heaved himself away from the shore. As soon as the boat was in deep water, he took his seat, and set both oars in the oar-locks he had carefully muffled with strips from an old shirt.

For a moment, he rested his hands on his knees, the oars rising like too-small wings from a cumbersome body, then he straightened his arms, dipped the oars cleanly into the water and in one smooth motion pulled his hands toward his chest. The first few strokes were even and graceful but then as a speck of pain like a grain of sand formed in his shoulder, the sweep of his left oar became shorter than his right. Each time he leaned against the oars, the pain grew until it was, in his mind, a bent shingle-nail twisted and turned in his shoulder socket.

With the exertion, a ball of gas formed in his stomach, making him uncomfortable. As quickly as a balloon being blown up, it expanded until his lungs and heart were cramped and he couldn't draw in a full breath. Although the air over the lake was cool, sweat ran from his hairline.

At his two-hundredth stroke, he shipped his left oar and pulled a coil of rope with a large hook from under the seat. After checking to see that it was securely tied through the gunwale, he dropped the rope overboard and once more began to row. Normally, he would have had a buoy made from a slender tamarack pole, a block of wood and some lead weights to mark his net, but he no longer had a fishing licence so his net had to be sunk below the surface where it could not be seen by the fish inspectors.

Five more strokes of the oars and the rope went taut. He lifted both oars into the skiff, then, standing in the bow, began to pull. The boat responded sluggishly but gradually it turned and the cork line that lay hidden under two feet of water broke the surface. He grasped the net, freed the hook and began to collect the mesh until the lead line appeared. For once he had been lucky and the hook had caught the net close to one end so there was no need to backtrack.

Hand over hand he pulled, being careful not to let the corks and leads bang against the bow, for on the open water sound carried clearly for miles. In the first two fathoms there was a freshly caught pickerel. As he pulled it toward him, it beat the water with its tail, making light, slapping sounds. His fingers were cramped, but Fusi managed to catch the fish around its soft middle and, with his other hand, work the mesh free of the gills.

It was then that the pain in his knee forced him to sit. Working from the seat was awkward and cost him precious time, but he had no choice, for the pain had begun to inch up the bone toward his crotch.

He wiped his forehead with his hand and cursed his infirmity. When he was twenty, he had thought nothing of rowing five miles from shore to lift five and six gangs of nets and then, nearly knee deep in fish, row home again. Now, he reflected bitterly, a quarter of a mile and one net were nearly beyond him. Externally, he had changed very little over the years. He was still tall and thin, his arms and legs corded with muscle. His belly was hard. His long face, with its pointed jaw, showed his age the most. That and his hands. His face was lined until it seemed there was nowhere the skin was smooth. His hands were scarred and heavily veined. His hair was grey but it was still thick.

While others were amazed at his condition, he was afraid of the changes that had taken place inside him. It was this invisible deterioration that was gradually shrinking the limits of his endurance.

Even in the darkness, he could see the distant steeple of the Lutheran church and the square bulk of the old folk's home that was directly across from his house. Emma, he thought grimly, would not be satisfied until he was safely trapped in one or carried out of the other.

He hated the old folk's home. He hated the three stories of pale yellow brick with their small, close-set windows. He hated the concrete porch with its five round pillars and the large white buckets of red geraniums. When he saw the men poking at the flowers like a bunch of old women, he pulled his blinds.

The local people who worked in the home were good to the inmates, tenants they called them, but there was no way a man could be a man in there. No whisky. Going to bed at ten. Getting up at eight. Bells for breakfast, coffee and dinner. Bells for everything. He was surprised that they didn't have bells for going to the toilet. Someone watching over you every minute of every day. It was as if, having earned the right to be an adult, you had suddenly, in some inexplicable way, lost it again.

The porch was the worst part of the building. Long and narrow and lined with yellow and red rocking-chairs, it sat ten feet above the ground and the steps were so steep that even those who could get around all right were afraid to try them. Fusi had lived across from the old folk's home for 40 years and he had seen old people, all interchangeable as time erased their identities, shuffling and bickering their way to their deaths. Now, most of those who came out to sleep in the sun and to watch the world with glittering, jealous eyes, were people he had known.

He would have none of it. He was not afraid of dying, but he was determined that it would be in his own home. His licence had been taken from him because of his age, but he did not stop. One net was not thirty, but it was one, and a quarter-mile from shore was not five miles, but it was a quarter-mile.

He didn't shuffle and he didn't have to be fed or have a rubber diaper pinned around him each day. If anything, he had become more cunning for, time and again, the inspectors had come and destroyed the illegal nets of other fishermen, even catching and sending them to court to be fined, but they hadn't caught him for four years. Every day of the fishing season, he pitted his wits against theirs and won. At times, they had come close, but their searches had never turned up anything and, once, to his delight, when he was on the verge of being found with freshly caught fish on him, he hid them under a hole in the breakwater and then sat on the edge of the boat, talked about old times, and shared the inspectors' coffee. The memory still brought back a feeling of pleasure and excitement.

As his mind strayed over past events, he drew the boat along the net in fits and starts for his shoulder would not take the strain of steady pulling. Another good-sized fish hung limp as he pulled it to him, but then as he slipped the mesh from its head, it gave a violent shake and flew from his hands. Too stiff and slow to lunge for it, he could do nothing but watch the white flash of its belly before it struck the water and disappeared.

He paused to knead the backs of his hands, then began again. Before he was finished, his breath roared in his ears like the lake in a storm, but there were four more pickerel. With a sigh that was nearly a cry of pain, he let the net drop. Immediately, pulled down by the heavy, rusted anchors at each end, it disappeared. People were like that, he thought. One moment they were here, then they were gone and it was as if they had never been.

Behind the town, the horizon was a pale, hard grey. The silhouette of rooftops and trees might have been cut from a child's purple construction paper.

The urgent need to reach the shore before the sky became any lighter drove Fusi, for he knew that if the inspectors saw him on the water they would catch him as easily as a child. They would take his fish and net, which he did not really mind, for there were more fish in the lake and more nets in his shed, but he couldn't afford to lose his boat. His savings were not enough to buy another.

He put out the oars, only to be unable to close the fingers of his left hand. When he tried to bend his fingers around the handle, his whole arm began to tremble. Unable to do anything else, he leaned forward and pressing his fingers flat to the seat, he began to relentlessly knead them. Alternately, he prayed and cursed, trying with words to delay the sun.

'A few minutes,' he whispered through clenched teeth. 'Just a few minutes more.' But even as he watched, the horizon turned red, then yellow and a sliver of the sun's rim rose above the houses.

Unable to wait any longer, he grabbed his left hand in his right and forced his fingers around the oar, then braced himself and began to row. Instead of cutting the water cleanly, the left oar skimmed over the surface, twisting the handle in his grip. He tried again, not letting either oar go deep. The skiff moved sluggishly ahead.

Once again, the balloon in his chest swelled and threatened to gag him, making his gorge rise, but he did not dare stop. Again and again, the left oar skipped across the surface so that the bow swung back and forth like a wounded and dying animal trying to shake away its pain. Behind him, the orange sun inched above the sharp angles of the roofs.

When the bow slid across the sand, he dropped the oars, letting them trail in the water. He grasped the gunwale, but as he climbed out, his left leg collapsed and he slid to his knees. Cold water filled his boots and soaked the legs of his trousers. Resting his head against the boat, he breathed noisily through his mouth. He remained there until gradually his breathing eased and the pain in his chest closed like a night flower touched by daylight. When he could stand, he tied the boat to one of the black pilings that was left from a breakwater that had long since been smashed and carried away.

As he collected his catch, he noticed the green fisheries department truck on the dock. He had been right. They were there. Crouching behind his boat, he waited to see if anyone was watching him. It seemed like a miracle that they had not already seen him, but he knew that they had not for if they had, their launch would have raced out of the harbour and swept down upon him.

Bending close to the sand, he limped into the deep shadow at the foot of the breakwater. They might, he knew, be waiting for him at the top of the ladder, but if they were, there was nothing he could do about it. He climbed the ladder and, hearing and seeing nothing, he rested near the top so that when he climbed into sight, he wouldn't need to sit down.

No-one was in the yard. The block was empty. With a sigh of relief, he crossed to the small shed where he kept his equipment and hefted the fish onto the shelf that was nailed to one wall. He filleted his catch with care, leaving none of the translucent flesh on the back-bone or skin. Then, because they were pickerel, he scooped out the cheeks, which he set aside with the roe for his breakfast.

As he carried the offal across the backyard in a bucket, the line of gulls that gathered every morning on the breakwater broke into flight and began to circle overhead. Swinging back the bucket, he flung the guts and heads and skin into the air and the gulls darted down to snatch the red entrails and iridescent heads. In a thrumming of white and grey wings, those who hadn't caught anything descended to the sand to fight for what remained.

Relieved at being rid of the evidence of his fishing—if anyone asked where he got the fillets he would say he had bought them and the other fishermen would lie for him—Fusi squatted and wiped his hands clean on the wet grass.

There was no sign of movement in the house. The blinds were still drawn and the high, narrow house with its steep roof and faded red-brick siding looked deserted. The yard was flat and bare except for the dead trunk of an elm, which was stripped bare of its bark and wind polished to the colour of bone.

He returned to the shed and wrapped the fillets in a sheet of brown waxed paper, then put the roe and the cheeks into the bucket. Neither Emma nor John were up when he came in and washed the bucket and his food, but as he started cooking, Emma appeared in a quilted housecoat covered with large, purple tulips. Her head was a tangle of metal.

'Are you satisfied?' she asked, her voice trembling. 'I've had no sleep since you left.'

Without turning from the stove, he said. 'Leave. Nobody's making you stay.'

Indignantly, she answered, 'And who would look after you?'

He grimaced and turned over the roe so they would be golden brown on all sides. For two weeks around Christmas he had been sick with the flu and she never let him forget it.

'Honour thy father and mother that thy days may be long upon this earth.'

He snorted out loud. What she really wanted to be sure of was that she got the house.

'You don't have to be like this,' she said, starting to talk to him as if he was a child. 'I only want you to stop because I care about you. All those people who live across the street, they don't. . . .'

'I'm not one of them,' he barked.

'You're 70 years old. . . .'

'And I still fish,' he replied angrily, cutting her off. 'And I still row a boat and lift my nets. That's more than your husband can do and he's just 50.' He jerked his breakfast off the stove. Because he knew it would annoy her, he began to eat out of the pan.

'I'm 70,' he continued between bites, 'and I beat the entire fisheries department. They catch men half my age, but they haven't caught me. Not for four years. And I fish right under their noses.' He laughed with glee and laced his coffee with a finger of whisky.

Emma, her lips clamped shut and her hands clenched in fury, marched back up the stairs. In half an hour both she and John came down for their breakfast. Under Emma's glare, John cleared his throat and said, 'Emma, that is we, think—' He stopped and fiddled with the knot of his tie. He always wore light grey ties and a light grey suit. 'If you don't quit breaking the law, something will have to be done.' He stopped and looked beseechingly at his wife, but she narrowed her eyes until little folds of flesh formed beneath them. 'Perhaps something like putting you in custody so you'll be saved from yourself.'

Fusi was so shocked that for once he could think of nothing to say. Encouraged by his silence, John said, 'It will be for your own good.'

Before either of them realized what he was up to, Fusi leaned sideways and emptied his cup into his son-in-law's lap.

The coffee was hot. John flung himself backward with a screech, but the back legs of his chair caught on a crack in the linoleum and he tipped over with a crash. In the confusion Fusi stalked upstairs.

In a moment he flung an armload of clothes down. When his daughter rushed to the bottom of the stairs, Fusi flung another armload of clothes at her.

'This is my house,' he bellowed. 'You're not running it yet.'

Emma began grabbing clothes and laying them flat so they wouldn't wrinkle. John, both hands clenched between his legs, hobbled over to stare.

Fusi descended the stairs and they parted to let him by. At the counter, he picked up the package of fish and turning toward them, said, 'I want you out of here when I get back or I'll go out on the lake and get caught and tell everyone that you put me up to it.'

His fury was so great that once he was outside he had to lean against the house while a spasm of trembling swept over him. When he was composed, he rounded the corner. At one side of the old folk's home there was an enclosed fire escape that curled to the ground like a piece of intestine. He headed for the kitchen door under it.

Fusi had kept on his rubber boots, dark slacks and red turtle-neck sweater, and because he knew that behind the curtains, eyes were watching his every move, he tried to hide the stiffness in his left leg.

Although it was early, Rosie Melysyn was already at work. She always came first, never missing a day. She was a large, good natured widow with grey hair.

'How are you today, Mr Bergman?' she asked.

'Fine,' he replied. 'I'm feeling great.' He held out the brown paper package. 'I thought some of the old people might like some fish.' Although he had brought fish for the last four years, he always said the same thing.

Rosie dusted off her hands, took the package and placed it on the counter.

'I'll see someone gets it,' she assured him. 'Help yourself to some coffee.'

As he took the pot from the stove, she asked, 'No trouble with the inspectors?'

He always waited for her to ask that. He grinned delightedly, the pain of the morning already becoming a memory. 'No trouble. They'll never catch me. I'm up too early. I saw them hanging about, but it didn't do them any good.'

'Jimmy Henderson died last night,' Rosie offered.

'Jimmy Henderson,' Fusi repeated. They had been friends, but he felt no particular sense of loss. Jimmy had been in the home for three years. 'I'm not surprised. He wasn't more than 68 but he had given up. You give up, you're going to die. You believe in yourself and you can keep right on going.'

Rosie started mixing oatmeal and water.

'You know,' he said to her broad back, 'I was with Jimmy the first time he got paid. He cut four cords of wood for 60¢ and spent it all on hootch. He kept running up and down the street and flapping his arms, trying to fly. When he passed out, we hid him in the hayloft of the stable so his old man couldn't find him.'

Rosie tried to imagine Jimmy Henderson attempting to fly and failed. To her, he was a bent man with a sad face who had to use a walker to get to the diningroom. What she remembered about him was coming on him unexpectedly and finding him silently crying. He had not seen her and she had quietly backed away.

Fusi was lingering because after he left, there was a long day ahead of him. He would have the house to himself and after checking the vacated room to see that nothing of his had been taken, he would tie his boat properly, sleep for three hours, then eat lunch. In the afternoon he would make a trip to the docks to see what the inspectors were up to and collect information about their movements.

The back door opened with a swish and he felt a cool draft. Both he and Rosie turned to look. He was shocked to see that instead of it being one of the kitchen help, it was Emma. She shut the door and glanced at them both, then at the package of fish.

'What do you want?' he demanded.

'I called the inspectors,' she replied, 'to tell them you're not responsible for yourself. I told them about the net.'

He gave a start, but then was relieved when he remembered they had to actually catch him fishing before they could take the skiff. 'So what?' he asked, confident once more.

Quietly, she replied 'You don't have to worry about being caught. They've known about your fishing all along.'

Suddenly frightened by her calm certainty, his voice rose as he said, 'That's not true.'

'They don't care,' she repeated. 'Inspector McKenzie was the name of the one I talked to. He said you couldn't do any harm with one net. They've been watching you every morning just in case you should get into trouble and need help.'

Emma stood there, not moving, her head tipped back, her eyes benevolent.

He turned to Rosie. 'She's lying, isn't she? That's not true. They wouldn't do that?'

'Of course, she's lying,' Rosie assured him.

He would have rushed outside but Emma was standing in his way. Since he could not get past her, he fled through the swinging doors that led to the diningroom.

As the doors shut, Rosie turned on Emma and said, 'You shouldn't have done that.' She picked up the package of fish with its carefully folded wrapping. In the artificial light, the package glowed like a piece of amber. She held it cupped in the hollows of her hands. 'You had no right.'

Emma seemed to grow larger and her eyes shone.

'The Lord's work be done,' she said, her right hand partly raised as if she were preparing to give a benediction.

1975

Clarke Blaise

b. 1940

Clark Blaise is a border-crosser. Born in North Dakota of an English-Canadian mother and a French-Canadian father, he moved frequently in his youth as his father failed in one business enterprise after another. Rarely completing a grade in any single school, Blaise lived in Florida, Georgia, New Jersey, Ohio, Kentucky, and Manitoba (where his mother still lives). He took a B.A. from Denison University in 1961 and then attended Harvard University (studying with Bernard Malamud) and the University of Iowa's Writers' Workshop, where he earned an M.F.A. in 1964. He taught English at the University of Wisconsin until 1966, when he accepted a job at Sir George Williams (now Concordia University). From 1978 to 1980 Blaise taught at York University and co-edited, with John Metcalf, the annual anthology *Best Canadian Stories*. Since 1981 he has taught at Skidmore College (Saratoga Springs, N.Y.) and the Iowa Writers' Workshop. In 1983 Blaise began a year of full-time writing on a Guggenheim fellowship while residing in Iowa.

Having grown up in the United States thinking of himself as a Canadian, Blaise has come to see himself as a permanent outsider, displaced in French and English Canada as well as in the U.S. His work has dealt extensively with this estrangement, transforming autobiographical incidents into parables of alienation. Confessional in tone, his narratives tend to reveal the innermost self of his narrators—a shadow self that embodies feelings of repressed guilt arising from displacement. Blaise's first collection of short stories, *North American Education* (1973), traces the lives of three characters (all resembling the author) who lack a home country and are unable to become part of any environment. *Tribal Justice* (1974) expands on this theme: the stories in this collection not only look at the alienation of such outsiders, but also at the way membership in any group—whether ethnic, racial, geographical, or religious—leads to some degree of social exclusion. Blaise's travel narrative, *Days and Nights in Calcutta* (1977), written with his wife, the novelist Bharati Mukherjee, continues this attempt to explore the experience of the outsider; the observations of Blaise, clearly an alien in India, are paired with those of Mukherjee who, through her marriage and the language in which she writes, has chosen alienation.

Blaise's first novel, *Lunar Attractions* (1979), is also autobiographical. It resembles a number of his earlier short stories in which the narrator reflects on his traumatic childhood. Blaise has described such narratives as ones in which 'an adult voice of unspecified age and circumstance describes a test that he failed years earlier, and the deeper chaos that has resulted. . . . The failure stems not from a lack of nerve or ambition or courage or even intelligence . . . but rather from a sudden contact with infinity' (Blaise's introduction to his stories in *New Canadian Writing 1968*). This notion of a failed struggle for enlightenment—which Blaise associates with philosopher Pascal and with the Jansenist Catholicism Blaise inherited from his father—is a feature of all his fiction. Unlike James Joyce's short fictions that offer sudden insights as small epiphanies, a Blaise story ends with an 'anti-epiphany'—a discovery, not of the unifying factor that will suddenly make sense of the chaos of life but of a subterranean void that throws the innocent world of childhood into confusion and despair.

The structures of Blaise's stories are determined by this moment of Jansenist realization that one's will is corrupt and one's environment depraved. He builds his narratives around parallels and echoes—using images (such as 'eyes') that draw together the apparently unrelated elements of the story. At moments of horrific discovery in these narratives such a central image is transformed into an emblem of infinite chaos, and the other images that have been associated with it become repugnant by association. Thus Blaise's stories do not follow the classic short-story structure of a single line of action. They are rather composed of disparate narrative threads that join not in a climax of event—little action takes place in a Blaise story—but in a climax of apprehension: the uncovering of a hidden 'unfathomable complexity, the insolent infinity that defeats our humanity' (New Canadian Writing 1968).

Eyes

You jump into this business of a new country cautiously. First you choose a place where English is spoken, with doctors and bus lines at hand, and a supermarket in a *centre d'achats* not too far away. You ease yourself into the city, approaching by car or bus down a single artery, aiming yourself along the boulevard that begins small and tree-lined in your suburb but broadens into the canyoned aorta of the city five miles beyond. And by that first winter when you know the routes and bridges, the standard congestions reported from the helicopter on your favorite radio station, you start to think of moving. What's the good of a place like this when two of your neighbors have come from Texas and the French paper you've dutifully subscribed to arrives by mail two days late? These French are all around you, behind the counters at the shopping center, in a house or two on your block; why isn't your little boy learning French at least? Where's the nearest *maternelle?* Four miles away.

In the spring you move. You find an apartment on a small side street where dogs outnumber children and the row houses resemble London's, divided equally between the rundown and remodeled. Your neighbors are the young personalities of French television who live on delivered chicken, or the old pensioners who shuffle down the summer sidewalks in pajamas and slippers in a state of endless recuperation. Your neighbors pay sixty a month for rent, or three hundred; you pay two-fifty for a two-bedroom flat where the walls have been replastered and new fixtures hung. The bugs *d'antan*[1] remain, as well as the hulks of cars abandoned in the fire alley behind, where downtown drunks sleep in the summer night.

Then comes the night in early October when your child is coughing badly, and you sit with him in the darkened nursery, calm in the bubbling of a cold-steam vaporizer while your wife mends a dress in the room next door. And from the dark, silently, as you peer into the ill-lit fire alley, he comes. You cannot believe it at first, that a rheumy, pasty-faced Irishman in slate-gray jacket and rubber-soled shoes has come purposely to *your* small parking space, that he has been here before and he is not drunk (not now, at least, but you know him as a pan-

[1]Of yesteryear.

handler on the main boulevard a block away), that he brings with him a crate that he sets on end under your bedroom window and raises himself to your window ledge and hangs there nose-high at a pencil of light from the ill-fitting blinds. And there you are, straining with him from the uncurtained nursery, watching the man watching your wife, praying silently that she is sleeping under the blanket. The man is almost smiling, a leprechaun's face that sees what you cannot. You are about to lift the window and shout, but your wheezing child lies just under you; and what of your wife in the room next door? You could, perhaps, throw open the window and leap to the ground, tackle the man before he runs and smash his face into the bricks, beat him senseless then call the cops . . . Or better, find the camera, afix the flash, rap once at the window and shoot when he turns. Do nothing and let him suffer. *He is at your mercy,* no one will ever again be so helpless—but what can you do? You know, somehow, he'll escape. If you hurt him, he can hurt you worse, later, viciously. He's been a regular at your window, he's watched the two of you when you prided yourself on being young and alone and masters of the city. He knows your child and the park he plays in, your wife and where she shops. He's a native of the place, a man who knows the city and maybe a dozen such windows, who knows the fire escapes and alleys and roofs, knows the habits of the city's heedless young.

And briefly you remember yourself, an adolescent in another country slithering through the mosquito-ridden grassy fields behind a housing development, peering into those houses where newlyweds had not yet put up drapes, how you could spend five hours in a motionless crouch for a myopic glimpse of a slender arm reaching from the dark to douse a light. Then you hear what the man cannot; the creaking of your bed in the far bedroom, the steps of your wife on her way to the bathroom, and you see her as you never have before: blond and tall and rangily built, a north-Europe princess from a constitutional monarchy, sensuous mouth and prominent teeth, pale, tennis-ball breasts cupped in her hands as she stands in the bathroom's light.

'How's Kit?' she asks. 'I'd give him a kiss except that there's no blind in there,' and she dashes back to bed, nude, and the man bounces twice on the window ledge.

'You coming?'

You find yourself creeping from the nursery, turning left at the hall and then running to the kitchen telephone; you dial the police, then hang up. How will you prepare your wife, not for what is happening, but for what has already taken place?

'It's stuffy in here,' you shout back, 'I think I'll open the window a bit.' You take your time, you stand before the blind blocking his view if he's still looking, then bravely you part the curtains. He is gone, the crate remains upright. 'Do we have any masking tape?' you ask, lifting the window a crack.

And now you know the city a little better. A place where millions come each summer to take pictures and walk around must have its voyeurs too. And that place in all great cities where rich and poor co-exist is especially hard on the people in-between. It's health you've been seeking, not just beauty; a tough urban health that will save you money in the bargain, and when you hear of a place twice as large at half the rent, in a part of town free of Texans, English, and

French, free of young actors and stewardesses who deposit their garbage in pizza boxes, you move again.

It is, for you, a city of Greeks. In the summer you move you attend a movie at the corner cinema. The posters advertise a war movie, in Greek, but the uniforms are unfamiliar. Both sides wear mustaches, both sides handle machine guns, both leave older women behind dressed in black. From the posters outside there is a promise of sex; blond women in slips, dark-eyed peasant girls. There will be rubble, executions against a wall. You can follow the story from the stills alone: mustached boy goes to war, embraces dark-eyed village girl. Black-draped mother and admiring young brother stand behind. Young soldier, mustache fuller, embraces blond prostitute on a tangled bed. Enter soldiers, boy hides under sheets. Final shot, back in village. Mother in black; dark-eyed village girl in black. Young brother marching to the front.

You go in, pay your ninety cents, pay a nickel in the lobby for a wedge of *halvah*-like sweets. You understand nothing, you resent their laughter and you even resent the picture they're running. Now you know the Greek for 'Coming Attractions', for this is a gangster movie at least thirty years old. The eternal Mediterranean gangster movie set in Athens instead of Naples or Marseilles, with smaller cars and narrower roads, uglier women and more sinister killers. After an hour the movie flatters you. No one knows you're not a Greek, that you don't belong in this theatre, or even this city. That, like the Greeks, you're hanging on.

Outside the theatre the evening is warm and the wide sidewalks are clogged with Greeks who nod as you come out. Like the Ramblas in Barcelona,[2] with children out past midnight and families walking back and forth for a long city block, the men filling the coffeehouses, the women left outside, chatting. Not a blond head on the sidewalk, not a blond head for miles. Greek music pours from the coffeehouses, flies stumble on the pastry, whole families munch their *torsades molles*[3] as they walk. Dry goods are sold at midnight from the sidewalk, like New York fifty years ago. You're wandering happily, glad that you moved, you've rediscovered the innocence of starting over.

Then you come upon a scene directly from Spain. A slim blond girl in a floral top and white pleated skirt, tinted glasses, smoking, with bad skin, ignores a persistent young Greek in a shiny Salonika[4] suit. 'Whatsamatta?' he demands, slapping a ten-dollar bill on his open palm. And without looking back at him she drifts closer to the curb and a car makes a sudden squealing turn and lurches to a stop on the cross street. Three men are inside, the back door opens and not a word is exchanged as she steps inside. How? What refinement of gesture did we immigrants miss? You turn to the Greek boy in sympathy, you know just how he feels, but he's already heading across the street, shouting something to his friends outside a barbecue stand. You have a pocketful of bills and a Mediterranean soul, and money this evening means a woman, and blond means whore and you would spend it all on another blond with open pores; all this a block from your wife and tenement. And you hurry home.

[2]In Barcelona *ramblas* are 'avenues' (elsewhere a *rambla* is a ravine).
[3]Pastry twists.
[4]Seaport in northeastern Greece.

Months later you know the place. You trust the Greeks in their stores, you fear their tempers at home. Eight bathrooms adjoin a central shaft, you hear the beatings of your son's friends, the thud of fist on bone after the slaps. Your child knows no French, but he plays cricket with Greeks and Jamaicans out in the alley behind Pascal's hardware. He brings home the oily tires from the Esso station, plays in the boxes behind the appliance store. You watch from a greasy back window, at last satisfied. None of his friends is like him, like you. He is becoming Greek, becoming Jamaican, becoming a part of this strange new land. His hair is nearly white; you can spot him a block away.

On Wednesdays the butcher quarters his meat. Calves arrive by refrigerator truck, still intact but for their split-open bellies and sawed-off hooves. The older of the three brothers skins the carcass with a small thin knife that seems all blade. A knife he could shave with. The hide rolls back in a continuous flap, the knife never pops the membrane over the fat.

Another brother serves. Like yours, his French is adequate. *'Twa lif d'hamburger'*, you request, still watching the operation on the rickety sawhorse. Who could resist? It's a Levantine treat, the calf's stumpy legs high in the air, the hide draped over the edge and now in the sawdust, growing longer by the second.

The store is filling. The ladies shop on Wednesday, especially the old widows in black overcoats and scarves, shoes and stockings. Yellow, mangled fingernails. Wednesdays attract them with boxes in the window, and they call to the butcher as they enter, the brother answers, and the women dip their fingers in the boxes. The radio is loud overhead, music from the Greek station.

'Une et soixante, m'sieur. Du bacon, jambon?'

And you think, taking a few lamb chops but not their saltless bacon, how pleased you are to manage so well. It is a Byzantine moment with blood and widows and sides of dripping beef, contentment in a snowy slum at five below.

The older brother, having finished the skinning, straightens, curses, and puts away the tiny knife. A brother comes forward to pull the hide away, a perfect beginning for a gameroom rug. Then, bending low at the rear of the glistening carcass, the legs spread high and stubby, the butcher digs in his hands, ripping hard where the scrotum is, and pulls on what seems to be a strand of rubber, until it snaps. He puts a single glistening prize in his mouth, pulls again and offers the other to his brother, and they suck.

The butcher is singing now, drying his lips and wiping his chin, and still he's chewing. The old black-draped widows with the parchment faces are also chewing. On leaving, you check the boxes in the window. Staring out are the heads of pigs and lambs, some with the eyes lifted out and a red socket exposed. A few are loose and the box is slowly dissolving from the blood, and the ice beneath.

The women have gathered around the body; little pieces are offered to them from the head and entrails. The pigs' heads are pink, perhaps they've been boiled, and hairless. The eyes are strangely blue. You remove your gloves and touch the skin, you brush against the grainy ear. How the eye attracts you! How you would like to lift one out, press its smoothness against your tongue, then crush it in your mouth. And you cannot. Already your finger is numb and the head, it seems, has shifted under you. And the eye, in panic, grows white as your finger approaches. You would take that last half inch but for the certainty, in this world you have made for yourself, that the eye would blink and your neighbors would turn upon you.

1973

Frank Davey

b. 1940

Frank Davey grew up in Abbotsford, B.C., until 1957, when he returned to Vancouver, the city of his birth, to study at the University of British Columbia (B.A., 1961; M.A., 1963). While at UBC Davey became part of a group of aspiring poets—which included George Bowering, Fred Wah, and Lionel Kearns—who shared an interest in the American Black Mountain poetry movement (especially the theories of Charles Olson). With Davey as editor and the others as contributing editors they founded *Tish* (1961-9), a mimeographed poetry magazine and newsletter that served as a monthly outlet for their own work and that of other writers in whom they were interested. The founding editors left the magazine after issue No. 19 (1963) to pursue separate interests; Davey later brought those early issues together for book publication: *Tish No. 1-19* (1975).

In 1963 Davey took a teaching position at Royal Roads Military College in Victoria, where he remained until 1969. After two years there he began a new magazine, *Open Letter*, to provide a forum in Canada for discussions of contemporary writing. He also published four books of poetry during this period: *D-Day and After* (1963), *City of the Gulls and Sea* (1964), *Bridge Force* (1965), and *The Scarred Hull* (1966). In 1966-7 he took a year away from his teaching to attend graduate school at the University of Southern California, completing his Ph.D. in 1968 with a thesis on Black Mountain poetry and poetics. In 1969-70 Davey was writer-in-residence at Sir George Williams (now part of Concordia University), and the following year he

moved to Toronto to join the Department of English at York University, where he still teaches.

Between 1970 and 1974 Davey published six new books of poems—*Four Myths for Sam Perry* (1970), *Weeds* (1970), *King of Swords* (1972), *Griffon* (1972), *Arcana* (1973), and *The Clallam* (1974)—as well as *L'An Trentiesme: Selected Poems 1961-70* (1972). Three of these books (*Weeds, King of Swords*, and *Arcana*) dealt with the collapse of his first marriage at the end of the sixties, while *Griffon* and *The Clallam* returned to a subject treated extensively in *The Scarred Hull*: shipwrecks and sunken ships. In 1971 Davey resumed editing *Open Letter* (having suspended its publication two years earlier), and in 1975 he joined bp Nichol and Michael Ondaatje as members of a new editorial board at Coach House Press. More recently Davey has published *Capitalistic Affections!* (1982), poems on comic strips as the myths of childhood, and he is working on *War Poems*—which has appeared in three pre-publication 'manuscript editions' (all 1979). In 1980 bp Nichol edited Davey's *Selected Poems: The Arches*.

Like a number of other Canadian writers, Davey has been especially interested in longer poetic forms. (In 1983 he published a critical chapbook called *The Contemporary Canadian Long Poem*.) His own books of poetry have all been loosely unified, most often in the form of the 'serial poem', a sequence held together by associations growing out of an image, object, or event rather than by a narrative or conceptual structure. Davey defines the serial poem as a loose sequence composed over an extended and indefinite period of time; without knowing where he will be led, the poet lets each poem suggest the next, while at the same time keeping himself open to new influences. These poems are a kind of phenomenological poetry—that is, they attempt to provide records of the poet's consciousness in the actual moment of discovering and giving voice to his material. Since by definition the serial poem can have no resolution, it must be abandoned rather than formally ended (as the subtitle to 'The Mirror', in the selection that follows, suggests).

This emphasis on process—part of the Black Mountain influence on the *Tish* poets—is closely allied to an emphasis on particulars. In a statement printed on the jacket of *Bridge Force*, Davey declared:

I tell only what I know, and speculate, never. Only with the validity of fact, and the form of the natural object, can a poem hope to survive in a world that admits only the real.

This concern with 'fact' has actually led Davey in several directions. In part it has resulted in his creation of a body of very personal, sometimes confessional, poetry in which the poet confronts his own past, even in its most intimate and least pleasant aspects. However, since Davey believes that 'there really can be no line between the external and the internal environment', the poet's facts come from *everything* he experiences and learns about, including the history and myths he inherits—sometimes unknowingly. Davey has engaged himself with the material of history, discovering its meaning in the ongoing present in his poetry about ships and shipwrecks. This use of the past suggests the importance for him of E.J. Pratt as a significant example of a poet who transformed history into long poetic works—although Davey rejects Pratt's use of traditional narrative, considering it inappropriate to the modern era.

If history is one kind of 'fact' that extends the poet's range, myths are another. Explaining the presence of myth in works such as *Arcana, King of Swords*, and *Weeds*, Davey remarked in an interview with George Bowering: 'All legend, all myth, I believe . . . is based on historical fact. You scratch a legend and you find a

real human being' (*Open Letter*, Fourth Series, No. 3, 1979). Indeed, for Davey, reality always takes on symbolic meaning because, as he has observed about the garden setting of his poem *Weeds*, 'All literal gardens are archetypal gardens.'

Whether responding to legend, to nautical history, or to events in his personal life, Davey's poetry is drawn together—as Nichol has remarked—by an overriding concern 'with relationships':

of man to woman, woman to man, captain to passengers, notions of responsibility & duty within a context of trust, & of how that trust is realized or betrayed. Sometimes the thrust is political or historical, sometimes entirely personal, but the issue is always there. (Introduction, Selected Poems: The Arches*)*

As well as being a poet and editor, Davey has also played an important role as a critic. He has written studies of individual writers and their work: *Five Readings of Olson's 'Maximus'* (1970), *Earle Birney* (1971), and *Louis Dudek and Raymond Souster* (1980). (Dudek—because of his own commitment to little magazines and small presses, as well as his experiments with loosely unified long poems—has always been an exemplary figure for Davey.) Davey is also the author of an important survey of the contemporary literary scene, *From There to Here: A Guide to English-Canadian Literature since 1960* (1974), which contains succinct accounts of sixty writers (along with bibliographies of primary and secondary material). This separate treatment of each writer, which makes neither connections nor generalizations, follows from Davey's opposition to 'thematic' criticism—that is, to the cultural interpretations of Canadian literature made by Northrop Frye and by the critics Frye has influenced, such as D.G. Jones and Margaret Atwood. In *Surviving the Paraphrase and Other Essays* (1983) Davey argues that thematic and cultural approaches, by ignoring the individuality of the artist and the freedom to choose 'among influences and traditions rather than being passively formed by them', lose sight of what makes each literary work unique.

Davey's criticism, however, contains its own generalizations and frameworks, deriving from his preferences for *avant-*

garde and post-modern writers over traditional and modernist authors. Davey considers most interesting those contemporary writers in Canada who see the world not as having an underlying static order, but as existing in a dynamic state of flux. To respond to this world, these writers turn away from a literature that is formal and closed and create one that internalizes and dramatizes the processes it is part of.

Davey's own poetry embodies this aesthetic. Despite the meditative tone of many of his poems—which conveys a sense of the poet's internalizing of his experiences—they never reach a still point; each moment leads instead to the next as the writer seeks 'To let one's words bespeak one's condition/at the moment of speaking. A poetry. I would be/that careful. That careful.' ('The Mirror')

From *Weeds*[1]
The Garden

My hours moving earth & leaves, about this garden. How they all, hold me. When Adam dwelld there, did his eyes too, fall away from his Eve? Or was it after, that he loved the wild roses he was leaving, the timid jackals from his doorway slinking. And I too, love those blooms. I stand among them in this city wind, not wishing to look back to house & window, wanting only, this soil on my skin, this traffic noise, these birds against my ears.

But Adam. Every day when he heard her scream behind him, did his mind flee, to wander there? But it would be no longer the garden. Yet why do my eyes yearn to hide here? What did he believe, when his heart dreamd of the old shelters? What is this place I am calling, garden?

[1]*Weeds* is a serial poem made up of twenty-six short prose poems. The selection here comprises the first poem, the fourth, the sixth, the eighth through the twelfth, the twentieth and twenty-first, and the twenty-fifth. (The concluding, twenty-sixth, poem is made up of the last sentence of the twenty-fifth poem repeated over the length of a page.)

The Bandit

A day spent bringing water to dry soil. So much dryness, & the weeds, thriving in the dust, grassblades piercing the aubretia,[1] chick weed, crowding past the alyssum. So much that happens, when let happen. Left alone, there would still be a garden. Camas, dandelions, cosmos, broom—blues & yellows rising all among the matted grass.

And what is the life of such a garden, the life, the way, the

[1]Usually 'aubrietia': small herb with purple or violet flowers, frequently used in rock gardens; 'chickweed': a hardy garden weed with a small white flower; 'alyssum': a spring garden flower (most often yellow) much favoured in English gardens and formerly believed to have curative properties; 'camas': blue-violet flower of the lily family, sometimes occurring wild; 'cosmos': ornamental garden plant with scarlet and purple flowers (in northern climates it can be grown only by starting it indoors and transplanting it after the danger of frost is past); 'broom': a European shrub with bright yellow flowers that has been naturalized in North America.

path of weeds and flowers? What is a weed?—a choice of
flowers, a forcing of a way. How far have I come, pulling
'weeds', upending stones, forcing, at the point of a hose, the
flowers from the garden?

Weeds

As tho weeds could stop growing. Pull up the weeds, show them
to daylight, sunlight, let the roots be seen for what they are, dry
them out, kill them, turn them to compost the old alchemical
trick, a weed, but in the service of the garden.

And the garden, it grows weeds. They spring from the very
rendings of the soil that mark where the old weeds grew. So
hard not to think of. 'A weed,' they say. Tear it up, tear it up,
the shock of weeds growing, of me following, weed to weed to
catch them all, & what, what they can mean for the garden.

The Reading

There is nothing that cannot be written. A maxim, told to
myself, in the morning. The eyes grow angry with reading. To
break the news gently, that I do feel, & do feel, variously.

To break the news gently. A requirement? the breaking? What
is it that is broken. Not the news. It is a world, its floss was
spun in a silver cup. She eats it, greedily. Now a broken world,
broken news. I am not who she dreamd I was. There are words
written. They are real. They steal the food from her mouth, snap
it. Shards of spun candy are tangled about a room.

What Is in the Sky Is Not Brown

To forget the ways. Despite her skin, despite the days my
fingers refuse its touch, the logic of not forgetting. The
reminders of love, old slippers on a bedroom floor, eyes in these
photos that she places about the house, to prevent, the
forgetting.

Yet I must, forget. The dishes in the sink, ooze scraps of five
meals, eaten in silence. The cat is huggd by each in turn. Deep,
in the refrigerator door, I can see myself, in porcelain. Sallow
cheeks, greying hair, my cheeks fragile as eggs, suckt. Her
voice. I turn. She again holds the cat, both, are brown, both,
hungry.

Mealtimes

My wife I suppose has taught me to nibble on raw hamburger.
Or I have learnd. On Sunday in the park the ducks bit each
other's bills in clashing for our bread. Snap of bone, on bone.

As if all were a room. As if this room were all. My loves, my
lovers, piling brick after brick at the door & window. No! I will
not stay. The walls of this chamber are paneld in raw flesh.
Bloody webs hang from the ceiling, float across my cheeks. A
raw deal, carvd out of the hollow within a handsome skull. My
skull. Mortgaged. Degrees of rotting meat.

Lord, love the selfish duck, tearing crumbs from the beak of
her mate.

The Place

The page is a rectangle borderd by cliffs. How far can one go.
Without leaving. Stay home. The world is flat. Not even a page
it is a notepad, write yourself a note, warn yourself there are
edges, edges, they will catch you, she, will not catch you, all of
it, is hers is her fault.

If she had caught you you would not be here, bouncing across
this narrow space. Not be here, physically, in this house where
the cat paces the hallways crying, wishing to be elsewhere but
afraid of the rain, not to be here, in this place that has become
who you are, a crying cat, continuous the rain.

A Yellow Page

How does a voice call? Who were the gardeners of
Gethsemane?[1] Here I, one hundred & fifty pounds, kneel on the
whirling crust of a planet of a backcountry sun. Raise spots of
color for her face, save leaves for compost, or amid the litter of
a desk, save scraps of words, old ink, a yellow page.

Who were the gardeners of Gethsemane? How long did they
labor, what voices raise? Were there footsteps, warning?
Flashings of light from the soil? I have feard for years now, the
long trajectories that are charted overhead, just as then, the
citizens trembled at the marching legions, their long shadows in
the garden. Later, not a stone unturnd.

But what else I fear. Who first will lift the stone? Who kiss?
Who kisst Eve the day before another garden vanisht from his
eyes?

---

[1]The garden of Gethsemane was the place to which Jesus withdrew to pray on the eve of his Crucifixion. He was betrayed there when Judas, bringing the Roman soldiers who took him prisoner, identified him with a kiss.

The Rock

A garden of flowers. I was digging in search of a garden of
flowers, when I struck a rock. Its extent at first was not clear,
only this: a layer of rock had interposed itself between the point
of my shovel & the garden. I dug, sod after sod from the sides,
searching for the edges, the lawn shrinking as the rock spread.
Then the shovel, catching, under the rock's lip, its shaft
bending.

Underneath the rock there was no garden of flowers. There is
a deep hole where there was to be a garden. At the hole's head
stands the rock. Yellowd grass & worms are rushing to its place
on the lawn.

Them Apples

Once there was a beautiful bird. I photographt its orange
necklace as it fed on the slatted top of an apple box, balanced on
the snow.

There are no more wooden apple boxes. Holes have been
drilld in the wood, the nails have been stolen. There are not even
orange feathers on the snow. Small grey finches dart to snap
crumbs from among swirling crystals. Icicles threaten the
doorway from the eaves. Inside, you & I divide the cutlery, the
dishes, knives, scraps of candle, cans of peas. The floor by the
window where I lie is cold. There are drifts mounting, & there is
snow flashing by the darkness of the tree trunks. I can see your
footprints, rounded furrows in the white lawn. How the snow,
rushes there, into you.

I Do Not Write Poems

I do not write poems, I do not even write you letters, telling you
of the winds inside my bones, of the words that stumble within
my flesh. I cannot sleep. I cannot sleep for the poems I do not
write, speaking, for the letters I do not write marching thru my
space, desiring, desiring your eyes.

How the words would destroy you, would send your heart
exploding its dark flesh, into your ankles & your brain. How
great these winds. How great the sentences that would drive &
drive these words to my hand, drive the razor blade to your
wrists, your blood into ponds for the cat, to lap from on your
kitchen floor.

Red

And where is love? Was a garden lost in its name? The lady lies
now on a rotting wharf, hangs traps for crabs. The planks of the
wharf are white from the sun. Her hands smell of dead fish.

And was a garden. Lost in the name of love. Two crabs are in
her trap, are gript, by her hand, across their shells. How they
flinch as she thrusts them into the steaming pot, contract, in the
bubbling water. And was a garden lost. The crack of the
skeletons. Orange entrails spew upon the rocks. For love?
Behold, a bowl of severd limbs. Chew, this morning's muscles
of the seafloor.

1970

The Mirror[1]
a serial poem abandoned 16 March, 1970

1. THE MIRROR

What I stand before. Not
God, not a crown, but
my own words, reproaching.

Their face is almost freckled.
The eyes are almost green.
The lenses smeard
with dandruff & dust.

Below, at belly,
a basin
fleckt with whiskers, calcimined   10
with toothpaste spit.

My words. Like you—
I am damned by them. The men
they would have murderd. The
countries stolen.

Under my four
plastic teeth, the supper's
half-chewd meat is rotting. A mammal's
dying has clutcht my tongue.

[1]This serial poem, printed here in its entirety, serves as a coda to *Arcana*; in the longer sequence that
precedes it and makes up the body of that book Davey finds correspondences between Tarot cards
('arcana' are the trumps of the Tarot deck) and events in his life during the period when his first marriage (to Helen) fails and he begins a new one and fathers a child.

2. THE WINDOWS

My eyes are roses, staring
from the trellis, white.
Description: today I scrub
the dining room's three rows
of twelve-paned windows.
And with the strokes
reflect, how the world
blooms. A sorcerer
I'd be, molding
squares of all I see   10
from bucket, soap,
two mushing piles of newspaper.

Yet would I avoid description?
So seldom I move to clean
these glasses which I wear.
I press myself, this poem,
this mouldering paper
so far within you.
That you would see.
That you would love me.   20
But not I? Is this
which I scrub, truly
window? How not
to end this
like another poem?

3. THE COLOR

The day I thot the snow was blue
was like the day I thot
Bob Creeley[1] was a friend. Colors

are not things, not qualities I could ever
make sense of. Depresst. Literally,
pusht down, blue, & that

the color of the ink of every poem when I write it.
And the snow on this windowledge
is white. On the sidewalk, brown. Why must

the snow be white, or brown. Why not   10
orange snow or red snow,
purple or blue? But

from November to April

---

[1](b. 1926); with Robert Duncan and Charles Olson one of the principals of the Black Mountain
poetry movement. Davey took a course from Creeley when he was a visiting professor at the University of British Columbia in 1962-3.

it is white & brown,
from November to April, & so

I say to me, to you
God save us that our poems
be not one color, & not only
two.

4. SURREALISM IS

Applying one's ass to the seat of a chair.
Ten poems a day. That was after
I stopt coughing up words & had to
roll my own.

A fear of silence.
When there are no goals scored
does no one cheer?

What if surrealism is a serious business?
Painting blue leaves on black velvet.
All these words, tax   10
deductible.

5. IS THERE NO CLIMATE

Is there no climate that is good for me? In Victoria
the flowers would not stop blooming. I was unaware
that the ground could freeze, that every stem
in the garden could lack leaves. And words too
flowd. Without work, or care.
Now Montreal, March 10, 1970, the day
on which my child is to be born, the ground
frozen since November, & the snow
still falling.

To let one's words bespeak one's condition   10
at the moment of speaking. A poetry. I would be
that careful. That careful. Does no one
believe me? Why are the words frozen? Have I
in my willfulness, making poems of events
& poems of ideologies, frozen
my tongue, frozen
the waters around my child's skin?

6. DIRECTION

The mirror
is not art. A daily
newspaper, or
an ordering of words, backwards,
reversed—

when my words are not art. To go
backward is not
art, to reverse one's field, it is
people who err, & people
who regret errors   10

who dream
of time machines. The mirror
sits in a chair, & sees
a world backwards.

What is
love
backwards?

7. DOES WHO

And should I move out, literally, move out
in this speech, in this speaking. How much
have I become
he, whom I pretended? When I calld
her sunshine, did I come to love? When I saild
my ships, did they make me their captain?
If you do not follow
your tongue, will it be with you
when your will ends?

If I had not yielded my tongue to the form   10
that poems have in anyone. In anyone's
textbook, galley, or chap. Giving poems
that have forgotten. Do I quit now? Does who
quit now?

8. THE TAROT

The writing has become a movement of the room
in which the cards are turning. Even this statement is now a habit, its six accents marching,
from place to place of working, toward the verbal.
Yet so many sounds cling to me. I could write
poems like such poems, even knowing that to be
like is to cease writing. Thus I kept liking.
The second girl I loved was built of simile.
Her breasts, her clothes, her friends, her way
in bed, I, her husband, writing pages of that
figure.   10

That was me. Or someone like me. When the poem
stops, do we make up lines to follow? If no one
speaks, will the poem be written? Over-written?
Unwritten? When the poem stops, I make up lines
to follow. Make up poems from lines I have heard,

overheard, followd. Here I go on, inking these
words on the paper, wondering if the poet is with
me, writing.

9. HABIT

Not to have it. Not to have the poem
when the habit won't let you have it.
Possesst by habit. A living that reproduces
the days of its living. Or poems that reproduce
the pages of past living. Not to live
but to be lived. Inhabited.

Let me not read poems. Let me not learn
poetics. Let me detest
images of my words in journals,
anthologies, in all those places   10
where habit is habit, let me not love
competence, heroism, idealism, I am not
competent, not heroic, not idealistic,
I cannot change a goddam tap washer, or cry
upon a photod corpse—
I am only
a writer, struggling to hear his own
words, speaking.

10. A PARENTHESIS
   For Michael

a child
bearing our breath away
& onward in that message,
a child is born
a child is born

& so begins
a measure—
enough,
a child is born
a child is born   10

11. WHERE ARE YOU GOING, MY PRETTY MAID?

What
a dumb question, I hadn't

expected even to meet you

sir, she sd.

12. FOR HELEN

Holding to your way, I discoverd
it wasn't.

Lesson: don't read maps, don't even
ask directions
everything they tell you has been copied,
they want you to buy

the new model. Forget
your diet plan, stop watching
American Bandstand
rehearsing your steps before the hall mirror.   10

13. THE HAT

or why I couldn't keep
the puck out of the net.

& look at your old photos
the clothes you
wore. Some one chose them

you say?

or how sociologists spend lifetimes
government grants. There is

explanation? You are

the man, woman
you intended? You have   10

a line for the end of this?

14. FAREWELL

I sit here naked within my clothes,
I am holding the table at which I am writing,
holding it from flame. Holding the meat which you see
as the flesh of my arm & hand
from putrefaction. None of this is magic.
My fear of not being loved
is not magic. My fear of being loved
so that dying in some aircraft's splinterd tumbling
I lose love, is also not magic.

The only process   10
is moving now onward. Causing breath
to follow breathing. I walk naked
within my clothes, within
this hostile air. I write these words
that someone, will remember me,
or at least finding me here
poisond, burnd, loved, unloved, will see words
moving.

1973

Gwendolyn MacEwen

b. 1941

Born in Toronto and raised there and in Winnipeg, Gwendolyn MacEwen published her first poem at seventeen in the *Canadian Forum* and left school a year later to become a writer. By the time she was twenty she had published privately two chapbooks, *Sela* (1961) and *The Drunken Clock* (1961), and two years later had her first commercial publication with *The Rising Fire*. She has subsequently produced seven poetry collections: *A Breakfast for Barbarians* (1966); *The Shadow-Maker* (1969), which won a Governor General's Award; *The Armies of the Moon* (1972); *The Fire Eaters* (1976); *The T.E. Lawrence Poems* (1982); and two volumes of selected poetry, *Magic Animals* (1975), which also contains a few new poems, and *Earthlight* (1982).

As well as writing poetry she has worked with a number of other literary forms. She has written two novels, *Julian the Magician* (1963) and *King of Egypt, King of Dreams* (1971), which reflect her on-going interest in the richness of myth and history from a variety of periods and cultures. (The Mediterranean and the Middle East have been of particular interest to her, and she has travelled extensively in those areas; *Mermaids and Ikons: A Greek Summer*, 1978, is a memoir of one journey.) Her collection of short stories, *Noman* (1972), although set in 'Kanada', also exhibits this predisposition for the foreign and the fantastic. She has also written plays and dramatic documentaries for CBC radio. She created a new version of Euripides' 'The Trojan Women' and with Nikos Tsingos, translated two long poems by Greek poet Yannis Ritsos (the play and translations appear in *Trojan Women*, 1981).

Beneath the fluid and rich surfaces of MacEwen's work is an unusual personal mythology constructed from sources as diverse as commonplace Canadian experience ('The Portage'), the bizarre romance of war *(The T.E. Lawrence Poems)*, and the mystery of the ancient past *(King of Egypt, King of Dreams)*. Out of the bits and pieces of various myths and legends, MacEwen creates paired oppositions, such as spirit and flesh, the magical and the mundane, male and female. These contraries are the basis of her world view, in which the occult and the everyday world exist together in harmonious simultaneity, and one must learn to move between them with ease.

Existing in all these realms is a recurrent figure that Margaret Atwood has identified as MacEwen's male muse or animus ('MacEwen's Muse' in *Second Words*, 1982). Sometimes a god incarnate, sometimes man in divine transmutation, this figure can ascend to universal levels or fall into the commonplace specifics of life and death. He appears as Icarus, Manzini, Julian, Noman, Akhenaton (the Egyptian pharaoh), and T.E. Lawrence.

MacEwen tends to use these figures as oracular I-narrators, and through a humorous blend of incantatory diction and cadences from the casual language of speech, she both affirms their vitality and undercuts their heroic attempts to exist simultaneously in the mythic and phenomenal worlds. As D.G. Jones has observed, MacEwen is a poet who can 'say then what most will not, that we are ambiguous, that our exorbitant hungers and satisfactions are both erotic and holy, that their incestuous relations may spawn a bestial phantasmagoria or project an angelic visitation . . .' (Introduction to *Earthlight*).

Icarus[1]

Feather and wax, the artful wings
bridge a blue gulf between
the stiff stone tower
and its languid god, fat sky.

The boy, bent to the whim of wind,
the blue, and the snarling sun
form a brief triumvirate
—flesh, feather, light—
locked in the jaws of the noon
they rule with fleeting liberty.   10

These are the wings, then,
a legacy of hollow light—
feathers, a quill to write
white poetry across the sky.

Through the mouth of the air, the boy
sees his far father, whose muscled flight
is somehow severed from his own.
Two blinking worlds, and Daedalus'
unbound self is a thing apart.

You, bound for that other area   20
know that this legacy of mindflight
is all you have to leave me.

The boy, Icarus, twists the threads of his throat
and his eyes argue with the sun
on a flimsy parallel, and
the mouth of the sun eager, eager,
smuggles a hot word to the boy's ear.

But flying, locked in dark dream,
I see Queen Dream, Queen Flight,
the last station of the poet   30
years above my brow, and

Something, something in the air,
in the light's flight, in the vaguely
voluptuous arc of the wings
drives a foreign rhythm into his arms,
his arms which are lean, white willows.

Icarus feels his blood race to his wrist

[1]Character from Greek mythology who escaped with his father Daedalus (the master craftsman and inventor) by means of wings made of wax and feathers. Forgetful of Daedalus's warning not to fly too close to the sun, which might melt the wax, or to the sea, which might get his feathers wet, Icarus soared too high and fell to his death.

in a marathon of red light. Swifter,
swift, he tears away the slow veil
from his tendons; the playful biceps   40
sing; they wish new power to the beautiful
false wings
and the boy loops up into tall cobalt.
His hair is a swirl of drunken light,
his arms are wet blades; wings wed with arms.

    You knew
    I would get drunk on beauty.
    The famous phantom quill
    would write me, pull me
    through the eye   50
    of needle noon.

Crete is a huge hump of a black whore beneath him.
Her breasts, two wretched mountains
tremble under his eye.
All is black, except the sun in slow explosion;
a great war strangles his vision
and knots his flying nerve.
Black, and fire, and the boy.

    You and your legacy!
    You knew I would try to   60
    slay the sunlight.

Look, Icarus has kissed the sun
and it sucks the wax,
feathers and wax.
The wings are melting!

The boy Icarus is lean and beautiful.
His body grows limp and falls.
It is cruel poetry set
to the tempo of lightning; it is too swift,
this thin descent.   70

On the lips of the Aegean:
globules of wax,
strands of wet light,

    the lean poem's flesh
    tattered and torn
    by a hook
    of vengeful fire . . .

Combustion of brief feathers

1961

A Breakfast for Barbarians

my friends, my sweet barbarians,
there is that hunger which is not for food—
but an eye at the navel turns the appetite
round
with visions of some fabulous sandwich,
the brain's golden breakfast
           eaten with beasts
           with books on plates

let us make an anthology of recipes,
let us edit for breakfast   10
our most unspeakable appetites—
let us pool spoons, knives
and all cutlery in a cosmic cuisine,
let us answer hunger
with boiled chimera[1]
and apocalyptic tea,
an arcane salad of spiced bibles,
tossed dictionaries—
           (O my barbarians
           we will consume our mysteries)   20

and can we, can we slake the gaping eye of our desires?
we will sit around our hewn wood table
until our hair is long and our eyes are feeble,
eating, my people, O my insatiates,
eating until we are no more able
to jack up the jaws any longer—

to no more complain of the soul's vulgar cavities,
to gaze at each other over the rust-heap of cutlery,
drinking a coffee that takes an eternity—
till, bursting, bleary,   30
we laugh, barbarians, and rock the universe—
and exclaim to each other over the table
over the table of bones and scrap metal
over the gigantic junk-heaped table:

by God that was a meal

1966

[1]a. Mythical firebreathing monster with the head of a lion, the body of a goat, and the tail of a serpent; b. a creation of the imagination or a foolish fancy.

Manzini:[1] Escape Artist

now there are no bonds except the flesh; listen—
there was this boy, Manzini, stubborn with
gut stood with black tights and a turquoise
leaf across his sex

and smirking while the big
brute tied his neck arms legs, Manzini
naked waist up and white with sweat

struggled. Silent, delinquent, he
was suddenly all teeth and knee, straining slack
and excellent with sweat, inwardly   10

wondering if Houdini would take as long
as he; fighting time and the drenched
muscular ropes, as though his tendons were worn
on the outside—

as though his own guts were the ropes
encircling him; it was beautiful; it was thursday; listen—
there was this boy, Manzini

finally free, slid as snake from
his own sweet agonized skin, to throw his entrails
white upon the floor   20
with a cry of victory—

now there are no bonds except the flesh,
but listen, it was thursday, there was this boy,
Manzini—

1966

---

[1]Manzini was an American magician whom MacEwen met in the mid-sixties; regarding Houdini (mentioned below), see p. 118, n. 1.

The Portage

We have travelled far with ourselves
and our names have lengthened;
    we have carried ourselves
on our backs, like canoes
in a strange portage, over trails,
insinuating leaves
and trees dethroned like kings,
    from water-route to
    water-route
seeking the edge, the end,   10
the coastlines of this land.

On earlier journeys we
were master ocean-goers
going out, and evening always found us
spooning the ocean from our boat,
    and gulls, undiplomatic
    couriers brought us
cryptic messages from shore
till finally we sealords vowed
we'd sail no more.   20

Now under a numb sky, sombre
cumuli weigh us down;
the trees are combed for winter
and bears' tongues have melted
all the honey;
    there is a lourd[1]
suggestion of thunder;
subtle drums under
the candid hands of Indians
are trying to tell us   30
why we have come.

But now we fear movement
and now we dread stillness;
we suspect it was the land
that always moved, not our ships;
we are in sympathy with the fallen
trees; we cannot relate
    the causes of our grief.
We can no more carry
our boats our selves   40
over these insinuating trails.

1969

[1]Sluggish, dull.

Dark Pines under Water

This land like a mirror turns you inward
And you become a forest in a furtive lake;
The dark pines of your mind reach downward,
You dream in the green of your time,
Your memory is a row of sinking pines.

Explorer, you tell yourself this is not what you came for
Although it is good here, and green;
You had meant to move with a kind of largeness,
You had planned a heavy grace, an anguished dream.

But the dark pines of your mind dip deeper   10
And you are sinking, sinking, sleeper
In an elementary world;
There is something down there and you want it told.

1969

A Lecture to the Flat Earth Society

With apologies to A.N.[1]

As president of this worthy organization
And having been entrusted with the task
Of saving the poor souls who dwell too near
The Edge of the Earth from falling into
The Primal Dark beyond,
I would like to say:

My God I've lived all my life right here
On the Rim, the Brink, the Final Boundary of fear
With the long flat continents of dreams behind me
And nothing ahead but the sweet and terrible Night   10
I long to fall into, but do not dare.

What can I tell you, who inhabit with me
The Very Edge of the Abyss? We have no bathysphere
To explore the depths, no means whereby we can collect
The Abysmal Eggs of those creatures of the chasm
Who dwell in darkness below our heels.

As president of this worthy organization
I want to point out, without arousing any fear
That we are doomed on this Disc which spins its insane dreams
Through space. And those of us who always lived too near   20
The Edge to begin with

[1]Alden Nowlan (see p. 336-7) helped to organize a Canadian branch of The Flat Earth Society, an organization whose adherents believe (or contend that they believe) that the earth is flat and that concepts that developed from the idea that the earth is round are inherently false.

Have the consolation of each other's company,
The certain knowledge that the Night is also beautiful,
The abundant Night which spews out constantly before us
As the rays of a half-forgotten sun strike us from behind
On our delicate and unwinged heels.

1972

The Real Name of the Sea

Everything would have been different
had I known it before. I would have had no fear
of tunnels, thunder, wind and water, also time,
which brought me always to the brink of being
and taught me how to love, and die.
(Sheer lightning found me cowering
hot and cold upon the floor; there were
some kinds of light I couldn't bear.
Even the candles lit for all the birthnights
of my life   10
were a blaze of boats in an ocean funeral)

I insisted that my terrifying cosmos
was not different from your own;
I promised you that it contained
all you had ever seen or done;
(for I had seen all things converge to one)
I asked you to hold the gold shell
of the burning sea to your ear
and hear the drowning children
call for their Viking fathers   20
and worldbreakers breaking
on the awful shores of love forever.

Everything would have been different
had I know it before. Thalassa[1]—
(whisper with me) *Thalassa*,
these last of the world's children
beg pardon at your shores.

1972

[1]Woman's name, from the Greek word meaning 'from the sea'.

The Golden Hunger

First the savage flower of the mind opens, catches flies and tigers and locks them in. My vowels burst like the lungs of divers gone beyond their depths. How to address you, who have a hundred times renamed me? The moon is yellow and terrifically full . . . (They were there, just a week ago, walking) . . . and the pale skyscrapers are altars I have erected for the night. After the dark fell you came again to rename me, composite god; behind your fluid masks there is always something that remains the same. Not a feature, but a *cast* to which the face always returns. I watch your expressions change, I wait until they resolve themselves into the face I remember. Through the eyes of all I know one mind looks out like a dark captured animal, seeing only what it wants to see. There is the pain of the miracle amid reality.

Another mouth is drawn above your mouth, my Teacher, and two other eyes above your own. Who would believe this ghost is the permanent guest of my blood? I dreamed I found a priceless Stradivarius[1] in my mailbox. What impossible concertos am I expected to play? The clouds have dissolved and the visited moon above me is an eye which watches as I bow.

1972

[1] A fine violin made in the workshop of the master instrument maker, Antonio Stradivari (1694-1737).

From *The T.E. Lawrence Poems*

The Real Enemies[1]

In that land where the soul aged long before the body,
My nameless men, my glamorous bodyguards,
                              died for me.
My deadly friends with their rouged lips and pretty eyes
            died for me; *my bed of tulips* I called them,
            who wore every color but the white
            that was mine alone to wear.

But they could not guard me against the real enemies—
Omnipotence, and the Infinite—
                     those beasts the soul invents   10
            and then bows down before.
The real enemies were not the men of Fakhri Pasha,[2] nor
Were they even of this world.

[1] The narrative voice of this poem, 'The Void', and the other poems in *The T.E. Lawrence Poems*, is that of Thomas Edward Lawrence (1888-1935), known as Lawrence of Arabia. Author, archaeologist, and soldier, Lawrence led a successful rebellion of the Arabs against the Turks during the First World War and became a near-legendary figure. He subsequently assumed the name T.E. Shaw and retired to self-imposed obscurity to write *The Seven Pillars of Wisdom* (1926), his account of his Arabian adventure.
[2] The leader of the Turkish forces.

> One could never conquer them,
> Never. Hope was another of them. Hope, most brutal of all.
>
> For those who thought clearly, failure was the only goal.
> Only failure could redeem you, there where the soul aged
> > long before the body.
> You failed at last, you fell into the delicious light
> > and were free. 20
>
> And there was much honor in this;
> > it was a worthy defeat.
> Islam is surrender—the passionate surrender of the self,
> > the puny self, to God.
> We declared a Holy War upon Him and were victors as He won.

The Void

The last truly foolish thing I did was some years ago
When I flew the Hejaz[1] flag from the pinnacle of All Souls;
I knew then that I was becoming an aging schoolboy,
> a master-prig with an ego as big
> as an ostrich egg. A pity,
> for I was still young.

Now I'm gray-haired, half-blind, and shaking at the knees;
There's something almost obscene about the few gold teeth
> I got in nineteen-thirty. What
> have I done, what am I doing, what   10
> am I going to do?
Days seem to dawn, suns to shine, evenings to follow.
I have burned all my bridges behind me; this is high, dry
> land.

I'm going around shooting the same camel in the head[2]
Over and over; I'm a pilgrim forever circling the Kaaba,[3]
> which has none of its sides or angles equal,
> for whatever that's worth.
Have you ever been a leaf, and fallen from your tree
> in Autumn? It's like that.   20

---

[1]District of Arabia (its capital is Mecca) from which the Arab revolt against Turkey began in 1916. 'All Souls': one of the colleges at Oxford University; Lawrence's family lived in Oxford and he graduated from Jesus College.
[2]In 'The Virgin Warrior', an earlier poem in the sequence, MacEwen alludes to Lawrence's first outing as a soldier during which, in excited confusion, he shot his own camel in the head.
[3]The most sacred Moslem shrine; located in Mecca, it is towards this shrine that Moslems face when praying and to which they must make at least one pilgrimage.

Poets put things like shirt-sleeves or oysters
Into their poems, to prevent you from laughing at them
      before they have laughed at themselves.
      I have put an ostrich egg in this one
      to amuse you. I have already laughed.

Where are my noble brothers, my bodyguards, my friends,
Those slender camelmen who rode with me to the ends
      of the desert? When does the great dream end?
      With my right wrist recently broken,
      I write this sad, left-handed poem.   30

1982

Michael Ondaatje

b. 1943

Philip Michael Ondaatje grew up in Ceylon (now Sri Lanka), speaking both English and Singhalese. At ten he joined his mother in England, where he received his secondary schooling and then, in 1962, he moved to Canada, which became his permanent home. As an undergraduate he attended Bishop's University and the University of Toronto, from which he earned a B.A. in 1965. After taking an M.A. at Queen's (1967), he taught English at the University of Western Ontario (1967-70) until he joined the faculty of Glendon College, York University, where he has remained.

Ondaatje began writing seriously at twenty, the year after he came to Canada; his first book of poems, *The Dainty Monsters* (1967), appeared some four years later. In 1969 he published a long poem, *The Man with Seven Toes*, a unified sequence of poems suggested by the experience of a woman who was shipwrecked off the Queensland coast of Australia. In the following year he combined poetry and prose in *The Collected Works of Billy the Kid: Left-handed Poems*, which won a Governor General's Award. Since then he has produced another book of short poems, *Rat Jelly* (1973), and the collection *There's a Trick with a Knife I'm Learning to Do: Poems 1963-1978* (1979), which is made up of selections from *The Dainty Monsters* and *Rat Jelly* plus nineteen new poems. It won him a second Governor General's Award.

Both Ondaatje's prose and poetry—even the short poems—evince his strong interest in narrative and the narrative form. *The Man with Seven Toes* and *The Collected Works of Billy the Kid* are full-length narratives, assembled from discrete pieces. The latter book, chronicling Billy's career and Pat Garrett's pursuit of him joins Ondaatje's own prose and poetry to quotations, an interview with Billy, and historical photographs. In 1976 Ondaatje published a novel, *Coming Through Slaughter*, about American jazz musician Buddy Bolden; like *Billy the Kid*, it is a portrait of an outsider driven to violence and self-destruction both by society and by himself. In his latest book, *Running in the Family* (1982)—which also mixes prose and poetry—Ondaatje constructs a narrative out of his family history, from its beginnings in Ceylon to his visit there in 1979. Ondaatje has also worked in other mediums. He adapted *The Man With Seven Toes*, *Billy the Kid*, and *Coming Through Slaughter* for the stage, and in the early seventies he made three films, including one on bp Nichol (*The Sons of Captain Poetry*, 1970) and another on Théâtre Passe Muraille's 'The Farm Show'. As well he has written a short critical study, *Leonard Cohen* (1970), and has edited three anthologies, including *Personal Fictions* (1977), a collection of short stories by Blaise, Munro, Thomas, and Wiebe; and the *Long Poem Anthology* (1979), a collection of several contemporary Canadian experiments with the long poem. He is also associated as an adviser and editor with Coach House Press.

The passage from Italo Calvino that Ondaatje chose as an epigraph to the new poetry in *There's a Trick with a Knife* suggests the difficulties of communication inevitably experienced by a person who crosses cultural boundaries: 'Newly arrived and totally ignorant of the levantine languages, Marco Polo could express himself only with gestures, leaps, cries of wonder and of horror, animal barkings or hootings, or with objects he took from his knapsacks—ostrich plumes, pea-shooters, quartzes—which he arranged in front of him . . .' Ondaatje's own sense of otherness often results in a poetry of vivid gestures (such as his wife's running her hands through her hair at the end of 'Billboards', or—the gesture turned violent—the bran-

dishing of the penknife in 'The Time around Scars', or the grandiose gesture of the poet's father in 'Letters & Other Worlds'), and through carefully realized physical objects (such as those named throughout 'Burning Hills'). The contrast between the psychic distance from his environment that is communicated in a reticent, at times coldly objective, voice, and the warmth and familiarity that arise out of his sharply etched depictions of everyday, domestic events, gives his work surprising emotional intensity. Just as Polo chose which objects to carry with him and which ones to take out of his knapsack, Ondaatje brings us a selected reality in the events and people he depicts. He pictures a rich but dangerous world in which vitality always carries with it the risk of being scarred—a world of violent beauty, like that of the Henri Rousseau paintings he admires. In Ondaatje's writing, destruction is as commonplace as creation and hate as available as love; his is a vision of lives lived in extremes. As he writes of family, friends, historical figures, or himself, he both weaves a gothic web of interrelations and juxtapositions and lays open these complexities through a brutally sensory language. The surgical precision of this writing holds both author and reader at a great distance from the subject: his characters are watched but not joined. There is everywhere in this work a buried internal conflict, the union of personal violence and tenderness simultaneously felt and carefully held in check.

The Time Around Scars

A girl whom I've not spoken to
or shared coffee with for several years
writes of an old scar.
On her wrist it sleeps, smooth and white,
the size of a leech.
I gave it to her
brandishing a new Italian penknife.
Look, I said turning,
and blood spat onto her shirt.

My wife has scars like spread raindrops   10
on knees and ankles,
she talks of broken greenhouse panes

and yet, apart from imagining red feet,
(a nymph out of Chagall[1])
I bring little to that scene.
We remember the time around scars,
they freeze irrelevant emotions
and divide as from present friends.
I remember this girl's face,
the widening rise of surprise.   20

And would she
moving with lover or husband
conceal or flaunt it,
or keep it at her wrist
a mysterious watch.
And this scar I then remember
is medallion of no emotion.

I would meet you now
and I would wish this scar
to have been given with   30
all the love
that never occurred between us.

1967

[1]Marc Chagall (b. 1887), Russian-born French artist whose paintings often have a quality of fairy-tale fantasy.

Elizabeth

Catch, my Uncle Jack said
and oh I caught this huge apple
red as Mrs Kelly's bum.
It's red as Mrs Kelly's bum, I said
and Daddy roared
and swung me on his stomach with a heave.
Then I hid the apple in my room
till it shrunk like a face
growing eyes and teeth ribs.

Then Daddy took me to the zoo   10
he knew the man there
they put a snake around my neck
and it crawled down the front of my dress.
I felt its flicking tongue
dripping onto me like a shower.
Daddy laughed and said Smart Snake
and Mrs Kelly with us scowled.

In the pond where they kept the goldfish
Philip and I broke the ice with spades
and tried to spear the fishes;   20

we killed one and Philip ate it,
then he kissed me
with raw saltless fish in his mouth.

My sister Mary's got bad teeth
and said I was lucky, then she said
I had big teeth, but Philip said I was pretty.
He had big hands that smelled.

I would speak of Tom, soft laughing,
who danced in the mornings round the sundial
teaching me the steps from France, turning   30
with the rhythm of the sun on the warped branches,
who'd hold my breast and watch it move like a snail
leaving his quick urgent love in my palm.
And I kept his love in my palm till it blistered.

When they axed his shoulders and neck
the blood moved like a branch into the crowd.
And he staggered with his hanging shoulder
cursing their thrilled cry, wheeling,
waltzing in the French style to his knees
holding his head with the ground,   40
blood settling on his clothes like a blush;
this way
when they aimed the thud into his back.

And I find cool entertainment now
with white young Essex, and my nimble rhymes.[1]

1967

[1] The 'Elizabeth' of this poem is Elizabeth I (1533-1603), who assumed the throne of England in 1558
following the reigns of her father, Henry VIII (1491-1547), her brother, Edward VI (1537-53), and
her sister Mary Tudor (1515-58). 'Philip' is Philip II of Spain (1527-98) who married Mary Tudor in
1554; 'Tom' is Lord Thomas Seymour of Sudeley (1508?-49), whose repeated attempts to compromise and marry the adolescent Elizabeth, as well as to overthrow his brother Edward Seymour, the
protector of Edward VI, led to his execution; 'Essex' is the second Earl of Essex, Robert Devereux
(1566-1601), soldier and favourite of Elizabeth, who was executed for attempting to incite an upris-
ing against the court. 'Uncle Jack' and 'Mrs Kelly' are characters invented by Ondaatje.

Near Elginburg

3 a.m. on the floor mattress.
In my pyjamas a moth beats frantic
my heart is breaking loose.

I have been dreaming of a man
who places honey on his forehead before sleep
so insects come tempted by liquid
to sip past it into the brain.
In the morning his head contains wings
and the soft skeletons of wasp.

Our suicide into nature.   10
That man's seduction
so he can beat the itch
against the floor and give in
move among the sad remnants
of those we have destroyed,
the torn code these animals ride to death on.
Grey fly on windowsill
white fish by the dock
heaved like a slimy bottle into the deep,
to end up as snake   20
heckled by children and cameras
as he crosses lawns of civilisation.

We lie on the floor mattress
lost moths walk on us
waterhole of flesh, want
this humiliation under the moon.
Till in the morning we are surrounded
by dark virtuous ships
sent by the kingdom of the loon.

1973

Billboards

'Even his jokes were exceedingly drastic.' [1]

My wife's problems with husbands, houses,
her children that I meet
at stations in Kingston, in Toronto, in London Ontario
—they come down the grey steps
bright as actors after their drugged four hour ride
of spilled orange juice and comics
(when will they produce a gun and shoot me
at Union Station by Gate 4?)
Reunions for Easter egg hunts
kite flying, Christmases.   10
They descend on my shoulders every holiday.
All this, I was about to say,
invades my virgin past.

When she lay beginning
this anthology of kids
I moved—blind but senses
jutting faux pas, terrible humour,
shifted with a sea of persons,
breaking when necessary
into smaller self sufficient bits of mercury.   20

[1]Willa Cather's comment on Stephen Crane (from 'When I Knew Stephen Crane', originally published in *Library*, 23, June 1900, and reprinted in *The Prairie Schooner*, 1949).

My mind a carefully empty diary
till I hit the barrier reef
that was my wife—
            there
the right bright fish
among the coral.

With her came the locusts of history—
innuendoes she had missed
varied attempts at seduction (even rape)
dogs who had been bred   30
and killed by taxis or brain disease.
Numerous problems I was unequal to.
Here was I trying to live
with a neutrality so great
I'd have nothing to think of,
just to sense
and kill it in the mind.
Nowadays I somehow get the feeling
I'm in a complex situation,
one of several billboard posters   40
blending in the rain.

I am writing this with a pen my wife has used
to write a letter to her first husband.
On it is the smell of her hair.
She must have placed it down between sentences
and thought, and driven her fingers round her skull
gathered the slightest smell of her head
and brought it back to the pen.

1973

Burning Hills

For Kris and Fred

So he came to write again
in the burnt hill region
north of Kingston. A cabin
with mildew spreading down walls.
Bullfrogs on either side of him.

Hanging his lantern of Shell Vapona Strip
on a hook in the centre of the room
he waited a long time. Opened
the Hilroy writing pad, yellow Bic pen.
Every summer he believed would be his last.   10
This schizophrenic season change, June to September,
when he deviously thought out plots
across the character of his friends.

Sometimes barren as fear going nowhere
or in habit meaningless as tapwater.
One year maybe he would come and sit
for 4 months and not write a word down
would sit and investigate colours, the
insects in the room with him.
What he brought: a typewriter   20
tins of ginger ale, cigarettes. A copy of *Strange Love*,[1]
of *The Intervals*, a postcard of Rousseau's *The Dream*.
His friends' words were strict as lightning
unclothing the bark of a tree, a shaved hook.
The postcard was a test pattern by the window
through which he saw growing scenery.
Also a map of a city in 1900.

Eventually the room was a time machine for him.
He closed the rotting door, sat down
thought pieces of history. The first girl   30
who in a park near his school
put a warm hand into his trousers
unbuttoning and finally catching the spill
across her wrist, he in the maze of her skirt.
She later played the piano
when he had tea with the parents.
He remembered that surprised—
he had forgotten for so long.
Under raincoats in the park on hot days.

The summers were layers of civilisation in his memory   40
they were old photographs he didn't look at anymore
for girls in them were chubby not as perfect as in his mind
and his ungovernable hair was shaved to the edge of skin.
His friends leaned on bicycles
were 16 and tried to look 21
the cigarettes too big for their faces.
He could read those characters easily
undisguised as wedding pictures.
He could hardly remember their names
though they had talked all day, exchanged styles   50
and like dogs on a lawn hung around the houses of girls
waiting for night and the devious sex-games with their simple plots.

Sex a game of targets, of throwing firecrackers
at a couple in a field locked in hand-made orgasms,
singing dramatically in someone's ear along with the record[2]
'How do you think I feel/you know our love's not real
The one you're mad about/Is just a gad-about

[1](1974), a book of poems by Victor Coleman (b. 1944); 'The Intervals': a long poem (1974) by Stuart MacKinnon (b. 1936); 'The Dream': 1910 painting by Henri Rousseau (1814-1910).
[2]*Elvis* (1956), which concludes with 'How Do You Think I Feel'; the second and third lines of Ondaatje's version differ from Presley's: 'Well I know your love's not real/The one I'm mad about. . .'

How do you think I feel'
He saw all that complex tension the way his children would.

There is one picture that fuses the 5 summers.   60
Eight of them are leaning against a wall
arms around each other
looking into the camera and the sun
trying to smile at the unseen adult photographer
trying against the glare to look 21 and confident.
The summer and friendship will last forever.
Except one who was eating an apple. That was him
oblivious to the significance of the moment.
Now he hungers to have that arm around the next shoulder.
The wretched apple is fresh and white.   70

Since he began burning hills
the Shell strip has taken effect.
A wasp is crawling on the floor
tumbling over, its motor fanatic.
He has smoked 5 cigarettes.
He has written slowly and carefully
with great love and great coldness.
When he finishes he will go back
hunting for the lies that are obvious.

1973

Letters & Other Worlds

'for there was no more darkness for him and, no doubt
like Adam before the fall, he could see in the dark' [1]

My father's body was a globe of fear
His body was a town we never knew
He hid that he had been where we were going
His letters were a room he seldom lived in
In them the logic of his love could grow

My father's body was a town of fear
He was the only witness to its fear dance
He hid where he had been that we might lose him
His letters were a room his body scared

He came to death with his mind drowning.   10
On the last day he enclosed himself
in a room with two bottles of gin, later
fell the length of his body
so that brain blood moved
to new compartments

[1] Translation from Alfred Jarry's *La Dragonne* (1943), cited in *The Banquet Years* by Roger Shattuck (1955).

that never knew the wash of fluid
and he died in minutes of a new equilibrium.

His early life was a terrifying comedy
and my mother divorced him again and again.
He would rush into tunnels magnetized   20
by the white eye of trains
and once, gaining instant fame,
managed to stop a Perahara[2] in Ceylon
—the whole procession of elephants dancers
local dignitaries—by falling
dead drunk onto the street.

As a semi-official, and semi-white at that,
the act was seen as a crucial
turning point in the Home Rule Movement
and led to Ceylon's independence in 1948.   30

(My mother had done her share too—
her driving so bad
she was stoned by villagers
whenever her car was recognized)

For 14 years of marriage
each of them claimed he or she
was the injured party.
Once on the Colombo docks
saying goodbye to a recently married couple
my father, jealous   40
at my mother's articulate emotion,
dove into the waters of the harbour
and swam after the ship waving farewell.
My mother pretending no affiliation
mingled with the crowd back to the hotel.

Once again he made the papers
though this time my mother
with a note to the editor
corrected the report—saying he was drunk
rather than broken hearted at the parting of friends.   50
The married couple received both editions
of *The Ceylon Times* when their ship reached Aden.[3]

And then in his last years
he was the silent drinker,
the man who once a week
disappeared into his room with bottles
and stayed there until he was drunk

[2]Religious ceremony celebrated by a parade.
[3]Capital of the British colony of the same name (Aden is now the capital of Southern Yemen).

and until he was sober.

There speeches, head dreams, apologies,
the gentle letters, were composed.   60
With the clarity of architects
he would write of the row of blue flowers
his new wife had planted,
the plans for electricity in the house,
how my half-sister fell near a snake
and it had awakened and not touched her.
Letters in a clear hand of the most complete empathy
his heart widening and widening and widening
to all manner of change in his children and friends
while he himself edged   70
into the terrible acute hatred
of his own privacy
till he balanced and fell
the length of his body
the blood screaming in
the empty reservoir of bones
the blood searching in his head without metaphor

1973

Pig Glass

Bonjour.   This is pig glass
a piece of cloudy sea

nosed out of the earth by swine
and smoothed into pebble
run it across your cheek
it will not cut you

and this is my hand   a language
which was buried for years   touch it
against your stomach

                        The pig glass   10
I thought
was the buried eye of Portland Township
slow faded history
waiting to be grunted up
There is no past until you breathe
on such green glass
                    rub it
over your stomach and cheek

The Meeks family used this section
years ago to bury tin   20
crockery forks dog tags

and each morning
pigs ease up that ocean
redeeming it again
into the possibilities of rust
one morning I found a whole axle
another day a hand crank

but this is pig glass
tested with narrow teeth
and let lie. The morning's green present   30
Portland Township jewelry.

There is the band from the ankle of a pigeon
a weathered bill from the Bellrock Cheese Factory
letters in 1925 to a dead mother I
disturbed in the room above the tractor shed.
Journals of family love
servitude to farm weather
a work glove in a cardboard box
creased flat and hard like a flower.

A bottle thrown   40
by loggers out of a wagon
past midnight
explodes against rock.
This green fragment has behind it
the *booomm* when glass
tears free of its smoothness

now once more smooth as knuckle
a tooth on my tongue.
Comfort that bites through skin
hides in the dark afternoon of my pocket.   50
Snake shade.
Determined histories of glass.

1979

Light

For Doris Gratiaen

Midnight storm. Trees walking off across the fields in fury
naked in the spark of lightning.
I sit on the white porch on the brown hanging cane chair
coffee in my hand midnight storm midsummer night.
The past, friends and family, drift into the rain shower.
Those relatives in my favourite slides
re-shot from old minute photographs so they now stand

complex ambiguous grainy on my wall.

This is my Uncle who turned up to his marriage
on an elephant. He was a chaplain.　　　　　　　　　　　10
This shy looking man in the light jacket and tie was infamous,
when he went drinking he took the long blonde beautiful hair
of his wife and put one end in the cupboard and locked it
leaving her tethered in an armchair.
He was terrified of her possible adultery
and this way died peaceful happy to the end.
My Grandmother, who went to a dance in a muslin dress
with fireflies captured and embedded in the cloth, shining
and witty. This calm beautiful face
organised wild acts in the tropics.　　　　　　　　　　20
She hid the mailman in her house
after he had committed murder and at the trial
was thrown out of the court for making jokes at the judge.
Her son became a Q.C.
This is my brother at 6. With his cousin and his sister
and Pam de Voss who fell on a pen-knife and lost her eye.
My Aunt Christie. She knew Harold Macmillan[1] was a spy
communicating with her through pictures in the newspapers.
Every picture she believed asked her to forgive him,
his hound eyes pleading.　　　　　　　　　　　　　30
Her husband Uncle Fitzroy a doctor in Ceylon had a memory
sharp as scalpels into his 80's
though I never bothered to ask him about anything
—interested then more in the latest recordings of Bobby Darin.[2]

And this is my Mother with her brother Noel in fancy dress.
They are 7 and 8 years old, a hand-coloured photograph,
it is the earliest picture I have. The one I love most.
A picture of my kids at Halloween
has the same contact and laughter.
My Uncle dying at 68, and my Mother a year later dying at 68.　40
She told me about his death and the day he died
his eyes clearing out of illness as if seeing
right through the room the hospital and she said
he saw something so clear and good his whole body
for a moment became youthful and she remembered
when she sewed badges on his trackshirts.
Her voice joyous in telling me this, her face light and clear.
(My firefly Grandmother also dying at 68).

These are the fragments I have of them, tonight
in this storm, the dogs restless on the porch.　　　　　50
They were all laughing, crazy, and vivid in their prime.
At a party my drunk Father
tried to explain a complex operation on chickens

[1](b. 1894), prime minister of the United Kingdom from 1957 to 1963.
[2]American pop singer of the fifties.

and managed to kill them all in the process, the guests
having dinner an hour later while my Father slept
and the kids watched the servants clean up the litter
of beaks and feathers on the lawn.

These are their fragments, all I remember,
wanting more knowledge of them. In the mirror and in my kids
I see them in my flesh. Wherever we are   60
they parade in my brain and the expanding stories
connect to the grey grainy pictures on the wall,
as they hold their drinks or 20 years later
hold grandchildren, pose with favourite dogs,
coming through the light, the electricity, which the storm
destroyed an hour ago, a tree going down by the highway
so that now inside the kids play dominoes by candlelight
and out here the thick rain static the spark of my match to a cigarette
and the trees across the fields leaving me, distinct
lonely in their own knife scars and cow-chewed bark   70
frozen in the jagged light as if snapped in their run
the branch arms waving to what was a second ago the dark sky
when in truth like me they haven't moved.
Haven't moved an inch from me.

1979

Sallie Chisum/Last Words
on Billy the Kid. 4 A.M.[1]

For Nancy Beatty

The moon hard and yellow where Billy's head is.
I have been moving in my room
these last 5 minutes. Looking for a cigarette.
That is a sin he taught me.
Showed me how to hold it and how to want it.

I had been looking and stepped forward
to feel along the windowsill
and there was the tanned moon head.
His body the shadow of the only tree on the property.

                                    *

I am at the table.   10
Billy's mouth is trying
to remove a splinter out of my foot.
Tough skin on the bottom of me.
Still. I can feel his teeth

---

[1]Written when *Billy the Kid* was in production at Stratford and added to a later production of the play.
Ondaatje views this poem as a kind of postscript to *The Collected Works of Billy the Kid*.

bite precise. And then moving his face back
holding something in his grin, says he's got it.

*

Where have you been I ask
Where have you been he replies

I have been into every room about 300 times
since you were here   20
I have walked about 60 miles in this house
Where have you been I ask

*

Billy was a fool
he was like those reversible mirrors
you can pivot round and see yourself again
but there is something showing on the other side always.
Sunlight. The shade beside the cupboard

*

He fired two bullets into the dummy
on which I built dresses
where the nipples should have been.   30
That wasnt too funny, but we laughed a lot.

*

One morning he was still sleeping
I pushed the door and watched him from the hall
he looked like he was having a serious dream.
Concentrating. Angry. As if wallpaper
had been ripped off a wall.

*

Billy's mouth at my foot
removing the splinter.
Did I say that?

*

It was just before lunch one day.   40

*

I have been alive
37 years since I knew him. He was a fool.
He was like those mirrors I told you about.

*

I am leaning against the bed rail

I have finished my cigarette
now I cannot find the ashtray.
I put it out, squash it
against the window
where the moon is.
In his stupid eyes.   50

1979

From *Running in the Family*

The Cinnamon Peeler

If I were a cinnamon peeler[1]
I would ride your bed
and leave the yellow bark dust
on your pillow.

Your breasts and shoulders would reek
you could never walk through markets
without the profession of my fingers
floating over you. The blind would
stumble certain of whom they approached
though you might bathe   10
under rain gutters, monsoon.

Here on the upper thigh
at this smooth pasture
neighbour to your hair
or the crease
that cuts your back. This ankle.
You will be known among strangers
as the cinnamon peeler's wife.

I could hardly glance at you
before marriage   20
never touch you
—your keen nosed mother, your rough brothers.
I buried my hands
in saffron, disguised them
over smoking tar,
helped the honey gatherers . . .

                    *

When we swam once
I touched you in water
and our bodies remained free,
you could hold me and be blind of smell.   30
You climbed on the bank and said

[1]One who peels the cinnamon bark, the source of the spice, from the trees.

this is how you touch other women
the grass cutter's wife, the lime burner's daughter.
And you searched your arms
for the missing perfume
                    and knew

            what good is it
to be the lime burner's daughter
left with no trace
as if not spoken to in the act of love   40
as if wounded without the pleasure of a scar.

You touched
your belly to my hands
in the dry air and said
I am the cinnamon
peeler's wife. Smell me.

Lunch Conversation

Wait a minute, wait a minute! When did all this happen, I'm trying to get it straight . . .

Your mother was nine, Hilden was there, and your grandmother Lalla and David Grenier and his wife Dickie.

How old was Hilden?

Oh, in his early twenties.

But Hilden was having dinner with my mother and you.

Yes, says Barbara. And Trevor de Saram. And Hilden and your mother and I were quite drunk. It was a wedding lunch, Babette's I think, I can't remember all those weddings. I know Hilden was moving with a rotten crowd of drinkers then so he was drunk quite early and we were all laughing about the drowning of David Grenier.

I didn't say a word.

Laughing at Lalla, because Lalla nearly drowned too. You see, she was caught in a current and instead of fighting it she just relaxed and went with it out to sea and eventually came back in a semi-circle. Claimed she passed ships.

And then Trevor got up in a temper and challenged Hilden to a duel. He couldn't *stand* everyone laughing, and Hilden and Doris (your mother) being drunk, two of them flirting away he thought.

But *why?,* your mother asked Trevor.

Because he is casting aspersions on you . . .

Nonsense, I love aspersions. And everyone laughed and Trevor stood there in a rage.

And then, said Barbara, I realized that Trevor had been in love with your mother, your father always *said* there was a secret admirer. Trevor couldn't stand Hilden and her having a good time in front of him.

Nonsense, said your mother. It would have been incest. And besides (watching Hilden and Trevor and aware of the fascinated dinner table audience), both these men are after my old age pension.

What happened, said Hilden, was that I drew a line around Doris in the sand. A circle. And threatened her, 'don't you dare step out of that circle or I'll thrash you.'

Wait a minute, wait a minute, *when* is this happening?

Your mother is nine years old, Hilden says. And out in the sea near Negombo David Grenier is drowning. I didn't want her to go out.

You were in love with a nine year old?

Neither Hilden nor Trevor were *ever* in love with our mother, Gillian whispers to me. People always get that way at weddings, always remembering the past in a sentimental way, pretending great secret passions which went unsaid . . .

No No No. Trevor *was* in love with your mother.

Rot!

I was in my twenties, Hilden chimes in. Your mother was nine. I simply didn't want her going into the water while we tried to rescue David Grenier. Dickie, his wife, had fainted. Lalla—your mother's mother—was caught in the current and out at sea, I was on the shore with Trevor.

Trevor was there too you see.

Who is Hilden? asks Tory.

I am Hilden . . . your host!

Oh.

Anyway . . . there seems to be three different stories that you're telling.

No, *one*, everybody says laughing.

One when your mother was nine. Then when she was sixty-five and drinking at the wedding lunch, and obviously there is a period of unrequited love suffered by the silent Trevor who never stated his love but always fought with anyone he thought was insulting your mother, even if in truth she was simply having a good time with them the way she was with Hilden, when she was sixty-five.

Good God, I was there with them both, says Barbara, and *I'm* married to Hilden.

So where is my grandmother?

She is now out at sea while Hilden dramatically draws a circle round your mother and says 'Don't you *dare* step out of that!' Your mother watches David Grenier drowning. Grenier's wife—who is going to marry three more times including one man who went crazy—is lying in the sand having fainted. And your mother can see the bob of her mother's head in the waves now and then. Hilden and Trevor are trying to retrieve David Grenier's body, carefully, so as not to get caught in the current themselves.

My mother is nine.

Your mother is nine. And this takes place in Negombo.

OK

So an hour later my grandmother, Lalla, comes back and entertains everyone with stories of how she passed ships out there and they tell her David Grenier is dead. And nobody wants to break the news to his wife Dickie. Nobody could. And Lalla says, alright, she will, for Dickie is her sister. And she went and sat with Dickie who was still in a faint in the sand, and Lalla, wearing her elaborate bathing suit, held her hand. Don't shock her, says Trevor, whatever you do break it to her gently. My grandmother waves him away and for fifteen minutes she sits alone with her sister, waiting for her to waken. She doesn't know what to say. She is also suddenly very tired. She hates hurting anybody.

The two men, Hilden and Trevor, will walk with her daughter, my mother, about a hundred yards away down the beach, keeping their distance, waiting until they see Dickie sitting up. And then they will walk slowly back towards Dickie and my grandmother and give their sympathies.

Dickie stirs. Lalla is holding her hand. She looks up and the first words are, 'How is David? Is he alright?' 'Quite well, darling,' Lalla says. 'He is in the next room having a cup of tea.'

1982

bp Nichol

b. 1944

Born in Vancouver, Barrie Phillip Nichol was raised there and in Winnipeg and Port Arthur (now part of Thunder Bay). He began writing poetry in the early sixties and, while attending the University of British Columbia in 1962 to obtain a teaching certificate, he became acquainted with the work of Earle Birney, bill bissett, and the poets of the *Tish* movement. Unhappy with the conventional lyrics he was then writing, Nichol found himself especially attracted to the visual experiments of Birney and bissett. After teaching Grade Four for part of a year, in Port Coquitlam, B.C., he left British Columbia to settle permanently in Toronto, where he began to work on visual poetry while employed at the University of Toronto library. In 1964 Nichol and David Aylward started *Ganglia* magazine and Ganglia Press; during the magazine's two-year existence it served as an outlet for west-coast writers who did not have Toronto publishers. After *Ganglia* ceased, Nichol began *grOnk* (1967-), a newsletter that continues to appear irregularly and is generally devoted to visual poetry. Having met lay-analyst Lea Hindley-Smith in 1963, Nichol joined her therapy-learning group and in 1967 became part of Therafields, a therapeutic community, where he lived and worked as a lay-therapist himself. He remained at Therafields until 1983.

Over the last two decades Nichol has published a large number of broadsides, pamphlets, and chapbooks in addition to at least thirty full-length books; *Selected Writing: As Elected*, a volume that includes some previously unpublished work, appeared in 1980. Nichol won a Governor General's Award in 1970 for four of his publications: *Still Water; The Cosmic*

Chef, an anthology of concrete poetry; and two booklets, *Beach Head*, a lyrical sequence; and *The True Eventual Story of Billy the Kid*, a prose piece—which was attacked in Parliament as pornographic. (Nichol has experimented with a wide range of unconventional prose narratives: *Two Novels*, 1969, which contains 'Andy' and 'For Jesus Lunatick'; *Craft Dinner*, 1978, a collection of short prose pieces written between 1966 and 1976; and the Gertrude Stein-like novel, *Journal*, 1978.) In 1972 Nichol and Steve McCaffery formed the 'Toronto Research Group' (TRG), which has regularly issued theoretical statements in Frank Davey's *Open Letter* about the nature of experimental poetry. Nichol now works as a full-time writer and editor (he is an editor for Coach House Press and Underwhich Editions as well as a contributing editor to *Open Letter*), while teaching creative writing part-time at York University.

Nichol is an experimental writer who has continually tried out new techniques or mediums in a search for more effective modes of expression. The several different directions his work has taken may all be found in his first collection of poetry, *Journeying & the returns* (1967; also entitled *bp*): inside its cardboard package is a record ('Borders'), a lyrical sequence ('Journeying & the returns'), an envelope containing visual poems ('letters home'), and a flip or animated poem ('Wild Thing'). 'Journeying & the returns', the most conventional part of the collection, is representative of Nichol's early, more traditional, lyric poetry (a selection of which appeared in Raymond Souster's anthology *New Wave Canada*, 1966), though it also anticipates Nichol's interest in extended forms: later collections (such as *Nights On Prose*

Mountain, 1969, *Monotones*, 1971, and *The Captain Poetry Poems*, 1971) and the on-going long poem *The Martyrology* are given structural unity through sequence and narrative form. The visual poetry in *Journeying & the returns* is explored further in *Still Water* (1970), *ABC: The Aleph Beth Book* (1971), *LOVE: A Book of Remembrances* (1974), among other collections. Nichol has also become one of the chief proponents of sound poetry in Canada. Since 'Borders', an early instance of this type of poetry, he has made a second record, *Motherlove* (1968), and helped organize The Four Horsemen, a performance poetry group whose members are Steve McCaffery, Paul Dutton, Rafael Barreto-Rivera, and Nichol himself. The Four Horsemen have appeared widely, giving improvisational 'readings' that range from pieces made entirely of non-verbal sounds to contrapuntal verbal sequences. There are several records of the Four Horsemen, and a film of Nichol in performance, *The Sons of Captain Poetry*, made in 1970 by Michael Ondaatje.

By experimenting with visual and sound poetry, while maintaining an interest in traditional forms (in which syntax continues to function as a carrier of meaning), Nichol seeks to synthesize new modes of poetry and prose. For his first visual poems he employed typed arrangements of words and letters to produce concrete poetry (letters, phonemes, words, and graphic figures arranged on a page in such a way as to elicit comprehension that is primarily visual rather than verbal or syntactic); later he introduced graphic designs made out of letters and combinations of drawings and letters or words. Since the mid-seventies Nichol's visual poetry has moved more and more to pure graphics, particularly to the cartoon. Unlike this visual poetry, which is primarily concerned with form, sound poetry evokes feeling by recovering the emotional possibilities of speech and human sound that were originally part of the oral tradition. Through the use of homonyms, unusual cadences and emphases, and (in group performances) the overlay of one utterance on another, sound poems free the rich oral qualities of poetry from the silence of the page.

Nichol claims that *The Martyrology* (1972-), his most ambitious and important work (five books and three sections of a sixth have been published so far), is 'where everything comes together'; it unites the visual and oral aspects of his work with the narrative and personal ones. In the whole of *The Martyrology* Nichol builds up a mythology that accounts for the structure of his universe by writing about 'saints' created out of broken-up or 'deconstructed' words (a word such as 'storm' becoming St Orm) whose story and nature are important to the narrator's own existence. Book I of *The Martyrology* provides the lives of the 'saints', while Book II focuses on the narrator and his perceptions of them. In the later books the external world becomes more important, but it is still seen in relation to these saints who, like gods, influence its operation. As *The Martyrology* develops, Nichol's tendency to deconstruct gives way to recombination. For instance, in Book 5, Chain 8, 'eyear' is a union of 'eye' and 'ear' while functioning also as the sound equivalent of 'a year'. Thus words become the means of examining sounds, and ideas cause new words to be formed. In such work Nichol sees himself as a researcher seeking to discover the nature of language by recreating its evolutionary process.

In many ways Nichol's work resembles that of the Dadaists, in whom he was interested as early as 1963. During and after the First World War these artists defied conventional expectations with their anti-art and called into question the definition of art itself, thereby challenging their audience to re-examine its preconceptions. By reordering and restricting language, visual image, sound, and form, Nichol makes his readers ask questions about the borderlines of art, forcing them to consider at what point the poem ceases to be a literary form and becomes mere sound or mere visual effect. He also invites us to reconsider the validity of distinctions between content and form. Even in the poetry of *The Martyrology*, which comes close to traditional writing, language itself—words, letters, syntax—is not only the source of meaning; it also creates form and is itself part of the poem's 'content'.

The Martyrology

From BOOK 1: 'THE SORROWS OF SAINT ORM'

my lady my lady

this is the day i want to cry for you
but my eyes are dry

somewhere i'm happy

not like the sky
outside this window
gone grey

---

this is the line between reality
when i hold your body
enter the only way i am   10

saint orm
keep her from harm

this ship journey safely

quick as it can

saint orm you were a stranger
came to me out of the dangerous alleys &
the streets

        lived in
that dirty room on
comox avenue   20

           me &
my friends
             playing what lives we had to
the end

         i want to tell you a story
in the old way
              i can't

haven't the words or
the hands to reach you

& this circus   this noise in   30
my brain
            makes it hard to explain
my sorrow

you were THE DARK WALKER
stood by my side as a kid

i barely remember

except the heaven i dreamt of
was a land of clouds
you moved at your whim

knowing i walked   40
the bottom of a sea

that heaven was up there
on that world in the sky

that this was death

that i would go there
when i came to life

how do you tell a story?

saint orm you were the one

you saw the sun rise
knew the positions of the stars   50

how far we had to go
before the ultimate destruction

as it was prophesied in REVELATIONS[1]
nations would turn away from god & be destroyed

told me the difference between now & then
when i could no longer tell the beasts from men

---

[1]See especially Revelation 11:18 and 16. Revelation also predicts that before the final destruction of the world it will be ruled by a man known as 'the beast' (13:11 ff.).

saint orm
grant me peace

days i grow sick of seeing

bring my lady   60
back from that sea she's crossed
tossed in a grey world of
her own

there is no beauty in madness

no sinlessness
in tossing the first stone

make her sea calm

bring her safe to
my arms

*   *   *

1972

From BOOK 3, Section VIII.

* * *

last take

late february 73   2070

dave & i look out towards the lion's gate[1]

years mass
                    events
we made it out between the lion's paws
rear shocks gone
swerving to avoid the bumps
spell of spelling cast around us
tiny ripples in the blood stream the brain stem's rooted in
a body place &
                    time   2080
the lion's month before us the lamb's born in
the door
          you are not permitted to open again
enter thru the lion's mouth the man's root gets planted in
not to be consumed
                         as tho the use of lips weren't speech
a doorway into the woman's soul intelligence comes out of
SCREAMING
               a complete thot
born from the dialogue between you   2090

or what comes forth from my mouth
born from the woman in me
handed down thru my grandma ma & lea
is what marks me most a man
that i am finally this we
this one & simple thing
my father Leo
my mother Cancer
                         she births herself
the twin mouths of women   3000
                    w's omen
it turns over & reverses itself
the mirrors cannot trick us

[1]The Lions Gate Bridge—connecting Vancouver with North and West Vancouver—is a mile-long suspension bridge that is flanked by two stone lions at either end.

our words are spun within the signs our fathers left
the sibilance of s
        the cross of t
there are finally no words for you father
too many letters multiply the signs
you are the one
        the unifying   3010
no signifier when we cannot grasp the signified[2]
saints in between
        the world of men
women
        the sign complete
the w & the circle   turning
add the E
        the three levels
linked by line
        or the two fold vision   3020
H to I
        the saints returned to this plane

the emblems were there when i began
seven years to understand
the first letter/level of
        martyrdom

CODA: Mid-Initial Sequence

faint edge of sleep
a literal fuzzing in the mind
as tho the edge of
what was held clearly   2030
became less defined
the penalty paid &
your father recognized
for what he is

for W

    HA!

the is

[2]Structuralists divide the 'signs' we use to communicate—the most prominent of which are words—into 'signifiers' (the arbitrary conveyors of meaning, such as the combinations of letters or sounds) and 'signified' (the underlying sense, the meaning intended).

orange

the vague light
closing the eye   2040

's lid

                    home plate

the late P
            destroyed
leaving only b
& n

beginning again

b n a

all history there

t here   2050

opposed against the suffering
we have yet to bear

last note

no t
no e

l as no

l body
l where
l w here

no w   2060
for w's sake

no is
          e
against the silent sleep

bushes

dawn

the r rises
brushes drawn
the whole scene

the w hole   2070
into which the world
disappears

d is a p
pear shaped

dear H
a p edges
into the sea

sun

the unenviable s

there is no desire for speech   2080

there is no desire to spell

each gesture
against the chaos
must be made well

there is stillness in the heart of the power
as there is stillness in the heart of the storm

between the w & the d
the in side of
the mind /
          / 's a quiet place   2090
from which the power unwinds

in vocation
i am
a singer

every letter
invokes a spell
ing is
the power
letters have
over me   2100

word shaping

addition of the l

within the difference
if exists

tensions a
polarity

who is moved or moves
a distinction a disparity

a.d.   a.d.
history's spoken in   2110
the first four letters

all e to z
outside the head's
measure of our kind

man's time

1976

From BOOK 5, CHAIN 8

out of the west the best rises
out of the east the beast
Leviathan[1]
      Utnapishtim's potential nemesis
a cloud of dust &
cliché in its sashay with the day-to-day
conversea in ation minor
variation
     recapitulation of
a to z themes   10

t hem e
    or e a
thrd yrs
    a vow the e makes with the l or a
capitulation
riddle read for writers: cap it!
what?
    —ulation—
ululation of its wake

roused from depths the deep   20
double e threads our speech
full power of the beast noise
voice
we cling to   silence

Thunder Bay   roar & crash the storms made
echoed off the cliffs
so loud you thot the giant'd wake[2]
slept over the lake
millenia
     trees had covered him   30
earth filled his pores
my mother'd hide in dread
took me to bed with her
protector from the storm

---

[1]A mythical sea-monster, sometimes identified with Satan (Isaiah 27:1). 'Utnapishtim': in Assyro-Babylonian mythology, the Noah-like figure (prominent in the Epic of Gilgamesh, c. 2000 B.C.) who, as the only human to know of the impending world-wide deluge, built a boat to house his family and the earth's animal life. After the flood, Utnapishtim and his wife became immortal.
[2]The Sleeping Giant, a rock formation in Thunder Bay harbour, is identified in Ojibwa legend with Nanabozho, the famous trickster; he is expected to wake in the future and come to the aid of his people.

St Orm we've not forgotten you
you speak with voice of wind
power to bend the limbs of trees & man
blow down anything stands in the way of your word's truth
spoke with force
against the coarse lie we call our 'civilization'   40

so i sing
stupefied by speech
brought under the spell eyear can bring
  ought   e   e   ing
thought   she sleeps   thing
emerges from the deep
the faceless dream
dreamt dreamer ter or
entered world of shifting imagery
we try to freeze   50
make shiftless
because we feel less than
stored imagery's full weight

torn apart too often
that divisiveness
an isolation to protect the feared for work
valued as self is valued
defended as you would your life
'he laid it down for art'
does art thank us?   60

Noel Coward[3] in the 1950's
'why must the show go on?'
the 'noble soul in torment' one does grow bored with
recognizing the romanticization
self-aggrandisement of one's own pain
we all fall prey to

you address the problems as they rise
prize what is most human as
worth the struggle
                the will to better   70
your self & others
hate that poverty of spirit ignorance breeds

---

[3](1899-1973); English dramatist, actor, and composer. Noted for his sophisticated songs and plays that were wittily critical of society, Coward was less popular in the fifties when the theatre was dominated by realistic drama; during this period he became a commercially successful cabaret performer.

Hannah Arendt[4] speaking of Eichmann
'the face of evil is ordinary'

we build it up
look for it in cops & robbers morality plays
ignore its presence in the day-to-day
out of our own naivete

the distortion or ignoring of what is obvious
(that structural scale must remain human)   80
leads to monumentalization
whatever the political belief
the ordinary man or woman is forgotten
because they are not known
sentimentalized or swept aside
noone takes the time to talk to them

noone t   t   t   t t   t t
seven crosses for our lack of humanity
          (akes)
seven crosses for our arrogance & pride   90
            (he ime)
seven crosses for our lack of humility
            (o alk o)
seven crosses for the people swept aside
                     (hem
'd in then

am id St Noise
the voices
ignorance
such lack of knowing   100
starts there

a beginning only
a tentative law or
exception
lets the self reveal itself
we claim despite our fear

                *   *   *

1982

---

[4](1906-75), German-Jewish philosopher and political theorist who escaped the Nazis and settled in the United States; in *Eichmann in Jerusalem: A Report on the Banality of Evil* (1961) Arendt argues that Adolf Eichmann (1906-62), the Nazi leader who was in charge of the execution of the Jews, represents the modern figure of evil: the rational, pragmatic bureaucrat who accepts immoral commands as part of life's banal routine.

From *Continental Trance*[1]
[From BOOK 6 of *The Martyrology*]

O
—
●

minus the ALL ABOARD

minus my father waving

minus the CN logo

minus my mother waving

minus seventeen years of my life
Ellie & me
our unborn child in her belly
heading east
out of Vancouver
July 27th   10
8 p.m.
nineteen eighty-
1.

O
—
●

the old guy who spoke to the porter just now said:
'my wife wanted to take this trip
before she takes her heavenly trip'

my grandma, 96, earlier today said:
'i don't think i wanta stay around too many more'

Ellie's sitting across from me
reading Peter Dickinson's *One Foot In The Grave*
& in the first draft of this poem i wrote:
'minus these coincidences
what is the world trying to tell me?'   10

minus—the word returns
—some notion of absence (not a life)
subtracting the miles travelled east
(minus mine—us)
loosing all notion of possession
aboard this mixed metaphor

---

[1]Printed as a separate book, *Continental Trance*, a sequence of thirty-three poems, is a section of Book 6 of *The Martyrology*. This selection comprises the first, fourth, twenty-fourth, twenty-fifth, thirtieth, thirty-first, and thirty-third poems.

●
—
○

'where is this poem going?'
'Toronto'

'what does it teach us?'
'how coincidence reaches into our lives &
instructs us'

the 19th century knew
any narrative, like life,
is where coincidence leads you

given, of course, the conscious choice of voice
the train of thot you choose   10

○
—
●

this next bit doesn't quite cohere

already past tense
or converted to a noun
when it's the bite of consciousness eludes you

the flickering light thru the trees
sets up an echo in my brain
petit mal
makes me want to puke

but the trees
so clustered   10
a bird could walk the branches
a thousand miles or more

it is a map of consciousness
what the light yields disgorges
perceived thru a pattern of branches
the birds fly free of

●
—
○

is this the poem i wanted to write?

it never is

it's a thing of words
construct of a conscious mind

governed by the inevitable end-rime
time

○
—
●

that's that tone

buried in the poem
a consciousness of its own mortality

or mine

a finality Homer

soon there's noone knows
whether your poem's your own

or if the name denoted a community of speakers
history of a race

(Ellie's an obvious we   10
draws our child's breath & her own)

i's a lie
dispenses illusions of plot

biography when geography's the clue
locale & history of the clear 'you'

$$\frac{O}{\bullet}$$

mist again at dawn

heading into Toronto
'end' translates 'home'

7 a.m.
August 2nd
1981

St Clair to Union Station
thru the junkyards, the backyard gardens,
decaying brick factories

scrawled across the one wall   10
I WANTED TO BE AN ANARCHIST

an ending
in itself
unending

Vancouver-Toronto
July 27 to August 2nd 1981

1982

Poets for Further Reading

DAVID DONNELL

The Canadian Prairies View of Literature

First of all it has to be anecdotal; ideas don't exist;
themes struggle dimly out of accrued material like the shadow
of a slow caterpillar struggling out of a large cocoon;
even this image itself is somewhat urban inasmuch as it suggests
the tree-bordered streets of small southern Ontario towns;
towns are alright; Ontario towns are urban; French towns are European;
the action should take place on a farm between April and October;
nature is quiet during winter; when it snows, there's a lot of it;
the poem shimmers in the school-teacher's head like an image
of being somewhere else without a railway ticket to return;   10
the novel shifts its haunches in the hot reporter's head
and surveys the possible relationship between different farms;
sometimes the action happens in the beverage rooms and cheap
hotels area of a small town that has boomed into a new city;
Indians and Metis appear in the novel wearing the marks
of their alienation like a sullen confusion of the weather;
the town drunk appears looking haggard and the town mayor
out ward-heeling and smelling women's hands buys him a drink;
a woman gets married and another woman has a child;
the child is not old enough to plow a field and therefore   20
does not become a focus of interest except as another mouth;
they sit around with corn shucks in the head and wonder
who they should vote for, the question puzzles them,
vote for the one with the cracked shoes, he's a good boy,
or the one who jumped over six barrels at a local dance;
the fewer buildings they have, the more nationalistic they become
like a man who has stolen all his life accused of cheating;
above all, they dislike the east which at least gives them form
and allows their musings and discontents to flower into rancour;
musing and rancorous, I turn down the small side streets of Galt,   30
Ontario, afternoon light, aged twelve, past South Water Street,

Born in St Mary's, Ontario, in 1939, DAVID DONNELL has been a resident of Toronto since the late fifties. Among his collections of poetry are *The Blue Sky* (1977), *Dangerous Crossings* (1980), and *Settlements* (1983).

not quite like Rimbaud[1] leaving Charleville,
my hands in my windbreaker pockets like white stones,
and promise myself once again that when I get to the city
everything will happen, I will learn all of its history
and become the best writer they have ever dreamed of,
I'll make them laugh and I'll even make them cry,
I'll drink their whiskey and make love to all their wives,
the words tumbling out of my mouth as articulate as the young Hector,[2]
the corn under my shirt awkward a little rough light brown dry   40
and making me itch at times

1983

[1] Arthur Rimbaud (1854-91), French Symbolist poet and adventurer who, after his father deserted his family, repeatedly ran away from his harsh mother and his home town, Charleville.
[2] Son of Priam, the Trojan King; most prominent in the *Iliad*, Hector was a warrior not an orator; his speech was blunt, impatient, and imprudent.

Hound

Hound is liver-colored and smooth after early morning run
laps up the bowl of water in the half-lit kitchen and sits
licking his lips as the blue and white pajama man drinks coffee.
The maples outside are turning yellow and most of the flowers are down.
He stretches like a sleek single muscle under the table
and points his long head at the ceiling lights the doorways
opening into the cool air and whiter light of other rooms.
This is the quiet moment at the beginning of every morning
looking out over the city hazing south and west
the big neon signs turned off for the day and the rough country   10
stretching green and brown to the north past tractors and groundhogs.
When he hurls himself against the door he makes the catch rattle
in the lock and the garage in the gauze curtain tilt sideways.

People who don't know anything about animals say that dogs
are reflexive and don't experience a contemplation of what they see.
Dogs have no names for things and no causal index for the way
in which the different parts of things are repeated.
The truck coming down the highway is a large oblong car.
A factory is a lot of houses put together and smells of grease.
Dogs do a lot of the same things that people do; they eat   20
run sleep run fall in love take an active interest in the world.
People eat work sleep get married and drink too much.
What fascinates me when he sits staring out over the yard
is the way the shapes of chicken gravel car tree announce themselves
without index cards and more fluidly than they come to me.
Calm is as calm as the wind rustling through trees in a poem
but the desperation in the eye of dog is more human than salesman.
The shape of tree in his mind is pure green and wet

flipped on his side reversed the tree is a green umbrella
whose roots have nothing in common with potatoes or root fences.   30
He knows my feet shoes I wear baths and the way I walk
more thoroughly than wife or the guys you work with.
My hands have no secrets from him my pockets are shadows
where my hands disappear from time to time and come out naked
smudged sweaty grain of tobacco empty since water and food
especially giblets liver the ends of a roast are kept in kitchens.

He follows me sometimes at a distance sniffing the wind ground
air and wherever I go is a definite point on a four-dimensional
map that has no words or tags or exploded diagrams.
The shape of a fire is enormous but contains images that   40
are discrete and go on to meadows rivers gravel driveways.
He knows my thick voice when I have a cold or a cigarette.
Dog is a museum of perfect objects banked in chemical reflexes.
I am lonely without him and the yellow air of the kitchen goes dull
until I hurl myself at the door and go out on the back porch
to gulp the air put the garage right side up wet tree on my cheek.
He sits there crooning tail wagging head quick as traffic
wanting to run chickens for later, this behavior on my part
as shadowy as my pockets and not sensible like dark or light.

1983

GARY GEDDES

Letter of the Master of Horse[1]

I was signed
on the King's authority
as master of horse.
Three days
            (I remember
            quite clearly)
three days after we parted.
I did not really believe it,
it seemed so much the unrolling
of an incredible dream.

---

[1]This poem, in the form of a letter home, describes the journey of a sailing ship—bound from Spain to the New World—which must pass through the horse-latitudes, an area of calms in the North Atlantic said to derive its name from the fact that ships becalmed there cast their horses overboard in order to save fresh water. The master of horse is the young man in charge of the horses being imported to the Americas.

Born in 1940, GARRY GEDDES grew up in Vancouver and Saskatchewan. He teaches at Concordia University and has been an editor of *Studies in Canadian Literature* and of several anthologies; he is also the founder of a small literary press, Quadrant Editions. Among Geddes' collections of his own poetry are *Letter of the Master of Horse* (1973), *War and Other Measures* (1976), and *The Acid Test* (1981).

Bright plumes, scarlet tunics,
glint of sunlight on armour.
Fifty of the King's best horses,
strong, high-spirited, rearing
to the blast of trumpets,
galloping
down the long avenida
to the waiting ships.
And me, your gangling brother,
permitted to ride with cavalry.   20

Laughter,
children singing
in the market, women
dancing, throwing flowers,
the whole street covered
with flowers.

In the plaza del sol
a blind beggar kissed my eyes.
I hadn't expected the softness
of his fingers   30
                    moving upon my face.

A bad beginning.
The animals knew, hesitated
at the ramps, backed off,
finally had to be blindfolded
and beaten aboard.

Sailors grumbled for days
as if we had brought on board
a cargo of women.

But the sea smiled.   40
Smiled as we passed
through the world's gate,
smiled as we lost our escort
of gulls. I have seen
such smiles on faces of whores
in Barcelona.

For months now
an unwelcome guest
in my own body.
I squat by the fire   50
in a silence broken only
by the tireless grinding
of insects.

I have taken
to drawing your face
in the brown earth
at my feet.
                    (The ears are
                    never quite right.)

You are waving,   60
waving. Your
tears are a river
that swells, rushes beside me.
I lie for days in a sea drier
than the desert of the Moors
but your tears are lost,
sucked
into the parched throat of the sky.

I am watched daily.
The ship's carpenter is at work   70
nearby, within the stockade,
fashioning a harness for me,
a wooden collar. He is a fool
who takes no pride in his work,
yet the chips lie about his feet
beautiful as yellow petals.

Days melt
in the hot sun, flow
together. An order is given
to jettison the horses,   80
it sweeps like a breeze
over parched black faces.

I am not consulted, though
Ortega comes to me later
when it is over and says:

        God knows, there are men
        I'd have worried less to lose.

The sailors are relieved,
fall to it with abandon.
The first horse is blindfolded,   90
led to the gunwales, and struck
so hard it leaps skyward
in an arc, its great body
etched against the sun.

I remember thinking
how graceless it looked,
out of its element, legs
braced and stiffened
for the plunge.

They drink long   100
draughts, muzzles submerged
to the eyes, set out like spokes
in all directions.
The salt does its work.
First scream, proud head
thrown back, nostrils flared,
flesh tight over teeth
and gums
            (yellow teeth,
            bloody gums).   110
The spasms, heaving bodies,
turning, turning.
I am the centre
of this churning circumference.
The wretch beside me,
fingers
knotted to the gunwales.

They plunge toward
the ship, hooves crashing
on the planked hull.   120
Soft muzzles ripped
and bleeding on splintered wood
and barnacles.
The ensign's mare
struggles half out of the water
on the backs of two
hapless animals.

When the affair ended
the sea was littered with bodies,
smooth bloated carcasses.   130
Neither pike pole nor ship's
boats could keep them off.
Sailors that never missed
a meal retched violently
in the hot sun. Only
the silent industry of sharks
could give them rest.

What is the shape of freedom,
after all? Did I come here
to be devoured by insects, or   140
maddened by screams in the night?

Ortega, when we found him,
pinned and swinging in his bones,
jawbone pinned and singing
in the wind: God's lieutenant,
more eloquent in death.

Sooner or later all hope
evaporates, joy itself
is seasonal. The others?
They are Spaniards, no more   150
and no less, and burn with a lust
that sends them tilting
at the sun itself.

Ortega, listen, the horses,
where are the sun's horses
to pull his chariot from the sea,
end this conspiracy of dark?

The nights are long, the cold
a maggot boarding in my flesh.

I hear them moving,   160
barely perceptible, faint
as the roar of insects.
Gathering,
gathering to thunder
across the hidden valleys
of the sea, crash of hooves
upon my door, hot quick
breath upon my face.

My eyes, he kissed my eyes.
the softness of his fingers   170
moving. . . .

Forgive me, I did not
mean this to be my final
offering. Sometimes the need
to forgive, be forgiven,
makes the heart a pilgrim.
I am no traveller,
my Christopher[2] faceless
with rubbing on the voyage
out, the voyage into exile.   180
Islanded in our separate
selves, words are
too frail a bridge.

I see you in the morning
running to meet me down
the mountainside, your face
transfigured with happiness.
Wait for me, my sister,
where wind rubs bare
the cliff-face, where we rode   190
to watch the passing ships
at day-break, and saw them
burn golden, from masthead
down to waterline.

I will come soon.

1973; rev. 1981

---

[2]A medal bearing the likeness of St Christopher (formerly the patron saint of travellers).

DAPHNE MARLATT

From *Steveston*

Imagine: a town

Imagine a town running
                (smoothly?
a town running before a fire
canneries burning
              (do you see the shadow of charred stilts
on cool water? do you see enigmatic chance standing
just under the beam?

              He said they were playing cards in the
Chinese mess hall, he said it was dark (a hall? a shack.
they were all, crowded together on top of each other.   10
He said somebody accidentally knocked the oil lamp over, off
the edge

      where stilts are standing, Over the edge of the
dyke a river pours, uncalled for, unending:

             where chance lurks
fishlike, shadows the underside of pilings, calling up his hall
the bodies of men & fish corpse piled on top of each other (residue
time is, the delta) rot, an endless waste the trucks of production
grind to juice, driving through

             smears, blood smears in the dark   20
dirt) this marshland silt no graveyard can exist in but water swills,
endlessly out of itself to the mouth

          ringed with residue, where
chance flicks his tail & swims, through.

1974

Born in Melbourne, Australia in 1942, DAPHNE BUCKLE MARLATT lived in Malaysia as a child. After immigrating to Canada in 1951, she studied at UBC in the early sixties (where she came into contact with the *Tish* movement) and then, after her marriage, in the United States for several years. In 1970 she returned with her son to Canada, settling again in Vancouver, where she teaches at Capilano College and works as poetry editor for *The Capilano Review*. Among her books are *Steveston* (1974), *What Matters: Writing 1968-70* (1980), and *Selected Writing: Net Work* (1980).

Coming Home

if it's to
get lost, lose
way as a wave
breaks

'goodbye'

i am not speaking of
a path, the 'right'
road, no such
wonderlust

weigh all steps   10
shift weight
to left or right to

a place where one
steps thru all erratic
wanderings down to
touch:

i am here, feel
my weight on the wet
ground

1980

At Birch Bay
for Roy
(thanks to Charles Olson)[1]

black, crow, leap up   fall, flap nervous wings against a steep
invisible. bank, against wind flutters, settle, has none of the
sweep & glide these gulls have open to this incessant
oncoming tide waves & foam wind
                                        Crow, rise &
(drop something rise & (drop, flutter, in to his own stress
landing against this wind, over & over. Cracking shells, having
learned this from the gulls?
                              thru time, in the rising
wind last night I dreamt, & see, now, like the crow what it is I   10
learn from you
            walking
                  walking the night as moon, moves out of

---

[1](1910-70), founder and chief theorist of the Black Mountain poetry movement, from which the *Tish*
group took much of its initial impetus. The quotations in the conclusion of the poem are drawn from
Olson's essay 'The Animate versus the Mechanical, and Thought' (*Additional Prose*, 1974).

cancer, out of sea & moon pre-eminent, walking the long. tiderow-
beach. alone: white shells, white backs of gulls on the further
strand, lift, onto the air, clapping wings at their
re-entry into the element, birds, know wind changes
fast as the moon, how tide makes sand disappear, no place to be
except the turbulent face of sea itself incessant. . .
                         It was you who   20
entered my dream, entered me, in the rising wind last night, in love
in the wash of opening seas we come together in : something about a
newborn you saw (rise & drop, rise &) drop   a long life line down
thru all these threshing seas, these birds, like refugees, are resting in
cloud earth sky sensorium   outside my dream, outside our dream—'ends &
boundaries,' or ' "space-activities" in Creation.' Within which, this
marvellous 'Animate' you teach me, along with the sweep & glide these
gulls possess   this (shell) their & our   one & only   world.

1980

ANDREW SUKNASKI

Homestead, 1914
(Sec. 32, Tp4, Rge2, W3rd, Sask.)[1]

i returning

for the third spring in a row now
i return to visit father in his yorkton shack
the first time i returned to see him
he was a bit spooked
seeing me after eleven years—
a bindertwine held up his pants then
that year he was still a fairly tough little beggar
and we shouted to the storm fighting
to see who would carry my flightbag across the cn tracks
me crying: *for chrissake father*   10
lemme carry the damn thing the
train's already too close!

now in his 83rd year father fails

[1]Land surveyor's designation locating a homestead: section 32, the fourth township north, second
range west of the third meridian (that is, about six miles east-northeast of Wood Mountain).

ANDREW SUKNASKI was born in 1942 near Wood Mountain, Sask., of Polish and Ukranian parents.
Since 1970 he has published a large number of chapbooks and collections of poetry; the best known
of these is *Wood Mountain Poems* (1973; rev. 1976), *The Ghosts Call You Poor* (1978), and *The
Land They Gave Away* (1982).

is merely 110 pounds now and cries while
telling me of a growing pain after the fall
from a cn freightcar
in the yard where he works unofficially as a cleanup man
tells of how the boss that day
slipped a crisp 20 into his pocket and said:
you vill be okay meester shoonatzki   20
dont tell anyvon about dis
commeh bek in coopleh veek time. . . .
father says his left testicle has shriveled
to the size of a shelled walnut
says there's simply no fucking way
he'll see another doctor—says:
the last one tried to shine a penlight up my ass
now son
no one's ever looked up my asshole
and never will   30
never
while we walk through the spring blizzard to the depot
i note how he is bent even more now
and i think: *they will have to break his back*
to lay him flat when he dies

in the depot
father guards my bag while i buy two white owl cigars
and return to give him one
we then embrace saying goodbye
and i watch him walk away from me   40
finally disappearing in the snowflake eddy near a pine
on the street corner
and then remember how he stood beneath a single lightbulb
hanging from a frayed cord in his shack
remember how he said
my life now moves to an end with the speed of
electricity

ii mother

her ship sails for the new land
and she on it
the fare paid by her brother in limerick saskatchewan   50

dancing in the arms of some young farmer
she remembers her polish village
the day her mother is fatally struck
by a car—
she remembers being 14
when world war one begins
remembers how she and another girl walk 12 miles
to work every three days
shovelling coal onto flatcars for sixteen hours
before returning home   60

along the boundaries of wolves (their eyes glowing
like stars on the edge
of the dark forest)
she remembers the currency changing as the war ends
her money and several years' work
suddenly worthless one spring day
all these things drift away from the ship carrying
her to the unknown
new land

iii father

arrives in moose jaw fall of 1914   70
to find the landtitles office
is given the co-ordinates for the homestead east
of wood mountain village—
and he buys packsack and provisions for the long walk south
sleeps in haystacks for the first few nights
(finally arriving in limerick
buys homesteader's essentials: axe saw hammer
lumber nails shovel gun bullets food
and other miscellaneous items)
he hires someone with a wagon and horses   80
to drive him to the homestead
builds a floor and raises one wall that day
and feeling the late autumn cold
nails together a narrow box in which to sleep
the first night

the following morning
he rises through two feet of snow to find
all his tools stolen (except for the gun bullets
and knife he slept with)
he searches for a spot on the hillside   90
to carve out with a blunted knife
a cellar
in which to endure the first few years—
he nails together a roof with a stone

philip well is his closest neighbour
and they hunt together
and through long evenings
play cards by light of the coaloil lamp
spin tales of old country wanderings
to survive 40 below winters till pre-emption time[2]   100
is up
when the landtitle is secured
and a more suitable shack is built—

[2]After a certain number of years a homesteader who had been given a pre-emption ticket, which entitled him to 'prove' himself on a section of land by building a dwelling and working the land, would
be certified a bona fide settler. The homesteader often made a number of payments during this time to
secure his title, the last one coming at pre-emption time.

father walks six times between moose jaw and
the homestead
till haggling civil bastards give him the title
each time
he carries a $10. bill sewn inside his pocket across
the heart

iv parting

the day i walked fearless between horses' trembling feet   110
my father watching with hands frozen
to a pitchfork
is clearer in my memory
than the day he and mother parted
—she leading the children through the fall
stubble to wood mountain

in the following years
all i knew of father was the lonely spooked man
whom i met each autumn
in the back alley behind koester's store   120
while winter descended from the mountains—
it seems he always came during the first storm
and tied his team to the telephone pole
(their manes and nostrils frosted)
he always pulled a side of pork from the hay
in the wagon
and placed it on my sleigh

parting
we never found the words
simply glanced at one another's eyes and turned   130
something corroding the love in my heart
until i left wood mountain one sunday afternoon—
running away to the mountains
for what i thought would be forever
until another spring
i returned to see father
eleven years later

v the funeral

sofie in winnipeg
sends each member of the family a telegram announcing
the death of sister eve   140

mother who is 66 at the time
rides a greyhound bus from moose jaw to brandon
all night
father and brother louis drive from yorkton
arrive in brandon the night before the funeral
and get a hotel room—

louis goes out and buys father a pair of pants
and a shirt
returns wondering: *how the hell will i get*
father out of that sweater he's sewn himself into?   150
back in the room
he goes to the bathroom and turns on the water
and returns to subtly introduce the idea to father
who will have no part of it
louis loses his temper and pulls out a pair of scissors
from a shaving kit
and wrestles father to the floor (cuts him out of
the old sweater
while father cries:
okay okay—i'll take a bath)   160

the following day
the family is all on edge
everyone wonders how mother and father will respond
to one another
after 18 years of silence—
louis drives father to the funeral chapel
where mother is already viewing their daughter
they park outside
and father nervously climbs out as the chapel door opens
(he freezes   170
while mother emerges and also suddenly freezes
both stand motionless for 30 seconds and then
begin to run toward each other
they embrace
and she lifts him off the ground
he is 79 at the time)

vi birth certificate

carrying it in my pocket now as father carried
the worn $10. bill across his heart for the landtitle
i have crossed bridges of cities
hoping to find salvation   180
have gazed into the dark rivers of
spring where others found love
hoping to glimpse the face of some god—
and stopped by grey-eyed policemen
produced identification and tolerated their jokes:
what do these letters and numbers mean kid?
where is this place?
is this all you have?

vii epilogue

my father once said:
i might have murdered you all and gone   190
straight to heaven

and having arrived at all these things now
what is to be done with you and love
father?
what is to be done now with that other man who
is also you?
that other man so long ago on a hot summer day
far too hot for man or beast
the day mother at the well with the rope
frozen in her hands watches louis   200
who has ceased haggling with you
sadly carrying a bucket of staples to the barn—
you father something frightening
slowly sweating and walking after him
you slowly raising a fence post above your thoughts
swimming in familiar rage
over that day's fence posts' improper spacing—
louis stopping suddenly for some reason
not looking back
but merely gazing across to tall wheat growing   210
beyond the coulee's black shadow
(you suddenly stopping too and seeming afraid
and then lowering the fence post
as you turn around and return to the picket pile
to continue sharpening poplar pickets
with your newly sharpened axe)
that other man beating mother with a rolling pin
by the cream separator one morning
she pregnant and later sleeping in the late afternoon
to waken from a dream while the axe rises   220
above her grey head
her opening eyes staring into the eye of death
you father slowly turning away once again frightened
and ashamed

you once warning us of that other man within you:
when these things happen to me
do all you can and help one another save yourselves
from me

that other man once sharpening mower blades
when brother mike plays and suddenly tips   230
a bucket of water used to soak blades—
that other man suddenly drowning in black rage
grabbing a long scarf from a coat hook in the porch
then seizing mike to knot the scarf around his neck
and around the end of the grindstone's pulley
bolted high in the porch corner
the trembling right hand slowly labouring to turn
the crude sandstone
(mother and sister sofie fortunately arriving just in time
to fight you and free your son)   240

father
i must accept you and that other dark man within you
must accept you along with your sad admission
that you never loved anyone in your life
(you must be loved
father
loved the way a broken mother loves her son
though he must hang in the morning
for murder)

viii suicide note

silence   250
and a prayer to you shugmanitou[3]
for something
to believe in

1976

[3]Coyote (Dakota Indian language).

ROBERT BRINGHURST

Deuteronomy[1]

The bush. Yes. It burned like they say it did,
lit up like an oak in October—except
that there is no October in Egypt. Voices
came at me and told me to take off my shoes
and I did that. That desert is full of men's shoes.
And the flame screamed *I am what I am.*
I am whatever it is that is me,
and nothing can but something needs to be
done about it. If anyone
asks, all you can say is, I sent me.   10

I went, but I brought my brother to do
the talking, and I did the tricks—the Nile
full of fishguts and frogs, the air opaque
and tight as a scab, the white-hot hail,
and boils, and bugs, and when nothing had worked right

[1]This poem is inspired by the biblical book of Deuteronomy, in which Moses makes farewell
addresses to his people on the eve of their entry into the promised land. The full account of the events
alluded to in the poem may be found in Exodus.

ROBERT BRINGHURST was born of Canadian parents in the U.S. in 1946 and grew up in Alberta, Montana, Utah, Wyoming, and British Columbia; he travelled and lived in the Middle East, Europe, and Latin America before settling in 1973 in British Columbia, where he operates Kanchenjunga Press. His books include *Deuteronomy* (1974), *Bergschrund* (1975), and *The Beauty of the Weapons: Selected Poems 1972-82* (1982).

we killed them and ran. We robbed them of every
goddamned thing we could get at and carry
and took off, and got through the marsh at low tide
with the wind right, and into the desert. The animals
died, of course, but we kept moving.　　　　　　　　　　20

Abraham[2] came up easy. We took
the unknown road and ate hoarfrost and used
a volcano for a compass. I had no plan.
We went toward the mountains. I wanted, always,
to die in the mountains, not in that delta.
And not in a boat, at night, in swollen water.
We travelled over dead rock and drank dead water,
and the hoarfrost wasn't exactly hoarfrost.
They claimed it tasted like coriander,
but no two men are agreed on the taste　　　　　　　　30
of coriander. Anyway,
we ate it, and from time to time we caught quail.

Men and half-men and women, we marched
and plodded into those hills, and they exploded
into labyrinths of slag. The air licked us
like a hot tongue, twisting and flapping and gurgling
through the smoke like men suffocating or drowning, saying
An eye for an eye, and on certain occasions
two eyes for one eye. Either way, you model me
in thin air or unwritten words, not in wood,　　　　　40
not in metal. I am gone from the metal when the metal
hits the mold. You will not get me into any image
which will not move when I move, and move
with my fluency. Moses! Come up!

I went, but I wore my shoes and took a waterskin.
I climbed all day, with the dust eating holes
in my coat, and choking me, and the rock cooking me.
What I found was a couple of flat stones
marked up as if the mountain had written all over them.
I was up there a week, working to cool them,　　　　　50
hungry and sweating and unable to make sense of them,
and I fell coming down and broke both of them.
Topping it all, I found everybody down there drooling
over Aaron's cheap figurines, and Aaron chortling.

I went up again to get new stones
and the voices took after me that time and threw me
up between the rocks and said I could see them.
They were right. I could see them. I was standing right
　　　　behind them

---

[2]Father of the Israelite nation who also led his followers to Israel (Genesis: 12-15); Moses here suggests that Abraham's journey was easier than his own.

and I saw them. I saw the mask's insides,
and what I saw is what I have always seen.   60
I saw the fire and it flowed and it was moving away
and not up into me. I saw nothing
and it was widening all the way around me.
I collected two flat stones and I cut them
so they said what it seemed to me two stones
should say, and I brought them down without dropping them.

The blisters must have doubled my size, and Aaron said
I almost glowed in the dark when I got down.
Even so, it seemed I was pulling my stunts
more often then than in Egypt. I had to,   70
to hold them. They had to be led to new land,
and all of them full of crackpot proverbs and cockeyed
ideas about directions. Aaron and I
outbellowed them day after day and in spite of it
they died. Some of weakness, certainly, but so many of them
died of being strong. The children stood up to it
best, out of knowing no different—but with no
idea what to do with a ploughshare, no
idea what a river is. What could they do
if they got there? What can they even know how to wish for?   80
I promised them pasture, apple trees, cedar,
waterfalls, snow in the hills, sweetwater
wells instead of these arroyos, wild grapes. . . .

Words. And whatever way I say them, words only.
I no longer know why I say them, even though
the children like hearing them. They come when I call them
and their eyes are bright, but the light in them is empty.
It is too clear. It contains . . . the clarity only.
But they come when I call to them. Once I used to sing them
a song about an eagle and a stone,[3] and each time   90
I sang it, somehow the song seemed changed
and the words drifted into the sunlight. I do not
remember the song now, but I remember
that I sang it, and the song was the law and the law
was the song. The law is a song, I am certain. . . .
And I climbed to the head of this canyon. They said
I could look down at the new land
if I sat here,[4] and I think it is so, but my eyes
are no longer strong, and I am tired now of looking.

1974

---

[3]The eagle and the stone (or rock) are both symbols of God. For Moses' song, see Deuteronomy 32:
1-32, particularly 11-13.
[4]Pisgah; because Moses called upon God on behalf of his people when they lost faith in the Desert of
Zin, he is not allowed to enter the promised land. (Numbers 20: 1-13; Deuteronomy 32: 51-2.)

Essay on Adam

There are five possibilities. One: Adam fell.
Two: he was pushed. Three: he jumped. Four:
he only looked over the edge, and one look silenced him.
Five: nothing worth mentioning happened to Adam.

The first, that he fell, is too simple. The fourth,
fear, we have tried and found useless. The fifth,
nothing happened, is dull. The choice is between:
he jumped or was pushed. And the difference between these

is only an issue of whether the demons
work from the inside out or from the outside   10
in: the one
theological question.

1975

These Poems, She Said

These poems, these poems,
these poems, she said, are poems
with no love in them. These are the poems of a man
who would leave his wife and child because
they made noise in his study. These are the poems
of a man who would murder his mother to claim
the inheritance. These are the poems of a man
like Plato, she said, meaning something I did not
comprehend but which nevertheless
offended me. These are the poems of a man   10
who would rather sleep with himself than with women,
she said. These are the poems of a man
with eyes like a drawknife,[1] with hands like a pickpocket's
hands, woven of water and logic
and hunger, with no strand of love in them. These
poems are as heartless as birdsong, as unmeant
as elm leaves, which if they love love only
the wide blue sky and the air and the idea
of elm leaves. Self-love is an ending, she said,
and not a beginning. Love means love   20
of the thing sung and not of the song or the singing.
These poems, she said. . . .
                    You are, he said,
beautiful.
          That is not love, she said rightly.

1982

[1]Woodworker's tool with a handle at each end of the blade, used to shave off surfaces.

MARY DI MICHELE

The City is a Village

Because the earth never blinks an eye,
I sit in my hotel room, throat
constricted with the desire
to communicate with silence.

The St Laurent wears her ice floes
like a corsage of crystal orchids,
like a dress in blue and white gingham.
The mountains are old men sitting,
reading the daily papers,
holding the lamps of dawn,   10
smiling into their beards.
Lights of the city seem to dim
like costume jewellery eclipsed
by the sun, now an amethyst,
the sky glowing with his violet caresses.
Here and now is the sun's new romance with the world,
each affair briefer,
as I count the years like a miser
stuffing them into a mattress,
lined with age, the body of an old woman.   20
I dream of a fresh nakedness,
reborn with the light that foams on the horizon.

And see what moves in the penumbra,
the near empty buses, the trucks
with sleep in their eyes, a boat
cutting her solemn way through the blue
ice to Lévis, goodbye again *la ville Québec*.

Inside, only the sound of pipes gargling,
so I must hear with my eyes,
the puckered lips of waves, kissing,   30
the ice cracking her bones,
and the startled coughing of cars
that incubate lives shivering
in the early morning, her eyes
still tender with night.

Why am I always alone
at sunrise, as I was born
one day in an Italian village,

Born in Luciano, Italy, in 1949, MARY DI MICHELE immigrated to Canada with her family in 1955. Since taking a B.A. from the University of Toronto (1972) and an M.A. in English and Creative Writing from the University of Windsor, she has worked as an editor and published three collections of poetry: *Tree of August* (1978), *Bread and Chocolate* (1980), and *Mimosa and Other Poems* (1981).

like the sun expelled from the dark
womb of my mother?

40

The still beating of my heart at rest
now is like the heart of this city,
and the traffic like the living
blood cells of that body metropolis.
The river banks exchange boats
like love letters,
letters in blue ice,
and my heart is barely beating,
as she whispers to herself,
half asleep,

50

in the blue grey morning.

1980

A Fiction of Edvard Munch[1]

More than death and death,
there is a malediction,
a pale green boy's sickness,
the way the organs start feeding on one another
when the body is starved for affection.

I can paint in the study the death of a sister
coughing blood into a porcelain, hand painted bowl.
When I paint this scene I paint the window into a corner of
the canvas,
I portray every detail of that corner, the ruddy, ruddy light,   10
every detail into the corner, I fill the canvas.
I paint the dark oak of the bed, the white sheets,
and a female face, my double, burning with fever,
a life already confined to the essence
of soft wax candles around a funeral bed.
She coughs into the bowl twelve summers and her thirteenth
winter
and no more.

So I paint the death of a sister,
so I draw the still life of objects,   20
furniture, rugs, drapes, woodpanels, a girl doll in a white
nightgown,
a clock on the mantel with the time fixed,
the affluence, the stubborn continuity of the material world

[1](1863-1944). Norwegian artist whose lithographs, woodcuts, and paintings express internal psychic torments and man's universal terror, loneliness, and anxiety; in this poem di Michele specifically alludes to Munch's painting. *Death in the Sickroom*, which was inspired by the death of his sister, and to his set of drawings, lithographs, and pastels on this theme, entitled *By the Deathbed*.

and a healthy income,
and the light, the light that translates all that
static show to the rhythm of music.

Walking the streets of Kristiana
I see the children of labour
crawl out of the slender darkness of mines   30
and into the tunnels of the street.
I do not know how to paint the darkness in darkness . . . yet . . .
how to paint black in black,
the details so few, a life nude,
a loaf of rye squeezed under a withered arm,
a pair of blue eyes, the wick still glowing,
in a coal encrusted face.

This I cannot paint so I go to the tavern
and talk about free love and unlocking all the doors of a
married woman's pleasure,   40
I can seduce, with my brush, a room;
it will surrender all of its vital parts,
but this woman that I meet so fatally,
makes me paint myself over and over,
as I paint the back she always has turned toward me,
and the head of buried gold I am forbidden to touch.

Finally, I realize that all details have to be erased.
Throw out the window, throw out the bed,
the canopies, the fragrant blue embroidery on a nightgown,
throw out the bowl and the pitcher,   50
throw out the serving woman holding them,
throw out the Good Book,
throw out the nicknacks,
throw out all the god damned accouterments of immortal
money
through which my family can avoid feeling directly any loss,
for what can be buried in rosewood and satin,
with the personal effects to be divided in lots among the poor
who are not afraid of disease.
Throw them all out and push the serving maid into my bed   60
to warm my numb, aristocratic toes, to jingle
the heart a little in the bank of the ribs.
I had to scrape my canvas clean
to begin again with a voluptuous death
posing naked on a bed.

1981

ROO BORSON

Blue

As I lay down to sleep
the pines stuck blackly up
like quills in a dog's lip
in the blue chasm of evening
and flowers withdrew
back of themselves like people interrogated.
Like big sad animals caged.

For I lay down in the big city to dream,
but fugitives ran through me.
Mothballs hung among old coats,   10
teeth collected in the bureau drawers,
trousers twisted on suspenders on the closet door.
Childhood, still confused, comes back imperfectly.
All night long ghosts try on the clothes,
packed close as cigarettes.
They are no one.

1980

The Creation

Black branches blown like oboes,
fallen bodies of men
drift across the moon.

In the purple forest the fungi,
unwanted ears and lips
left here
where no one comes
except in loneliness
talking and listening forever
as they capsize into the ground.

The owl that can't be located
begins again
the low note of a flute.

Up a treetrunk ants file
bearing what perishes.

Born in the United States in 1955, ROO BORSON immigrated to Canada in 1972 and has lived in Vancouver and Toronto. She has published three collections of poetry: *In the Smoky Light of the Fields* (1980), and *A Sad Device* (1981).

Of human houses I remember
mantelpiece ornaments,
and speech, that club-footed habit.

Water seeps out of the loam
like a man's ugliness
weeping at itself,
and in the lavender dawn the falls leap
like women leaping, one after another,
out of their bodies.

1980

Gray Glove

Among branches
a bird lands fluttering,
a soft gray glove
with a heart.

The land at twilight.
Swamp of black mist.
A first planet. A swordtip.
The bird chanting
in a jail of darkness.

This is the last unclassified bird,   10
the one one never sees,
but hears when alone, walking.

You can see how far I've gone
not to speak of you.
Birds have made a simple bargain
with the land.

The only song I know
is the one I see with my eyes,
the one I'd give up my eyes
in order for you to hear.   20

1981

ERIN MOURÉ

It Is Only Me

For Aline Kouhi Klemencic

Say there is a woman
in the locked-up cornfield.
She is making a desert for herself, not me.
Like the poet[1] said: Fumbling the sky's queer wires,
asking for
mercy, abstract collusion, a kind of awe;
she hikes across the frozen furrows in mid-November
ready to observe nearly anything,
self-consciously, as if the turned dirt
would see her singing,   10
would answer with arguments on Kandinsky[2] & Klee.

At least she can't hear
the saxophone playing scales in the next room,
taking the colours out of the air;
they become discordant sounds & no longer answer.
The words stay silent on the page, their usual selves,
picking lice from under their collars,
not yet torn, or interested, or censored,
or even free.
There are never enough groceries, does the woman   20
know this in the strange field?
Probably she has thought of it before, a few minutes,
but now the long furrows
are turning her over & over, like a leaf
in the wind.

Never mind the sound,
the saxophonist is in another country, its mountains
stop him from reaching her.
It is only me, with my bad language, my long distance whisky:
I see her far away, it is very cold, I am   30
calling her out of her field.

1983

---

[1]Al Purdy; in lines 3 to 5 Mouré alludes to his poem 'Wilderness Gothic' (see pp. 57-58).
[2]Wassily Kandinsky (1866-1944), Russian painter and pioneer of abstract expressionism; Kandinsky
and the Swiss abstract painter Paul Klee (1899-1940) were members in Germany of the *Blue Rider*
group of artists and colleagues on the Bauhaus faculty.

ERIN MOURÉ was born in Calgary in 1955; she lives in Vancouver and works full-time for the railroad.
Her collections of poetry are *Empire, York Street* (1979), *The Whisky Vigil* (1981), and *Wanted Alive*
(1983).

Barrington

For Tony Klemencic

There was the hard day you told us of,
nineteen stories into the sky; with your grey
shirt-sleeves rolled, the metal box filled
with tools, hammers,
fixing some thing on the roof of the building.
You couldn't tell us what.
Or if it was sunny.
If it was the shingles, or something to do with the drains.

You told us you worked with an old man, that between
his hands & the tools there was   10
no withholding.
All day you tried to work as he did, moving slowly
across the roof like a cat
high up into the daylight.
For you this happened;
for us it is just an image like a film, you & this man
nineteen floors up the building on Barrington,
the light is hard, all your arms move together,
tacking the roof, feet spread over it,

you & the workman high above us in the sky.   20

Then you told us what you dreamed then,
that the roof was done, you both
had turned your arms back thru the sleeves of your jackets,
& locked the tools, when
the old man jumped off the side of the building.
Holding his box of tools, that evening.

& we see you as you tell it, awake with our glasses of beer
on the twelfth floor of the same building, where you live,
gazing with you
into the dark where the old man fell.   30
How he fell, you told us: like a lamp, like a skiff of paper,
easily, you dreamed him falling like a seed,
slowly, ready to land.
Waiting for you.
& you jumped after him, you too with your tools.

It was like jumping off a stair, you said, when you landed.
You had seen the whole city thru its haze, the sun
pushing the lake into the towers, the light
as it sparked
each window in your long floating,   40
nineteen stories to the street & the old man outside the door.

Then we take our beer again, the same grainy film
of your dream runs past us, its defiance of the layered city,
the people in their houses along Barrington
eating dinner,
& your jacket floating, sunset, the hard speck that was
the box of tools, & your wild trust of the man,
that carried you down to us

1983

Reading Nietzsche

The pitcher with his thin arm
winds up the world.
He is a boy in a peaked cap   called Nietzsche,
Every church is a stone   rolled onto the
tomb of the man-god, he says gently,
his pitch wobbling in the spring heat above the lawns.

I walk near him,
I am the inheritor:
I am as sad as my Mother climbing steps from the basement,
turning out the light.   10
I have my Father's old anger inside me;
like my grandfather I am jealous of hard earth,
of the house I built   that fell
years later, a home for bees.
On the other side I am the grandfather who refused love.

Also I am my grandmother with cancer, I am
my grandmother of whom I know nothing,
I am cousins who married & raised children to fix cars.
I am the thin girl, too, pedalling a tricycle
madly down 36th Ave. on Easter morning, bonnet blown off in the wind. 20
Lawns brown & wet, the snow melted in Calgary.

I too was raised.
in the Church that *prevented the   Resurrection,*
by force.
The sunlight hides in my roads, pushes
a thrown baseball into the lawn;
the neighbours continue stupidly with their lives, & I with mine.
Scientists discover cures for   my family,
radiation therapy, shock, inexplicable
paths of love—   30
                    where one day I saw, alone,
the insistent boy Nietzsche in his baseball cap frowning,
who didn't remember me,
whose reading ruined everything, who hadn't known
Madness, yet

1983

INDEX

About Geneva (Gallant), 76-81
Advice to the Young (Waddington), 28-9
After Reading 'Albino Pheasants' (Page), 19-20
After the Explosion (Macpherson), 296
Afterword to *The Journals of Susanna
Moodie* (Atwood), 471-2
Albino Pheasants (Lane), 497
Alive or Not (Purdy), 64
Alphabet, The (Reaney), 175-6
Anagogic Man, The (Macpherson), 292-3
And the four animals (Watson), 2-3
Another Night with Telescope (Cohen), 350
Another Space (Page), 18-19
Apex Animal, The (Avison), 37
Arras (Page), 16-17
At Birch Bay (Marlatt), 616-7
At the Edge of the Jungle (Lane), 496
Atwood, Margaret, 454-6
    Afterword to *The Journals of Susanna
    Moodie*, 471-2
    Departure from the Bush, 467-8
    Disembarking at Quebec, 461-2
    Dream: Bluejay or Archeopteryx, 473-4
    Dream 2: Brian the Still-Hunter, 469-70
    First Neighbours, 463-4
    Further Arrivals, 462-3
    Last Poem, 480-1
    Making Poison, 481-2
    Marrying the Hangman, 477-9
    Paths and Thingscape, 465-6
    Planter, The, 464
    Pre-Amphibian, 457
    Procedures for Underground, 472-3
    Progressive Insanities of a
    Pioneer, 459-61
    Reincarnation of Captain Cook, The, 458
    Resplendent Quetzal, The, 482-91
    Siren Song, 476-7
    Strawberries, 482
    This is a Photograph of Me, 456
    Tricks with Mirrors, 474-6
    Two Fires, The, 466-7
    Variation On The Word *Sleep*, 480
    Wereman, The, 465
Autobiology (Bowering)
    Raspberries, The, 377
Avison, Margaret, 32-3
    Apex Animal, The, 37
    Butterfly, The, 35

Butterfly Bones; or Sonnet Against
    Sonnets, 37
    Light (I), 41
    Light (II), 42
    Light (III), 42-3
    Meeting Together of Poles and
    Latitudes (In Prospect), 38
    Neverness, 33-4
    Perspective, 35-6
    Snow, 36
    Strong Yellow, for Reading Aloud, 39-41
    Tennis, 39

Bandit, The (Davey), 549-50
Barrington (Mouré), 633-4
Beautiful Creatures Brief as These
    (Jones), 275
Because I Never Learned (Lane), 493
Bicycle, The (Reaney), 173-4
Billboards (Ondaatje), 573-4
Blaise, Clarke, 542-3
    Eyes, 543-7
Blue (Borson), 630
Boatman, The (Macpherson), 292
Boldt's Castle (Souster), 70-1
Borson, Roo, 630
    Blue, 630
    Creation, 630-1
    Gray Glove, 631
Bowering, George, 374-5
    Autobiology
        Raspberries, The, 377
    Desert Elm, 378-84
    Harbour Beginnings & That Other Gleam,
    376
    Thru, 376-7
Breakfast for Barbarians, A (MacEwen), 562
Bringhurst, Robert, 623
    Deuteronomy, 623-5
    Essay on Adam, 626
    These Poems, She Said, 626
Broadcaster's Poem, The (Nowlan), 343
Broken Globe, The (Kreisel), 98-105
Burning Hills (Ondaatje), 574-6
Butterfly, The (Avison), 35
Butterfly Bones; or Sonnet Against
    Sonnets (Avison), 37
Butterfly on Rock, Introduction
    (Jones), 282-7

Cadence, Country, Silence: Writing
  in Colonial Space (Lee), 521-32
Canadian January Night (Nowlan), 342
Canadian Love Song (Nowlan), 338
Canadian Prairies View of Literature, The
  (Donnell), 607-8
Cariboo Horses, The (Purdy), 52-3
Child Blowing Bubbles, A (Dudek), 46
Children of Bogota, The (Lane), 495
Chinese Boxes (Page), 20-1
Cinnamon Peeler, The (Ondaatje), 583-4
City in Canadian Poetry, The (Mandel), 128-37
City is a Village, The (di Michele), 627-8
Cohen, Leonard, 346-7
  Another Night with Telescope, 350
  For Anne, 348
  From *The Energy of Slaves*
    Welcome to these lines . . . , 352-3
  I Decided, 353
  I Decided, 353
  In the Bible Generations Pass . . . , 350
  Kite Is a Victim, A, 349
  Priests, 352
  Suzanne Takes You Down, 350-1
  You Have the Lovers, 348-9
Coming Home (Marlatt), 616
Coming Suddenly to the Sea (Dudek), 46-7
Continental Trance (Nichol), 603-6
Country Full of Christmas (Nowlan), 341
Country North of Belleville, The (Purdy), 53-5
CPR Station—Winnipeg (Lane), 502
Crazy Riel (Newlove), 428-9
Creation (Borson), 630-1
Cry Ararat! (Page), 13-15

Dancer (Nowlan), 337
Dark Pines under Water (MacEwan), 565
Davey, Frank, 547-9
  Bandit, The, 549-50
  Garden, The, 549
  I Do Not Write Poems, 552
  Mealtimes, 551
  Mirror, The, 553-8
  Place, The, 551
  Reading, The, 550
  Red, 553
  Rock, The, 552
  Them Apples, 552
  Weeds, 550
  What Is in the Sky Is Not Brown, 550
  Yellow Page, A, 551
Day of Atonement: Standing (Mandel), 117
Death of Harold Ladoo, The (Lee), 507-20
Departure from the Bush (Atwood), 467-8
Desert Elm, 378-84
Deuteronomy (Bringhurst), 623-5
Diamond Sutra, The (Jones), 280-1

di Michele, Mary, 627
  City is a Village, The, 627-8
  Fiction of Edvard Munch, A, 628-9
Disembarking at Quebec (Atwood), 461-2
Donnell, David, 607
  Canadian Prairies View of Literature, The,
    607-8
  Hound, 608-9
Doors of Perception (Mandel), 125-6
Double-Headed Snake, The (Newlove), 430
Dream: Bluejay or Archeopteryx (Atwood),
  473-4
Dream 2: Brian the Still-Hunter (Atwood),
  469-70
Dream Within Dream (Reaney), 172
Dudek, Louis, 43-5
  Child Blowing Bubbles, A, 46
  Coming Suddenly to the Sea, 46-7
  From a Library Window, 45-6
  Old Song, 47
  Poetry Reading, 48
  Tao, 49
  Torn Record, A, 48
  Within the Walls of the Visible, 48

Easter Egg, The (Reaney), 182-224
Eight Pears (Souster), 74
Elizabeth (Ondaatje), 571-2
Energy of Slaves, The (Cohen)
  Welcome to these lines . . . , 352-3
Eschatology of Spring (Webb), 236
Essay on Adam (Bringhurst), 626
Eurynome I (Macpherson), 290
Eurynome II (Macpherson), 291
Eyes (Blaise), 543-7

Fiction of Edvard Munch, A (di Michele),
  628-9
First Names and Empty Pockets (Kinsella),
  386-97
First Neighbours (Atwood), 463-4
First Stirring of the Beasts, The (Nowlan), 340
Fisherman, The (Macpherson), 293
Flight of the Roller-Coaster (Souster), 70
Flying a Red Kite (Hood), 251-9
For Anne (Cohen), 348
For Eve (Jones), 276-7
For Fyodor (Webb), 234-5
For Mstislav Rostropovich with Love (Page),
  21-2
Four Small Scars (Newlove), 428
F.P. Grove: The Finding (Kroetsch), 244-5
From a Library Window (Dudek), 45-6
Further Arrivals (Atwood), 462-3

Gallant, Mavis, 75-6
  About Geneva, 76-81

Ice Wagon Going Down the Street, The,
    81-96
Garden, The (Davey), 549
Geddes, Gary, 609
    Letter of the Master of Horse, 609-14
Get the Poem Outdoors (Souster), 72
Glass Castle, The (Webb), 229
God Is Not a Fish Inspector (Valgardson),
    534-41
Golden Hunger, The (MacEwen), 567
Gray Glove (Borson), 631
Green Plain, The (Newlove), 437-40
Green Stakes for the Garden (Thomas),
    399-402

Handful of Earth, A (Purdy), 65-6
Harbour Beginnings & That Other Gleam
    (Bowering), 376
Hodgins, Jack, 440
    Lepers' Squint, The, 441-53
Homestead, 1914
    (Sec. 32, Tp4, Rge2, W3rd, Sask.)
    (Suknaski), 617-23
Hood, Hugh, 250-1
    Flying a Red Kite, 251-9
    Woodcutter's Third Son, The, 259-73
Houdini (Mandel), 117-18
Hound (Donnell), 608-9
Hustler, The (Lane), 494-5
Hymn to Dionysus (Nowlan), 341

Icarus (MacEwen), 560
Ice Wagon Going Down the Street, The
    (Gallant), 81-96
Icons (Waddington), 27-8
I Decided (Cohen), 353
I Decided (Cohen), 353
I Do Not Write Poems (Davey), 552
If It Were You (Page), 8-9
Imagine: a town (Marlatt), 615
Initram (Thomas), 402-14
In My 57th Year (Mandel), 126-7
Instructions (Mandel), 123-4
In the Bible Generations Pass . . . (Cohen),
    350
I Thought There Were Limits (Jones), 275-6
It Is Only Me (Mouré), 632

Jones, D.G., 273-4
    Beautiful Creatures Brief as These, 275
    Diamond Sutra, The, 280-1
    For Eve, 276-7
    From 'Kate, These Flowers . . . (The
        Lampman Poems)', 277-9
    Introduction to Butterfly on Rock, 282-7
    I Thought There Were Limits, 275-6

Kate, These Flowers . . . (The Lampman
    Poems) (Jones), 277-9
Kinsella, W.P., 385-6
    First Names and Empty Pockets, 386-97
Kite Is a Victim, A (Cohen), 349
Kreisel, Henry, 97
    Broken Globe, The, 98-105
    Prairie: A State of Mind, The, 105-14
Kroetsch, Robert, 237-8
    F.P. Grove: The Finding, 244-5
    Poem of Albert Johnson, 243-4
    Stone Hammer Poem, 238-42
    Unhiding the Hidden: Recent Canadian
        Fiction, 246-50

Lament for the Dorsets (Purdy), 59-60
Lane, Patrick, 492
    Albino Pheasants, 497
    At the Edge of the Jungle, 496
    Because I Never Learned, 493
    Children of Bogota, The, 495
    CPR Station—Winnipeg, 502
    Hustler, The, 494-5
    Long Coyote Line, The, 503
    Murder of Crows, A, 501
    Stigmata, 498
    Thinking on That Contest, 500
    Unborn Things, 493-4
    Weasel, 503
    Witnesses, The, 499-500
Last Poem (Atwood), 480-1
Laurence, Margaret, 137-8
    Place to Stand, A, 165-8
    Tomorrow-Tamer, The, 139-53
    To Set Our House in Order, 154-64
Lecture to the Flat Earth Society, A
    (MacEwen), 565-6
Lee, Dennis, 504-5
    Death of Harold Ladoo, The, 507-20
    From 'Cadence, Country, Silence:
        Writing in Colonial Space', 521-32
    When I Went Up to Rosedale, 505-6
Lepers' Squint, The (Hodgins), 441-53
Letter of the Master of Horse (Geddes), 609-14
Letters & Other Worlds (Ondaatje), 576-8
Light (Ondaatje), 579-81
Light (I) (Avison), 41
Light (II) (Avison), 42
Light (III) (Avison), 42-3
Like the Last Patch of Snow (Souster), 73
Long Coyote Line, The (Lane), 503
Looking for Strawberries in June
    (Waddington), 25-6
Lost Child, The (Reaney), 174
Lost Salt Gift of Blood, The (MacLeod),
    414-26

Lost Soul, A (Macpherson), 295
Lunch Conversation (Ondaatje), 584-6

MacEwen, Gwendolyn, 559
  Breakfast for Barbarians, A, 562
  Dark Pines under Water, 565
  Golden Hunter, The, 567
  Icarus, 560
  Lecture to the Flat Earth Society, A, 565-6
  Manzini: Escape Artist, 563
  Portage, The, 564
  Real Enemies, The, 567-8
  Real Name of the Sea, The, 566
  Void, The, 568-9
MacLeod, Alistair, 414
  Lost Salt Gift of Blood, The, 414-26
Macpherson, Jay, 288-9
  After the Explosion, 296
  Anagogic Man, The, 292-3
  Boatman, The, 292
  Eurynome I, 290
  Eurynome II, 291
  Fisherman, The, 293
  Lost Soul, A, 295
  Notes & Acknowledgements, 299-300
  Old Age of the Teddy-Bear, 298
  Old Enchanter, 291
  Orion, 296
  Substitutions, 294-5
  Surrogate, 297
  Third Eye, The, 290
  Thread, The, 289-90
  Visiting, 297-8
Making Poison (Atwood), 481-2
Mandel, Eli, 115-16
  City in Canadian Poetry, The, 128-37
  Day of Atonement: Standing, 117
  Doors of Perception, 125-6
  Houdini, 117-18
  In My 57th Year, 126-7
  Instructions, 123-4
  Meaning of the I Ching, The, 118-20
  On the 25th Anniversary of the
      Liberation of Auschwitz, 120-3
  Two Part Exercise on a Single Image, 116-17
  Ventriloquists, 127-8
Manzini: Escape Artist (MacEwen), 563
Marlatt, Daphne, 615
  At Birch Bay, 616-17
  Coming Home, 616
  Imagine: a town, 615
Married Man's Song (Purdy), 63
Marrying the Hangman (Atwood), 477-9
Martyrology, The (Nichol)
  From Book 1, 589-93
  From Book 2, 594-9
  From Book 5, 600-2

Marvell's Garden (Webb), 226-8
Masks of Childhood, From the Preface to
    (Reaney), 180-1
Mealtimes (Davey), 551
Meaning of the I Ching, The (Mandel), 118-20
Meeting Together of Poles and Latitudes
    (In Prospect) (Avison), 38
Message to Winnipeg, A (Reaney), 177
Mirror, The (Davey), 553-8
Moons of Jupiter, The (Munro), 314-26
Mouré, Erin, 632
  Barrington, 633-4
  It Is Only Me, 632
  Reading Nietzsche, 634
Munro, Alice, 300-1
  Moons of Jupiter, The, 314-26
  Something I've Been Meaning To Tell You,
      301-14
Murder of Crows, A (Lane), 501
My Lessons in the Jail (Waddington), 24-5

Naked Poems (Webb)
  Suite I, 230-1
  Suite II, 231-2
Naming of Albert Johnson, The (Wiebe),
    366-73
Near Elginburg (Ondaatje), 572-3
Neverness (Avison), 33-4
Newlove, John, 427
  Crazy Riel, 428-9
  Double-Headed Snake, The, 430
  Four Small Scars, 428
  Green Plain, The, 437-40
  Prairie, The, 436
  Ride Off Any Horizon, 433-6
  Samuel Hearne in Wintertime, 431-2
Nichol, bp, 587-8
  From Continental Trance, 603-6
  Martyrology, The
    From Book 1, 589-93
    From Book 2, 594-9
    From Book 5, 600-2
Nineteen Thirties Are Over, The (Waddington),
    29-30
Notes & Acknowledgements (Macpherson),
    299-300
Notes on a Fictional Character (Purdy), 56-7
Nowlan, Alden, 336-7
  Broadcaster's Poem, The, 343
  Canadian January Night, 342
  Canadian Love Song, 338
  Country Full of Christmas, 341
  Dancer, 337
  First Stirring of the Beasts, The, 340
  Hymn to Dionysus, 341
  On the Barrens, 344-5

Sleepwalker, The, 338-9
Survival, 342
Temptation, 339
Nurselog, The (Purdy), 66-7

Old Age of the Teddy-Bear (Macpherson), 298
Old Enchanter, The (Macpherson), 291
Old Song (Dudek), 47
Ondaatje, Michael, 569-70
   Billboards, 573-4
   Burning Hills, 574-6
   Cinnamon Peeler, The, 583-4
   Elizabeth, 571-2
   Letters & Other Worlds, 576-8
   Light, 579-81
   Lunch Conversation, 584-6
   Near Elginburg, 572-3
   Pig Glass, 578-9
   Sallie Chisum/Last Words on Billy the Kid.
      4 A.M., 581-3
   Time Around Scars, The, 570-1
On the Barrens (Nowlan), 344-5
On the 25th Anniversary of the
      Liberation of Auschwitz (Mandel), 120-3
Orion (Macpherson), 296

Page, P.K., 4-5
   After Reading 'Albino Pheasants', 19-20
   Another Space, 18-19
   Arras, 16-17
   Chinese Boxes, 20-1
   Cry Ararat!, 13-15
   For Mstislav Rostropovich with Love, 21-2
   If It Were You, 8-9
   Photos of a Salt Mine, 11-13
   Portrait of Marina, 10-11
   Preparation, 17
   Stenographers, The, 6
   Stories of Snow, 7
Paths and Thingscape (Atwood), 465-6
Pause (Purdy), 52
Perspective (Avison), 35-6
Photos of a Salt Mine (Page), 11-13
Pig Glass (Ondaatje), 578-9
Place, The (Davey), 551
Place to Stand On, A (Laurence), 165-8
Planter, The (Atwood), 464
Poem of Albert Johnson (Kroetsch), 243-4
Poetry Reading (Dudek), 48
Portage, The (MacEwen), 564
Portrait of Marina (Page), 10-11
Prairie, The (Newlove), 436
Prairie, A State of Mind, The (Kreisel), 105-14
Pre-Amphibian (Atwood), 457
Preparation (Page), 17
Priests (Cohen), 352
Procedures for Underground (Atwood), 472-3

Progressive Insanities of a Pioneer (Atwood),
      459-61
Purdy, Al, 49-50
   Alive or Not, 64
   Cariboo Horses, The, 52-3
   Country North of Belleville, The, 53-5
   Handful of Earth, A, 65-6
   Lament for the Dorsets, 59-60
   Married Man's Song, 63
   Notes on a Fictional Character, 56-7
   Nurselog, The, 66-7
   Pause, 52
   Roblin's Mills (2), 61-2
   Trees at the Arctic Circle, 55-6
   Wilderness Gothic, 57-8
   Winter Walking, 51

Queen Anne's Lace (Souster), 72

Reading, The (Davey), 550
Reading Nietzsche (Mouré), 634
Real Enemies, The (MacEwen), 567-8
Real Name of the Sea, The (MacEwen), 566
Reaney, James, 168-70
   Alphabet, The, 175-6
   Bicycle, The, 173-4
   Dream Within Dream, 172
   Easter Egg, The, 182-224
   From 'A Message to Winnipeg', 177
   From the Preface to Masks of Childhood,
      180-1
   Lost Child, The, 174
   School Globe, The, 170-1
   Starling with a Split Tongue, 178-9
   Table of Contents, A, 179
   Writing and Loving, 175
Red (Davey), 553
Reincarnation of Captain Cook, The (Atwood),
      458
Resplendent Quetzal, The (Atwood), 482-91
Richler, Mordecai, 326-7
   Summer My Grandmother Was Supposed to
      Die, The, 327-36
Ride Off Any Horizon (Newlove), 433-6
Roblin's Mills (2) (Purdy), 61-2
Rock, The (Davey), 552
Rooke, Leon, 354-5
   Sixteen-year-old Susan March Confesses to
      the Innocent Murder of All the Devious
      Strangers Who Would Drive Her Down,
      355-63

Sallie Chisum/Last Words on Billy the Kid.
   4 A.M. (Ondaatje), 581-3
Samuel Hearne in Wintertime (Newlove),
      431-2
School Globe, The (Reaney), 170-1

Siren Song (Atwood), 476-7
Sixteen-year-old Susan March Confesses to the
    Innocent Murder of All the Devious
    Strangers Who Would Drive Her Down
    (Rooke), 355-63
Sleepwalker, The (Nowlan), 338-9
Snow (Avison), 36
Something I've Been Meaning To Tell You
    (Munro), 301-14
Souster, Raymond, 68-9
    Boldt's Castle, 70-1
    Eight Pears, 74
    Flight of the Roller-Coaster, 70
    Get the Poem Outdoors, 72
    Like the Last Patch of Snow, 73
    Queen Anne's Lace, 72
    Trillium Returns, The, 73-4
Spots of Blood (Webb), 235-6
Starling with a Split Tongue (Reaney), 178-9
Stenographers, The (Page), 6
Stigmata (Lane), 498
Stone Hammer Poem (Kroetsch), 238-42
Stories of Snow (Page), 7
Strawberries (Atwood), 482
Strong Yellow, for Reading Aloud (Avison),
    39-41
Substitutions (Macpherson), 294-5
Suknaski, Andrew, 617
    Homestead, 1914
        (Sec. 32, Tp4, Rge2, W3rd, Sask.),
        617-23
Summer My Grandmother Was Supposed to
    Die, The (Richler), 327-36
Surrogate (Macpherson), 297
Survival (Nowlan), 342
Suzanne Takes You Down (Cohen), 350-1

Table of Contents, A (Reaney), 179
Tall Tale, A (Webb), 228-9
Tao (Dudek), 49
Temptation (Nowlan), 339
Tennis (Avison), 39
Ten Years and More (Waddington), 31
Them Apples (Davey), 552
These Poems, She Said (Bringhurst), 626
Thinking on That Contest (Lane), 500
Third Eye, The (Macpherson), 290
This is a Photograph of Me (Atwood), 456
Thomas, Audrey, 398-9
    Green Stakes for the Garden, 399-402
    Initram, 402-14
Thread, The (Macpherson), 289-90
Thru (Bowering), 376-7
Time Around Scars, The (Ondaatje), 570-1
To Friends Who Have Also Considered Suicide
    (Webb), 233-4
Tomorrow-Tamer, The (Laurence), 139-53

Torn Record, A (Dudek), 48
To Set Our House in Order (Laurence), 154-64
Trees at the Arctic Circle (Purdy), 55-6
Tricks with Mirrors (Atwood), 474-6
Trillium Returns, The (Souster), 73-4
Two Fires, The (Atwood), 466-7
Two Part Exercise on a Single Image (Mandel),
    116-17

Unborn Things (Lane), 493-4
Unhiding the Hidden: Recent Canadian Fiction
    (Kroetsch), 246-50

Valgardson, W.D., 533
    God Is Not a Fish Inspector, 534-41
Variation On The Word Sleep (Atwood), 480
Ventriloquists (Mandel), 127-8
Visiting (Macpherson), 297-8
Void, The (MacEwen), 568-9

Waddington, Miriam, 23-4
    Advice to the Young, 28-9
    Icons, 27-8
    Looking for Strawberries in June, 25-6
    My Lessons in the Jail, 24-5
    Nineteen Thirties Are Over, The, 29-30
    Ten Years and More, 31
Watson, Sheila, 1-2
    And the four animals, 2-3
Weasel (Lane), 503
Webb, Phyllis, 225-6
    Eschatology of Spring, 236
    For Fyodor, 234-5
    Glass Castle, The, 229
    Marvell's Garden, 226-8
    Naked Poems
        Suite I, 230-1
        Suite II, 231-2
    Spots of Blood, 235-6
    Tall Tale, A, 228-9
    To Friends Who Have Also Considered
        Suicide, 233-4
Weeds (Davey), 550
Wereman, The (Atwood), 465
What Is in the Sky Is Not Brown (Davey), 550
When I Went Up to Rosedale (Lee), 505-6
Wiebe, Rudy, 364-5
    Naming of Albert Johnson, The, 366-73
Wilderness Gothic (Purdy), 57-8
Winter Walking (Purdy), 51
Within the Walls of the Visible (Dudek), 48
Witnesses, The (Lane), 499-500
Woodcutter's Third Son, The (Hood), 259-73
Writing and Loving (Reaney), 175

Yellow Page, A (Davey), 551
You Have the Lovers (Cohen), 348-9